# Footprint

## Libya

### The travel guide

### Handbook

**James Azema**

*The palm tree is a priceless treasure,*
*The lands where it grows will always*
*be settled.*

Proverb from the Fezzan

النخلة كنز ما يغلاش

برّ النخلة ما يخلاش

**Libya Handbook**
First edition
© Footprint Handbooks Ltd 2000

**Published by Footprint Handbooks**
6 Riverside Court
Lower Bristol Road
Bath BA2 3DZ. England
**T** +44 (0)1225 469141
**F** +44 (0)1225 469461
**Email** discover@footprintbooks.com
**Web** www.footprintbooks.com

ISBN 1 900949 77 6
CIP DATA: A catalogue record for this
book is available from the British Library

In USA, published by
NTC/Contemporary Publishing Group
4255 West Touhy Avenue, Lincolnwood
(Chicago), Illinois 60712-1975, USA
T 847 679 5500 F 847 679 2494
Email NTCPUB2@AOL.COM

ISBN   0-658-01455-2
Library of Congress Catalog Card
Number on file

**Credits**

**Series editors**
Patrick Dawson and Rachel Fielding

**Editorial**
Editor: Sarah Thorowgood
Maps: Sarah Sorensen

**Production**
Typesetting: Richard Ponsford, Emma
Bryers and Angus Dawson
Maps: Robert Lunn, Claire Benison and
Alasdair Dawson
Colour maps: Kevin Feeney
Cover: Camilla Ford

**Design**
Mytton Williams

**Photography**
Front cover:  Art Directors and Trip
Back cover:  Getty One Stone
Inside colour section: James Azema, Ed
Aves, Art Directors and Trip, Eye
Ubiquitous, Images Colour Library,
Impact Photos, Pictures, Robert Harding
Picture Library.

**Print**
Manufactured in Italy by LEGOPRINT

# Libya

SICILY

GREECE

CRETE

TUNISIA

*Mediterranean Sea*

□ **TRIPOLI**

○ Nalut

Khums

○ Gharyan

Misrata

Al Bayda ○

Derna ○

Marj ○

Tobruk ○

Benghazi ○

○ Mekhili

Burdi ○

**BENGHAZI**

Syrte ○

TRIPOLITANIA

○ Sidra

ALGERIA

Ghadamès ○

EGYPT

Raguba ○

○ Gialo

*Libyan Desert*

*Ubari Sand Sea*

Sabha ○

AL KHALIJ

○ Murzuq

*Jabal Akakus*

Ghat ○

FEZZAN

○ Gatrun

*Murzuq Sand Sea*

*Rebiana Sand Sea*

*Tropic of Cancer (23°30')*

Awenat ○

NIGER

SUDAN

CHAD

N

0   km   100

0   miles   100

# Contents

*Right*: human footfall on the natural perfection of a dune crest.

A foot in the door

# A foot in the door

Libya is North Africa without the hassle of the Tunisian resort or the pressure and poverty of Egypt or Morocco. Tripoli, its capital, and second-city Benghazi are really rather sleepy places: the focus of daily life is based round the family and people do not tend to define themselves by their jobs; there are no great cultural events in the western sense of the term; and even organized sport is pretty limited. Visiting the modern cities, you get a feel for Libya's Third Way: a unique brand of Islamic-tinted socialism. And despite (or perhaps because of) the capricious nature of the government, Libyans are a generally kind and helpful people. (Libya is a very safe country to travel in – apart from the crazy driving). But what makes Libya truly special is its great 'set-piece' sights: the classical ruins smothered in wild flowers in spring that litter the north of the country and the fierce, stark and shimmering desert landscapes further south, where prehistoric rock art has miraculously survived to tell a tale from a very different time.

**Tripolitania, Cyrenaica & Fezzan**

The area now covered by Libya was first united as an Italian colony in the 1930s. Three disparate regions, Tripolitania, Cyrenaica and Fezzan, were brought together and eventually became a state (independence was achieved in 1951). However, Libya is a land with quite a past. In the southwestern deserts of the Fezzan, the cliffs of the Jabal Akakus and the Messak Settafet are a fragile gallery of prehistoric rock art. The remains of ancient cities in the eastern region of Cyrenaica would not be out of place in Greece or Turkey. And in Tripolitania, the western province where most of Libya's population resides, you will find the sprawling ruins of Roman Leptis Magna. The home town of a second-century emperor, local lad made good, endowed with monuments as grandiose as any to be found in Rome itself.

**Ancient highways & colonization**

These sites are separated by huge distances. To visit them in a single trip requires long transfers, still almost exclusively by road, across austere and arid landscapes. The situation may change as air transport, hard hit by the embargo, improves but for now, Libya is still defined by great land journeys – as has always been the case. In Libya, the Mediterranean comes closest to sub-Saharan Africa. For caravans carrying slaves, gold and ivory, Tripoli was a favoured destination right up until the mid-19th century. Muslim pilgrims from western North Africa journeyed along the Libyan coast on their way to the Islamic holy cities of Arabia. In the 1930s, Italy completed the Litoranea, a modern highway running from Tunisia to the Egyptian frontier. This is the backbone of modern Libya, linking the narrow coastal strip where 95% of the population lives. Using public transport, the independent tourist can travel the width of the country, visiting the ancient ruins en route.

**Introducing modern Libya**

So Libya, North Africa's second largest country, petrol rich and one-time rogue state extraordinaire, is opening up to tourism. It was in the mid-1990s that western tourists began to visit the country once more. The Italian and German off-road vehicle brigade headed for the deep Sahara, and travel companies began running coach tours to the spectacular archaeological sites of the north. With the suspension of sanctions, (originally imposed because the Libyan regime's alleged ordering of two international terrorist attacks on airliners), the country is beginning to open up to the outside world. Although it is probably too early for major expansion in tourism, serious investment will no doubt be on the cards once the Lockerbie trial is over. Leader Colonel Gadhafi is gradually acquiring a patriarchal aura with his promotion of development and unity in Africa, and a new, more technocratic generation is slowly beginning to emerge in government. And in an age of unstoppable globalization, international confidence is slowly returning.

*Left*: Logan's run aesthetic. The 1970s Planetarium, Tripoli. **Below**: Tripoli. The carpet sellers' day is never done. (Stylized gazelles are a popular motif on rugs).

**Above**: At the bakery, Fjeij, down in the Fezzan. **Left**: One of the Dhat al Imad towers looming over the old Tobacco Factory, Tripoli.

6

*Right*: Eroded statuary, Leptis. **Below**: A great limestone reef of ruins. View of Sabratha-on-Sea.

*Above*: The great Severan Basilia, Leptis Magna. *Right*: The ample forms of one of the Dioscuri stand guard over the stage of the theatre, Leptis Magna.

# Tripolitania

Tripoli is a rather bizarre sort of place. The façade is Mediterranean in feel. However the Italian and Levantine influences combine with hints of oil emirate, splashes of Mali – and a strong totalitarian undertow. The Castle Museum is a great starting point and a perfect example of this mix. One time stronghold of the Knights of Malta, stormed by the Ottomans, and then restored by the Italians, Tripoli's citadel now contains a concentrate of Libyan history and culture, from prehistoric flints, mosaics and ancient sculpture to Berber jewellery and threadbare costume. In the neighbouring old town, you will find mosques, restored houses and vines snaking over the peeling walls of souks. Nearby on picturesque Shari'a Rashid are cheap hotels, *shwarma* stalls and Algerian immigrant cafés. At the food market you can pick up a bottle of *rob* (pressed date juice) or a macaw. Away from the narrow streets of the *madina*, Tripoli has some splendid 1930s Italian rationalist buildings. The colonizers sought to develop the city as an elegant winter resort and avenues of apartment buildings have survived from this time. The café in the Gazelle Park, is a main focus point – a place to smoke a peaceful hubbly-bubbly pipe and play backgammon on a summer evening. Heading seawards, five chunky towers, the Dhat al Imad complex, are the embryo of a future business district and nearby is swanky Burj al Fatih, a glass and granite shopping mall and temple to the new Libyan consumerism. But this is also the hub of immigrant Tripoli, a place where you will hear the languages of Africa as well as Arabic. Colourfully swathed Malian women have every cosmetic requisite and remedy on their pavement stalls whilst be-turbaned Sa'idis from Upper Egypt wait for work.

**Tripoli of the West, influences Arab, Italian & African**

The real glory of Tripolitania is Roman Leptis. Coach loads of visitors drive out from Tripoli, but are easily absorbed in the stone labyrinths of the site. After a eucalyptus-shaded compound, you descend a flight of steps to ancient street level. A massive, elaborate arch comes first. Its purpose? Pure propaganda, all-glory to the Severan family who revamped the city in the early 3rd century AD. Then comes a bath complex, once stuffed with sculpture but now chiefly famed for its marble multi-seater latrines. The heart of the city is the New Forum, flagship project in a grandiose remodelling scheme launched by the Emperor Septimus Severus. For an idea of the wealth acquired by Leptis in its heyday, consider that these granite columns were brought all the way from Egypt, the marble from Greece, and the sculptors from Pergamum. There is a magnificent theatre, too. Today, however, much of the attraction of Leptis is the site's bucolic calm. Huge chunks of Roman building rise here and there; rustling reed-beds fill the great port where the galleys moored; Redstarts flit across the theatre stage; lizards flicker over the stones and when the heat gets too much, you can go for a swim on the nearby beach.

**The grandeur that was Leptis Magna**

An altogether more compact site lies west of Tripoli. Sabratha is best known for its soaring Roman theatre – a careful archaeological re-assembly – and the great early Christian peacock mosaic in the museum. And in the uplands above the Tripolitanian coastal plain, the amateur of all things archaeological will find other traces of the Roman presence. Of these outlying sites, the most impressive must be Ghirza, easily visited as a day trip from Misrata. Here lay the ancient frontier, where Roman settlers, entrenched in their fortified farmhouses, faced nomad raiders. Out in the rock desert, the sense of isolation is intense. Camp out at night here to watch the stars but remember that the Arabs and early travellers held Ghirza in awe: it was the petrified city, the Medusa's terrible gaze had turned a thriving community to wind-worn stone. Here you begin to sense the arid emptiness of the Libyan interior, reaching out and away into Africa.

**Theatrical Sabratha & Ghirza, a petrified city**

8

**Below**: A hungry lion sinks its claws in. Mosaic in the museum at Tolmeita. **Right**: A Byzantine fortified Church surrounded by wild flowers at Torca.

**Above**: Temple of Zeus, Cyrene.
**Right**: A desirable Hellenistic residence, the Palace of the Columns, Tolmeita.

# Cyrenaica

Hundreds of kilometres of highway separate Tripolitania from Cyrenaica, Libya's eastern region. Heavily populated in ancient times, this is a land of open uplands and vistas of deep valleys, thick with fragrant Mediterranean woodland and green all year round. One 19th-century traveller compared it to a fine *jardin anglais*. Cutting through the heart of Cyrenaica is the Wadi al Kuhouf gorge, whose cliff-face caves were inhabited in prehistoric times. The region was also a hideout of fierce Sanusi freedom fighters in the early 1930s. Their leader, 'Umar al Mukhtar, is immortalized in a portrait on the meccano-type bridge down in the gorge.

**Green uplands with an ancient past**

Closer to Crete than either Tripoli or the Nile Valley, the highlands of Cyrenaica were chosen by the ancient Greeks as their first settlement overseas. One town, named for the nymph Cyrene, a noted lion-strangler, became a major Hellenic city. Partly unearthed in the 20th century, Cyrene descends a hillside in terraces. In spring, the humpy unexcavated areas are smothered in wild flowers and (for the moment) the sounds, the wind in the trees and the birdsong, are as rural as they were in ancient times. In this moist African upland, the Greeks found the perfect place for a city. Citizens could gaze from temple terrace northwards across their farmlands to the wine-dark sea beyond. Cyrene can be secretive, too. Off the Sacred Way are perfectly preserved cave baths. Though the spring water has been diverted, neat niches are ready still for bathers' sponges, soap and oil lamps. And concealed by rustling pine trees, the Temple of Zeus is gradually being reassembled, its tumble of carved blocks and column drums challenging archaeologist puzzle maniacs. Cyrene also had a port, ancient Apollonia, 15 km away. Here a pocket-sized ancient theatre now sits next to the sea, ready to host some ancient drama.

**Hellenic Cyrene**

The ancient sites of Cyrenaica are almost too numerous to mention but Christianity was also important in the region in its early days (St Mark was a local). East of Apollonia, on a wild and beautiful coast, early churches have been uncovered: at Ra's Hilal the basilica overlooks a sweeping bay, while at Latrun, twin churches were found right next to the sea. Here sugar-white marble columns carved with crosses tell of the early Christian community's wealth. At Qsar Libia, west of Al Bayda, two massive stone-built basilicas were unearthed in the 1950s. The famous 50-panel mosaic found there reflects tolerant times: there are portrayals of the pagan spring Castalia and Orpheus, pagan equivalent of Christ the Good Shepherd, along with the Pharos of Alexandria, light of learning in the ancient world.

**A cradle of early Christianity**

The Jabal Akhdar is the highest and the coolest part of Libya, and has some magnificent trekking country (and yet more interesting ancient sites) waiting to be discovered. At Slonta, high on a windswept upland, is a tiny pre-Greek sanctuary, sole survivor of an obscure Libyic cult. Carved into the limestone, human heads peer gargoyle-like from under a rocky overhang. In the juniper-scented outback you will find Roman mausolea and farmsteads, Ottoman strong-points and the austere Italian 1930s rural settlements.

**By-ways and independent tourism**

For some, the journey to eastern Libya is a pilgrimage. Fighting raged here during the Second World War and Benghazi alone changed hands five times. At Tobruk, in far Marmarica, four cemeteries are the last resting place of those who gave their lives in the desert campaigns. There are two cemeteries for the British and Commonwealth fallen, plus a small one for the graves of the Free French who fell at Bir Hakeim. Perhaps most impressive of all is the German war memorial, its austere ochre-stone fortress and great silent courtyard a sobering reminder of the terrible destruction wrought here.

**Pilgrimages to the war graves**

Essentials

2

# Essentials

2

# Planning your trip

## Where to go

Libya has much to offer the traveller. However, given the distances between the main points of interest, you will probably have to be selective. The country has three regions with points of interest: **Tripolitania**, with the main city, Tripoli, Roman sites and the Jabal Nafusa, the **Fezzan**, with its spectacular landscapes, two main areas of rock art and the lakes of the Ubari Sand Sea, and finally **Cyrenaica**, again with a number of fascinating classical sites. A visit to the war cemeteries of Tobruk in the far east of the country could be tacked on to a visit to Cyrenaica.

With the UN embargo on international flights, getting into Libya was not always easy in the 1990s. However, French and Italian travel companies began offering packages to the main classical sites in Tripolitania and Cyrenaica, and German and Italian off-road enthusiasts began to travel in the Libyan South. The situation continues to be fairly favourable to tourism, although there is still a shortage of decent hotels, notably in Cyrenaica, and a number of UK-based travel companies are now offering organized tours in Libya. (Note that tourist visas can only be issued to UK passport holders via a Libyan travel company.) This is still the easiest, but by no means the only, way to see the country. Several Tripoli-based tour companies can set up four-wheel drive and camel circuits in the Libyan South. Travelling under your own steam by public transport is also possible, but slower, as buses and service taxis do not always go to isolated tourist sites. In the desert, the services of a guide or travel agency of some kind are essential unless you have your own transport, good maps and equipment.

Five packed days would be ample to get a feel for Tripoli and cover the two main Roman sites of Leptis Magna and Sabratha, both easy day trips from Tripoli. A very intensive ten-day trip would enable you to do these coastal sites, and get down south to the Akakus Mountains, visiting the Berber sites in southern Tripolitania en route. **If you have a week or ten days**

In Tripolitania, start by visiting **Tripoli**, with its old madina and Italian-planned new town, and two fine Roman sites, **Sabratha**, halfway between Tripoli and the Tunisian frontier, and **Leptis Magna**, near Khums about 90 minutes' drive east of Tripoli. Along with Oea, ancestor of modern Tripoli, these were the three cities (tri-polis) of the region in ancient times. Those with an interest in Berber culture should go up into the **Jabal Nafusa**, south of Tripoli. Here there are once-isolated citadel villages and the fortified granaries at **Nalut**. Beyond the Jabal Nafusa, hard by the Tunisian frontier, is the tiny oasis settlement of **Ghadamès**, the so-called 'Pearl of the Sahara'. From Ghadamès, the Akakus is a long four-wheel drive trip south across the desert.

In a two-week trip, you could take in two of the country's three regions, say either **Tripolitania** and **Cyrenaica**, or Tripolitania and the vast desert region of the **Fezzan**, the southwestern quarter of Libya. Until recently, oasis farming and herding livestock to seasonal pasture was the way of life here. To avoid a long drive south, try to get a flight to Sabha and then drive down the Wadi al Hayat to **Germa**, which makes an ideal base for excursions to the **Dawada Lakes** in the **Ubari Sand Sea** and the prehistoric rock carvings of the **Wadi Matkhandush**, in the Messak Settafet. Further to the southwest, either Serdeles (**Awinat**) or **Ghat** are the bases for excursions into the spectacular **Jabal Akakus**. Desert camping is a fine experience and almost inevitable if you want to see the finest examples of prehistoric rock art around the **Wadi Teshuinat** in the Akakus. There is a small airport at Ghat, and when regular flights are resumed, this region will be much more easily accessible to visitors. **If you have two weeks**

| | |
|---|---|
| If you have three weeks | On a well planned three-week trip, the visitor can cover both Tripolitania and the highlights of the Fezzan, as well as taking in the main classical sites of Cyrenaica. Ideally, one would fly from Tripoli to Benghazi to avoid a 12 hour bus journey. (Travel by bus is preferable to braving the often suicidal tendencies of the Peugeot share-taxis.) In Cyrenaica, **Al Bayda** is the most central and convenient place to use as a base, not least because it is one of the few places with a decent hotel. Day excursions can be made west and east from Al Bayda, taking in **Teucheira**, **Ptolemaïs** and **Qasr Libia** (to the west), and **Apollonia**, **Ra's Hilal** and Derna (east). **Derna** has some small hotels, and might be worth an overnight stop if making the long haul east to **Tobruk**, a destination for those seeking to visit the graves of relatives who gave their lives in the Second World War. |

| | |
|---|---|
| Longer expeditions | For many Europeans, longer desert expeditions have come to be the big draw in Libya. Petrol is cheap, and there are thousands of square kilometres of desert landscape to roar across in four wheel drive vehicles or off-road motorcycles. Major attractions include the Dawada Lakes in the Ubari Sand Sea and the crossing from the northeast Jabal Akakus to the southern side of the Messak Settafet. For those with reliable vehicles, the **Ghadamès to Ubari** crossing is one possibility. The remote, extinct volcano of **Waw al Namus**, in the eastern Fezzan, also draws visitors. Certain Libyan agencies now offer trips to the **Tibesti** on the Chadian frontier and to the remote mountain of **Awinat** in the far southeast. (Just over the frontier in Egypt is the Gilf al Kabir Massif.) |

| | |
|---|---|
| Distances | Note that distances in Libya are enormous for those used to Europe: Tripoli to Ghadamès is around 650 km, Tripoli to Sirte 500 km, and if you are thinking of doing Cyrenaica, Sirte to Benghazi is another 500 km. It is clear then that the UN-imposed embargo on air transport hit Libya hard, so for the moment, a long drive south (basically, a day each way) across the Sahara is inevitable to reach the Fezzan. This situation is changing, however, as *Libyan Arab Airlines* updates its fleet and obtains spare parts for its planes. |

## When to go

The best times to go are spring and autumn, especially if you intend to head down into the Sahara. The summer is extremely hot and makes visiting remote desert sites and Berber settlements hard work. The problem with winter is that the desert gets very cold at night and the days are shorter. However, a winter trip to the Roman sites would be fine, and the climate on the Tripolitanian coast is perfect between November and January. March to May are ideal for visiting Cyrenaica. The winter there can be wet and the days are short, which needs to be borne in mind if you are planning on taking in lots of sites.

## Tour operators

With a minimum of intelligence, it is perfectly possible to visit all the main classical sites **without** the over-priced services of a tour company or travel agency, despite what you might be told. However, for the more remote desert sites, you will have to use an agency, as these are places to which few Libyans ever go. You can either buy a package trip from a European tour company, generally at great expense, or contact a travel agency in Tripoli, of which there are many today, some with considerable experience.

However, in order to get a visa (see below), you may well need the services of a tour company in order to get an invitation telexed to the Libyan People's Bureau (embassy) in your home country.

*Africa Tours*, Dhat al Imad, Tripoli T021-3613037, F3613036, and Sabha T071-625594, F621778.

*Al Ula Aviation and Tourism*, 59-61 Shari'a Mizran, T021-3336190, F4446280. Nicely decorated premises but of no help to the independent traveller. A bums-on-seat type agency working for the Italian charter market.

*Asslum Tours*, Burj Al Fatah, 2nd floor, suite 13, Tripoli. T021-3351112, F3351113, mobile T09-12127023, assllum@hotmail.com. Adil is their 'expert'.

*Azar Tours*, POB 101/510, Shari'a Jamal Abd al Nasser, Coast Road, Zuwara, T025-24821. European agent mobile T49-177-2886866, F0049-40-3603198115, www.angelfire.com/az/azartours

*Bab al Madina Tours*, Tariq Gargaresh km 9, Regatta Village, office 101, POB 91578 Tripoli. T021-4832689, F4807306/4836164. Can organize specialized archaeological trips.

*El Mwassem*, 50 Shari'a al Massira al Kubra, Tripoli. POB 214, T021-3339316/3341884, F3341883. Contact person: the pleasant and capable Mohamed Zagloot, mobile T09-12127770. Speaks French and some English and Italian.

*Fezzan Tours*, POB 81495, Tripoli. T021-3335556, F3339438, mobile T09-12141247. Mukhtar is their contact man. Mr M. Bughrara, who can arrange for visas from the UK, (see 'visas' below) uses this agency for invitation telexes. A long established company.

*Les Voyages*, French tour operator with office in Tripoli, T/F021-3351124. Can arrange visas and trips. See below for details of office in France.

*Libyan Arab Tourist Co*, on Mizran St, (contact Salem Azzabi), T021-4448005.

*Libyan Tourism Treasures*, 25 Shari'a Istanbul, Tripoli, T021-4449199, F3339486 (postal address POB 5144 Tripoli) has had good reports from visitors.

*Oea Tours*, now located on Shari'a Awwal September, just one block up from Fergiani's Book Shop, 3rd floor. POB 91749 Tripoli. T021-33338237, F3338369, oeatours@hotmail.com They also have a branch in Ghadamès, T0484-2991, F2291.

*Robban Tours*, 212 Shari'a Jamahiriya, PO Box 84272, T021-4441530, F4448065. Contact: Mr Hussein Founi.

*Wings Travel and Tours*, just off Green Square, on the corner with Shari'a al Baladiya, postal address PO Box 1736 Tripoli, T021-3331855/3341655, F33330881/3341654, wingstravel@yahoo.com. Specialize in tours to the Roman sites but can also set up desert trips. Manager Yousef al Khatali speaks good English and knows his country well.

*Akakus Tours*, based in Ghat. T0274-2804/2318/2938. Agency which can set up desert circuits for fit (and fairly wealthy) travellers taking in the remote rock-art sites of the southwestern regions.

*Imazighan Agency*, T0274-2780. Organize camel trips into the desert.

There are also some experienced individual guides working in Ghat. Try **Sajid Ali Abd al Salam**, who has lots of experience working with Italian groups, T0724-2434/ 2486/2487.

Of the UK-based travel companies, *Exodus* and *British Museum Tours* run excursions to Libya in spring and autumn, taking in desert and Roman sites. The price of these tours is often high, with a 14-day circuit priced at around £1500.

*Arab Tours Ltd*, 60 Marylebone Lane, London W1M 5FF, T020-79353273, F74864237. Not very helpful. Have an expensive tour to Egypt which takes in some of Libya.

*British Museum Traveller*, 46 Bloomsbury St, London WC1B 3QQ, T020-74367575, traveller@bmcompany.co.uk, www.britishmuseum.co.uk. Run a couple tours to the main archaeological site of Libya each year. Two weeks all-inclusive costs around £2250.

*Caravanserai Tours*, 1-3 Love Lane, Woolwich, London SE18 6QT, T020-88556373, F020-88556370, www.caravanserai-tours.com. Probably the best of the bunch.

*Dragoman*, Camp Green, Debenham, Suffolk, IP14 6LA, T01728-861133, st@dragoman.co.uk, www.dragoman.co.uk. Offering tours, treks, safaris and expeditions.

*Encounter Overland*, 267 Old Brompton Road, London SW5 9JA, T020-73706845, www.encounter-overland.com

*Exodus Tours*, 9 Weir Road, London SW12 0LT, T020-86755550 (sales and reservations), F86730859 (brochures and factsheets), sales@exodustravels.co.uk. Expensive.

*Prospect Music and Art Tours*, 454-458 Chiswick High Road, London, W4 5TT, T020-89952151, F87421969.

France-based
*Allibert*, T0033-1-76452226, F40211621. Walking and camel safaris in the Fezzan. Groups are on the large side for what should be small, more personal journeys in the desert.

*Association Zig-Zag*, 54, rue de Dunkerque, 75009 Paris, T0033-1-42851393, F45263285, www.zig-zag.tm.fr. Small agency which covers Chad and Niger as well as Libya.

*Fun Aventure*, 127 chemin d'Artaud, 83500 La Seyne-sur-Mer, T0033-94942623. Small company specializing in off-road travel (four wheel drive vehicle and quad bikes).

*Hommes et Montagnes*, 125, Jean Jaurès, BP 223, 38506 Cedex Voiron (Isère), T0033-4-76661443, F76054320, www.hommes-et-montagnes.fr. Walking and camel safaris in the Akakus. Owners Jean-Louis and Odette Bernezat travelled the Fezzan thoroughly before setting up their tour company. Probably the best agency. Run trips lasting from one week to a month. Organize a lot of *à la carte* journeys, and have run journeys for American groups. Also do Tunisia and Mauritania.

*Les Voyages*, 37 rue Battant, 25000 Besançon, T/F0033-3-81812124, Mobile 685160260. In Tripoli: T/F021-3351124. Can organize visas, too.

*Jean-Claude Bourgeon*, Saharan guide, BP 10, 07230 Lablachère, T0033-75366518. Small group tours and personal itineraries into the Libyan Sahara.

*Point Afrique*, T0033-1-47736264, www.point-afrique.net Organizes cheap flights to 'forgotten' parts of Africa. Does a charter flight from Marseille to Sabha in Libya. Also does Agadez in Niger, Gao in Mali and Er-Rachidia, Morocco.

*Tamera*, 26, rue du Boeuf, 69005 Lyon, T0033-4-78378888, F78929970, www.tamera@asi.com. Advertises circuits in the Fezzan with direct flights to Sabha. Small, personal company, can do *à la carte* trips for a handful of people.

*Terre d'Aventure*, long established agency, soon to be listed on the Paris stockmarket. Said to cut corners, largish groups, up to 15 people. (Small groups of 6 to 7 are more expensive). Libya is not really their speciality – they have no local team at present.

Italy-based
*Antichi Splendori Viaggi*, Via Vanchiglia, 22/a, 10124 Turin, T0039-11-8126715, F8123542, email antichi@aerre.it.

*Osservando il Mondo*, Via Boves, 5, 25124 Brescia, T/F0039-30-3541719.

Malta-based
*Iram Tours*, 103/1 Saint Bartholomew St, Qormi, QRM07, Malta. Libyan contact numbers T00218-213335914, F00218-214444595, iram@maillink.net.mt.

*Sahara Guide*, 13 Our Lady of Angels Street, ZBG 02 Zebbug, T/F00218-356462065, saharaguide@waldonet.net.mt.

## Language

Arabic is the official language throughout Libya. Given the Arab nationalist leanings of the government under Colonel Gadhafi, Arabic is regarded with some pride as a cultural emblem. Immediately after the 1969 revolution or coup d'état, all foreign language signs were removed, including street names, shop names, signposts and indications on official buildings. The result is that it is difficult for non-Arabic speakers (or readers) to make use of written signs. The answer to this problem, other than learning the Arabic script and some vocabulary before travelling, is to be very patient when asking your way until help is volunteered by a source you can comprehend. In normal circumstances Libyans are helpful to foreigners and will point out routes and other destinations. Unfortunately, however, it is only the older generation who have

Essentials

Essentials

☞ *Useful Arabic sign words*

| | |
|---|---|
| street / shari'a | شارع |
| square / maydan | ميدان |
| hotel / funduq | فندق |
| bank / masraf | مصرف |
| restaurant / mat'am | مطعم |
| travel agency / maktab li-ssafar wa siyaha | مكتب للسفر والسياحة |
| resthouse / istiraha siyahiya | استراحة سياحية |
| city centre / markaz al madina | مركز المدينة |
| archaeological service / maslahat al athar | مصلحة الأثار |

colloquial English, French or Italian since the quality of foreign language teaching has fallen and fewer Libyans travel abroad than previously (Tripoli City is the easiest place for the non-Arabic speaker). But, to make you feel better, remember that locals sometimes have to ask their way too, as a lot of streets do not have names and in Tripolitania, none of the towns have name signs as you arrive in them either.

The private commercial sector is likely to be best aware of **English** and **Italian**. **French** is understood widely by the older generation in the west and southwest of country (Ghadamès and Ghat), and much spoken by immigrants from sub-Saharan Africa. Italian is still an occasionally used language in the Tripoli area. English can be used in Cyrenaica and Al Khalij where there are many oil industry workers who have rubbed shoulders with English-speaking personnel. But these language difficulties should not put you off travelling in Libya since the Libyans themselves are so helpful and patient. A few words or phrases in Arabic will ease the way considerably. The **Arabic** of Cyrenaica resembles that of Egypt a great deal, and an Egyptian phrase-book could be useful here, especially as there are large numbers of Egyptians and Sudanese working in the service sector. Tripolitanian spoken Arabic is very close to Tunisian. Rudimentary French will often be enough in Tripolitania too when speaking with Algerian, Moroccan and Tunisian immigrants.

**Berber** is spoken as a first language in some rural areas, especially the Jabal Nafusa. **Tamashek**, related to Berber, is spoken by the few Tuaregs in the region of Ghadamès and in the Fezzan, where there are also many residents originally from Mali and Niger. In the far south, around the Tibesti Mountains, the **Tibu** language is the lingua franca.

# Before you travel

Travellers from all but Arab and certain African countries need a visa to get into Libya. These are normally issued at the Libyan people's bureau, embassy or consulate in the relevant overseas country. Until the late 1990s, visa allocation for UK nationals was closely controlled and mainly confined to those with bona fide jobs in the country. Things are more relaxed now and **except** for US or UK citizens, obtaining a visa creates few problems. For a UK passport holder, it is essential to obtain an invitation from a Libyan official agency, travel company or individual in order to get your visa (see list of tour operators above). Note that it is technically still illegal for US citizens to go to Libya. (Americans who have Libyan stamps in their passport may have to 'lose' their passport and obtain a replacement before returning to the US). Generally speaking, however, there is a gradual relaxation of visa controls as tourism grows, albeit very slowly, in economic importance.

**Obtaining a visa**  Tourist visas cost around US$50 (45DM + 16DM translation fee for German passport holders; £20 for UK nationals). They are valid for entry for 3 months from the date of issue, and allow a month's stay in Libya. (In mid-2000, one UK agency was charging a visa fee of £100, the cost of the visa being obviously linked to the number of middle-men. The paperwork required by the People's Bureau can also change unexpectedly. But, with any luck, the gradual improvement in UK and USA-Libyan relations may simplify this rather complicated visa process.) You can obtain a visa either as a member of an organized tour group or as an independent traveller. The latter option can be very slow indeed so allow plenty of time to apply for your visa before you wish to travel. Note that you can only apply for your visa in your country of nationality. Europeans who happen to be in Egypt or Tunisia and wish to travel on to Libya cannot obtain visas there.

In early 2000, one of the simplest ways for independent travellers to obtain a visa for Libya was to go via ***Allied Tickets and Visas***, a UK-based company at 17 Marshfield House, Grove Road, Drayton, Portsmouth PO6 1QA, T01705-362835, F01705-785388, M0795-7769610, mbughrara@hotmail.com. This agency will organize the invitation telex from Tripoli and the translation of passport details. The procedure can be terribly slow, however.

All visitors to Libya must have the essential data on their passport translated into Arabic (which is filled in on a form stamped towards the back of your passport). If you are travelling as part of a tour group then the travel company will almost certainly deal with this (and the rest of the procedure) for you.

As an **independent traveller**, the proceedure is as follows:
**1**. Non-Arabic passports must be stamped with an official Arabic translation of the personal details of the individual's passport. In the UK the Passport Office 7-78 Petty France, London SW1, T020-72793434 will do this as a matter of routine on presentation of the passport. The Libyan embassy in Malta can also provide a visa and Arabic translation. Later at the People's Bureau (see 3 below), they will fill in the form with your details in Arabic.
**2**. You then need to obtain an invitation from a travel company in Tripoli. Contact a travel company, (see list above) and give them all your passport details. The company will then send a telex of invitation to the People's Bureau in your home country.
**3**. When they have done this, you can go to People's Bureau with 2 photos and visa fee. You will have to fill in a green form to hand in along with your passport and in addition to all this, you may also be required to show proof of an air-ticket reservation. In 2 weeks, the visa should be ready.

Essentials

*Libyan embassies abroad*

**NB** *A Libyan embassy is referred to as a Libyan people's bureau (here: LPB). (In practice, you need to go through an agency to get a visa, see below).*

**France** *Consulate 2 rue Charles Lamoureux, 75016 Paris T0033-1-47047160. For southern France, consulate at 6 boulevard Rivet, 13008 Marseille T0033-4-91716702*

**Italy** *LPB, Via Nomentana 365, Rome, T0039-6-86320951. Also consulate Via Baracchini 7, Milano, T0039-2-86464285.*

**United Kingdom**. *LPB, 54 Ennismore Gardens, London SW7, T020-74868250.*

*See page 38 for foreign embassies in Tripoli*

**4**. Once in Libya, even if you are going to travel independently, the tour company will want you to contact them and pay a fee, possibly as much as $100. They will register your passport for you with the authorities (fee 5LD) and are in fact responsible for you during your stay.

Once in Libya, if you need an **extension** beyond the normal visa period, the immigration police should be informed and the fact noted in your passport. (In Tripoli, you go to the Jawazat, a sort of immigration office on Shari'a Ashrin. Taxi-drivers know where it is). Tourists may extend their visas by one month, twice, at a cost of 5LD each time. This is a time-consuming procedure, however, and it is probably easier to leave the country and come back on a fresh visa. Note again that regulations are subject to change.

What to take  Travellers always tend to take too much. It is true that few hotels have a reliable laundry service, but cheap clothes are readily available. A travel-pack will survive the holds of rural buses and sitting on the roof-rack of a share taxi. If you acquire many items on your travels, there is plenty of cheap luggage available for sale in Libya, so you do not need to worry about transportation. (Many Tunisians, for example, frequently travel down to Libya to bring cheap merchandise back).

Regarding **clothing**, outside summer you will need woollens or a fleece for evenings. Longish cotton skirts are a good idea for women travelling in rural areas. Women visiting cities alone should have an item of smartish clothing. In the towns, Libyans like to dress well if they have the money. Many don't, so a smart appearance is appreciated. (In many outlying settlements next to remote archaeological sites, a lot of poverty is apparent.)

If you are aiming to travel to the Fezzan, stout walking shoes are a good idea, as getting to some of the rock art sites requires a little scrambling. If planning to bivouac out in the desert, you will need a warm sleeping bag. The penetrating cold of the Sahara at night is a well-known phenomenon, so bring your warm undergarments – long johns are a good idea. Wear layers of clothing at these times.

*Always take more money & fewer clothes than you think you'll need*  Everybody has their own preferences, but listed here are those most often mentioned. These include an inflatable travel pillow for neck support. You should also take waterproof clothing and waterproof treatment for leather footwear and wax earplugs, which are vital for long bus trips or noisy hotels. Also important are rubber-thong Japanese-type sandals, which can be worn in showers to avoid athlete's foot, and a sheet sleeping-bag to avoid sleeping on filthy sheets in cheap hotels.

*Remember PMT – passport, money, tickets*  Other useful things to take with you include: a clothes line, a nailbrush, a vacuum flask, a water bottle, a universal bath and basin plug of the flanged type that will fit any waste-pipe (or improvise one from a sheet of thick rubber), string, electrical insulating tape, a Swiss Army knife, an alarm clock for those early-morning bus departures, candles (for frequent power cuts), a torch/flashlight, pocket mirror, pocket calculator, an adaptor, a padlock for the doors of the cheapest hotels (or for tent zip if camping). The most security-conscious may also wish to include a length of chain and padlock for securing luggage to bed or bus/train seat.

A list of useful medicines and health-related items is given at the end of the 'Health' section. To these might be added some lip salve with sun protection, and pre-moistened wipes (such as 'Wet Ones'). Always carry toilet paper, which is especially important on long bus trips. Contact lens wearers: should note that lens solution can be difficult to find in the more remote areas of Libya.

Duty free goods are available at the main airport departure lounge at Tripoli airport, **Customs** purchasable in foreign currencies only. A range of cigarettes, cigars, perfumes, watches and travel goods can be found – but no alcohol. No other tourist facilities of this kind are available.

**Compulsory currency purchase** For those coming in on a work visa or as part of an organized group, there is no obligation to change currency on arrival. However, in late 1999, individuals coming in as tourists were **sometimes** required to change $500 into local currency at Tripoli International Airport. Here again this regulation was not applied all across the board and on occasion, group members will be required to change this sum.

**Import-export bans** Libya has a stringent ban on the import of alcohol of any kind. It is a pointless risk taking in beer, spirits, or indeed drugs. Severe penalties can be imposed and at the very least passengers can be incarcerated pending deportation. It is rather easier to carry books and newspapers into the country than formerly, though sensitivities remain and it is best not to carry literature which might be misunderstood or thought to be anti-Libyan. Firearms cannot be imported without special permission. Radio transmitters and electronic means of printing will attract official attention and should clearly be for personal use only.

On leaving Libya make sure that you have no antiquities. The Libyan authorities take unkindly to the illegal export of bits of their ancient monuments and penalties for infringement can be ferocious.

Immigration and sometimes currency declaration forms are needed on arrival. The **Registration** forms themselves are in Arabic but English translations are available on the plane. **on arrival** Only the Arabic question form should be filled in (with answers in English or French). Copies of the forms should be carefully retained since they will be requested on exit. Visitors should make sure they are registered at the local foreign passport office within five days of arrival, otherwise they can be stopped and held. Worse, they can be delayed on departure, even missing flights if officials are convinced that malpractice rather than ignorance is the cause of the problem.

For most foreigners **see note about registration below**, registration takes place in Tripoli at the Passport Office on Shari'a Ashrin, a 15 minute walk from Shari'a Umar al Mukhtar. (The street carries no name plaque.) Ask your taxi driver for the *Jawazat* (Passport Office). The building, just off a major roundabout, is easily relocated after one visit. There are numerous foreigners coming in and out, and you need to find the staircase, to the right of the main door, taking you upstairs to a room like a post office with lots of counter windows. You will be asked for a copy of the telexed invitation from your employer or travel agency in Tripoli, and the registration fee of 5LD. In practice, your travel agency or employer will take care of this formality, so you won't need to sort this out yourself. Sometimes, the big hotels (eg Bab al Bahr in Tripoli) register guests on arrival.

Essentials

### Currency in Libya, 2000

*One of the features of travelling in Libya is the need to carry large wads of green dinar notes. To avoid confusion, the main notes and coins are as follows:*

#### Notes

*10LD Highest value note. Green with profile portrait of national resistance hero. 'Umar al Mukhtar, fortress at Sabha on flip-side, extract from declaration of people's rule. Any major transaction needs lots of these.*

*5LD Green and reddish-brown. Image of camel suckling her young.*

*1LD Blue note with picture of mosque. (There is also an older, green 1LD with views of a mosque.*

*.5LD Purple brown, images of industry, irrigation and wheat.*

*.25LD Blue-green, images of arch and column at Leptis Magna and the citadel at Murzuq, traditional mosaic (zlij) patterns.*

#### Coins

*These are rare but you will come across round, 50 dirham and 100 dirham coins dated 1975, bearing the eagle, preferred symbol of Arab republics and emblem of the Jamahiriya. More picturesque are the scalloped-edge 50 dirham and 100 dirham coins from 1979, bearing an image of a horseman and with values indicated in Middle Eastern Arabic numerals.*

**Travellers with own vehicle** For those travelling with their own vehicle in the southwestern parts of the country, registration formalities are slightly different from those above and are explained below in the 'Getting there' section. Basically, you need to register with a tourist agency in either Sabha or Ghat who will deal with your passport registration. A tourist card (list of vehicle passengers) issued by such an agency is necessary for visiting off-road sites in the Fezzan.

Departure tax There is a departure tax at **land borders**. Leaving by air, embarkation cards will be filled in with the help of attendants. There is also sometimes a currency control. Only small amounts of Libyan currency may be exported, preferably less than 10LD. Any excess Libyan dinars should be changed back into hard currency.

The departure tax on leaving Libya by **air** was 3LD. Only Libyan currency is accepted. At Tripoli airport, from which the majority of flights leave Libya, there is a special counter for buying the exit stamp before passing through to the passport and customs formalities. Without a stamp you will be sent back to start the entire process again.

Insurance For those travellers not already equipped with travel or other insurance, there are facilities available in Libya directly through the **Libyan Insurance Co** or the **Libya Travel and Tourist Co** shop in Tripoli, T021-3336222.

## Money

Currency The Libyan dinar is the standard currency which is divided into 1,000 dirhams. Notes in circulation are 10, 5, 1, 0.50 and 0.25LD; coins 0.10 and 0.05LD. Travellers may have to fill in a currency form on arrival (cash and travellers' cheques) and present it together with official exchange receipts on departure. The system is not watertight nor fully implemented but is perhaps best observed. Make sure you keep receipts from the banks and it is a sensible procedure to make sure that you do not leave the country with either more than a few Libyan dinars or more foreign currency than you arrived with.

## Sample prices, late 2000

For the western tourist, Libya can actually be quite cheap. The following prices are for late 2000.

Decent hotel, 20LD to 55LD a night
Meal in cheap restaurant, 4LD to 6LD
Hot, mince-meat sandwich, 1LD
Loaf of bread, .05LD, i.e. 50 dirhams, practically free.
1 litre of imported fruit juice, 2LD
1.5 litre Kufra table water, 1.25LD
Black coffee, .5LD
Zabadi natural yoghurt, .25LD
Imported yoghurt, .75LD
Imported chocolate (Kit-Kat) 1LD
Long-distance bus ride, Tripoli to Benghazi, 13.5LD
Medium-distance share taxi ride, Benghazi to Al Bayda, 6LD
Individual taxi ride in Tripoli, 5LD
Museum or archaeological site entrance, 3LD
Imported guide books at Fergiani Bookshop, 50LD to 70LD
A good quality burnous (traditional cloak) 70LD
A day's four wheel drive hire 250LD.

**Banks** There are banks at Tripoli airport, which are open 24 hours. All the principal banks will exchange travellers' cheques and currency notes at the official rate of exchange. Note that there is no longer any black market in currency. Coming in from Tunisia, you can generally change money at Ben Gardane, the last major town before the border at Ras Ajdir. There are plenty of banks in Tripoli, Benghazi and all the main coastal places. In Fezzan, things are more problematic: there are a couple of banks in Sabha, one in Ghadamès, and none in Ghat, so make sure you change your money before going south in order to avoid wasting time. If hotles do have a Bureau de Change, will only take US dollars.

**Exchange rates** In early 1999, the official exchange rate was very unfavourable to the visitor, i.e. 0.35LD to the $US. On the black market, the exchange rate ranged between 3 and 3.5LD to the $US. In summer 2000, the official exchange rate was aligned with the black market one, $US1 buying you 1.9LD, and £1 being equivalent to 3.06LD.

**Credit cards** International credit cards are very rarely used. Cash is the normal medium of exchange and most shops are not equipped to handle credit cards of any kind. Credit cards at hotels are best if not of US origin, though generics such as Visa and Mastercard are normally suitable.

**Cost of living** Libya is an oil economy and it mainly imports its necessities from abroad and prices tend to reflect this external reliance to a certain extent. The distribution system and a high level of mark-up by some shopkeepers means prices of certain goods are high. Specialist western foods and commodities like Libyan mutton are very expensive. Eating out is pretty cheap in the small popular cafés, even if you are having a full meal. Fresh vegetables and fruit are moderately priced. Pharmaceuticals, medical goods and imported high-tech items can be expensive. Personal services such as dry cleaners can prove expensive. Travel is extremely cheap by internal air services, although the quality of service may not be what you are used too. Travel by bus and share taxi is extremely cheap but hotels are few and the even fewer good quality hotels are expensive for what they are. These costs are offset, however, by the generosity of the Libyans in rural areas in finding accommodation for visitors in public buildings. (For those travelling before the end of black market currency in early 2000, costs were very low).

# Getting there

Until mid-1999, travellers bypassed the UN air embargo on Libya by flying to Malta or Tunisia and continuing their journeys by land, using buses or shared taxis, or by sea on the regular ferry run from Malta. Heavy traffic at the Tuniso-Libyan border meant long waits, and boat from Malta was the best way to get to Tripoli. Shortly after the suspension of the embargo, direct flights from certain European destinations and Tunisia were resumed.

## Air

*Libyan Arab Airlines* is the main carrier. The embargo on the transfer of arms and strategic materials to Libya by the USA for its alleged involvement in state terrorism in the early 1980s led to a huge depletion of the LAA fleet, which is ageing and inefficient, but the company looks set to purchase a large number of new aircraft.

*Air Malta, Alitalia, British Airways, Egyptair, KLM, Lufthansa*, and *Swissair, Syrian Airlines* and *Tunisair* all have flights to Tripoli. Most are on a once or twice a week basis. There are no direct flights to Libya from the USA or Canada at the moment. Flights to Libya from African points of origin used to include Accra, Algiers, Cairo, Casablanca, Khartoum, Ndjamena, Niamey and Nouakchott, but only flights from Alexandria, Cairo and Casablanca had been resumed at time of going to press. From the Middle East, there are scheduled flights to Tripoli from Amman, Damascus and Dubai. Little by little, air links with most of these destinations will be re-established as Libya seeks to re-establish itself internationally.

In normal conditions foreign visitors by air are advised to have reserved firm flights for departure since it is not always easy to get return flights booked inside Libya. The fare structure for flights used to be extremely polarized. *LAA* is also expensive and not easy to get discounts for. From the UK, the cheapest flights are with *Air Malta* via Valletta. In summer 2000, the cheapest London to Tripoli return fare was around £400.

**Airport information**  Note that there are two airports in Tripoli, the main international airport at **Ben Ghashir** 27 km south of the city centre and the former Wheelus Airfield, renamed **Maatiqa**, 4 km east of the city centre, following the coast road. Flights for Benghazi may leave from this airport. To get to the international airport, a place in a share taxi from Bab Jedid will cost you 2LD (allow plenty of time). It is better, however, to take a normal taxi, which will cost you between 15 and 25LD, depending on how rich you look. The airport has banks and a restaurant on the main concourse.

**Airlines in Tripoli**
*Tripoli area code: 021*

Many of the main airline offices are located in the Dhat al Imad Towers, just outside the madina near the new *Corinthia Hotel*. Others are located on the streets fanning southwards from Green Square (ex-Piazza del Castello). Airline office working hours are likely to be Sun-Thu 0830-1400.

*Air Malta*, in Libya: Tower 5, Floor 1, Dhat al Imad, Tripoli T3350578/9 (reservations) T3605288 (airport office), F3350580; and Floor 1, Sidi Hussein Complex, Benghazi, T061-9080205/6, F9080205. **In Malta:** T662211, kmsales@airmalta.com.mt. **In UK:** T0845-6073710, F020-87857468, ticket-office@airmalta.co.uk. **In Australia:** 64 York St, Sydney, T2-9329111, F2-92903306. **In USA** T212-9838504, F212-9838508.
*British Airways*, African Union Organisation Road, Borg Al Fatih, Floor 19, T3351277/78/79, www.britishairways.com..
*Emirates*, Dhat al Imad, tower 5, floor 5, T3350591.

*Libyan Arab Airlines*, has two main city centre offices: one is just off Shari'a Awwal September, on your right at a main junction as you head south, T4442442 (not far from ex-Cathedral), and the other is on Shari'a Umar al Mukhtar, T021-602091, on your left as you leave the city centre, almost opposite the Fair Ground entrance and near the Oasis Oil Company building.

*Lufthansa*, Dhat al Imad, tower 4, 12th floor, PO Box 91518, T3350375/3350377, F3350378. Airport office T3619516, F3619517. (5 flights a week).

*Swissair*, Dhat al Imad, tower 3, floor 4.

*Syrian Airlines*, just behind the Funduq (Hotel) al Kabir, T4446715/4446716.

*Tunisair*, 6 Shari'a Haiti, T021-333750. Close to Maydan al Jaza'ir and the ex-cathedral.

Essentials

## Train

Unfortunately, Libya's small railway system was gradually dismantled after the Second World War and there are no services within Libya. However, a new high-speed littoral railway was proposed in 2000 to link Egypt, via Libya, with Tunisia.

## Road

There is plenty of cheap public transport from **Tunisia** to Tripoli. The best option from Tunisia is to take a share taxi from one of the major eastern towns, i.e. Sfax, Gabès or Houmt Souk to the Tuniso-Libyan frontier at Ben Gardane / Ras Ajdir. Passengers may cross the frontier on foot and then take a Libyan domestic bus or taxi. If flying from Tunis to Djerba, another option is to take a private car with driver from just outside the airport to the frontier. This may cost up to 100LD a head, depending on how many passengers are in the car. Since flights to Tripoli resumed, traffic on the Djerba to Tripoli route has fallen away, and there may be a considerable wait.  *From Tunisia*

Once in Libya, there are two main **bus** transport companies, one engaged principally in long-distance international services and the other plying between Libyan cities and towns. A place in a share taxi is normally cheaper than a luxury bus and departures can be more frequent. However, considerable waits can be involved while the taxi fills up. Driving standards are variable among taxi drivers and passengers need good nerves. But basically, taking a share taxi is easier and quicker than waiting for the bus. Once over the border, if a bus is preferred, take a share taxi from Ras Ajdir to the nearest town (Zuwara) and take the bus from there to Tripoli in more comfortable conditions.

When leaving Tripoli for Tunisia or Egypt, you can use the *Libyan International Bus Company* which has an office behind the Tripoli madina off Shari'a Umar al Mukhtar to the west of the old citadel, in an area now being cleared of buildings and being reconstructed. Buses tend to leave Tripoli very early in the morning, not later than 0800. Passengers should be at the bus station by at least 0700. While the air embargo was in force, buses tended to fill up quickly and leave as soon as all seats were taken (see Tripoli transport section, page 88, for more details).

**Louage (share taxi) stations in Gabès, Tunisia**  The louage and bus station are next to each other at the top end of Ave Farhat Hached, by the entrance to the oasis. **Houmt Souk (Djerba)** louage and bus station are in the centre of Houmt Souk, capital of Djerba. Information on T05-650399. Ordinary taxi from airport to Houmt Souk 5 Dt. **Sfax** the main louage station is 10 minutes' walk southwest of the city centre, down Ave Habib Bourguiba. The train station is at the other end of the Ave Bourguiba, a good 20 mins' hike from the louage station. **Tunis** louages for Libya leave from a small car park just off Rue Jazira on the east side of the madina (old town) of Tunis. To get there, start facing the old Sea Gate at the top of Avenue de France. Go left down Rue Jazira for 200 m, the taxi park is on your right 20 m off the street, behind a small square with lots of shoe repairers. One-way fare Tunis from to Tripoli, 35DT, 70LD.

Rather than take a share taxi the whole way from Tunis to Tripoli, you may want to do the journey in short hops. Tunis to Sfax will cost you 10DT, journey time on a good day around 3 hrs.

**Tripoli to Tunisia** Taxis to Djerba (Tunisia) leave from Shari'a al Rashid near the bus station and cost 25-40LD, depending on the number of passengers and the journey takes 4-5 hours, depaending on border controls. One option is to take a Libyan share taxi just as far as the frontier, then pick up a Tunisian louage on the other side. Sfax to Tripoli is a popular run.

**In your own vehicle** It is possible to take one's own vehicle into Libya, and large numbers of German and Italian off-road enthusiasts head down into the Sahara every winter with their latest model four-wheel drives and all-terrain bikes. The practicalities for taking a vehicle into Libya are as follows, though border procedures and paperwork are subject to change.

**Shipping a vehicle from Europe to Tunis** It is not possible to ship a vehicle direct to Tripoli from Europe at the moment, although there has been talk of a new ferry service between Italy and Libya. The current solution is to ship your vehicle to Tunis and drive to to Libya. Numerous ferries operate across the Mediterranean carrying both vehicles and foot passengers. Prices vary according to the season. Main points of departure are Marseille, Genoa, and Palermo, arrival is at Tunis port, La Goulette. In summer, certain ferries run from Toulon and Naples, and there is a hydrofoil from Trapani to Kelibia on the Cap Bon peninsula, southeast of Tunis. In summer, there will be long waits at passport control and customs in the port at La Goulette. Also expect to have considerable difficulty buying a ferry ticket at short notice in Tunis in the summer. The *Compagnie tunisienne de navigation* (CTN) has an office for this purpose on the rue de Yougoslavie, downtown Tunis, behind the French Embassy.

The following companies do the Marseille/Genoa to La Goulette run: *CTN* (Compagnie tunisienne de navigation) and *SNCM* (Société nationale maritime Corse-Méditerranée (61 boulevard des Dames, 13002 Marseille, T4-91563030, 12 rue Godot-de-Mauroy, Paris T1-36679500; c/o *Tirrenia*, Ponte Colombo, Genoa T010 258041; c/o *Southern Ferries*, 179 Piccadilly, London, W1V 9DB, T020-74914968).

In summer, *Linee Lauro* does one sailing a week from Naples to Tunis (Piazza Municipio 88, Naples T081-55133520) while *Tirrenia Navigazione* operates the hydrofoil service (Corso Italia 52/56 Trapani, T0923-27480, c/o Touraffic 53 ave Habib Bourguiba, Tunis, T01-341488). Note that the hydrofoil – which calls in at Pantelleria on the way – is subject to the vagaries of the weather, and crossings may be cancelled early and late in the season.

**Tunis to the Libyan border** European registered vehicles are allowed into Tunisia for up to three months. The driver must present a *carte grise*, a *green card* (insurance certificate), and an international driver's licence. If the vehicle you are driving does not belong to you, Tunisian customs will ask for a legally certified letter from its owner authorizing you to use the vehicle. In practice, it is advisable to come in one's own vehicle. Driving in Tunisia, the highway police seem to accept any European licence when they make spot checks.

Should part of your group prefer to travel by air, *Tunisair* is the Tunisian national carrier, with regular flights from almost all western European capitals. From London, there are flights fom Heathrow to Tunis (*Tunisair*), and Gatwick to Tunis (*GB Airways*). Contact numbers: *Tunisair* in London, T020-77347644, F77346763; in Tunis (reservations) T1-700700. Cheap tickets to Tunisia available through *Tunisia Direct*, 53 London St, Southport, Merseyside, PR9 0TH, T01704-531999, F501533. There are plenty of cheap charter flights to Tunisia.

Leaving the port at La Goulette, you can head straight across the causeway for Tunis. Head directly into the town centre. At the Clock Roundabout, take fourth exit (at 15 minutes to the hour), and after crossing several sets of lights and tram tracks, go right onto a busy stretch of dual carriageway. After 200 m the road veers left after an Agil petrol station. Follow road round to right. A junction follows where you need to take the left hand fork onto the main dual carriageway south out of the city. This eventually becomes the Tunis to M'saken autoroute. There are three toll points. After M'saken, just south of Sousse, (approximately 1¾ hours from the capital), the autoroute ends and the road becomes slow single carriageway. Sfax is 3 hours' drive from Tunis. After Sfax, the road is emptier, although there can be tail-backs because of slow moving lorries. A pleasant place for a stop is Maharès, about 50 km south of Sfax. Gabès, a major port is the next settlement, 406 km from Tunis. After passing through Medenine, the frontier is reached at Ben Gardane, 559 km from Tunis. If you need to phone, there are *taxiphone* (public phone shops) here – look out for the blue and white signs. As you approach the border, there will be a number of checkpoints staffed by the smartly turned out and generally courteous Tunisian highway police (Garde nationale, khaki uniforms).

Note that camping out in the region close to the frontier is not a good idea. The nights are damp and Garde nationale patrols will ask you to move on if they think you are too close to the border.

**Border formalities for vehicles** The border is open 24 hours a day, and can be particularly busy during the month of Ramadhan and in summer. When you reach the Libyan border at Ras Ajdir, avoid joining the queues of Tunisian cars. Park and head to the police cabin with your passport and the green form. The passport will be stamped and the entry date may be written in by hand. Next move onto the next stage, a customs check under a large hangar. There is generally no full search of tourists' vehicles. (Share-taxis may be searched twice or more by separate teams of customs officers). It is not compulsory to declare GPS equipment. Video cameras (but not ordinary cameras) must be declared, however.

Next there is a slightly complicated process (which may change) in order for you to have the right documents to drive in Libya (insurance, carnet de passage and licence plates). First, change two lots of money separately to pay for your insurance and Libyan licence plates. On foot, go to the insurance office in a small building just after the check point on leaving the border zone. The insurance office keeps a bureau de change receipt. Next rent your Libyan license plates for your vehicle (60LD, ie circa $35) in the customs area. When you leave Libya, 50LD will be given back to you when you return the plates and the paperwork. Try to have some wire handy to tie the plates on securely. Next you need a carnet de passage from the *Libyan Automobile Club* office, also in the customs area, which costs 30LD. You give this carnet back when you leave Libya.

Note that there is nothing to tell you what the sequence of formalities actually is. However, everybody is courteous and one does eventually get through. Never, ever even consider shouting. Remember, 'it's not personal, it's just paperwork' and be thankful you don't have to live with this sort of bureaucracy all the time.

**Tourism Card** Officially, any tourist travelling in Libya with a personal vehicle must have a tourism card issued by the appropriate authorities. This card is essential if you are travelling to sites off the beaten track. If you are travelling off-road in the Fezzan, the tourist card will be issued at Sabha (for the Wadi Mathkhandush and the Edeyen Murzuq) or in Ghat for the Jabal Akakus. The General Tourist Office in Sabha on Shari'a Jamal Abd al Nasser under the arcades opposite the main police station issues this card (cost 5LD per head). Group tourist cards, basically a list in Arabic of all those travelling in the vehicle with passport numbers, are now issued. The same office can also register your passport, a procedure compulsory for all visitors to Libya within five days of arrival. In Ghat, the Central Office of the Tadrart Akakus National Park located in the town's main administrative building issues tourist cards (cost 10LD per head). In practice, a tourist agency in the town, of which there are several, can issue a card and register your passport with the authorities.

**By sea from Malta**  The overnight ferry from Valletta in Malta uses modern vessels, usually the *MV Garnata* of 3,672 dwt, with other passenger vessels, the *MV Toletela* of 3,671 dwt and the *MV Garyounis* of 3,423 dwt. Sailing times change monthly and travellers should check with the **General Maritime National Transport Co**, Shari'a al Mqaryef, almost opposite the Caffè del Commercio in Tripoli, T021-3334865 or via **Seamalta** in Malta on T00356-25994212, Tx12101321. Currently the boat departs 1900 from Valletta and costs US $150 one-way, or 1900 from Tripoli from the port in front of *Hotel al Mehari*. From Tripoli to Valletta costs 66LD one-way, 102LD return and the journey takes 12 hours. There are agents for GMNTC in Tunisia, Morocco, Turkey, Italy, Germany, Belgium and Holland.

There can be considerable queues in front of the GMNTC office in Tripoli. It may be better to try one of the travel agencies on Shari'a Mizran. Try *Waha Tourism Services*, T4444552. Foreigners have in the past been required to pay for their tickets in dollars.

# Touching down

## Airport information

**Tripoli International Airport**  Direct flights to Tripoli from abroad resumed in 1999. The main airport in Tripoli is at Ben Ghashir some 24 km from the centre of Tripoli, but some planes come into the smaller Maatiqa local airport just 4 km east of the city, near the beach.

Coming into the main concourse of Tripoli Airport, there is an information box on your right, next to the big departures / arrivals board. Opposite, on the other side of the concourse, are the banks, open 24 hours a day, and the *maktab barid* (post office), from which you can make phone calls. (Give the man at the counter the telephone number written on scrap of paper, he gets number, you take call in cabin indicated and pay after call). The loos are at the far right hand end of the concourse, to the right of the small café.

When you return to this airport to leave the country, departures are to the left hand of the concourse as you come into the building. Internal flights (*rihlat dakhiliya*) check-in is outside and round to the left. Departure tax chits are bought from a desk to the right of the departure gate.

A bus service is available to/from the main hotels and down-town Tripoli (27 km). Service taxis are also on hand for the run into the city, and are probably a better, if more expensive option if you have a lot of luggage (you will probably have to pay between 10LD and 15LD for the ride to a city centre hotel). Various people with private cars hang around just outside the airport hoping to drive arriving people into town. (Given that Libya's state sector salaries are frozen, this is a good way for people to make a bit of extra cash.) Note that taxis in Tripoli centre do not use meters and the general charge is 5LD for any run. Trips to the western suburbs are more expensive (15LD).

At the moment, **internal flights** cannot be reliably reserved from all *Libyan Arab Airlines* offices abroad. At the moment, there are reasonably priced flights (56LD return) to Benghazi (1 hour) and Sabha (75 minutes). In pre-embargo days, there were internal flights to Ghadamès (75 minutes) and Tobruk (1¾ hours). These will no doubt resume in the near future as LAA acquires spare parts and new planes.

**Benghazi Airport**  Benghazi Airport is outside the city at Benina, a short taxi ride away. There is a daily flight in from Tripoli.

## Touching down

**Electricity** *Libyan electricity services use a standard 240V system for power. Take an international adaptor plug as socket sizes can vary. Electric power is available in all but the most isolated of settlements.*
**Hours of business** *Working hours vary from summer 0700-1400 to winter 0800-1300 and 1600-1830 in private offices. Official agencies run on a basic day of 0800-1400, though it is always* better to start communications with official offices and banks before 0900 since they can become busy or officials can be in meetings at later times. Shops open from approximately 0900-1400 and again from 1630-2030, depending on area and trade.
**Official time** *GMT -1.*
**Weights and measures** *Libya uses the metric system.*

Essentials

## Port information

The ferry service from Malta run by the *General National Maritime Travel Company* comes into the port in the early evening, arrival time 1900, weather permitting. The port is located east of the city centre, just below the Hotel Mehari and a five minute taxi ride from the Hotel Kabir and the city centre (cost 5LD) along the main coast road, Shar'ia al Fath. The Dahra bus station is just five minutes taxi ride from the port and the main land transport hub at Bab al Jadid is 15 minutes away by taxi, depending on the traffic, on the far side of the old town. Information on departures and arrivals is hard to obtain, but you could try T021-3334865, the main port operations number.

## Frontier information

There is no tourist information at the Tuniso-Libyan border at Ra's Ajdir. First major settlement is at Zuwara, 60 km from the border. Note that the border crossing from Tunisia near Nalut is closed to tourist traffic at the present time. *Tuniso-Libyan border*

The border between Egypt and Libya at Amsad is 386 km from Tobruk, the nearest major town with decent hotel accommodation. The small coastal village of Al Burdi is 23 km from the border. *Egypto-Libyan border*

## Tourist information

Libya is only now awakening to the potential of tourism. Facilities are few and far between. Local tourist offices exist but are generally under-staffed and ill-informed. They rarely have useful information, maps (but see below) or guides. At present the best sources of help and information are the new private travel agencies springing up across the country. They have enterprise and initiative and understand the needs of foreign travellers. In Tripoli contact the **Libyan Travel and Tourist Co**, T3336222 which has an office on Shari'a Mizran close by the *LAA* head office. Other area offices are mentioned in the regional sections within the book and a full list of Libyan tour agencies is given in the 'Planning your trip' section. These are the best source of information. *See page 50 for a list of maps of Libya*

Be warned that while private travel agencies can provide some information and perhaps transport, some may imply that without the 'official guides' which only they can provide, there may be problems with the police. Certainly this is not true, although some sites may have a *murshid siyahi* (tourist supervisor) who may trail round with groups to ensure that video cameras are not being used and that no photographs are taken of new finds.

Essentials

 *Libyan Months*

Working hard against globalization, Libya has its own calendar, which starts with year zero in 570 AD, the year of the Prophet Mohamed's birth. Making a stab against the hegemony of the Latinate European calendar, Libya also has its own months, which are a combination of the ancient agricultural calendar with some nationalist overtones they are as follows:

**Aynar**  January in traditional calendar
**Al Ma'**  Water

**Al Rabi'a**  Spring
**Al Tayr**  Birds
**Al Nuwwar**  Blossoms
**Al Sayf**  Summer
**Nasser**  After Egyptian president Jamal Abd al Nasser
**Hannibal**  Great Carthaginian general
**Al Fatih**  lit, 'the Opening' as 1st September date of revolution
**Al Temour**  Dates
**Al Harth**  Ploughing
**Kanoun**  Brasero

## Rules, customs and etiquette

**Dress**  Basically, western visitors to Libya should not offend Muslim sentiment by wearing scanty clothing. In any case, outside the main hotels or private transport the need is to be sheltered from the sun, the sand and the glare. Remember that the sun is extremely strong in summer, so cover up to prevent sunstroke and sunburn. (Libya is the country with the world's highest recorded temperature.) It is also a good idea to wear clothes that enable you to keep your key documents on your person.

**Tipping**  Tipping is not widespread in Libya and is only expected by those giving personal services in hotels, cafés and restaurants. The normal rate is 10%. For small services in hotels use quarter and half dinar notes. At the airport only use porters if you are heavily weighed down with luggage then tip at half a dinar per heavy bag. Taxi drivers should, unless there is actually a working meter and then perhaps in any case, give a price before starting the journey. Tips for Libyan drivers are not the rule but will be accepted. Foreign drivers in Libyan employ tend to be more demanding of tips. **Do not** get drawn into bribing officials at any level since it is a sure way of increasing difficulties and possible delay. Although the chain of command is not always very clear in the Libyan bureaucracy, things do eventually get sorted out. Patience is the rule.

**Photography**  The sand deserts, arid rock formations and fine ruins of classical antiquity mean you can leave Libya with photographs worthy of the National Geographic Magazine. (The best light is probably in the autumn). However, there are certain things you must be careful of. Do not photograph military installations, and take care in photographing women: preferably, if you are male, do not photograph women at all. The camera still carries the feeling of intrusion in some areas. Use of video cameras at ancient sites is forbidden.

**Religion**  Sunni Islam is the dominant religion in Libya, although there are Ibadite Berbers in some of the western rural areas. Surprisingly perhaps, historic mosques in Tripoli old town are not off-limits to the non-Muslim outside prayer times. However, always remember that mosques in Libya are first and foremost places of worship, and those who are clearly not of the faith will be intruding if they try to slip in during prayers. Libya, despite its revolutionary credentials, takes religion very seriously.

## Safety

Basically, there is no real security problem in Libya, although travellers report occasional rumours of isolated violence and there are reports that there is a growing drug use problem in Tripoli and Benghazi. The odd brawl causes more noise than damage and walking through the streets is generally safer than in Europe. After dark, and indeed at all times everywhere, foreign nationals in Libya are advised to carry their passports, or at the very least a photocopy of the key pages. Libyans are used to foreigners in their midst but their visitors are almost exclusively male. Foreign women need, therefore, to dress and act sensibly, especially in Tripoli, to avoid arousing undue interest.

A woman travelling alone in Libya must appreciate that this is a totally segregated society, women sit apart and eat apart from, or after, the men. On long-distance buses the driver will organize space for the women. As no one is prepared to speak it can be very lonely. The biggest problem is getting a room in a hotel without a male companion. The bus driver may feel obliged to introduce you to the hotel receptionist thereby giving some respectability, otherwise only the expensive hotels will accept women alone: take this into account when budgeting for a trip. One advantage of a woman being of no significance is the lack of problems at check points and compared with Egypt the lack of hassle. On the whole men do not touch (as in Egypt) or make 'charming' remarks (as in Tunisia). However, eventually the sheer masculinity of society and the feeling of isolation caused by the lack of communication may well makes women travelling on their own find leaving the country a welcome relief.

**Women travelling alone**

In Tripoli, there are a significant number of women sex workers, based in café-cum-telephone shops in the Umar al Mukhtar area. They are generally of North African origin. Unaccompanied younger women with Mediterranean looks may be taken as belonging to this category in certain hotels in Tripoli and Benghazi. (Avoid the Funduq Qasr al Jazira in Benghazi, for example).

A special warning is necessary to travellers tempted to travel to the Tibesti in the southern Fezzan. This zone close to the Aouzou strip was a war zone until recently. Travelling off the road in Aouzou, you risk offending the Libyan security officials – which is fair enough, given the recent conflict. Travel in this area should only be with official knowledge. Any abandoned or scattered armament or ammunition should not be touched. Consult with Tripoli or Sabha-based travel companies on the possibilities of travel in this remote region.

**Warning: travelling in the Fezzan**

# Where to stay

Libya is thinly provided with hotels (Arabic: *funduq*, pl. *fanadiq*), even in the populated northern coastal area. (According to the current figures, the country only has around 15,000 hotel beds). This is mainly a result of years of state control when tourism was discouraged. The slow re-establishment of the private sector is making for a revival in the hotel trade at the middle to lower end of the market. Tripoli, in practice the main business centre, can boast a few top quality international hotels. Despite the prices they charge, these are not really 'A' grade standards. (In terms of standard, they equate with a good European two/three star or a Tunisian three star.) In **Tripoli**, tourist groups tend to be parked in the *Funduq al Mehari*, T021-3334090/94) or the *Al Kabir*, T021-444950/58. Although it does not have such a wide range of facilities, the older *Funduq Al Waddan*, T021-3330041/45 is just as good, and the Maltese-managed *Tripoli Corinthia*, opening in 2001, T021-353233141, F356239732, (check www.corinthia.com) should be better than all of them. *Funduq al Nahar al Sina'i*, Shari'a Tariq, T021-4444948/3334645, F4444690, near the Bourguiba Mosque, Bab Jadid, Tripoli is a good mid-range option, as is the *Funduq Bab al Bahr*, next to Dhat al Imad, T021-3350676/0710, F3350711. In **Benghazi**, the two top hotels used by groups are the *Funduq Tibesti* (T061-9090016/7, F9097160) and the *Funduq Uzu* (T061-95160).

**Hotels**
See inside front cover for breakdown of hotel price codes.
Hotels are marked on maps with a symbol ■

Essentials

Outside the two main cities, standards are entirely variable and the comments made in the relevant sleeping sections of this booko should be read with care. Heading east, the best hotel near **Leptis Magna** is the *Hotel Zliten*, T0521-620121, F620120, which opened in 1998. At **Khums**, the town closest to the ruins, the Italian hotel, *Funduq al Siyahi*, T031-621140 is back in service. The best mid-range option in **Misrata** is the *Funduq Saferous*, T051-629620, on the main square. (Tour groups to Misrata use the *Hotel Goz al Tik*, T051-613333/614614, F610500.) The best hotel to use as a base for touring the **Jabal Akhdar** is the *Funduq Qasr al Bayda*, Al Bayda T084-6334555, F633459. In **Tobruk**, the *Funduq al Masira* (T078-25761) is used by tour groups. In the **Fezzan**, the *Dar Germa*, Germa, T0729-2396 (if line in service) is probably the best of a not very distinguished bunch.

On the coast, there are a number of often well provisioned beach clubs with residential facilities and holiday villages. They are designed for Libyan families, and are occasionally used for official visitors. Holiday villages are booked well in advance in summer and many close out of season. You may be lucky, however, and get a place in summer. In general, the beach clubs are best approached through a Libyan travel agent or a Libyan state organization for sports, youth or scouts. Possibilities in Tripoli include the *Ghornata Holiday Village*, Gargaresh, T4773942 and the *Regata Holiday Village*, Al Ghiran, west of Gargaresh, (generally occupied by foreign company employees, however).

**Youth hostels** Libya has a plenty of youth hostels. They are basic and highly variable in standard. Hostels such as those at Sabratha, Gargaresh (west Tripoli suburbs) and Cyrene (Shahat) are acceptable, others are depressing (down-town Tripoli and Khums) and not really what you would expect of a youth hostel at all. Pressure on housing from large numbers of foreign workers has meant certain hostels being turned into migrant worker hostels (eg at Misrata). In principle, both women and men can stay in youth hostels. In practice, these are men-only institutions. In any case, major towns have hotels cheap enough for women budget travellers.

The locations, numbers of beds and telephone numbers of the better youth hostels are given in regional sections. Opening hours are 0600-1000 and 1400-2300 unless otherwise stated. In all there are 25 youth hostels in Libya. The minimum age is 14. Some hostels have small rooms as well as dormitories. If you do not have a youth hostel card, the overnight charge is 5LD including sheets; breakfast is 0.5LD, lunch 2.5LD and dinner 2LD. The *Libyan Youth Hostel Association* is at 69 Shari'a Amr ibn al As, (aka Shari'a al Wadi) POB 8886, Tripoli, T021-4445171, F3330118, Tx20420 LYHA. (Shari'a Amri ibn al As runs from near Green Square southwards.) They can provide a full, up-to-date list of hostels currently functioning.

Better hostels include the following: *Fjeij Youth Hostel*, Fezzan. T0728-2902. 129 km west of Sabha on the main route to Germa and Ubari, a long, low building visible from the road. Well run, but no a/c. *Gargaresh Youth Hostel*, on right of Gargaresh road, 5 km from centre, next to sea. T021-4776694. *Khums Youth Hostel*, T031-21880. To be avoided really, but you might be stuck for accommodation after a visit to Leptis Magna. Three km from city centre in the *hayy al riyadi* (sport city). Only in real need. *Sabratha Youth Hostel*, T024-24139. Close to the ruins. Big building over on your right near a water tower as you approach the ruins. Hostels at Misrata, Surman and Zawiya are best avoided.

It is also possible to stay in the dormitories of secondary schools with boarding facilities during school holidays. This is best arranged officially in advance, otherwise through the local *baladiya* (municipality offices).

**Camping** For Libyans, camping is not hugely popular, except as a mass venture organized by state institutions. Private camping is less usual except near Mediterranean beaches.

Here there are picnic sites which double as camping areas. They are crowded on public holidays but otherwise little used. Certain areas near to military camps and oil company installations are closed to all camping, so comply with any *mamnu' al dukhoul* (keep out) notices. Do not camp close to private farms or housing without an invitation to do so. Whenever possible seek permission from local farmers or land owners before setting up camp.

In the **Saharan regions** camping is a popular option for tourists travelling with own off-road vehicles or motorcycles or on organized camel or four wheel drive trips. If doing a north-south vehicle crossing of the Hamada al Hamra and the Ubari Erg from Ghadamès down to Serdeles (Awinat), you will have several nights bivouacking out in the desert. Down in the Fezzan, at Serdeles and near Germa, there are camp sites which offer simple bungalow or hut-type accommodation as well as camping. At the sophisticated end of the scale, an Italian travel agency has built an elaborate *Out of Africa*-type permanent campsite in the Wadi Awis area of the Akakus National Park (winter only, bookable only through Italian tour companies operating in Libya). One or two hotels (see *Dar Germa*, Germa) have large compounds which provide safe camping facilities. Also at Germa, the *Erawin* camp site, Zinchekra, T0729-2413, had a good reputation a few years ago. At the present time, there is no official operational campsite in Ghat. The *Winzrik Travel Agency* operates camp sites, Tripoli phone number T021-3611124/5. Jadid Gabraoun, Fezzan, T0728-2726 in the Dawada Lakes at Gabaraoun, and at Ghadamès and Zwila.

# Getting around

## Air

There are daily connecting flights between Benghazi and Sabha, transiting via Tripoli. (In early 2000, return inter-city flights from Tripoli to Benghazi and Tripoli to Sabha both cost 56LD.) Regular flights for Ghadamès, Ghat and Al Bayda have yet to be laid on. Generally people book, as demand for flights is high, given the long road journeys which are the only alternative. In the past, overbooking was common. To book, you have to go to the *LAA* office in person.

*See also individual town's transport sections*

**NB** the UK Foreign Office has advised travellers to Libya **not** to use internal airlines as a lack of spare parts prevents satisfactory safety standards. However, travellers have found the planes (Boeing 737s) in use in Libya to be perfectly satisfactory. The country looks set to purchase a number of Airbuses in the near future.

## Road

The bus service is excellent and extremely cheap. There are good quality a/c inter-city services and more interesting crowded local buses. Buses tend to win out over share taxis on longer routes as they are safer, there being at least three drivers taking turns at the wheel. Starting in Tripoli, buses leave from the bus station in the Al Dahra neighbourhood, 10 minutes' walk from the *Hotel Qasr Libia*, and from the area behind the Bourguiba Mosque off Shari'a Rashid. The main international bus companies have offices here. For major inter-city and international journeys, ie Tripoli to Benghazi, you will need to buy your ticket the day before (cost 13.5LD). Domestic buses from the Al Dahra station are all *General Express Travel Company* (*Sharika 'ama li-naql al sari'*) buses (green and white with squashed bird logo).

**Bus**
*For more information on bus services from Tripoli see page 88*

There are no rental facilities for boats and only a limited few individuals own boats for pleasure purposes. It is occasionally possible to hire small fishing boats with their

**Boat**

owners for an hour or a day. Visits to Farwa Island, for example, near Zuwara are feasible by this means. The opening of new water sport tourist sites for foreign tourists such as at Farwa Island will make boat hire easier in the future.

Car hire    Car hire for self-drive in Libya is not reliable. Vehicles on offer are often old and not in great condition. Whilst they are suitable for use in town, they should not be taken on long journeys without thorough pre-travel checks, especially of tyres and suspension. Among the best hire locations are the main hotels, where agents have desks in the foyer. Hire rates for cars are high and vary quite a bit, especially outside of Tripoli.

Of the car hire offices in the Tripoli, the most reliable seems to be the one at the *Hotel Waddan*, Shari'a Sidi Issa, just off Shari'a al Fath, T021-3330041/2, F4445601. Wajdi Hattab, head of reception, speaks good English and is very helpful here. In late 2000, *Al Waddan Car Hire* was quoting prices of 75LD per day plus 25LD per km. A deposit of between 500 to 1,000LD was required, and you can have a driver for 30LD per day, too. The cars used are new Daewoo Celios. Contact person: Ahmad al Wigha in the Hotel al Waddan. The car hire desk at the *Funduq al Kabir*, Shari'a al Fatah, T021-4445940, F4445959, has no English-speaking staff, which can lead to protracted discussions at the reception desk. They also want to keep your passport when you hire a car, which effectively means you can't travel. The *Hotel Safwa*, Shari'a Baladiya, heading for Garden City, T4448691, F4449062, reception staff speak English and might be able to sort something out (T021-3334422/4592). Ultimately, most main sites can be visited by share taxi, and if you have a number of isolated sites to get to, then the best option will be to take a private car with driver for the day.

Motoring    Great effort has gone into creating the road system in Libya and very few areas of the country are now inaccessible. Petrol stations are fairly well distributed but only on the main through roads. Driving is on the right, as elsewhere in North Africa. Drivers are supposed to wear seat belts and these may be checked at police control points on entering and leaving Tripoli. International driving licences are normally required though, in most cases, easily understood (English or Italian) foreign licences might be accepted. There is no equivalent of the *Automobile Association* services in Libya but passing motorists are normally very helpful.

**Fuel distribution** There are state-owned petrol stations in every town and at most key road junctions. Make sure that you fill up regularly rather than relying on stretching your fuel supply, since occasionally a station might be out of use for lack of deliveries or a cut in the electricity supply. This is especially true in the Saharan regions, where running out of fuel is not merely a nuisance, but can be fatal. Drivers should always be aware of the enormous distances between settlements in southern Libya and have fuel, water, food and clothing reserves at all times.

## Distances from Tripoli

**West of Tripoli**
Zawiya 43 km
Sabratha 67 km
Zuwara 110 km
Ras Ajdir and Tunisian border 170 km
**Jabal Nafusa and Ghadamès**
Gharyan 88 km
Yefren 160 km
Nalut 360 km
Ghadamès 585 km
**East of Tripoli**
Khums 120 km
Zliten 157 km

Misrata 211 km
Sirte 454 km
Ajdabiya 854 km
Benghazi 1,015 km
Al Bayda 1,212 km
Tobruk 1,226 km
**South of Tripoli**
Mizda 175 km
Qaryat 305 km
Sabha 776 km
Ubari 980 km
Ghat 1,340 km

Essentials

**High accident rate**  Driving standards in Libya are truly appalling, and the accident rate is high by international standards, although to be fair, few countries have leapt from the gentle age of the oasis and pack animal to four-lane highways so quickly. In the highways coming into Tripoli, note that drivers cut across the central reservation with seemingly suicidal abandon. You need to drive defensively to ensure that you are not involved in accidents, especially those involving injury to humans, for which you may well be deemed culpable. Drivers can be held in jail for long periods and the settlement of law suits against drivers guilty of dangerous driving leading to death or injury of a third party can be protracted and difficult.

**Warning: off-road travel in the interior**  This should only be undertaken with a full tank and a spare petrol supply. **Never** leave the black top road unless there are two vehicles in the party. A reliable and generous water supply should also be taken. This is especially important in summer when exhaustion and dehydration can be major problems if vehicles need digging out of sand. During winter 2000, a French group undertook a 17 day crossing with camels of the Erg Murzug in southern Libya. On day two, they sighted a lorry out in the sands. The engine had given up; the passengers, immigrants from sub-Saharan Africa, had been perfectly desiccated by the sun and wind as they crouched by the vehicle.

In Tripolitania too, care is needed in off-road driving since there are difficult sand dune areas and other regions where soft sand can quickly bog down anything other than a four-wheel drive vehicle. However, even in far-flung parts of the Jefara Plain, the traffic is quite regular and people are never far away. Note that in the central Jefara there are large areas of military installations which are best avoided.

**Cycling**  Travel by bicycle is a little unusual. Off the main track, cycling is definitely for mountain bikers only, and there are probably some splendid circuits to be developed in the Tripolitanian Jabal. When cycling you should be well marked in brightly coloured clothing. Puncture repair shops exist in the towns alongside the main roads at the point of entry, though they mainly deal with cars and light motorcycles rather than bicycles. In the countryside, repair of cycles will be difficult but the profusion of small pick-up trucks means that it is very easy to get a lift with a cycle into a settlement where you can get your repairs done.

**Hitchhiking**  Libya is a country of great distances, and many people do not have cars. Thus hitching a lift is a perfectly acceptable and acknowledged means of getting from A to B, and locals will pay a small sum for the service. As a foreign traveller, however, you might

Essentials

find yourself being picked up for free out of sheer curiosity. Hitchhiking is not really a viable option in the south, though, since traffic can be very irregular. Carry water and other safety supplies.

Taxis **Within cities** Individual taxis are more expensive, more flexible and generally more comfortable over the same distance than the local bus. The taxis do have meters but on the whole, any taxi ride in Tripoli costs 5LD. A short hop in Benghazi will cost 2.5LD.

**Inter-city** Shared taxis (which are larger) are a very popular mode of travel, and they leave for a particular destination as soon as they are full. In Tripoli, the taxis leave from large stands between Shari'a Umar al Mukhtar and the sea. They ply for hire normally on a shared basis but can be had for an individual or private group with suitable haggling over the price. These taxis can look quite decrepit but generally get to their destination. The seven passenger Peugeot 504 is the most popular long distance car.

When taking a long-distance taxi, first identify a car going to your destination. The seemingly chaotic mass of vehicles at an inter-city taxi station (*agensiya*) has a logic of its own, and people will generally be helpful. Cars for each town are parked in a given area, and drivers holler out their destinations. When you have located a car going to your destination, the driver will take you to the reservations window (*shubak al hijz*), where your name and passport number will be added to the vehicle passenger list. In some towns, this is where you pay. Sometimes there is no *shubak*, and you pay the driver directly. An official share-taxi driver, on a long run, has to have a list of passengers to show at road blocks. (A vehicle is more likely to be stopped if there is a military person on leave travelling in it). In Tripoli, at the main taxi-park just off Shari'a al Rashid, there are a number of small agencies which can organize reservations, including *Sharikat al madina li-safar* and *Sharikat Ibn Batuta*.

**Where to sit in a Peugeot 504?** Travelling long distances in Peugeot 504 share taxis means you have to choose where you sit carefully. If you are tall, the most comfortable place is in the front, although if the run is not too long, there will be two passengers up front next to the driver. The middle seat in the back row is generally deemed the most uncomfortable, while for short people, the back row is probably the best option. If you want a more comfortable ride, another option is to pay for two places. This also gives you the added benefit of your vehicle being able to leave earlier.

Walking In Libya, hiking is to be approached in the knowledge that it may attract curiosity and possibly disbelief. Maps of good scale for walking eg better than 1:50,000 are very rare and thus travel has to be by sight lines, compass work and common sense. In many areas of the Jefara sighting to topographic markers on the Jabal can be used or lines on the taller minarets in the small towns are distinctive guides. Dogs are not a general problem in Tripolitania except near large farms where they are used for security purposes. Carry a stout stick and have some stones for throwing at approaching aggressive dogs – this is how the Libyans deal with this problem.

In the Fezzan, visiting the Jabal Akakus in winter can involve some pleasant walking. Travel agencies in Tripoli and Serdeles (Awinat) can set up trips to the main rock art locations with camels carrying the baggage and, more expensively, with four wheel drive back up to transport tents and camp-fire fuel. Groups can hike between the main sites, all of which are highly accessible, bivouacking out in the wadis at night.

# Keeping in touch

Internet access is spreading slowly in Libya. However, Tripoli now has a small number of public internet access centres. Try the area south of Green Square and Gargaresh district. In the downtown area try the following: *Echonet*, Funduq al Kabir, Shari'a al Baladiya side; *Haïti Internet*, 102 Shari'a Haïti, T3332789; *Libyan Telecom and Technology*, Tower 4, Dhat al Imad, open 0900-14000 and 1630-2030. Cost 4LD/hr. *Main Public Library* in former People's Palace, just south of Maydan al Jaza'ir. The *Ibn Durayham Cyber Club*, (*Nadi Internet*) T4441723, 4441912, is in part of the basement, access from outside of building, right hand side as you face the main entrance. There is a form in Arabic to fill in, passport-size photographs needed. There is a 25LD permanent membership to pay, hourly fee is 7LD. However, if you are staying for a longer time, you can buy blocks of time cheaper. They may let you off without paying the membership if it's just a one-off visit.

**Internet**

Independent Libya inherited a good postal system. *Poste restante* and post office box facilities are available in the main cities at the respective central post offices. The service to and from Europe, costing .350LD for a letter, takes about 7 to 10 days in normal circumstances. Internal mail is cheap, and for in-city letters, fairly fast and efficient. Libya produces a great range of collectors' stamps and there is a philatelic counter in Tripoli main post office on Maydan al Jaza'ir, to the left of the former cathedral.

**Postal services**

Phone calls, both within Libya and abroad are easy to make from one of the numerous public phone shops, referred to as *markaz khadamat baridiya*. (In downtown Tripoli, these can be found under the arcades on the streets south of Green Square and on Shari'a Umar al Mukhtar.) You write your number on a piece of paper and give it to the person at the cash-desk. They put you through and call out the number of the booth where you take your call. You pay afterwards. A short local call gets charged at 1LD. Faxes can be sent from the same call-shops.

**Telephone services**

Full telephone facilities also exist at post offices in all towns and most villages. Internal calls are straightforward, though there can be some waiting time for a public line at the post office. International calls from all points can be difficult since there are restricted numbers of lines. You may be asked to show your passport if making an international call. The Tripoli post office is still quicker than trying international calls from private telephones. In coming international calls, by contrast, get through comparatively easily.

Fax and telex facilities are also available from luxury hotels and the main post offices which are advertised as being open 24 hours a day but suffer from the constraint on telephone lines. Late night automatic fax facilities in private offices are useful if available through friends (or friends of friends).

**Fax and telex**

The Libyan media are powerfully controlled from the centre. This situation is changing only very slowly and the media still reflect the wishes of the régime. This does not make for good entertainment. The programming in Arabic leaves a lot to be desired, and most Libyans watch videos or foreign satellite stations. There is a half-hour local news broadcast in French and English each evening. The radio channel carries programmes of western music from time to time. The State produces daily broadsheets in French and English together with Arabic language newspapers. If you are very lucky, you may find an out-of-date foreign news magazine at one of the street markets near the Dhat al Imad towers in Tripoli.

**Media**

Essentials

*Embassies and consulates in Libya*

Essentials

*In summer 2000, Australia, Canada and South Africa had no embassy in Libya, although Canada had plans to open diplomatic representation in the near future. All addresses are for Tripoli unless stated otherwise. (Tripoli code 021)*

**Austria**
Shari'a Khalid ibn Walid, Dahra
T4443393, 4443379, F4440838.

**Bangladesh**
Hayy Dimashq, opp. Al Khadra Hospital.
T900856, T/F4906616.

**Belgium**
Dhat al Imad, tower 4, floor 5,
T3350115, F3350116, 3350118.
Represents USA interests too.

**China**
Shari'a Monastir, Tariq Gargaresh.
T4832914, 4833193, F4831877.

**Cyprus**
60 Shari'a Al Dhul, Bin Ashur.
T3600499, F3613516.

**Czech Republic**
Shari'a Ahmad Lutif, Bin Ashur.
T3615436, F3615437.

**Finland**
Shari'a al Qadisiya, Ghat Sha'al.
T4831132, F4836065.

**France**
Embassy, Shari'a Bani al Ahmar, Hay al
Andalus (Tariq Gargaresh).
T4778267, 4773807, F4778226.
**Commercial section**, Dhat al Imad, tower
1, 15th floor.
T3350340, F3350339.
**Cultural section**, Shari'a Karatchi, nr
Maydan al Jaza'ir.
T/F3375567.

**Germany**
Shari'a Hassan al Mashari.
T4448552, 3330554, F4448968.

**Greece**
18 Shari'a Jallal Bayar.
T3336689. Consul T3336978, F4441907.

**Hungary**
Shari'a Talha bin Abdallah, Bin Ashur.
T3618218, 3618220.

**India**
16/18 Shari'a Mahmud Shaltut,
Garden City.
T4441835, 4441836, F3337560.

**Italy**
1 Shari'a Wahran, nr Shari'a al Fatih.
T3334131, F3330365.
**Consulate** in Tripoli T333630, F3330365.
**Consulate in Benghazi** T061-9092331 /
9093484, F061-9099806.

**Japan**
Dhat al Imad, tower 4, 13/14 floor.
T3350056, 3350055.

**Korea**
Shari'a Ben Gardane, Gargaresh.
T4831322, 4831323, F4831324.
**Commercial section**, Dhat al Imad,
tower 4, floor 16.
T3350418.

**Malta**
13 Shari'a Ubay ibn Ka'ab.
T3611881/2, F3611180.

# Food and drink

## Food

Although Libya is very short on little boutiquey Parisian restaurants, there are plenty of cheap eateries near the centres of most settlements. Outside Tripoli, restaurant and popular café opening hours are limited. In the evening eat before 2100 or risk finding eateries closed. As Libyans prefer to eat at home, restaurants tend to be for foreigners and travellers. The exception is in the use of cafés in the towns where males, mainly

**Morocco**
*Shari'a Bashir Al-Ibrahimi.*
*T4441346.*

**Netherlands**
*20, Shari'a Jallal Bayar.*
*T4441549, 4441550, F4440386.*

**Nigeria**
*Shari'a Narjis, Hay al Zuhur.*
*T4443036, 4443037, F4443035.*

**Norway**
*Dhat al Imad, tower 4, floor 10.*
*T/F3350348, F3350343.*

**Pakistan**
*Shari'a Huzyfa ibn al Yaman.*
*T360041, 3600411.*

**Philippines**
*Tariq Gargaresh, km 7.*
*T831925.*

**Poland**
*61 Shari'a Bin Ashur.*
*T607619, F3615199.*

**Russia**
*10 Shari'a Mustapha al Kamal.*
*T3330545, 3330546, F46673.*

**South Africa**
*The South African ambassador to Tunisia*
*is accredited to the Jamahiriya as well.*
*7 rue Achtart, Nord-Hilton, Tunis, BP 251,*
*1082 Citi Mahrajane, Tunis.*
*T1-800311, F1-796742,*
*sa@emb-safrica.intl.tn*

**Spain**
*36 Shari'a Amir Abd al Qadir, Garden City.*
*T3336797, 3333275, F4443743.*

**Sweden**
*(Consulate general only)*
*c/o Ericsson Camp, Qasr Bin Ghashir.*
*T022-30800, F022-30805.*

**Switzerland**
*Shari'a Bin Ashur, Badawi Area.*
*T3614118/19, F3614238.*

**Turkey**
*Embassy, Shari'a Zawiya Dahmani, Tripoli.*
*T3337717, F3337686.*
**Consulate in Benghazi**
*Shari'a Wadi Zine, Matruq, villa 5.*
*T061-2230002.*

**United Kingdom**
*(Chancellery in temporary premises near*
*Hotel Mehari)*
*T3343630, F3343634.*
**Commercial section**
*Burj al Fatih,*
*T3351084/5/6, F3351082.*
*britcom@lttnet.net*

**United Nations Development**
**Programme**
*67-71 Shari'a Turkiya.*
*T3330852/3/4.*

**United States of America**
*Represented by Belgium (see above)*

**Venezuela**
*Zanqat Abu Gfifa, Bin Ashur.*
*T3600408/0, F3600407.*

Essentials

younger males, gather to meet their friends and socialize. On Fridays and holidays, Libyans picnic and buy food from beachside stalls. On long cross-country journeys, you will find yourself eating at an *istiraha*, one of the numerous roadside café or snack places. At these sorts of eateries, you can fill up for under 5LD a head.

Tripoli has a handful of star restaurants, among them *Al Shira'a* (The Sail) T021-4775123, on the corniche in Gargaresh. (This is the former *Gazelle*, which was dramatically closed in 1997 when overnight it was decided to knock down its premises, the former Banca d'Italia.) Also in Gargaresh, *Wajda* in the Regata Tourist Village has a good name, T021-4832314. Perhaps the best place to try Libyan

**Good restaurants in Tripoli**

*Alcohol-free Libya*

Libya once upon a time had a wine industry, with the Tarhuna region producing some very palatable red wines. The country also had a brewery, producing the heavy Oea beer but this is all in the past now. Libya is now a dry country, and it is unwise to try to bring any alcohol into the country. As a foreigner abide by Libyan rules. Nevertheless, home-brewing is said to be flourishing. The only safe place for a foreigner to drink, however, is a non-Muslim country's embassy compound – should you happen to be invited.

traditional cooking is *Al Sharqi*, close to the Al Naqa Mosque in the old town. If in the sector close to the embassies, there are a couple of restaurants behind the fomer cathedral. Try *Al Nakhla* for snacks on Shari'a Mqaryif or possibly *Al Snabel* on Shari'a Karatchi, just opposite the French Cultural Centre. On Maydan al Jaza'ir, *Al Murjan*, T3336307, a fish restaurant, has a good name. If on business, there are a number of restaurants in the Dhat al Imad towers or the panoramic restaurant on the top floor of the Burj al Fatah, Tripoli's skyscraper. If entertaining at one of the best places, prices will be of the order 30 – 50LD a head.

**Libyan cuisine** Libyan cooking has a mixture of Mediterranean influences. There is something of an Italian legacy with pastas still being very popular, particularly macaroni. Local dishes include *couscous*, with a bowl of boiled cereal as a base carrying large pieces of mutton and some potatoes. The best traditional forms of *couscous* in Libya use millet as a cereal though now most meals come with wheat. *Bazin* is a Libyan speciality, a hard, paste-like food made of water, salt and barley and is really not recommended except to the gastronomically hardy. *'Aish* is a similar food made from the same ingredients but slightly softer and prepared differently. *Shurba* (Libyan soup) is delicious but highly spiced. For the rest, the range of meals is not quite as sophisticated as in Tunisia, with Italian influences being greatest in Tripolitania and rather more Arab dishes (less macaroni!) in Cyrenaica. Family life is kept separate from public acquaintances, and invitations to eat in a Libyan home are rarely given. As a foreigner, if you are invited into a Libyan home you should feel very favoured.

The offerings in cafés and restaurants are generally very limited and mainly made up of various hot meat, chicken and vegetable stews either with potatoes or macaroni. In the main hotels, cuisine is 'international' and very bland. Good dates and excellent oranges can be bought cheaply. Other seasonal fruit including apricots, figs and almonds are all good value. Also look out for honey at roadside stalls near Khums and in Cyrenaica.

**Drink** It should be emphasized that **alcoholic drinks** are banned in Libya. Offers of illegal liquor should be avoided even in private houses unless its provenance is beyond doubt. Local brews or 'flash' can be of questionable quality. Traditional brews of *bukha* (a form of arak), or *laghmi* (fermented date palm sap) are illegal. Otherwise, Libyans drink local **sodas**, most of which are not always reliable copies of lemonades, colas and orange drinks available worldwide. *Bitar* is a sort of sweet dark soda, faintly like coke, while Pepsi is widely available. Imported **non-alcoholic beer** is also available in bottles and cans, price 1.5-2LD. In season, real **orange juice** can be bought from stalls on the streets. Take a bottle opener since most drinks are in glass bottles. The local tap **water** throughout much of Libya is slightly brackish. For drinking, buy bottled water such as *Moyyah Ben Ghashir* (Ben Ghashir water) or *Moyyah Kufra*. If you want to say "a bottle of water, please", ask for *shisha moyyah, min fadhlik*.

Libyans like their **tea** heavily boiled, thick and sweet, often with mint or nuts in a small glass. If you want English-style infused tea, ask for *shay kis* (tea from a teabag) *bil* *leben* (with milk). Coffees include the inevitable Nescafé (ask for 'Nescafé') with or without milk and Turkish (sometimes called 'Arabic') coffee. With the latter, specify whether you want it *bis-sukar* (sweet) or *bidun sukar* (unsweetened).

# Shopping

Petroleum is Libya's main export, rather than manufactured goods. The country consumes large amounts of consumer goods and little is left of the pre-industrial craft production system. There will be few calls on your wallet for artefacts or craftwork. In southwestern Libya, especially in Ghadamès and Ghat, a few handmade items are available. Touareg leather-work, woven palm frond articles and small rugs have a certain individual charm. Look out too for the elegant metal shapes and geometric designs of Touareg jewellery. Stamp collectors will find a vast range of splendid stamps available from the main post offices in Tripoli. If looking for paintings, try the *House of Art and Legacy*, a gallery in the ground floor of the Hotel al Kabir, Tripoli. There are one or two dusty antique-cum-curio shops on Shari'a M'qaryif in downtown Tripoli with bits of silver, old post cards and African wood carvings.

One possible purchase is traditional men's clothing. For this, you can try the main clothes souk in the old town of Tripoli or a small textiles souk just off the main square at Misrata. Look out for cloaks, waistcoats and the *chechia*, a black tasselled felt cap rather like a fez. Be warned, however, prices are high. A good *abaya* (the men's light-weight traditional cloak) is 150LD, while a *burnous* (thick cloak) will go for 70LD. Misrata is definitely the best place for textiles – look out for the *jard*, the thick, cream, wool cloak worn by older Tripolitanian men, even on the hottest days. Misrata also produces beige, red and black carpets with geometric gazelles and other motifs. The craft souk on the left inside Bab al Manshiya, just off Green Square, also carries a stock of these. In Libya's Saharan towns, you will come across tailors from the Sahel countries, and if staying a few days, might be able to have an African shirt or robe run up for yourself. Good quality African batik cloth (most of it dyed up in the Netherlands!) is on the expensive side, however.

**Traditional clothing**

Film is generally available for 35 mm cameras and most other types of film can also be found in Tripoli. *Kodak* and *Fuji* brands are readily available in the capital. Check the 'sell by date'. For specialist and video film try to bring reserves from outside. Beyond Tripoli and Benghazi film supplies cannot be guaranteed. For buying film in Tripoli, there is a handy shop just behind the Funduq al Kabir on a small, tree-planted square.

**Film**

# Holidays and festivals

Libya, as a Muslim country, observes all the main Islamic festivals as holidays. These are moveable feasts. As the Muslim year is a lunar year, it is shorter than the Gregorian solar year. Hence, it moves forward by 11 days every year. Ramadhan for the year 2000 will be mainly in December, in 2001 it will move forward to start in mid-November. Fridays are days of rest.

In addition there are several national holidays
**2 March** Declaration of the Jamahiriya.
**11 June** Evacuation of foreign military bases.
**26 October** Commemoration of the fight for independence.
**1 September** Anniversary of the 1969 Revolution.

Essentials

 ## Why fast for a month?

The ninth month of the Islamic calendar, Ramadhan is the month of fasting (siyam), the fourth pillar of Islam. Ramadhan, the holiest month, was when the Qur'an was revealed to Mohamed (and to the whole universe) and fasting during this time is compulsory for all Muslims. For a whole lunar month, from daybreak to sundown, they neither eat nor drink and sexual abstinence is strictly observed. The day's fasting ends with iftar, generally a great family occasion when wives and mothers do their best to produce splendid meals. Not everybody can go without eating and drinking all day, and Islam defines categories exempt from the ritual fast: pregnant and menstruating women, children and travellers, the severely ill, the very old, and the mad. However, if you are able to fast and fail for any reason, then you have to try to make up the lost day's fasting outside Ramadhan. At the end of the month, the fast is concluded by the zakat al fitr, a sort of personal alms tax to compensate for any minor deviations from the fast. The zakat is set every year by the highest religious authority in the country. Defined as a certain number of sa'a (cubic measures) of wheat, for example, or the equivalent cost in money, the zakat must be given to the poor before the great prayers marking the end of Ramadhan.

During Ramadhan, the rhythm of daily life completely changes in Libya – and indeed in all Muslim communities. In Libya, the fast is very strictly observed in public. All cafés and restaurants are closed during the day. (In neighbouring Tunisia many cafés remain discretely open, and the fast is generally much less strictly

observed in Egypt). For those finding the fast difficult, there are medical programmes on the television vaunting the merits of Ramadhan. The month is particularly hard on nicotine and caffeine addicts who have to start the day without their fix (and deal with appalling headaches and mood-swings). As evening approaches, an expectant quiet descends on towns. Long distance inter-city buses pull into istiraha restaurants for passengers to break the fast. Televisions are on in all households and eateries, broadcasting Qur'anic recitation; all are waiting for the evening call to prayer indicating that eating can begin.

But why have a whole month's fasting? The idea is for all Muslims to be aware of what life is like for the poor. Ramadhan evenings are supposed to be spent in prayer and meditation, in tajahud (spiritual endeavour). The mosques resound with tarawih, special night-time prayer vigils, held after the last prayer of the evening. However, modern Ramadhan tends to be a time when city people overeat. The nights of Ramadhan are an occasion for families to go out together – and do some serious shopping. The reversal of night and day seems to stimulate a consumer frenzy, and the end of the month has become a sort of 'Muslim Christmas'. At 'Id al saghir, the festival marking the month's end, kids are taken round to see friends and relatives, all togged out in brand new clothes. On Green Square in Tripoli, the tradition is to have your kids photographed in all their finery. Enterprizing individuals bring up shiny motorcycles, horses, thrones and Disney-type figures for the souvenir photo-call.

Note also that other holidays may be declared. Unpredictably, the frontier can be closed for Libyans during Christmas and the New Year.

There are now a couple of festivals for the tourist industry. Ghadamès has its date festival annually in mid-October, while Ghat has a sort of Touareg festival, generally held in late December.

# Sport

Libya is not a country with a great international sporting profile. Surprisingly perhaps, the Green Revolution has never set great store on sporting achievement. Perhaps mass-spectator sports have been discouraged because they could provide opportunities for demonstrations against the régime. Nevertheless, Libyan men are very keen on football, and thanks to satellite television enthusiastically keep up with the ups and downs of European and South American football teams. The Italian league in particular is followed with much gusto. An area in which Libya excels is horse-riding, and Libyan horsemen are a regular feature of the Festival of the Desert held in Douz in southwest Tunisia every Christmas and New Year.

# Health

There are many well qualified doctors in Libya, practically all of whom speak some English. Nevertheless, as many of Libya's doctors were trained in the former Eastern Block, their English may not be very fluent. Medical care is free to all Libyans, although the availability of medical care does diminish somewhat away from big cities. However, at least you can be reasonably sure that local practitioners have a lot of experience with the particular diseases of their region. The local pharmacy (*saydaliya* in Arabic) should be able to provide you with names of recommended doctors and primary care facilities. Hopefully, you will not need any more medical care than this. Note, however, that for serious illnesses Libyans transfer to private hospitals (*polycliniques*) in neighbouring Tunisia which offer a more sophisticated service, the cost of which is generally covered by the Libyan State. Outside the major towns, availability of pharmaceutical products can be patchy. This used to be blamed on the embargo. It was (and is) more likely the result of a badly managed distribution system. Thus if you have special needs, make sure you bring an adequate stock of your medication with you.

If you are a long way from medical help, a certain amount of self medication may be necessary and you will find that many of the drugs that are available have familiar names. However, always check the date stamping and buy from reputable pharmacists because the shelf life of some items, especially vaccines and antibiotics is markedly reduced in hot conditions.

With the following precautions and advice you should keep as healthy as usual. Make local enquiries about health risks if you are apprehensive.

## Before you go

Take out medical insurance. You should have a dental check up, get spare glasses and, if you suffer from a long-standing condition such as diabetes, high blood pressure, heart/lung disease or a nervous disorder, arrange for a check up with your doctor who can at the same time provide you with a letter explaining details of your disability. Check the current practice for malaria prevention. At present, there is no malaria risk in Libya.

## Medicines and what to take

General items: Antiseptic ointment; Condoms; Contact lens solution; Contraceptive pills; Disposable needles (?); Foot powder; Insect repellant / anti-mosquito device; Sachets of rehydration salts; Plasters; Sun cream and after-sun cream; Small scissors; Tampons; Travel sickness tablets; Water sterilizing tablets.

*A little Arabic for medical emergencies*

*Chemist:* al saydaliya
*Doctor:* al tabib, al duktour
*Hospital:* al mustashfa
*Clinic:* al mustawsaf
*Broken:* mekessar
*Blood:* dumm
*It hurts a lot:* youja' halba / ktir
*I vomit all the time:* nerudd dayma
*I have diarrhoea:* kirshi yijri
*A lot:* halba *(Tripoli)*; ktir *(Cyrenaica)*

*A little:* shweyya
*I have something in my eye / my foot:* 1ndi haja fi aynaya / saqaya
*I need to see a doctor:* yilzimni nshouf duktour
*Is there a clinic in this town?:* fi mustawsaf fi-l-bled?
*Take me to the nearest doctor (pharmacy) please:* hizzni aqrab duktour (saydaliya) min fadhlik

Medicines: Against diarrhoea: Immodium or Lomotil tablets, and an anti-bacterial like Intétrix (available in Tunisia); Headache tablets; Inhalers (asthmatics); Malaria tablets (if considering travelling down into Chad or Niger); Powder or gel for gastric pains (Actapulgite or Polysilane).

**Inoculations**   Smallpox vaccination is no longer required. Neither is cholera vaccination, and there have been no outbreaks of the disease for years. Yellow fever vaccination is not required for either Libya (or Tunisia if you are coming in by land). Cholera vaccine is not effective which is the main reason for not recommending it.

The following vaccinations are recommended:
*Typhoid (monovalent)*: one dose followed by a booster in 1 month's time. Immunity from this course lasts 2-3 years. Other injectable types are now becoming available as are oral preparations marketed in some countries.
*Poliomyelitis*: this is a live vaccine, generally given orally and the full course consists of three doses with a booster in tropical regions every 10 years.
*Tetanus*: one dose should be given with a booster at 6 weeks and another at 6 months and 10 yearly boosters thereafter are recommended.
*Hepatitis A and B*: see below.

**Children** should, in addition, be properly protected against diphtheria, whooping cough, mumps and measles. Teenage girls, if they have not yet had the disease, should be given rubella (German measles) vaccination. Consult your doctor for advice on BCG inoculation against tuberculosis. The disease is still common in the region. North Africa lies mainly outside the meningitis belt and the disease is probably no more common than at home so vaccination is not indicated except during an epidemic.

## Staying healthy

**Desert heat**   Full acclimatization to high temperatures takes about two weeks and during this
**& cold**   period it is normal to feel a degree of apathy, especially if the relative humidity is high. Drink plenty of water (up to 15 litres a day are required when working physically hard in hot, dry conditions), use salt on your food and avoid extreme exertion. Tepid showers are more cooling than hot or cold ones. Large hats do not cool you down but they do prevent sunburn. Remember that, especially in the mountains, there can be a large and sudden drop in temperature between sun and shade and between night and day so dress accordingly. Clear desert nights can prove astoundingly cold with a rapid drop in temperature once the sun has gone down. Loose fitting cotton clothes are still the best for hot weather; warm jackets and woollens are essential after dark in some desert areas, and especially at high altitude.

These can be a great nuisance, although the serious diseases such as malaria and yellow fever that insects can carry, are not found in Libya. When camping out, the best way of keeping insects away at night is to sleep off the ground with a mosquito net and to burn mosquito coils containing Pyrethrum. Aerosol sprays or a 'flit' gun may be effective as are those little plug-in anti-mosquito devices. (Check that you have enough 'mats' for your stay, and note that Libya uses a range of plug fittings. Do you have an adaptor?).

You can use personal insect repellent, the best of which contain a high concentration of Diethyltoluamide. Liquid is best for arms and face (take care around eyes and make sure you do not dissolve the plastic of your spectacles). Aerosol spray on clothes and ankles deters mites and ticks. Liquid DET suspended in water can be used to impregnate cotton clothes and mosquito nets. Wide mesh mosquito nets are now available impregnated with an insecticide called *Permethrin* and are generally more effective, lighter to carry and more comfortable to sleep in. If you are bitten, itching may be relieved by cool baths and anti-histamine tablets (but take care with alcohol or when driving), corticosteroid creams (again take great care with this and never use if there is any hint of sepsis) or by judicious scratching. Calamine lotion and cream have limited effectiveness and anti-histamine creams have a tendency to cause skin allergies and are therefore not generally recommended. Bites which become infected (commonly in dirty and dusty places) should be treated with a local antiseptic or antibiotic cream such as Cetrimide, as should infected scratches.

Skin infestations with body lice, crabs and scabies are unfortunately easy to pick up, especially if you are staying in the cheap hotels. (Such establishments can be pretty grubby in Libya). Use Gamma benzene hexachloride for lice and Benzyl benzoate for scabies. Crotamiton cream (Eurax) alleviates itching and also kills a number of skin parasites. Malathion lotion 5% is good for lice but avoid the highly toxic full strength Malathion used as an agricultural insecticide.

Practically nobody escapes this one so be prepared for it. Most of the time intestinal upsets are due to the unsanitary preparation of food. Do not eat uncooked fish or vegetables or meat, fruit with the skin on (always peel your fruit yourself) or food that is exposed to flies. Eating large quantities of summer fruit such as grapes is not a good idea. Tap water is generally safe in large towns in Libya but drink bottled water (*moya Kufra* or *moya Ben Gashir* are the two main brands) to be on the safe side – it is cheap and can save much misery. If your hotel has a central hot water supply this is safe to drink after cooling. Ice for drinks should be made from boiled water but rarely is, so stand your glass on the ice cubes, instead of putting them in the drink.

If travelling out in the desert, you will probably be carrying most of your water with you from base. In any case, dirty water should first be strained through a filter bag (available from camping shops) and then boiled or treated. Bringing the water to a rolling boil at sea level is sufficient but at high altitude you have to boil the water for longer to ensure that all the microbes are killed. Various sterilizing methods can be used and there are proprietary preparations containing chlorine or iodine compounds. Pasteurised or heat treated milk is now widely available as is ice cream and yoghurt produced by the same methods. Un-pasteurised milk products including cheese and yoghurt are sources of tuberculosis, brucellosis, listeria and food poisoning germs. You can render fresh milk safe by heating it to 62°C for 30 mins followed by rapid cooling or by boiling it. Matured or processed cheeses are safer than fresh varieties.

**Diarrhoea** is usually the result of food poisoning, occasionally from contaminated water (including seawater when swimming near sewage outfalls). There are various causes – viruses, bacteria, protozoa (like amoeba) salmonella and cholera organisms. Diarrhoea may take one of several forms, coming on very suddenly or rather slowly. It may be accompanied by vomiting or by severe abdominal pain and the passage of blood or mucus when it is called dysentery. Although your intestinal flora will adapt as you travel in Libya, you are at risk of getting diarrhoea when you eat poorly cooked food. Note that diarrhoea can also spead quickly within tour groups.

**Diagnosis and treatment** All kinds of diarrhoea, whether or not accompanied by vomiting, respond favourably to the replacement of water and salts taken as frequent small sips of some kind of re-hydration solution. There are proprietary preparations consisting of sachets of powder which you dissolve in water or you can make your own by adding half a teaspoonful of salt (3.5 grams) and four tablespoonfuls of sugar (40 grams) to a litre of boiled water. If you can time the onset of diarrhoea to the minute, then it is probably **viral or bacterial**. The treatment, in addition to re-hydration, is Ciprofloxacin 500 mgs every 12 hours (but note that one day's treatment of this is as good as five – worth knowing, in view of its cost). The drug is now widely available as are various similar ones.

If the diarrhoea has come on slowly or intermittently, then it is more likely to be **protozoal**, ie caused by amoeba or giardia, and so antibiotics will have no effect. These cases are best treated by a doctor, as is any outbreak of diarrhoea continuing for more than three days. If there are severe stomach cramps, the following drugs may help: Loperamide (Imodium, Arret) and Diphenoxylate with Atropine (Lomotil).

Giving plenty of mineral water to drink plus rehydration salts can be, especially in children, a lifesaving technique. As there is some evidence that alcohol and milk might prolong diarrhoea, they should probably be avoided during and immediately after an attack. There are ways of preventing travellers' diarrhoea for short periods of time when visiting these countries by taking antibiotics but these are ineffective against viruses and, to some extent, against protozoa, so this technique should not be used other than in exceptional circumstances. Some preventives such as Enterovioform can have serious side effects if taken for long periods.

Diarrhoea can lead to your having a very sore and fragile-feeling stomach. Here powders taken mixed with mineral water ('stomach liners') may be helpful. A pharmacy may sell you Actapulgite powder (Laboratoires Beaufour), or an equivalent, which can be very effective in calming gastric pains and diarrhoea. Dimeticone, commercialized by *Laboratoires Upsa* as Polysilane Gel, is another effective gastric calmer.

Basically, to **avoid** diarrhoea always be careful what you drink - go for mineral water and fizzy drinks. Beware of unwashed fruit. If you are going to be travelling in remote areas, carry Lomotil and Immodium, something for stomach pains (Actapulgite or equivalent) and an anti-bacterial drug like Intétrix, available at pharmacies throughout Tunisia and Libya. Self-medication is not a good thing, but sometimes a necessity. If symptoms persist, see a doctor as quickly as possible when you get to a town.

**Mental pressures** The mental pressures facing the traveller in Libya are rather different to those experienced by travellers in other North African countries with a long tradition of tourism. Most travellers to Libya have to go in organised groups, which limits time for contact with the locals to a minimum. However, if travelling alone in Libya for a long period of time, the lack of hassle, compared with other North African countries, is refreshing – at first. But eventually the lack of international newspapers and contact begins to get oppressive. And one becomes aware that people have to watch what they say very carefully. One should never put anyone, either Libyan or foreigner, on the spot by mentioning politics in public. The results could be disastrous for your stay, and most definitely worse for the person who has to stay in Libya. Few western women travel alone in Libya at the moment. For them, it ultimately becomes oppressive to be travelling in a land where women have such a limited public presence.

● ● ● ● ● ● ● ● ● ● ● ● ● ● ● ● ● ● ● ● ● ● ● ● ● ● ● ● ● ● ● ● ● ● ● ● ● ● ● ● ● ●

### *Infected blood products in Libya?*

*Late 1999 saw a number of Bulgarian medical personnel who were employed in Libya accused of deliberately infecting Libyans with HIV. What actually happened is unclear, and the people accused were held for a long period of time without trial. It may be that Libya had acquired infected blood products*

*from a foreign source and that these products had been unwittingly used to treat patients in the Libyan health care system. The truth of the matter may never be known. If travelling in a group to Libya, it may be as well to make sure that at least one of the party has a stock of clean disposable needles.*

● ● ● ● ● ● ● ● ● ● ● ● ● ● ● ● ● ● ● ● ● ● ● ● ● ● ● ● ● ● ● ● ● ● ● ● ● ● ● ● ● ●

Being in a place where your first language is not spoken for a prolonged stay can also be a trying experience. Remember, they're not trying to be unhelpful, it may just be too difficult for them to make sense of your approximate Arabic. Whatever you may think, many people, even those with many years of schooling, have had very little English in Libya. You may communicate better in English or broken French with African immigrants who, despite their lowly jobs, are often very well educated.

## Other risks and more serious diseases

This is common throughout North Africa, and Libya has a large population of low-income migrants from sub-Saharan Africa, some of whom may be in poor health and therefore carrying infectious hepatitis. Travelling on an air-conditioned bus you are at little risk of hepatitis, however. The disease seems to be frequently caught by travellers probably because, coming from countries with higher standards of hygiene, they have not contracted the disease in childhood and are therefore not immune like the majority of adults in developing countries. The main symptoms are stomach pains, lack of appetite, nausea, lassitude and yellowness of the eyes and skin.

*Infectious hepatitis (jaundice)*

Medically speaking there are two types: the less serious, but more common, is **hepatitis A** for which the best protection is careful preparation of food, the avoidance of contaminated drinking water and scrupulous attention to toilet hygiene. Human normal immunoglobulin (gammaglobulin) confers considerable protection against the disease and is particularly useful in epidemics. It should be obtained from a reputable source and is certainly recommended for travellers who intend to live rough. The injection should be given as close as possible to your departure and, as the dose depends on the likely time you are to spend in potentially infected areas, the manufacturer's instructions should be followed. A new vaccination against hepatitis A is now generally available and probably provides much better immunity for 10 years but is more expensive, being three separate injections.

The other, more serious version is **hepatitis B** which is acquired as a sexually transmitted disease, from a blood transfusion or injection with an unclean needle or possibly by insect bites. The symptoms are the same as hepatitis A but the incubation period is much longer.

You may have had jaundice before or you may have had hepatitis of either type before without becoming jaundiced, in which case it is possible that you could be immune to either hepatitis A or B. This immunity can be tested for before you travel. If you are not immune to hepatitis B already, a vaccine is available (three shots over 6 months) and if you are not immune to hepatitis A already then you should consider vaccination (or gamma globulin if you are not going to be exposed for long).

This is not a significant risk in Libya. Protection against meningococcal meningitis A and C is conferred by a vaccine which is freely available.

*Meningitis*

Essentials

AIDS In North Africa AIDS is probably less common than in most of Europe and North America but is presumably increasing in its incidence, though not as rapidly as in Sub-Saharan Africa, South America or Southeast Asia. Having said that, the spread of the disease has not been well documented in the North African region; the real picture is unclear, especially in Libya, where cities such as Tripoli and Benghazi have a floating population of female sex workers from the other North African countries. The disease is possibly still mainly confined to the well known high risk sections of the population ie intravenous drug users, prostitutes, children of infected mothers and possibly gay men. Whether or not heterosexual transmission outside these groups is common or not, the main risk to travellers is from casual sex. The same precautions should be taken as when dealing with any sexually transmitted disease.

The AIDS virus (HIV) can be passed via unsterile needles which have been previously used to inject an HIV positive patient but the risk of this is very small indeed in normal circumstances. It would, however, be sensible to check that needles have been properly sterilized or disposable needles used. Check whether the medical centre you are being treated at is using disposable needles anyway. The chance of picking up hepatitis B in this way is much more of a danger. The trouble with carrying disposable needles oneself is that customs officials may find them suspicious. The risk of receiving a blood transfusion with blood infected with the HIV virus is greater than from dirty needles because of the amount of fluid exchanged. Supplies of blood for transfusion are now largely screened for HIV in all reputable hospitals so the risk ought to be very small indeed. Catching the AIDS virus does not necessarily produce an illness in itself; the only way to be sure if you feel you have been put at risk is to have a blood test for HIV antibodies on your return home.

Snake bites & other stings If you are unlucky enough to be bitten by a venomous snake, spider, scorpion, lizard, centipede or sea creature try (within limits) to catch the animal for identification. The reactions to be expected are fright, swelling, pain and bruising around the bite, soreness of the regional lymph glands, nausea, vomiting and fever. If in addition any of the following symptoms occur, get the victim to a doctor without delay: numbness, tingling of the face, muscular spasms, convulsions, shortness of breath or haemorrhage. Commercial snake bite or scorpion sting kits may be available but are only useful for the specific type of snake or scorpion for which they are designed. The serum has to be given intravenously, so is not much good unless you have had some practice in making injections into veins. If the bite is on a limb, immobilize it with a splint and apply a tight bandage between the bite and body, releasing it for 90 secs every 15 mins. Reassurance of the bitten person is very important because death by snake bite is in fact very rare. Do not slash the bite area and try and suck out the poison because this kind of heroism does more harm than good. Hospitals usually hold stocks of snake bite serum. The best precaution against snake is to not walk in snake territory with bare feet, sandals or shorts and watch where you sit. Snakes on the whole are more frightened of large galumphing animals like humans, and will tend to disappear as they approach.

Avoid spiders and scorpions by keeping your bed away from the wall and look under lavatory seats and inside your shoes in the morning. In the rare event of being bitten, consult a doctor.

Beach nasties If swimming in an area where there are poisonous fish such as stone or scorpion fish (also called by a variety of local names) or sea urchins (*retzi*) on rocky coasts, tread carefully or wear plimsolls or jellyshoes. The sting of such fish is intensely painful and this can be helped by immersing the stung part in water as hot as you can bear for as long as it remains painful. This is not always very practical (take care not to scald yourself) but it does work. Otherwise head for a GP to get a painkilling shot. In areas of the Tripolitanian coastline where the weaver fish hides in the sand in shallow water, just its spine protruding for you to step on, local pharmacies should stock the relevant painkillers.

The burning power of the sun in Libya is phenomenal, especially in the desert. Strong sunlight may damage exposed skin. In the short term, burning can be severe, and even dangerous to children and some adults. There may also be a long term risk of skin cancer and certain individuals, if exposure is prolonged or repeated, are potentially at risk. Those with very fair skin, especially with blonde or red hair and those who hardly tan should be particularly careful about protecting themselves. Babies under 6 months should be kept out of the sun as much as possible. Try to avoid the beach between 1100 and 1500 when the burning power of the sun is at its height.

Sunburn and heat stroke

Normal temperate zone suntan lotions (protection factor up to seven) are not much good. You need to use the types designed specifically for the tropics or for mountaineers or skiers with an SPF, sun protection factor (against UVA) of between 7 and 15. Certain creams also protect against UVB and you should use these if you have a skin prone to burning. Glare from the sun can cause conjunctivitis so wear sunglasses, especially on the beach.

Protective clothing including a light weight hat is a useful precaution and essential for children. The closely knitted fabric made from 80% polymide and 20% elastane will help protect a child's skin from damage. Be sure to apply sun lotion every one to two hours especially after swimming and towel drying. Sprays and roll-on sun screen products make putting lotion on more fun and are easier for children to use.

There are several varieties of heat stroke. The most common cause is severe dehydration. Avoid this by drinking lots of non-alcoholic fluid and adding some salt if you wish.

**Athletes foot** and other fungal infections are best treated by exposure to sunshine and a proprietary preparation such as Tolnaftate.

Other afflictions

**Intestinal worms** do occur in unsanitary areas and the more serious ones, such as hook-worm, can be contracted by walking bare foot on infested earth or beaches.

**Leishmaniasis** is a parasitic disease present in all countries around the Mediterranean, especially in rural areas. It is transmitted by sandflies that tend to bite at dawn and dusk. The cutaneous form causes a crusty sore or ulcer that persists for several months. The rare, but more serious, visceral form causes a persistent fever. Protect against sandfly bites by wearing impregnated long trousers and a long sleeved shirt, and DET on exposed skin. Sleep under and impregnated bed net. Seek advice for any persistent skin lesion or nasal symptom.

**Prickly heat** is a common itchy rash avoided by frequent washing and by wearing loose clothing. It can be helped by the regular use of talcum powder to allow the skin to dry thoroughly after washing.

**Rabies** is endemic throughout Libya. Remote rural communities invariably seem to have savage dogs in their vicinity. Their main role is to guard sheep and goats. However, they can go beserk as an outsider walks by. If you are bitten by a domestic animal, try to see a doctor at once. Treatment with human diploid vaccine is now extremely effective and worth seeking out if the likelihood of having contracted rabies is high. A course of anti-rabies vaccine might be a good idea before you go. In any case, steer clear of rough-looking dogs.

## When you get home

If you have had attacks of diarrhoea whilst away, it is worth having a stool specimen tested in case you have picked up amoebic dysentery. If you have been living rough, a blood test may be worthwhile to detect worms and other parasites.

Essentials

# Further reading

**Bookshops & bibliographies**
*See also Selective Bibliography at the end of the book*

There is a dearth of good material on Libya in English – or other languages for that matter. In the UK, you could call in at the *Librairie du Maghreb*, in central London, 45 Burton St, T020-73881840. In Tripoli, you should look in at the *Fergiani Bookshop*, on Shari'a 1st September (aka Awwal Sabtambar). Here you can obtain a useful Arabic/English *Atlas of Libya*. Fergiani also reissues early 20th-century travel writing on North Africa in English under the Darf Publishers imprint. A starting point for researching material on Libya is **RI Lawless'** 1987 excellent annotated bibliography, *Libya*, Oxford: Clio Press. On historical background, see **RB St John's** *Historical Dictionary of Libya* (1991, Methuen, NJ: Scarecrow Press). There are some interesting travel books from the 1950s which might be found by digging around in second-hand bookshops.

**Other sources of information**

The *Society of Libyan Studies*, c/o Institute for Archaeology, 31-34, Gordon Square, London WC1H 0PY is a 'British institute abroad', mainly involved in archaeological research. The society's journal is edited by Dr Andrew Wilson, Magdalen College, Oxford, OX1 4AU. *Africa Intelligence*, 142 rue Montmartre, F75002 Paris, T1-44882610, F44882615 provides up-to-date economic and political information on North Africa.

**Research centres**

It is currently difficult for scholars other than archaeologists to get permission to do research in Libya. In Tripoli, a visit to the library-cum-research centre located in a converted former Jewish school, the Dar Ahmad Nayib al Ansari, Shari'a al Akwash, Old Town, will prove useful. The building houses important archives on the history of Tripoli, including books, papers, theses, and sound recordings. (Open 0900 to 1300, 1600 to 1900, closed Fridays, entrance free). The *Organisation and Administrative Project for Tripoli Old Town*, housed in the Old Tobacco Factory near the Bab Jedid taxi station might by of help, PO Box 10332 Tripoli, T021-36725, F31069. Also you could visit the *Markaz al Jihad*, a research centre just off Shari'a Rashid, behind the Central Food Market, in the Shari'a Umar al Makhtar direction.

In Tunis there are three research centres all of which have some Libya-related material, namely the CEMAT, the IBLA and the IRMC. Part of the American Institute of Maghreb Studies, the *CEMAT (Centre d'études maghrébines à Tunis)* on impasse Manubréa, rue d'Angleterre, near place Barcelone, T1-246219, (dir. Jean Jeffers-Mrad), has a full collection of all the MA and PhD theses on North African subjects produced in English in Canadian, USA and UK universities over the last 30 or so years. There are numerous dissertations on Libya in the collection. The *IBLA (Institut de belles lettres arabes)* T1-560933, down an alley behind the Haoua Mosque (Jami'a al Haoua) on place du Leader, Médina of Tunis, has a small research library (David Bond/Jean Fontaine). Try also the *IRMC (Institut de recherche sur le Maghreb contemporain)*, at 20, rue Mohamed Ali Tahar, Mutuelleville, 1002 Tunis, T1-796722, F797376, This French-funded centre has a large collection of North Africa related material and produces a researchers' newsletter.

**Maps**

There are no useful maps of Libya actually available on sale in the bookshops of Tripoli. In London, *Stanfords* bookshop, 12-14 Long Acre, London, WC2E 9LP, T020-72403611, should have a copy of the *GEO Projects* Map of the Socialist People's Libyan Arab Jamahiriya, scale 1: 3,500,000, also available from GEO Projects, PO Box 113, 5294 Beirut, T00961-1344236, F353000. In fact, the most detailed maps of Libya available were produced by the Russians in the 1970s on 1:200,000 and 1:500,000 scale. Unfortunately, they are labelled in the Cyrillic script only. Sheets can be purchased from *Därr Expeditionsservice Gmbh*, Theresien Strasse 66, Germany D800333, T0049-89-282032, F282525. For those in France, the Soviet maps can be consulted at the *Institut géographique national*, 2 ave Pasteur, 94160 St Mandé (just east of Paris near the Bois de Vincennes), T1-43988000. Otherwise, the best available maps are the *Michelin Carte routière et touristique*, Afrique du Nord et de l'Ouest, sheet 953 (1/4,000,000 scale) and *Cartographia's Libya* (1,200,000 scale). Other larger scale maps are hard to find, although may be available, with patience, from the Secretariat for Planning.

**Books on ancient sites**

Look out for the following: **DEL Hayes'** *The Antiquities of Tripolitania*, (Tripoli: Dept of Antiquities, 1981). If visiting the ancient sites of Cyrenaica, take **R Goodchild**, *Cyrène and Apollonia* (Tripoli: Dept of Antiquities, 1963). Dar Fergiani publishes its own guide to Leptis Magna.

**Anthropology**

**EE Evans-Pritchard**, *The Sanusi of Cyrenaica,* (Oxford: Clarendon Press, 1949). In Tunisia, interesting ethnographic and historical material can be found in back numbers of the journal produced by the *Institut de Belles Lettres Arabes* (IBLA), place du Leader, Tunis-Médina.

**Cities**

**P Ward**, *Tripoli, Portrait of a City* (Oleander Press, 1969). On Tripoli, Francophones have **JC Zeltner**, *Tripoli, carrefour de l'Europe*, (Paris: L'Harmattan, 1992). On Italian colonial planning and architecture, look out for *Colonial Constructions: architecture, cities and Italian imperialism* by **M Fuller**, (London: Routledge-Spon, forthcoming).

**Desert**

**C Scott**, *Sahara Overland* (Hindhead: Trailblazer, 2000). A must for really serious desert addicts. Off-piste routes into the Akakus and beyond. Those who read French have the annual *Guide bleu du Sahara*, (Paris: Hachette).

**Fiction**

**Muammar Gadhafi**, *The Village … the Village, the Earth … the Earth and the Suicide of the Astronaut*, (Sirte: Dar al Jamahiriya, 1996). Short stories by the Raybanned supremo himself. Available chez Fergiani in Tripoli.

**History**

*JM Abun-Nasr*, *A History of the Maghrib in the Islamic Period,* (Cambridge: CUP, 1987, third edition). Not an easy read, but undoubtedly the fullest account in English of northwest African history from seventh century AD on. **L Anderson**, *The State and Social Transformation in Tunisia and Libya, 1830-1980,* (Princeton, NJ: Princeton University Press, 1986). **CR Pennell**, *Piracy and Diplomacy in Seventeenth Century North Africa,* (London: Associated University Press, 1989). High-level academic work on piracy in early modern Tripoli. **E Rossi**, *Storia di Tripoli e della Tripolitania dalla conquista araba all 1911*, (Roma: Istituto per l'Oriente, 1968). **H Serrano Villard**, *Libya: the new Arab kingdom of North Africa*, (Ithaca, NY: Cornell University Press, 1956).

**Modern Libya (general)**

Start with Muammar **Gadhafi**'s three part *Green Book*, available in the major European languages and provided as a free pillow-book in all the major hotels. Creative political thought from the Guide of the Revolution. Of the more recent academic material, **D Vandewalle**, *Libya since Independence*, (London: I.B. Tauris, 1998). Essential reading for anyone seeking to understand contemporary Libyan politics. Vandewalle is one of the most respected analysts of contemporary Libya. Also useful are **M Djaziri**, *Etat et société en Libye* (Paris: L'Harmattan and Mansour O, 1996). **El Kikhia**, *Libya's Qadhafi: the politics of contradiction*, (Gainesville: University of Florida, 1997). A range of academic viewpoints can be found in a recent (1995) collective volume edited by **D Vandewalle**, *Qadhafi's Libya, 1969-1994*, New York: St Martin's Press.

Rather less up-to-date is work by **J Davis** and **M-J Deeb**. See for example **J Davis**, *Libyan Politics: tribe and revolution*, (Berkeley: University of California Press, 1987); and **M-J Deeb**, *Libya's Foreign Policy in North Africa*, (Boulder, Colorado: Westview Press, 1991). See also **J Wright**, *Libya: a modern history* (Baltimore: John Hopkins University Press, 1982).

For those who read French, **A Martel**, *La Libye, 1835-1990, essai de géopolitique historique*, (Paris: PUF, 1991), provides a broad introduction to the country, even if it is impressionistic in places.

Modern Libya
(foreign policy)

**B Lanne**, *Tchad-Libye: la querelle des frontières* (Paris: Editions Karthala, 1982); **R Lemarchand**, *The Green and the Black: Qadhafi's policies in Africa* (Bloomington: Indiana University Press, 1988); **RB St. John**, *Qaddafi's World Design: Libyan foreign policy 1969-1987*, (London: Saqi Books, 1987).

Travelogues

**M Berenson**, *A Vicarious Trip to the Barbary Coast* (London, 1938). Aristocratic jottings on Cyrene, Tripoli and elsewhere. **H Clapperton**, *Difficult and Dangerous Roads* (London: Sickle Moon, ISBN 1-900209-06-3, 2000). Account by the 19th century British explorer of his travels in the Fezzan and elsewhere in the Sahara. Thoroughly recommended as a companion book when travelling in southern Libya. You have it easy. **N Danziger**, *Danziger's Adventures* (London: Harper Collins, 1992). Contains an entertaining piece about a weekend in Tripoli-sur-mer. **K Holmboe**, *Desert Encounter* (London: Harrap, 1936). Interesting reading on colonial Libya. Holmboe was an Arabic-speaking Muslim Dane who travelled through Libya in the 1930s, and portrayed the brutal treatment inflicted by Italy on the people whose land they had occupied. This was not to the colonial authorities' liking, for Holmboe was asked to leave. **P Diolé**, *Saharan Adventure* (New York: Julian Messner, 1956). Described as 'a natural sequel' to the author's earlier *Undersea Adventure*. From Fort Polignac to Sabha at a time when the French still (just) ruled the roost in the Sahara. **W McArthur**, *Auto Nomad in Barbary* (London: Cassell, 1950). Account of a drive from Tanger to Alexandria in the late 1940s. Attitudes to the Other as displayed by a white British male travelling with his wife in a Wolsey 18/85. Tripoli and Benghazi a world away from oil and revolution. **G Williams**, *Green Mountain* (London: Faber, 1968). Time out (for expats) in an idyllic Cyrenaica recounted by a former university lecturer. Strong on atmosphere.

Libya on
the web

You could try approaching Libya on the web via www.libyaonline.com Also try: www.geocities.com/Athens/8744/mylinks1.html.

**Desert** www.sahara-overland.com, www.sahara-info.ch (Swiss site in German), www.sahara.it (in Italian), www.j.mann.taylor.clara.co.uk/153.html The website of the *153 Club*, formed by Saharan travellers and named after the Michelin map no. 153 which covers the Sahara. Membership open and they produce a newsletter.

**Tour operators** www.angelfire.com/az/azartours Recommended by desert specialist Chris Scott.
www.caravanserai-tours.com Organizes a range of tours to Libya. Has a good name.

Tripolitania

# Tripolitania

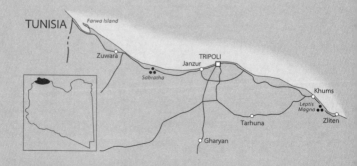

The main reasons for visiting Tripolitania are the spectacular Roman sites of **Leptis Magna** and **Sabratha**. **Tripoli** has an atmospheric decaying madina (with some mosques worth visiting), and a fine early 20th-century city centre built by the Italians. The Castle Museum in Tripoli provides a concentrate of ancient history, with fine statuary and mosaics from the Roman sites of Tripolitania along with finds from the Greek cities of Cyrenaica. If you are not heading down for the Fezzan, the museum also gives you a chance to get an overview of pre-historic rock art in Libya's far southwestern province.

Four days should be enough to cover these sites – say one and a half days for Leptis, a day for Tripoli and a long half-day for Sabratha – although some tour groups will have to cram Tripoli and Sabratha into a single day. For those with plenty of time and their own transport, Tripoli can make a good base for long day trip up into the Jabal Nafusa and the Jabal Gharyan.

# History and background

**Geography** The arid region which the Romans defined as Tripolitania, 'land of the three cities', stretched from Arae Philaenorum in the east right round to Tacapae (Gabès) in modern Tunisia. The three cities in question (and focus of this chapter) were Leptis Magna, Sabratha, and Oea (now lost under Tripoli old town). Back in ancient times, as today, Tripolitania was essentially pre-Saharan in climate. Close to the coast, cultivation is possible in spring-fed oases. A wide plain, the Jefara, stretches inland from Tripoli to the escarpment of the Jabal Nafusa in the south, and west right up to the Tunisian island of Djerba. In the border region, the arid plain is broken by wide salt flats. Eastwards of Tripoli, the plain narrows where the eastern spur of the Jabal Nafusa tails down towards the sea. A good part of the Jefara is really desert, and if you come into Tripolitania from the Tunisian side, you cross flatlands of salt bush and spiny shrubs before the landscape becomes greener around Sabratha. Unfortunately, 20th-century urban sprawl has got the better of many of the coastal oases.

**Roman Tripolitania** Under the Romans, the area was famous for its great plantations of olive trees, despite frequent drought. Emperor Hadrian won life-long support in the region by timing his visit in 128 AD at the end of a particularly harsh five year drought. Rainfall had to be carefully husbanded, and the Romans became champions at building cisterns (as at Leptis Magna) and dams across the wadis. The bas-reliefs from the Ghirza mausolea show that grain crops were cultivated in quite arid regions. The region may also have been the transit point for wild animals destined for the bloody spectacles of Roman amphitheatres.

As the ruins testify, Tripolitania was a prosperous place under the Romans. Public life centred on magnificent forums surrounded by marble-columned temples. There were bathing complexes and gymnasia, amphitheatres and theatres for entertainment. But although the physical form of the cities was Roman, the population maintained traditions and beliefs from earlier times. However, as the Romanization of the province developed, especially in the late second to early third centuries AD, Libyic and Punic deities took on a Roman face.

## Tripolitania

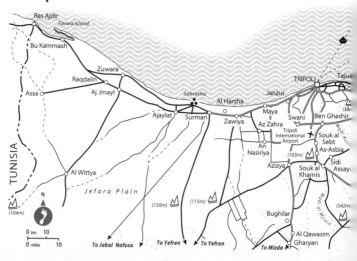

# Tripoli     طرابلس الغرب

*Tripoli has all the pleasant features and inconveniences of a modern Mediterranean town. There are flyovers and a cargo port, sprawling suburbs of villas and blocks of flats, and a palm tree-lined corniche. The heart of Tripoli is its somewhat melancholy old town, where a triumphal arch to Marcus Aurelius bears witness to a grand Roman past. Under the Ottomans and the Qaramanlis, the old town grew wealthy through the Saharan caravan trade. For a while, piracy also helped fill the coffers of Tripoli's rulers. Today, the original inhabitants have left the old town for the comforts of Garden City, amongst other places, and new towers are rising on the Corniche. The souks are sleepy, and Tunis-style tourist herding has yet to come. But although many government secretariats and the faculties of the Al-Fatah University have been moved out, the transfers have not changed the fact that Tripoli is still the real political centre of Libya. The People's Congress meets in Tripoli and Colonel Gadhafi is for the most part resident there.*

*Phone code: 021*
*Most numers in Tripoli are 7 digits, although there are still a few 6 digit numbers*

Tripolitania

## Ins and outs

International flights arrive at Ben Ghashir, the main airport some 24 km from the centre of Tripoli (although some planes leave from the smaller local airport just 4 km from downtown Tripoli – so check). A fast highway leads into the city and taxis are a cheap (10LD) and quick way into town, although a bus service is available. (You may find a private car to run you into town for 15LD.) On departure, you should leave plenty of time to get to the airport in case of official arrivals or downtown traffic congestion. The *Libyan Arab Airlines* central office is located on Shari'a Haiti. For details of flights to Tripoli, see 'Essentials' section page 24.

**Getting there**
*See also transport section page 88*

    Tripoli is well served by direct buses, mini-buses and share-taxis from all major destinations in Libya. There are international buses from Damascus, Amman, Cairo and Alexandria. Travelling by bus, you will come into one of two bus stations: the Mahatat al Dahra, just south of the neighbourhood with the embassies, or, more informally, into one of the streets near the Dhat al Imad towers on the sea front. All the share taxis and mini-buses come into a couple of open areas heaving with public transport vehicles between Dhat al Imad and the madina.

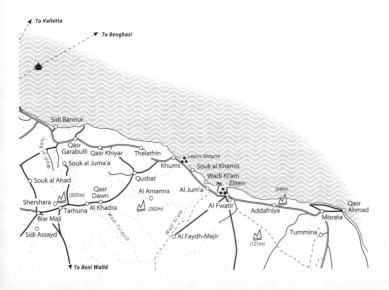

Tripolitania

## 24 hours in and out of Tripoli

*Dubbed 'Bride of the Sea', Tripoli is a distinctive sort of city: North African with a strong Levantine flavour, Italian without the Campari. There is a strong African presence, while a 1930s elegance lingers in the central avenues. Arabic-only street signs may indicate a will to build a pan-Arab identity but foreigners are nevertheless generally welcome.*

*The main sights of Tripoli can easily be covered in a long half-day. All the main hotels (apart from the Mahari and the Safwa) are within 10 to 15 minutes' walk of the **Jamahiriya Museum** on Green Square, the city's focus point, and the **madina** (old city). With an early start, you could cover both in a morning. A thorough tour of the museum takes a good 90 minutes. In the old city, make sure you see the **Ottoman clock tower** and the **copper workers' souk**, the **Gurgi Mosque** and the **Aurelian Arch**. A pleasant stroll up Shari'a M'qaryif from Green Square will take you to **Maydan al Jaza'ir** and the former **cathedral**. A few blocks further south is the former **Governor's Palace**.*

*After a morning in the city centre, you could speed off west to the ancient Roman site of **Sabratha**, right on the coast at the town of the same name. A thorough visit including the site museums merits at least 2 hours and you might*

*squeeze in time for a quick dip after your exertions. Otherwise, in Tripoli itself, there are one or two more sights for hard-core architecture enthusiasts, including the 1970s **Planetarium** and the **Mosque at Tajura**, 30 mins drive away east of the capital. (Locals head east to the beaches after Tajura: swimming in the sea at Tripoli is not recommended.) Also just about feasible as a hurried day trip from Tripoli are the sprawling Roman ruins at **Leptis Magna**, near Khums, 90 minutes' drive east of Tripoli. Be warned: the site is enormous, and the museum of great interest, too.*

*If you are spending an evening in Tripoli you might be tempted by a meal at one of the city's posh fish restaurants (in descending order of price, Al Fursan al awa'il at the Furousiya, Bou Sitta, Al Shira'a in Gargaresh, Dendishi in Hayy al Andalus, or Al Murjan on Maydan al Jaza'ir. NB avoid the restaurant on the top-floor of the Burj al Fatih). Another option, less painful on your wallet, is to take a hubbly-bubbly pipe at the café-cum-snack restaurant in the Gazelle Park, (next to the Hotel Al Kabir), or at the café opposite the Clock Tower in the Old Town. If you need to check your emails, the easiest **cyber-centre** to find is the one in the Hotel al Kabir, ground floor, rear side of the building.*

Note that the old coast road into Tripoli is very crowded with shopping traffic and local people and should be avoided in the rush hours. As you come into the outer suburbs, Tripoli centre is only 5 km away but it can take 30 mins or more to complete the journey across the Wadi Mejenin bridge and then into the centre via Shari'a Umar al Mukhtar.

**Getting around**    There are mini-buses running all over the city and though taxis are very expensive (5LD for the shortest trips – this is a standard fare, there are no metres), in the heat they might be an attractive option to those with some distance to travel. Outlying parts of Tripoli can be reached by share taxis at very reasonable rates. In practice, the tourist will be able to walk around the city centre. A taxi will be necessary to see the planetarium or to get out to Gargaresh.

Traffic can be a problem in Tripoli, despite the magnificent flyovers and ringroads. At peak times, 0730-0900, 1330-1430 and 1800-1930, roads are choked and extra time must be allowed for travelling to appointments and particularly to the airport or bus stations.

### Tripoli oasis in the 17th century, Consul Anthony Knechts' view

"The territory about the city from one sea coast to the other and to the distance of about five or six miles is laid out in gardens and garden houses, beyond those gardens begins the desert, where nothing can be seen but yellow sand, in constant motion like the waves of the sea. These gardens with the white walls of the houses in them, shaded with multitudes of date palm trees, yield a beautiful prospect from the town. The Tripolines have little notion … of gardening; fine walks, flower beds, groves and other such ornament is looked upon as a waste of so much useful ground, and regularity in planting and sowing as a deviation from the practice of their ancestors. For in their gardens they have nothing but a confused mixture of date trees and shrubs above, with cabbages, beans and all kinds of greens growing beneath and sometimes barley and wheat intermixed … The soil being nothing but sand requires constant watering at least twice a day, so there is never a garden but has a well dug in some part, commonly in the middle for that purpose. The water is drawn up in buckets by the help of a crane turned by horses or bulls, and emptied into a receptacle whence it is conveyed by little rills through all parts of the garden. This manner of watering is the only means to render the ground fertile and preserve their fruits in their gardens (which by having high walls about them are sheltered from an overflow of sand from the desert). Yet it would not answer in the open desert which is in almost constant agitation, and as these gardens can furnish but a small portion towards the necessary subsistence of the inhabitants, they immediately after the October and April showers sow their corn in the desert and have a sure harvest within a month after. And even those rains often fail, which is the cause why there is an almost constant scarcity of corn and of course all kinds of provisions in Tripoli."

*Quoted in **Richard Pennell**'s detailed account of Tripoli based on the journal of English consul Thomas Baker,* Piracy and Diplomacy in Seventeenth Century North Africa *(London: Associated University Presses, 1989)*

Tripolitania

## History and background

Tripoli's Greek and Phoenician past is lost in the mists of time. No doubt the **Roman Oea** site was ideal for a trading post, having an excellent natural harbour and the additional advantage of an oasis nearby. Settled by the Romans, the Phoenician settlement of Wy't was to become a major town, Oea, as is shown by the impressive Aurelian Arch and the chunks of ancient buildings, mainly columns, capitals and paving-stones, recycled in the mosques. Ancient Oea was the second city of the region after Leptis, and probably covered more or less the same area as the madina today. The layout is regular, with one major street running roughly north-south (the *cardo*), and three important south-west to north-east streets (*decumani*). The size and splendour of the one surviving monument, the Arch, would suggest that this was a wealthy city indeed. Today, with large sections of cluttered madina now demolished, there is an opportunity to find out what lay below the medieval and early modern town.

After the Severan period, Leptis seems to have fallen into decline. Perhaps the magnificent harbour silted up too quickly. As at Sabrata, a small population subsisted in a walled core at the heart of the vast imperial city. Oea remained important, however, and was automatically adopted by the Arab-Muslim invaders as their centre in the region. As compared with its rivals, it had the best protected (and deepest harbour), with off-shore reefs offering protection from the northwesterly winds. And nearby, along the coast, were luxurious villas were Oea's rich indulged themselves with a spot of conspicuous consumption (see mosaic from Tajura in the Castle Museum).

Tripolitania

### The Noble Arthur Herbert Esquire Admiral of his Majesty's Fleet in the Mediterranean Seas visits Tripoli, November 1681

*An English consul displays the prejudices of his time during the visit of an admiral to Tripoli.*

"*This afternoone upon the Begh's invitation the Admiral came in his Barge just into the Wash of the shore to the Eastward of the Towne, where a considerable Body of horse appeared, and exercised for about three howers; The Begh with others of the best qualitie drew themselves up neere ye Admiral and saluted him, whilst the Captain of the Port attended him in his Briganteene, The Dey himself being upon the Battlements of the Castle, where hee caused to be spread abroad a very great Flagg of Greene Silk most Richly wrought with Gold, a Respect wherewith the Turks most Solemne Festivals have not been known to bee honored. Towards the evening as the Admiral went off, the Dey saluted him with five peeces of Cannon Shotted. This most honorable way of Reception (considering the haughtinesse of these People and their national hatred and contempt they have for Christians) was never yet showne, (and truly I believe will never bee) to any Christian Admiral whatever.*"

*Extract from* The Journal of Thomas Baker, English Consul in Tripoli, 1677-1685, *quoted in Richard Pennell (1989)* Piracy and Diplomacy in Seventeenth Century North Africa *(London: Associated University Press)*

**Medieval Tripoli**  Tripoli fell to the Arabs in 643-644. The Byzantine defences were razed to the ground, and a mosque, one of the first in Tripolitania, was constructed. The town was dubbed Trablus, a deformation of Tripoli. The street plan survived, the Roman *insulae* were gradually covered with new building. Little has survived of medieval Tripoli, however, thanks to frequent invasions and uprisings. In the mid-12th century, the Normans of Sicily were the dominant power in the region, occupying Tripoli from 1146 to 1158. Although the Mamluk sultans of Egypt claimed on occasion to rule as far as *Trablus al Gharb* ('Tripoli in the west', to distinguish it from Tripoli in the Lebanon), their authority was never effective. Later the town was loosely attached to the Hafsid rulers of Tunis. In the 16th century, the town became a pawn in the great trans-Mediterranean Hapsburg-Ottoman power struggle. Falling to the Spanish forces led by Pedro Navarro in 1510, Tripoli was finally taken by the Turks in 1551.

**Spaniards, the Knights of St John and Ottomans**  Tripoli fell to the Hapsburgs after much fighting in 1510. Navarro proceeded to construct a citadel using the latest Renaissance military architecture, adapted to resist an artillery siege. Older building was torn down, including the Great Mosque and a 13th-century college, the Madrasa al Mustansiriya, to supply construction materials. A moat was excavated to separate citadel from town. Smaller forts were constructed to guard approaches to the anchorage.

Once the situation was stable in Tripoli, Navarro launched attacks on the islands to the west, Djerba and Kerkennah, in present day Tunisia. The Djerbans resisted strongly, and Tripoli was to remain a Spanish outpost. In 1511, responsibility for the town was given to the viceroy of Sicily. But the garrison required heavy subsidies for little military or economic gain. Spain then came up with the idea of giving it to the Knights of St John, a religious order founded in 1113 for the defence of Jerusalem, then in crusader hands, against Muslim attacks. Jerusalem had been lost in 1187, and over time the Knights had become a naval force, based in Nice and Viterbo. Eventually, in 1535, they accepted the offer to garrison Tripoli, along with Malta.

The Knights' position was untenable. They were separated by 350 km of sea from their main base in Malta. As of 1531, the Ottoman forces began to build up a base at nearby Tajura, and in 1551, despite the Knights' decision to build up their forces in Tripoli, the citadel fell to the Ottoman fleet. Two years later, the formidable corsair captain Dragut was named governor of the town by Sultan Sulayman.

Under Dragut, Tripoli became an Ottoman provincial capital and a centre for the Sublime Porte's operations in the western Mediterranean. Dragut was governor for 12 years. He rebuilt the walls and added a further fort, the Borj al Trab, on the north side of the madina. (A large water-tower occupies the site today). On the site of the demolished Great Mosque, he built himself a splendid residence, now vanished, the Saray Dragut. Djerba and the Tripolitanian tribes were brought to heel with modern firearms, and made to pay a regular tribute.

After the death of Dragut in 1565, Tripoli was ruled by pashas appointed from Istanbul. Most only ruled briefly, for real power lay in the hands of the janissary troops. There were frequent uprisings by the local tribes, and the politico-military situation was rarely stable.

### The Qaramanlis of Tripoli

By the beginning of the 18th century, Tripoli, like other Ottoman outposts, had a large class of *kulughlis*, descendants of Turkish soldiery and local women. In 1711, the *kulughli* commander of the cavalry, Ahmad Qaramanli, seized power. The janissary troops were massacred, and the Ottomans were unable to re-establish their authority. Eventually, great expressions of loyalty and many substantial presents led to the Sultan naming Ahmad Qaramanli governor of Tripoli. The dynasty remained in power until 1835, when, in reaction to French expansion in Algeria, the Ottomans renewed direct rule of the province.

In the mid-18th century, Tripoli achieved a measure of prosperity under

Ahmad Qaramanli's son, Ali Pasha. Corsair activity, mainly against the ships of the Italian states, brought considerable wealth to the town, while problems were carefully avoided with major powers like France and Britain by the signing of trade treaties. European merchants set up shop, attracted by the trans-Saharan trade. It was at this period that the fortifications of Tripoli reached their greatest extent. Within the walls, new mosques, including the Qaramanli Mosque, and fine residences went up, the souks were reconstructed. Outside the tight confines of the old city, new neighbourhoods developed as early as the 18th century and possibly before that. It is known from the letters of the European consuls such as Tully, resident in Tripoli during Qaramanli times, that a thriving community existed on the Manshiya, an area of flat ground immediately outside the old city. Here troublesome members of the traditional military class lived side by side with farmers and traders.

*Madrasa Othman Pasha*

**Tripoli in the second Ottoman period** Tripoli was of considerable importance to the Ottomans in the 19th century. With Algiers lost, and Tunis and Cairo effectively independent, the region was a last chance for re-asserting Ottoman rule, increasingly under pressure from independence movements in Greece and eventually the Balkans. Reforms which the Sublime Porte had already implemented in the central regions of the Empire were introduced. Energetic Ali Ridha Pasha, governor from 1867 to 1870, gave Tripoli a public park and a fine clocktower (still visible today), and restored the Citadel Mosque. In December 1870, Tripoli acquired its first modern *baladiya* or town council. For the first time, local rates were used to finance infrastructure development. The institution was to survive into the Italian period, even though the governors who succeeded Ali Ridha were not of the same ilk, viewing their postings as an opportunity for quick self-enrichment.

**20th-century Tripoli** At the turn of the 20th century, the skyline of Tripoli of Barbary with its pointy-topped mosques and great citadel was still very much as it had been two centuries earlier. Oasis gardens were within a few minutes' walk of the town, great caravans from the desert arrived in the open space below the walls of the citadel. In 1911, with the arrival of the Italians, things began to change – and fast. A new town took shape along the old caravan tracks, and in under 30 years, the population rose from 30,000 to 100,000.

In 1912, the Italian government sent out a civil engineer to produce a development plan, drawn up with all the latest hygienist theories on the city in mind. The madina was left untouched, although certain sections of the fortifications were torn down, and a new town of wide streets and modern apartment blocks laid out. The great open area south of the madina was paved over to become the Piazza Italia, today's Green Square. From there the new town's streets fanned out southwards and westwards. Works began to modernize the port and build a railway line from Tripoli to Ain Zara.

It was under governor Giuseppe Volpi that the foundations of modern Tripoli were laid. Volpi had a great interest in heritage. He had the Aurelian Arch restored, along with parts of the city walls and a number of mosques and historic buildings in the madina. In the new town centre, on corso Vittorio Emanuele III (today's Shari'a M'qariyef), a new municipality building and law courts went up. Works started on the cathedral and the governor's palace. In 1923, the Tobacco Factory was opened, just northwest of the madina, overshadowed today by the Dhat al Imad towers.

In 1925, Emilio De Bono replaced Giuseppe Volpi as governor. Under De Bono, works on the cathedral, the governor's palace, the Banca d'Italia and other major public buildings were completed. Despite the amount of public money pumped into these splendid buildings, private investment lagged behind. Italian investors proved reluctant to put money into real-estate projects in Tripoli. Under governor Pietro Badoglio (1928-1934) a new city plan came into force in 1931. In 1934, Italo Balbo became governor of Libya. He manifested a great interest for all things architectural. It was Balbo who commissioned the fresco in the Church of San Francesco in Dahra and those in the governor's palace in Tripoli.

**Post-1969 urban expansion** This pleasing early 20th century urban form was broken by the revolution of 1969. In an attempt to diminish the apparent colonial heritage and European influence, all street names were changed, the cathedral converted to a mosque and signs not in Arabic removed. The character of Tripoli was changed by massive population growth during the 1970s and 1980s, combined with an influx of Libyans from elsewhere in the country. Tripoli's population grew five-fold to reach 600,000 in 1990. Extensive new suburbs grew up on all sides, many ill-planned and the city became the core of a large metropolitan area which spread out into the neighbouring oases to encompass major satellite settlements such as Tajura to the east.

The removal of some civil service personnel to other sites together with a fall in prosperity in the late 1980s eased some of the traffic congestion but expansion of the city continues, with people commuting 60-80 km into the city from outlying towns. Huge new ringroads were built to cope with the expansion of traffic.

Today, downtown Tripoli consists of a number of fairly discrete zones. At its **Tripoli today**
heart is the Green Square, overlooked by the great walls of the Castello. Behind this much-restored citadel lies the 40 ha madina, the oldest part of town. Running south of Green Square are parallel streets of early 20th century building, once the commercial heart of Tripoli. Two major public buildings, the former Cathedral and the splendid former Governor's Palace provide a focus for this neighbourhood. East of this area lies the Dahra, first developed by the Italians in the 1930s and now largely rebuilt. Here are embassies, hotels, and modest residential blocks. Still further east, along the coast road, are the main ministries. Running west from Green Square is Shari'a Umar al Mukhtar which takes you out toward the roundabout for the first ringroad and upmarket Gargaresh. Finally, to return to the vicinity of the madina, a new business district is taking shape with the Dhat al Imad towers, the Burj al Fath and the future Hotel Corinthia.

There was an exodus of the traditional families from the old city after Inde- **Preserving**
pendence in 1951. Families moved to occupy houses and apartments vacated **historic Tripoli**
by the departing Italians to take advantage of better sanitation, water supply and other facilities. By the mid-1970s the situation had deteriorated to such an extent that the majority of residents in the old city were immigrant workers from overseas. Neglect of the old buildings enabled damp to get into their fabric and many fell to ruin. The *bayt li-sakinihi* policy ('the house belongs to its occupier') did nothing to help things. Old families basically had to abandon their old property to sitting tenants. All motivation for basic repair work disappeared. Eventually a conservation authority was established in an attempt to halt the rot. In addition to the establishment of a research workshop and library in the old city, the main mosques and a number of other buildings have been restored, including the former British consulate and a Jewish school.

*Tripoli near the arch of Marcus Aurelius*

Change is in the air today as Libya's **Trends in the**
economy begins to open up. Large **late 1990s**
sections of rotting building in the northwestern part of the madina have been torn down and there is little sign as to how (and when) they will be redeveloped. In the 1990s, some of Tripoli's finest buildings were demolished. (The Real Teatro Miramare

Tripolitania

had already gone thanks to Second World War bombardment.) Two of the finest hotels, the neo-Moorish Grand Hotel and the Albergo del Mehari were replaced by characterless modern blocks. The arrival of the waters of the Great Man-Made River had some unfortunate results. The pressure was so great that the water-mains burst, flooding parts of the down town area. Surprisingly in such a wealthy country, Tripoli also lacks a municipality able to provide a decent level of urban services. Old cars rust in side streets, garbage piles up, there are unpaved streets. However, if the city ever decides to develop some form of cultural tourism, many of the ingredients are there: a pleasant city centre, a wealth of historic buildings, and an extremely fine museum.

## Sights

For anyone interested in urban history and architecture, Tripoli has much of interest. A rushed day would enable you to see the **Tripoli Museum**, the **madina** and get a feel for the early **20th-century city**. Two days at a more leisurely pace would be better, allowing you plenty of time for photographs.

# Tripoli

Related maps
A Tripoli Médina,
page 70
B Southeast of Green
Square, page 79
C Shari'a Rashid &
around, page 83

Tripoli also makes a good base for side-trips to **Sabratha** and **Leptis Magna**, the latter just 90 minutes away by car. All the tourist hotels are handily located for exploring madina and town centre (the *Funduq Mehari*, overlooking the ferry-terminal in the Dahra neighbourhood is the most distant). In the madina, make sure you see the **Qaramanli House** (restored city residence with traditional furnishings), the old **French** and **British consulates**, and the **Aurelian Arch**. Also look out for the **copper souk** just below the Ottoman clock tower, and have a look at the **Gorgi Mosque**. For low-life, cosmopolitan Tripoli, explore the cafés along **Shari'a 'Umar al Mukhtar**, drift along **Shari'a Rashid**: visit the 1930s fruit and vegetable market and head up to the chaotic mini-bus and taxi ranks near the great Dhat al Imad towers. Here you will find street sellers from Chad and Mali, shoe-repairers, tall Sa'idi workmen from Egypt and all the nationalities that Libya's 'open-door to Africa' policy sends up to Tripoli.

Tripolitania

## The Jamahiriya Museum

Tripolitania

*Opening days can be unreliable, with the whole museum closed for works for days on end. 'Come back to tomorrow', they say at the door, which is frustrating when you go back 3 days in succession to find the museum still closed.*

Housed in the **great citadel** which dominates Green Square, the Jamahiriya Museum is essentially concerned with the archaeology and ancient history of Libya. The first museum in the building was put together by the Italians under Italo Balbo. Today the collection covers the Phoenician, Greek and Roman periods well and has an expanding amount of material on the Islamic period. The top floor is devoted to modern Libyan history and a selection of craftwork, musical instruments and jewellery. Unfortunately, large areas of the Castle are off-limits. If open to visitors, the upper walls afford a fine view to the sea and across the town. ■ *Open (in theory) weekdays 0800-1400, last admissions 1300, closed Mon, Fri afternoons only, 1400 to 1600, last admissions 1700. Entrance 3LD.*

**The castle**
The massive fortified building housing the Jamahiriya Museum, known in Arabic as Al Saraya Al Hamra (lit: 'the red palace'), occupies a site known to be pre-Roman in the eastern quadrant of the city. As is appropriate for such an ancient building, the castle is a complex labyrinth of rooms, courtyards and passages. It was here in the 1530s and 1540s that the Knights of St John planned their outpost of Christendom. However, when things began to look really black for the knights, they suggested to Charles V that they dynamite the whole castle complex. The emperor rejected this idea, however, and ordered Giovanni Valletta, later responsible for fortifying Malta, to reinforce the fortress at Tripoli. France came up with the funds but unfortunately the galley carrying the cash was captured by the corsair-pirate Dragut. Work stalled and in 1551 the castle fell to the forces of Sinan Pasha. Subsequently home to beys, deys and other exotic Ottoman officers, it was in Tripoli Castle that the Qaramanli dynasty held court until 1835.

The castle was extensively rebuilt on a number of occasions, most recently in the 20th century when it was remodelled by the Italians. Restoration works began in 1922, sponsored by governor Count Volpi, to designs by Brasini. The bastion of St George (on your left, as you stand facing the museum entrance) was heavily restored, while arches were erected along the bastion of St James (right of the entrance). An inscription in Latin on the outside wall records that Volpi sponsored the works, while next to it is a sundial and a bas-relief of St George and his dragon. In the 1930s, a large number of fine pieces of ancient statuary were assembled in the castle, not without considerable difficulty. Eventually, the city's first museum was set up in the bastion of St George, in the offices of governor Italo Balbo. In the near future, with a bit of luck, more of the castle will be open to visitors.

**Entrance hall**
*The loos are on your left, just after the statue of Antonius, as you come into the first hall.*

Some of the Museum's prize pieces are in display in the ground floor entrance hall. On your left as you go in is a whole **Roman mausoleum from Ghirza** (fourth century AD), the frontier settlement out in the desert south of Misrata. There is some well-observed detail in the bas-reliefs: look out for the man climbing a palm tree to pick dates. The crucial detail on this piece of funerary architecture? A false door with a chain carved in stone.

*Castello de Tripoli*

Opposite the mausoleum is an immense second century AD **mixed-technique mosaic** from the Roman villa at Dar Buk Ammera, Zliten, the ancient equivalent of a Wilton carpet. Here *opus sectile* (coloured marble marquetry) is used alongside detailed imagery in *opus vermiculatum*. The central panels of the mosaic are given over to a Cousteau-collection of fish and other denizens of the deep. Less peacefully, the border is given over to gory gladiatorial scenes, full of detail. Also on this side of the hall, you have an oversized reproduction of Tripoli in the 17th century. The moat, constructed by the Knights of St John, is clearly visible. Finally, observe the statue of Capitoline Venus, found in the Hadrianic Baths at Leptis Magna in 1924. And in 1939, Italo Balbo gave the statue to Air-Marshall Goering as a present on his visit to Libya. Happily, in 1999, it was returned to Libya by the Italian government, a gesture in the general rapprochement between the two countries.

Two further second-century Roman copies of Greek originals decorate the niches in the entrance hall. These statues, from the Hadrianic Baths at Leptis, were typical decorative features in bathing complexes. To the right is a copy of Praxiteles' **Diadomenos**, a portrait of an athlete tying the ribbon of victory round his brow, a copy of a fourth century BC original. In the statue on the left, of **Apollo-Antinous**, a Roman cult is grafted onto a Greek body. The statue, a copy of Praxiteles' Apollo of Delphi has all the attributes of the sun god. The head though is of Antinous, Hadrian's lover. Born in the undistinguished province of Bythinia, until his tragic death Antinous was the emperor's confident, travelling with him the length and breadth of Rome's domains, even bringing rain to Carthage after a long drought. For Hadrian, Antinous was the gift of providence. He soon became the object of a cult, shrines were dedicated to him and the new town of Antinopolis was named for him in Egypt. But it was in Egypt that Antinous was to perish, drowning in the waters of the Nile.

The first main hall has a big map of Libya up on the wall. Press buttons to light up the ancient sites, trade routes, museums etc.

**Prehistoric Libya (Rooms 1-4)**

Rooms 2 to 4 deal with prehistoric Libya. There are real-size **casts and copies of rock carvings and paintings** from the Messak Settafet and the Jabal Akakus, displays of flints and simple, wavy-line pottery. Look out for the oldest skeleton discovered in the Akakus, dating from 3,400 BC and discovered in 1958 in the Wadi Teshuinat. Lying in the foetal position, the body is accompanied by funerary offerings.

Room 5 deals with the main settlements of the ancient Berber tribes of Libya. Look out in particular for the **cast of the sanctuary at Slonta**, Cyrenaica. There is also material from Zinchekra in the Wadi al Hayat, cradle of the Garamantian civilization, including curious stone grave altars, and fragmentary evidence of daily life in Ghirza in the third and fourth centuries AD. Room 6 is devoted to Punic settlement in Libya. (Punic is the adjective used to refer to Phoenician / Carthaginian culture in the central and western Mediterranean). There is a votive stela bearing a stylized female figure, the sign of Tanit, mother-goddess of Carthage. Look out also for a rather nice standstone lion, discovered in 1930 on Farwa Island, and the heads of Punic Gods from the port area of Leptis Magna.

**Libyan tribes and Punic settlement (Rooms 5 & 6)**

By far the most spectacular part of the Jamahiriya Museum is that devoted to Greek and Roman antiquity. The **Cyrene Rooms** contain models of the Temple of Zeus and the Agora in Cyrene. In a side room to the left is a statue of the Three Graces from the *frigidarium* of the Roman baths in the Sanctuary of Apollo. The marble of these Graces (reassembled) has preserved the shiny

**Greek and Roman times rooms 7-9**

Tripolitania

marble patina buffed up in the sculptor's workshop. Note the two funerary statues from Cyrene (fourth century BC), one of which is faceless. Such statues, common in the necropolises of Cyrene, are thought to represent Persephone, goddess of the Underworld, wife of Hades. The large statue is of Minerva, easily recognized by the owl on her arm, plus spear and shield.

As you move into the next hall, you pass some examples of the Romans' taste in statuary, including, on your right, a colossal Dionysus, god of fun, in a state of advanced inebriation, accompanied by a young satyr and a panther. This was discovered in the Old Forum at Leptis Magna and may have been the cult statue from the Temple of Liber Pater. To the left is Fortuna.

The large **Leptis Gallery** (room 9) divides into three sections. The first section, centring on a model of the Severan Forum, contains a large amount of sculpture from the Old Forum, most of it from the Temple of Rome and Augustus. By dedicating such pieces, the inhabitants of Leptis demonstrated their loyalty to the Julio-Claudian dynasty. The colossal pieces go back to the early first century, the smaller pieces are mid-first century AD. After a Venus, n the left are portrayals of Tiberius, Augustus' son-in-law and successor, Claudius, Tiberius' nephew, and Agrippina the Elder, Augustus' granddaughter. To the right is a colossal statue of Ceres, goddess of the harvest, shown with the rotund features of Livia, Augustus' wife. Look out too for a fine head of Germanius, son of Severus. And finally, there is splendid mosaic of the four seasons from the Villa Dar Buk Ammera at Zliten.

Moving through to the second section, there are a couple of colossal imperial heads: Tiberius on the left and Augustus on the right. (Life-like portraiture was the Roman contribution to sculpture.) In the niches, are portrait statues of two Leptis Magna notables, Iddibal Caphada Aemilius, on the left, and Annobal Rufus, on the right, who gave their home town a couple of fine monuments, respectively the Chalcidicum and the Market. You will also find the inscription, in Latin and Neo-Punic, which decorated the entrance to the theatre at Leptis.

In the centre of the second Leptis Room is a large **mosaic** with geometric motifs from the **Villa of the Nereids at Tajura** in the western suburbs of Tripoli. The central section features the head of a sea god, Amphitrite. To the left of the mosaic is a series of imperial portraits (second century AD), mainly from the theatre at Leptis, while to the right is more statuary from Leptis and a case with some very fine glassware.

On either side of the passage taking you through to the third Leptis room is a further selection of sculpture from the Hadrianic Baths at Leptis, perfectly preserved from pillaging when the vaulted roofs of the baths collapsed. To the right is Apollo playing his lyre, while to the left is Marsyas, who had such confidence in his musical abilities that he dared to challenge Apollo to a duel. He lost and met an unfortunate end. A seated muse seems to be listening to their musical competition. (NB traces of the original paint can still be seen on Apollo's eyes.) Also in this selection is Hermes with a child Dionysus, and up in a niche, the behelmeted god of war, Mars. The statue is a copy of a now lost Greek original by Polycleites. On the left, the female figure beyond Marsyas is Isis, wearing a diadem set with sun and moon.

The third part of the Leptis Room, dominated by a large photograph of the theatre at Sabratha, centres on a scale-model of the forum at Sabratha. Here again is more material bearing witness to the Roman taste for sculpture, including a resting satyr, copy of a Greek original by Praxiteles. There is a mosaic showing Orpheus bewitching the beasts with his music, and four mosaic panels from the Villa of the Nile (second century AD) at Leptis. To the left of the Orpheus mosaic is the mosaic which gave the villa its name, showing the Nile as a bearded man riding a hippopotamus, processing towards an altar

● ● ● ● ● ● ● ● ● ● ● ● ● ● ● ● ● ● ● ● ● ● ● ● ● ● ● ● ● ● ● ● ● ● ● ● ● ● ● ● ● ● ● ●

### Souks and Funduqs

*Old Tripoli has a number of funduqs; entrepôt hostels' where merchants lodged their goods and animals around large courtyards. From the 13th century, trade developed considerably, both between the Middle East and North Africa and with the Christian nations of Europe. In the case of the European nations, trade was regulated by treaties which specified that there should be special accommodation reserved for Christian merchants in the main coastal towns. These hostels came to be referred to as funduqs, an Arabic term derived from the Greek* pandokeion, *inn or hostel. The word gained currency in the languages of the medieval western Mediterranean,* fondech *in Catalan,* fondaco *in Italian and* fondigus *in Latin. Such hostels were commonplace in the Mediterranean trading cities, and the funduqs of the Christian nations are the ancestors of the consulate and trade missions. In Tripoli, as elsewhere, the funduqs played an important role in the life of the city. Here the main merchants would store and dispatch large amounts*

*of goods, and from here trans-Saharan traders would muster their caravans.*

*The manufacturing and retail souks or markets of old Tripoli were run by guilds of craftsmen producing items for daily use. Hand-made pottery, metalwork, traditional clothing and jewellery were made and sold in these souks. Trade still continues under vaulted brick ceilings, though very few goods are now manufactured in situ and the traditional specialization of the souks has largely broken down. In 1982, the souks of Tripoli received what might have been a mortal blow: it was decided, as part of a campaign against private business, to close them down and replace them with state-owned supermarkets. The closure lasted for five years but growing difficulties in supplying people's needs forced the government to back down on its anti-private business stance. The souks of Tripoli were re-opened, and together with the vast number of informal traders operating off Shari'a Rashid, they now do thriving business.*

● ● ● ● ● ● ● ● ● ● ● ● ● ● ● ● ● ● ● ● ● ● ● ● ● ● ● ● ● ● ● ● ● ● ● ● ● ● ● ● ● ● ● ●

bearing the words 'good fortune' in Greek. Satyrs play music, a joyful crowd moves along with the hippo. No doubt the scene is part of a celebration to attract the god's good graces. In a glass case as you leave this section, look out for a fountain in the form of a sleeping cupid – obviously the ultimate in second-century AD home decoration.

You now continue the visit on the **second floor**. A narrow corridor with third and fourth century mosaics, including a nice hunting scene with big cats, takes you to the staircase leading to the next floor.

In the first hall (room 10) are some of the smaller pieces of sculpture from Leptis, including a statue of Caracalla as a child, a Venus and portraits of Faustina, wife of the emperor Marcus Aurelius. There is a fine statue of a priestess of Isis, again from the Hadrianic Baths. This section of the museum also contains some fine Roman portrait busts and coins. Look out also for the case of Roman ceramics and mirrors, along with some tiny statues. From the upper section here you also have a good view down into room 9 with its Amphitrite mosaic.

Taking a narrow corridor to your right, you come to room 11 with the **bas-reliefs from the Arch of Septimius Severus**, a strident demonstration of political loyalty from third century Leptis Magna. The emperor is shown in a chariot, accompanied by officers. A crowd of barbarian prisoners precede him. Another section of bas-relief shows Julia Domna, Syrian wife of Septimius, burning incense on an altar. To the left, as you come in, is a relief designed to show the harmony reigning in the imperial family, between Septimius and his two sons, Caracalla and Geta.

**Byzantine times** The last room in this section (room 13, with yellow and beige walls) is dedicated to the Byzantine period. There is masonry from the basilica at the Al Khadhra, Tarhuna, up in the Jabal southeast of Tripoli, and photographs of some of the mosaics from the church at Qasr Libia in Cyrenaica.

The second floor of the museum (when open) is devoted to **Islamic buildings and traditional lifestyles**. There is a photograph of the finds at Madinat Sultan, the oldest mosque in Libya, and another of the Naga Mosque, the oldest surviving in Tripoli madina. Look out too for the fine scale-model of the Tripoli Castle (where you are at present). Vanished (or vanishing) ways of life are represented in the form of a *zriba* (palm frond hut from the Dawada Lakes), a reconstruction of a room in a Ghadamès house and a Touareg tent. There are also displays of country women's jewellery, Touareg craftwork and traditional costumes.

# Tripoli Madina

Sidi-Abul-Wahhab Mosque

Water Tower

Sidi-Salem Mosque

Aurelian Arch

Funduq Zumit

Gurgi Mosque

Old French Consulate C18th

Zanqa des Français

Zanqat Al-Meiroo

Dar Nuwayji

Méddersa Ottoman-Pacha C17th

Old Jewish School

Zanqa Al-Akonach

Place des Nazaréens

Draghut Mosque

Sīh Al Fatih

Old Bank of Rome

Hammam Draghut

Bab Sidi Al Haddar

Mahmud Mosque

Santa Maria degli Angeli

Zanqat Al Rish Errich

Crossroads 4 Columns

Qaramanli House

Shaib al Air Mosque

Zanqa Soug

Zanqa Arbaâ-Arsat

Dorouj Mosque

Zanqa Soug Al-Harrara

Kharrouba Mosque

Bab Jedid

Bab Zenata

N

0 metres 50
0 yards 50

Tripolitania

The top floor deals with **contemporary Libya**, presented with photographic displays. The Cyrenaican resistance to Italian occupation is well represented: there are photos of the capture of **national hero Umar al Mukhtar**, as well as the trunk of the tree from which he was hanged. Next comes a section on Colonel Gadhafi and his contribution to the construction of the modern Libyan state (the colonel shown at various important events, presents received from foreign nations), plus sections on the oil industry and the Green Book, Gadhafi's master work, published in the 1970s, which develops the Third Universal Theory, an alternative model to capitalism and communism. The visit comes to close with a display of somewhat threadbare wild animals, insects, and birds.

**Contemporary times**
*It is not always possible to visit this floor.*

## Historic Tripoli

The historic neighbourhoods of Tripoli divide into two discrete sections, the oldest area, the **madina** or **medieval walled town**, built on the site of the original Roman settlement, and the **20th-century city centre**, centring on Shari'a al Fatah and the Maydan al Jaza'ir, south of the madina. A moderately structured meander of 2½ hours would enable you to do the madina justice. The avenues of the central area are a place for strolling, too. An hour and a half's wandering enables you to see the main streets, cathedral, former governor's palace and get as far as the Church of San Francesco up in Dahra.

Most people start their visit to the madina of Tripoli from Green Square. Happily for the rushed visitor, the main sites and photo- opportunities are close together, and two parallel streets (Shari'a Arba'a Arsat and Souk al Mushir/Souk al Truk) take you up to the northeast corner where there is a concentration of interesting buildings. If time is limited, make sure you see the souks around the Naga Mosque, the Qaramanli House, the Church of Santa Maria degli Angeli, the Arch of Marcus Aurelius, and the Gurgi Mosque.

Beginning on Green Square, two gateways give access to the madina. Take the left hand, higher gate, **Bab al Manshiya**, which takes you through into the street called Souk al Mushir. The first sight on your left is a small

**Exploring the madina of Tripoli**

*Mediterranean Sea*

Tripolitania

Al Truk
F Ezzhar
Zanna Souq Al Mushir
Zaouia Al-Khadria
An-Naga Mosque
Ahmed pacha Qaramanli Mosque
Zandat Al-Helga
Funduq Al-Bacri
Castle & Jamahiriya Museum
Green Square
Bab Al-Menchia
Bab Hurria

Tripolitania

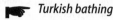 *Turkish bathing*

*If you have plenty of time in Tripoli, try to visit one of old town's two hammams (Turkish baths). No Roman settlement in North Africa was without its thermae, and the Turkish bath seems to be a survival/adaptation from ancient times, particularly widespread in Syria, Tunisia and Turkey. In Tripoli madina there are two hammams, the **Hammam Dragut**, close to the mosque of the same name (see above), and the **Hammam al Halga**, not too far from the Naga Mosque and the souk. To get to Hammam al Halga, from Green Square, enter Shari'a al Mushir in the old town; take first left, proceed and then follow street round to right, turn left again, then first right after 30 m down a short alley; the hammam is the green door on your right with the plaque with opening times in Arabic above it. (Men: Tuesday, Wednesday, Friday).*

***Hammam Dragut**, dating back to the 16th century, is the more spectacular (open for women Mondays to Wednesdays, men other days). In its time, it must have been Tripoli's premier bathing establishment, considering itself on a par with the great hammams of the Levantine cities and a sign, along with the tapering Hanefite minarets, that Ottoman urban culture had arrived. Today, although basically clean, it is frequented essentially by poorer locals and migrant workers (many of the decaying madina dwellings have poor plumbing or inadequate bathrooms). You enter through a narrow passageway (where you might sit and cool off before leaving the hammam), and come into a large square domed room, where you change your clothes. If you want to be*

*slightly upmarket, you could change in a **maqsura**, one of the side rooms, which in the hammam's heyday would have been most luxuriously appointed.*

*A corridor off the main 'changing room' takes you into the hot room. You can lie on a heated raised central platform, or sit and sweat in one of the side chambers. When you have built up a sweat, you'll notice that as you rub yourself, little mucky twists of dead skin form. After rubbing with a rough bath glove by an expert masseur, these can be washed off. Then you can soap yourself and wash with cooler water.*

*Note that for men, modesty is de rigueur, (ie you change under a towel). The Islamic concept of the 'awra, (basically the region below navel and above knees), means adult men don't uncloth themselves fully in front of each other. (No running around in thongs on Libyan beaches, please). Boys go with their mothers to the hammam until they reach puberty. Then they are excluded from the world of women. Traditionally, their first visit to the men's hammam was an essential rite of passage. For women in Arab Muslim cities the hammam was an opportunity for gossip, laughter and identifying suitable brides for their sons. Sometimes brides will rent the whole hammam for their big pre-wedding wash.*

*Equipment for a hammam visit: swimming shorts, towels (fut, sing. **fouta**), rough bath glove (**kessa**), shampoo, flipflops (so you don't burn your feet on the hot marble floor). Terminology: **tayyab** (masseur for men), **harza** (masseuse), **taksila** (athletic, pre-wash stretching, men only).*

tourist souk with carpets from Misrata. (This leads through to a cloistered courtyard where there are some small touristy shops, and eventually to the Souk al Sagha, the Jewellers' Souk). Off Souk al Mushir, the first street on your left is occupied by jewellers, too. Next on your left is the eastern side of the **Ahmad Pasha al Qaramanli Mosque**, visitable outside prayer times. (Remove shoes and behave appropriately for a place of worship). The mosque, the largest in the old city, was inaugurated in 1738, and must have been the key part of Ahmad Qaramanli's campaign to establish himself as a legitimate ruler. Inside the central prayer hall, the decoration is dense: the lower surfaces of the walls are covered with polychrome ceramic tiles, higher sections faced with elaborately carved stucco. The prayer hall, like most older Libyan mosques, is roofed with 25 small domes, the two domes over the fine *mihrab* being more elevated and carrying stucco work. The tombs of Ahmad Pasha and many of his family lie in a separate room with a large domed roof of spectacular design. The distinctive minaret is octagonal in the Turkish style.

Next on your left after the mosque is the **Funduq al Zahar** ('the Orange Flower Hostel'), one of Tripoli's numerous *funduqs* or merchant's entrepôt-inns. The poetic name derives from the time when great sacks of orange flowers, raw material for the making of perfume and orange flower water, a crucial element in Middle Eastern patisserie, would be brought into the city for sale. Today, more prosaically, this funduq provides workshop space for the many jewellers whose shops are nearby in the neighbourhood. There is a small café at the entrance.

At the end of Souk al Mushir, an arch leads into the square in front of the **Clock Tower**, a minor piece of Ottoman Baroque erected by the city's first municipality and completed in 1898. (A small café with hubbly-bubbly pipes just on your right as you come through the arch might be a place to stop at some point.) To the right of the square, you have the back of the splendid **Bank of Libya** buildings. Have a peek down the narrow street to the left of the clocktower, where you will find the industrious **copper workers**, assembling large metal spheres and crescents, final flourish for any self-respecting minaret.

Just after the Clock Tower, turn left, and then take the first right onto **Souk al Truk**, the Turks' Souk, partly covered with lattice-work roofing. This will take you right up to the northeast part of the madina where there is another concentration of monuments. On your way up Souk al Truk, look out for the elaborate door of the **Shaib al Ain Mosque** on the right. (The tiny *Madina Hotel* is on the left, a little further on). The next main photo stop comes with the **Dragut Mosque** (another pointy-topped Turkish-style minaret) on the right. The **Hammam Dragut** is just before the mosque down a side-street on the right, and

## Dragut Mosque

Turba (tomb)

Courtyard

Turba (tomb)

Turba (tomb)

Prayer Hall

Minbar

Courtyard

Ablution

Entrance

Hammam

Main room (chagig)

Entrance

Hot room

Cubic

Tripolitania

if you turn right after leaving the mosque, you can head for Bab al Bahr (the Sea Gate), which now has a fine metal gate with Arabic slogans stressing the importance of education (perhaps commemorating the fact that that it was through this gate that Colonel Gadhafi would come on his way to school).

The **Dragut Mosque** was built in the late 16th century by the celebrated pirate Dragut, governor of Tripoli from 1553 to 1565. It was to have been part of a much larger complex, but unfortunately Dragut died during the siege of Malta. Dragut's body was brought back to Tripoli for burial in his mosque, and the minaret, plus the neighbouring hammam were completed under his successor Iskandar Pasha. In the Second World War, the mosque was damaged during a bombardment. Reconstruction works altered the building, adding an extra nave and widening the street at the expense of the mosque. The great Dragut also had a large palace complex in the centre of the madina, between the former British Consulate and the Turkish prison.

After the mosque, turn left out of the Sea Gate and head along the side of the madina towards the **Mosque of Sidi Abd al Wahhab**, which sits by itself next to the busy main road between port and madina. Keeping this mosque on your right, turn left into the old town towards the **Arch of Marcus Aurelius**. A four-square stegosaurus of a building, this solid monument is practically all that survives of the splendours of Roman Oea. In many ways it resembles that other piece of strident street furniture, the great *quadrifons* Severan Arch at Leptis Magna. An old Tripoli proverb links the survival of the arch to the survival of the city. In the early 20th century, the arch housed a cinema. The Italians inevitably decided to spare no pains in restoring it. The northeast and southwest façades of the arch had niches for statuary to impress people entering and leaving the neighbourhood. The dedication at the top mentions that the arch, built on public land, was funded by a leading magistrate, Caius Calpurnius Celsus, and dedicated in 163 AD by the proconsul of Africa and his legate to Marcus Aurelius and Lucius Verus, co-emperors of the day. Obviously, a career in Roman law brought considerable financial gains, as the building is entirely faced in marble. The narrower façades feature figurative bas-reliefs, the wider façades are plainer.

The bas-reliefs gave the sculptors, no doubt Greek and imported, a glorious excuse to let their imaginations run riot. On the narrower façades you can see Apollo and Minerva, twin tutelary deities of Tripoli, racing to the assistance of the Roman armies in their chariots, that of Apollo drawn by sphinxes, while Minerva has some pretty fierce female griffons. Look out too for the symbols of Apollo (tripod of Delphi, crow), and Minerva (shield, lance, helmet and owl).

Discovered in the vicinity of the arch were the remains of the **Temple to the Genius of the Colony** of Oea. Among the marble remains laid out near the arch are bas-reliefs from the temple pediment. Apollo and Minerva stand on either side of a woman wearing a high cylindrical headdress, possibly a personification of Tyche, goddess of Fortune. Once more,

## Gurgi Mosque

*To Aurelian Arch*

Entrance

| | |
|---|---|
| 1 Minaret | 3 Minbar | 5 Tombs |
| 2 Prayer Hall | 4 Mihrab | 6 Madrasa |

Apollo is identifiable thanks to his Delphic tripod and serpent. On the surviving left-hand end of the pediment can be seen one of the Dioscuri (the twin brothers Castor and Pollux, all muscles and holding back a champing steed).

After examining the Aurelian Arch, you should definitely have a look at the **Gurgi Mosque**, perhaps the best known of the Tripoli mosques, built comparatively recently in 1833 by one Mustapha Gurgi (a mamluk originally from Georgia in the Caucasus, hence the family name), who was responsible for Tripoli's fleet. The plan closely resembles that of the Ahmad Pasha al Qaramanli Mosque. The unusual octagonal minaret with two balconies is the tallest in old Tripoli. Inside is the usual square prayer hall, decorated with tiles. The group reciting the Qur'an would sit up in the elaborate *sidda* (wooden balcony-like structure), at the back of the prayer hall. Note too the marble marquetry work of the *minbar* (preacher's 'chair'). If you are pressed for time, the Gurgi Mosque is the one to visit, and there is a kindly warden to show you round.

A few metres south of the Aurelian Arch, to the left down a side street, is the **former French Consulate** (founded 1630), currently being restored. The building is representative of the fine homes of 18th- and 19th-century Tripoli. A short flight of steps leads to the colonnaded gallery which gives access to the main reception rooms. France maintained a significant presence in Tripoli from the 18th century, with certain consuls, notably one Charles Féraud in the 19th century, leaving fine accounts of the life of the city. France moved out of the building in 1940. The intention is to turn the building over to some sort of cultural use, once works are completed. (If you continue down this street, you will come to Shari'a Arb'a Arsat (Street of the Four Columns), which takes you straight back towards Green Square).

If you have time, then you can do a quick loop up from the Aurelian Arch to the Water Tower and back down to a street leading to the central madina. With the port and the arch behind you, head right up a side-street, then left uphill towards the Water Tower. On your left, you will pass the 15th-century **Mosque of Sidi Salem**. Despite its cylindrical, pointy-topped minaret, this is one of the older mosques in Tripoli. The **Water Tower** is on the highest point of the madina where Dragut built his Borj al Trab (Earth Tower), to look out over the approaches to Tripoli. The area, today much dilapidated, is still referred to as **Al Qubba** ('the Dome'), after the Monument to the Fallen, now demolished, put up by the Italians in 1923-25 to those who died during the conquest of Libya. Below lies the main coast road, leading west towards Dhat al Imad. From the Water Tower, head back towards the central madina

Heading west from the Gurgi Mosque (away from the Aurelian Arch) along Shari'a al Akwash, are another couple of restored buildings. Just before the first major street running right (Zanqat al Ispanyol), a plaque on the wall on the left tells you that here is the restored **former British Consulate**, now restored by the Old Tripoli Conservation Authority and referred to as **Dar Abd al Khaliq al Nuwayji**. Inside the rooms have been converted to exhibition space and offices. There is also a small library. The house was originally built in 1744 as a residence for Ahmad al Qaramanli. Later, it came to house the British Consulate, a function which lasted until 1940. Restoration took place between 1987 and 1993. Abd al Khaliq al Nuwayji was one of the main movers behind the restoration project.

Another 75 m or so further west on Shari'a al Akwash, on the right, facing a cleared expanse of land, is another building of interest, **Dar Ahmad Nayib al Ansari**, the restored **Jewish School** which today houses important archives on the history of Tripoli. The school was originally known as the Sarousi House of Prayer (or something like this, in Italian). Abandoned in 1967 after the Arab-Israeli War which put paid to so many centuries-old Jewish

Tripolitania

• • • • • • • • • • • • • • • • • • • • • • • • • • • • • • • • • • • • • • • • • •

☞ *Tripoli madina neighbourhoods*

*Old Tripoli is criss-crossed by streets going back to the old Roman chequer-board layout. Basically, there are a number of separate quarters or humat: Baladiya, near the castle, Bab al Bahr ('Sea Gate') to the northeast, the Hara, as the old Jewish quarter was called, and Humat Gharyan). Off the narrow streets criss-crossing the madina run blind alleys. While the piece meal development of the city produced a random street pattern, the blind alleys that resulted were useful for creating defensible areas controlled by extended families or ethnic groups. In this way, attackers or casual passers-by would not intrude on family life. Generally unroofed, the through streets in Tripoli old city have buttresses at intervals which help to hold up the walls on either side of the alley and provide some shelter from the sun. Walls facing the public alleys are for the most part plain with few windows, a device to increase privacy and deter curiosity. Doorways to houses and interior courtyards are remarkably ornate in contrast to the tall plain walls around them. Massive arches are used, while the doors themselves are often high, sometimes studded and provided with ancient locks.*

• • • • • • • • • • • • • • • • • • • • • • • • • • • • • • • • • • • • • • • • • •

communities in the Middle East, the building fell into disrepair until it was decided to convert it into an archive centre. Works lasted from 1990 to 1994. Generally, the staff are happy to show visitors around. For any researcher, the place is a mine of sources, including some interesting oral archives, consular documents and all the university dissertations and theses written in English and other languages on Libyan themes. The building bears witness to the early interest taken in modern education by Tripoli's Jewish community. ■ *Open 0900 to 1300, 1600 to 1900, closed Fri. Entrance free.*

After visiting the former British consulate, head back towards the Aurelian Arch for a few metres and turn right (south) down a street which will bring you to the **Church of Santa Maria degli Angeli**, undergoing extensive restoration in the late 1990s. Here you are at the heart of the madina, close to the site of the original Great Mosque and that of an extensive palace put up by Dragut in the mid-16th century. The large church comes as something of a surprise in such a Muslim city. Close by (turning left as you face the church), is the former ***bagnio*** (prison) put up by Uthman Pasha in 1664 to stock Christian captives awaiting ransom (room for 700 prisoners). Though pirate activity was at its height in the 17th century, the income generated was irregular. Therefore there was a need for such a building to house prisoners until the right price could be negotiated for their release. There is a small café opposite the chuch.

Christian orders were given permission to assist the prisoners as of 1613, and a small chapel was put up on the site of the present church. Entirely rebuilt in the early 18th century, the church was destroyed once more in 1829. The present building, 70 m long, 20 m high, dates from 1891. Its size bears witness to the growing prosperity, confidence and numbers of Christians in Tripoli at the time, and the freedom of worship existing in the Ottoman domains. Santa Maria degli Angeli was the city's cathedral until 1928, when the large neo-Lombard style Cathedral of the Sacred Heart was completed up in the new town. With restoration works nearing completion, Santa Maria looks set to take on a new role as an art gallery, although given the large number of Christian migrant workers, it might also become a place of worship once more.

Turn right out of the church, and at the first junction, go right on the main street (Shari'a Arba' Arsat) running back south. The tall, crumbling building on the corner which would look very much at home in Naples or Palermo was home to the **Banco di Roma**. Continuing straight ahead, after about 100 m

Tripolitania

you will come to the **Crossroads of the Four Columns**, so-called because of four pieces of Roman masonry inserted picturesquely into the street corners. Such recycling was commonplace when the Arabs were building their first cities in North Africa, and the mosques of Tripoli have numerous columns and capitals from Roman temples. Just south of the Four Columns, the entrance to the **Dar Qaramanli** is on your right. Note that if you turn right (west), at the Four Colums, Shari'a al Gharyan/souk al Harara brings you out at Bab Jadid on the western side of the old town.

A pleasant, patrician residence, the **Dar Qaramanli** has been restored and converted to a museum. The courtyard, surrounded by galleries on two levels displays the wealth and prestige of a branch of the Qaramanli family, rulers of Tripoli in the 18th and early 19th century. For most of the 19th century, the building housed the Tuscan Consulate. Off the courtyard are narrow living rooms. The more splendid, private apartments, furnished with period furniture, are on the first floor. The tiled alcove room (Dar al Kabu) has a couple of splendid, if uncomfortably seated, wax Qaramanlis in period dress, the male with a soaring turban and full beard. The large brass UFO-like object on the floor is a *daghar*, an incense burner, much-used during wedding parties. Next on the circuit is a chamber with period musical instruments, followed by a room where women stitched sequin designs on velvet cushions, no doubt an appropriate accomplishment for upper-class Tripoli women in times gone by. Finally, in another long narrow room, you will find further wax-work dummies dressed to represent each period of Tripoli's long history. From Roman soldier to British Tommy, they await a carnival to spring into action. From the terrace, you can view the mosques, minarets and bell-towers of the old city – and look down into streets and courtyards of urban decay.

Turn right out of Dar Qaramanli to head back towards Green Square. Keeping straight ahead, you will eventually come to the narrow and busy Shari'a al Halga. Prefer, however, to head for the **Naga Mosque**, taking the third turn left, follow round to the right after 50 m, continue straight ahead for a further 80 m and you will go left again. Ahead of you is the odd, 'hanging' or rather semi-cantilevered (to use the technical term) minaret of the **Zawiya al Khadria**. The mosque entrance is just round the corner on the right.

*Naga* is one of the many terms for camel in Arabic, and the **Naga Mosque**, the oldest surviving in Tripoli, is so-called because (so the story goes) the citizens of Tripoli met the great Arab conqueror Amr ibn al As with a camel-load of valuables to buy the survival of the city. Ibn al As refused to accept the gift and requested that the goods be used to fund the construction of a mosque. Another version has it that the mosque was built by the Fatmids. In 912, Fatmid caliph Al Mu'izz, travelling from Mahdiya (in Tunisia) to establish his rule in Egypt, was so well received by the inhabitants of Tripoli that he gave them a camel-load of treasure to extend and embellish the mosque. The present structure is the result of numerous refurbishments down the centuries, the last major rebuilding programme being undertaken in 1610-1611 at the orders of Safar Dey. Unsurprisingly, the plan of the mosque is slightly irregular. In its ascetic simplicity, it contrasts greatly with the other, more elaborate mosques of the madina. The sanctuary makes use of columns from varied sources, many Roman. Column capitals are sometimes used as column bases. The roof of the mosque is comprised of 42 brick-built domes. And the short square minaret has a spiral stairway of palm wood and plaster.

Turning right out of the Naga Mosque, you are just a couple of minutes from Green Square. (Leaving the mosque, go right and then left, and you are back on Shari'a al Mushir). You can now either explore the souks located in this neighbourhood, or take a look at the Ahmad Pasha al Qaramanli Mosque, if you still have time. Another possibility is to embark on a wander down Shari'a al Halga and through the busy narrow streets taking you to Shari'a al Rashid and its fruit and vegetable market.

## Exploring early 20th-century Tripoli

Basically, your explorations of Tripoli's 20th-century architectural heritage will take you through three neighbourhoods. Immediately south of Green Square is the **heart of the early 20th-century town**. To the east is the **Dahra neighbourhood**, home to embassies and a couple of the better hotels. Southwest of the old city, between Shari'a Rashid, Shari'a 'Umar al Mukhtar and the western coast road, you have a sort of **inter-zone**, a place of shabby apartment blocks, lorry parks and immigrant cafés. Here is the Tripoli fairground, also dating back to the Italian period, and the city's monument to economic liberalization, the shiny Burj al Fatih.

**From Green Square to the National Library** Apart from the flood-lighting, the wide expanse of Green Square is much as it was left by the Italians, although there is infinitely more traffic. Look out for the bronze sea-horse fountain, have an espresso at the Caffè Commercio, founded 1923. The two columns next to the Citadel are topped respectively by a ship, for Tripoli, and a rearing horseman, for Libya's independence. (Originally, there was the She-Wolf of Rome.) Running south of Green Square, arcaded shopping streets are home to a handful of chic shops, a bookstore and miscellaneous cafés and eateries. Fine examples of 1920s and Italian official building survive very nicely, though the tarmac in the streets is often in a rough and ready state. The smooth-faced 1930s architecture, which would have been swept away long ago in many countries, is happily free of advertising. To the east, a small area of Dolce Vita chic villas gives way to the offices and apartment blocks of the Dahra neighbourhood.

With the Castle Museum behind you, the streets leading away from you are, from left to right, the coast road (ex-Lungomare, today Shari'a al Fatih), Shari'a al Baladiya, Shari'a Mohamed Al M'qaryef, Shari'a Awwal Sebtambar (1st September), and Shari'a Mizran (aka Shari'a al Wadi). Take **Shari'a Mohamed M'qaryef** (ex-corso Vittorio Emanuele III) which runs directly from Green Square to the former cathedral on Maydan al Jaza'ir, ex-piazza della Cattedrale. This square was the great set-piece of 1930s Tripoli. The cathedral, built in a sort of Romano-Lombard style, was completed in 1928, but partly remodelled by governor Italo Balbo's *architetto numero uno*,

National Library
Tripoli
arch: Meraviglia
Mantegazza

## *Libya: a few useful facts*

*Surprisingly, Libya's capital has a Shari'a Haiti (Haiti St). The reason for this is that it was thanks to the Haitian delegate's vote that the UN decided to give Libya its independence in 1951. Most cities also have a Shari'a al Fatih, a 1st of September St, (aka Shari'a Awwal Sabtambir), this being the day in 1969 that a group of*

*young army officers overthrew the Sanusi Kingdom of Libya.*

*And finally, the Libyan year is neither Islamic (starting with the Prophet Mohamed's migration or hijra from Mecca to Medina) nor, of course, Christian. The Libyan calendar starts in 570, year of the Prophet's birth.*

Florestano di Fausto, who also designed the other buildings on the square, the imposing **Post Office** (on your left as you face the cathedral), and the magnificent **INPS building** with its soaring portico (opposite the cathedral, nice café next to fountain in courtyard). Two shopping opportunities on the square are the Post Office (heroic Libyan stamps) and the Patisserie Snawber in the arcades on your right as you face the cathedral (sticky Levantine delights).

Take the street immediately to the left of the cathedral (snack stops in restaurants on this street) and you will come out facing the palm trees and splendid orange domes of the former **Palazzo del Governatore**, some 500 m away. The palace, in a simplified neo-Saracenic style, designed by architect Meraviglia-Mantegazza, was completed in 1931. Since independence, the building has been successively Royal Palace, Palace of the People, and National Library. (Internet access available from basement, round the corner on your right as you stand facing the building.) The gardens, all pergolas and palms, must have been very fine in their day. Travelling up the eastern side of the palace you come to the Shari'a ibn Ashur which cuts through one of the better residential districts, the Garden City being to the east and newer property to the west.

After the Governor's Palace, you need to head back towards Green Square. With the palace behind you, go left along the main street (Shari'a Al Nasser), and take the first right (Oil Secretariat on corner). You are now on **Shari'a**

*Tripolitania*

# Southeast of Green Square

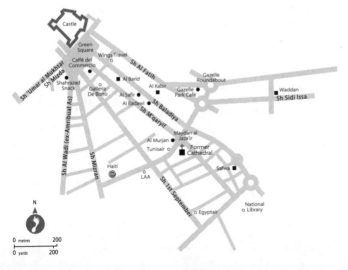

**Awwal Sebtambar**, aka Shari'a Al Fatih, ex-via Costanzo Ciano. Heading back to the centre, you will pass the long, two-storey neo-classical façade of the Ottoman **Arts and Crafts School** on your left, and, closer to Green Square, the arches of the splendid **Galleria De Bono** on your right. This is as near to walking through a wedding cake as an architectural experience gets, plaster mouldings and fioritures à gogo. There is a small open-air café in the marble-paved precinct, the Café Karama, and a handy photocopy shop. Also look out for the Fergiani Bookshop on your left, near the Galleria. Back on Green Square, you could turn left up Shari'a Umar al Mukhtar, ex-corso Sicilia.

**Al Dahra: functionalist architecture and a church** The sights in this part of the city are really for people with plenty of time. A fast walker with an hour or so to spare can do Green Square to the Church of San Francesco and back. Leaving Green Square and keeping the port on your left, there is a wide expanse of open ground where Tripoli lads play football of an evening. The large concrete tubes are a monument to the Great Man-Made River. (Look out for public art on irrigation theme). With Funduq al Kabir on your right, head towards the Gazelle Roundabout, marked by a rather charming little fountain: a bronze young woman reaches an arm uncomfortably up behind her to scratch the neck of her pet gazelle. (There is a pleasant café under the pergolas of the park, too.) Turn right, and then left after a semi-abandoned 1930s building on the corner, up a street with evergreen shade trees. Cross the dual carriageway, and the **Hotel al Waddan**, easily recognizable by its curious chimney feature, is on your left. (*Waddan*, by the way, means mouflon – a type of mountain sheep – in Arabic). Continue straight ahead, to the junction where the *Funduq Qasr Libya* is on your right. Turn right, uphill, and you will find the back of the Catholic **Church of San Francesco** on your right. This is the seat of the Archbishop of Libya. The austere building, its white façades picked out with terracotta trim, goes back to the 1930s. Inside are frescoes by Achille Funi and, behind the altar, a painting of Saint Francis venerating the Madonna, given in 1857 by Ferdinand II, King of the Two Sicilies, to the Church of Santa Maria degli Angeli (now de-consecrated) in the madina. After visiting the church, you can either head back to the Funduq Qasr al Libya, where there are generally cabs waiting, or continue uphill on Shari'a Khalid ibn Walid to the next main junction (Going left here you come to the main inter-city bus-station.) Turn right onto Shari'a al Nasr to head towards the 1930s Governor's Palace, about 500 m distant. On the left, you could look into a fresh food market to get a feel for everyday local life. The neighbourhood over to the left (south) is Garden City.

**Around Shari'a Umar al Mukhtar & Shari'a Rashid** Just as you leave Green Square, heading west on Shari'a Umar al Mukhtar, the large piece of arcaded functionalist building on your right is another Florestano di Fausto achievement, not to be photographed, however, as it houses something to do with State security today. You now have a good 15 minutes' trek before you reach the former Fiera di Tripoli, the **National Fairground**. Along Shari'a al Mukhtar are shops selling cheap clothes and household electrical goods and busy café-cum-public phone shops, where Moroccan women ply the world's oldest profession in a speak-easy atmosphere. On your left, shortly before a major junction, you will pass a church which wouldn't look out of place in a provincial town in northern Italy. Keep heading straight on, and you will eventually reach the entrance to the fairground, easily identifiable by its great pylons – like something from an Egyptian temple. Retrace your steps to the main junction, and go left, then right. The aim is to cut through a neighbourhood of small apartment blocks to reach the Shari'a Rashid. The area is full of immigrants, many from North Africa. There are cheap restaurants catering for North African workers, selling tea like they make it back home in Morocco; a poster of long-distance runner Hichem Guerrouj gives a touch of national pride. Eventually you come out on an open area with a few taxis. Opposite, on the far side of Shari'a Rashid are the white arcades and dome of the 1930s **Municipal Market**. Here are stalls selling field-fresh produce, much from Tunisia just across the frontier. There are more exotic things on sale too, parrots and macaws, tortoises and chameleons, even a hawk or two.

Further up the Shari'a Rashid, you come to the city's main public transport hub. To your right, on an area opposite the former **Italian Tobacco Factory**, is a chaotic expanse of share-taxis and mini-buses. Continuing towards the **Abraj Dhat al Imad** (a group of squat skyscrapers), you pass through a crowded pavement market. African women have everything for your beauty routine, spread out on plastic sheeting: hair-creams and portions of henna powder, fluorescent plastic combs and handfuls of gravely incense to chuck on a brasero. Others specialize in underwear, gas-lighters, and chirping alarm-clocks, everything the traveller could need. Shoe-repair boys sit in the shade of a building, a white-turbanned elder has bundles of *swak* twigs, Touareg toothpaste.

Cross the hectic dual-carriageway to the Dhat al Imad towers, home of the Islamic Call Society. Here you will find oil company and airline offices, and a couple of restaurants. The area has been marked for tower block development. Nearby the **Burj al Fatih** gleams green and white, Tripoli's most recognizable skyline feature. Inside is a luxurious shopping mall with escalators and shiny granite floors, sign that a new entrepreneurial Libya is taking shape? With the city sprawling ever further out into whatever remains of the oasis, up is the way to go. Here 21st-century Libya is building a business district with a waterfront profile. With thousands of social-housing units now constructed, the Man-Made River flowing, maybe oil money will be used to create prime business property.

If you're a walker, you would need a good couple of hours to walk out to the Planetarium from the centre and back again. Best to get a taxi in the late afternoon, and possibly walk back. Travelling by car, from Green Square a fast **dual carriageway** runs south and then east. Built over the former Lungomare, part of the former harbour area and adjacent to new wharves, it takes you past Al Dahra and on to the main area of state secretariats. For part of its length, it is called Shari'a al Fatih (originally Shari'a Adrian Pelt, named after the UN official who sponsored Libyan Independence in 1951). On this section, you pass close to a number of embassies, before the dual carriageway branches left to run past the tower-block Funduq al Mehari. Continuing along the cliff top highway, you have splendid views of the port. To your right, the two small domed structures are the eighteenth century **Qaramanli Tombs**. In the southermost of the two tombs are buried the sons of Yousef Pasha, ruled 1798-1832. The real aim of this excursion, however, is the **Planetarium**, Qubbat al Kawakib, a fine piece of 1970s building (designer Ulrich Müther) to the right of the highway, shortly after the royal blue domes of the Guest Palace. The Planetarium's low dome is surrounded by concrete sail-like structures which bristle up towards the heavens. Getting onto the building's terrace, you find that the pointy parts are a sort of concrete claustra. If visiting in the evening, mind the stray dogs that kip out on the terraces.

**East of the centre: past Al Dahra to some outlying sights**
See photograph of the Planetarium, page 5

With time on your hands on a Tripoli summer evening, you could take a taxi over to the planned Museum of Islamic Art, to be housed in the former Villa Volpi. The building, on your left down a side street near the main hospital, started life as an oasis summer palace of the Qaramanlis. The building was face-lifted by Comte Volpi's architects, the gardens were replanted.

**South of the centre: the Islamic Art Museum**

Tripolitania

Eventually, the villa became the Tripoli home of Volpi's daughter Anna-Maria Cigogna. The grounds, a fragment of the old oasis, have children's slides and play areas, plus an open-air café with Mickey Mouse murals. The Islamic Art Museum is still very much a figment of a heritage consultant's imagination. However, you can peek into the courtyard of the villa.

**Christian & war cemeteries** The cemetery for foreign Christians – (Al Maqbara al Masihiyya) – lies between Shari'a Jamal Abd al Nasser and Shari'a Al Jamahiriyah. The British and Commonwealth Cemetery is located 2 km west of Tripoli, 400 m south of the main road.

**Beaches** It is best to avoid the city centre beaches. The *masayif* (summer 'resorts'), small concentrations of concrete blocks near the Bab al Madina hotel are practically all male. Popular weekend trips include Farwa Island and Sabratha, west of Tripoli. The so-called Check Beach, at petrol station 207, north of the road, about ten minutes east of Tajura, was originally reserved for foreigners. (Carpark, 2LD per person access.) The narrow band of sand under the crumbly cliff gets packed with parasols, a café-restaurant pumps out house music all day long. To get there under your own steam, get a micro-bus from Dhat al Imad for Tajura Swahli, and ask to be let off at the appropriate petrol station. The farther you get from Tripoli, the better (and more difficult to reach) the beaches get. Those at **Bsis** and **Ghanima**, after Garabulli, have a good name.

## Essentials

**Sleeping**
*Phone code: 021*

*Single women may be refused accommodation in some of the mid-price hotels if they do not look respectable enough*

Tripoli is only moderately endowed with hotels, adequate for a country with little commercial tourism but a large immigrant worker population. Business visitors are fairly well catered for with 5 or so large hotels in Tripoli centre. Cheaper accommodation is difficult to find when arriving in the evening, so try to book ahead.

**Hard currency hotels** None of the hotels in this category really merit their classification. The Mehari and the Kabir cater for official visitors and the tour bus trade. The new Corinthia Hotel, next to Dhat al Imad, will no doubt be Tripoli's premier address when completed sometime in 2001.

**A** *Al Mehari*, Shari'a Al Fatah, 14 storey building overlooking the harbour, close to the main government secretariats and embassies, T3334090/6, Tx22090. Pool, best service in Tripoli, some say. US$215 a night for a double room, must be paid in US dollars, but not really A grade. Has better currency change desk than the Al Kabir (which is slightly better, however). There is a nice-ish local café over road from entrance. Very handy for ferry to Malta. NB rooms may be requisitioned when an official delegation is in town, whether you have a reservation or not. **A** *Funduq al Kabir*, Shari'a al Fatah, close to Green Square, the tall building is good landmark, T4445940, F4445959. 2 restaurants, buffet, café, very close to the madina and conveniently central with facilities close by (see below), expensive car hire, travel agency. Currently US$200 a night for a double room, which must be paid for in dollars, but it is not really A grade standard by a long shot. Currency desk would only exchange dollars in summer 2000. *DHL* office in same building, T3331133, on the right side of the building as you face the main entrance. The *Echo Cybercentre* is nearby on Shari'a Baladiya at the rear side of the building, along with couple of moderately acceptable restaurants, the best of which is *Al Safir*. Very handy for pleasant *Gazelle Park* café (turn right out of main entrance).

**B** *Funduq al Wahat*, on Shari'a Umar al Mukhtar. Ugly tower block, but handy for the *Libyan Arab Airlines* office and the Tripoli Fair Ground T3612021/2039, F3612041.

Tripolitania

Unpleasant reception insists on dollar payment. Prefer *Funduq al Waddan* over in Dahra in this price category. *Bab al Bahr* is also much better.

**Ordinary hotels  Near fairground off Umar al Mukhtar**: just west of Tripoli Fair Ground, between Shari'a Umar al Mukhtar and the sea, there is a concentration of mid-price hotels.

**C** *Hotel al Jawda*, off Shari'a Umar al Mukhtar near the Corniche, T4446908. A recent hotel, 50LD a night. Identify by blue and yellow sign over entrance. **C** *Funduq al Nahar* (Man-Made River Hotel), Shari'a Tariq (turn left at the Bourguiba mosque as you face the Towers at the top of Shari'a Rashid). Easily identifiable by orange awnings on roof terrace. T4444948, 3334645, F4444690. A/C and TV in all rooms. Single room 44LD, double 71LD. (At this price, Bab al Bahr or Waddan are better). Very handy for buses etc.

**D** *Hotel Atlas*, southwest of old town at top of Shari'a Umar al Mukhtar on a small square to the right, T3336815. Simple but clean rooms with and without shower. Around 20LD a night. Its drawback is that there is quite a bit of traffic noise in the summer because it is on the main road, however, it is handy for reasonable eateries nearby on Umar al Mukhtar. **D** *Funduq Bahr al Abiad* (*Hotel Mediterranean*), T4860246. 200 rooms, with bath, half a/c, roof terrace (currently closed), clean-ish. Best to have own sheet and pillow case. Rooms have carpet on floor and walls, very hot and sweaty in summer, mosquitoes, no A/C. Rooms at 10LD, 15LD and 20LD a night. **D** *Hotel Lula*, seafront to the southwest of the madina, T3331013. (Closed at the last count). Was on the grotty side, restaurant, café, room with bath, breakfast included. 20LD a night. Prefer Hotel al Jawda if possible.

# Shari'a Rashid & around

Mediterranean Sea

MADINA

Al Kurnish Rd

Dhat al Imad (5 Towers)

Taxis/Micros to Sabratha, Tajura & Yefren

Taxis to Al Khums (Garage Tunis)

Bourguiba Mosque

Al Kurnish Rd

International Bus Agencies

Sh Rashid

Taxis to Tarhuna

3

Micros to Gargaresh

Taxis to Ben Ghashir

Maydan Swayhli

Micros/Taxis to Gharyan, Jadu, Nalut & Tiji

1

Burj al Fatih

Sh Umar al Mukhtar

International Fairground

Sh Al Ma'ari

Sh Tariq

4

LAA

2    8    5    Sports Centre

N

0 metres  200
0 yards   200

■ **Sleeping**
| | | |
|---|---|---|
| 1 Al Hani | 4 Al Wahat | 7 Bab al Madina |
| 2 Al Jawda | 5 Atlas | 8 Bahr al Abyad |
| 3 Al Nahar | 6 Bab al Bahr | (Mediterranean) |

Tripolitania

### At the sandwich shop

*At the average cheap Tripoli eatery, you pay at the till first, acquiring a coloured chit or plastic jeton which you then give to the guy serving your sandwich or drink. Prices are extremely cheap, and as the choice is limited, pointing will generally do to get you what you want. The usual sandwich fillings are shawarma, lahm mafroum (hot minced beef), falafel (oil-fried chickpea and garlic balls, an Egyptian speciality) or klayat djaj (chicken kidneys fried with onion). You will be asked whether you want your sandwich with chopped salad or harissa (spicy red-pepper paste, liberally spooned out of a plastic box). Roast chicken is usually available, too: ask for **nuss djaj***

*(half chicken) or **ruba' djaj** (quarter chicken) generally served with **batata** (chips) or **rouz** (rice). In this case, you are having a **wajba khafifa**, a light meal.*

*Surprisingly for a country with so much coastline, fish does not figure on the menus of cheap eateries to any great extent. Fish is called hout or **samak**, and if available tends to come fried (**muqli**) or grilled (**mashwi**). On the drinks front, there is generally **asir** (fruit syrup or juice), which comes in various lurid colours. Or you can have a **shishat moyya** (bottle of water). Small bottles of still water are not always available, so you may have to go for a litre of Kufra or a small bottle of fizzy Bin Ghashir.*

**Near Shari'a al Rashid   D** *Hotel al Mamun*, Shari'a al Mamun, near the main bus and taxi station, very handy for both old city and central Tripoli, no phone. Kind of seedy – bring own sheet. Fills up quickly. 25LD a night. **E** *Funduq al Barid*, in Shari'a al Baladiya, behind the Funduq al Kabir, in the Green Square direction, T333 2509. 12LD a night, acceptable but noisy in summer when you have to sleep with windows open. Handy for downtown services. **E** *Funduq al Hani*, located close to Maydan al Swahli, T3332173. Very convenient for public transport and cheap. Twin room without bath 15LD, with bath 20LD. No a/c. To get there, start at Maydan al Swahli. With the post office on the left, go straight ahead on Shari'a al Kindi. Take second right, Funduq al Hani is on left. **F** *Tourist Hotel*, in the old town. As you head up souk al Truk, away from Green Square, a steep staircase on the left takes you up to this hotel. (Hooray! Sign on wall outside is in Latin letters.) 5 small rooms round a patio, beds allotted as people arrive. Pleasant, helpful reception. Tiny shower room not for the nervous (the electric immersion heater is very close to the shower). Not really for women travelling alone. Very hot and sweaty in the humid Tripoli summer.

There are also migrant workers' hotels with **shared facilities** (category **D/E**) in the streets around the Shari'a Rashid. More or less clean, often noisy, these hotels are ideal for those needing to leave early with inter-city share taxis. Similar hotels can also be found in the triangle between Shari'a Umar al Mukhtar, Shari'a Rashid and Shari'a Tariq. Perhaps the best is **D** *Funduq Trablus*, Shari'a al Rashid (parallel to Shari'a al Mamun), on your left as you leave Dhat al Imad and main taxi station behind you, a couple of blocks before market (identify at night by large, multi-coloured sign), T4441093/5. Clean rooms, very reasonable but eat elsewhere. 30LD a night. NB Cheap hotels in this area not a good choice for women travelling alone, as there is a risk of being mistaken for one of the many sex workers.

**Dhat al Imad   C** *Funduq Bab al Bahr*, multi-storey building close to the five Dhat al Imad towers, Tripoli's main business centre, on the Corniche, T3350676, F3350711. 45LD a night for a single room with a/c, essential if you are here to work and need a good night's sleep. Probably better than the *Hotel al Kabir*, and certainly far better located if you need to visit clients in Dhat al Imad. Small pool. Run by the Social Insurance Fund's hotel investment department, hence good management. Will register passport for new arrivals. Much used by business travellers and local organizations.

**C** *Funduq Bab al Madina*, next to the Bab al Bahr, T608051. Sea views but very much a third choice in this category. No a/c, so pretty humid in summer as right next to the sea.

**Dahra A** *Safwa*, Shari'a Baladiya, heading for Garden City, T4448691, F4449062. Rooms 120LD a night. Reservations necessary. A popular business hotel. Pleasant café garden. Reasonable restaurant and handy for Maydan al Jaza'ir area restaurants, UNDP offices and *Libyan Arab Airlines* on Shari'a Haiti. **C** *Al Waddan*, Shari'a Sidi Issa, just off Shari'a al Fath, T3330041/2. Good location in the old 1930s centre. At 60LD a night, this is a better price than the hard-currency hotels. Often full, so try to reserve. Nice management, English speakers at reception. Will organize transfer to airport. Car hire office on ground floor. Handy if you have business at Zweitina Oil Company, just opposite. **D** *Qasr Libya* (*Libya Palace*), Shari'a Sidi Issa, T3331181. Rambling, 6-floor hotel in the Dahra area. Service and cleanliness of fair standard, busy, if slightly seedy, reception area, some quiet rooms with a/c, travel agency. Rather Eastern-bloc feel. 25LD a night for single with double bed. Just under 1 km from the old town. Frequented by Libyan and other business travellers. Rooftop restaurant. Very close to British Embassy, *Hotel al Waddan* and *Zweitina Oil Company*. 10 mins' walk to Dahra inter-city bus station. Recommended in this price category. **D** *Funduq Yousser* in the street leading up to the main entrance of the Church of San Francesco), parallel to Shari'a Sidi Issa. What the French call *un hotel de passe*. Prefer the Qasr Libya. Handy for bus station.

Outside Tripoli there are several **tourist villages** which can offer accommodation on request, but which are often very full in the vacation periods. Try the *Gharnata Holiday Village*, T4773942, at Gargaresh, although reservations will be very difficult in the summer. Most of the tourist villages really function for the families of the locally employed expatriate community.

**Youth hostels** *Tripoli City*, 69 Shari'a Amr ibn Al-As, T4445171. About 50 m off Green Square, on left opposite cinema. Dormitory accommodation. The rather rundown headquarters building of the *Libyan Youth Hostel Association*. Not a good option at all. *Gargaresh*, Shari'a Gargaresh, 5 km south of Tripoli, T4776694. Open 0700-2400, 200 beds, meals, family room, laundry, airport 20 km, harbour 2 km. Booking recommended.

**Camps** Expatriates in Tripoli for a lengthy stay will be drawn to one of the camps out in the Gargaresh district. These are owned and run by international companies to house their personnel. *Gharnata Complex*, in Gargaresh, T4773942. A holiday camp-type place, which gets crowded in summer. 27LD/double. *Regatta*, expatriate enclave beyond Gargaresh in the Al Ghiran neighbourhood, T4832314. Home to the Wajda Italian restaurant. *7th October Camp*, Hay al Atar, Gargaresh, T4780308, 4775335, F4775335. Tennis courts and a reasonable swimming pool.

Until recently, Tripoli had few restaurants. However, over the last 5 years or so, the situation has improved considerably. Hotels such as the *Al Kabir* and the *Al Mahari* have more than one restaurant, which though 'dry' are perfectly adequate. For a view over Tripoli, there is the restaurant at the top of Burj al Fatih. For something more elaborate, you could try an evening out at one of the fish restaurants like the *Shira'a* or the *Dandashi* in the Gargaresh area. In the city centre on, or just off, Shari'a Umar al Mukhtar and on the main streets leading southwards off Green Square there are plenty of cheap eateries which are hygienic, on the whole. The area around Maydan Al Jaza'ir has a number of good restaurants, including the *Murjan* and the *Sanabil*. If you have a micro-bus to catch, there are stand-up shawarma places on Shari'a Rashid. The large number of customers means that plenty of food is being cooked and served, making these small eateries safe to eat in.

**Eating**

Tripolitania

**Expensive** *Al Shira'a*, ('The Sail') on the seafront at Gargaresh, T4775123. A pleasant place with terrace overlooking the sea. This is where businesses entertain their clients. Good seafood – but not cheap at around 50LD a head. (Fish is charged by the kilo, usual price 25LD per kilo). *Al Sharqi*, in Tripoli old town, under 5 mins' walk from Green Square. Serves local dishes, closed Fri. Ask your way – the restaurant is not far from the Naqa Mosque (Jam'i al Naqa). *Dandishi*, popular new fish restaurant on the main Gargaresh road. *Mat'am Dhahabi*, (*Golden Restaurant*) on the 3rd floor in Tower 3 of the Dhat al Imad complex, T3350069. *Mata'am al Fursan al Awa'il* (Restaurant Les Cavaliers), newly opened with Italian management, near the Hippodrome. Ask taxi driver for restaurant near the *Furusiya*, Bou Sitta. Prices circa 30LD a head. Excellent spaghetti fruits de mer. Highly recommended. *Murjan* ('Coral'), under the arcades at 2, Maydan al Jaza'ir, opposite the Main Post Office, T3336307. A new fish restaurant. Specialities include *tajine hraymi* (fish baked with potatoes) and *sharmoula* (fish oven-baked with natural salt). Also paella and a good choice of fresh fish. Efficient Moroccan service. Cost, say 25LD for a really good feed. Cheaper than the Gargaresh fish restaurants. A welcome addition to Maydan al Jazai'r, already a stylish section of the city centre with its 1930s rationalist architecture. *Safir*, Shari'a Baladiya a few mins' walk from Green Square, T4447064. Popular restaurant serving Middle Eastern and North African food. Handy location just behind the Hotel al Kabir. *Wajda*, Regata Holiday Village in the Gargaresh district, west of Tripoli, T4832314. A fine Italian restaurant.

**Mid-range**  Al Jarra KTV. Coffee shop and restaurant, Younis Building, Gargaresh Rd, T4839402, on left before Regatta (on right) as you head west. Philipino-run karaoke restaurant in an area with a large expatriate population. Badwan, tiny Lebanese restaurant on Shari'a Baladiya, just behind the Funduq al Kabir. Nothing much to recommend it except its proximity to Tripoli's largest hotel. Sanabil (Chez Camille), 16, Shari'a Karatchi, nearly opposite the French Cultural Centre, T4440479. (Following Shari'a M'qaryif uphill from Maydan al Jaza'ir, Shari'a Karatchi is on your left near the top). Despite its unprepossessing façade, a popular centrally located restaurant under Lebanese management.

**Cheap**  Try Shari'a Mizda, a cheerful street with pavement restaurants between Shari'a Umar al Mukhtar and Shari'a al Wadi, aka Shari'a 'Amr ibn al As. A large blond Moroccan lady presides over the main café restaurant. Smoke a *chicha* and have a game of backgammon after your kebab. On the corner of Green Square and Shari'a al Wadi, the *Shahrazad* serves the usual sandwiches. The unsigned restaurant with the wooden façade, also on Green Square, is best avoided. There are plenty of stand-up cheap eateries on Shari'a al Rashid and near the Dhat al Imad/Garage Tunis bus station, and on Shari'a Umar al Mukhtar. If you need somewhere air-conditioned to sit and eat, there is the *Arous al Bahr*, almost directly opposite the Funduq al Nahar. They do both sandwiches and pâtisseries.

**Cafés**  On a summer evening, the café in the Gazelle Park is a pleasant place for a snack. They do *shawarma* sandwiches and *sfayih*, unleavened bread with mince meat. Try also the former *Caffè del Commercio* at the corner of Green Square and Shari'a al M'qaryif. If you want a croissant, ask for a *brioche*, generally served with a jam and butter filling. In summer, there are sandwich stalls on the Corniche, too.

**Entertainment**  Tripoli is not exactly blessed with concert halls and sports facilities. However, rest assured, things are much better than they were in the bleak 1980s, when the local Islamic socialist ideology was at its height. The city centre corniche gets quite lively in summer, with mini fun-fairs and small restaurants much frequented by families. There is even live music by local bands, attracting an all male crowd, however. On 1st September, African bands and dancers dance on the corniche to celebrate the anniversary of the revolution. In summer, families go to the beach if they can't get abroad. For the wealthy, leisure activities are similarly limited: the beach, a barbecue at a farm in winter, or the odd trip to a restaurant. If you like chess and backgammon, you'll probably be able to get a game at the café in Gazelle Park near Funduq al Kabir. Another option, if in Tripoli for a long stay, is a trip to the zoo (*hadiqat al hayawanat*).

**Shopping**

Shari'a 1st September and Shari'a Mohammad M'qaryif have shops with clothes and other consumer goods, travel agents, and an abundance of cafés. 2 more streets fan out from Green Square and the adjacent traffic island. Shari'a Mizran and Shari'a Amr ibn al As carry small scale commercial activity, bakers, general goods shops, traders and others. Joining these streets to Shari'a 1st September and Al-Fatah area are cross links, the most important of which is Shari'a Tahiti. Shari'a Umar al Mukhtar leads off Green Square directly running southwestwards. On the right is a red-marble faced building, the Secretariat of Justice, with the rest of the street given over to trading houses, Arab restaurants, cafés and shops. On the right the street opens up on the site of the *Tripoli Fair ground* used for international exhibitions. Shari'a Umar al Mukhtar ultimately gives access to the main western suburbs such as *Gurgi* and the former European villa area of *Giorgim Poppoli* with its supermarkets, beach clubs and tourist centres. Shari'a Ibn Ashur has dry cleaning, a pharmacy, a bakery and grocery stores. Throughout the central business and inner residential districts there are excellent doctors' surgeries, chemist shops, food stores, general goods shops, bakeries and small cafés. There are some popular restaurants, though these are almost entirely confined to the streets off and adjacent to the streets fanning out of Green Square. The poorer residential suburbs have small scale facilities and often no doctors, though pharmacies are common. The larger suburbs with pre-existing commercial centres such as Gurgi have a full range of facilities.

If it is reading material you require then the main bookshop is *Fergiani's* near the roundabout off Green Square on Shari'a 1st September with a 2nd shop in Shari'a Al Jamaririyah near Eliarmuk Square. Try also *Dar Al Hadara* close to *Fergiani's* at 90 Shari'a 1st September, for books in Arabic and English on scientific subjects.

**Sports**

There is a football team – dates and times of games are advertised in the Arabic press. The main opening for sport for visitors to Tripoli is swimming, snorkelling and scuba-diving in the sea along the coastline. For medium-to-long stay travellers it might be worth joining a beach club, most being on the Gurgi side of the city. Each club is marked with a large board which, though in Arabic, makes it quite clear that it is a sports centre. It is advised that enquiries are made personally at the gate, through a state agency or, most easily, through a travel agent.

**Tour companies & travel agents**

There are a number of tour companies in the main avenues leading from Green Square. *Africa Tours*, Dhat al Imad, tower 3, ground floor. T3613037, F36123036. Also offices in Sabha, T071 625594, F071 621778. *Al Faw Tours*, POB 13355, Tripoli. T/F4802881. *Asslum Tours*, Burj al Fatih, floor 2, office 13. POB 71098 Tripoli. T3351112, F3351113, mobile 0912127023. *Fezzan Tours*, POB 81495 Tripoli. T3335556, F3339438, mobile 091 2141247. Contact Mukhtar. *Libyan Travel & Tourist Co*, Shari'a Mizran headed by Salem Azzabi T4448005. *Oea*, Shari'a 1st September, POB 91749 Tripoli, T3338237, F3338369. Good reputation. Also have a branch in Ghadamès, T0484-2991, F0484-2291, oeatours@hotmail.com. *OUM Ghozlan Tourism*, T4835419, F4835407, injaz@ittnet.net. *Robban Tours*, main offices out of town centre. Ring Hussein al Founi on T4441530 or 4448065. Can organize a driver to take you up the to Jabal Nafusa or elsewhere. *Tecnis Travel*, offices in the reception area of the Hotel Bab al Bahr, T3350526, F3350525, mobile 091-2139207. Postal address: POB 91218, Dhat al Imad, Tripoli. Manager Ali Shibli. *Wings/Al Jinah*, conveniently located right on Green Square, almost directly opposite the entrance to the Castle Museum. No sign, but look out for tour company stickers on the windows, T3331855, F3330881, wingstravel@yahoo.com General manager is Abd al Karim al Yussufi. Wael Harrus speaks good English and can advise on tours to the South and elsewhere.

**Transport**  **Local**  Transport within Tripoli is by one of the ubiquitous black-and-white cabs or by yellow and white micro-bus. By cab, all trips in central Tripoli cost 5LD, regardless of the distance. For Gargaresh, you pay 10LD, more for Janzur. For the airport, expect to pay 15LD. Micro buses from Maydan al Swahli, off Shari'a Rashid, do the Hayy al Andalus / Gargaresh and Gorgi run, for the moderate sum of .5LD. Micro buses can be flagged down on all main routes through the city.

**Car hire**  If you are short on time and are not confident in driving in Libya, one option is to take a private car (*sayyara makhsousa*) with driver to take you to Leptis or the Jabal Nafusa. This is by no means a cheap option if you are by yourself, but the driver will wait while you tour a site. A half-day trip to Sabratha will be around 150LD. Preferably go through one of the tour agencies, who will find you a driver with a reliable car. The other option is to look out for one of the drivers who hang out around the *Hotel al Kabir* (there are car hire offices at the hotels Kabir and Waddan, at the Kabir they speak no English). You could also try *Al Salama Car Rental*, which has several offices: Tripoli International Airport, T3618947, Funduq al Waddan, T3330041/45, mobile 091-2145370, F4449526.

**Air**  Currently there are *LAA* domestic flights from Tripoli to Benghazi and Sabha, very reasonably priced at 56LD for a return trip. There is heavy demand for flights, however. Reserve in advance at the *LAA* offices on Shari'a Haiti or Shari'a Umar al Mukhtar, close to the Hotel al Wahat.

**Road**  There are two main centres for catching public transport to leave Tripoli, namely the Dahra Bus Station (modern and organized) and the more chaotic Garage Tunis / Shari'a Rashid area.

**Dahra Bus Station**  Buses of the *National Rapid Transport Company* operate out of the Mahatat Dahra, a modern bus station located 5 mins' walk from the Hotel Qasr al Jazira. Buses do the following routes: Tripoli to **Benghazi**, Tripoli to **Ghadamès**, Tripoli to **Sabha**. (The company also does Sabha to Ghat, reservations to be made in Sabha). For more distant destinations, you need to buy your ticket a day in advance. The domestic bus ticket office is close to the café-restaurant, at the back of the station. Window (*shubak al hijz*) 1 does tickets for Benghazi, window 2 does other destinations. Departures as follows: Tripoli to **Benghazi**, 0700 and 1000 everyday, 13.5LD; Tripoli to **Sabha**, 0500 everyday, 13LD; Tripoli to **Ghadamès**, 0800 everyday, 8LD; Tripoli to **Nalut** 0700 and 1300 everyday, 3.5LD. Return buses from these destinations leave at the same times. However, if the bus is not full, they will leave later. At Dahra, note that the Benghazi buses generally go from the 'platform' closest to the café and magazine sellers. The next platforms are for **Derna** and **Sabha**. **Ghadamès** is the 4th quay, Gharyan and Mizda the 5th.

The **international** section of the Dahra Bus Station is over to your left as you stand facing the domestic ticket office. It is easily identifiable by the colourful international line coaches with their blue / yellow / brown livery. There are services to Egypt (both Alexandria and Cairo) and Tunisia. Tripoli to **Cairo**: Mon (Libyan bus) depart 0700, arrive Cairo Tue circa 1200; Thu (Egyptian bus) dep 0900, arrive Fri 1400. Ticket 65LD one way. Tripoli to **Alexandria**: Tue only, dep. 0700, arrive 1000 the following day. 55LD one way. Tripoli to **Tunis**: every day except Sat, dep. 0400, 20LD one way (return from Tunis 27 Dt)

**Garage Tunis / Shari'a Rashid** Tripoli's main public transport terminus is in the Shari'a Rashid area. Here you will find Peugeot 504 inter-city share taxis and micro-buses for local and international destinations. Vehicles go when they are full. Some international coach services go from this neighbourhood, as well as the desert bus for Niger. The handiest decent hotel in this area is the *Funduq al Nahar*, Shari'a Tariq. Also close by are the hotels Bab al Bahr and Bab al Madina.

*The Bourguiba Mosque, the one with the arcades on Shari'a Rashid is a key reference point in this area*

There are four main 'sections'. **Micro-bus station opposite Dhat al Imad**: seemingly chaotic, this is a heaving mass of yellow and white micro buses. There are departures for **Sabratha** and **Tajura**. On the far side, closest to the main coast road, Peugeot 504s depart for **Yefren**, 3.5LD. **Shari'al Ma'ari**: the first main street on your right as you leave Dhat al Imad behind you. (Turn right before the Bourguiba Mosque.) From here there are long distance coach departures, look out for offices opposite social housing project. Peugeots and micro-buses for **Jadu** and **Nalut** go from waste ground opposite the unfinished mosque next to Burj al Fatih. **Garage Tunis**: so named as buses for Tunis used to leave from here. Another area heaving with vehicles, just next to the ramparts of the madina. Peugeot 504s for **Khums** (**Leptis Magna**), 3.5LD, go from the ranks farthest from Dhat al Imad. There are 2 international reservation offices on this square. **Maydan Swahli**. On same side of Shari'a Rashid as Bourguiba Mosque. Maydan Swahil, micro-buses for Gargaresh and Janzur, is a block west off main street. Departures for **Tarhuna** on Shari'a Rashi, about 50 m before you reach the central market on your left.

**Boat** For the moment, the only passenger ferry from Tripoli is for **Malta**. Services have been reduced since the end of the embargo. At present, there are boats for Malta on Thu and Sun. In principle, one should be able to buy a ticket at the *National Maritime Company Office* in the first building on your left on Shari'a Mohamed al M'qaryif , on your left as you leave Green Square. (Look out for sign with blue lettering and ship.) In practice, you need to go to the port or through a travel agency. You could try ringing the main switchboard at the port, T3331710. The best way is to turn up at the ferry terminal, just below the *Hotel Mahari*, a few days before you wish to travel. On day of travel, be at port at 1600, boat leaves at 1800 (usually). Return ticket 115LD, single 70LD.

**Airline offices** The vast majority of the airline offices are handily located in the Dhat al Imad complex. Some of the Arab airline companies (*Egyptair, LAA, Syrian Airlines, Tunisair*) are in the shopping streets south of Green Square. *Air Malta*, Dhat al Imad, tower 5, floor 1. T3350578/79/81. Frequent daily services between Tripoli and Valletta. *British Airways*, Burj al Fatih, tower1, floor 19. Use lifts 4 and 5. Sales T3351277/82, F3351283. Airport 3605332, F3605313. (There were difficulties with the phones in summer 2000.) Office hours Sat-Thu 0830-1430. Flights London to Tripoli 3 times a week. *Alitalia*, Dhat al Imad, T3350297/98, 3350300, F3350306. Chaotic offices in Dhat al Imad, tower 3, floor 1. *Austrian Airlines*, Dhat al Imad, tower 3, floor 6. T3350241/42/43. F3350244. Three flights a week between Tripoli and Vienna, Wed/Fri/Sun. *Egyptair*, top of Shari'a 1st September, on corner with Shari'a Calcutta (on your left as you come from Green Square). T3335781/82, F3332806. Flights between Cairo and Tripoli on Mon/Thu. *Korean Airlines*, Dhat al Imad, tower 4, floor 13. T 3350301/02, F 3350302. No flights as yet (summer 2000). Libyan Arab Airlines. Two main offices. Down town on Shari'a Haiti, a short walk from Maydan al Jaza'ir. Main office on Shari'a Umar al Mukhtar, on left opposite the Tripoli International Fairground, T3337500 open 0730-1630. Phone reservations not generally possible. Queue and hope. *Swissair*, Dhat al Imad, tower 3, floor 4. *Tunisair*, Shari'a Haiti, a couple of doors away from Maydan al Jaza'ir. T3350095/96, 3337750, F3350097. Flights between Tunis and Tripoli on Mon/Thu.

**Directory**

*There is no phone directory for Tripoli*

**Banks** Banks are generally open 0800-1400, in the central shopping zone. However, many of the central area banks do not (as yet) deal with currency exchange for tourists. Both the hotels Al Kabir and Al Mahari have currency exchange facilities. In Funduq al Kabir, the bureau de change is just next to reception. Despite a display board with currency exchange rates for the dinar and main European currencies, they only take dollars. The *Mahari* is more flexible. If you are in the hotels Bab

*Tripolitania*

al Bahr or Bab al Madina, use the bank on the ground floor of Dhat al Imad, tower 1, easily recognizable by its yellow and green logo (*Masraf al Tijara wa al Tanmiya*). They generally take dollars only, but have been known to take other currencies. If you are really stuck, then jewellers and tourist shops in the souk and on Shari'a 1st September will generally provide a discreet exchange service for francs, Deutsch-marks, dollars, lire and pounds. For information, the following are the main central area banks. Masraf al Umma is conveniently on the roundabout adjacent to Green Square and the others are on the main roads leaving the square. *Masraf al Umma* , Shari'a Umar al Mukhtar, T3334031. *Central Bank of Libya*, Shari'a Gamal Abd al Nasser, T3333591. *Jamahiriya Bank*, Shari'a Mohammad Magariyef, T3333553. *Libyan National Arab Bank*, Shari'a 1st September. *National Commercial Bank*, Green Square, T3337191. *Sahara Bank*, Shari'a 1st September, T3332771. *Wahhadah Bank*, T3334016.

**Communications** Main Post Office: this is found on Maydan Al-Jaza'ir opposite the former cathedral and has telecommunications facilities. Telephone: Note that old 5 digit numbers beginning with 3 place 33 in front, beginning with 4 place 44 in front. Most Tripoli numbers are now 7 digit, although some of the old 6 digit numbers are still in use. **Private call centres**: The easiest way to phone out of Libya is from one of the numerous public phone offices. Try for instance Shari'a Mohamed al M'qaryif, under the arcades, a few doors up from the former Caffè del Commercio on Green Square. There is another behind the Central Market on Shari'a Rashid, on the street to the right of the Markaz al Jihad research centre. Write your number on a scrap of paper and the operator will dial your number. Take call in cabin, pay after. **Internet**: Tripoli is now well endowed with cyber-cafés. The easiest to find is *Echo-Net*, in the same building as the Hotel al Kabir, on the ground floor on the Shari'a al Baladiya side of the building. 4LD an hour, stays open late. Also in the central area, try *Markaz Haiti*, T3332789, 3332776, F333328450, 102 Shari'a Haiti, near the Libyan Arab Airlines office. (Turn right off Shari'a 1st September as you come up from Green Square, cyber centre is on your right.) The *Sigma Internet*, generally crowded, 2.5LD / hour, is on a side street third left off 1st September as you leave Green Square (or second left after the Galleria De Bono). A cyber-centre was scheduled to open in Burj al Fatih, first floor. The one on the ground floor of Dhat al Imad, tower 4, was not functional summer 2000.

**Embassies** See box in Essentials chapter page 38.

**Hospitals and medical services** Chemists: in all shopping areas chemists are normally marked with a red crescent sign. Chemists have a duty rota which is normally reliable, but travellers with special needs are advised to bring their own stores. In the central area, there is a handy chemists on Shari'a al Mizran, not far from Green Square, on the right. Another good chemists is located on Shari'a Rashid, on your right between two small restaurants as you turn off Shari'a Umar al Mukhtar. **State-run hospitals**: there are several large, fairly well-equipped hospitals. The main general hospital (*Al Mustashfa al Markaziya*) is in the Bin Ashur district, T 3605001. A secondary hospital is at Al Khadra (the old military hospital). Another possibility is the Tripoli Medical Centre, out by the Al Fatih University, T 3608366/69. **Private medical services**: in severe emergencies, it will be best to contact one of the private clinics. The best equipped is the *Al Afiya Clinic*, T 2233051/4, managed by Dr Fawzi Addala and his brother Dr Nouri Addala. This clinic is located close to the airport, and so is ideal for emergency evacuation. The former SAMI clinic ('*Ayada Sami al Khasa*) , in a side street between the Gargaresh and Gorgi roads, near the Philippino School, works mainly with private companies. It belongs to International SOS, of which BUPA is a member. A central clinic which has a good reputation is the Brothers' Clinic (*Masahhat al Akhwa*), T 4442496, F 4442498, located at Neflin, just east of Dahra. If based in the hotels Bab al Bahr or Bab al Madina, the *Dhat al Imad Clinic*, tower 1, ground floor, T 3350461/62 might help. Oil company personnel and those employed in diplomatic missions generally make use of the *11 June Clinic*, the National Oil Company facility.

# Around Tripoli

West Tripoli suburbs: tourist villages

**Janzur** is on the old coast road running west out of Tripoli, as is the **D** *Janzur Tourist Village*, T4890430, right on the coast, mainly new, with a wide range of accommodation including bungalows and apartments. Facilities available include sailing, tennis, cinema, children's play room, shops, clinic. The village is signposted in Arabic as *Madina Siyahia Janzur*.

Booking at tourist villages is not easy from a distance since they are run by state organisations and are not aimed at the foreign visitor. Persistence in seeing the on-site manager might be the best way to get accommodation. Their big disadvantage is their isolation from the city though bus or shared taxi transport is available on the old coast road 500 m south of the beach club sites. Charges per night vary with the season and the quality of the complex between 15 and 35LD. If you really want a beach holiday, you would be better advised to hop over the frontier to Djerba in southern Tunisia, where accommodation is of the beach-resort type expected by an international clientele.

# Tuniso-Libyan border to Sabratha via Zuwara

As a consequence of the UN air embargo from 1992 to 1999, plus an easing by Libya of border controls, there is a considerable flow of commercial heavy traffic as well as private cars and taxis on the road from the Tuniso-Libyan border to Tripoli. Whether this will ease up as air traffic develops following the lifting of the embargo remains to be seen. Although there seem to be only the slightest of restrictions on movements of goods and people for Arabs, the volume of traffic is such that large queues can build up on both sides. The border post has few facilities other than a petrol station and a small café on the Libyan side. Once through the frontier from Tunisia the road connects as a single lane highway along the coast from Farwa to Zuwara.

## Farwa Island

The island of Farwa lies just offshore, close to the border at Ras Ajdir. The island is approached either by a rough causeway built at the time of the construction of the nearby Bu Kammash petrochemical/refinery complex, or by ferry from a pier at Bu Kammash village to the west of the plant. The ferry, run by local fishermen, is an occasional rather than a regular service. There are sea police and customs officials at both the pier and the causeway to control movement and those at the pier can be helpful in retaining a boatman.

The island, 12 km long and 2 km at its widest, is basically flat with a few dunes. There are palm groves which have been tidied up in the central section of the island. (There is perhaps a tourist complex to be built). The sand is fine grained and silver coloured. Excepting the view of the petrochemical plant, the site is absolutely first class.

Shortly after Bu Kammash, at the Farwa road restaurant, easily spotted on the left, there is a turn off left onto the old coast road, which will take you to Zuwara some 35 km further on. This is a slower option than the main, busy highway.

## Zuwara   زوارة

Moving eastwards, Zuwara is an expanding if unexciting town, approximately 100 km from Tripoli and 60 km from the border with Tunisia. In the 1930s, the town was the terminus of the coastal railway from Tripoli, and the old central square still has a little architecture from the days of Italian Libya. Today, the main employer is the petrochemical complex at Bu Kammash. Most commercial and municipal activity is concentrated in the centre of the town on the old road 1 km to the north of the new dual carriageway coastal highway. The town extends to the seashore with lots of new villas.

**Sleeping** There are only a couple of accommodation options at Zuwara. **C** *Funduq al Salam*. A new hotel, next to the football stadium. Acceptable, 30LD a double room. **E** *Istiraha Siyahiya al Zuwara* (*Zuwara Tourist Resthouse*), in the middle of the town adjacent to the square. A cheap, small hotel. Also has a small restaurant. No camping facilities are reported near Zuwara, although along the coast there are plenty of good camping places in woodlands or on the coast. Ask permission if possible before setting up camp.

**Transport** **Road** The shared taxi/bus services to east and west along the coast road are very frequent. Express buses with a/c on Tripoli to Tunis run can be stopped in Zuwara. Ordinary inter-urban service buses can be caught to Tripoli.

**Directory** **Communications** **Post Office:** this is near the clinic on the old road. **Medical services** First aid: the Red Crescent clinic is on the old road.

**Zuwara to Sabratha** From Zuwara travel east via the modern road to **Sabratha**, 97 km from Tripoli. The Zuwara to Sabratha stretch of road is narrow and still single carriageway and is known to be particularly dangerous since traffic is dense and undisciplined. Coastal mists can be a problem because local drivers tend to ignore such hazardous conditions.

## Modern Sabratha

*Phone code: 024* One of Libya's most important ancient sights, the excavated Roman town of **Sabratha**, is situated roughly midway between Zuwara and Zawiya. On your way to the Roman site, you will pass through the rapidly expanding modern town of Sabratha which has all basic services. There is some new industry and many large villas extend down from the old coastal road towards the ruins. The new **Faculty of Arts of Zawiya University** is located here.

**Local beach** At Telil there is a good sandy area with shallow water, popular with Libyan families. The beach is served by black top dual carriageway from the main road from junction west of Sabratha city.

**Sleeping** **F** *Funduq Sabratha* on corner of main road only 100 m from Tourist Information, on second main roundabout as you come in from the west. Very primitive but quite clean 8LD pp/night. **F** *Funduq Siyahi*. The former tourist hotel, on the avenue leading to the ruins. Avoid if at all possible.

**Camping** Camping is banned in the woodlands around the archaeological site. Camper vans are often allowed to park up next to the *Arous al Bahr* restaurant on the carpark beside the ruins.

**Youth hostel** 1 km northwest of town very close to the ruins (look out for large building next to water tower), T24139. 160 beds, kitchen, meals, family rooms, laundry, open 0700-2400. 5LD per night, booking is recommended between May and Aug, but this is one of the better-run hostels.

**Eating** The *Arous al Bahr* restaurant is next to the ruins at the side of the large car park immediately outside the archaeological compound, open all year round. The restaurant caters for Libyan and foreign visitors including large groups.

**Tour agencies** Try *Sabratha Tours*, T2292, F24010. In a block of flats on the main road, not far from the former church.

The main taxi stand is over the road from the church on the main road. Private cars for **Transport**
the short hop to the ruins park up next to the taxi stand. **Petrol** is available in town
and at the road junction for Ajaylat, 7 km west of Sabratha.

# Ancient Sabratha    صبراتة

*Sabratha began life as a Carthaginian trading post. With its excellent natural
harbour on a long, straight coast, it became a permanent settlement in the fourth
century BC to act as a terminal for the trans-Saharan trade. Under the Romans,
development continued, although not on anything like the scale of Leptis Magna.
Italian and British excavations, a small museum with fine mosaics, bearing witness to a revival after the Vandal invasions, sculpture and a spectacularly reconstructed Roman theatre, let alone its magnificent coastal location, make it well
worth a visit.*

Tripolitania

## Ins and outs

The ruins of Sabratha are easily visited as a day trip from Tripoli. Take a share-taxi from **Getting there**
the chaotic stand immediately over the road from the Dhat al Imad towers to new
Sabratha (1.75LD) on the main road, journey time around 50 mins, depending on traffic as you leave Tripoli. Taxis park up in an area just over the road from an old Italian
church. To reach the ruins take a second taxi or a private car (say 2LD) for the short ride
to the ruins, down the road immediately to the left of the church, down what was
once an avenue of fine cypress trees. This distance is walkable, say 15 mins, and you
may be able to hitch a lift back to the main road after your visit. If travelling in your
own vehicle, there is plenty of parking next to the site.

There appear to be no guides available but there are publications and artefacts on **Getting around**
show at the museum. Entrance 3LD, open from 0800-sunset daily, museum closed **& practicalities**
Mon. It is best to avoid visiting on Fri, when lots of local families come to picnic and
stroll among the ruins. Other days are less crowded. Do not use videocameras. You
will need a good 2 hrs to do the site justice. For a post-visit swim, try the beach to the
east of the site near the temple of Isis. Next to the carpark there is the Arous al Bahr
('Bride of the Sea') restaurant. You might also consider a dip in the sea beyond the
Temple of Isis, although in principle this is *mamnou'* (forbidden).

## History and background

Sabratha was one of the three great cities of Roman Tripolitania, along with
Leptis and Oea (Tripoli). Unfortunately for the historian, however, there are
few mentions of Sabratha in the works of ancient authors. Excavations in the
late 1940s revealed evidence that there had been a seasonal Punic trading post
before the actual stone city was built. The early settlement was located here
because the coast is protected by a low reef lying some 100 m offshore, creating
a shallow basin adequate for the needs of the low-draft trading ships of ancient
times. In the third and fourth centuries BC, the city grew up in a haphazard
fashion, buildings growing up on narrow streets. As of the second century BC,
Sabratha seems to have grown richer, becoming a major population centre.
The imposing mausoleum B testifies to the wealth of Sabratha at this time.

In the first century BC, the dominant culture at Sabratha seems to have been **Hellenistic**
Greek. The urbanized area was divided up *per strigas*, into blocks running in **Sabratha**
strips, according to a grid plan. Some archaeologists believe that a major

*Justice at Sabratha*

*Wealthy Apuleius, rhetorician and author of one of the only two surviving Roman novels, the* Metamorphoses *(aka The Golden Ass), was brought to trial at Sabratha around 157 AD. The speech he made in his defence, the* Apologia, *has survived. Apuleius had persuaded an extremely rich widow to marry him, and quickly found himself accused of seducing her by witchcraft by her relatives who had no doubt been expecting a large inheritance. With brilliant rhetoric, he managed to get himself acquitted. He managed to tear the prosecutor's credibility to shreds, informing the audience that the unfortunate man was a dancer at the theatre in addition to being married to a prostitute. From his* Apologia, *it appears that Apuleius believed in the powers of magic – and felt that everyone else certainly did, too.*

*Roman law by the second century AD was an elaborate system with rules binding on all, even the emperor. Along with the cult of the emperor, it was a central element of Roman rule. Every Roman town worthy of its status had a basilica where cases were tried. Across the empire, it was accepted everywhere that trials should be public, and that cases should be decided through rational discussion on the basis of earlier decisions. In the late second and third centuries AD, jurists began to produce formal legal codes. The process accelerated under Diocletian in the late third century. Under Justinian in the sixth century, an accessible* Digest *of the vast corpus of Roman law was compiled and it was through the rediscovery of this work in the 11th century that Roman law entered medieval European legal systems.*

earthquake provided the opportunity to go about some major renewal schemes, creating a new main square and neighbourhoods to the south on the regular layout found in many Hellenistic cities. Another indication of this Greek influence is that the Alexandrine god Serapis was worshipped at Sabratha.

**Roman Sabratha** Another earthquake shook Sabratha sometime between 65 and 70 AD, destroying much of the city – and providing a superb opportunity for the Romans to do some rebuilding on a grand scale. Under Marcus Aurelius and his son Commodus, major building works were undertaken in the city centre, destroying parts of the original Punic city. By the late second century AD, Sabratha had monuments decorated with statuary and fine marble – including a spectacular theatre with seating for 5,000 people. New residential neighbourhoods went up between coast road and the Mediterranean. (As compared with Leptis Magna, a particular feature of Sabratha is the amount of housing uncovered in areas to the south and east of the Forum.)

**The wealth of Sabratha** Also under Commodus or possibly Septimus Severus, new port facilities were constructed with the usual thoroughness of the Roman engineers. Undoubtedly, the port was the main reason for the town's success, generating large volumes of trade (as images of merchant ships on the walls of both homes and public buildings indicate). The city exported oil and grain, along with valuable luxury products from sub-Saharan Africa such as ivory. The merchants of Sabratha had offices on the great square at Ostia, Rome's port. The mosaic sign for Sabratha has an elephant, symbol of the ivory trade no doubt.

**The end of monumental Sabratha** Tripolitania was hit by severe earthquakes between 306 and 310 AD, and again in 365 AD. Archaeological evidence suggests that the city never really recovered. Rubble was used for restoration work. The central temple of Liber Pater

Tripolitania

## Sabratha pays homage to Rome

*On the fine marble stage front of Sabratha's theatre, the central bay has a scene telling of the city's loyalty to Rome. Though the figures have almost all been defaced, symbolic meaning can be picked out. Rome, a female figure dressed as an Amazon warrior, shakes hands with high-crowned Sabratha, who bears a shallow dish and a horn of plenty. To the left and right of the two female figures are high ranking military, seemingly wearing triple plumed helmets. Their right hands are raised, palm facing outwards.*

*Sabratha is clearly swearing loyalty to Rome. On either side of this allegory are sacrificial scenes. To the right, priests can be seen leading a bull towards an altar bearing fruit, bread and pine-cones. To the left, we can see a bearded man pouring a libation at an altar. Some see this as an image of Septimius Severus. The young man facing the spectator is therefore his son, Caracalla. He is assisted by a priest, on the far right, and possibly by Caracalla's father-in-law, Plautinus, another powerful figure, on the left.*

Tripolitania

was hard hit, restored by the mid-fourth century only to be hit by the second earthquake. Basically, the temples never returned to the worship of the old gods: Christianity was already gaining ground. In fact, prior to the Vandal invasions, the city prospered, although the monumental grandeur of its forum had gone forever. Less dependent on imperial favour, Sabratha survived rather better than splendid, more extravagant Leptis.

**Byzantine city**

By the fourth and fifth centuries AD, Sabratha had a large Christian community – and a splendid complex of basilicas to match, built on the eastern edge of the city. By the first half of the 5th century, the Christians were sufficiently numerous to be taking over the old heart of the city: the main imperial basilica became a church. After the fifth century Vandal occupation, the Byzantines retook Sabratha in 533. A considerably smaller city, only 17 ha, was enclosed by walls with towers (constructed from recycled masonry), protecting the port, the old centre and neighbouring residential areas.

After the end of Byzantine rule in North Africa, there is little information about the fate of Sabratha. It is thought that the city survived after the first Arab invasions of the early 640s for at least a century – as rare Islamic coins discovered on the site and graffiti in the cella of the Antonine temple indicate.

**Rebuilding Sabratha**

Serious archaeological work on Sabratha got going in 1927. Giacomo Guidi ran the excavations from 1928 to 1932. In 1932, Guidi turned his attention to rebuilding the theatre, a task continued by his successor Giacomo Caputo as of 1937. The whole building had been destroyed by earthquake. Guidi and Caputo were lucky enough to find most of the original masonry and the result is a building which gives the visitor a very real feel for what a Roman theatre must have been like. The aims of the Italians were not entirely innocent, however. Such reconstructions were designed to demonstrate that the Kingdom of Italy was heir to the Roman Empire, and therefore very much 'at home' in the its colony of Libya.

## Touring the site

A visit to Sabratha divides up nicely into four stages. You start with the **Roman Museum** (and the Punic one, too, if open). Then take a look at Mausoleum B, before continuing down a paved street into the central **Forum** of the ancient city. Heading east, you pass a couple of basilicas to reach the **Temple of Isis**.

(Still further east is an amphitheatre). Finally, you head back inland towards the imposing mass of the **Theatre**, the monument closest to the entrance gate.

**Roman Museum**  The entrance is by the Roman Museum. (Down a path to the left is the **Punic Museum**, often closed.) The rather majestic Roman Museum, designed by Giacomo Guidi in 1934, houses the fine mosaics from the Basilica of Justinian, and a number of frescoes, and marble and bronze statues. The central mosaics hall is open along with the two wings which have just reopened.

In the courtyard for the Roman museum, the visitor is greeted by four statues of priests, dedicated to Jupiter-Serapis, from the third century AD. If still in position, the statues round the portico include, from left to right, a headless Venus, a headless sacrifiant (third century AD), Flavia Domitilla, wife of Vespasian and native of Sabratha.

Inside, the key find is the **mosaic from Justinian's Basilica**, discovered in 1925. A field of tendrils, scattered with birds in muted browns and blues, soft whites, yellows and beiges is packed with Byzantine Christian symbolism. A great vine root shoots forth a double helix enclosing a peacock (facing the visitor), the human soul imprisoned in the body (a caged bird) and a great

# Sabratha

peacock spreading its tail, symbolizing the soul's salvation. A phoenix represents the resurrection. The mosaics with geometric motifs displayed on the walls were originally situated left and right of the main mosaic. The column bases, pulpit and other marble pieces are copies of the originals which are still in situ in the basilica. Note the Christian oil lamps in the glass cases.

In the West Wing of the museum are numerous objects from the excavations, including glass, lamps, and bone hairpins. The East Wing, left of the portico, has mosaics and statuary. In the first hall are mosaics from the Ocean Baths with the words *Bene lava* ('Wash well') and *Salvum lavisse* ('In washing lies health') There is also a late mosaic from the *triclinium* of a villa at Sabratha, showing the Triumph of Dionysus, always a popular theme for dining rooms. Dionysus and Ariadne ride in a chariot drawn by two panthers, accompanied by a tambourine-banging maenad and Pan. In the second hall are more statues and mosaics, including a rather nice portrait of the god Ocean in a hexagonal frame. Look out too for a bronze portrait of the emperor Philip the Arab (244-249 AD) and a mosaic of Diana as moon goddess. The excavations yielded large amounts of fresco fragments, a good indication of the wealth of Sabratha.

Tripolitania

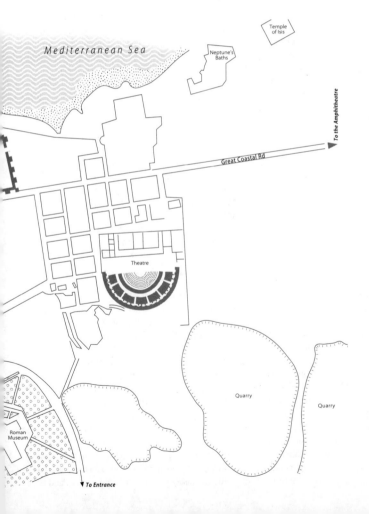

*Mystery cults and Egyptian influence*

As of the first century AD, a number of cults of Egyptian origin developed in Rome, thanks to the presence of merchants and imported slaves. One of the most popular was the cult of **Isis**, mother goddess of the cow-horn headdress. Her cult had been present in North Africa from Punic times, and Isis features on Punic grave markers. She probably had a significant place in the religious world of the Carthaginians. Herodotus mentions the fact that the nomad Libues avoided eating beef. Still according to Herodotus, the women of Cyrene did not eat beef out of respect for Isis. Temporarily banned by Augustus after the conquest of Egypt in 31 BC, the cult of Isis was soon flourishing in Rome. In Greece, Isis became identified with Demeter, looking after crops and harvest.

Isis is sometimes shown as a cow-headed woman. As a mother goddess, she is often represented suckling her son Horus. The cult statues of the goddess showed her wearing a cape with a special knot just below the breasts. Her hair spirals down in long corkscrew locks. She is generally young and svelte, and bears the symbols of her cult, a sistrum (rattle) and a situla, a sort of pail. Women in particular identified with the compassionate, motherly nature of Isis. She was also important to seafarers: there was an annual festival of the navigium Isidis, celebrating the end of the winter storms when ships could put to sea again. (In Petronius' Satyricon, at one point the hero steals a cloak and rattle of Isis from a wealthy shipowner). Temples to the goddess have been discovered across Roman North Africa. Isis enjoyed imperial favour under the Flavian emperors (69 to 96 AD). Septimius Severus (193-211) showed sympathy for eastern cults, as did Elogabalus.

Another divinity from Egypt was **Serapis**, a Hellenised version of Osiris and Apis, the bull god. The cult of Serapis, also present at Sabratha, was instituted by Ptolomey I at Alexandria. According to one recent writer, he was the only ancient deity invented by a committee, to please Greeks and Egyptians. Generally shown as an enthroned figure in long, flowing robes, he is a bearded patriarch, rather like Zeus/Jupiter. Great locks of hair fall on his strong forehead.

The worship of Isis and Serapis, unlike other cults popping out of the eastern Mediterranean in the first and second centuries AD, was a tolerant sort of affair. One could attend Isis' ceremonies and still take part in official cults or continue with local gods. Her worship had none of the 'all or nothing' side of Christianity and Judaism. Thus Isis, who in many ways was all things to all worshippers, was a highly successful international goddess, venerated across the empire.

**Mausoleum B** Walk northwest along the main thoroughfare. On your left, is a residential neighbourhood with a couple of mausolea, generally referred to as Mausoleum A and B. (Only the base of mausoleum A exists.) The pointy-topped **Mausoleum B** is particularly interesting and was totally rebuilt by Italian archaeologists. Punic-Hellenistic in style, 23 m high and dating from the third or early second century BC, the building was totally destroyed in one of the earthquakes which shook Sabratha in the fourth century AD. Post-earthquake, the stone was recycled, so in order to reconstruct the building, the archaeologists had to dismantle a Byzantine tower and some house remains. Original pieces from the upper part are in the Punic Museum.

Originally, this mausoleum must have been a rather jolly building, covered in red and blue stucco. It looks like the sort of post-modern street furniture that architect Michael Graves might design for an American campus. Egyptian features include a false door topped with an asp's head. The metopes (panels on the frieze above the columns) displayed a mixture of Egyptian and Greek symbolism: the god Bes taming lions is rather Egyptian, while Hercules taming the Nemean lion is very Greek. On the three consoles ('shelves'), supported by lions there would have been statues of *kouroi*, heroic youths in the Greek mode. In many ways, this mausoleum resembles the Libyco-Numidian Mausoleum at Dougga in Tunisia, although the Dougga mausoleum has a square rather than a triangular plan.

After the mausoleum, return to the main street, and pass through the site of the **gate** in the **Byzantine walls** to reach the old core of the city. As in other Roman cities in North Africa, in the unsettled fifth century AD the inhabitants withdrew into a well-fortified core.

Cross the main street (*plateia*) and you come to the monumental centre of Sabratha. On the left is the **South Temple**, 'of the unknown deity' (second century AD) before you reach a small square. This wider area has the **Antonine Temple** (166-169 AD) up five steps on the right and the **Judicial Basilica** on the left. The remains of the basilica show that it has been much changed since the original building of the first century AD. Next you come to the forum and its granite columns. To the east side of this is a podium, the remains of the East Temple or **Temple of Liber Pater** (an ancient fertility god associated with Bacchus, god of wine). Four massive re-erected columns make identifying this temple easy. Opposite the Temple of Liber Pater, if you stand facing west, is the **Capitol**, and the **Temple of Serapis**. The Capitol, early first century AD, was Roman rather than Greek in design, ie columns at the front only. There was a high platform for orators, and flights of steps at the corners. To the south side of the forum was a large basilica or court house dating from the first century AD.

Thus at the height of Roman rule, the centre of Sabratha had some very fine buildings indeed. The earliest temples are probably the Capitol and the Temple of Serapis. The Temple of Liber Pater is thought to have gone up later, on a site occupied by older building. In the early stages, most Sabrathan building had used a soft, crumbly yellow sandstone, generally faced with a stucco rendering. In the second century AD, imports of fine stone from elsewhere in the empire started, and existing buildings acquired marble columns. At the same time, the South Forum and Antonine temples went up. The latter, still with much shattered white marble paving and magnificent cipolline marble columns in situ, provides a good viewpoint over the central area.

*The central core of Sabratha*

*Tripolitania*

church, Sabratha

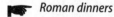

### Roman dinners

All that survives of the Roman dining room today are fine mosaic floors on mythological themes and the occasional fragment of painted fresco. To judge by the mosaics, the dining room could be a splendid affair – as indeed it had to be, since the banquet was most important social event in the wealthy villa owner's calendar, an opportunity to get friends and political and business contacts together. In addition to the frescoes, the standard triclinium would have had draperies and niches for statues. Furniture would have been limited to couches placed along three sides of the dining area. Guests would recline and the food would be placed in front of them on low tables.

On the Roman menu were egg dishes, salads, and fish and meat accompanied by rich sauces. Dormice were a delicacy, as was garum, a sort of fish paste manufactured all over the empire. Many of the vegetables familiar worldwide today, such as the potato and the tomato, were unknown. Nevertheless, wealthy Romans tended towards conspicuous consumption at the dinner table. The early Latin novel The

Satyricon, composed by Petronius in the first century AD, contains a merciless dissection of nouveau riche dining habits at the home of one Trimalchio, so wealthy that he had a clock in the dining room and a special trumpeter to tell him how much longer he had to live. A magpie in a golden cage greeted guests, and before dinner Alexandrian boys washed the guests' feet with ice cold water, performing a quick pedicure at the same time where necessary. The menu chez Trimalchio was as elaborate as the welcome, including sweet and sour hors d'oeuvre (hot sausages on a silver gridiron with damsons and pomegranate), fish in peppery sauce and a hare with wings attached so it looked like Pegasus. Vulgarity definitely got the upper hand at the end of the meal. Trimalchio's chef had artistic tendencies, and his masterpiece for this particular banquet was a goose, surrounded by fish and game, all made out of pork. Just for the record, Italo Balbo, Italian governor of Libya in the 1930s, is said to have enjoyed mock Roman banquets in the Turkish governor's palace in Tripoli.

On the seaward side of the Forum are the remains of **Justinian's Basilica** – dismantled in the 1920s by archaeologists, as the building's importance was only realised later when mosaics were found. (Note that the term basilica, originally denoting a great hall used as law court, came to denote a church in Byzantine times.) Behind the Temple of Liber Pater, to the northeast, are the second century **Forum Baths** (aka Seaward Baths), chiefly notable for a nearby luxurious hexagonal latrine. This is the largest bath complex at Sabratha, though nowhere near as splendid as the great Hadrian's Baths at Leptis. (For the Roman *thermae* specialists, the other baths are a set of private baths, near the Punic museum, the so-called Theatre Baths, just off the Decumanus, north of the Theatre, and Neptune's Baths, close to the Temple of Isis.)

**Eastern area** Some 10 minutes' walk east of the central area are the remains of the **Temple of Isis**, easily identified by its columns. This is most isolated set of ruins, right next to the sea. Look out for the second century AD **Ocean or Neptune's Baths**, close to the sea about 40 m west of the temple. A densely worked mosaic paving can be seen in situ here in the *tepidarium*. The missing central hexagonal medallion is the portrait of the god Ocean to be seen in the site museum. At these baths, one of four complexes discovered at Sabratha, the visitor can also see the *caldarium* with its raised hypocaust flooring and special hot air ducts.

At the **Temple of Isis**, columns have been re-erected, to give an idea of the former dimensions of the building. The temple was constructed under Augustus and extended under Vespasian, 69-79 AD. The cult of Isis was just one of a number of eastern Mediterranean cults which gained popularity in ancient Rome with the arrival of slaves and merchants from the new provinces of the Empire. Elaborate rites and shared meals were a feature of mystery cults. Isis was portrayed with curving cow horns set with a solar disc, and is sometimes shown with her son Horus – rather like the Virgin Mary and Jesus. Visiting Sabratha's Temple of Isis, you can imagine a procession arriving in the temple, bearing palm branches and led by priests in embroidered garb. Apuleius in *The Golden Ass* describes just such a scene.

The main entrance to the temple was on the east side, there being a large hall and a double line of columns open to the sea. Little remains apart from some steps. On the north side, part of the foundations are visible. Behind the temple, to the west, some small chambers are visible, no doubt for the worship of other deities. Of the actual temple, some columns are standing and rooms which would have been under the *cella*, the room housing the statue of the goddess.

Several hundred metres east from the Temple of Isis lies the **amphitheatre** (second century AD), located, as was the custom, remote from the main core of the city. (Blood-letting and the sound of general violent mayhem were not allowed to disturb the *dignitas* pervading the Roman forum.) As at Leptis, the amphitheatre occupies a hollow carved out of a low rise. The entrance is through the restored west gate. In the middle of the arena, two impressive underground galleries meet each other at right angles, and the niches into which temporary wooden flooring would have been fitted are clearly visible. Such galleries are a feature of most amphitheatres. Here wild animals would have been kept in cages which would be hauled up at an appropriate moment during an afternoon's entertainment.

Sabrathans could enjoy less bloodthirsty entertainment at their magnificent **Roman Theatre** theatre. Along with sculpture and rhetoric, theatre was one of the Greek arts adopted by the Romans. Initially, comedy and tragedy were popular. However, gradually the emphasis shifted to farce and mime, and music and dance came to be a part of theatrical entertainment. Every self-respecting Roman town had to have a **theatre**, though not generally on such a spectacular scale as the one at Sabratha. It is most definitely the site's most striking monument and is still used occasionally for open air shows. Located to the east of the site, next to the quarries which provided the stone for much of the town, the theatre at Sabratha is the largest in Roman Africa – and easily the most impressive today, due to the re-assembly work undertaken by Italian archaeologists in the 1930s. The semi-circular orchestra area was excavated out of the rock, while the majority of the building was constructed with great blocks of stone hewn from the quarry that lies south of Sabratha.

During the reconstruction, 96 of the original columns were put back into place, recreating a spectacular three-storey galleried backdrop to the stage. The stage platform or *pulpitum* is over 40 m wide, and fronted by a white marble frieze featuring mythological characters including the Three Graces and personifications of Sabratha paying allegiance to Rome. Insufficient material was available to reconstruct the final or attic storey of the backdrop, which would have supported a canopy to protect the stage and improve the sound. The theatre had three tiers of seating, enough to accommodate an audience of 5,000 and wide promenade galleries behind, where the fashionable Sabrathans would have discussed the productions of the day – or enjoyed theatrical gossip.

The wealth of Sabratha can be gauged by the luxurious fittings of the theatre. The stage-front columns came from diverse sources. Many were of white marble, others were black or cipolline marble. There are columns with vertical grooves, others with spiral grooves. Some column capitals are carved with

Tripolitania

masks, including a Gorgon, a bacchante and a lion. Behind the stage were large chambers, ancient 'green rooms', richly decorated with polychrome marbles.

Sabratha, like Leptis, is lucky enough not to have been built upon or heavily quarried by later civilizations. Finally abandoned in the mid-eighth century as Arab rule took hold in North Africa, it is vast and visitor-free enough to allow you to slip back to ancient times in your imagination. With any luck there will be some new investment to open the Punic Museum on a regular basis, too.

## Sabratha to Tripoli

After visiting Sabratha, continue on to **Zawiya**, 40 km from Tripoli, where should you need to stop there is a **youth hostel**, 80 beds, breakfast included, other meals available, family rooms. The hostel is located some 50 m from the main mosque, next to a football ground.

After Zawiya, the road to the east becomes a dual carriageway through palm groves, sprawling urban development, and plantations of olives, oranges and pine trees. Many commuters as well as large numbers of vehicles moving to the frontier or the chemical plants at Bu Kammash use this high speed road which can be EXCEPTIONALLY DANGEROUS at rush hours and at major road junctions. (Traffic cuts left across the dual carriageway with little regard for oncoming vehicles.) Nonetheless this route is to be preferred to the narrow, more tortuous single track coastal road slightly to the north of it.

Entry to the Tripoli suburbs and the city itself on this route is through the Gurgi district and an exceptionally complicated (and basically unsigned) network of flyovers and roundabouts. Head for the Dhat al Imad towers, and with luck you will find yourself on Shari'a Umar al Mukhtar, heading directly to Green Square and the seafront adjacent to the Castle. You will have more luck if you are heading for the airport, which is indicated with aeroplane symbols on the sign boards.

# East of Tripoli to Leptis Magna via Khums

The main coastal highway runs from Tripoli eastwards via Khums and Misrata. The road links all the major coastal towns and passes through one of the richest agricultural zones of the country. The main reason for following this route is of course to visit Leptis Magna, perhaps the most imposing Roman ruin in North Africa.

The drive to Leptis Magna takes over an hour (90 minutes is good time, depending on the traffic at Tajura). Out of Tripoli, you have the choice of either taking the old coast road or the modern highway. Buses and taxis leave Tripoli on the coastal main highway. A dual carriageway leaves Tripoli city via Bab Ben Ghashir and travels through dense developments of villas and small houses, mainly expensive properties built on former oasis gardens. There are old square, single storey, whitewashed farmsteads interspersed with modern villas. Occasional small whitewashed domed shrines, the tombs of *marabouts* (Islamic holy men), are visible. Around 32 km east of Tripoli, at **Tajura**, is E *Madinah Siahiah Tajurah* (*Tajurah Tourist Village*). The beach is popular with Libyans on Friday but is otherwise quiet. (Km 32 is its local name.) The tourist village is an old development and open to all-comers. After Tajura are some pleasant beaches that get extremely crowded during summer weekends. **Sidi Bannur** is the most popular. Next to the petrol station207 on the north side of the road is Check Beach, which is very popular with expats. You need to buy a ticket (2LD) for access to the beach and parking.

Sixty kilometres out of Tripoli is **Qasr Garabulli**, on the old coast road. There is now a bypass, but you can take the spur into town for petrol and other services. Former Italian farmsteads can be seen among the dense, recent Libyan housing.

East from Qasr Garabulli is fine farming country with orchards and olives and almond plantations. At **Qasr Khiyar** there are roadside shops on the main highway, cafés and petrol. Also along the main road other than in the smaller settlements there are plenty of roadside cafés. In season there are lots of roadside sellers of fruit, olive oil, pressed date syrup and honey.

*Despite the lack of signs, Qsar Khiyar is identifiable by petrol station 209, south of the road on the east side of the settlement.*

Thelathin (literally at the Km 30 mark), is a tiny settlement built around a mosque (a shop and café are adjacent). There is a fine area for swimming on the coast just north of the road and in season, succulent oranges are on sale at the roadside. A good black top road runs to it then goes on to a rocky seashore 2 km below. Khums town lies approximately 20 km to the east over the forested ridge. The road runs through some attractive hilly countryside. There is a military police (red beret) checkpoint at the turn-off for Tarhuna (115 km from Tripoli, 67 km from Khums). Khums is 5 km further on, after one more checkpoint.

**Thelathin**

*Tripolitania*

## Khums الخمس

With new buildings going up, and many incomplete, Khums is not a very pretty sight. The Friday market is held in the street leading to the old harbour. The main town has expanded considerably in recent years. Some Italian and British military and civilian landmarks still exist, with the army barracks left as they were at the end of the war. There is a cinema on the left of the street opposite the taxi ranks. Old houses were demolished to make room for a large new town council building just below the cinema. Look out for the **Mosque of Ali Pasha** with its curious dome. A palm-lined street with a few old Italian buildings leads to the sea and the recently re-opened *Hotel Touristique* (*Funduq Siyahi*). A sandy beach leads along the coast to the ruins of Leptis.

There is a vast extension to the town from the army barracks east along the coast towards Wadi Lebda and between the coast and the bypass comprising mainly poor quality housing with few services for the traveller. Chalets have been built along the sea shore towards Leptis Magna. The modern port is located on the west side of the town. There is some industry including a cement plant.

*Phone code: 031*

*Care is needed at all times when driving in Libya, but this is especially the case when arriving in Khums. On the outskirts, slow-moving vehicular and pedestrian traffic makes the main highway very dangerous.*

Not much choice here. **C** *Funduq Naggaza* located in the countryside a few kilometres from the sea, turn off main road about 17 km from Khums, T26691/2. Pleasant, but not easy to get to without own transport. The side road is easily missed as you come from Khums. As the road curves left, the turn off is on your right, just after a hill with a communications antenna. (Look out for a sign – a dark orange arrow on a white background with green Arabic lettering.) The hotel is 2 km down the side-road and has no restaurant, a huge disadvantage in such an isolated place. 30LD double room. **D** *Funduq Khums al Kabir* , on the main road, on your left as you come from Tripoli, T23333. Cheap, but close-passing traffic makes it noisy. Breakfast included, also quantities of cockroaches. 20LD for a double. **D** *Funduq Lebda*, T21252. The closest to the ruins, just 2 km away and only about 200 m from the inter-city taxi station.

**Sleeping**

**Youth hostel** *Sports City*, 3 km southwest of centre, T21880. 160 beds, meals. Mucky and cheap.

**Transport** The share-taxi and minibus station is on the main market square. The journey time from Tripoli is around 90 mins. A place in a share taxi from Tripoli costs 3LD. Buses stop in the town centre near the taxi rank and on the main road at the *Khums Hotel*. Ancient Leptis is only a couple of kilometres from the town.

# Leptis Magna لبدة

*Note that Leptis was designated a World Heritage site by UNESCO in 1982*

*The ruins of Leptis Magna, second Roman port in Africa, must be among the most extraordinary ancient sites in the Mediterranean. Situated at the mouth of the Wadi Lebda immediately to the east of the modern town of Khums, the town is still a place of great splendour. There is a noble triumphal arch and vast baths, famous in antiquity. The city exported huge quantities of olive oil and grain, and benefited from the largesse of a third century emperor, Septimius Severus, a local lad made good. Perhaps the most impressive site of all is the spectacular forum complex, supreme example of architecture in the service of the imperial ideology triumphant. In early modern times, sands invaded the site, preserving it for 20th-century archaeologists to discover.*

## Ins and outs

**Getting there**
*See also Khums transport above*
Khums is the nearest town to Leptis and the site is accessible from there on foot (2 km walk) and by local taxi/private car.

**Getting around** The sight is to be visited on foot. Approximately 4 km west of Khums is a minor site, the Villa Silin (see below) with fine mosaics. Permission to visit and an accompanying guide can be obtained at entrance to Leptis at no extra charge.

The site is open daily 0800-1730, 3LD adult, although access is always possible. There is a good museum (opened Jul 1995), entrance 3LD, hrs 0800 to 1200 and 1400 to 1700, plus café-eatery next door. As Leptis is easily the most important Roman site in Libya, and probably in eastern North Africa, it receives large numbers of visitors. It certainly merits a full day, although this is not an easy experience at the height of summer. Guidebooks, maps and lots of postcards of the site and others in Libya are generally available. There are guides available for a fee (5LD seems to be a minimum) who are comprehensible in the main European languages.

You may feel tempted to take a dip after doing your bit for cultural tourism. The site wardens say that swimming off the site is forbidden. However, a quick dip in the sea from the beach near the Hunting Baths might be possible. On a quiet summer's day, there's no on around to stop you. Local lads do spectacular dives off a chunk of masonry from the Roman lighthouse.

**Warning**
*Travellers have reported being detained (in one case for an entire day) by police for pointing their camera in the wrong direction whilst taking pictures at Leptis.*
Warnings that the ruins must not be touched nor artefacts taken away must be taken very seriously since successful prosecution can lead to imprisonment. Any seller of ancient items to be found on the site is obviously operating illegally. If you have a bag, this might be inspected as you leave the site. Note also that video cameras are absolutely forbidden. Just opposite the site entrance, in the old museum building, is the local tourist police station.

## Exploring Leptis

Although Leptis Magna is a large archaeological site it is not particularly complex since the best elements date from a fairly specific period. All the important buildings can be reached adjacent to, or just off the main paved monumental road from, the present entrance through the newer parts of the site. A full

## Who were the Severans?

The names of emperors **Septimius Severus** (193-211) and **Severus Alexander** (222-235) pop up regularly at Roman sites throughout Tunisia and Libya. At Dougga in Tunisia, there are triumphal arches to both these rulers. What was so special about them? Fast rewind to the late second century AD, when Rome went through a particularly difficult patch under Emperor Commodus. From 180-193, Commodus lived a life of debauchery in Rome, renaming the city Commodiana and spending his time showing off his brute force fighting with wild beasts in the colosseum. Eventually, he was strangled by a wrestling partner. In the power struggle that ensued among the military, one Septimius Severus, an aristocrat from Leptis Magna came out on top after four years of civil war.

Septimius Severus was the right strong man at the right time. He realized that the Empire faced some formidable enemies, notably on the eastern frontier, and hence was to rule from the frontier provinces. He added Mesopotamia to Rome's dominions, and expanded the army, adding two new legions and opening up the career structure to soldiers from the ranks. His dying words to his sons are said to have been "Do not quarrel with each other, pay the troops, and despise the rest."

Septimius Severus did not forget his African origins. In 202-203, he overwintered in Africa. He had huge works undertaken at Leptis Magna. Along with Leptis, Carthage and Utica were given immunity from provincial taxes. The emperor had acquired huge properties in Africa Proconsularis, the lands of senators whom he had executed for their support of rival Clodius Albinus. This no doubt gave him the resources for his considerable largesse towards Africa's cities, recognized by the construction of triumphal arches.

Unfortunately, Septimius Severus' sons **Caracalla** and **Geta** were not of the same stuff as their father. Dynastic infighting followed, with Caracalla murdering Geta, only to be murdered by his own troops. **Elagabalus**, (218-222), was also murdered after a short reign decadent by even Rome's standards, and his cousin, the young **Severus Alexander**, succeeded in 222. (He too was eventually murdered by the army.) The Severan dynasty disappeared, and 26 emperors followed in fifty years. But though the mid-third century proved to be a time of chaos in Rome, the provinces of Africa continued to prosper. Septimius Severus had broken the power of the warlike desert tribes, Numidia had been made a separate province and the defences reorganized.

Despite the vast sums spent on building programmes and the army, the Severan period saw a development which was to have long lasting effects for Europe. Septimius Severus named a certain Papinian praetorian prefect. Along with jurists Ulpian and Julius Paulus, he laid the bases of the Roman law which was eventually codifed by the emperor Justinian in the sixth century. And under Caracalla, an edict was issued granting Roman citizenship to virtually all free men in the Empire.

Tripolitania

inspection would require at least a full day – and rather longer for visitors with a specialist interest since Leptis Magna is well preserved and has an unequalled range of buildings from the classical period. In summer the site is very hot, and the sight might best be seen in a series of visits when the heat is less oppressive. This presupposes over-nighting in one of the unprepossessing hotels in nearby Khums, or if you have own transport, at the *Funduq Naggaza*, west of Khums. The small *Funduq Siyahi* is probably the best bet. Tour groups often use the *Funduq Zliten* in the nearby town of the same name, east of Khums.

Basically, there are six main areas (and the museum) to cover at Leptis, namely the **Severan monumental centre**, the **Old Forum**, the **Theatre and around**, outlying **buildings to the west**, the **port**, and **outlying sites to the**

Tripolitania

### Carnage under the sun: Romanity and spectacle

The level of 'Romanity' of a city was defined by the presence of an amphitheatre. Such buildings of public entertainment existed across the Roman Empire, and have been found as far east as modern Iraq. The Colosseum of Rome and the amphitheatre at Capua were the largest, while the one at the sleepy Tunisian town of El Jem is among the best preserved. In modern Libya, Leptis Magna had a sizeable amphitheatre, as did Ptolemaïs.

It is difficult to see where the Roman practice of public slaughter came from – the Greeks were far too refined for such practices. The populace of the Empire developed a taste for the *munera*, the bloody spectacles provided as bounty by the magistrates or as a tribute to the deceased. Pliny in his Natural History tells the tale of the amphitheatre's origins. In 53 BC, in Italy, a candidate for the tribune's office in search of votes came up with a new electioneering technique: two semi-circular wooden theatres were set up back-to-back, mounted on a swivel. Thus two plays could be put on simultaneously. But the gimmick came in the afternoon when the two theatres were swung round on their pivots to form an oval where a **munus** or gladiatorial show was held.

Under Augustus, the munus became an important (and sinister) way for rulers to interact with the ruled. The primitive wooden structures gave way to magnificent stone buildings and the word amphitheatrum was coined to describe these settings for various brutish "sports" – depicted in gory graphic detail in the mosaic floors of the ancient Roman home. In addition to the hoplomachia or gladiatorial fights, there were re-enactments of various myths (Pasiphae and the bull, amongst others...), and in the later Empire, the adepts of Christianity, then viewed as a dangerous sect with secret ceremonies, were a particular target (blood spilling onto the ground and the disguising of Christian martyrs as initiates of Caelestis would transform torture into sacrifice). Damnatio ad bestias (being condemned to the beasts), however, was reserved for common criminals and certain prisoners of war, ie the Garamantes taken prisoner in first century AD expedition, see mosaic in entrance hall of Tripoli Museum.

The huge resources devoted to shipping rare beasts to Rome for slaughter is testimony to the importance of the amphitheatre shows, and also evidence of the wealth of the Empire – and the extent to which this wealth could be squandered. No doubt certain Tripolitanian fortunes were built on this trade. The inhabitants of the province, to go by the mosaics, preferred venationes or the exhibition and "hunting" of wild beasts. (Visit the Hunting Baths at Leptis for their wall frescoes of leopards and venatores.)

Today's visitor to Leptis Magna can clamber up into the highest parts of the seating and look down into the arena just as the Roman spectator would have done. Mercifully the slaughter of people and beasts is no longer considered great entertainment, and little disturbs the quiet of the great stone crater apart from the clicking of camera shutters. The nearby sea offers the tempting prospect of a cooling dip after a surfeit of ruins.

**east and south**. If you are pressed for time, then you will probably only be able to cover the monumental centre, the Old Forum, the Theatre and the museum. The Hunting Baths, outside the city walls to the west, should be taken in if you have more time, as should the wharves. The other outlying sites are more of specialist interest, although the amphitheatre, to the east, is most photogenic.

## Stone for Leptis

*The visitor to Leptis is struck by the profusion of coloured marbles used by the architects of Leptis. No expense was spared to ship in the finest marbles possible, including grey-green cipolline (onion-grain) marble. From Egypt came 112 red-granite columns for the basilica and temple. Marble was used for columns, entablatures (frieze elements), veneers and paving. Look out for the fine Pergamene column capitals. Generally, marble was carved at the quarries to save overloading the ships. Only the finishing touches were added in situ. Communication between designers and stone-masons must have been very good.*

*Leptis was lucky too in that it had excellent building stone nearby, namely a hard limestone, used for places where there would be much wear and for facing with carved detail, and a rather softer sandstone, used in other areas. Both sorts of stone came from a quarry nearby at Ra's al Hammama, 5 km inland to the south. Archaeologists think that the large blocks used for the harbour were quarried nearer at hand.*

*Unusually for the Romans, there is little use of brick and that great innovation, concrete, at Leptis. However, the latter was used for the vaulted roofing in both main sets of baths.*

Tripolitania

## History and background

Leptis Magna was the dominant city in the region, just as important as Carthage at the height of its influence under the Severan emperors in the early third century AD. Thanks to burial under the shifting sands of its coastal location, the site survived in an excellent state of preservation down to the present. The city really took off with a lavish building scheme launched under Septimius Severus, though even before that town's wealthy citizens had put up some impressive public buildings. The building projects conducted under the Severans were without precedent, however. In terms of scale, planning and exotic materials, the construction programme was quite extraordinary, stamping the town with imperial glory. It is the remains of this scheme that the visitor comes to see today, architecture in the service of the ideology of the Roman state.

**The importance of Leptis Magna**

Leptis is unique. It is a superb example of ancient town planning. Making your way around, you become aware that the buildings were integrated with great care. Because of the sand, pillaging did not really start until the 17th century, and then only in a very limited sort of way. The quality of the building materials, imported from all around the eastern Mediterranean is unique as well. Another extraordinary feature is the huge number of inscriptions that have survived. This means that archaeologists are in an extremely strong position. Though the inscriptions are often in obscure language, they are far more reliable clues to the city's past than finds from painstakingly dug trenches. Finally, Leptis, like Sabratha and Cyrene, was the object of major restoration work undertaken by the Italians. As such ambitious schemes are no longer seen as valid, if Leptis were discovered today, the results would be far less spectacular from the lay visitor's point of view.

The origins of Leptis Magna are not known with certainty. It is probable that a Berber settlement first existed at the site which was later developed by Levantine traders from Tyre and Sidon. As these seafaring traders hauled their boats up onto the beach, they no doubt appreciated the protection from storms given by a number of tiny islands at the mouth of the Wadi Lebda. So far the only traces of this Phoenician presence to have been found are graves under the stage of the

**Early days**

### Exporting Leptis to England

Back in the 17th century, wily consuls and other wheeler-dealers realized that there was money to be made by exporting classical masonry from North Africa to Europe. Six hundred columns were excavated at Leptis and sent to France for use in Louis XIV's new palaces at Versailles and Paris. (Three large cipolline marble columns which were too heavy for the barges remained near the shore, still visible today.) By the 19th century, rulers like the Bey of Tunis were granting permits for the mining and export of material from sites like Carthage.

In 1816, Colonel Hammer Warrington, British consul-general in Tripoli and a close friend of the Prince Regent, persuaded the Pasha of Tripoli to give the Regent whatever remained of ruins at Leptis. The booty was assembled at the waterside at Leptis in the summer of 1817, and in the autumn was loaded onto the storeship Weymouth. The load included 22 granite columns, 15 marble columns and 10 fine capitals. The material reached Spithead in March 1818, only to be abandoned in the courtyard of the British Museum.

Eventually in the 1820s, Sir Jeffrey Wyatville, architect of the reconstruction of Windsor Castle, was to create an elegant ruin for the prince, now King George IV. The gardeners sought to encourage a feel of antique romance by allowing suitable undergrowth to climb over the stones. But fashions changed, and the ruin's origin was forgotten. In fact, the Windsor Leptis Magna ruin was the last and largest major ruin to be constructed (if that is the term) in England. The English and French were not the only ones to acquire bits of Leptis: the Ottomans had a taste for luxury, and Lepcitan marble can be seen in the Museum of Istanbul and certain palaces.

Roman Theatre. Greeks also appear to have been at the site. In Carthaginian times the people at Lebda paid tribute of one talent per day, reflecting a certain prosperity based on a trading hinterland stretching deep into Tripolitania and Sirte. By the time of the Third Punic War (149-146BC) there were approximately 10,000-15,000 inhabitants in the city. Leptis was a flourishing town open to the Mediterranean with fully developed urban institutions.

Apart from the protection for ships, another factor favouring the development of Leptis was rainfall. Dry farming is possible in the region, and there are oases with springs nearby. In the nearby hinterland is the fertile Jabal M'sellata, and a short way to the east is the fertile region of the Wadi Ki'am. The Leptis region thus had many reasons to commend it over the oases further west.

In 107 AD Leptis set up formal relations with Rome and, despite the disruption caused by attacks from tribes from the desert interior, the city continued to develop. Leptis gained full rights to Roman citizenship as a *colonia* under the Emperor Trajan (98-117 AD). The early Roman period saw the construction of basic harbour works and a forum close by the original Punic settlement. Over the second century AD, Leptis expanded.

**Roman prosperity** The fortunes of Leptis Magna were greatly improved in 193 AD when Septimius Severus (193-211 AD) was made Emperor of Rome. Born at Leptis in 146 AD, his vast public works programme no doubt created considerable prosperity and the population grew to 60,000-80,000 people. The peace of Tripolitania was ensured after the emperor put down the most warlike tribes of the region in 203.

Septimius Severus travelled restlessly across his domains, crushing a rebellion here and attempting new border conquests in other regions. The winter of 202-203 AD saw him at Leptis. He had grown rich by confiscating the property of his rivals and enemies, and so was able to launch major building works to embellish his home town (rulers never seem to forget their hometowns). The

## Leptis or Lepcis Magna?

There are two spellings of the city's name. **Leptis** is the version to be found in the ancient texts, and the one preferred by historians in the past. **Lepcis**, however, is the name most widely found on inscriptions in the city. This is a more or less exact transcription of the city's original Punic name, based on the consonants L-P-Q-Y. The epithet **Magna** appears to have been added in the first century AD, to distinguish the town from the obviously smaller **Lepti Minus** on the coast of the Sahel region in modern Tunisia. The inhabitants of Leptis were of mixed Berber and Punic stock. Though heavily Romanized by the third century AD, they clearly continued to use the more local name Lepcis.

best builders and sculptors of the day were brought over, a new forum and an immense temple were constructed, dedicated to the city's protecting gods. The harbour was extended, water supply improved, and an elaborate triumphal arch erected. Leptis became one of the finest cities of the empire.

**The decline of Leptis**

However, with its overblown public buildings, Leptis was very much an artificial creation. After the fall of the Severans in 235 AD, the city began a slow but inexorable decline. The remains of the so-called Late Roman Wall show that the city had shrunk considerably. Built between 250 and 350, it was the city's first stone fortification, and indicates an increasingly hostile surrounding environment. Some major buildings outside this wall, including the Hunting Baths, continued to function. Although there was something of a revival under Diocletian and Constantine, Leptis probably suffered later from a decline in the Saharan trade

## Leptis Magna overview

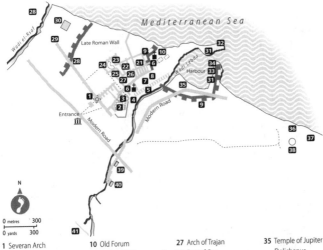

| | | | |
|---|---|---|---|
| 1 Severan Arch | 10 Old Forum | 27 Arch of Trajan | 35 Temple of Jupiter |
| 2 Hadrianic Baths | 11-20 (See Old Forum map) | 28 Port of Oea | Dolichenus |
| 3 Palaestra | 21 Temple of Serapis | 29 Arch of Marcus Aurelius | 36 Eastern Baths |
| 4 Nymphaeum | 22 Market | 30 Hunting Baths | 37 Circus |
| 5 Colonnaded street | 23 Sanctuary of the Divine | 31 Quay of Severan Port | 38 Amphitheatre |
| 6 Byzantine church | Emperors | 32 Lighthouse | 39 Reservoir |
| 7 Imperial Forum | 24 Theatre | 33 Doric Temple | 40 Reservoir |
| 8 New Basilica | 25 Chalcidicum | 34 Signalling tower | 41 Roman Dam |
| 9 Byzantine wall & gate | 26 Arch of Tiberius | | |

Tripolitania

and the silting of the mouth of the river. A five year period of attacks by the Asturianii, a regional tribe, beginning in 363 AD brought great problems.

**Vandals and Byzantines**

In 455 AD the Vandals arrived and took Leptis, demolishing the wall and leaving the city eventually in the hands of the Berber Zenata tribe. The city lay in the shadow of the ever-advancing dunes, and the citizens retreated into a small core area. In 533, the Byzantines under Belisarius restored Roman rule. They put up new fortifications which confirmed the city's decline: only the harbour and the two forums lay within the walls. The Byzantines were put under heavy pressure from all sides. They had a major war against the Sassanian Empire on their hands in the east. In Libya, they suffered from attacks by the Zenata. Finally the Arab invasions of 643-644 AD ended Byzantine power. The later incursions of the Beni Hillal and Beni Sulaim led to the completed abandonment of Leptis Magna in the 11th century.

**The rediscovery of Leptis**

In succeeding centuries, coastal sand dunes overwhelmed the site, preserving it from destruction during the succeeding centuries. The result is that the site is below the present ground level with access via a steep flight of steps. Most of the excavations at Leptis were undertaken in the Italian period when the monuments, preserved from damage by encroaching sands, were unearthed. Work began under Bartoccini in 1923, and was particularly intensive under Guidi (1928-36). The excavation and re-erection of Roman monuments was extremely important to the Italian colonial enterprise, proving as it did the Latinity of Tripolitania – and hence Italy's right to be there. In the 1990s, teams from France, Italy and the UK (King's College, London) undertook excavations at Leptis, with work being co-ordinated by the Libyan Department of Antiquities.

## Touring the site

A rushed minimum tour focuses on the monumental centre, plus (time allowing) the Hunting Baths and the Museum. Enthusiasts will find time to have a good look at the port and tramp over to the amphitheatre, and maybe up the Wadi Lebda to look at the Roman cisterns.

**The monumental centre**

*The numbers in brackets are coded to refer to different maps:*
*LM: Leptis Magna overview*
*HB: Hadrianic Baths & palaestra*
*OF: Old Forum*

This is the glory of Leptis, home of many photo opportunities. Here you will find the great monuments of the 20-year Severan rebuilding scheme, including a fine colonnaded street, a massive nymphaeum, a brand new forum and basilica, and a lavish arch, the starting point of the tour of the central area.

The **Arch of Septimius Severus** (LM1), completed 203, lies at the end of a short avenue leading from the entrance. It was built at the intersection of the *cardo* and the *decumanus maximus* to commemorate the visit of Septimius to his native town. The four-faced limestone structure was covered in sumptuously carved panels in marble. At the top of the arch and on the inside were haut-relief panels to the glory of Septimius Severus and his family. The whole repertoire of Imperial propaganda is used; a monument to democracy this is not, and as it was three steps above street level, it functioned as a piece of street furniture, a landmark in a cityscape. Winged victories carrying crowns and palm branches fly in the corners left and right of the actual arch, while the pilasters are decorated with vines featuring mythical figures. These details are thought to be the work of craftsmen from Asia Minor. The hauts-reliefs (now on display in Tripoli Museum) show a distinct Levantine influence.

Head east from the arch (right from the site entrance) towards the Baths of Hadrian and the Palestra. The area on your left is thought to have been the red-light district, as a large number of oil-lamps featuring erotic motifs were found there. (Look out for stones with phallus symbols.) The **Baths of Hadrian** (LM2) (Italian: *terme*), are an enormous construction covering approximately 3 ha, including the outbuildings. This was one of the largest bath houses built outside Rome itself. The baths were constructed in 123-127 AD and improved and extended at various later dates. Excavations at the baths were begun in 1920 by Dr P Romanelli. This was a splendid establishment, built to a regular, symmetrical plan.

The baths are best approached through the **Palaestra** (LM/HB3), the sports' hall for the baths, comprising an open rectangular area surrounded by a portico of 72 columns. There are five doorways into the baths, two on the north aspect leading from the palaestra. To the south two more doorways open onto a corridor parallel to the fascia. Behind lies the **frigidarium** (HB2). In the centre of the frigidarium is a small monument dedicated to Septimius Severus, possibly commemorating the grant of full Roman rights to the city by that emperor. At the east and west sides of the *frigidarium* are two highly decorated **pools** (HB4&5) with parts of the black granite facing still intact. Immediately south of the frigidarium is the **tepidarium** (HB6) and its lateral pools. From here, the ancient bather would have proceeded into the **caldarium** (HB7) or warm room, which had under-floor heating. This room leads on by two doors to two steam-rooms, the *sudatoria* or *laconica*. Behind the caldarium you can see the remains of the boiler rooms and the water tanks. The baths also had a nice pool, near to which are two sets of luxurious and well conserved marble latrines.

The Severan **Nymphaeum** (LM4), with its high semicircular walls and fountain basin stands at the south end of the **colonnaded street** or **Via Colonnata** (LM5), as the Italian archaeologists called it, connecting the Hadrianic Baths with the port. As you head harbourwards along this street, the most important chunk of Severan rebuilding, the **Imperial Forum** (LM7) and the **New Basilica** (LM8) lies on your left.

*Tripolitania*

*The heart of Severan Leptis*

# Hadrianic Baths & palaestra

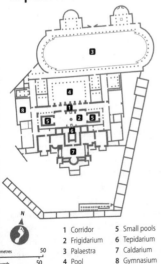

| | |
|---|---|
| 1 Corridor | 5 Small pools |
| 2 Frigidarium | 6 Tepidarium |
| 3 Palaestra | 7 Caldarium |
| 4 Pool | 8 Gymnasium |

0 metres 50
0 yards 50

The **Nymphaeum** (LM4) or Temple of the Nymphs, another finely decorated early third century AD structure, backs onto the Wadi Lebda. It makes a nice feature on the square which marks the beginning of the Via Colonnata (LM5). There are niches for statues, a pool and seven fountains. Note the brick, rubble and mortar structure now visible behind the stone facing. The building was named the Belvedere Mussolini when the dictator visited Leptis in 1926. Behind the Nymphaeum, a stairway leads to the top of the building, whence there are good views over the site. Back on the square, look out for the small **Byzantine church** (LM6) on your left as you look down the Via Colonnata. This was one of four put up by Justinian in the mid-sixth century.

The **Via Colonnata** (LM5), 420 m long, 50 m wide, is the main street of

Severan Leptis, and was built on the dry bed of the diverted Wadi Lebda. It links the bath and leisure areas to the port. Along the street ran a double portico with 125 columns with Pergamene capitals. The Via Colonnata is one of the finest examples of Roman urbanism. Similar streets can be found in the Syrian cities of Bostra and Palmyra, and in Gerasa in Jordan. Much excavation work still remains to be done on the second part of the street, which runs up past Hadrian's Baths.

The early third century **Imperial Forum** (LM7) or *Forum novum severianum* and **New Basilica** (LM8) lie at the heart of Severan Leptis Magna. The Forum is a spectacular sight, despite the ravages of time and looters, and today takes the form of a vast (100 m x 60 m), masonry-strewn area enclosed by high walls. Originally, there were porticoes with Pergamene columns like those of the Via Colonnata. The Forum, dominated by a temple to the gens Septimia, the Severan family, resembles Trajan's Forum in Rome. Septimius Severus clearly wanted his home town to rival the capital of the Roman world in splendour. (The trend is far from dead, of course. Numerous overweening 20th-century rulers have sought to do the same for their home towns, ie Houphouët-Boigny at Yamassoukro, Bourguiba at Monastir.) On a practical note, the planners solved the problem of an irregular site by inserting lines of shops (*tabernae*) on the south and east sides. Look out for the Forum's main decorative feature, stone Medusa and nereid heads, which once stared down from the pendentives (sections between the tops of the arches).

Abutting the Imperial Forum is another expensive Severan public building, the **New Basilica** (LM8), which was a court of justice under the Romans, before being converted to use as a church. This basilica is a large (92 m x 40 m) hall, with semi-circular areas (*exhedrae*) at either end. Colossal Aswan granite columns lined both sides of the hall, supporting the roof. Column capitals were elaborate Corinthian. The *exhedrae* are flanked by finely carved pilasters featuring the myth of Hercules. Look out for Hercules strangling the Nemaean lion, Hercules holding the giant Antaeus off the ground, the centaur Chiron and Hercules with one of the nymphs of the Hesperides.) These hauts-reliefs resemble those at Hadrian's Baths in Caria, and suggest that the craftsmen came over from Asia Minor. An inscription tells that the building was completed under Caracalla in 216 AD. Originally, there would have been several trials going on in the building at the same time. Whether the acoustics in the high-ceilinged hall were suitable for multiple trials is another matter.

When the Byzantines converted this basilica to a church, they put the altar at the southeast end. A cross-shaped baptistery was put into the side room at the northwest end. A sort of pulpit, in the middle of the hall, was made by the Byzantines from recycled column capitals.

**The Old Forum and around**

*Numbers 11-20 and the code 'OF' refer to the Old Forum map*

Some of Leptis' older monuments lie to the northwest between the Severan Forum and Basilica and the sea. Look out for the well preserved four-square **Byzantine Gate** (LM9), which was constructed using much recycled masonry. From this gate, you proceed along the *cardo* into the **Old Forum** (LM10), which dates from the Augustan age. Moving clockwise around this forum, from your left as you come in the *cardo*, there is a selection of major buildings for public worship, including a **former temple later transformed into a church** (OF11), a **portico and altar to Antoninus Pius** (OF12), the **Temple of Liber Pater** (OF13), the **Temple of Augustus and Rome** (OF14), the **Temple of Hercules** (OF15), the stela to Caius, son of Hanno, the **Curia** (OF16) and, over on the eastern side, the **Old Basilica** (OF17) (38m x 92m) which like its later, Severan counterpart, takes the form of a rectangular, colonnaded hall, though without the semicircular recesses at either end. Finally, just to the right of the *cardo* before entering the Old Forum is a small **temple** to orgiastic goddess **Cybele** (OF18). In the middle of the forum can be seen a **Byzantine baptistery** (OF19) and a semi-circular structure or **exhedra** (OF20).

This exhaustive selection of places for worship and administration (the Old Basilica) gives an idea of the importance of the Old Forum. Re-paved with white marble in the first century, thanks to the generosity of a local dignitary, it was surrounded by a portico on three sides. In its day, it must have been a truly impressive urban space, with great temples rising around it. The most important of these were the ones dedicated to **Augustus and Rome** (OF14), and to **Liber Pater** (OF13). This latter temple was rebuilt in marble in the second century. Unfortunately, only the podium and a few steps have survived. It was linked to the neighbouring Temple of Augustus, likewise rebuilt in marble. Access to this temple was by two lateral flights of steps. A neo-Punic inscription visible on the forum, originally placed over the entrance to the *cella* (inner chamber) records that the temple was completed under Balayton and Bodmelquart, suffetes of Leptis, and that it contained statues to Augustus, the goddess Rome, Tiberius and other members of the Julio-Claudian family.

Heading back towards the site entrance, to the north west of the *cardo* is an area of important public buildings, including the **market** (LM22), the **Sanctuary of the Divine Emperors** (LM23), the **Theatre** (LM24), and the **Chalcidicum** (LM25). On your way there, you may pass a small **Temple to Serapis** (LM21), testimony to the presence of an important Alexandrian colony in Leptis. (Certain of the statues from the Serapeum are on display in the Leptis Museum.) On the *cardo* next to the Market is the **Arch of Tiberius** (LM26), while close to the Chalcidicum is the **Arch of Trajan** (LM27). **The theatre and around**

The **market** was another luxury building (LM22), put up by a wealthy citizen of Leptis, one Annobal Tapapius Rufus, son of Himilkon, who had held the posts of both *suffect* and *flamen* (priest of the imperial cult). No doubt he

*Tripolitania*

## Old Forum

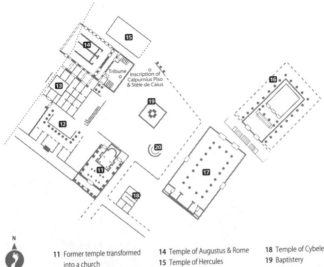

N

0 metres 10
0 yards 10

11 Former temple transformed into a church
12 Portico & altar to Antonius Pius
13 Temple of Liber Pater
14 Temple of Augustus & Rome
15 Temple of Hercules
16 Curia
17 Old Basilica
18 Temple of Cybele
19 Baptistery
20 Exhedra

had seen the great building projects of Rome, whence he drew inspiration for redeveloping the market. In the middle of the market esplanade were twin round kiosks (or *tholoi*). These were surrounded by octagonal porticoes. Look out for sales counters, including those of the fishmongers (?) with their dolphin decorations. Also visible, west of the northwest kiosk or *tholos*, is a copy of a stone table for checking measurements. In use in the first century AD were the Punic cubit, the Alexandrian cubit and the Roman foot. In the northwest kiosk arcade, also look out for a deeply grooved stone, no doubt once used as a well-head stone. Between the two kiosks is a pedestal on which stood a statue to a certain Porphyrius, so honoured for having brought four live elephants to Leptis. The most chic market of its kind in the Roman world, Leptis market as you see it today was partly re-assembled after the Second World War. The granite columns date from an improvement scheme under the Severans.

After the market, take a look at and photos of the two honorary **arches**, one to **Tiberius** (LM26), and the other to **Trajan** (LM27). The latter was put up c. 109 AD to celebrate Trajan's granting the status of *colonia* to the city. Abutting Trajan's Arch is the **Chalcidicum** (LM25), a large rectangular site surrounded by a portico, put up in 11-12 AD, in the reign of Augustus, by (as usual) a local dignitary. It may well have been another market area, perhaps for wild beasts, as statues of elephants were found there. The name Chalcidicum derives from an altar dedicated to Venus Chalcidica situated in the line of stalls along the southern side of the market.

After the Chalcidicum proceed to the really rather splendid **Theatre** (LM24). Ready to host a Greek tragedy, it occupies a commanding position in the western side of the city. Facing northeast, with a diameter of 70 m, the theatre has a

# Theatre

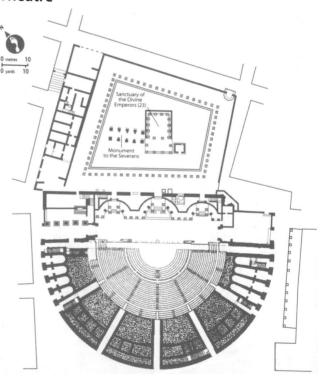

stage backdrop with a fine array of costly columns. On the entablature (horizontal stones above the columns), east, ancient inscriptions are clearly visible. *Proscaenium columnis et marmoribus*, the wording unimaginatively begins. Beyond the stage is a view over the columns of the nearby Temple of the Divine Emperors to the sea. The stage is flanked by twin, white-marble statues of the Dioscuri, who look as though they put in hours and hours in the weights room. (The Dioscuri, Castor and Pollux, were the sons of the nymph Leda and Jupiter, who transformed himself into a swan to make this particular conquest. The Dioscuri announced to the Romans their victory at a major battle by making their horses drink at the fountain of Jupiter, on the forum.)

Atop the seating area was a portico, of which certain elements have been re-erected. Also above the seating, in the middle at the top, was a small temple, probably dedicated to Ceres. Such temples were customary in early Roman theatres, a sign of the link between spectacle and religion. The cult statue from the temple, now in Tripoli Museum, shows the goddess as Tyche (Fortune), personifying the city with a crenellated crown.

After the Theatre, cross the street behind the stage to the **Sanctuary of the Divine Emperors** (LM23) with its grey granite columns, a monument dedicated to the worship of the *Dei Augusti*, the emperors who became gods after their death. Once again, this is a building put up at the expense of a local notable. Obviously disposable income in Roman Leptis had to go into something, and where better than grand projects symbolizing the merchant community's desire to be part of the expanding Roman State.

**Outlying monuments: west of the centre**

If you start back at the Severan Arch, you can head west up a long paved street to visit some outlying monuments. Some 300 m up the street is the **Oea or West Gate** (LM28), part of the late Roman wall. Here an earlier triumphal arch has been integrated into a later defensive system. Another 700 m on is the **Arch of Marcus Aurelius** (LM29). The most important building in this western sector, however, is a bath complex, the so-called **Hunting Baths** (LM30), about 500 m west of the Old Forum. To judge by their size, they were part of a palatial villa complex. Totally buried under the dunes, they are in an excellent state of preservation. One theory goes that the baths were never finished and they are thought to have been under construction at the time of the Vandal invasions. Upon their rediscovery, archaeologists had only to strengthen the vaulting and put glass in the windows. Like other palaces and bathing establishments, the Hunting Baths were not designed with the outsider in mind; the results of aesthetic efforts are to be seen on the inside only. In terms of structure, the vaults and domes, erected thanks to early concrete technology, are supported on massive rubble stone and mortar walls.

The baths were approached by a narrow corridor which led into the *frigidarium*, decorated with splendid wall paintings. There is a splendid leopard hunt: the *venatores* Inginus, Nuber, Ibentius and Bictor can be seen fighting with fierce beasts with names like Rapidus and Fulgintus ('Lightning'). Another feature is a fine Nilotic scene. From the *frigidarium*, one moves into the twin, octagonal *tepidaria*, after which come twin hot rooms. Outside the baths on the southern side the remains of water tanks and the boiler rooms are visible.

## Hunting baths

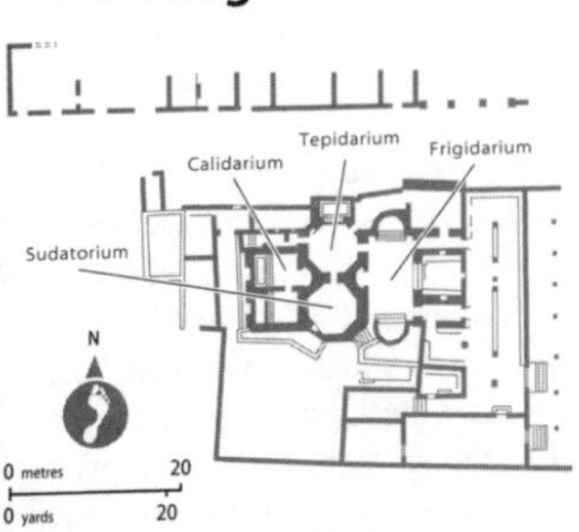

**The Port area** The extension of **harbour** and related facilties at Leptis was the practical heart of the Severan redevelopment scheme, an expansion which was to make the port one of the largest in the Roman Mediterranean, rivalling Ostia and Carthage. Under Nero, **quays** (LM31) had been constructed on the northwest bank of the Wadi Lebda estuary. However, the port suffered from chronic silting up, and in the early third century it was decided to divert the wadi in order to prevent new port facilities from being rendered useless by further silting. The islets protecting the approaches to Leptis harbour were linked up and two large new breakwaters were constructed, protecting a vast new harbour of over 100,000 sq m. A splendid **lighthouse** (LM32) went up on the northern breakwater (base still visible), while over on the smaller, eastern breakwater was a small **Doric temple** (LM33) in Hellenistic style and a **signalling tower** (LM34). This is the most visible part of the port today, and the moorings are clearly visible.

On a calm day, stones marking the start of a further breakwater/quay running out 300 m into the sea can be seen. This area has been explored by a French underwater archaeology project directed by Prof. André Laronde. Some of the finds are on view in the site museum.

The historical record shows that Leptis port handled many thousands of tonnes of olive oil and food grain every year. For centuries, it was a vital point with produce being shipped out from the empire's North African granary to Rome. After Leptis was abandoned, the Wadi Lebda assumed its former course, and the Severan port silted up.

Also of note in the port area are the remains of a **Temple to Jupiter** (LM35) and the **Eastern Baths**, currently under excavation (LM36).

**Outlying monuments: east and south** Out on the far eastern edge of the site are two further monuments, the circus (LM37) and the fine amphitheatre (LM38).

The **circus** (LM37) was completed in 112 under Trajan and forms an extremely elongated narrow horse-shoe, 450m in length and 100m wide, aligned parallel to the coastline. It is as yet not fully excavated but the starting gates can clearly be seen at the city end, while the monumental arch and the circular terminus is at the eastern end. There are two tunnels at ground level carved apparently through solid rock. There are tiers of seats rising from the base around the arena, with places for an estimated 23,000 spectators.

The **amphitheatre** (LM38) immediately south of the Circus in the same complex, is thought to date from 56 AD and has been well excavated by Italian archaeologists. It is slightly elliptical in shape with widest points 100m and 80m. It had seating for 15,000 people. At the top of the seating area (*cavea*) was a small temple or *sacellum* to Artemis. The location for the amphitheatre was carefully chosen. The construction was carefully fitted into a hollowed out rise. Proximity was such that spectators could have walked over to the circus from the northern part of the *cavea*. No doubt the location and the crater-like nature of the amphitheatre meant that noise from bloodthirsty combats and the slaughter of wild beasts did not disturb the life of the town. (For graphic illustration, see the Hunting Baths, above.)

Real enthusiasts of Roman urbanism will need to take a look at a couple of practical features on the Wadi Lebda, namely two well-preserved **reservoirs** (LM39 and LM40) and a **Roman dam** (LM41). The **reservoirs** lie beyond the Khums to Zliten road. The larger northern reservoir (LM39) has five parallel vaulted cisterns. Arrangements are the same in the southern reservoir (LM40), where they are more visible. To enhance rain-gathering capacity, a low wall surrounded the roof, and the tops of the vaults had ridges to speed up run-off. Much further up the wadi, the **dam** was part of the Severan port development works, built to divert water from the Wadi Lebda westwards to the Wadi Rsef. Constructed in concrete with buttresses, it was strengthened on a number of occasions.

**The Museum at Leptis**

With two floors and some 20 rooms, the Museum at Leptis, near the site entrance (3LD entrance), is organized chronologically. As well as containing finds from ancient Leptis, it presents a number of other sites in the region (notably the Villa Silin, see below and Ghirza), before taking the visitor right up to the present. A huge image of Colonel Gadhafi looks over the central hall and its stone elephant. The first rooms take you back to Phoenician and Punic Leptis, with objects from the excavations near the theatre. Then you have a series of rooms dedicated to the development of Roman Leptis. Look out for statues of Serapis, two beautiful heads of Isis with glass-paste eyes, onyx funerary vases and a foot from a bronze statue of Septimius Severus. Part of the Misrata horde is also on display, as are the lower bas-reliefs from the Severan Arch.

**Eating**

There is a small restaurant between the entrance to the site and the museum. With your own transport, you could try the road restaurant, 100 m east of the present entrance, on the turn off for the new highway to Tripoli and opposite the old entrance to the site.

## Excursion from Leptis: the Villa Silin

The plutocrats of Leptis were not ones to skimp when it came to accommodation. All along the Tripolitanian coast, they built themselves fine villas, rediscovered by 20th-century archaeologists. One of the finest, the well conserved Villa Silin, a few kilometres west of Khums, off the main road towards the sea, is easily visited as an excursion from Leptis, and there is a hotel nearby which has had some good reports (*Funduq Naggaza*, T031-26691/2) but does not serve food. The Villa Silin is a little awkward to find, however, being on an isolated part of the coast. The easiest way is to ask at the ticket window or museum at Khums, where you get an authorization. If you have your own car, a guide from either office will come with you. (The disadvantage of this arrangement being that you have to take them back to Khums/Leptis after the visit.) It is not actually very clear whether an authorization is required to visit. If you just turn up without passing via Leptis beforehand, there may be a kindly warden on hand to let you in.

# Villa Silin

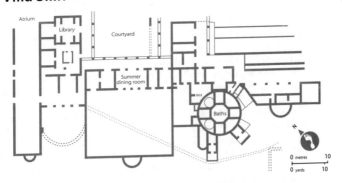

To get to the Villa Silin from Khums, take the main black-top road for Tripoli. At the turn-off inland for Tarhuna, there is a check point. Some 5 km after this junction, there is an unmarked turn to the right. After 10 km of this narrow road, you come to a rough track. The villa lies close to the sea 2 km down this piste, which is just about accessible in an ordinary car. Look out for the dome of the baths and vaulted roofs. Generally, the villa area is wired off, though the access gate is usually open. The warden should be on hand to give you access to the interior.

The Villa Silin was discovered in 1974 (and so does not unfortunately feature in Denis Haynes thorough *Antiquities of Tripolitania*). The location is superb, and in its day (second century AD), the 20-room villa must have been one of the choicest pieces of Tripolitanian real estate. Happily, it was covered by the dunes and remains extaordinarily well preserved. Today, the villa is visited for its mosaics and surviving bits of fresco. There are hunts and scenes of public spectacle, including acrobats and a chariot race. So-called Nilotic mosaics provide an exotic touch, with pygmies fighting crocodiles. More peacefully, there are storks and ducks, and a sea-nymph playing with a triton.

Of the other villas discovered, the **Villa Dar Buc Ammera** near Zliten (see chapter 4) is unspectacular. Fragments of the painted frescoes, now in Zliten Museum, are worth a look, however. At Tajura, just east of Tripoli, the remains of the **Villa of the Nereids** are unfortunately off limits for the foreseeable future, as the site is inside a military zone. The mosaics are visible in Tripoli Museum.

# Eastern Tripolitania: Khums to Zliten

Moving east from Khums and Leptis Magna, you can take the old road through the palm oases. The road is single lane black top, often running at a higher level than the adjacent market gardens and palm groves. **Beware** of local traffic emerging abruptly from side roads and of the road surface in wet weather, when the black top becomes notoriously slippery. There are often small scale road works on this route, too. Motorists and others wishing to avoid the oasis route can take the new road which passes 1 km further inland between the palm groves and the main area of the former Italian La Valdagno agricultural estate to Wadi Ki'am.

However, for those with time, the **oasis route** is more interesting. After Leptis, the oasis, here called the **Sahel al Ahmad**, has numerous modern farmhouses. Farming continues in *suani* (small walled irrigated traditional market gardens) but little effort is put into farming at present. The principal spring field crops in the gardens are wheat, barley and broad beans. The crops are mainly thin but the palm canopy remains for most part in good trim, providing welcome shade. **Souk al Khamis** (lit: 'Thursday Market'), some 7 km from Leptis is the main settlement. From here the old road runs on through palm groves to the intersection with main highway.

**Wadi Ki'am** is Tripolitania's only flowing river, known to the ancients as the Cinyphus. Here a well established agricultural estate spreads out on both sides of the road. The original farm was a mere 120 ha of 2 ha plots fed by irrigation from the impounded stream of a spring source in the Wadi Ki'am. There is now an extension of reclaimed land under orchards and trees from Wadi Ki'am west to join up with old Sahel al Ahmad oasis and ex-La Valdagno.

There are two routes from Khums to Zliten (distance 33 km), beyond the bridge over the Waid Ki'am. (NB There is a check point at the intersection of old road and new highway.)

## An inland route: Khums to Tripoli via Tarhuna

For those with plenty of time in Libya, there is an inland route back to Tripoli from Leptis Magna via Tarhuna and Gharyan. Though the highway is occasionally narrow, it takes you up into the eastern hills of Tripolitania, the Jabal M'sellata and the Jabal Gharyan. (West of the latter town, the Jabal Nafusa region begins.) Before arriving at Gharyan, there is some hill agriculture, including plantations of almond and olive trees, a couple of former Italian settlements and even the odd isolated Roman site. With stops, you have a journey which takes half a day. Driving at normal speed, this route will take over two hours.

From Khums travel west on the main highway to Tripoli but take the Tarhuna road at the first left-hand junction. It is 67 km to Tarhuna from this junction. The road follows more or less the line of an old road but is a good width now. Take care on this road as it is dangerous, with mixed traffic and many curves as the road rises towards the town of **Qusbat**.

Today the main town of the Jabal M'sellata, **Qusbat** has been much extended in an undistinguished sort of way, spoiling whatever charm the place once had. There are most facilities, including a hospital but there is no hotel and travellers interested in walking in the M'sellata should stay in Khums.

From Qusbat continue on the main road to Tarhuna. The road passes through scenic open landscape with ex-Italian olive and almond plantations at **Qasr Dawn** (ex-Mazzoni) and **Khadra** (ex-Breveglieri). Qasr Dawn has a hospital, police, school and shops. Look out for Roman remains beside the road. **Breveglieri** was built during the last phase of Italy's agricultural colonization projects. Situated at the heart of a large agricultural estate, the village's buildings were built around three sides of a small piazza, with all the usual components (municipality, post-office, case del Fascio, police station, school and market). Just opposite was a suitably positioned symbol of Italianness in the form of the undistinguished foundations of some Roman building.

## Tarhuna    ترهونة

Tarhuna is home to the Faculty of Law of Al Nasser University, located north of the town towards Shershara. Cinema, shops, *Libyan Arab Airlines*, and hospitals are among the facilities in the town. Modern building has destroyed the town's character. The famous *Lady of Gharyan*, a wall painting on the barracks wall in the town painted by a US soldier in the Second World War, has sadly disappeared. Tarhuna's excellent wines are also no longer to be found. Leave Tarhuna towards Shershara.

For archaeology enthusiasts, an unexcavated site (ancient **Mesphe**?) on a track 8 km northeast of Tarhuna might merit a visit. Known locally as **M'deina Doga**, the site is located in an olive grove. Haynes (1965) mentions remains of bath-houses and colonnaded buildings in his short description of the site.

**Sleeping** If you need to sleep over, there is a **youth hostel**, c/o Education Department, Tarhuna, 20 beds, breakfast available, kitchen.

**Shershara** The much visited spring at Shershara has now stopped flowing as water has been diverted away and the local water table has fallen. A small stream now comes in through a narrow upper valley with dense trees. It flows under the road which acts as an Irish bridge and there is a tiny fall of water on rocks below the roadway. The lower valley is green but marred by rubbish. What was a very beautiful area is now very disappointing.

**Sleeping** The hotel at Shershara, *Funduq Shershara*, is in a poor state: the rooms are not now used, but there is a restaurant and café. The staff do their best but the general effect is not very good. The hotel has no water from time to time. Tea and a selection of cold soft drinks are available. Open 0800 to 2100.

**West of Tarhuna and back to Tripoli** After Tarhuna you have a choice of roads, northwest to Tripoli, west to Gharyan or south to Beni Walid. The main road from Tarhuna out to the northwest leads down to Tripoli, while an alternative route leads west to Gharyan and the Jabal Nafusa. The Tripoli road is fast but winding. There is a junction outside Tarhuna which permits a direct link from the petrol station at Biar Maji to Beni Walid 90 km to the south, and a second junction to Qatamah, 32 km from Biar Maji. **Youth hostel** in former *Beni Walid Hotel*, T0322-2415, 30 beds, meals available, shop. From Bani Walid, it is possible to continue south and then west via Nisma to Mizda, on the main Tripoli to Sabha road.

The road to Tripoli goes on to **Souk al Khamis**, approximately 75 km from Tarhuna. Here there is a large roadside market, post office, police, shops and other basic facilities. Reaching **Souk al Sebt** there are more roadside shops, a petrol station and other services.

At **Ben Ghashir** the road leads off at a junction to the international airport link. Also from this point there is a dual carriageway to Tripoli, slow with heavy traffic. Roadside orange sellers are found in the spring season. Farm tractors and vehicles are plentiful on this dangerous road, mixing with fast traffic. It may be better to take the dual-carriageway, airport to Tripoli route, generally faster, if not necessarily much safer.

## Tarhuna to Gharyan

Further along the Tarhuna to Gharyan route, there is a rather minor Roman attraction approximately half-way between the two towns, namely the site of ancient **Thenadassa** at modern **Ain Wif**. The site lies approximately 40 km southwest of Tarhuna, 15 km west of the former Italian village of Tazzoli, and 2 km south of the main road, on high ground overlooking the east side of the Wadi Wif. (The modern track from the Wadi Hammam runs right past the site.) Thenadassa was an outpost on the lines, garrisoned by a detachment of the 3rd Augustan legion under the Severan emperors. There are the unspectacular remains of a fort, a church and the site of an important altar to Jupiter, first recorded in 1925. The limestone altar, dedicated by the commanding officer of the garrison, is now in Tripoli Museum. The remains of the baths lie some 300 m west of the main site.

After Ain Wif, the road continues west, meeting the main Gharyan to Tripoli road a few kilometres north of Gharyan. From this junction, you head back into Tripoli, rather more than an hour's drive away, via Azizya and Al Suani.

Misrata and Syrtica

4

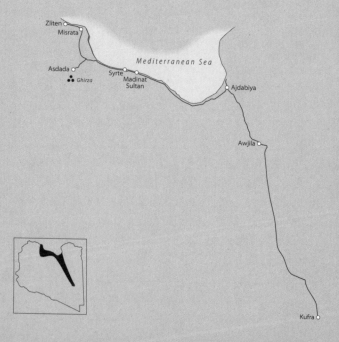

*Easternmost town in Tripolitania,* **Misrata** *comes as a bit of a surprise with its wide clean avenues and tree-planted squares. A quiet sort of place, it makes a good base for excursions to ancient* **Ghirza** *and other desert outposts of Romanity, or to nearby* **Zliten***, with its extravagant mosque and museum famous for its painted Roman frescoes. South of Misrata, the 1930s coast road runs for hundreds of desolate kilometres eastwards to Benghazi, through the flat and featureless lands of Syrtica. Even from the windows of an air-conditioned coach, this is a frightening sort of desert. For much of the way, the highway is a slender ribbon of tarmac running straight across the plain. The scenery changes from arid lands and coastal flats south of Misrata to low-growing salt bushes. Near Syrte are plantations of tamarisk and attempts at irrigated agriculture. Goats and camels can be seen grazing out in the scrub. (If driving in winter take care: the camels like to come and sit on the road to warm their tummies. Sand-blasted car wrecks are reminders of the dangers of this desert route. All along the roadside are old car tyres illustrating the decay of vulcanised rubber in its various stages.)*

*    **Syrte** (future capital of all Africa?) may be a place to stop. Its concrete conference hotel and People's Palace hint at a Brasilia in the making. Nearby at* **Madinat Sultan** *are Islamic remains and a reminder of an ancient frontier: two heroic statues are all that remains of the triumphal arch erected by the Italians to celebrate completion of the Litoranea. Still in heroic mode, in eastern Syrtica the visitor will glimpse vast oil refineries and infrastructure belonging to the* **Great Man-Made River Project***.*

# History

In ancient times, the wastes of Syrtica were a very real barrier to movement along the North African coast. For the Greeks and Carthaginians, they represented the frontier between Hellenic Cyrenaica and the Punic lands further west. The classical writers held the Syrtican desert very much in awe. It was the home of the Nasamones, a people who lived by preying on shipwrecks, and of snake-haired, petrifying Medusa and the Gorgons. (Medusa features prominently in sculpture at Leptis Magna.) In the seventh and eighth centuries AD, the Arab armies moving west to Byzantine Africa had no fear of snakes and other beasties of the burning sands. They were carried along by dromedaries, the great strategic advance in Middle Eastern campaigning of that time.

More recently, in the mid-20th century, Syrtica saw much military activity. In the Second World War, the Allied and Axis armies slogged across the region. The triumphal arch put up by Italy to celebrate the completion of the Litoranea highway was nicknamed Marble Arch by the British soldiers heading westwards towards Tripolitania. In his war memoire *Alamein to Zemzem*, poet Keith Douglas waxed lyrical about the desert flowering after rain. The military vehicles rumbled forward, and "the sweet scent of the flowers would come up to your nostrils even in a tank turret, moving along; it could overcome all the odours of machines."

In the 1960s, eastern Syrtica became a centre for the oil industry. October 1961 saw a major pipeline come into service at Marsa Brega. Oil had been discovered 180 km inland at Zaltan, and a pipeline was constructed to bring the precious liquid to the new tanker terminal. Further exploration revealed more deposits to the south and east of Marsa Brega. Pipelines were constructed up to Tobruk, and in Syrtica to further oil installations at Ra's Lanuf and Zuweitina, south of Benghazi.

After the revolution in 1969, the Libyan authorities began to look for ways to strengthen the country's unity, overcoming the sharp division between the two major regions of Tripolitania and Cyrenaica. A new province, Al Khalij (literally, the Gulf), was created, named for the Gulf of Syrte, comprising the coastal lands from Syrte to Zuwetina and a wide swathe of desert down to Kufra and Al Awinat near the Sudanese frontier. Syrte, it was decided, would be the new capital, situated halfway between the two lead cities of Tripoli and Benghazi and close to the main oil towns. Being Colonel Gadhafi's home town, Syrte had much to recommend it. In early 2000, it was named as the (potential?) capital of a new, Libyan-sponsored, Saharo-Sahelian Federation.

# Misrata    مصراتة

*Phone code: 051* *In the minds of most Libyans, Misrata is the country's best organized town, a pleasant place of wide avenues centring on a couple of pleasant tree-planted squares. Apart from some large sand dunes and the wacky Goztlik monument-museum, there is not a lot to see. Nevertheless, Misrata is a suitable place to stay for exploring the Roman sites of eastern Tripolitania. It also makes a good stop-over on the long slog between Tripoli and Benghazi. Finally, in a country short on shopping opportunities, textile lovers will find high quality blankets and carpets on sale in the souk.*

## Ins and outs

Misrata lies north of the main east-west coastal highway, nearly 250 km east of Tripoli and 825 km west of Benghazi, and is easily accessed by public transport. Travelling by share-taxi, you may be set down at one of the exits from the highway if the car is going on to another destination. Private cars will stop to run you into the town for a dinar or two. Syrte to Misrata is 265 km. **Getting there**

The main inter-city taxi station is located on a large area of open ground close to the main square where the cheap hotels are located. For the beach, take a taxi. Otherwise all the central sights are within 10 minutes walking distance of each other. Zliten and Ghirza are easy day trips from Misrata. Leptis Magna, 75 km away, could also be a day trip from Misrata. **Getting around**

## History and background

Misrata & Syrtica

Misrata could have been a soulless sort of place. There was very little in the way of local building prior to the arrival of the Italians, just a small settlement with souks in a coastal oasis. In the 1920s and 1930s, Misrata became the centre of Italian colonisation in eastern Tripolitania. A new town was laid out on a grid pattern, and all the usual public buildings put in. Municipality, church (now a mosque), and old grand hotel are still visible today, and the pine trees on the old central square have reached a graceful maturity. One of Italy's governors of Tripolitania, Giuseppe Volpi, in need of ennoblement, was to take the title of Conte di Misurata. No doubt it sounded sufficiently Italian to create an air of ancient aristocracy for the holder – whose first fortune had been made generating electricity for Istanbul. For the record, it was Volpi who led the 1922 Italian re-conquest of Tripolitania, and it was under Volpi's governorship (1921-25) that Italian agriculture began to be developed on Jefara plain.

The expansion of Misrata from the 1970s was prodigious. Population growth within the town grew with mass migration from the rural areas. In part, Misrata has taken off thanks to the development of the steel industry. The construction of the two iron and steel mills created employment and the ensuing demand for local services has generated a real sense of growth in the area. **Steel town**

The power of the steel mill authorities is considerable and has helped to unify the town. The old marina was extensively redeveloped to take shipping coming to service the industrial plant with raw materials and other goods. The result is that today the city is the administrative and education capital of eastern Tripolitania. Most ministries have local offices there. Schools, hospitals and colleges are located in the new town. The town centre has the usual shops, cafés and restaurants. A large number of immigrant managers and labourers live in the town and this is reflected in a fairly cosmopolitan atmosphere in the cafés.

Misrata is thus an orderly sort of place, and there seems to be less riotous self-build construction in progress here than elsewhere. There were clearly some enlightened folk in the urban planning department in the 1970s. The main square next to the souk, set with wooden pergolas and planted areas, recalls the well-designed central areas of certain Moroccan cities.

Organized, clean Misrata is the place where new legislation gets tested. Misratans are proud of their town. Other Libyans, however, tend to see Misrata's cleanliness as reflecting the local personality: Misratans are held to be people with a good head for business, and popular mythology relates their financial acumen to the town's once influential (but now vanished) Jewish community.

## Sights

Although Misrata is not exactly well endowed with things touristic, there is enough to fill a leisurely half-day. There are the souks and the strange Goztlik monument-museum, designed as a giant spinning top, and the town is really quite a pleasant place to wander. If you have time, take a look at the sand dunes on the west side of the town, said to be among the highest coastal dunes in the world.

**The souk** Off the main pedestrian square, Misrata has the usual souks selling mass-produced clothes and shoes. More interestingly, every Tuesday, Thursday and Sunday there is a cloak and carpet auction under the vaults of the old cloth souk. Potential buyers stand in front of the narrow, lock-up shops; sellers walk back and forth, shouting their prices, while a senior merchant seated at one end records the sales. The most striking items are the carpets. The best buys, however, are the fine cream wool blankets, winter day-wear for any self-respecting Tripolitanian male. This souk is also the place to purchase an *abaya*, the stylish cloak, often trimmed in gold thread, worn by Libyan men on special occasions.

**Gozltik Monument** The Borj Gozltik, the 'Tower of the Dunes' is one of the more curious monuments in Libya, a science fiction piece of architecture straight from the rotring pen of some 1970s architect with inter-planetary vision. Situated next to the hulking Hotel Gozltik, the tower is an apparition from *Logan's Run*. You half expect to meet people in red jumpsuits and jetpacks running along a walkway pursued by cybermen. In fact, the tower is a monument to the Libyan resistance to the Italians. Somewhat more peacefully, you will now find locals and their children enjoying the garden below the monument. Beneath the tower there is a small museum, with a collection of coins, ceramics and some information on a Roman shipwreck discovered off Khums during the construction of the port. Also there are collections of amphorae and funerary urns from Dafniya. If you do not have time to get to the Fezzan, then the photos here of the Jabal Akakus and the Wadi Matkhandush will be of interest. One final point of interest here is a circular room containing a display of coins from the Misrata Horde, a treasure of some 100,000 tiny Roman coins dating from the early forth century AD and discovered in 1981. (Most of the treasure is on display at the site museum of Leptis Magna).

## Essentials

**Sleeping** Misrata has some clean, simple hotels – and plans for more luxurious accommodation. The Maltese Corinthia group looks set to build a new holiday village on the coast, which should make Misrata more of a tourist destination. The centrally located Funduk Siyahi and Funduk Saferous are just five minutes' walk from the share taxi station. **B** *Hotel Gozltik*, T613333/614614, F610500. Large, modern and generally as well run as the larger hotels in Tripoli; booking is advised, rates as for those in the capital (twin room 45LD), large restaurant and other facilities including a small shop and hairdressers and a travel agency. Make sure you can pay in dinars not dollars. Contact point for the *Winzrik Travel Agency*, T631941 for arranging trips to Ghirza. **D** *Funduq Siyahi*, T619776. Centrally located hotel dating from the 1920s, which must have been very fine in its day. Café on ground floor, helpful reception. High-ceilinged rooms with en-suite shower. Street-facing rooms on the noisy side. Ask to see room first – in summer you may have to move your bed to avoid a/c unit blasting cold air directly at you as you sleep. Some triple rooms, most doubles. **D** *Funduq Saferous*, entrance on the main tree-planted square opposite the old municipality building, T629620. Hotel in 1930s functionalist building close to share taxi station. Pleasant rooms, quieter and cleaner than Funduq Siyahi (25LD for a double), but most without ensuite shower. Good café on ground floor. **D** *Al Jazira Holiday Village*, 7 km out of Misrata, T631940/631925. Rooms (around 15LD for a double) with sea view. Open for the summer only, reservations essential. This is the best place to swim around Misrata. **E** *Funduq Dhat al Ramla*, above a line of shops on a roundabout not far from the centre. With the People's Palace to the left behind you, proceed straight ahead and the hotel is five mins' walk on your left, T619250. Far from being an ideal choice. *Youth hostel*, 4 km west of centre. Open 0700-2300, 120 beds, family rooms, meals, kitchen, laundry, bus 400 m. On the grubby side, more of a migrant workers' hostel than youth hostel.

For a western-type menu you might use the Hotel Gozltik. Otherwise, Misrata is rather lacking in great gastronomic experiences. Try the *Samarcanda*, close to the Hotel Gozltik. Otherwise the main drag running between the main square and the People's Palace has plenty of small eateries and grocer's shops. There is a small shawarma restaurant in the same block as the Hotel Saferous, and a recommendable Tunisian-run roast chicken grill place in the souk – head straight into the souk from the main square and take first left. **Eating**

*Winzrik Tourism Service Company*, Misrata Office, T/F631941, or contact the manager Umar Muhammad al Naas on T619503. Address PO Box 209, Misrata. Can set up Ghirza trips, at a price. **Travel agencies**

**Share taxi** There are planty of departures for **Zliten**, **Khums** and **Tripoli** throughout the day, but fewer departures for **Benghazi**. All departures are from the open ground near the main square. **Transport**

For completeness sake, Tauorga, some 40 km south of Misrata, is situated in the middle of a swamp formed by the great Tauorga salt lake and was reputed to be a refuge for escaping slaves. The town is located on a set of springs, which provides water for agriculture, including a modern farm settlement set up by the government. **Tauorga**
تورغاء

## Misrata to Zliten

The dual carriageway leading west to Zliten passes through oases. The once thinly populated coastal strip is now increasingly busy. Close to the road, large new block-like family houses, great chunks of concrete among the palms, can be seen. Today the trend is to treat the oases as amenity areas rather than working farms. Further from Misrata, the palms give way to rich agricultural estates established by the Italians. Close to Misrata in the **Zawiat al Mahjub** district is the former estate of the pre-Fascist Governor of Tripolitania, General Volpi.

One of the largest estates was at **Dafniya** where the orchard groves of olives and almonds cover what was originally thin pastureland. At Dafniya there is a checkpoint, petrol station, shops and recreation area in the shade of large pine trees. Here you can see the buildings of the old Villagio Garibaldi with its disaffected church and piazza. After independence, the Italian rural development effort was continued by the Libyan Government with new areas reclaimed and ex-Italian estates taken over by Libyan farmers.

# Zliten زليطن

*Phone code: 0521* If you have half a day to spare, an easy half-day trip from Misrata is Zliten, a sleepy place with a small museum, important for its Roman frescoes. However, Zliten has well and truly lost any feel of the pleasant oasis settlement it once was. The city has expanded in all directions. Although the square in front of the museum has a couple of nice examples of early 20th century architecture, including the old municipality with its clock, in late 1999, both buildings were in a parlous state, and the one-time Piazza Vittorio Emanuele III had turned into a rubbish dump. In fact central Zliten as a whole, apart from the area close the Shrine of Sidi Abd al Salam, is down-at-heel. There are numerous new apartment blocks, but the rubbish just piles up in the street. Next to the main taxi rank, poor looking Tuareg and Malians wait to mend shoes next to yet another semi-abandoned public garden. Car carcasses stand rusting in the street. Coming from neat and proper Misrata, the contrast is surprising.

**Getting there & around** Arriving at Zliten from the Misrata direction, you turn right off the highway for the town centre. The journey time from Misrata is about 40 mins, and the cost 1.5LD by share taxi. Zliten is also only 37 km east of Khums. Share taxis stop on a scruffy central street a block away from the main square, where the museum is located, and five mins' walk from the shrine of Sidi Abd al Salam. Whilst in Zliten, the ruins of the Villa Dar Buc Ammera are just five mins' drive out of town on the coast.

**Sights** With its multiple domes and minarets, from a distance the modern **Mosque of Sidi Abd al Salam** looks like a Disney version of an Arabian nights palace. In fact, it houses the shrine of the region's holy man, one Sidi Abd al Salam al Asmar. Born in 1455 of a local chief and one Sayida Salima, a saintly woman who spent every night in prayer, Sidi Abd al Salam was educated at Qussabat. He grew famous for his piety and ascetic lifestyle, existing on a diet of flour and barley. In his retreat, a spring burst forth, and this was held to be his first miracle. Much later in life, in 1562, Sidi Abd al Salam returned to Zliten. He passed away at the ripe old age of 120.

The mosque today is a recent creation and your chance to see a major display of Moroccan craft decorative techniques. The entrance to the shrine includes elaborate geometric *zlij* mosaic work. Above the *zlij* ceramic, the tops of columns and walls are covered with stucco carved with decorative designs. In the traditional Moroccan house or mosque, such decoration is reserved for courtyards and rooms within a building. Here, its use on a massive scale is all about the respect born by modern Libya for one of its most pious men. At

ruined municipality & mosque, Zliten

Zliten's museum, there are some black and white photographs of the mosque before restoration. It was altogether a much simpler affair, a low building with whitewashed walls in keeping with the ascetic character of its founder. In the Zliten area are other *marabout* tombs (best visited with a local inhabitant) famous for their fertility improving qualities, hence a number of pilgrimages.

Zliten's most interesting archaeological remains are to be found in the **Zliten Museum**, which opened in 1994 in the former Albergo delle Gazelle. The museum, chiefly notable for its fragments of exquisite Roman frescoes, is easily recognizable by the two ceramic gazelles above the main entrance. (The austere façade is a 'must photograph' for adepts of 1930s Italian functionalist architecture). ■ *If you arrive late, then the warden sleeps in the museum: as you stand in front of the museum entrance, go right and knock on the first window on the right hand side of the building, where the caretaker lives. Hopefully, he'll be kind enough to let you have a look. Entrance ticket is 1LD. The museum is actually quite tiny and can easily be covered in 15 minutes.*

The frescoes from the Villa Dar Buc Ammera are housed in a room to the right of the former reception. No doubt the dining rooms of Petronius' Satyricon had such decoration. There is a rather splendid sea procession with nymphs on seahorses, a winged Nike with a palm branch for some victor, nicely executed vignettes of antelopes, Pegasus and a Gorgon. There is also a Nile scene. The Egyptian landscape was to be popular for centuries – see also a later mosaic at Qasr Libia, Cyrenaica. No doubt it brought just the right touch of the exotic to a living area in a Roman home.

Less importantly, the museum also has some plaster castes of sculpture from Leptis, and there are some cases of Roman ceramics from tombs in the Zliten area. There is the usual room with damp and moth-eaten examples of regional craftwork, so after the frescoes, head for the **Villa Dar Buc Ammera**.

The villa is on the coast, and any taxi driver on the main square will take you there and back for 5LD, waiting while you explore. (There is no entry charge). The remains are not spectacular, and the original isolation of the site has gone with the construction of company holiday villages close by. The villa occupies a superb site right on the coast, and it looks as though sea erosion carried away part of the building. No doubt there was an elegant terrace overlooking the sea. The site was excavated by Italian archaeologists early last century, and some superb mosaics, now in Tripoli Museum, were discovered here. However, today's lay visitor will find the low rubble walls not all that easy to understand.

At the entrance to the site, the remains of a small bath complex can be distinguished, including two tubs, one round and the other square. A narrow corridor, paved with bricks laid in herring-bone pattern, led to the main part of the villa. Further to the west are the living quarters, housed in a long, rectangular block. A 20m long corridor gives access to rooms of various sizes, which can be imagined by the surviving low foundations. The Mosaic of the Four Seasons and that of the Amphitheatre Games in Tripoli Museum came from this part of the house. A geometric mosaic and some areas of *opus sectile* paving can be found, left in place but covered by a thin layer of sand for protection from the elements. Finally, look out for a vaulted passageway, parallel to the main corridor and right next to the sea. This probably served as a cistern.

As noted above, the old hotel *Albergo delle Gazelle* was converted into a museum in 1994. Today there are two acceptable accommodation options in Zliten: **B** *Hotel Zliten*, T620120/1/2. Large, new hotel used by tour groups as a base for visiting Leptis Magna. 35LD for a double room. **D** *Funduq al Waha*, on the main road from highway to town centre, T623426. Grotty hotel with rooms for 20LD a night. Ideally, take a hotel in Misrata in preference to this option.

**Sleeping**

Misrata & Syrtica

**Eating**    There are eateries in the ground floor of the building opposite the taxi rank.

**Transport**    **Share taxi**  Plenty of departures for **Misrata**, **Khums** and **Tripoli** from the central square, a couple of blocks from the museum.

# Ghirza

*The tombs of Ghirza are one of the legendary sites in Libya. Out in the desert to the south of Misrata are colonnaded stone mausolea. The four-square buildings, receptacles for the ashes of Roman grandees, and only slightly eroded by the desert winds, remain as monuments to a time when Tripolitania was a good deal greener. Locals find petrified Ghirza to be an eerie place, where djinn (and scorpions) lurk under the rocks. The original inhabitants were turned to stone, they say. This version of the Medusa myth has yet to be confirmed, and bold, romantic souls may want to spend a night under the stars near the ruins. Others may be content to gaze on the reconstructed tomb from Ghirza in the Jamahiriya Museum, Tripoli.*

## Ins and outs

**Getting there**    Ghirza is best visited as a day-trip from Misrata. A car with driver can be organised from the Hotel Goztlik, price in 1999, 200 to 250LD. Self-drivers need to know that the drive is long (186 km), but not complicated, and that a strong saloon car can do the trip. As there are sections of piste, a four-wheel drive is preferable, as is a local guide who knows the landscape well. The drive takes about 1 hr 45 mins.

To reach Ghirza, head south from Misrata on the main coast road. (Distances given from flyover 3 km from town centre). After the dual carriageway ends, the road is lined with mature trees for some kilometres. (A few Italian houses survive). After 22 km there is a check point, and an Italian village with a ruined church tower. After 82 km, you come to a flyover in open country (the Asdada turn-off). Turn right here and 17 km further on you turn left at a crossroads onto a road running alongside a branch of the 'river'. Follow this for 80 km. The asphalt stops after 22 km, but the surface is pretty good and you can drive at normal speed. 179 km out of Misrata, after a series of small conical hilltops to the right, you turn right at a rusty petrol barrel complete with Arabic inscription. After 7 km of rough road, you come to the new village of Ghirza, about 1 km north of the main ruins, which can be reached by a driveable track. The site is located at the meeting of the wadis Zemzem and Ghirza.

Note that the main mausolea are situated at GPS 30°56'49" N / 14°33'05" E. A very thorough visit of the site warrants at least 3 hrs, although most visitors will be happy with considerably less.

## History and background

Ghirza was rediscovered by Europeans in 1817, when the English admiral Smyth visited the site. The earliest written record goes back to the Arab historian Al Bakri, writing in the 11th century: "Three days travel from Qasr ibn Maymun stands a stone idol on a hill, which is called Guerza even today; the Berber tribes of the neighbourhood make sacrifices to it. They address prayers to it to be cured of sickness and they believe it has the power to increase their wealth. This idol lies three days' travel from Waddan." (Had Al Bakri actually been to Ghirza?) The mention of an idol leads us to the origins of the name Ghirza. Ancient historians have speculated that the name may derive from Gurzil, a local god mentioned by Corippus, a Latin poet of the sixth century

AD. Corippus mentions the Laguatan, a Syrtican people who in battle would send a bull charging at their enemies; this bull they believed to be born of Ammon and a cow. And from this ancient writer we move into animal worship in an obscure corner of the classical world.

Ghirza is thought to have grown up in the third century AD as a settlement on the Limes Tripolitanus, the frontier between Roman lands and the nomad tribes of the desert. Agriculture would seem to have been the lifeblood of Ghirza. The bas-reliefs from the mausolea, some of which can be seen in the entrance area of Tripoli Castle Museum, portray a prosperous rural community. There are flocks, farmers ploughing, sowing and reaping, and illustrations of the main crops: grapes and dates, figs and corn.

Travellers began to visit Ghirza in the 20th century – and certain bas-reliefs were taken to Istanbul. The first excavations were undertaken by British teams in the 1950s. (A good account of some of the monuments can be found in D.E.L. Haynes' scholarly work, *The Antiquities of Tripolitania*).

## Exploring Ghirza

Today the ruins of Ghirza centre on a series of fortified farms of the kind frequent in Roman Tripolitania. Parts of some stand to full height, with doors and window openings clearly visible. Within are courtyards and rooms with holes for beams and so forth. The buildings are essentially functional, the masonry somewhat on the coarse side. Two main groups of buildings are visible, separated by a minor dry wadi. The north cemetery, which has the most impressive tombs, is to the west, across a further subsidiary wadi. The main wadi extends to the south of the site, and it is along this that the southern cemetery, some 2 km away, is located. Follow the wadi, noting the regular lines of stones that divide the bed into 'fields': these are the remains of Roman dams meant to break the force of flood water and retain it, thereby preventing soil erosion. (This *jasur* system is still in use in parts of southern Tunisia, notably the Matmata region.) After 1½ km, you cross to the eastern side and climb diagonally towards the ridge: you should emerge near the group of tombs, two of which are still stand to considerable height and can be clearly seen from the southernmost section of the ancient settlement. Despite the proximity of the new 'river' (some 5 km away), the rough stony terrain seems totally empty.

# Ghirza: main settlement, field system & mausoleum tombs

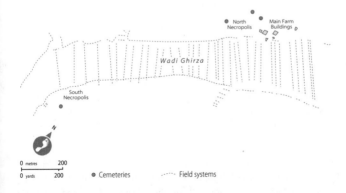

Misrata & Syrtica

Misrata & Syrtica

### Burial at Ghirza

Archaeologists think that the early Libyic peoples had a cult of death and the after-life very similar to that of the ancient Egyptians. The dead were buried, never cremated, and remained extremely important for the living – as is still the case in the Dogon country of Mali and in parts of Madagascar. Mausoleum C in the northern cemetery carries a votive inscription in which Nimir and Maccurasan, who paid for the building, express the hope that their parents, Chullam and Varnychsin may visit their children and grandchildren. The dead remained part of daily life, a benevolent presence no doubt, and ancestral links required careful cultivation. Some of the Ghirza mausolea have grooves through which libations could be poured into the cella. Elsewhere in Libya, visitors interested in all things necrological will want to see the Greek tombs at Cyrene and Tocra. (Grave offerings can be seen in the museum at Tocra.) Down in the Fezzan, in the Wadi al Hayat, are the vast burial areas of the nomad Garamantes.

**Tomb building** Ghirza's most outstanding feature are its elaborate tombs. Ennobling the desert horizon, they come as a surprise in this remote place, a Père Lachaise in the Tripolitanian hinterland. It is likely that other Roman settlements in the region had similar chunky limestone monuments to the dead – but which proved to be a handy source of building stone for later peoples. The native Libyic cult of the dead seems to have survived under the Romans, and temple tombs were clearly a way of stressing the social pecking order in frontier outposts like Ghirza. While pre-Roman religion in the region left few temples, the grafting of Rome onto Libyic traditions produced spectacular funerary architecture. The names of certain tomb inscriptions at Ghirza show that these were local families. However, they were folk keen to display their Roman credentials. With Corinthian capitals, pilasters and columns, plus plaques in Latin, the most splendid tombs pretend to be distillations of Romanity (and are more than just a little nouveau riche in their ostentation). Two of the tombs in the northern necropolis have votive inscriptions which also list construction costs.

**The North Necropolis** In the northern necropolis, a little way south of the fortified farms, lie three fine examples of the temple tomb. They are referred to by archaeologists as **mausolea A, B,** and **C**. Tomb A is largest and is the one without arches, while B and C are taller and have arched galleries. In all three examples, large stone blocks form a platform reached by a short flight of steps. In mausoleum A, a colonnade runs round all four sides of the platform, and in the middle sits the *cella* (tomb chamber). An elaborate false door 'opens' into the cella, and above it sits the dedicatory plaque, protected by a pair of eagles.

All the tombs were decorated with elaborate bas reliefs. Tomb C has scenes of daily life (a man carrying an amphora, another feeding a camel, a third playing the lyre), and lively vignettes of hunting (horsemen in pursuit of ostriches, dogs chasing antelopes), along with agricultural life. All these mausolea have elaborate pilasters and column capitals, local stone-carvers' variations on the Corinthian type. Rosettes and friezes of vine leaves and pomegranates may symbolize abundance or just be decorative fillers.

The dating of the tombs is uncertain, but they are thought to go back to the fourth century AD.

**The South Necropolis** Less spectacular than its northern counterpart, the southern necropolis at Ghirza also has an obelisk tomb. This 'desert needle', which collapsed during an earthquake in 1935, was subsequently restored by archaeologists. The

### A legendary meeting in Syrtica

The two main halves of Libya, Tripolitania and Cyrenaica, meet at the coastal settlement of Syrte, on the gulf of the same name and now a place of some political importance as the centre of Libyan government. Back in ancient days, Syrte was the meeting point of the Greek and Punic worlds, of the Pentapoli, five federated Hellenic towns to the east and Punic trading posts to the west.

As in all such cases, there is a suitably explanatory legend. Hellenic Cyrene and Carthage were at war. To define the frontier between them, a pair of brothers set out from each city, and the boundary would be marked at the spot where they met. The laid-back Cyrenaican brothers made slow progress, unlike the fleet-footed Carthaginians. The result was that the two pairs met at Syrte, not so very far from Cyrene. The Cyrenaicans, seeing that their city would lose considerable territory should the boundary be at Syrte, proposed a deal. They offered their lives for the race to be re-run – or the Carthaginian pair would give its lives at Syrte and the boundary would stay there. The Carthaginians preferred the second solution, and for their self-sacrifice were named the philanoi, the 'lovers of praise', by the Greeks and an altar was put up to them.

Centuries later, in the 1930s, a coastal highway was completed. The colonizing Italians erected a triumphal arch near Syrte to commemorate the classical legend and celebrate their newly declared colony, Libia. No trace of the monument survives today.

small mausoleum which can be seen in Tripoli Castle Museum also comes from this cemetery.

### Excursion to the Roman mausolea at Wadi Nefed

The Roman mausolea in the Wadi Nefed is another excursion which can be done from Misrata. The first part of the journey is as for Ghirza, heading south on the main road from Misrata, and after leaving Tauorga, taking the second turn right for Asdada, easily recognizable by a road bridge in the middle of nowhere crossing the main road. Head for Asdada, and after around 40 km, you will come to a track on your left. After some 20 km of rough piste, you will see the first of the Roman obelisk-type mausolea to your right.

This excursion is a must for enthusiasts of Roman funerary architecture. The presence of such elaborate tombs in the today's arid Wadi Nefed bears witness to the wealth of the area's landowners in Roman times. The two mausolea at **Qasr Umm al Ahmad** in the Wadi Nafed are among the best preserved in the country. The southern mausoleum survived almost intact from ancient times, while the northern mausoleum was recently restored. Rising to a height of 16 m, it is an impressive monument.

## Syrte سرت

*Phone code: 054*

From rather unpromising beginnings, Syrte, ancient Macomedes-Euphranta, has joined the ranks of purpose-built African capitals. Until recently it was also known as Qsar al Zaafran, on account of the saffron produced there. Apart from being a half-way house on the long slog between Tripolitania and Cyrenaica, Syrte has little to offer the visitor. Architecturally, there is nothing to qualify the city for a prize as a new African Brasilia. However, journalists dealing with Arab affairs will almost certainly wind up visiting Syrte sooner or later, as it is here that the annual Popular Congresses of the Jamahiriya are held.

Misrata & Syrtica

It may well be that Syrte will be the new capital of Libya. Colonel Gadhafi was born 20 km from Syrte, at Qasr Abu Hadi, and first attended school there at the age of 10. However, despite an extensive public works programme and the fact that major meetings are held there, the city never quite seemed to catch on as capital of Libya. In 1998, Al Bayda, up on the Cyrenaican plateau, was declared capital. Currently plans are afoot for a vast airport at Syrte. Perhaps, the Libyan political imagination intends Syrte to be the capital of a trans-Saharan federation. For the moment though, ministries, embassies and oil company HQs remain firmly fixed in Tripoli and Libya's civil servants are said to be unwilling to leave the comforts of the old capital.

**Sleeping** Syrte is not the easiest place to find a bed and during major political meetings, the hotels can be block booked by the government. There are two 'quality' hotels and couple of smaller options. **A** *Hotel Qasr al Mu'tamarat*, on the southern edge of the city, T60165. A large conference centre hotel (as its name in Arabic suggests). Around $120 a night for a double room. **C** *Hotel Mehari*, 3 km out of Syrte, T60104. A better option than the above, close to the sea with a bit of a garden. Used by travel agencies. Make sure you can pay in local currency, otherwise it will work out very expensive (40LD a night, double room). **C** *Hotel Medina*, Centrally located close to the People's Palace (Qasr al Sha'ab), T60160. Has nothing to recommend it. **Youth Hostel**, on the corniche, generally full, 5LD a night.

**Eating** As regards eating, there are plenty of cheap eateries in the central area for roast chicken and couscous.

**Transport** **Share taxi** Departures for **Benghazi**, **Misrata** and **Tripoli**. Taxis can fill up quickly and as Syrte is a small place, there are not many of them. Make an early start.

# East from Syrte to Benghazi

Heading eastwards from Syrte, the landscape improves slightly. There are plantations of eucalyptus, more settlements, and eventually even a major Great Man-Made River site. There is some dual carriageway before the road narrows once more. To the south of the road, sections of the Man-Made River track can be seen, marked by lorry tyres.

## Madinat Sultan

More interestingly, some 50 km out of Syrte, there are the remains of a small early Muslim town, Madinat Sultan. (Some 5 km further on, the unimportant and scattered settlement of **Sultan** is reached, not to be confused with another Sultan much further east near Benghazi). Located roughly halfway between Cyrenaica and the pleasant coastal oases of eastern Tripolitania, Madinat Sultan is thought to have been founded by the Phoenicians under the name of Charax. Like Ajdabiya further east, it would have been an important staging post for the caravans coming up from the Fezzan, meeting the east-west trade between the Middle East and the Maghreb. Known as 'Sort' by the early medieval Muslim writers, the town was completely abandoned by the 13th century. The Beechey brothers visited Madinat Sultan in 1821, but it was not until the early 1930s that an Italian captain, one Luigi Cerrata, wrote the first detailed account.

The recently excavated ruins of Sultan can be visited, even if they are a little difficult to **Getting there** locate. Basically, 49½ km east of the eastern roundabout on the Syrte by-pass, look out for a three-part arch and metal gate in a compound wall set well back from the road to your left. There are no signs. Another indication: the museum is 6 km east of a checkpoint. (If you are coming from the Benghazi direction, the museum compound is on your right 519 km from Al Maqrun, outside Benghazi, and 359 km from Ajdabiya).

Just to your right within the compound is a concrete building containing a few **The site** sparse finds from the excavations, including coins, glass and fragments of pottery. The caretaker may also point out the remains of what was one of the earliest mosques in Libya, a couple of kilometres further on towards the sea. More spectacularly, two great bronze statues lie on their sides among the dust and weeds. These sinewy figures are the **Philanoi Brothers**, the 'lovers of praise' (see box), whose altar once upon a time marked a frontier in this region. (See 'Graret Gser al Trab', below.) The statues once lived high above the Tripoli – Benghazi road, a feature of a great arch celebrating the completion of the Litoranea in 1936 and demolished under the present régime. (On older maps, the original site of this construction, 681 km from Tripoli, is marked as Marble Arch, from the nickname given to it by British soldiers in the Second World War.)

The **Arco dei Fileni** was the high water mark of the Italian presence in Libya – and for this very reason had to go. Designed by Florestano di Fausto, one of the leading architectural lights of the colony, the building, over 25 m high, resembled an Egyptian temple pylon in its massive simplicity. The Philanoi bronzes lay horizontally above the actual arch, one on each side. Above them were three tiers of bas-reliefs, portraying camels, farmers and soldiers, the Italians working alongside the Libyans and the meeting of King Victor Emanuel III and Mussolini – in short, a full display of fascist symbols which cannot have been very easily visible from the road 20 m below. History does not relate who had the idea of bringing the old legend of the Philanoi out of the classical texts. Perhaps it was Italo Balbo, fascist Italy's glamorous aviation minister, sent to Libya as governor in 1934, who was behind this exercise in reinventing Greek mythology.

Despite their demotion, the statues have a certain melancholy (perhaps kinky?) fascination. These Philanei throw their over-muscled arms up as if to parry a sword blow; their huge feet have lost a few toes. Dust storms have given a rough patina to the metal. Inspired by Greek legend, the bronzes have a sense of movement worthy of Hellenistic statuary. They are tortured cup-bearers, nothing like the poised *kouroi* created by the sculptors of fifth-century Athens. With an eye to realism, the 1930s sculptor gave them the lean lines and elongated legs of long distance runners. But this still does not explain why it was felt appropriate for the fascist Italian state to use such grim models of self-sacrifice.

Leaving Madinat Sultan behind, there are many more flat and uninteresting **Graret Gser** kilometres to go before Benghazi, nearly six hours in fact, if you are travelling **al Trab** by bus. A good 50 minutes after Syrte, at **Jawda**, there are red dunes and more eucalyptus. Off the main road, near Ra's al Ali, there is a site for archaeological enthusiasts, Graret Gser al Trab, which on the basis of recent archaeological discoveries is thought to be the ancient frontier between Tripolitania and Cyrenaica. Close to the foot of the Jabal Allah, at the bottom of the Gulf of Sidra, the remains of a Roman monument have been discovered. Consisting of four columns bearing statues of the Emperor Diocletian (284-305 AD) and his three co-rulers, the monument marked the imperial Roman presence at the altars of the Philanoi. Later travellers believed that the twin humps of the Jabal Allah marked the burial place of the two mythical brothers.

Misrata & Syrtica

*Graziani destroys the tribes*

*By 1930, the Italian government felt the campaign to pacify Cyrenaica had dragged on too long. General Rodolfo Graziani was sent in to end resistance, which he did efficiently and with utmost cruelty. The tribes that submitted, the sottomessi, were rounded up and corralled in camps close to Italian strong points. The idea was that the resistance would have to follow the population, even if communication with them had become hazardous – and that the wild terrain of the Jabal Akhdar, the rebel stronghold, would require less surveillance. In spring 1930, nomad tribes were thus moved down to the plain between Tolmeta (modern Dirsiya) and Benghazi, and a territorial gap created between resistance fighters and their kinspeople.*

*But the rebels did not begin to surrender and notwithstanding the creation of the camps, the people continued to help the resistance. Italian geo-political strategy had to shift up a gear. Leading sheikhs were arrested and interned in Italy. More disastrously for the nomads, it was decided to reduce links with the guerrillas by moving the camps to the coastal steppelands between Benghazi and Al Agheila, at the bottom of*

*the Gulf of Syrte. The new camps were surrounded by double-barbed wire, food was rationed and grazing strictly monitored by troops. Special permits were needed to leave the camps. Graziani later wrote that the government had been determined to reduce the people to the most miserable starvation if orders were not obeyed. At Al Agheila, a special camp was set up for the families of rebels and 'trouble-makers'.*

*The deportation strategy was successful, accompanied as it was by a switch in Italian military strategy from pitched battles to guerrilla war using a battalion of Eritrean troops. Mussolini and Graziani took a risk with Italy's international reputation – which initially paid off. Few foreign correspondents were likely to find their way to isolated Syrtica to report on the horrors of fascist Italy's first concentration camps. The guerrillas were thus deprived of supplies and human support; constant armed pressure was maintained. But there were longer term results. Some would say that the people of eastern Libya's first contact with a modern nation was so terrible that it created a long-lasting reticence towards modern structures of government.*

**Ra's al Naluf & Al Brayqa** Some 2½ hours east of Syrte, you reach the oil refineries of Ra's al Naluf and its airport, after which there are views of white dunes over to the north. You will pass the buildings of a large university. The next major settlement, Brayqa, formerly Brega, is another key point of the Libyan oil industry. After Brayqa (244 km to Benghazi), the road runs further inland, and the landscape becomes more steppe-like. In 1938, the Italian authorities came up with a Plan for the Intensive Demographic Coloniszation of Libya: bore holes were planned to tap deep groundwater and enable the Jabal Akhdar nomads and their flocks displaced by Italian settlement to survive in arid eastern Syrtica. Good though the winter grazing may be, the prospect of summer in Syrtica is not one to be relished. Next on this desolate stretch of the Litoranea, Ajdabiya, about an hour and 40 minutes' drive from Benghazi (160 km), where there are some Islamic remains, is a possible stopping point of interest.

**Ajdabiya** Ajdabiya, also spelt Agedabia on the older Italian maps, has been identified as **اجدابيا** the Roman Corniclanum. As the site had drinking water, it became a staging post in an otherwise arid region. Later part of the Byzantine Empire, the settlement was most important in the early centuries of Islam. It is thought that it was sacked during the Hilalian invasions of the second half of the 10th century, after which it fell into decline before being revived under the Ottomans as a minor administrative centre. During the truce between the Italians and the Sanusiya, from 1917 to 1922, Ajdabiya was an important Sanusi centre. Under the terms of the 1920 Al Rajma Accord, the Sanusi leader received the title of Sanusi Amir, and became head of an autonomous administration covering the oases of Jaghbub, Awjila, Jalu and Kufra; Ajdabiya was his capital. In 1923, when the truce broke down, the Italians believed that by seizing Ajdabiya they would defeat the Sanusi movement. Referred to by General Bongiovanni as the *roccaforte della Senussia*, Ajdabiya was easily taken in April 1923. The Sanusi resistance, however, was not to be ended so easily and fighting continued until the early 1930s. Ajdabiya became an important Italian military outpost.

There are two sites of importance which recall old Ajdabiya. Firstly, the remains of the **mosque**, built in the early 10th century, are located on the Jalu road. The plan of the building can be distinguished. There was a large rectangular courtyard with underground cistern. The minaret was on the north wall. Latin inscriptions on some of the blocks indicate a building erected by recycling material from an earlier Roman settlement. Secondly, and more spectacularly, the ruins of the **palace fortress** are worth a look, close to which is the Municipality, a white Italian building with detail picked out in green. Of the palace a vaulted chamber survives – thanks to restoration works in 1952. Built like the mosque in the 930s under the Fatimid caliph Abu al Qasim, the palace was probably the residence of a regional governor. The surviving massive walls indicate a building put up at a time of some prosperity.

After Ajdabiya, the road runs across a flat and desolate plain to Benghazi, some **Ajdabiya ro** 150 km to the north. You pass through Madinat Sultan 38 km after Ajdabiya and **Benghazi** the turn off for **Suluq**, once upon a time a great camel market and final station on the extinct narrow gauge railway line from Benghazi. A few kilometres before Benghazi, the road is shaded with eucalyptus once more and the sprawling buildings of the University of **Qara Younes** can be seen to the left. Downtown Benghazi is reached after an impressive network of roundabouts and flyovers.

## Excursion from Ajdabiya into the Khalij region

From Ajdabiya it is possible to journey southeast into the desert, to Awjila, Jalu and eventually the remote oasis of Kufra, although it is unlikely that the average visitor will have the time or the inclination to head this way. Head south out of Ajdabiya, past the grain silos. There is now 280 km of desert to cross before you reach Awjila. The underground presence of the Great Manmade River is indicated by breather pipes and inspection covers.

For centuries, the oasis of Awjila (written Ojla in the Italian spelling) was a stop **Awjila** on the caravan route from Egypt and Cyrenaica to the Fezzan. Thanks to the electric pump, modern irrigated agriculture has arrived in the desert and Awjila, like nearby Jalu (aka Gialo), produces market garden crops for consumption in Benghazi 400 km to the north. The original oasis is suffering from neglect, however. The old quarters of Awjila contain two of Libya's oldest mosques, the Jami'a Al Kabir or Great Mosque, and the Sidi Abdallah Mosque. The old town also has a small ethnographic museum located in a restored house.

Awjila's history is obscure. Along with the rest of the region, the oasis submitted to the invading Arab armies of Uqba ibn Nafi' in the seventh century. The legend goes that one Abdallah ibn Sarth, said to be a brother of the third caliph, Uthman, and leader of the Arab conquest of Cyprus, died here. In Ottoman times, Awjila fell into decline and its monuments disappeared under the sands. The size of the mosques shows, however, that in pre-industrial times

Misrata & Syrtica

## The Long Range Desert Group

During the First World War, the British Army in Egypt used light car patrols driving Model T Fords and Rolls Royce armoured cars to penetrate the Libyan desert and protect the western flank from attacks by armed groups of Sanusi warriors. These patrols were the predecessors of the Long Range Desert Group (LRDG) of the Second World War. Originally established in June 1940 as the Long Range Patrols under British Army Command in Cairo, the LRDG was the brainchild of R A Bagnold. He assembled a team of men with great experience of desert travel in order to harry the Axis forces behind their lines in eastern Libya. Early recruits came from the New Zealand Command and it was the New Zealanders who were to form the core of the LRDG.

Each patrol originally had two officers and around 30 men supported by 11 trucks, equipped with heavy machine gun and anti-aircraft guns, though this complement was later halved. Essential skills for LRDG members were signalling, navigation and intelligence-gathering,

map-making and the ability to work out routes through the desert. The LRDG patrols, based in the oasis of Siwa in western Egypt, headed out into Libya to gather information on enemy movements between Aujila, Jalu, Kufra and Awaynat. On 1 March 1941, the Free French general Leclerc captured Kufra oasis from the Italians and it became the LRDG's main base.

During 1942, the LRDG was used in association with the Major David Stirling's parachute raiders and other commando groups to attack Axis airfields behind enemy lines. The group also kept a close watch on General Rommel's troop movements in the days leading up to the Battle of El Alamein in late 1942. After the defeat of the Axis armies at this battle, the LRDG was involved in operations to cut off German forces retreating west towards Tunisia. In 1943, when the North African campaign finally moved into Tunisia, the role of one of the most skilled and courageous sideline groups of the Second World War came to an end.

the oasis was home to a flourishing community. The low-lying **Great Mosque** is said to go back to the early days of Islamic rule. With its numerous domes, it looks like nothing so much as a giant mud-coated egg-box. A commemorative plaque at the entrance records the visit of Colonel Gadhafi. The interior is gracefully minimalist. There is practically no decoration, apart from a few Quranic verses carved here and there on the walls. The sculptural forms have an almost African feel.

To build their mosque, the faithful in this distant oasis came up with a mod-ular solution. The walls are of small limestone blocks, held together with clay mortar and covered with a dried-mud rendering. There were basically five gal-leries available for prayer, running north-east to south-west. In some of the galleries, each section is covered with a conical dome constructed from palm branches and covered with a mud rendering. Two tiny courtyards allow light into this payer hall. The building has an austere simplicity, no doubt condu-cive to meditation.

Awjila's other sight is the **Sidi Abdallah Mosque**, located on the south side of the old neighbourhoods. This too is a semi-underground mosque featuring egg-shell domes. Tiny openings in the domes allow light to filter into the prayer hall below. The building is the ideal solution in a region of intense dry heat, dazzling light and scarce construction materials. The small building with the green dome nearby is the **tomb of Abdallah ibn Abi Sarh** (died 647 AD), governor of Egypt and one of the Arab chiefs who took part in the early Arab-Muslim invasions of North Africa.

## A wedding at Awjila

*Attracted by the romance and mystery of the desert, 19th century traveller James Hamilton visited Cyrenaica in the early 1850s. Before heading east to Siwa in the Egyptian desert, he found time to visit the oases of Jalo and Augila (modern spelling: Awjila), then key stopping places on the caravan route down to the Fezzan. He left an entertaining and often well-observed account of local customs, including marriage feasts.*

*"Here, when the camel knelt at the door, before the howdah containing its precious burden was removed from its back, a sheep's throat was cut over its right knee, in manner of sacrifice. The Sheikh, after many ineffectual hints which I would not understand, at last boldly begged of me a sash woven with gold which he had one day seen me wear; this he wished to form part of the corbeil, and in letting him have it I took the opportunity of inspecting the ornaments destined for the bride. They consisted of two pairs of broad silver bands to be worn as bracelets, weighing respectively ten and fourteen ounces, and a*

*pair of very curious silver earrings of Tunis make. They were in shape like the young moon, two inches and a half in diameter, two-thirds of the circumference being covered with filigree bosses, from which five pear-shaped filigree pendents hung, each earring weighing 160 grammes. I felt a great curiosity to see the cartilage capable of supporting such a weight. The marriage feast was diversified by dancing to the sound of the drum, and a curious double clarinet, formed of the leg bones of the eagle or vulture, which discoursed sweet music in the tone of a very broken-winded bagpipe. The dancing, like that of the Egyptian Alnach (in whom youth, good looks and sex hardly excuse the peculiar style), was here performed by a hideous man, and was utterly disgusting. When the bride had entered the house, the festivities were terminated by a discharge of fire-arms, and the company retired, to meet again the next evening, and to renew the eating and dancing."*

**James Hamilton**, *Wanderings in North Africa (London: John Murray, 1856)*

Before you head out for Kufra, make sure you have adequate petrol. Though the next station is at **Bir Bu Zarraygh**, 353 km out of Awjila / Jalu, petrol frequently runs out in these remoter regions, as in the Fezzan. South of Awjila the road strikes straight across the desert to Kufra, some 600 km away. At Bir Bu Zarraygh, there is a checkpoint at the turn-off for the Sudanese frontier. The road is not of the same quality of those elsewhere in Libya, the large sections of tarmac laid directly onto the sand take a hammering from heavy lorry traffic. At Kufra, terminus of the road, there is a control point at the junction where roads from different parts of the oasis meet. Any visitor not on official business or work will be subject to much questioning.

**Awjila to Kufra**

## Kufra الكفرة

Little remains of old Kufra. In 1895, Sayyid al Mahdi, son of the Sanusi order's founder, moved his headquarters from Jaghbub to Kufra, so inevitably the settlement was to be the site of important resistance to the Italians. Under the Sanusiya, Kufra grew in importance, forming the base for the spread of the order's influence into Saharan Africa. However, Sayid al Mahdi was worried about competition from the French, and in 1899 moved his headquarters still further south, to the oasis of Quru, down between Borku and the Tibesti.

It was not until 1931 that the Italians got around to occupying Kufra. The Cyrenaican tribes had largely been defeated, and there was little strategic interest in occupying such an outpost oasis. For General Graziani, Kufra was "la

**Italian occupation of Kufra**

Mecca della Senussia", and made it a point of honour that this distant centre of resistance be crushed. Sledgehammer Italian armoured columns were sent from Jalu, Waw al Kabir and Zalla to crush the nut of Sanusi resistance, and in January 1931 the Italian flag flew over the Kufra oases. Fleeing caravans were machine-gunned out in the desert on the orders of Graziani. Henceforth, Kufra was to be an important re-fuelling point for aircraft flying down to Italian East Africa.

**Kufra today**   Kufra today has rather lost its isolated oasis feel. The water table has fallen, the palm groves have declined in economic importance, and new family residences are going up on the once-precious oasis land. A brand new quarter, Kufra al Jadida has gone up with mosque, market and modern housing. Outside the settled areas are the great Kufra farming schemes, the pride of modern Libya. Huge wheeled gantries irrigate great circles of wheat out in the desert. Aerial photographs show a landscape which could have been created by an extra-terrestrial. Whether wheat produced in this way is cost effective is another matter. Whatever, the agricultural scheme and attendant investment to expand the town have created activity in Kufra, providing work for migrants from the Sahel countries and Sudan.

Cyrenaica

5

Cyrenaica

The word 'Libya' does not conjure up images of fertile plains and cypress trees, thick maquis and deep gorges, yet Cyrenaica has all these, plus a good crop of ancient sites. East of **Benghazi**, Libya's second largest city, lies the **Jabal Akhdar**, the Green Mountain, a wild upland crossed by gorges and strewn with ancient remains. Here the visitor will come across Roman forts and mausolea, Byzantine churches, and the abandoned villages of 20th-century Italian colonization. While many civilizations have left their mark on the Jabal Akhdar, only the Bedouin Arabs were to survive. Close to the burgeoning city of **Al Bayda** (an ideal base for exploring the region), is the most spectacular site, **Cyrene**, the first Greek colony overseas, a place of mythic resonance founded where the spring of Apollo bubbles forth. Partly reassembled by 20th-century archaeologists, it is a place of great beauty, a must on anyone's itinerary, together with its port, ancient **Apollonia**. Amateurs of archaeology will want to see the Greek coastal settlements at **Tolmeita** and **Tocra**, too, while east of Apollonia, the north-facing coastline has been worked jagged by the sea. This stretch of coast saw a flowering of early Christianity: there are basilicas at **Ra's Hilal** and **Natrun**, while up in the mountains lie the remains of the church of **St Mark** the Evangelist. Cold and rainswept in winter, the Jabal Akhdar is best visited in spring when flowers soften the stones of the ancient sites.

Cyrenaica

# Background

The area referred to by modern geography as Cyrenaica is essentially a high plateau, bounded on the north by steep cliffs facing the Mediterranean. To the south, the plateau runs gently down to the Sahara. Until the nineteenth century, Europe knew little of Cyrenaica – it was also referred to by another ancient name, Barca, which properly refers to the steppe south of Benghazi. But for many Europeans with a classical education, Cyrene had a familiar ring (as Pindar put it, "Cyrene, sweetest garden, I crown you with song"). The region was one of the wealthiest in the ancient Mediterranean. The Beechey brothers, who travelled from Tripoli to Derna in 1821-22, noted that "Many spots of more than ordinary interest were comprehended within the limits of Syrtis and Cyrenaica: scenes of mythology, haunts in which the poets of Greece and Rome had loved to linger." To the generations of the Second World War and after, Cyrenaican place names such as Benghazi were familiar, too. Unlike Tripolitania, the region also resisted Italian colonization with determination and ferocity. In modern Libya, Cyrenaica is the easternmost province, and its inhabitants are called *shargawa*, easterners, from the Arabic *sharq*, east.

## Geography

The region referred to as Cyrenaica here covers three sub-regions: Benghazi and the coastal plain north and east of it; the Jabal Akhdar; and the coastal plain running east of Apollonia. Cyrenaica is surrounded by desert on three sides, hence in ancient times the most accessible civilization was to the North, across the Mediterranean, in Crete and Greece, only 400 km away.

Benghazi is surrounded by the *barr*, arid steppe. The Jabal Akhdar, literally, 'the Green Mountain', so-called because of the dense evergreen woodland of the region, rises to the east. A large section of the western Jabal Akhdar is taken

# Western Cyrenaica

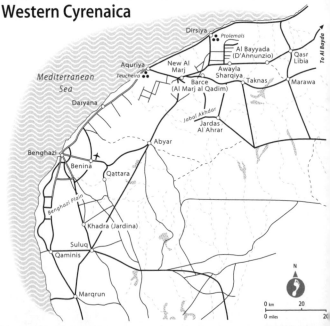

## On Cyrenaican place names, ancient and modern

The place names of Cyrenaica's classical sites can be a little confusing, to say the least. A number of places can be referred to by three names: the original classical name, a recent Italian version of the same, and a current Arabic version. The present guide generally uses the Arabic name (most useful for asking directions), with the classical name in brackets. The potentially confusing names the visitor will probably come across are as follows, in the order ancient name, Italian name, and Arabic name:

Hadrianopolis, Driana, Daryana
Teucheira, Tocra, Al Aquriya
Ptolemaïs, Tolmeta, Al Dirsiya
Balagrae, Beda Littoria, Al Bayda
Apollonia, Susa, Marsa Susa
Cyrene was until recently referred to as Grena, the Arabised version of Cyrene, but is now known as Shahat.

up by the fertile Al Marj plain (the Arabic *marj* means grazing land). Further east is the second level of the Jabal Akhdar, between 500m and over 875m above sea level, often thickly wooded and cut by ravines. Annual rainfall here, especially around Cyrene, can reach 500mm. This was the favoured land chosen by the Greeks for settlement. The soil is rich, red and clayey, as anyone who visits ancient sites on a wet winter's day will find. To the north, below the steep cliffs of the plateau, lies a narrow belt of Mediterranean farmland. To the south, the forest and farmland gives way to juniper bush maquis and pre-desert scrub with some winter grazing.

## History

The Cyrenaican coast was known to humankind in prehistoric times, as the finds at the caves of Hauea Fteah show. However, it was Greek civilisation that really put Cyrenaica on the map in ancient times. Links were developed with Greece and Egypt rather than with the western Mediterranean. The Greek link began when a group of people from the island of Thera came across to the North African coast to found a colony, the first founded by the Greeks in the southern Mediterranean. After a number of abortive attempts, they settled at Cyrene, high on a well-watered plateau, in 631 BC (see below). Successful Cyrene was to found other colonies in the region, most notably Apollonia, its port, and Euhesperides (near the site of modern Benghazi) – in the late seventh and early sixth centuries BC. A Greek dynasty, the Battids (named for Battus, founder of Cyrene), was to rule until 440 BC. Then for a century and a half there followed a period of democratic government, ending with Cyrenaica's voluntary submission to Alexander in 332 BC. It was around this time that the term Pentapolis, 'the five cities', came to be used for Cyrenaica, the five leading federated cities in question being Cyrene, Apollonia, Ptolemaïs, Taucheira, and Euhesperides.

After the death of Alexander, Cyrenaica came under the Ptolomies of Egypt. Their rule was never very stable until 246 BC, when a Cyrenaican princess, Berenice, married Ptolemy III. But with the end of the Ptolemies in 96 BC, the region passed to Rome, finally becoming a Roman province in 76 BC, linked with Crete. Cyrenaica was badly affected by a Jewish revolt in 115-17 AD, which was severely suppressed by Trajan. It was left to Hadrian to repair the damage, which he did with his usual energy and thoroughness. He founded Hadrianopolis on the coast between Berenice and Taucheira, while Cyrene was expanded, becoming a city in which both imperial and local deities were worshipped.

**A province of imperial Rome**

Cyrenaica

Under Diocletian, Cyrenaica was split into two provinces, Upper Libya with the cities of the Pentapolis, capital Ptolemaïs, and Libya Sicca (Dry Libya), covering the more arid lands to the south and east, which eventually had its capital at Darnis, modern Derna. In 365 AD, the region was hit by a severe earthquake. Cyrene in particular suffered, especially as it was no longer capital. The established order was dying, Christianity and a new rural land-owning class was pushing aside the old religion. Its success is testified to by the number of Byzantine basilicas and strong points in Cyrenaica, (make time to visit Qasr Libia at the very least). Under Justinian, a number of cities were refortified, and the region was used as a base for reconquering Vandal-occupied lands further west.

**The Arab-Muslim invasion** Eventually, in the seventh century AD, Byzantine rule gave way to an invasion from the east. In 643, the Muslim Arabs invaded North Africa under 'Amr ibn al 'As, governor of Egypt. The Byzantine armies were unable to halt their advance, and Cyrenaica became part of the new Islamic empire. The old settlements do not seem to have been abandoned completely, as Arabic inscriptions found at Cyrene show. But in the eleventh century, nomad Arab tribes from Upper Egypt were unleashed on the former Byzantine lands of Cyrenaica, Tripolitania and Africa and the once proud cities of Greek North Africa disappeared from the map until the arrival of travellers in the nineteenth century.

For the Middle Ages, information on Cyrenaica is scarce. The region is hardly mentioned in the chronicles of the Crusades by either Christian or Muslim writers. Benghazi (Berenice) survived as the seat of a minor emirate, while Ptolemaïs, now Tolmeita, maintained a certain importance as a supply port for vessels following the coast. But the region did produce one thing which the merchant city states of Italy needed: animal hides and wool. In 1216, Genoa concluded a treaty with Benghazi obtaining a monopoly on trade with Cyrenaica. An Italian missionary, Corrado d'Ascoli, was sent by the future Pope Nicolas IV to explore the region, and was by his account highly successful. It may be that Christian communities still survived at the time in remote parts.

**The Ottomans arrive in Cyrenaica** The 15th century was a time of constant conflict in the Mediterranean between Ottomans and Habsburgs. A vast military and diplomatic game was played across the coasts and islands, especially intense in the central Mediterranean. Once Tripoli, Sfax and Tunis were confirmed as Ottoman possessions, Cyrenaica, halfway between Egypt and Tripolitania, could hardly be ignored. Qasim Pacha of Tripoli, overthrown in 1632, made his way back to Constantinople via Cyrenaica. Noting the fertility of the land – and that there was apparently no central authority – he resolved to use it as a base for reconquering Tripoli. The Grand Vizier supported his resolve, for Cyrenaica was definitely within the Sublime Porte's sphere of influence. The tribes of the region were not to surrender their autonomy so easily, however, and the situation was complicated by internal rivalries in the Ottoman camp. Eventually, after 1711, Cyrenaica as a dependency of Tripolitania was to come under the rule of the Qaramanlis, who ruled independently of Constantinople.

After the fall of the Qaramanli dynasty in the early 19th century, Cyrenaica returned, nominally at least, to Turkish rule. Benghazi developed as an important town, while up on the plateau and the southern steppe, a new authority developed, that of the Sanusiya *tariqa* (brotherhood), a regional religious movement which gave the nomad tribes a structure more deeply rooted in Islam. Through a network of *zawias* (usually translated as 'lodges'), the Sanusiya brought basic Islamic learning and a new order to the rural communities of Cyrenaica and oases across the Sahara. The Sublime Porte, however, became increasingly worried about the growing power of the Sanusiya, and in 1879 the Province of Benghazi was established in order to manage Sanusi influence more closely.

But Ottoman authority was weak in the region, and when Italy decided to used force to create a North African empire, Cyrenaica as well as Tripolitania was in the firing line. Italian troops landed at Tobruk, Derna and Benghazi in October 1891, forcing the Turkish garrisons to withdraw inland. On 12 March 1912 at the Battle of Swani al Rani, the Arabo-Turkish forces were destroyed in the Benghazi region. Geo-political events elsewhere made the situation even more favourable to the invading Italians: the Turks became embroiled in a war in the Balkans, and with the withdrawal from Derna of Turkish patriot Enver Bey, the Sanusiya were the main structured force in the region. Italy, however, became increasingly preoccupied with the situation in Europe, and was obliged to rein in her North African ambitions. The First Italo-Sanusi War ended without Italy being able to satisfy its territorial ambitions.

**Italy versus the Ottomans**

For Cyrenaica, Italians and Senusiya reached a *modus vivendi* in April 1917. In 1919, the Statutes for Tripolitania where applied to Cyrenaica as well. In 1921, a further agreement gave the amir new privileges. However, Mussolini's seizure of power in Italy seemed to promise a change in Italian policy, and in January 1923, the amir fled Ajdabiya for Egypt leaving his brother Muhamad al Rida behind to represent him. From then on things worsened for the inhabitants of Cyrenaica as the Italians undertook to bring the whole region under their control in what historians refer to as the Second Italo-Sanusi War. Although Muhamad al Rida surrendered in 1928, and the oases of Jarabub and Jalu came under Italian control, fighting lasted until 1931.

In the late 1920s, the Italian armed forces had made considerable material advances since the 1911-12 campaigns. They now had planes and columns of armoured vehicles. The fighting was small scale, however: by late 1926, the Italians still had no more than 20,000 mainly native troops in the field; the Sanusi probably never had more than 1,000 men involved in operations at any one time. There were hundreds of minor incidents in the rough terrain of Cyrenaica but never a pitched battle. The towns played no part in resisting Italian rule, and it was mainly the more isolated, southern tribes which led the fighting. Basically, the *saf al bahr*, (lit: 'the sea party'), who already had a long history of co-operating with the Turks, were drawn into the orbit of the Italian administration. The *saf al fawqi* (lit: 'the upland party'), who had had little contact with formal government, resisted Italian encroachments fiercely. An unpleasant civil war developed in which Italy encouraged rifts between the co-operative tribes (the *sottomessi*) and the *ribelli*. Bedouin Muslim solidarity tended to be more significant, however. The Italian forces faced an unpredictable, shifting enemy which had thorough knowledge of the terrain.

**The Italian conquest of Cyrenaica**

In the event, in 1930 Italy sent out General Graziani to try to clean up in Cyrenaica – which he did with extreme cruelty. Large numbers of civilians were rounded up and parked in unsanitary concentration camps on the arid steppes south of Benghazi. Many died of disease – and the fighters on the plateau lost an important source of supplies. It then remained for Graziani to seek out what was left of the resistance groups, now confined to the forests of the high plateau. Finally, in September 1931, the last experienced leader, Umar al Mukhtar, was captured and, after a summary trial, hanged in front of a crowd of notables and bedouin at Suluq. The dignity with which Umar al Mukhtar met his fate did nothing for Italian popularity.

Cyrenaica

Cyrenaica

###  *Italo Balbo*

Flying ace Italo Balbo was one of the few attractive figures thrown up by the Italian fascist régime. A war veteran who had served with the Alpini, he was often compared to a Renaissance mercenary chief. Energetic and educated, he had a zest for adventure, charm, polish and a goatee. In 1933, after leading a successful mass flight from Rome to Chicago he was promoted to the status of air-marshal. In short, Italo Balbo was a potential rival to the Duce. Thus in 1934, he was shuttled off to Libya as governatore to reduce his visibility - and hopefully fail. When Balbo took over, the Italian population in Tripolitania was barely 30,000, ie 5.7 % of the total.

The new governor found himself at the head of two impoverished provinces. In Cyrenaica, the Italians were heartily detested. Balbo set about demonstrating that the repression was over. He organised Mussolini's 1937 entry into Tripoli as 'protector of Islam', the aim being to win over the Muslim population with pageantry and tangible gains produced by co-operation. Balbo also launched an impressive public works programme.

Paternalist, he surrounded himself with his pilots, junior officers and friends from his native Ferrara, including a team of highly competent architects and planners. However, his task in Libya was not an easy one. Although he wanted to create a model colony, he ended up building on inherited policy.

Towards the end of the 1930s, as Mussolini moved towards Germany, Balbo became reconciled with the Italian monarchy. On 28 June 1940, he died in an air crash at Tobruq, reputedly shot down by Allied forces. The circumstances of his untimely death have never been fully elucidated.

Balbo was often compared to Maréchal Lyautey, the aristocratic resident-general who shaped French policy in Morocco from 1912 into the 1920s. Like Lyautey, Balbo professed a deep respect for local culture and was interested in heritage and building. Ultimately, his lasting contribution was architectural. Thanks to Balbo, Tripoli became a handsome city with fine functionalist architecture, much of it still visible today.

**Italian colonization in the late 1930s** With the zaouias of the Sanusiya in ruins and the bedouin reduced to poverty, Italy could set about occupying the best land for colonial farmers. In fact, the process of seizing Sanusi lands had already begun back in 1923. In 1930, all property belonging to the *tariqa* was to be registered in the name of the colony. The process of colonisation was speeded up from 1934 under Italo Balbo's governorship. The ENTE distributed some of the most fertile land in Cyrenaica to Italian small-holders. Further land was allotted to agricultural development projects for Arab farmers. A series of new settlements were built at strategic points on the plateau, and at Awayla Sharqiya, Massa and Umar al Mukhtar the 1930s village centres, each with a church, municipality and house of the fasces, are clearly visible, while nearby in the countryside are the small farmhouses built for the colonists from the Veneto and elsewhere. The old colonial place names have long since been forgotten. Indeed there was hardly time for the settlers to begin to put down roots: the Second World War swept away the detested Italian presence in Cyrenaica.

**Cyrenaica since the 1950s** As cradle of the Sanusiya, Cyrenaica was likely to be favoured by Idris, the descendant of the Sanusi leadership who became king of independent Libya. Benghazi was the first capital of the United Kingdom of Libya. However, Al Bayda, founded in 1840 by Sheikh Muhammad ibn Ali al Sanusi was a far better symbolic choice. King Idris moved the capital there in the 1950s, and splendid new federal buildings were put up in a sort of Ottoman administrative style.

However, Libyan realpolitik meant that Tripoli became capital, then Syrte, before Al Bayda was declared capital once more in 1998.

Neither of Cyrenaica's major cities has really been able to challenge the predominance of Tripoli in Libyan life, although Al Bayda expanded at a vertiginous rate in the 1990s and Benghazi is important as an oil town. There are large numbers of Egyptian migrant workers in the province, and correspondingly fewer Maghrebis. Despite its numerous classical sites, there are not the hotels to accommodate large numbers of tourists, and independent tourists are a bit of a surprise. It remains to be seen whether the tourist industry will develop in a region which has much to offer. The roads run through often stunning empty landscape, the coast is essentially unspoiled and the ancient sites are particularly lovely in the spring.

# Benghazi    بنغازي

*Named after a distant Muslim mystic, one Ibn Ghazi, Benghazi is a 20th century creation, snared in a net of flyovers and ringroads, equipped with stadiums, corniche and tower block hotel. Despite the bombardments of the Second World War much of the old Italian town centre has survived. (The cathedral has become a mosque). The atmosphere is resolutely Middle Eastern, however. Benghazi is a magnet for Egyptian, Sudanese and other migrant workers, the closest major city to the oil settlements of Syrtica. A working city, it has little to offer the visitor in search of the picturesque. If travelling by public transport, it makes a good base for day trips to the Greek sites of Tocra and Tolmeita.*

*Phone code: 061*

Cyrenaica

## Ins and outs

**Getting there**
Benghazi can be reached by air and road from Tripoli. The airport is at Benina, some 18 km outside the city. There should be flights to Benghazi from Kufra, too, and Egyptian flights from Cairo. Buses also run to Benghazi from Alexandria and Cairo and buses and share taxis from Tripoli, Misrata, Al Bayda and Derna. A taxi into the city from the airport costs around 10LD. Buses and share taxis arrive at stations close to each other, outside the old centre. A taxi to one of the central hotels should cost around 2.5LD from the bus station.

**Getting around**
The sites of central Benghazi are easily covered on foot. Should you wish to go to Tocra or Tolmeita, you will need to take a taxi or bus – ask for a taxi to take you to the *agensiya*, local term for the main public transport hub.

## History and background

Of Benghazi, Second World War poet Keith Douglas wrote: "… it is always astonishing to me how close you can go to a town which has been completely gutted, before it begins to look like a ruin. We saw only the Arabian beauty of white square buildings, the squat domes and the slender fingers of minarets and towers. The whole city had the appearance of a mirage." Douglas was unwittingly right but the city he saw from afar was an Italian 20th-century creation, all whitewashed apartment buildings; the domes were probably those of the cathedral. And today the old Benghazi, heavily bombed by Allies and Axis (it changed hands no less than five times during the Second World War), is a small neighbourhood in a sprawling town given a summary structuring by fast highways. Nevertheless, Benghazi is said to be built close to the site of the mythical Garden of the Hesperides.

The oldest settlement in the Benghazi area, Euhesperides, goes back to the sixth century BC, and was probably founded by migrants from Cyrene. The town is known to have resisted a Persian expedition to conquer the nearby Greek settlement of Barce, and during the fifth century, it remained a Greek strongpoint, frequently attacked by the local population. Later, in the third century BC, the Greeks created a new settlement, named Berenice after the wife of Ptolemy III, Euergetes, on a promontory linked to the land by a narrow ridge. (The name Berenike, later transformed into Benghazi, actually derives from the Greek *pherenike*, 'bringer of victory'.)

Roman influence followed when the last of the Ptolomies left his lands to the people of Rome. Later, under Byzantine rule, the emperor Justinian had the walls and baths rebuilt. The city fell to the invading Arab armies led by 'Amr ibn al As in 642 AD, after which it disappears from history for some 600 years. In the 1200s, the small settlement became an important player in the trade growing up between Genoese merchants and the tribes of the hinterland. In 16th century maps, the name of Marsa ibn Ghazi appears. Around 1450, a holy man was buried in the local cemetery, and his piety was sufficient to give the village a name.

Benghazi was too useful a port to be ignored by the Ottomans. In the late 16th century a fort was built by the Turks, and in 1638 the dey of Tripoli sent out a governor and a garrison. During the second period of Turkish rule, Benghazi was to expand and become the major settlement in a region otherwise dominated by nomad tribes. In 1911, the town was the point of

Cyrenica

# Benghazi overview

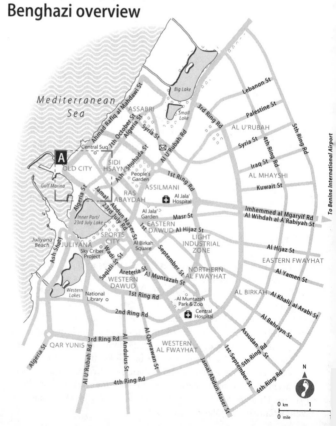

Related map
A Benghazi centre,
page 152

disembarkation for Italian troops. The conquest of the province named Cyrenaica by Italy was to be long and hard. Benghazi nevertheless acquired all the trappings of an Italian town: cathedral, theatre and municipality, apartment buildings with an Arab touch. At one end of the *lungomare*, twin tall columns provided supports for symbols of Italy: Lion of San Marco and She-Wolf of Rome. Today, they are topped with a caravel and a galleon, symbols of Benghazi's modern importance as a port.

## Sights

Benghazi is not one of the most pretty places in North Africa. Nevertheless, the street of the central area, with occasional tree-planted squares and some interesting bits of building have enough to keep the visitor occupied for a couple of hours. A further minor attraction is the excavations at Sidi Khrebish, north of the centre.

Heading north along the sea front on Shari'a Rafik al Mahdawi, you come to the former lighthouse, a chunky building which resembles the minaret of the Great Mosque of Kairouan in Tunisia. Just next to the lighthouse is the cemetery of Sidi Khrebish where archaeologists are bringing to light the remains of ancient Berenice. The Department of Antiquities has an office behind the lighthouse, and one day there may be a museum.

*Sidi Khrebish, the ruins of Berenice*

Berenice was of course the second Greek foundation in the area, the first being Euhesperides. Close to well-protected lagoons where ancient boats could be drawn up onto the beach, Berenice was ideally placed for trade, and no doubt exported silphium, the medical plant which brought fame and fortune to Cyrenaica. The excavations at Sidi Khrebish have uncovered a small temple to Asclepius and Igea, along with the foundations of a number of small courtyard houses dating back to the second century BC. Towards the end of the second century BC, the city seems to have experienced a period of crisis, and it was not until the late first century AD that prosperity returned. Larger houses decorated with mosaics were put up in the Sidi Khrebish neighbourhood. In the sixth century, a church was built using recycled material from an old temple. For the moment, however, the location of Berenice's agora and main temples is unknown.

Benghazi has two corniches: the north corniche (Shari'a Rafik al Mahdawi) faces the open sea, while the western corniche faces the calmer waters of the port. Here are two of the finest examples of Italian building. The **Hotel Berenice** (now Funduq Qasr al Jazira, not recommended), and next to it the **former cathedral**, (at present a mosque), easily recognizable by its twin domes. But Benghazi's belle époque is long gone, and the promenade is deserted after dark, outside the summer months – apart from visitors seeking entertainment of a dubious kind in a garden 'bar' by the hotel. Follow the corniche to the twin columns, turn right onto Shari'a al Mukhtar (ex-Via Roma) and a few metres down a one-way street you come to a tree-planted square, the former Piazza del Re, where you will find small but optimistically grand Italian buildings from the 1920s and 1930s: the former theatre, the Banca d'Italia and government offices. Continuing straight ahead up Shari'a al Mukhtar, you eventually come to the neo-Moorish **town hall**, complete with clock and crenellations. A pleasant fruit and vegetable **market** can be found in a shaded square to the right of this street as well.

*Downtown: mosques & the 20th century city*

Near the town hall is Benghazi's oldest mosque, the **Jami' al Kabir** (Great Mosque), also referred to as Jami'a al 'Atiq. The mosque was founded by one Abd al Sami al Qadi around 1400, and was restored on a number of occasions.

*Cyrenaica*

The building as it stands at the moment was extended by Ottoman governor Tahar Pasha (1893-1904), restored under Italian rule and recently refurbished. On the square behind the Jami' al Kabir is another historic mosque, the **Jami' Osman**, which also has a distinct Ottoman feel. Over the prayer hall, there is a large central dome, plus smaller corner domes and longer vaulted domes on the sides. Neither the Jami' al Kabir nor the Jami' Osman has a courtyard, however, as is generally the case in North African mosques. The Osman Mosque, like the Great Mosque, was closed for restoration works until recently, and it is to be hoped that the general scrape and paint of redecoration has not destroyed the original decoration – as has too often been the case in other historic mosques in Libya.

**A hero's mausoleum and two war cemeteries** In the Sidi Hussein area, east of downtown, is the **Mausoleum of Umar al Mukhtar**, Libyan national hero. (For fine portrait, see 10LD banknote). Umar al Mukhtar was hanged at Suluq, south of Benghazi, and in fact he is buried there. Given the fact that Benghazi changed hands so many times in the Second World War, it is hardly surprising that there are two war cemeteries, one French and one British. Heading south out of Benghazi, take the road which runs under the Tripoli motorway flyover; the French cemetery is on the right, the British on the left.

## Essentials

**Sleeping**
Phone code: 061, 7 figure numbers

**A** *Hotel Tibesti*, T9802931, 9092033. Tower block (15 floors) hotel used by main tour groups, named for plateau on the frontier between Libya and Chad. Horribly expensive if you have to pay in dollars ($240 for a double). **A** *Hotel Uzu*, on the far side of the lagoon from the downtown area, T9095160/66. The number 2 tour group hotel. Not very exciting and expensive at $150 a night for a double.

# Benghazi centre

*Cyrenaica*

# £4000 worth of holiday vouchers to be won!

**... that can be claimed against any exodus, Peregrine or Gecko's holiday, a choice of around 570 holidays that set industry standards for responsible tourism in 90 countries across seven continents.**

## exodus

The UK's leading adventurous travel company, with over 25 years' experience in running the most exciting holidays in 80 different countries. We have an unrivalled choice of trips, from a week exploring the hidden corners of Tuscany to a high altitude trek to Everest Base Camp or 3 months travelling across South America. If you want to do something a little different, chances are you'll find it in one of our brochures.

## Peregrine

Australia's leading quality adventure travel company, Peregrine aims to explore some of the world's most interesting and inaccessible places. Providing exciting and enjoyable holidays that focus in some depth on the lifestyle, culture, history, wildlife, wilderness and landscapes of areas that are usually quite different to our own. There is an emphasis on the outdoors, using a variety of transport and staying in a range of accommodation, from comfortable hotels to tribal huts.

## Gecko's

Gecko's holidays will get you to the best places with the minimum of hassle. They are designed for younger people who like independent travel but don't have the time to organise everything themselves. Be prepared to take the rough with the smooth, these holidays are for active people with a flexible approach to travel.

To enter the competition, simply tear out the postcard and return it to Exodus Travels, 9 Weir Road, London SW12 0LT. Or go to the competition page on www.exodus.co.uk and register online. Two draws will be made, Easter 2001 and Easter 2002, and the winner of each draw will receive £2000 in travel vouchers. The closing date for entry will be 1st March 2002. If you do not wish to receive further information about these holidays, please tick here. ☐ No purchase necessary. Plain paper entries should be sent to the above address. The prize value is non-transferable and there is no cash alternative. Winners must be over 18 years of age and must sign and adhere to operators' standard booking conditions. A list of prizewinners will be available for a period of one month from the draw by writing to the above address. For a full list of terms and conditions please write to the above address or visit our website.

To receive a brochure, please tick the relevant boxes below (maximum number of brochures 2) or telephone (44) 20 8772 3822.

| exodus | Peregrine | Gecko's |
|---|---|---|
| ☐ Walking & Trekking | ☐ Himalaya | ☐ Egypt, Jordan & Israel |
| ☐ Discovery & Adventure | ☐ China | ☐ South America |
| ☐ European Destinations | ☐ South East Asia | ☐ Africa |
| ☐ Overland Journeys | ☐ Antarctica | ☐ South East Asia |
| ☐ Biking Adventures | ☐ Africa | ☐ India |
| ☐ Multi Activity | ☐ Arctic | |

**Please give us your details:**

**Name:** -------------------------------------------------

**Address:** -------------------------------------------------

-------------------------------------------------

-------------------------------------------------

**Postcode:** -------------------------------------------------

**e-mail:** -------------------------------------------------

**Which footprint guide did you take this from?**

-------------------------------------------------

**getaway tonight on www.exodus.co.uk**

**exodus**
*The Different Holiday*

**exodus**
*The Different Holiday*

getaway tonight on
www.exodus.co.uk

exodus
The Different Holiday

exodus

9 Weir Road
**LONDON
SW12 0BR**

BUSINESS REPLY SERVICE
Licence No SW4909

**C** *Hotel Umar al Khayyam*, on the old corniche, T9095110. Perhaps the best choice in this price bracket. Rooms with view of sea or overlooking square. 25LD double room. Good value. **C** *Hotel Qasr al Jazira*, on the corniche, at the far end from the twin columns, next to the old cathedral, T9096001. Once upon a time this was the Grand'hotel Berenice, as some of the light switches still indicate. Time has been cruel, however. North African women sex-workers ply their trade from the ground floor café. The rooms are of the sort where you'd rather sleep in your clothes, the electrics are dodgy in the bathrooms. Still, if nostalgia takes you … 25LD a night for a double room.

**D** *Funduk Anis*, in the downtown area: find the main post office on Shari'a Umar al Mukhtar, then facing the PO, go down the street to the left of it, T9093149. Acceptable at 20LD a night. Less decrepit than *Qasr al Jazira*. **D** *Funduk Khordabi*, behind the Tibesti on Shari'a Abd al Nasser, T9096997. Small moderately seedy hotel. 15LD a night.

**E** *Funduk Siyahii* Cheapie on the sea front, Shari'a Ahmad Rafiq al Mahdawi, 8LD.

**Youth Hostel**, T2234101. Situated on the south side of the lagoon, next to the sports complex and the main stadium. Clean but fills up quickly in summer. 5LD a night.

Benghazi has little in the way of exciting restaurants. *Shahat*, the Italian restaurant of the Hotel Tibesti on 13th floor. On the eastern sea front try *Muhammad al Kwaly* for sea view and fresh fish. Try the *Mata'm Turki* (Turkish restaurant) next to the small park on Shari'a Abd al Nasser. Try the shawarma sandwich stall at the Shari'a Jamal Abd al Nasser end of Shari'a Amr ibn al 'As. | **Eating**

*OUM Ghozlan Tourism*, T61-2228782, F61-2235459, injaz@itt.net. *Shallal (Waterfall)* *Travel Agency*, T016-9095912 (they also have an office in Al Bayda, T637234, F633457). | **Tour operators**

**Air** Benghazi Airport is 18 km outside the city at Benina. *Libyan Arab Airlines* have an office in the city centre not far from the tomb of Umar al Mukhtar. | **Transport**

**Bus and share taxi** Buses come into a large international bus terminal, located at a busy crossroads. For Al Bayda and other Cyrenaica destinations, the main share taxi station is the low building with small minaret just over the road (loos here). Share taxis for Misrata and Tripoli go from an informal taxi stand diagonally across the intersection from the main taxi station. To get there from city centre take local taxi and ask for *mahatat al bujawat* (lit: the Peugeot station) or the *agensiya*.

**Consulates** Italian Consulate on Shari'a 'Amr ibn al 'As, T9092331. **Communications**  Post office: | **Directory**
In town centre on Shari'a Umar al Mukhtar. Small public telephone shops can be found in town centre, on Shari'a Abd al Nasser and elsewhere. **Places of worship**  Catholic church of Shari'a Umar al Mukhtar near the post office. Congregation mainly Philipine, Korean and Sudanese.

Cyrenaica

# Northeast of Benghazi: Aquriya (Teucheira) and Dirsiya (Ptolemaïs)

Of Hadrianopolis, the sixth city of Cyrenaica, there remains only a place name, Daryana, an undistinguished settlement 25 km northeast of Benghazi. However, if you are based in Benghazi, the ruins of Teucheira (modern Aquriya) and Ptolemaïs (Dirsiya) are an easy day trip from the city. Based in Al Bayda and equipped with a hire car, you could cover Teucheira, Ptolemaïs along with Qasr Libia and Qasr Bani Gdam in a long but full day trip. Both Aquriya and Dirsiya are easily reached by share taxi from Benghazi for a few dinars. (Distances: Benghazi to Aquriya 61 km, Aquriya to Dirsiya 38 km.) Dirsiya is a very minor town today, so there are correspondingly fewer share taxis on the empty road from Aquriya. It may be best to make an early start and travel from Benghazi to Al Marj al Jadid, changing there for Dirsiya.

## Aquriya (Teucheira)  العقورية (توكرة)

Ancient Teucheira is one the least excavated sites of Cyrenaica, a pleasant classical backwater. This is what a site looks like before archaeology begins. The site centres on a sort of Gothic folly, next to which is the museum with several rather exquisite finds. There is a sunken necropolis with inscriptions in neat Greek characters. All tombs were pillaged and later turned into desirable troglodyte homes. The palms and the nearby village square give an oasis feel to Teucheira. On the western edge of the city, the Byzantine wall is clearly visible, its giant blocks spilling into the sand.

**Getting there**  Aquriya is an easy 61 km drive from Benghazi, 38 km from Dirsiya. Coming from Benghazi, you leave the main highway for the town. Look for the main telecommunications mast, and turn down a narrow street left (if coming from town centre) or right (if coming from Dirsiya), towards the sea. You pass through the Italian village square and reach the site gateway, a large stone arch, some 100 m further on towards the sea.

## Aquriya (Teucheira)

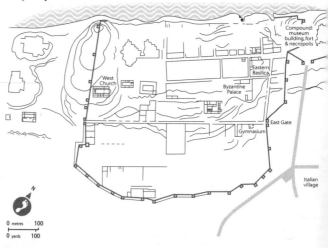

*Labels on map:* Compound: museum building, fort & necropolis; West Church; Eastern Basilica; Byzantine Palace; East Gate; Gymnasium; Italian village

0 metres 100
0 yards 100

*Side tab:* Cyrenaica

Teucheira was one of the five cities of the Pentapolis, founded in the late sixth **History &** century, as the discovery of a sanctuary to Demeter and Kore in 1963-65 indi- **background** cates. It was a commercially important town, as the quantity of imported Greek ceramics discovered at the site shows. In Ptolemaic times, it was renamed Arsinoë-Cleopatris, for the mother of Ptolemy II, Queen Arsinoë and her daughter, and re-planned. An artificial harbour was built, along with walls and a gymnasium. On the basis of inscriptions, there is known to have been a temple to Liber Pater and Apollo. In Byzantine times, with insecurity growing, the walls were rebuilt. Teucheira was the last site of Byzantine resistance in Cyrenaica after the seventh century AD Arab-Muslim invasion. In 643 AD, governor Apollonius withdrew there with his troops into hastily improvised fortifications. The troops of 'Amr ibn 'As, governor of Egypt, stormed the defences, and an era in Cyrenaican history came to end. Were the Byzantines so demoralised – or unpopular – that even the thirty towers of Teucheira's walls could not be properly defended?

Teucheira is the most neglected of the sites – not that any are as well tended as **Exploring** they should be. Little has been excavated, despite Professor Goodchild's plans **the site** a few decades ago. Vegetation hides the walls. Points of interest include an ancient quarry, just southwest of the museum, and the necropolis. Like the other classical sites in Cyrenaica, it bears traces of redevelopment as the centuries passed and conditions changed.

The main area to explore is to the left of the entrance arch. After the arch, follow a driveway, lined with fossilized trunks and ancient masonry, which curves left to reach the 'fort' and museum. The fort is a vaguely medieval folly-monument put up by the Italians, and the museum is an undistinguished hangar just beyond it, to the left. On both sides of the driveway are sunken areas of funerary chambers carved out of the living rock. As you make your way into the actual site, look out for the **Eastern Basilica**, with some column bases in local limestone and paving, and, to the south of it, a Byzantine official building of some kind, partially excavated. Again, south of this, a large rectangular basin was found, probably a font used for mass baptism. Nearby was a chapel with mosaics. The **Greek gymnasium** is thought to have been just on the south side of the main east-west street running across the city. In the western sector, remains of further basilicas have been discovered. Large stone blocks indicate the foundations of the **great walls** which once surrounded Teucheira, partly built from demolished Hellenistic building. At the beach end of ancient Teucheira, the sea is eroding into the site. Pottery shards and stones protrude from the damp earth.

After walking the site, take time to look at the necropolis before heading to the museum. The folly-fort was once a private residence. A plaque records the names of the Italian troops who died during the First Italo-Sanusi War of 1911-13. There is a view of the site from the small tower.

Teucheira Museum is well worth visiting. There is a handy site plan on the wall **The museum** as you enter. The best pieces are in the left-hand inner room. Look out for Greek cratera with vivid images including a lively cock fight, and some (so-called) amphorae with graceful goats. The cratera are truly beautiful with their delicate handles and fluidly painted images. In the case at the far end of the room is a tall Corinthian (the label says) terracotta vessel featuring a winged Our Lady of the Beasts, along with a slender-necked oenochoe (wine flask). Finds like these must make hours of slaving in dusty trenches worthwhile for archaeologists. The museum also has cases full of tiny pieces of grave furniture (pottery lamps and other vessels). Fragments give an idea of the beautiful quality of the craftwork. Teucheira must have been a rather rich place to afford to import such fine tableware. ■ *At the museum, you will probably find the warden to pay the 3LD entrance fee to the site, and another 3LD for the museum (no photography allowed). Opening hours are 0900 to 1730 in winter, 0900 to 1930 in summer. On no account point your camera at the 'new excavations'. Teucheira unfortunately has an extremely unpleasant* murshid siyahi, *('tourist guide'), who guards his patch with ferocity. Films have been confiscated with much shouting on the slightest suspicion of a sneak picture of a minor newly discovered remain.*

## Dirsiya (Ptolemaïs)    الدرسية (طلميثة)

Situated between the Mediterranean and the steep slopes of the Cyrenaican plateau, Ptolemaïs was the rich port of ancient Barce. You approach the site via the dilapidated main street of the Italian village of Tolmeita. (A wrecked cargo vessel lies in the shallows, the former church is roofless.) In its heyday, merchant Ptolemaïs was extensive, and much still remains to be excavated. Behind the museum sheds in their grove of tamarisk trees, the site spreads south to the foot of the escarpment, a vast shard bed set with partly re-erected monuments: Roman palace, Byzantine basilica and fine gateway, and a gymnasium, under which lies a dank network of cisterns. Eucalyptus trees provide shade for goats and the odd donkey making the best of the stony grazing land.

**Getting there**  Without your own transport, Dirsiya (Ptolemaïs) is not the most accessible of sites. A small coastal settlement, it is not actually on the way to anywhere. If you are based in Benghazi, you will probably have to take a share taxi or inter-city bus to Al Marj al Jadid, and a second taxi down to Ptolemaïs. Another option would be share taxi to Aquriya (Teucheira), after which you might try hitching along the coast road to Ptolemaïs. An early start would maximize your chances of getting a lift. The ancient site is on the far east of the modern settlement. At the end of the pot-holed main street of the old Italian village you will find the museum and ticket office to your right in a small garden of tamarisk trees.

**History and background**  Ptolemaïs is much more recent foundation than nearby Teucheira. It would have been the main port for nearby Barce, up on the first fertile level of the plateau inland. However, the discovery of Greek ceramics from the seventh and sixth centuries BC indicates that there was an early settlement on the site. The name Ptolemaïs indicates a Hellenistic foundation, of course, as does the regular grid street pattern. Under Diocletian, Ptolemaïs became the capital of the province of Libya Superior. Increasing insecurity on the plateau may have been the reason for moving the capital down from Cyrene. This was a well protected city, with the Hellenistic walls being restored during the Roman period in the third century AD. (Ancient fortifications enthusiasts look out for the well-preserved Teucheira Gate.) Ptolemaïs remained the capital until the mid-fifth century AD, and it was described as rich and well populated by historians Synesius and Procopius. Many important late-Roman buildings have been discovered.

**Visiting the site**
*Numbers in brackets refer to the plan opposite*
If you have your own transport, Ptolemaïs really merits half a day, and could be combined with a circuit including Teucheira and Barce. If you have a full day, then you could combine things archaeological with a dip in the sea next to the site. Note that for the moment, there is no hotel at Dirsiya.

The ruins excavated so far make a convenient circuit. Starting with the museum, you do the central area (**Via Porticata**) first, including the **Palace of the Columns** (8), take in the **Gymnasium** (10) and the **Odeon** (14), cut west

Cyrenaica

to the **Basilica** (16) and the **Teucheira Gate** (15), and head back to the museum via the **amphitheatre** (17). If you are pressed for time, make sure you don't miss the great cisterns under the gymnasium floor. With plenty of time, you will be able to have a look at the **Eastern Fort** (not shown on map), the **Palace of the Dux** (7) and the site of the collapsed bridge to the east.

Head into the site from the museum (1) to start your circuit of monuments at **Main** the reconstructed remains of **Constantine's Arch** (2), erected 312 AD. You **monuments** then pass down a paved street, along what would have been a colonnade providing shade for a gallery of shops. With chic, blue marble, grey granite and Corinthian column capitals, this **Via Porticata** would have been Ptolemaïs' premier address. On the south side is a small audience chamber, the so-called Doric Hall, (third century AD), named for the Doric frieze which decorated it. Next you reach a crossroads where there was a **four-column monument** (5) (a *tetrastylon*, to use the jargon). Dating from the fifth century AD, the columns would have been topped with honorific statues. To your left (north), are the excavated remains of a **large courtyard residence** (6), while at five-past the hour is the fortified **Palace of the Dux** (7) (sixth century AD). The

*Cyrenaica*

# Ptolemaïs

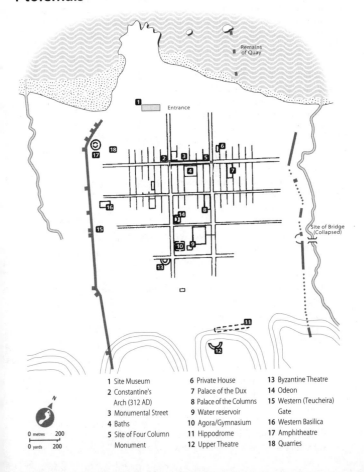

| | | |
|---|---|---|
| **1** Site Museum | **6** Private House | **13** Byzantine Theatre |
| **2** Constantine's Arch (312 AD) | **7** Palace of the Dux | **14** Odeon |
| **3** Monumental Street | **8** Palace of the Columns | **15** Western (Teucheira) Gate |
| **4** Baths | **9** Water reservoir | **16** Western Basilica |
| **5** Site of Four Column Monument | **10** Agora/Gymnasium | **17** Amphitheatre |
| | **11** Hippodrome | **18** Quarries |
| | **12** Upper Theatre | |

0 metres 200
0 yards 200

Cyrenaica

courtyard residence, dating from the first century AD, has a three-apse hall where fragments of fine marble paving are visible. This building is thought to have been the governor's residence due to the presence of large fragments of porphyry, a stone generally reserved for imperial buildings.

*Numbers in brackets with PC codes refer to Palace of the Columns plan*

Next on the list of monuments to visit is the so-called **Palace of the Columns** (8), easily the most decorated ruin at Ptolemaïs. It is thought to date from the second/first century BC, and was much remodelled in Roman times. The palace occupies a whole block, over 600 sq m. No doubt it was the main residence of the regional governor for centuries. The main apartments of this palace include a two-level galleried courtyard (PC1), built around a rectangular pool and, at the north side of the building, the *oecus aegyptius*, the Egyptian living room (PC6), to use Vitruvius' terminology. This fine reception room had colonnades and vast windows and fine mosaics. To the south end of the main courtyard was the Medusa Room (PC2), so-called because the mosaic in *opus vermiculatus* displayed in the museum was found there. Other small rooms off the courtyard were for servants, while below the *oecus aegyptius*, baths and shops at a lower level can be distinguished (PC8-11). Note that there has been much archaeological re-assembly work here: many of the column drums are concrete. The overall impression is none-the-less impressive, however.

Next stop after the Palace of the Columns is the **gymnasium** (10), clearly marked by re-erected columns. Thought to date from the second century BC, the building was restyled in Roman times. However, the most impressive construction work here is underground, for beneath the paving of the gymnasium are great vaulted chambers, eight running north-south (50 m long), and nine running east-west (20 m long). These are generally held to have been **cisterns**. Ptolemaïs, like Apollonia, was dependent on an aqueduct for its water supplies, and the city had to have enough water in reserve to withstand siege and drought. The northeast side of the gymnasium had a rather sumptuous rostrum, set with columns topped with Ionic capitals, no doubt used for the display of honorific statues. There are a number of access points for the

# Palace of the Columns

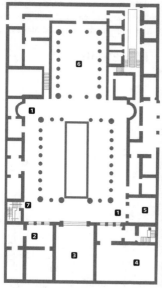

**Noble floor**

0 metres 10
0 yards 10

**Lower floor**

1 Main courtyard gallery
2 The Medusa room
3 Summer dining room
4 Winter dining room
5 Kitchen
6 Oecus aegypliius
  (Egyptian room)
7 Stairs to upper floor
8 Small courtyard
9 Calidarium
10 Tepidarium
11 Frigidarium
12 Shops

cisterns in the gymnasium floor: the absent-minded and those with small children should watch out for unprotected 'hatches' with drops of several metres to the mud floor several metres underground.

After clambering out of the gymnasium cisterns, take a look at the semi-circular mini-theatre close by. This was the **bouleuterion** or odeon (14), the former town council chambers. One archaeological theory runs that this theatre was remodelled in the fourth/fifth century AD for use as a setting for aquatic entertainments – which seems a little unlikely given the great distances across which water had to be brought to the city. Nevertheless, the lower area in front of the semi-circular seating could have been filled with water. There was a special central box for local bigwigs to enjoy water fights, Roman synchronised swimming or whatever.

After the bouleuterion, strike west across the shardbeds for the looming mass of the Western Basilica and the Teucheira Gate. The fifth century AD **Teucheira Gate** (15) is an impressive piece of solid Byzantine building. As is the case of other Roman gates, the road runs straight through into the city. Roman vehicles did not have pivoting axles, so elaborate chicane gates were too difficult for them to manage, despite being better from a defensive point of view. Graffiti in Greek, Latin and Arabic can be seen on the great masonry blocks of the gate.

The **Western Basilica** (16), a sixth century AD construction, is the next point of call. This was heavily restored under Italian archaeologist Giacomo Caputo. The only basilica excavated so far at Ptolemaïs, it is a solid, austere building with three parallel naves. At the end of the left-hand (north) nave, there is a small domed chamber built to a trefoil plan, no doubt the place for the display of icons blackened by candle smoke. The building had vaulted roofing rather than a lighter tiled roof held up by a wooden structure, hence the thickness of the basilica's walls. The building is entered from the north side, and steps in the southwest corner lead up onto the walls. The contrast with the showy Roman temples with their marble statuary and airy colonnades could hardly be greater. Later Arabic graffiti on the wall behind the altar reads 'There is no God but God and Mohamed is his Prophet'.

The final stop before heading back to the museum should be the **amphitheatre** (17), located between the western wall and a quarry (18) and looking for all the world like a great bomb crater. Slightly elliptical in shape, the amphitheatre has yet to be excavated. With 35 rows of seating (measuring 48 m by 45 m), it ranks among the largest Roman public buildings in Cyrenaica.

### The museum (1)

Rather more extensive than the museum at Teucheira, the collection at Ptolemaïs has some very fine pieces indeed. (Contemplating the sculpture on display in the shade of the tamarisks outside, you can recover after tramping round the ruins.) The museum has three main display rooms with interesting sarcophagi, sculpture, mosaics and unusually some information panels in Italian. There doesn't seem to be any particular structure to the displays – but the luxury decorative items on show testify to the wealth of Ptolemaïs. The museum will be fine indeed when funds are made available.

Just inside the **East Room** (on your left as you go into the museum), you will find the marble feet of a statuette of the Three Graces (unusually the highly polished original finish has survived), next to which is a rather chunky Roman leopard (possibly iron). There is a grand second century AD sarcophagus lid with a deceased couple portrayed as though reclining on a cushioned couch and part of a sarcophagus featuring scenes from the legend of Meleager. There are some stone Arabic inscriptions.

In the **Central Room**, look out for the finely executed mosaic fragments of fish and fighting cocks (very Conran shop), as well as the famous Medusa Head mosaic. Along with the statue of Artemis, they came from the House of the Columns. There is also a marble tablet from the Via Porticata indicating the prices of certain goods as laid down in an edict issued by Diocletian in 301 AD.

Among the other important pieces are parts of a fountain featuring eight dancing meneads, once a choice piece of urban street furniture on the Via Porticata. The girls are prancing along in their fluttering cloaks, waving tambourines, the thyrsus (wand) and ivory crowns, as is appropriate for adepts of Dionysus. The room also features a rather crude mosaic portraying Orpheus and the beasts. The statuary includes a torso of Hercules, a body builder gone slightly to seed in this version, and a tall female figure, the front to scale, the profile too narrow – hence this was carved with a niche in mind.

Other sights As you leave Dirsiya, there is one more spectacular ruin to take in, the large square **Hellenistic mausoleum** (second century BC?) to your right as you head back to the junction/check point. This was the main burial area for the city, and the mausoleum is most impressive for its huge scale. Surrounded by fields, the buildings were erected on a rock base, concealed by steps long vanished. Today only the lower part of the structure remains, and a few fragments of the second storey. In terms of form and plan, the building may be thought of as similar to the Mausoleum of Halicarnassus in present-day Turkey. Round the mausoleum are makeshift livestock pens of cactus, corrugated iron and barbed wire. The mighty indeed have fallen.

Finally, just after the turn off onto the Aquriya road, there is a modern monument, right next to the sea, a structure put up to commemorate the place where the young officers met to plan the overthrow of the monarchy in 1969. Note that Radio Benghazi was the first to announce the news.

# From Benghazi to Al Bayda

*There is no accommodation at all on this route until you reach Al Bayda, except one run-dawn hotel at Al Marj* **Al Bayda**, sometime capital of Libya, and the jumping off point for visiting Cyrene, lies about two hours' drive east of Benghazi. The well built road takes you across the most fertile lands of the eastern Cyrenaican plateau and into the uplands of the **Jabal Akhdar**, of which one nineteenth century traveller wrote: "… the country is a most beautifully arranged jardin anglais … perhaps the most lovely sylvan scenery in the world." There are a number of pleasant distractions en route for Al Bayda, including the Byzantine mosaics at **Qasr Libia**. A side-trip to the former Italian settlement of **Barce** (Al Marj al Qadim) will please those in search of colonial remains.

Keeping on the main road rather than turning off for Aquriya (Tocra), you head up onto the first 'terrace' of the Jabal Akhdar. The road has been widened and straightened in places; the original Italian-built road wound up the scarp slope more slowly. The vegetation changes – there are Aleppo pines and juniper – and then you are on the Barce plain. Lines of tall dark cypresses protect the fields of market garden crops and orchards from winter winds.

**New Al Marj** is the major settlement of eastern Cyrenaica, with all the usual panoply of concrete building. There are restaurants at the road side as you leave on the eastern side of town, and a cheap hotel, the **E** *Funduq al Marj*, T067-2475, run-down and close to the mosque. This is not really a stop. If you have a hire car, it is better to use Al Bayda or Benghazi as a base for visiting Ptolemaïs (Dirsiya).

### Rain at Tocra in 1852

"… I had intended to spend some days here, and to open a large number of tombs, whose position I had conjectured from the hollow sound the ground above gave out when struck; but the rains had now set in, descending every night in torrents, and frequently lasting all day; so that no working was possible, and in the small tents a dry spot could not be preserved. The discomfort produced by the rain, however, was even exceeded by the by the destruction it brought to books and instruments; I therefore left Tocra, and firmly resolved that my first purchase in Benghazi should be one of the hair tents of the Arabs, which, though not quite impervious to rain, are yet the best protection one can have against it. As used in this country, they are generally about eighteen feet long, by fifteen broad, the roof formed of long strips of coarse hair-cloth woven by the women. The roof is sometimes made in white for winter use; but more generally it is brown, earthy colour, with stripes of black and white. No cutting out or other fashioning is necessary, for the cloth, being sufficiently elastic, accommodates itself to the slope of the roof. Two poles, three feet apart, support the tent, giving in the centre a height of about seven feet, while the corners and edges are stretched by cords, and supported by slender spars, at about half this height from the ground. Three sides are closed by strips of the same stuff, rudely attached to the roof by wooden pins, the fourth - that turned to leeward - being left open. In summer the sides are removed, and branches are used to replace them, while, in general, an older roof is substituted for the better one used in winter. With a little management, they might be comfortable enough, and, with the exception of the great weight of the hair-cloth of which they are formed, would be very convenient for travelling, are exposed to no great accidents which could not be remedied on the spot, and are less liable than cotton tents to rot when packed up wet."

From **James Hamilton's** Wanderings in North Africa (London: John Murray, 1856)

After New Al Marj, a possible side trip is to Barce, Al Marj al Qadim. Heading east, look out for a right turn off the main road at a place where there is a checkpoint, just 5 km out of New Al Marj. In fact, a severe earthquake destroyed much of Barce in 1963, and Al Marj is the town put up to replace it. (If you are coming up from Dirsiya, then you need to go right at the T-junction with the main road, then left a few kilometres in the Benghazi direction at the checkpoint.)

## Barce (Al Marj al Qadeem)  المرج

Of the ancient town of Barce nothing remains today. The Greek city was founded by a group of emigrants from Cyene in 560 BC. A second wave of immigration from Greece had placed severe strains on society in the original city, so a new city was established by the brothers of Archesilaos II of Cyrene. Endless squabbling and intriguing by Barce with the Persians, who at the time had a presence in Egypt, meant Barce lost its independence to Cyrene by the end of the sixth century. The city remained an important farming centre, no doubt supplying produce to Ptolemaïs, and was still significant at the time of the Arab invasion when it was renamed Al Marj (lit: 'grazing land'). For the Arab armies that had just crossed the desert west of the Nile Valley, it was a welcome surprise no doubt to come across such a fertile land. In the nineteenth century, the Turks built a castle at Al Marj.

As the centre of the finest farming land in Cyrenaica, Al Marj was to become **Barce** once more for the Italians. The new settlement was the terminus of the railway up from Benghazi. There was a church and a municipality in the

### The mystery of silphium

A notable architectural detail at Al Bayda's **Shrine of Aesclepius** are the rather elegant column capitals featuring silphium, the plant which brought fame and wealth to Cyrene – but about which we know nothing today in botanical terms. Silphium was much in demand in the ancient Mediterranean: its sap was used both as a medicine and a dressing, and it came to be the emblem of Cyrene, even featuring on coins. One legend went that Aristaeus, son of Apollo and the nymph Cyrene, introduced silphium into the region. It became the basis for Cyrene's prosperity, and was exported under royal supervision. A sixth-century cup now at the Bibliothèque nationale in Paris shows King Archesilaos watching over the weighing and loading of silphium for export. One line of thinking runs that Euhesperides in western Cyrenaica, a region with little farming potential, was founded as a silphium port.

The plant certainly had wondrous properties, if the ancient authors are to be believed: it was good for the coughs, the chest, and as a cure for snake bite. Pliny mentions that mixed with wine it had dramatic results on serpents (who are in fact very fond of wine); it caused them to explode. Unfortunately, silphium has disappeared today, although who knows, there may be a small colony surviving in some damp and isolated corner of Cyrenaica.

rationalist style, the Albergo Moderno and all the trappings of provincial Italian life. But the earthquake put an end to the town; the Turkish fort toppled over, many lives were lost. Today the trains no longer steam up the plateau to Barce. The Via Principe Umberto is in a parlous state, and poor migrant workers have made themselves homes in the least ruinous buildings.

## East of Barce

Back on the main highway, heading for Al Bayda, the next 'major' place is the agricultural settlement of **Awayla Sharqiya** (ex-**Villagio Maddalena**), established in 1936. North of the road you have a large piazza with the former church, which has an unusual truncated pyramid façade. On the outskirts are Italian farmhouses. The next former Italian port of call is 43 km on from Al Marj. **Al Bayyada** (stress on the first 'a', not to be confused with Al Bayda), started life in the 1930s as the **Villagio Gabriele d'Annunzio**, named for the flamboyant aviator-poet who is said to have kept five mistresses all at one time, in addition to writing purple verse in a strain unfashionable today (q.v. 'To a torpedo boat in the Adriatic'). The somewhat imposing centre of D'Annunzio rises around a ball-topped column to the left of the road, and arranged around the square you will find church, Casa del fascio and municipality. The inscription under the column has not been obliterated (yet), and reads: '1863-1938, Gabriele d'Annunzio. Diede ala ci sogni, alle speranze, ai cimenti'. Dreams, hope and ambitions in Al Bayyada today are probably as they were when the settlement was started, focusing on rain, crops and the availability of tractor parts.

A further 15 km on from Al Bayyada and you come to the easily missed turn-off for Qasr Libia, ancient Olbia. Driving eastwards, the road rises slightly to approach a small settlement, divided by the road as it runs through a cutting. Turn off left and drive up the road parallel to the main road for a few metres, then turn left again onto a road heading north. A couple of kilometres down the road, and you will see the crenellated buildings of Qasr Libia on a low, wooded rise to your left. Go left and take the first right up the track to the site. There is a museum but if it is closed, you may have to bang on the metal gate. (They are used to coach parties rather than individual travellers showing up.) Entrance 3LD, no photos of the mosaics please.

At Qasr Libia, work on a road in the late 1950s accidentally revealed two ancient basilicas. The main or western basilica, part of the main block of buildings among the trees, still has a large mosaic in situ. The more surprising mosaic, however, was found in another (eastern) basilica down the slope. The pavement was composed of fifty individual figurative panels, all now moved to a display hall next to the western basilica.

The eastern basilica mosaic is undoubtedly the finest early Christian find in Cyrenaica. The panels were originally placed in rows of five, and the original arrangement can be seen in a photocopied Illustrated London News article (14 December 1957), framed on the wall. There are birds, beasts and fish, and a number of symbolic figures and buildings. You can pick out Orpheus and his lyre – hardly surprising on a mosaic full of animals, the rivers Tigris and Euphrates, Gheon and Fison, (the four rivers of Paradise in the Book of Genesis), and the female figures symbolising Ktisis (Creation), Kosmesis (Beautification) and Ananeosis (Renovation) – which might refer to the development of the church buildings. More unusually, there is the pagan Fountain of Kastalia and the Pharos of Alexandria. The peacock is of course a typical early Christian symbol, and the panels featuring buildings may symbolise the expansion of Olbia. Paganism has not gone completely overboard: there is a rather jolly satyr of the sort which was no doubt lurking round the Cyrenaican gorges and juniper woods in classical times.

One theory holds that the Pharos symbolises the light of the true faith. A gigantic statue can be seen atop the building, along with something that looks vaguely like a signalling mirror. Originally to the right of this panel was another one with two sailors in a boat – heading for Alexandria? Or just the True Faith?

In the middle of the mosaic was a further panel with a short text declaring that the mosaic was completed in the third year of Bishop Makarios' office, ie 539/540 AD. Of the panels with buildings, the middle of the top row carried the image of the entrance gate to a fortified town, probably Olbia, with the words Polis Nea Theodorias. The thinking is that the basilica was part of an urban expansion scheme named in honour of Theodora, wife of Justinian. (Qasr Libia would appear to be a deformation of Olbia.) She was a popular empress, featuring prominently in the ceiling of the church at Ravenna.

In the middle of the panel display hall is a rather splendid late mosaic with a Nilotic scene in the middle. A farmer is trying to pull his precious cow away from a crocodile, which has got its jaws on the beast's nose as it tried to drink. Whether further marvels of Byzantine interior decorating have survived under the hillocky terrain around the basilica remains to be seen. A ruined monument to local independence fighters stands next to the carpark, above some rock tombs, now used as sheep pens.

Heading east from Qasr Libia, the next major ancient site is Qasr Bani Gdam, also referred to as Bu Migdam. The impressive fifth/sixth century fort stands by a turn left off the main road on the final ridge before the winding drop down into the Kuhuf Gorge. The fort is one of the more impressive Byzantine buildings in the region, controlling access to the canyon. After the fortress, head down the winding gorge road with care, as local drivers who know the road too well are wont to attempt perilous overtaking. There are occasional 'viewpoints' to pull over into, complete with broken park benches. The gorge is spanned by a Meccano-type bridge (put up by the British army?), on which hangs a picture of 1930s resistance hero Umar al Mukhtar. Climbing up out of the gorge, high up on your left, you will glimpse the new suspension bridge, scheduled to come into service in the near future. Up in this sides of the gorge can be seen the ledges and overhangs where early humankind would have sheltered from the elements. (NB *kuhuf* is Arabic for caves.)

**Massa to the coast**
After the Kuhuf Gorge, the road winds up onto the highest part of the Jabal Akhdar, with occasional views of open country to the south. At **Massa** is another Italian settlement, the former **Villagio Luigi Razza**, founded 1934, with its odd church tower and piazza to the left (north) of the road. Razza was a leading farmworker unionist who campaigned intensively for agricultural colonization in Cyrenaica. Here a detour down to the coast is possible: a road runs north from Massa to the coastal town of **Haniya**, passing an ancient settlement before dropping down the escarpment to the coastal plain. By the dunes, the Wadi Kuhuf reaches the sea. From Haniya, a coast road runs east to **Ra's al Hammama** where there are sandy beaches and an abandoned resort. From Ra's al Hammama, it is a 25 km drive north up the escarpment to Al Bayda. From Massa it is only another 17 km across rolling countryside to Al Bayda.

## Al Bayda    البيضاء

*Phone code: 084*
The rapidly expanding town of Al Bayda may well be your base for exploring the ancient sites of Cyrenaica. The town's name derives from Al Zawiya al Bayda ('the White zawiya'), ie the whitewashed building which housed the Sanussi lodge established in 1840 by Mohamed al Sanussi, founder of the Sanussi *tarika*. The Italians established a farming settlement here named Beda Littoria in 1933, of which a few buildings survive fairly unaltered towards the western side of town.

**Sights**
Although the town has few sights, it is exceptionally well placed for exploring the Jabal Akhdar. You could, however, take a look at the remains of the **Sanctuary of Aesclepius** on the western outskirts. The sanctuary is about 35 minutes' walk from central Al Bayda, and is located to the right (north) of the main road running west, just before you reach the university buildings to the left. Look out for ancient masonry and a fence to the right of the road. There is a concrete 1950s entrance with iron gate, and a flight of steps leading to the shattered ruins of a modern fountain. A short way after these modern remains, the temple stones nestle at a lower level, grey and lichen covered. Be careful where you point your camera here, as there is an unmarked police post over to the northwest of the ruins behind the trees.

Al Bayda corresponds to the ancient Balagrae. Dating back to the fourth century BC, the Sanctuary of Aesclepius was no doubt one of its major cult centres. The remains visible today go back to the second century BC. The sanctuary consisted of a large courtyard, about 30m by 30m, surrounded by colonnades, with the main door on the east side. Fragments of an inscription referring to the emperor Hadrian were found in the courtyard. On the south side of the sanctuary is another door, where fine columns with capitals featuring stylized silphium plants have been re-erected. To return to the main door, there is a pocket theatre just opposite it. This might well have been used for ceremonies associated with the cult of Aesclepius. In the lower front of the stage are niches which no doubt accommodated some form of statuary. During the excavations, a fine alabaster head and shoulders of Serapis was discovered in a well on the site, so eastern cults had taken hold in ancient Balagrae as well.

After visiting Aesclepius' Sanctuary, you may want to have a look at the fine red-washed 1950s (?) university buildings over on the other side of the road, easily recognisable by the minaret clock tower. These large, formal buildings would not look out of place on some English provincial university campus, bar an Islamic dome or two. Unless you are on official business of some kind, the faculties will be off limits.

The rest of Al Bayda has little worth seeing. The eastern suburbs have construction fever. Low-rise apartment buildings sprouted out of the farmland in the 1990s, highways and flyovers were built, and large mosques. This is a young town. Hordes of children fill the streets at school's-out. There is plenty of room for football games between the shabby housing blocks. However, this doesn't make the city any more attractive on a bleak Cyrenaican winter's day. The town centre has a few cafés and video arcades by way of entertainment.

**Sleeping**

The only hotel, for the moment, at Al Bayda is the **C** *Funduq Qasr al Bayda*, PO Box 213 Al Bayda, T633455/8, F633459. A 4-storey block right on the main road through town. 35LD for a single room with breakfast. Spotlessly clean rooms with electric heater, en-suite showers and unlimited hot water. Dinner pretty undistinguished – cheaper to eat out (if you eat in, you're stung for LD15 for dinner). In the summer, if you need to leave the windows open, the street facing double rooms may be noisy. The back facing rooms are all *jinah*, ie suites, so you may have to pay more for quiet. Try to reserve in advance at busy times of year, as the hotel is much used for over-nights by tour groups. The only other options in the region are the holiday village at Susa (Apollonia), summer only, or the youth hostel at Shahat near the ruins of Cyrene.

**Eating**

As you leave the *Funduq Qasr al Bayda*, cross the main road and head left. There are two restaurants a few metres down the road, the *Batriq* (Penguin), and a small chicken grill place. Both are cheap and clean, and tend to close early. In the other direction (west), on the same side of the road as the hotel, is a garden café popular with local youth.

**Shopping**

Plenty of small grocer shops opposite the hotel. Arcade shopping for cheap clothes on street south of main street.

# Al Bayda area

**Travel agencies**

The *Shallal (Waterfall) Travel Agency*, T637234, F633457 (they also have an office in Benghazi, T016-9095912), is in premises adjoining the hotel. (Turn right out of hotel lobby.) Can arrange, at a high price, for car and driver to tour region's sites. OK if there are several of you.

**Transport**

Share-taxis coming in from Benghazi will let you off almost anywhere on the main street through Al Bayda. The *agensiya* station for share taxis is on the east side of town. (Coming from the town centre, turn right at the 'globe monument' on the main dual carriageway. The *agensiya*

Cyrenaica

is about 50 m up on your right, recognisable by the usual battered Peugeot estate cars.) Coming into Al Bayda from Derna, get set down on the main road and pick up an Iveco mini-bus into town. If you want to find a car and driver for the day, head for the main square next to the Post Office, recognizable by telecom mast.

**Directory**  **Communications**  For international calls, the best solution is a call-shop, not far from the main square. **Pharmacy**  Several in central Al Bayda. There is one almost immediately opposite the hotel *Qsar al Bayda*.

# Cyrene    شحات

*At the edge of a once-wild upland, the ruins of ancient Cyrene are one of the great ancient sites of North Africa, on a par with Leptis Magna and Sabrath, Morocco's Volubilis, and Dougga and El Jem in Tunisia. When the first Greek settlers arrived, as advised by their oracle, they found forested hillsides, a clear spring, and a plain below: the ideal place to build a city. Despite the nearby urban sprawl of Shahat, the ruins retain a country air. "Cattle feed among the ruins of Cyrene, and its whole air is infinitely more rural than civic", wrote 19th-century travellers, the Beecheys. The site surprises by its sheer extent. It was settled for over 1,200 years, and bears the marks of revolt, earthquake and rebuilding. There are colonnades lovingly re-assembled by archaeologists, and carefully cleared mosaics, market squares and pocket theatres. But Cyrene does not have the planned pomposity of Roman Leptis: there are concentrations of soft yellow stone ruins, but also great areas of hillside still to be excavated. Cyrene is all about discontinuity and resettlement. And even if ruins are not your thing, then the beauty of the site, the pine trees, the wild flowers in spring, the views to the distant Mediterranean, will all make the visit worthwhile.*

# Cyrene

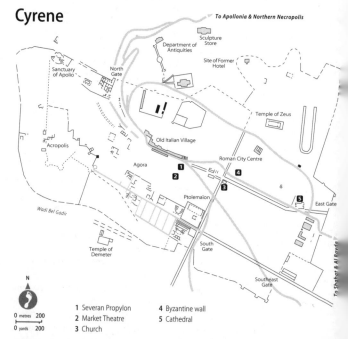

*To Apollonia & Northern Necropolis*

Sculpture Store

Department of Antiquities

Site of Former Hotel

Sanctuary of Apollo

North Gate

Temple of Zeus

Acropolis

Old Italian Village

Roman City Centre

Agora

**1**

**2**

**4**

**3**

Ptolemaïon

**5**

East Gate

*Wadi Bel Gadir*

Temple of Demeter

South Gate

Southeast Gate

*To Shahat & Al Rovda*

N

0 metres  200
0 yards  200

1 Severan Propylon
2 Market Theatre
3 Church

4 Byzantine wall
5 Cathedral

Cyrenaica

## Ins and outs

Cyrene is easily reached by public transport from Al Bayda. Take one of the small Iveco minibuses heading east along Al Bayda main street, making sure that it is going to Shahat, which is the modern settlement next to the ruins. The minibus will go left at the first checkpoint, and set you down just before the pine woods and ruins begin, about 1.5 km further on. (Cost of ride, .5LD). In winter, there are few minibuses running late, so you might have to hitch or walk back to the main crossroads.

**Getting there**

There are basically two entrances to the ruins, the main one with a ticket office being about 20 mins' walk down the road on your left. Here you go straight into the heart of the original Greek settlement.

**Getting around & practicalities**

The ruins are closed on Mon, but open at all other times, ticket 3LD. Having said that, even if you arrive late, you should be able to climb through a fence near the Agora or over the ticket office gate to explore at your leisure.

The best guidebook to Cyrene is Professor Richard Goodchild's *Cyrene and Apollonia. An historical guide*, a pocket-sized publication which is available from the Fergiani Bookshop in Tripoli (but not in Al Bayda or Cyrene).

## History and background

Callimachus referred to Cyrene as a "deep-soiled town", and no doubt farmland and the presence of water were the reason the Greeks settled here. In fact, it was not their first attempt at settling on the African coast. Advised by the oracle of Apollo, a group of colonists from the island of Thera (Santorini), left their homes to found a new city. The reasons were the usual ones: Thera's resources were inadequate for an expanding population, civil strife was making life untenable on the island. Initially the colonists settled on the island of Plataea, in the Gulf of Bomba (eastern Cyrenaica). This proved inadequate, and two years later they founded a second settlement on the African coast, at Aziris, east of Derna. But here again, resources were inadequate, and the locals persuaded the Therans to head for a new site, where water was plentiful as, in Herodotus' words, 'there were holes in the sky'. They were led up onto the plateau to the site of Cyrene, where under their leader Battos, a city was founded close to the Spring of Apollo, spreading up onto the easily defended slopes of the Acropolis hill. Although the area was already settled by a local tribe, the Asbisti, the two communities came to get on well. Herodotus recounts that the locals began to imitate the new arrivals, and both sides benefited from working together.

This legendary foundation of Cyrene goes back to 631 BC, during a period which saw the foundation of numerous Greek cities overseas, in particular in the central Mediterranean. From its initial core, the city then expanded southeast, into the Agora area, where the tomb of King Battos provided a focus point. The city was structured by two main streets, the Sacred Way, running from the Sanctuary of Apollo up to the Agora, and the so-called Street of King Battos, a straight avenue from the Ptolemaïon/Agora neighbourhood to the Acropolis. To judge by the size and number of the sacred buildings, Cyrene in the fifth century BC would have had a population of several tens of thousands, whose livelihood came from stock raising, farming and the sale of the valuable silphium plant. By way of a comparison, the Temple of Zeus at Cyrene is marginally larger than the Parthenon at Athens. A port, named Apollonia for the tutelary deity, grew up to serve the city 15 km away down on the coast.

**Early Cyrene: seventh to fourth centuries BC**

The fourth century BC saw the construction of the Temple of Artemis, a second temple to Apollo up on the Agora, and the embellishment of the cult-altars

Cyrenaica

## Libya, 'dripping rain'

*The name Libya derives from the Greek, and means 'dripping rain'. In Greek myth, Libya was the daughter of Zeus and Io. The story goes that Cyrene, a strong maiden adept at wrestling with wild beasts and protecting flocks on Mount Pelion, attracted Apollo's attention. He carried her off in his golden chariot, to the site of what was to become the city of Cyrene. There Aphrodite greeted them – and had them bed down in Libya's golden chamber. Apollo promised Cyrene that she would reign over a well-watered, pleasant land, where she could enjoy her hunting. This land was no doubt the Jabal Akhdar, the Green Mountain. Cyrene then bore Apollo a son, Aristaeus. The Greeks of Cyrene in eastern Libya held Aristaeus to be their ancestor – and named their port Apollonia, in honour of his father.*

with marble. Eastern influences became manifest, a sanctuary to Isis was built on the Acropolis. This was a slick and prosperous time for Cyrene: new Athenian-style porticoes went up on the Agora, the Sanctuary of Apollo acquired a *propylaea* and a fine treasury for war booty. Great necropolises began to fill the northern slopes below the city, cliffs of funerary pigeonholes in stone.

**Hellenistic and Roman Cyrene**  In 331 BC, Cyrenaica submitted to Alexander the Great. It was under his successors, the Ptolemies of Egypt, in Hellenistic times, (roughly the third and second centuries BC), that Cyrene reached its greatest extent. Theatres and the great gymnasium, the Ptolemaïon went up, temples were refurbished, fountains were embellished – and a fortified city wall, 5.5 km long, was constructed, with square towers to reinforce the weak points. The large square block of the Ptolemaïon brought structure to the Agora area, which was re-planned in a series of square blocks. Cyrene was no doubt a shining example of Greek urbanism, ruled in a benevolent sort of way from Alexandria. Eventually, the city and its hinterland were bequeathed to Rome.

Under Roman rule, the Ptolemaïon became a forum. The nearby Agora acquired further monuments, including a capitol. In the Sanctuary of Apollo, fine baths and new propylaea were constructed, while the Temple of Apollo was remodelled, proof of the Roman State's respect for the main local deity. However, Romanization was the order of the day: the conversion of the Sanctuary Theatre to amphitheatre bears witness to the arrival of brutish Roman taste in public entertainment.

In 115 AD, Cyrene was sacked by Jewish rebels. The Emperor Hadrian, a great builder forever on the move across his dominions, undertook the reconstruction of the city. The Agora was repaved and the basilica in the new forum refurbished. By the end of the second century AD, the majority of Cyrene's public buildings had been restored – with the exception of the vast Temple of Zeus. Unfortunately, the region was hit by earthquakes in 262 AD and, more seriously, 365 AD. Cyrene was no longer capital, and some commentators consider that it suffered a loss in population. It may have continued to function as a sort of summer capital and the construction of a number of churches in the fifth century testify to continued activity. The great days were over, however. The Byzantine Empire was exhausted by war in the East and internecine religious struggles. Cyrene awaited a dénouement of some kind – which came from an unexpected quarter, the oases and wastes of Arabia.

**The rediscovery of Cyrene**  After the Muslim-Arab invasion of the seventh century, Cyrene continued to exist in a sort of half-life. Soon, however, it disappeared from history, until its rediscovery by French consul Lemaire in 1705. To Europeans with a classical education, Cyrene was a commonplace, familiar from the Greek poets. From Pindar they knew of the Sacred Way, "gravelled, flat and straight, resounding with the pounding of horses hooves". Other travellers soon followed in Lemaire's footsteps: Cervelli of Pisa made the first map, Paolo della Cella of Genoa, accompanying the Pasha of Tripoli on a punitive expedition against mountain rebels, recorded inscriptions.

In the early nineteenth century, other travellers followed, including the English Beechey brothers, Pacho and Müller, and Barth. They filled diaries and made sketches, turned into picturesque engraved plates in the illustrated weeklies which appeared in European capitals in the nineteenth century. The first accurate survey was made by two British officers, R.M. Smith and E.A. Porcher, published as *The History of the Recent Discoveries at Cyrenaica* in 1864. They procured numerous sculptures and inscriptions for the British Museum, perhaps the most famous being the bas relief of the Nymph Cyrene strangling a lion while the goddess Libya crowns her. In 1910, an American, Richard Norton, began serious archaeological work on the necropolis, while Italians Federico Halbherr and Gaetano Sanctis travelled through the region recording the ancient sites. The archaeological world became aware that there were splendid finds awaiting in Cyrenaica.

A thunderstorm revealed the first major find: in 1913, the Italian army ensconced itself on the heights of Cyrene; on the night of 27 December, a violent storm washed away much topsoil in the Sanctuary of Apollo, revealing the famous Venus of Cyrene. An archaeological mission was established, although until the 1930s, security for the Italians was uncertain. The first excavations were undertaken by the Italian army, protected by a fortified wall. The Sanctuary of Apollo and the Agora were brought to light, the city began to emerge from the hummocky, scrub-covered hillsides. Little rail lines ran through the ruins to remove soil, while a fine hotel was put up to house the beautiful people visiting the ruins. After the Second World War, excavations continued, and the task of re-assembling the great Temple of Zeus was started. With the end of the embargo, prospects look good for a resumption of archaeological research work on a significant scale. Hopefully, there will be enough imagination to give Cyrene the museum it so merits.

*Venus of Cyrene and the city rediscovered*

## Exploring Cyrene

The ruins are extensive, and you may not be able to cover everything in one day. Basically, there are four main sections, the **Sanctuary of Apollo** and around, near the main ticket window, the **Ptolemaïon and Agora district**, closest to Shahat, the **Temple of Zeus**, and finally, the **Northern Necropolis**, down off the old road to Apollonia. There is no site museum, but if you are with a well-organized group, you should be able to get into the sculpture store. Tour groups sometimes do the site in two half-day visits, combining with a half-day to Apollonia and the coast. If you were really pressed for time, it is difficult to say what the "must sees" actually are, as all three major areas of ruins are beautiful and important.

*The codes in brackets refer to various maps and plans in the section*
*C: Cyrene*
*SA: Sanctuary of Apollo*
*P: Ptolemaion Quarter*
*A: Agora Neighbourhood*

## The Sanctuary of Apollo

The original Greek settlement grew up around a spring which bubbled forth onto a terrace overlooking the coastal plain. The extensive remains brought to light bear witness to centuries of urban life, from Greek to Byzantine times. The area is full of clues and reminders to Cyrene's history. The entrance to this

*See map Sanctuary of Apollo next page - codes in brackets refer to the map*

area is a metal gate next to the ticket window. Following the path, you will see a wall on your left behind which are the extensive remains of Trajan's Baths (SA1), (see the end of the section on the Sanctuary neighbourhood for their description). Just before a milestone (SA2) commemorating repairs to the road under Hadrian in 118 AD, you head right into the heart of the ancient city. (If you carry on straight ahead, the Sacred Way leads up past the Greek Baths to the upper levels of Cyrene).

**Baths and ceremonial colonnades** As you turn right you will have a short colonnade, the Greek propylaea (SA3), on your right; to your left is an unidentified temple, followed by the entrance to the Byzantine Baths (SA4). The Greek propylaea is composed of four Doric columns, restored to support a complete entablature (sort of lintel). This colonnade symbolized the entrance to the Greek city, and was put up by one Praxiades, a priest of Apollo, in the fourth century BC. At the foot of the building are marble (sacrificial?) tables with beasts' feet. Later, in Roman times, the entrance to the precinct was re-modelled with a baths, and a new propylaea (SA6) was built further on to the right.

The Byzantine Baths were built on the site of the palaestra of Trajan's Baths after their destruction by earthquake. A vestibule leads to the cold baths, and then further north, the hot rooms. Successive alterations and rebuilding means that the ruins are not easy to interpret. Just after the bath is the Roman propylaea (SA6), erected under Trajan or Hadrian. Opposite is one of the finest ruins at Cyrene, the Strateghion (SA5), dating from the late fourth century

# Sanctuary of Apollo

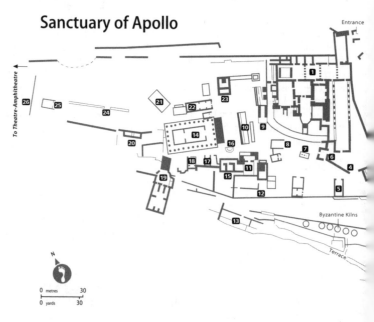

1 Trajan's Baths
2 Hadrian's commemorative milestone
3 Greek propylaea
4 Byzantine Baths
5 Strateghion
6 New (Roman) propylaea
7 Hellenistic fountain
8 Temple of Hades
9 Possible temple of the Diosauri
10 Altar of Apollo
11 Temple of Jason Magnus
12 Flight of steps
13 Fountain of Apollo
14 Temple of Apollo
15 Sanctuary of Apollo
16 Fountain of the Nymph Cyrene
17 Greek fountain
18 Temple of Isis
19 Grotto of the Priests of Apollo
20 Paved terrace
21 Unidentified temple

Cyrenaica

BC. The Strateghion is what the Romans would later refer to as a *donarium*, a sort of treasury designed to house war booty. The name Strategion derives from the fact the building was dedicated by three *strateghoi*, citizens designated by the city to lead the Greek armies. Under the Romans, the building received a second dedication, this time to the Emperor Tiberius, by a leading citizen, one M. Sufenas Proculus.

Continuing towards to the Temple of Apollo, there is a **Hellenistic fountain** (SA7) and the **Temple of Hades** (SA8), where a statute of the god of the Underworld was found. To the right lie **Trajan's Baths** (SA1). More significant is the long, marble-faced **Altar of Apollo** (SA10). These stone-built altars were refaced with white marble in the fourth century BC, and would have been the site of animal sacrifices to the city's patron god. Under the Byzantines, when paganism was no longer the flavour of the day, the marble was reused to pave the Byzantine Baths. Twentieth century Italian archaeologists restored it to its original position.

**Monuments to Apollo**

Remodelled on three occasions during its long history, the **Temple of Apollo** (SA14) is the most significant monument of the sanctuary area, easily recognised by its great columns, looking for all the world like great stone oil drums stacked atop each other. The temple was rebuilt after destruction by earthquake in 365 BC, and a second time after the Jewish revolt of the second century AD. The smooth columns standing today belong to this most recent rebuilding, and were re-erected in modern times. Inside the temple, the lower floor levels of phases one and two of the temple can be seen. The second century AD floor was held up on Doric columns from the first temple, laid horizontally in the foundations. In 1861, a sensuous and colossal Hellenistic statue of Apollo Citharedus (Lyre-playing Apollo) was discovered in the temple – and can now be seen in the British Museum in London.

Just to your left as you stand facing the entrance to Apollo's Temple is another emblematic monument of the city, the **Fountain of the Nymph Cyrene** (SA16). To the modern mind, the fountain's theme, 'Cyrene strangling a lion', from whose mouth water poured forth, is rather un-nymph-like. However, Apollo was so struck by her beast-handling skills that he consulted the centaur Cheiron on what to do. The wise old centaur advised marriage, and Apollo bore Cyrene off to green and well-watered Libya to consummate the union. The original statuary is in the Cyrene sculpture store.

Running parallel to the cliff face behind the Fountain of the Nymph is a series of buildings, including the

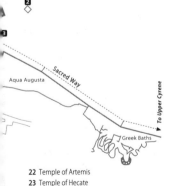

22 Temple of Artemis
23 Temple of Hecate
24 Wall
25 Unidentified temple
26 Nicodaemean wall

Cyrenaica

Temple of Jason Magnus (SA11), the **Sanctuary of Apollo** (SA15), a **Greek fountain** (SA17), and the **Temple of Isis** (SA18). Behind the Temple of Jason Magnus, a flight of steps (SA12), runs up to the **Fountain of Apollo** (SA13). From here a narrow terrace runs east towards the Sacred Way, overlooking the Sanctuary neighbourhood. The Fountain of Apollo originally came bubbling out of the hillside. The spring lay deep in the hillside at the end of a long tunnel, now off-limits.

Back down in the sacred precinct, behind the Temple of Apollo to the south-west and abutting the cliff-face is the **Grotto of the Priests of Apollo** (SA19). From here you may proceed west along a paved terrace (SA20), past a wall (SA24) and an unidentified temple (SA21) to the **Nicodaemean Wall** (SA26) and the **Theatre-Amphitheatre**, a short way beyond.

**The Theatre-Amphitheatre**

The Theatre is one of the oldest buildings of Cyrene, although its original dates are unclear. The earliest surviving parts are the stage foundations and the seating close to the orchestra, both Hellenistic. In the second century AD, the taste for displays of beast-baiting, carnage and fighting reached Cyrene, and this beautifully located theatre was converted into an amphitheatre with a semi-circle of extra seating being added to the north. Seats closest to the arena were replaced with a wall, and a tunnel added around the ring to provide space for spectacle performers to move around. The vulgar displays of carnage could not be allowed to sully the Sanctuary of Apollo, however, and so one Nicodaemus built a wall (SA26) to separate the two some time in the late second or third centuries AD.

After the Theatre and its view across the plain, you can return towards the centre of the sanctuary, taking in a selection of ruins north of the Temple of Apollo, namely another **unidentified temple** (SA21), the **Temple of Artemis** (SA22), and the **Temple of Hecate** (SA23). Artemis was sister of Apollo, and her cult, associated with hunting and nature, was no doubt strong on the game-rich plateau of Cyrene. The temple has a fine carved entrance, indicative of the importance of Artemis to the city. Before you leave the Sanctuary neighbourhood, you must not, however, miss Trajan's Baths (SA1).

**Trajan's Baths (SA1)**

This large bath complex covered the northeastern section of the Sanctuary neighbourhood. Built under Trajan by one C. Memmius, the baths were subsequently restored by Hadrian, only to be abandoned after an earthquake in 365 AD. They were later replaced by a new Byzantine bath complex next door, put up on the site of the former *palaestra* or exercise hall. Access to Trajan's Baths today is via the *frigidarium* or cold room. The bather would then proceed to the warm rooms to the *caldaria*, located right next to the furnaces. Remains of the hypocaust floor system, which allowed hot air to circulate under paving supported on brick pillars, can still be seen.

The Baths were the source of some of the finest sculpture found at Cyrene, some of which used to be visible in a small museum and some of which is on show in Tripoli Museum. It was in Trajan's Baths that a statue of Aphrodite 'rising from the foam', dubbed the Venus of Cyrene, came to light after heavy rains in the winter of 1913, thus beginning the great Italian excavation campaigns in the city. Among the finds were a statue of Alexander the Great, the Three Graces, a Hermes and a Faun with the child Dionysos.

**Along the Sacred Way**

After the elegant Baths, no doubt the social centre for ancient Cyrene, head back past the Strateghion (SA5) towards the Greek Propylaea (SA3), and the Sacred Way, which will lead you to the upper terrace of the city, past the **Aqua Augusta**, a fountain presented to the city by Proconsul Vestalis in the reign of

Augustus. This consists of a practical arrangement of water tanks cut out of the rock. The so-called Sacred Way had a portico, running along the south side of the valley leading to upper Cyrene. The base of two parallel walls can still be seen today. Further up the valley, the track gets rougher, and on your right you have the surprising Greek Baths, set in caves under the cliff face. The Baths consist of sit-in tubs, above which were niches for oil lamps and bath gear; they probably date from Hellenistic times. These baths were abandoned when water was diverted for the Aqua Augusta Fountain below.

One final point of interest in the Sanctuary area: the five circular Byzantine kilns, situated below the cliff behind the Strateghion. These kilns were no doubt used by the Byzantine Christians to reduce large amounts of marble statuary to lime.

After visiting Apollo's Sanctuary, you can either head up the road, past the old Italian village, and continue your visit in the Agora and Ptolemaïon areas or you can clamber up along the Sacred Way, perhaps scrambling back onto the road near the village. To the right of the road as you head uphill and eastwards are the carefully assembled remains of a **propylon** dating from Severan times (C1), behind which is the **Market Theatre** (C2). The friezes of the propylon carried imperial propaganda in bas-relief, representations of the Emperor Severus and his sons Geta and Caracalla. After the propylon, the road forks, while the former Roman road ran straight ahead. At a crossroads that was the centre of the Roman town, are the remains of a **basilica** (C3), and a **Byzantine wall** (C4). If pressed for time, take the right hand fork after the Severan propylon and keep bearing right. The great walls of the Ptolemaïon will soon come into view.

**From Apollo's Sanctuary to the Ptolemaïon**
*See map 'Cyrene', page 166*

Cyrenaica

## The Ptolemaïon neighbourhood

The Ptolemaïon is one of the most spectacular monuments at Cyrene, rivalled only in scale by the Temple of Zeus. Constructed as a magnificent sports ground for the city by Ptolemy VIII (second century BC), this Hellenistic building is a vast porticoed enclosure (96 m x 85 m), with great gates to the east (P1a) and south (P1b). Before excavation work, very little of the building was visible. In the 1930s, the Italians re-assembled the walls and colonnades. The central area was used for physical and military exercises by the young men of Cyrene. Along the northern portico were covered training areas, while a walled-in running track, the **Portico of the Herms**, (P11) was a continuation of the southern portico. Under the Romans, the gymnasium was converted into a forum, while the buildings on the north side (P3) became law courts. Under the Byzantines the former gymnasium's dignity was further lowered when the area was converted into a fortress. In the middle of the exercise area is a **temple** (P2), recognizable by its steps and raised base, thought to have been dedicated to Julius Caesar. The basilica (P3) conversion goes back to Hadrian, c120 AD, and niches for Roman statues can clearly be seen.

Leave the Ptolemaïon via the magnificent southern portico. You are on the southeast to northwest axis referred to by archaeologists as the **Avenue of King Battos** (P5). The street starts with **propylaea**, a ceremonial gateway (P4) at the eastern end. Just inside the propylaea, to the left, are the remains of a **private courtyard house** (P6). Next along, behind the foundations of a line of shops, is a **theatre** (P7). Beyond the theatre, the enthusiastic can pick their way over the stones to a **Temple of Venus** (P8), and some **small altars** (P9), perhaps dedicated to Heracles and Hermes, gods favoured by athletes. Then you come to the low ruins of what must have been one of the most magnificent constructions in Cyrene, the **House of Jason Magnus** (P12), dating from the second or early third centuries AD. Clearly visible are the courtyards of the official quarters (P13) and the private area (P14). There is a fine geometric *opus sectile* mosaic in the summer dining room on the south side of the official patio. There was a fine colonnade, with statues of the nine Muses between the columns.

After the House of Jason Magnus, return towards the Street of King Battos. Note the **Temple of Hermes** (P15) with its dedicatory mosaic offered by one Januarius, slave of Tiberius Jason Magnus, in the reign of the emperor Commodus. You can now observe the 130m long **Portico or Stoa of Hermes and Heracles** (P11). Originally, this was a roofed passageway, with a central line of columns and windows flanked by busts of Hermes and Heracles on the street facing side. In more unsettled Byzantine times, the outer wall was heighten to function as part of the defences of the city.

Just north of the Stoa is a fine little **Roman theatre** (P10) with vaulted access corridors leading to the seating from an outer semi-circular passage. Marble columns can be seen lying in the orchestra area. In its day, this must have been quite a prestige venue. At the western end of the Stoa, on the same side as the theatre, the visitor will find the **House of Hesychius** (P16), whose name can be found in a marble mosaic. This private residence dating from the fifth century AD testifies to the continued vitality of Cyrene (as a summer capital?), at a time when Ptolemaïs had become capital of the Pentapolis. The final stop in this section of the city is the **Hall of the Muses**, so called for the mosaic floor discovered there depicting the heads of the Muses. The street carries on into the Agora neighbourhood.

## Ptolemaïon Quarter

| | | |
|---|---|---|
| **1** Ptolemaïon | **5** Avenue of King Battos | **11** Portico of the Herms & Heracles |
| **a** East Gate | **6** Private courtyard house | **12** House of Jason Magnus |
| **b** South Gate | **7** Market Theatre | **13** Official quarters |
| **2** Gymnasium Temple | **8** Temple of Venus | **14** Residential areas |
| **3** Judicial Basilica | **9** Small altars | **15** Temple of Hermes |
| **4** Eastern Propylaea | **10** Roman Theatre | **16** House of Hesychius |

Cyrenaica

## The Agora neighbourhood

The Agora esplanade was the centre of public life in Cyrene, containing a concentration of public buildings and temples to rival that of the Sanctuary of Apollo on the lower terrace. It would seem to have started as a market which grew up around the founder's tomb. Over the centuries, it became extremely elaborate, with fine porticoes and monuments added as the city grew in wealth. Various administrative buildings, including the archives, were installed here. Pride of place went to two huge marble altars, symbols of civic pride and piety.

Entering from the Ptolemaïon area, the left (south) side of the Agora is fronted by a series of public buildings, including the **Hall of the Medusa** (A2), the **Prytaneum** (A3), where banquets would be given to official guests, the **Capitol** (A4), and the **Archives** (A5). Excavations in 1919 brought to light lists of the archivists and thousands of the clay seals used to authenticate documents. The archives were functioning in the first century AD, only to be destroyed in the Jewish revolt of 115AD. The nearby Capitol was in use in the second century AD. (A statue base dated 138 AD was discovered there.)

The **Western Propylon** (A7) closes the Agora end of the Street of King Battos (compare with the Eastern Propylon). The two propyleia defined the city's central area in the Roman period. Closer to the esplanade is a fourth century **Temple of Apollo** (A8), its marble decoration testifying to the wealth of Cyrene at the time.

*Cyrenaica*

## Agora neighbourhood

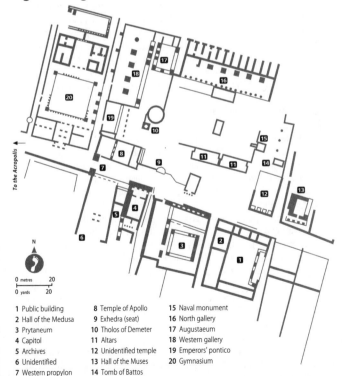

| | | |
|---|---|---|
| **1** Public building | **8** Temple of Apollo | **15** Naval monument |
| **2** Hall of the Medusa | **9** Exhedra (seat) | **16** North gallery |
| **3** Prytaneum | **10** Tholos of Demeter | **17** Augustaeum |
| **4** Capitol | **11** Altars | **18** Western gallery |
| **5** Archives | **12** Unidentified temple | **19** Emperors' pontico |
| **6** Unidentified | **13** Hall of the Muses | **20** Gymnasium |
| **7** Western propylon | **14** Tomb of Battos | |

The actual esplanade is charged with symbolism. The striking round construction (A10), originally thought to be the tomb of founder King Battos, was in fact a sanctuary to the fertility goddess Demeter and her daughter Core, who became Queen of the Underworld under the name Persephone. The colossal seated figure identified as the goddess Demeter was found here. The sanctuary dates from Hellenistic times, possibly third to second centuries BC. Note that a short way south of the Agora (see main map, page 166), Cyrene also had a Temple to Demeter. Note the nearby round marble base with dedicatory inscription to the goddess Libia.

In the middle of the esplanade are great **ceremonial altars** (A11), once entirely faced with white marble. Here whole oxen would have been roasted in honour of the various deities. Hard by the altars is the building thought to be the **Tomb of King Battos** (A14). The poet Pindar mentions that the tomb of Battos is on the agora at Cyrene, so this would seem to be a reasonable guess. The late Hellenistic **Naval Monument** (A15) is another example of civic pride, celebrating some sea victory or other. A female statue of victory rises up on the prow of a galley. The statue is often compared to the Victory of Samothrace, now in the Louvre.

As the Agora filled up with pieces of commemorative urban art, more mundane market functions were moved aside, no doubt housed in areas like the shops beyond the **North Gallery** (A16), also known as the North Stoa, or in premises inserted into the great **Western Gallery** (A18) Originally built for ceremonial purposes, this barn-like edifice had a ridged roof held up by a central row of columns. Finally, just west of the Agora is another large public building thought to have been a **gymnasium** (A20). The great courtyard with its Ionic columns certainly seems to fit the bill.

After the Agora area, the so-called Street of King Battos continues west for some 100 m to the eastern gate of the **Acropolis**, which had a single wide entrance, flanked by two square towers. Little of the Acropolis has been excavated. If you proceed right to a corner tower, then left for some 20 m, you will come to the remains of the Sanctuary of Isis, completely excavated in 1935. From here you can cut straight down hill towards the valley, eventually intersecting with a rough track which will bring you into the Sanctuary of Apollo.

## The Temple of Zeus and around

Of all the religious buildings in Cyrenaica, the Temple of Zeus at Cyrene must be one of the most spectacular. Its golden stone Doric columns have been largely re-erected, and the temple's massive bulk sits in a quiet pinewood, well aside from the monument-packed central quarters of the city. The temple is reached by a narrow road running right shortly after you enter the zone of the ruins from the south.

The temple would seem to go back to the sixth century BC, although major reconstruction work was undertaken in Roman times due to the destruction wrought by the Jewish revolt of 115 AD. At 70 m in length and 17 m wide, the temple is slightly larger than the Parthenon of Athens and the Temple of Zeus at Olympia. In fact, the cult statue of the Father of the Gods, twelve times life-size, was modelled on Phidias' statue of Olympian Zeus, seated on his throne. The feet and arms were in marble, the rest in plaster. Of the head of this statue, no trace has been discovered. A head of Zeus, in all likelihood from the statue of the first temple, was re-assembled by archaeologists and may be seen in the Sculpture Store. The rebuilt temple was destroyed by the earthquake of 365 AD, and further vandalised by the Christians. It would seem that the large 'cathedral' near the East Gate (**5** on main plan), took its place as chief centre of worship in Byzantine times.

Cyrene
South Entrance
Roman Forum

It was the British Royal Engineers who first re-erected one of the temple's columns, back in the 1950s. The reconstruction campaign was started seriously in 1967 by the Italians. The Temple of Zeus as it stands today is the result of much dedicated work by archaeologist Sandro Stucchi, architect Claudio Frigerio and their teams. The scaffolding still in place suggests that the task is to be continued. One can but marvel at the destructive energy released during the Jewish revolt to overturn such a massive building. The re-assembly of the Doric columns means that today's visitor is seeing the temple broadly as it looked pre-115. Hadrian's restoration created a smaller walled building within the original precinct. Only the statue was more colossal, dwarfing a gallery of Corinthian capitals holding up a sort of viewing platform which allowed worshippers to be close to the upper parts of the statue. The massive base where the cult statue would have been located can still be seen today.

Those interested in classical building will note that the original Greek architects, though lacking in arches and domes, had a number of optical tricks up their sleeves to produce a refined result. The blocks composing the three-step temple base are slightly curved, while the columns lean ever so faintly inwards. This slight 'correction' was to ensure that the columns appeared straight to the viewer.

Recent excavations have given researchers a better idea of the area around the temple. There were *donarii*, (rooms for leaving gifts), and three *hestiatoria*, banqueting halls, suggesting that the sanctuary received large numbers of visitors.

## The necropolis

Cyrene's necropolises are extensive and spectacular. The tombs of the dead occupy the hillsides looking north towards the Mediterranean. No doubt the ancient Greeks, like their modern counterparts, had an annual feast for tending the homes of the deceased. There are around 1,200 shared tombs, and several thousand individual sarcophagi. With the collapse of the old religious ways in Byzantine times, grave robbing became legitimate, and few tombs were to escape desecration. The vast extent of the robberies would seem to indicate that valuable grave goods were left in the tombs and sarcophagi as a matter of course. The cemetery areas are extensive, and scrambling around them is probably only for the really dedicated. There are four main areas: the Eastern Necropolis, on either side of the approach road to the ruins from

Shahat, now increasingly submerged by new building; the Southern Necropolis, along the ancient road to Al Bayda (ancient Balagrae); the Western Necropolis, in the Wadi Belgadir, and the Northern Necropolis, the most rewarding with rock cut tombs in the steep hillsides along the ancient road to Apollonia. Probably the most impressive – and most accessible group of tombs lies in the valley just below the Sculpture Store. There are fine early rock cut tombs in the Western Necropolis, too.

The necropolises of Cyrene give a very real idea of the Greek conception of death – and the evolution of Greek funerary architecture. Many of the early tombs have Doric temple façades cut out of the living rock. Later, in Hellenistic times, the fashion grew for circular tombs (there is a good example next to the Sculpture Store). Certain graves were topped with a base inscribed with the deceased's name and a bust of a veiled or faceless female figure symbolising Persephone, goddess of the Underworld. As pressure on land grew, whole hillsides were covered with tiers of tombs. In modern times, the local nomad population found that the tombs made splendid dry quarters during the cold, wet winter months. Today, however, the tombs of ancient Cyrene are for the most part empty, apart from nesting redstarts and the occasional snake.

## Essentials

**Sleeping**  If you have the funds, the *Hotel Qasr al Bayda*, T084-633455/8 (see above Al Bayda) is preferable to the **Youth Hostel**, T085-12102, the building to your left, down behind the petrol station, just before the pine trees and the ruins begin properly. The advantage is that you are really close to Cyrene. The disadvantage is that it gets crowded, often with migrant workers. Cheap, 5LD. Rumour has it that new tourist accommodation is to open near the ruins 'soon'. Back in the 1960s, Cyrene had a famous hotel, 'one of the pleasures of Libya' according to Philip Ward, author of two travelogues on the country. Bernard Berenson sung the praises of the Grand' Albergo agli Scavi too: "The hotel here is as much as possible like the Brussels house of the Stoclets in splendour of marble and semi-precious stone but, on the whole, finer as architecture. The central hall is a great cupola. The furniture is du dernier chic". Never mind, in summer a cool breeze still drifts through the pines of Cyrene.

# Susa (Apollonia)    سوسة

*High on the plateau, Cyrene needed a port, and Apollonia was created to serve this need. Today's visitor will find a quiet, listless sort of place: ships lie rusting in the port, in the museum nothing has changed in thirty years apart from the travel company stickers on the door. Fortunately for the archaeologists, modern Susa hardly impinges on the ancient town that sits within a neat oblong of ramparts, parallel to the sea. There is a bijou theatre, and three basilicas, evidence of the town's rebirth in Byzantine days. As the coast has sunk since ancient times, much of Apollonia is now submarine. The waves crash against the reefs offshore, remains of quarried coastline which once defined an elaborate dual port.*

## Ins and outs

**Getting there**  Susa (Apollonia) is a small place, so there is not a great deal of transport going there and an early start is advisable. The town is about a 30 minute drive from Al Bayda, via Shahat. From Al Bayda, one option is to take an Iveco minibus from the main street to the post office (*al barid*) just before the trees around the ruins at Cyrene begin. Wait under the eucalyptus trees where the road forks right and try to hitch a lift. (You may have to pay). There are also infrequent buses down to Susa from this point. To return to Al Bayda, you can try hitching back up to Shahat from the main road. Getting to Susa from sparse settlements east along the coast road (Ra's Hilal) is more difficult, as traffic is light.

Modern Susa is laid out on a grid pattern. The museum is in a 1930s building, the for- **Getting around**
mer municipality, on the main square. The site is easily found – go down the road running to the right of the museum, heading towards the sea. Look out for the rundown modern lighthouse atop the southwestern corner tower of the ancient ramparts. The site entrance, a rusting gate, is on your right. If the warden is not kipping in his hut, you can usually get in. Do not miss the theatre at the far eastern end of the site.

## History and background

Coming from Al Bayda, you first glimpse Apollonia/Susa as the road sweeps through a cutting high on the plateau. Far below lie flat red-soil farmlands next to the sea, a holiday village, Susa and its port, and the Mediterranean stretching northwards till sea meets sky. Waves break white against small islets just off-shore, and there should be a fleet of galleys coming in from some distant Hellenic city-state.

The wild coast close to Cyrene offered few easy landing points for ancient vessels. In any case, the sea was too wild in winter for fragile Greek boats, which had to be drawn up on the shore. Originally there was a simple port, the site was chosen back in the seventh century BC as there was a small natural cove protected from the prevailing winds by some islets. Then in Hellenistic times (first century BC), the port became a full city, named Apollonia for the patron deity of its mother town. In the fourth century BC, works were undertaken to improve protection against the north winds. An inner (western) port was created, with access by a narrow channel protected by two towers. Ships could be moored here or pulled up into dry dock. On the far eastern extremity of the islands, a lighthouse was built. These port arrangements were further improved in Roman times.

Apollonia was thus developed as a good anchorage, while to the landward side a long and carefully designed fortified wall, following the line of the land, was constructed. Drinking water was a big practical problem, however. Water had to come via an aquaduct from a spring 3 km away. Unless the garrison was especially strong, supplies could easily be stopped – hence the presence of numerous cisterns within the walls. Apollonia thus never had more than a maximum of 15,000 inhabitants. The town was the final point on both Greek and Roman road systems – there were no ancient roads along the coast, east-west communications being across the plateau.

A gradual sinking of the coastline became apparent in Byzantine times, and today the ancient port installations are submerged. The Byzantines undertook extensive quarrying of earlier constructions, no doubt toppled by the earthquake of 365AD, for their building needs. The result is that apart from the theatre, baths and city walls, little remains of the earlier periods in the city's history.

Dating back to 1897, the modern settlement of Susa was founded to house Greek-speaking Muslim refugees from Crete. The Italians extended the tiny village, adding church and bank, pasta and ice factories and even a small airport. Today, Susa is a backwater. The old Italian buildings are largely neglected, although there are a fair number of new villas going up – summer places or second homes for Susa people who have done well elsewhere.

Cyrenaica

## Visiting Apollonia

A rushed visit to Apollonia and its museum would take an hour. Two hours would be preferable, giving you time to relax and maybe have a quick paddle – although be warned, the rocky waters, so clear and tempting, can be treacherous. Don't miss the pocket **theatre** at the far east of the site, and take a look at the **Byzantine port installations**, also towards the eastern end of the site. There are the usual **Roman baths**, and **three basilicas**, witness to the importance of Apollonia in Byzantine days. After the vast expanses of Cyrene, Apollonia is an interesting, digestible site, where the changes to the built fabric over time are easily read. Like most other ancient places in Cyrenaica, it has material for a far more interesting museum. ■ *You start at the western end of the site. Ticket 3LD, from man in concrete box at metal gate.*

## The site

*The codes in bracket refer to the plan on Apollonia*

The visit starts with the **Western Gate** (AP1). To the right of the entrance gate is the **Western Basilica** (AP2), and a Byzantine construction, of which the massive arches survive, thought to have been a **Christian martyr's tomb** (AP3). The layout is appropriately cross-shaped. You then head east towards the **Central Basilica** (AP4), to the shore side of which is an interesting **Byzantine industrial site** (AP5). Numerous communicating cisterns can be seen, along with cisterns. Part of the area has crumbled into the sea, but the surviving ruins suggest that this was an industrial area, possibly used for processing fish or dying cloth.

## Apollonia

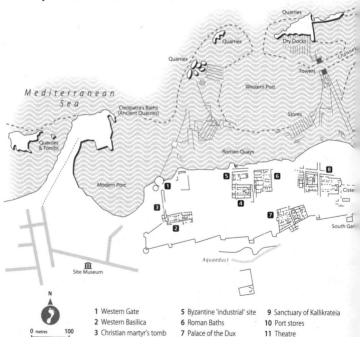

1 Western Gate
2 Western Basilica
3 Christian martyr's tomb
4 Central Basilica
5 Byzantine 'industrial' site
6 Roman Baths
7 Palace of the Dux
8 Eastern Basilica
9 Sanctuary of Kallikrateia
10 Port stores
11 Theatre

0 metres 100
0 yards 100

Cyrenaica

Just beyond the Central Basilica is a **Roman bath complex** (AP6), built **The Baths** between 75 and 125 AD. The Romans grafted their bath complex onto an earlier Hellenistic gymnasium, of which they kept the colonnaded courtyard and central plunge pool (*natatio*). The complex was largely destroyed by the earthquake of 365. Eroded column drums have been put back in position; Doric, Ionian and Corinthian capitals testify to the wealth of Roman Apollonia.

After the baths, inland, to your right, are the complex remains of the **Palace of** **A Byzantine** **the Dux** (AP7), thought to have been the residence of the Byzantine governor of **palace** the city. Columns and a couple of arches on the main courtyard have been re-erected. This palace was built in the sixth century AD, when Apollonia, then Sozusa, was capital of Libya Pentapolis. The discovery of a marble copy of the Edict of Anastasius on the military reorganisation of the province in 500 AD has led archaeologists to suppose that this was the governor's residence. Off the central courtyard, ceremonial rooms can be identified: a private chapel, north of the courtyard, a council chamber (east) and an audience hall with apse (south).

One of the finest monuments at Apollonia, however, is the **Eastern Basilica** **The Eastern** (**AP8**), excavated in the early 1920s and easily identified from afar by its cipolline **Basilica** marble columns. The entrance is on the north side of the building. After a small portico, the worshipper would enter the main nave. To the left of the eastern (altar) end of the nave was a baptistery, easily identified by its trefoil layout. In the centre of the baptistery are the remains of a font. Fragments of mosaic paving can still be seen in situ. The finest mosaics from this church, comparable in quality to those at Qasr Libia, can be seen in Apollonia Museum. A few metres to the east of this basilica is another religious site, the **Sanctuary of Kallikrateia** (9). Despite damage caused by later quarrying work, three small altars carved into the rock and a funerary chamber can be seen.

Some 50 m further to the east, next to the shore, is **port storage area** (**AP10**). There are storerooms, while the vaulted structures were probably cisterns. Nearby are four circular vats, hollowed out of the rock. These were probably used for macerating fish to make *garum*, the fish paste so highly appreciated by the ancient Romans. Still further east along the present shoreline, a French underwater archaeological mission discovered fish tanks, richly decorated with marble and statues. In 1998, statues were discovered here including a drunken Dionysos with satyr and a colossal portrait of one of the Ptolemies. There is probably much of interest still down in the glass-clear waters of Apollonia's ancient harbours.

Cyrenaica

**The**
**best-preserved**
**theatre**
The final monument on this circuit is the **theatre** (AP11), uncovered in the early 1960s and the best preserved theatre of its kind in Cyrenaica. Situated outside the walls, the theatre would seem to have been built in Roman times, albeit to a Greek model. (A dedicatory plaque on the stage wall declares it to have been built under Diocletian in 92 AD.) The theatre was largely dismantled in Byzantine times, the stones being recycled in other buildings. Finally, just southeast of the theatre, is yet another quarry area, partly re-used as a necropolis at a later date. Further exploration along the coast will bring you to other tombs and the remains of a Greek fortress.

**Apollonia**
**Museum**
'O temps suspends ton vol', some wag has inscribed in the visitor's book at Apollonia Museum. Little seems to have changed since the 1950s. The caretaker can generally be summoned from his iron bedstead inside. He will willingly find current for the lights. The neon buzzes and flickers alarmingly in the closely shuttered rooms. There are some fine pieces here, from Ra's Hilal as well as Apollonia. Happily the yellowing labels are in English – a legacy of Professor Goodchild's day?

**Hippolytus' tale**
At the entrance, you cannot miss a large **Roman sarcophagus**, carved with hunting scenes in bas relief. Dating from the late Antonine/early Severan period (late second, early third century AD), the sarcophagus carvings tell the myth of the hunter Hippolytus. Phedra, wife of Theseus, conceived a great desire for Hippolytus, who refused her advances. Phedra went for unpleasant tactics, accusing him of raping her. Unfortunately, Hippolytus had sworn to his old nurse that he would say nothing of his mother-in-law's vile behaviour. Thus his father cursed him, rousing a monster from the deep. The creature scared the lights out of the horses drawing Hippolytus' chariot. The horses panicked, Hippolytus lost control, and was dragged to death as the vehicle careered along the beach. Thus ends another Greek dysfunctional family tale. On the front of the sarcophagus, Phedra can be seen with her servants; Hippolytus was in the middle, while the old nurse, kneeling, and the hunting companions to the right. On the rear side of the sarcophagus is a hunting scene with a wild boar.

Also in the entrance area of the museum are **mosaics of Ktisis and Kosmesis** from the basilica at Ra's Hilal. In Byzantine times, such representations seem to have been popular for churches, Ktisis symbolising 'foundation' and Kosmesis 'beautification'.

**Funerary**
**remains and**
**mosaics**
In the corridor to the left of the entrance hall is a case of terra-cotta figurines and vessels, all votive offerings. Some of the figurines represent the goddess Artemis holding a silphium plant in the right hand. In the far room to the left are more **Byzantine mosaics**. Look out in particular for the panel featuring **Noah and his ark**, and some nice panels featuring a leopard and a serpent, both from the Eastern Basilica at Apollonia. There are also some fine marble plaques from the basilicas at Atrun, and a marble reliquary from the chapel of the Palace of the Dux.

**Statuary,**
**inscriptions and**
**local life**
To the right of the entrance hall is a small room containing some pieces of **Hellenistic statuary** and another with funerary busts. Also to be seen are some fragments of the Edict of Anastasius from the Palace of the Dux. To the right is a room with cases of the usual slightly mouldy pieces of traditional craftwork.

## Essentials

Not much choice here. The last guest left the *Albergo Roma* long ago and the devel- **Sleeping** opment of sleepy Apollonia as the summer resort for Al Bayda is just a profitable idea lurking in a building contractor's mind for the moment. There is only one (summer) accommodation option, a tourist village to the west of town, turn left at the check-point as you come down from the plateau. The **C** *Susa Holiday Village*, T0853-2365 or 084-26551 is always full in summer, reservations essential. In winter it tends to close down. Rooms 20LD and 30LD. Not terribly clean.

# Excursions south and east of Al Bayda

## Al Bayda to Lamluda via Slonta

If you have time and can arrange to hire a car, there is a pleasant excursion into the undulating empty countryside south of Al Bayda, taking in a former Italian village, the strange cult site of **Slonta** and the fort at **Gaygab** (also spelt Geigab). This route brings you out onto the main Al Bayda to Derna road near Lamluda, whence you could cut across the plateau northwards to Ra's Hilal.

Heading west out of Al Bayda centre, turn left (south) where the pine avenue begins. At the end of the built up area, fork right onto the lower road (where there is much rubbish by the roadside for the goats to eat). At the first checkpoint, there is a staggered junction: go right, and then left almost immediately. Some 5 km on you will pass a **minor archaeological site** with a few rock tombs to the right, an indication of the region's economic vitality in classical times. Heading south, 11 km further on, you will see the substantial remains of a **Byzantine fortified building** surrounded by a lesser wall. There is a double cistern to the southwest. The building occupies an impressive position commanding views over a wild moorland. The road eventually runs into a gentler shallow valley, and single storey Italian farmhouses appear, some abandoned, others used as outbuildings for newer farm buildings alongside. You come to a T-junction with checkpoint, where you turn right and head up towards **Umar al Mukhtar**, the former Villagio Mameli, visible on a ridge 1 km up the road. The village has a large square – or piazza one should say – dominated by an impressive former church with triple portico and pitched roof. The whitewashed buildings have received touches of official green. The formality of the square fits well with the austere countryside of this, the highest part of the Jabal.

# The Eastern Jabal Akhdar

Cyrenaica

**Slonta** After a short pause at the village, head back down to the T-junction, where you go straight ahead. Follow the road, which after a few kilometres will bring you to the village of Slonta, chiefly famed for its mysterious **grotto-sanctuary**. As you reach the village, you will see a small area of one-storey social housing to your left. Either turn left where the dual carriageway ends, before housing or turn left uphill after the housing. The sanctuary is about 50 m uphill behind a breeze-block wall set with a metal door. Visitors are not terribly frequent, and you might ask at the café on the main square for the caretaker's whereabouts.

The grotto of Slonta is one of the more obscure archaeological sites of Libya. Once the key has been found, the metal door creaks open to reveal a small space a few metres square, open to the sky, around which run low limestone ledges. These are carved with faces and animals, some much eroded. A round base suggests that this was once a sort of cave, its roof supported by a pillar. (The presence of other small caves on the hillside, some used as animal shelters, would seem to support this hypothesis.) Broadly speaking, from left to right, the carvings are as follows. On the left-hand (western) side, as you come in, the carvings are difficult to interpret. Moving to the right, behind the pillar at the back, is a strange horizontal snake, around which human faces and animals can be distinguished. Next along to the right, back in a corner, are some faintly sinister human heads with bulging eyes. Then, further forward, is a sort of block: on top are carved what look like four pigs, (an offering to some unknown deity?), while round the sides are small figures, some with a hand on the head. Finally, on furthest right as you stand facing the carvings is a group of figures (four adults and two children?). Next to it is another group with a large head and a female figure in a long robe.

No one knows who made the carvings of Slonta. Was it some of the region's original Berber inhabitants, influenced by incoming Greeks? The shrine lay on one of the most important routes in ancient times leading from Barce via Cyrene to Darnis. It is the only surviving cult site of the pre-Greek population, and as such fascinated travellers in the nineteenth century. The nature of the cult has aroused much speculation – was the pig a sacred animal to these people? Whatever, the images have an eerie fascination, and even on a bright spring day, the small staring faces looking out from under a rock can send a shiver down the spine.

Sadly, the dancing figures and gargoyles of Slonta have been exposed to the elements for far too long. There have been some crude attempts at 'repair' with concrete, but in all honesty the Antiquities Department should get its act together to protect the site properly. Note that if you do not have time to make it to Slonta, then you can still see a representation of the site at the Jamahiriya Museum, Tripoli.

**Gaygab** After Slonta, the road continues east towards **Faydiya** across one of the highest parts of the Jabal Akhdar. You cut straight east through Faydiya heading for Gaygab, where there is a **small fort** built in 1852 by the Turks and Abu Bakr Bey Haddud, head of the Barasa tribe, who was named local governor by Constantinople. The fort is on your left, about 75 m from the road, as you drive into the village. Inside is a small natural history and local life museum where the clock slowed and stopped sometime in the late 1950s. No-one seems to come here any more, and display rooms around the courtyard are firmly shuttered. The museum displays exude the enthusiasm of committed local history enthusiasts. There are fossilized tree-trunks, and a very scholarly case of dusty orange-tip butterflies, a mastodon's tusk and a big diorama of local animals. (The leopard, poor thing, is terribly mangy now.) There are large numbers of stuffed birds, local costumes and harnesses, tent assembly equipment, and a rusting chunk of machine gun. A case of small arms and bayonets contains only labels. The neon lights flicker and hum, and it is a relief to get back out into the courtyard, graced by a few small lichen-patched statues. Gaygab's worthy local council has lost the taste for displaying knowledge to its inhabitants.

After Gaygab, continue east along the main road, which eventually forks. Take the left hand fork and head north for the main Al Bayda – Derna road, which you will intersect at Lamluda.

## Lamluda to Susa (Apollonia): uplands and a wild coastline

This drive takes you across a beautiful empty stretch of upland and down to what is perhaps the most beautiful stretch of coast in Cyrenaica. In a day, you could reasonably cover the **basilicas at Ra's Hilal and Natrun** (Al Atrun), along with the ancient site of **Apollonia**. (Heading back up to Al Bayda via Shahat to complete a loop, you could also take a look at the Greek necropolis of Cyrene.) There are two sites up in the Jabal escarpment on this route, the remains of **St Mark's monastery** and the great **Hawa Al Ftea cavern**. As the monastery is a substantial uphill hike, it might best be combined with a long day out including the two basilicas.

A few kilometres after the Cyrene crossroads and Al Abraq airport, you come to another crossroads, where the remains of ancient **Lamluda** are visible immediately on your left (see page 187). You turn left at this junction, and head north across almost empty plateau land. Just beyond a ridge, several massive blocks of stone, (the remains of an ancient mausoleum?) come into view. You go left at the fork here, and continue across open country. Eventually, you will see two almost complete Hellenistic mausolea, the **Snibat al Awila**, one on each side of the road. Dating from the second century BC, they were shored up by Italian archaeologists in 1935. Continue to follow the road and fork right at the next junction. Drive carefully, as the road runs steeply down the steep sided Wadi Gla'a, to come out on the coast road to the east of **Ra's Hilal**, 'Cape of the Crescent Moon'. It might be best to start with the basilica at **Al Atrun** (also referred to as Natrun) some 15 km east along the coast.

For Al Atrun, heading east from the Ra's Hilal junction, you turn off left, **Al Atrun** seawards, down a minor road when you come to an area of small fields set with palm trees to your left. There is plenty of water here, and you can see why the Byzantines chose this site for a basilica. The road turns right, you pass between fields, and there are new houses under construction. (If you pay attention, the basilica's re-erected columns are just about visible from main road and side road.) After about 100 m, stop at the eastern end of the sequence of houses on your left, and tramp along a field drain for 50 m towards the sea. Then, low and behold, you will see the sugar-white columns of the Basilica of Atrun, ancient Erythron. The original white marble facing has been arranged on the ground like a giant jigsaw puzzle, the columns have neatly carved crosses and some splendid Corinthian capitals. There was fine mosaic paving, too. The building is very different in tone to the grim-walled basilica of Qasr Libia. In winter, the waves crash against the rocks below. In summer, the local *shabab* dive off the cliffs into stiller waters, a drop of a good 6 m. On the cliff face just east of the basilica are numerous tiny openings: once tombs or troglodyte summer homes? Atrun has a wonderful unspoiled feel– but for how long?

The next important early Christian site on this coast (the church of Wadi **Wadi Margus** Margus) is up in the escarpment. The turn off for the track leading up to the site is 6 km after Ra's Hilal, on your right as you go east. (You might ask at the

Cyrenaica

police station in Ra's Hilal to get them to show you the turn off. Otherwise, ask at one of the small houses at the roadside near the mouth of the wadi. A caretaker might turn up.) The site is an 8 km walk up in the hillside. Whether this church, high up in the gorge, was actually founded by St Mark is a moot point. St Mark was born in Cyrene, and after the death of Christ returned to his native land. Then he headed for Egypt to spread the word, and was martyred there.

**Ra's Hilal** Driving west to the coast road junction, the peninsula of Ra's Hilal is clearly visible, providing a sheltered anchorage – just the place for an ancient settlement on a wild coast. Just after the junction with the road from Lamluda, there is a small settlement on your right, between road and sea. This was founded by the Italians as **Al Fajr** (Alba), in the late 1930s, as part of their attempt at settling the nomads in organized farming schemes. The village met little success at the time. Today, the neat original village centre with souk and mosque are still in place. Nearby is a holiday village, rather Soviet Block in feel.

The early Christian site of Ra's Hilal is on the headland. Going west, head uphill on the coast road from the old Italian village. There is a turn off right onto the headland after a few 100m. Head down a track, to your right, where there is an abandoned lighthouse. The site is about 100m down the track, on your right but invisible from the track because of the scrub and trees. There is a concrete storage building and the usual metal gate, carefully tied shut with a bootlace. The basilica has one of the most beautiful locations on the coast. After prayer, worshippers would have gathered on the east-facing porch of their church with its splendid views of sea, coast and mountain. Below the church is a semi-abandoned sheltered harbour, no doubt with some good swimming. The three-nave church itself, with altar to the west, still has some marble marquetry flooring in place, and must have been real bijou in its day. It was here that the mosaics of Ktisis and Kosmesis in the Apollonia Museum were discovered. There is a baptismal font in the left chapel, and a well with cistern next to the entrance. Various turfy, bushy humps in the enclosure suggest more collapsed buildings. Stones with Arabic inscriptions, now in Apollonia Museum, indicate that the building continued in use after the Islamic conquest.

After Ra's Hilal, head along the coast road in the direction of Susa, 20 km to the west. The road has been much widened and improved. In the past, the old road, crossing the poor, windswept terrain of the coastal plateau, was much effected by wadis in flood sweeping the tarmac away. The next site along here is the cave of **Hawa Ftea**, a few kilometres east of Susa. Prehistoric finds from the cave, reputedly the largest in North Africa, are on display in the Jamahirya Museum in Tripoli. The cave, a great gaping opening in the Jabal escarpment, looks north towards the sea. Here early humankind built its communities, safe from marauders and beasts up on their rocky ledges.

After your scramble up to Hawa Ftea, Susa-Apollonia is the next stop. If you have made good time, it may be possible for a last dose of ancient ruins before sundown (see Apollonia above for details).

## The eastern Jabal Akhdar: (Al Bayda to Derna)

East of Al Bayda, the road heads across the plateau for Derna, easternmost city in Cyrenaica, passing through a couple of former Italian villages before dipping down the Jabal Akhdar escarpment to Derna. On reaching the Cyrene (Shahat) crossroads, there is an opportunity for a side excursion to the **Roman cisterns at Safsaf**. At the crossroads, turn right. After 0.7 km, there is another crossroads, where you go left. Safsaf lies 7.5 km further on. The cistern is to the left (northeast) of the road, in front of a modern wall; there are houses to the right. At over 300 paces long, the carefully engineered single unit construction is impressive. Although much of the barrel-vaulted roof is intact, with regular holes for drainage, the interior is largely silted up. The cistern bears witness to the Romans' excellent water management skills, and the extent to which it was necessary to plan for water in a region where, despite the generally abundant winter rains, there could be supply problems in the summer. The road leads on to the former village of Battisti and thence to Faydiya.

After the Shahat/Safsaf crossroads, you head east across open country, passing the Al Bayda airfield at Al Abraq to the right. Next point of note are the as yet un-excavated remains of **Lamluda** to the left (left turn here to head north for Ra's Hilal). Lamluda, Roman Limnias, was probably a major settlement in ancient times, to judge by the stones still standing. Some of these would have been doorposts, others uprights as used in the *opus Africanum* construction system. After Lamluda, the road then passes through the former Italian village of Giovanni Berta, now **Qubba**, a spruce sort of settlement which greets you with a big blue and yellow *marhaban* (welcome) sign. There are blocks of flats picked out with green on the left, and the old Italian buildings of Berta among the eucalyptus trees on the eastern side of the settlement. Here in classical times there was plenty of water and a fountain dedicated to Apollo. Both Luigi di Savoia (back towards Lamluda) and Berta were among the first settlements put up by the Ente per la colonizzazione della Libia. After Qubba, the road continues to the east across rolling countryside to **Ayn Mara**, after which it winds spectacularly down to **Derna** on the coastal plain. There are fine views of the sea. All that is missing are islands specked with white villages. The breakers crash against some reefs off-shore. Arriving at Derna, there is a checkpoint, generally fairly strict, before the final approach to the town through a desolate zone of *terrains vagues* and semi-abandoned public buildings. At the checkpoint, you can also turn left to follow the coast road west along to Karsa, Natrun, Ra's Hilal and Susa (Apollonia).

Cyrenaica

Marmarica

6

Marmarica

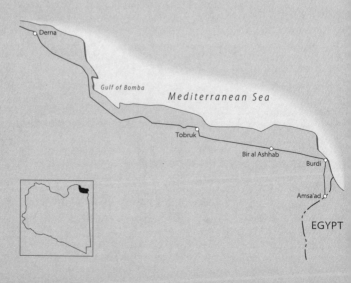

The easternmost region of Libya was dubbed Marmarica by the first European travellers sometime in the 18th century. The term is used variably but basically refers to the isolated and arid region stretching east from Derna to the Egyptian frontier. Here life was essentially nomadic. Rainfall is insufficient for more than a sparse population, and sedentary life was impossible until modern times outside a few rare oasis settlements like Derna.

East of **Derna**, the Jabal Akhdar gives way to an arid coastline, although the sands of the Bay of **Bomba** might be a worthwhile detour. There would be little reason to come here, had not some of the fiercest battles between the Allies and the Axis been fought here during the Second World War. Near **Tobruk** in easternmost Libya, four war cemeteries commemorate the dead on both sides. If you are travelling through to Egypt, you will pass melancholy **Al Burdi** before reaching the undistinguished border town of Amsa'ad.

Marmarica

# Derna    درنة

Phone code: 081 Easternmost town in Cyrenaica, Derna makes a good stopping point on the long drive east to Tobruk. The first Greek settlements were in this region, and within living memory it was a pleasant coastal oasis sitting between the scarp of the Jabal Akhdar and the sea. In the 1930s, it was 'la perla della Cirenaica'. Derna has a port and seaside promenade, two large mosques, a small souk, and inland, just up the Wadi Derna, a waterfall. The cascade comes pounding out of a low cliff, a surprising sight in the ochre-arid valley.

## Ins and outs

**Getting there**  By public transport, Derna is easily reached from Al Bayda and Tobruk. Journey time from Al Bayda share-taxi station is around 70 mins, cost 3LD. From Tobruk, journey time to Derna is over 3 hrs, distance 163 km. Susa is just 70 km from Derna, but there are no (or few) share taxis on this route. Best to try and hitch. By public transport, Derna is an easy day trip from Al Bayda. There are a few buses, but share taxi is the quickest means of transport for short hops in this region.

**Getting around**  Share taxis will let you out close to the town centre, or at the *agensiya*, a short walk east out of town overlooking the port. Everything can easily be covered on foot, apart from the *shallal* (waterfall), about 5 km up the Wadi Derna. Take a local taxi, which will cost you 5LD for a quick round trip with a short photo stop at the falls.

## History and background

Ancient Darnis comes insignificantly into history as a Greek settlement, mentioned by Ptolemey. Perhaps it was too unsafe an anchorage to attract major settlement, perhaps the access from the plateau was too difficult and the ports at Apollonia, Ptolemaïs and Teucheira quite sufficient for ancient needs. In Byzantine times, Derna was a little luckier, having its own bishop, and was no doubt the scene of internecine struggles between Catholics and Donatists. There was fierce fighting here during the Arab conquest, but it was only with the arrival of Muslim settlers from Spain in the late 15th century that Derna began to take shape as a town. In 1600, under the rule of an Ottoman governor, one Muhammad Bey, development continued apace, and merchants from Tripoli came to trade. A public works programme created a new mosque and channelled the wadi that divides the town.

**The USA versus the Qaramanlis: dirty dealings in Derna**  Derna's moment of historical glory was in 1805, when the United States of America and the Qaramanli dynasty of Tripoli clashed over piracy in the Mediterranean. The story is one of complex local politics and secret deals. Under Yussef Qaramanli (r1797-1805), Tripoli became something of a Mediterranean power. Piracy took off in a big way, and in 1797, the Ottomans sent a present of two warships to Tripoli. By 1805, Tripoli had 24 warships, many captured from European nations. The Americans thought that Yussef Qaramanli's brother, Ahmad, governor of Derna, would make a pliable ally if made Governor of Tripoli. This US vision of Mediterranean politics turned out to be on the simplistic side, however (this was not to be the only occasion on which US foreign policy was to come a cropper in Libya). Ahmad, re-installed in Derna by the Americans after fleeing to Egypt, proved unable to raise an effective army, and before long the town was besieged by tribal warriors and forces from Tripoli. In the event, the Americans concluded a treaty with Yussef Qaramanli in June 1805,

## Deportation from Derna

In the 1930s, Danish Muslim traveller **Knud Holmboe** visited Cyrenaica. Italian repression was at its height, and with the assistance of East African troops, the fascist military went about putting an end to all possible resistance in the region with relentless thoroughness. General Graziani gave no quarter, all prisoners being hanged or shot. ("When Arabs were to be hanged - and that happened nearly every day in Benghazi - all patriotic Italians went out with cameras to secure lasting records of the execution of traitors"). As all telegrams were censored, European public opinion had no idea what was going on.

Holmboe travelled across Cyrenaica, aiming for Egypt. Unfortunately, the Italian military authorities got wind of his pro-Arab sympathies, and he got stuck in Derna, where he was refused permission to leave. He quickly got to know the locals, arousing Italian suspicions by frequenting both mosque and local cafés. First hand, he observed a crass and cruel occupation: blind misunderstanding, denunciations and summary executions. Eventually, Holmboe too was arrested and thrown into Derna gaol. However, unlike the four sheikhs in the cell next door, he survived and was deported. His travels appeared in the book Desert Encounter (London: Harrap, 1936). They remain the sole published eyewitness account of colonial barbarism in Libya available in English.

evacuated Derna, and paid a large ransom for a US ship captured by Tripoli in 1803, the start of the trouble in the first place.

After all this excitement on the international stage, the rest of the 19th century was quiet for Derna: plague struck in 1816, and the population fell to the 500 mark.

In October 1911, Derna once more made the international headlines, being one of the five Libyan towns seized by Italy. The Ottomans withdrew and resistance took shape under Turkish officers, in training camps at Gharyan, Benghazi and near Derna. Libyans, both Sanusis and non-Sanusis, enlisted. The Derna camp was particularly effective, run by one Enver Pacha, ably assisted by Mustapha Kamel, the future Kamel Ataturk. Enver Bey was to leave a diary of his time in the region. The camp brought new hope to the region, organizing some schooling and a bank. Over 350 sons of local sheikhs were sent to Constantinople for military training. Eventually, however, Enver Bey was forced to return home to take an active part in the Balkan War. **Enver Bey, local hero?**

In the event, Ottomans and Italians negotiated a peace agreement, made public in October 1912, leading to the withdrawal of Turkish officers and troops from Libya. But via Enver Pasha, the Ottomans left a glimmer of hope. Near Derna, in November 1912, Enver Pasha handed a message to the Sanusi leader, Sayyid Ahmad al Sharif, in which the Sultan entrusted him with the leadership of Libya, making him responsible for its defence against foreign aggression. Thus from late 1912, the Sanusis referred to their amirate and, for the first time, to a Sanusi government.

Under the Italians, Derna had a brief period as a fashionable resort for Cyrenaica. A fine hotel was constructed, the *Grand'Albergo Derna*, in an austere modernist style which must have fitted well with the vernacular building of the oasis settlement. (Mussolini is said to have stayed there.) In the 1960s, travel writer Ward described Derna as "a beautiful town, with palms overlooking the streets and the sound of water everywhere". But reinforced concrete and modern politics arrived. In the 1990s, Derna was a hotbed of Islamic revivalism. Opposition was put down; the escarpment where the fundamentalists **The Pearl of Cyrenaica**

Marmarica

took refuge was torched. Out of season, Derna feels very much like 'the seaside town they forgot to close down'. A road bridge stops in mid-flyover, unidentified public buildings stand empty on the coast road, the promenade's concrete umbrellas no longer look like cutting-edge urban design. Still, here and there are hints of the old Derna, palm trees and vine arbours, bougainvillaea draped across courtyards in the souk. The main square with its ficus trees and arcades is pleasant on a summer evening.

## Sights

Derna town and the waterfall can be toured in a couple of hours. The Wadi Derna, subject to flash flooding and so carefully channelled by concrete engineering works, divides the town in two. If you come in from the east side, down the main street, the first main site is the large and modern **Mosque of Sidi Zuhayr**, just opposite a market. This is the last resting place of one Zuhayr ibn Qays al Balawi, who, along with 70 warriors, died here. Back in the seventh century, Sidi Zuhayr and his men headed west to Kairouan, (in present day Tunisia), to avenge the death of the Muslim general Uqba ibn Nafi'. But on their return east, they found the Byzantines lying in wait at Derna. The Muslim forces were overwhelmed by superior numbers. Initially buried up in caves in the hillside, the warriors were later given a worthy burial place in the mosque dedicated to Sidi Zuhayr. Next to the tombs is a well whose water is said to have miraculous properties.

Over the wadi in the western half of town, the number two sight is also religious, the **Great Mosque** (Al Jami' al Kabir) or **Mosque of Muhammad Bey**, named for the Ottoman governor who had it built in 1689. The building is easily located, being on the square behind the main hotel. This mosque was one of the largest in Libya, with the roof of the prayer hall formed by 42 small domes. But like so many of Libya's mosques, it endured extensive remodelling in the late 20th century. The plan is the same, however. The minaret dates from 1901 after the collapse of the original construction.

As you stand on the square facing the Great Mosque's arcades, the arched entrance to the souk is on your left. (The *Funduk Jabal al Akdhar's* entrance is behind you, to the right.) Exploring further, you may find a small square with a fountain featuring vines and a piece of ancient masonry, vaulted passageways, jewellers, the odd stall with local craftwork and as per usual lots of imported shoes and clothes. A fig tree peers over a wall.

**Waterfall on the Wadi Derna** All taxi drivers will assume you will need to nip up to the **waterfall on the Wadi Derna**, the town's chief touristic claim to fame. For most of the year, the wadi is dry, the sort of place where small boys play football, the odd goat roots in the rubbish and plastic bags blow in the wind. The road on the west bank of the wadi leads inland some 5 km to the waterfall. After about 2.5 km, at the start of the gorge, you cross the wadi to the east bank. The road narrows, running under the cliffs between hedges of reeds and oleander. There are tiny orchards of pomegranate, orange and almond trees. In summer, the cascade and around is popular with picnickers from town. You can stand on the concrete bridge to catch the cool spray. Children try to spot where the rainbow begins as the water comes over the cliff.

## Ali Ridha Pasha and the Tobruk project

In the late 19th century, the Ottoman Empire was under pressure from all sides. Nationalist movements menaced the Sublime Porte's hold in the Balkans while in the southern Mediterranean, the French were well established in Algeria. French influence had grown in Tunisia too which, in principle at least, was an Ottoman vassal state. Thus Tripoli of the West became an outpost from which the Porte tried to save what little influence it had left in North Africa. The modernizing reforms or tanzimat, already operational elsewhere in the Empire, were introduced.

From 1867 to 1870, a far sighted governor, Ali Ridha Pasha al Jazayri tried to take the reforms further. He had the harbour at Benghazi dredged with French technical assistance and developed elaborate plans for a new port at Tobruk. With the opening of the Suez Canal, a new port on the inhospitable coast between Alexandria and Benghazi would clearly be a viable proposition. A large quarantine facility was constructed, along with a barracks and warehouses. Families were settled, a Catholic order was offered land to build a hospice, the idea being to attract Maltese immigrants. In 1869, Ali Ridha Pasha himself set sail for Tobruk to supervise the works.

However, the Ottoman port of Tobruk was not to be. Concessions had been granted to French nationals, thus arousing other powers' suspicions. British manoeuvrings in Istanbul changed the Porte's vision of Ali Ridha's development activities. He was portrayed as using the same methods as the French had used in colonizing Algeria, which would create the risk of the tribes rebelling against the Ottoman government. (Already, despite the common bond of Islam, the Turks were seen as an outside imperial power.) Ali Ridha was requested to refrain from further ambitious innovations, and finally, in May 1870, was recalled to Istanbul without explanation.

Marmarica

## Essentials

**D** *Funduq Jabal al Akhdar*, off the main square, T22303 or 23858, F25858. Lobby with 1930s mosaic floor intact, magnificent domed reception area. Some of the accommodation is in the form of 2-room suites with sagging armchairs. Check that water works in your room. Cleanliness doubtful. Did you bring a sheet and towels? Reception does its best but doesn't have much idea really. **D** *Funduq al Madina*, T25401. Very centrally located, a few paces from the main square. (Down a side street to your left as you face the mosque arcades and souk entrance.) Respectable, used by people travelling between the Egyptian frontier and Benghazi. The best option. **E** *Funduq Ifriqiya*. Barracks-like building just over the road from the *agensiya* share taxi station. Prefer *Funduq al Madina*. **E** *Funduq al Bahr*. T26506. On the sea front. Restaurant nearby. Best avoided. Emergencies only.

**Sleeping**
*Compared with Al Bayda, Derna is well provided with hotels*

There are a few eateries near the sea front and near the souk with the usual Egyptian cooking. Try the restaurant near the *Funduq al Bahr* close to the seafront.

**Eating**

Share taxi connections for **Al Bayda**, **Benghazi** and **Tobruk** from the share taxi station on the eastern outskirts of town.

**Transport**

# From Derna to Tobruk

The road heads out for Tobruk onto an arid plateau, the easternmost outpost of the Jabal Akhdar. Some 10 km from Derna is the left turn for Sidi 'Awn. Another 7 km further on is the turn off for Martuba. The coast dips southwards, and some 60 km from Derna are the sea and sands of the **Gulf of Bomba**. Unfortunately, the peninsula is off-limits to civilians. Out in the sea is the **Island of Plateia**, where the Greek settlers landed for the first time in the seventh century BC. If you want to head back into Cyrenaica, then there is a turn taking you back towards Al Marj 75 km from Derna. After this highlight, there is some 90 km of arid, largely flat terrain to cross before you reach Tobruk, passing through the road-movie settlement of Qurdaba. The **Acroma Knightsbridge British cemetery** is west of Tobruk, just before a check point. If travelling by share Peugeot, the taxi station in Tobruk is next to the football ground.

## Tobruk    طبرق

*Phone code: 087*  Though built on a sort of promontory next to its port, Tobruk was probably never very picturesque. Even though it was one of the few natural harbours on the Marmarican coast, Tobruk attracted little interest before the 19th century. Some writers consider it to be the ancient town of **Antipyrgos**. Neither the Mamluk dynasties of Egypt nor the Qaramanlis of Tripoli bothered with it. In the early 1870s, Ottoman governor of Tripoli Ali Ridha Pasha came up with a major port development scheme, eventually abandoned. Tobruk was eventually developed by the Italians as they needed some sort of settlement at the eastern end of the Litoranea. It became famous for the poundings it received during the Second World War. The city changed hands five times as the Allies and the Axis struggled for supremacy in the western Egyptian desert in the autumn of 1942. This was a key time in the war. At the same time, the Allies were landing in Morocco and Algeria, and a few weeks later Stalingrad capitulated.

Post-war rebuilding has not produced anything distinguished. Tobruk now has a flourishing souk. Migrant workers from Egypt and further east pass through. In the middle of Tobruk, near the souk, is the bunker from which generals planned their manoeuvres. You may also find a few bits of Second World War artillery and (unless it has been moved), the wreck of a US Airforce plane.

The main reason for getting all the way to Tobruk are the **four war cemeteries** (Knightsbridge Acroma, German, Commonwealth and French). It is rumoured that the bunker in Tobruk itself will be converted into a museum. There is also an abandoned Italian war cemetery near Burdi, close to the Egyptian frontier.

**Sleeping**  **C** *Funduq al Masira*, near the road running towards the border, T25761/2/3. Very similar in all respects to another 1970s monster, the *Hotel Gozltik* in Misrata. Absurdly expensive if you have to pay in dollars changed at the official exchange rate. Otherwise reasonable at 40LD a night.

There are other small hotels near the souk patronized by immigrant workers travelling between Egypt and their places of work in Libya.

**Eating**  Plenty of cheap eateries near the souk. Otherwise try the *Mat'am Bab al Bahr*, on the bay near the football ground.

**Travel agencies**  *Antipyrgos*, in the Funduq al Masira, T25761, F25709. Has various tours on offer, including the ancient sites of Cyrenaica and the oases of the eastern Libyan desert.

# The war cemeteries

Most European visitors to this part of the world will be making a pilgrimage of kinds to one of the war cemeteries, maintained to the memory of those who fell during the bloody campaigns of the Second World War. All four can easily be visited as a day trip from Tobruk. The German cemetery, an austere ochre stone fortress, is certainly the most impressive. There are no rigid opening hours. On the whole, if you turn up at a reasonable time, the caretaker can be found in his house nearby.

For the record, around 27,000 soldiers fell in Libya during the Second World War, including 11,000 Italians, 8,500 British and Commonwealth, 6,000 Germans, and 128 French. After the carnage, the survivors buried the dead as best as they could. War poet James Walker (RAF) wrote of the graves at Tobruk that most were anonymous; "With stones heaped over them to keep their bones/ Longer, a little, from jackals and raven."

**Knightsbridge Acroma Cemetery**

Coming in from the west, the Knightsbridge Acroma Cemetery is the first one you reach, some 20 km before Tobruk. It is not very well signed. Look out for a mosque on the right and some tamarisk trees. The cemetery is about 200 m from the road. A drive planted with ficus trees leads to the entrance, and the caretaker lives in a house opposite the cemetery. He has a book with the names of all those who gave their lives, 3,670 of them. A great cross protects the cemetery, 'Their name liveth for ever more' reads the inscription on the central mausoleum.

**Commonwealth War Cemetery**

The Commonwealth War Cemetery at Tobruk is 4 km to the east of town, to the left of the main road for Alexandria. At the entrance is the long-silent bell of HMS Liverpool. Long lines of simple white stones bear the heartfelt words of family members. There are Australians, British, Czechs, Indians, Irish, and Libyans, Christians, Jews, and Muslims buried here. You will find a memorial to the Australian dead, the Stone of Remembrance, and the Cross of Sacrifice.

**French War Cemetery**

Smaller than the others, the French War Cemetery is 6 km southeast of Tobruk, near the intersection of the Tobruk to Alexandria road and the road leading to the airport and across southern Cyrenaica to Adjabiya. A small building styled like a Saharan fort marks the entrance. Despite its small size, this is an important cemetery, commemorating the stiff resistance put up by the Free French Forces at the Battle of Bir Hakeim, out in the desert 90 km south of Tobruk. For more than a week, from 27 May to 10 June 1942, some 3,000 men managed to block the advance of Rommel's Afrika Korps, thus enabling the British forces to pull back into Egypt in good order. Originally, the bodies were buried at Bir Hakeim. However, when the graves at Bir Hakeim and elsewhere in the desert were desecrated during the Algerian War of Independence, they were moved up to this purpose-built cemetery at Tobruk. Those buried here are a cosmopolitian mix: there are African, French, Indochinese, and North African names. Here and there are the graves of legionnaires, some with Germanic sounding names. Carved in marble is the story of the heroic resistance at the Battle of Bir Hakeim.

**German Cemetery**

With its massive stone walls and round towers, the German Cemetery looks out over Tobruk like a medieval fortress. Built in 1954-1955, this is an unforgettable austere memorial to the folly of war. At the entrance, the inscription reads: 'From the German people to its soldiers who fell in Libya and their Field-Marshall Rommel'. Inside is a great courtyard, at the centre of which is the basin for the eternal flame, held up by four kneeling angels. Arcades run round three sides of the courtyard. On the walls are inscribed the names of all those who fell at Tobruk. All are equal in death in this austere monument: the names, picked out in white mosaic on a dark ground, run in alphabetical order.

As for the Italians, they no longer have any war graves in Libya at all. In 1972, the Libyan government asked for all graves to be removed from national territory. Some 9,000 Italian soldiers now lie in the **Sacrario Militare dei Caduti d'Oltremare** in Bari, southeast Italy.

## To the Egyptian frontier

From Tobruk, the road heads monotonously east to the frontier at Ams'ad. Some 70 km from Tobruk you pass through **Bir al Ashhab**, near which Umar al Mukhtar, the Libyan resistance hero, was born. The next settlement of any interest is **Al Burdi**, ex-Porto Bardia, 112 km from Tobruk. (Here there is a check point and a restaurant just after.) Turn off the main road to explore what remains of the former Italian village. The cliffs are magnificent, the waters of the bay deep and blue. In spring, there will be fishing vessels moored down below.

The **Libyan-Egyptian border** lies 129 km from Tobruk. It can take just two hours to get through or as long as eight. Between the two border posts is 1 km of no-man's land, which you can cross on foot or in a share taxi, price 1LD.

Marmarica

# The Jabal Nafusa and Ghadamès

7

# The Jabal Nafusa and Ghadamès

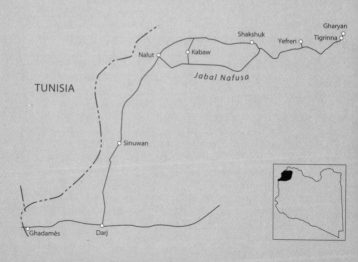

On the high plateau south of the Jefara Plain, the Jabal Nafusa has many resemblances with the Jabal Abyad over the border in Tunisia. Visited for its crumbling traditional Berber villages and fortified granaries, and for its spectacular arid landscapes, the rushed visitor to Libya, may think that this region, though beautiful, is not really a priority. The great Roman and Greek sites of Tripolitania and Cyrenaica and the desert landscapes and rock art of the Fezzan require a lot of time, and given the distances involved, it is difficult to do them justice in under three weeks. However, an organized tour taking in Ghadamès, will inevitably show you something of the Jabal Nafusa. So if you do have the time, there are some interesting corners and atmospheres well worth exploring.

**Gharyan**, 86 km south of Tripoli, is the region's main settlement, while **Nalut**, conveniently about halfway between Tripoli and Ghadamès, is at the far western end of the Jabal Nafusa. Other Berber settlements such as **Kabau** and **Yefren** are generally on visitors' itineraries for their ruined citadel villages and fortified granaries. But old villages are being gradually abandoned, and unfortunately the new settlements, sprawling and concrete built, have little accommodation on offer. Many people visit the sights of the Jabal Nafusa as day trips from Tripoli or as stops on the long drive southwest to the town of **Ghadamès**, with its unique earthen architecture and oasis calm. Once a halt on the trans-Saharan trade routes, it is now an essential stop on the four-wheel drive itinerary.

# Background

**Geography**

*Travellers heading for the Jabal Nafusa generally start at Tripoli. Note that in spring 2000, the Tunisian southern frontier post at Dehibat was closed for tourists. Travel on to Algeria from Libya is not feasible at the moment.*

The Jabal Nafusa is the highest part of a long plateau which runs from broken foothills, starting near Khums on the coast, in a long arc round into Tunisia. The Jabal starts at Qusbat, some 20 km to the southwest of Khums and rises to the Jabal Msellata and Jabal Tarhuna (see Tripolitania chapter, page 119), the best watered region (annual rainfall 300 mm) where the Italians founded agricultural estates. Next comes the Jabal Gharyan and the Jabal Nafusa, both largely 600 m above sea level. The scarp slope rises sharply from the Jefara Plain, reaching a maximum height of 900 m in places. In ancient times, this was a wooded and populous region, if sixth-century poet Corippus is to be believed.

To the south, the plateau dips gradually into a set of rough basins, the largest of which lies around the town of Mizda (reputed to be the home of sorcerers, weavers of spells and holy men). The Hammada al Hamra, a vast level-topped plateau, is reached after climbing another scarp to the south of Mizda.

**Climate**

The Jabal has a climate quite different from the Jefara. Rains are slightly less reliable than the northern plains and diminish rapidly from the crest of the scarp to the south. Most places have over 250 mm of rain per year (generally between October and March), although fluctuations are enormous. Winters are quite cold and snow and frost can be experienced on occasion. Air temperatures throughout the year are lower than on the Jefara. Both winter dress and sleeping bags need to be heavier and windproof. The evenings and nights in the summer are far more comfortable than in the plains.

**Traditional economy**

The agricultural year in the Jabal Nafusa starts in September, with land preparation and sowing. Most rainfall comes between October and March, however, both autumn and spring rains can fail. Thus the region's people have developed a mixed system of agriculture, raising flocks and practising low-yield agriculture.

Traditionally, dry cereal farming, albeit with very low yields, and fruit tree cultivation, especially olive trees and figs, were the main forms of agriculture. The Berber communities practised transhumance, and in a wet year, the pre-desert plateau, the Dahar, provided good winter grazing for flocks of sheep and goats. A small number of folk would remain behind in the hilltop settlements, while the majority would travel with flocks in search of pasture. There were exclusively pastoralist tribes too, who would obtain their needs in

# Jabal Nafusa

grain and dried fruit as part of a 'protection fee' with sedentary groups or by bartering meat and wool with them. Certain Berber groups would grow barley and some wheat on more fertile land on the Jefara Plain in the shadow of their mountain homes.

The Jabal economy has proved remarkably versatile. Agriculture survives in most areas and remains concentrated on growing cereals and rainfed orchard crops. Figs and apricots are still famous on the Jabal. Deep artesian wells now supplement meagre rainfall on land at the foot of the escarpment. The greatest source of funds for the Jabal groups is, however, remittance income from members of the family living elsewhere, usually in Tripoli or in other coastal towns. Even permanent residents of Tripoli have houses in their old tribal homes and a great deal of investment flows back to the Jabal villages in this way.

**The Jabal Nafusa today**

The region has reasonable hotels at Gharyan and Nalut. The 1930s hotel at Yefren is closed. Problems with accommodation can arise at Ghadamès at peak times of year (Christmas and Easter). Bring a sleeping bag – there have been cases of severe overbooking.

**Accommodation difficulties**

# South from Tripoli to Gharyan and the Jabal Nafusa

The Tripoli-Gharyan route (distance 86 km, driving time just over an hour), gives you an ideal cross-section of the landscape and climates from the Tripolitanian coast and up into the Jabal foothills.

The road south to Gharyan leads not only to the Jabal Nafusa, and from there to Ghadamès, but also down to the Fezzan, via Mizda, Qaryat and Sabha. The road heads through the long tentacles of the Tripoli suburbs. There are dense farmstead settlements out to the **Swani Ben Yadim** turn off. The road is dual carriageway and busy with traffic, mostly local. After the Swani Ben Yadim and Ben Ghashir towns/oases, the highway runs through a countryside of trees and orchards, often very green in spring, with pasture in uncultivated places. The two-lane highway leads from Swani Ben Yadim to Zahra and onward to the main town of Aziziya.

Aziziya, 41 km from Tripoli, has a petrol station, post office, hospital and several banks all situated on the main street or immediately adjacent in the few principal side roads. From Aziziya, it is 221 km to Nalut on the west end of Jabal Nafusa via the route at the foot of the Jabal Nafusa, a straight and fast single carriageway.

**Aziziya**

**العزيزية**

Heading towards Gharyan, the road remains dual carriageway and a few kilometres south of Aziziya the landscape opens up rapidly and the trees thin out. This is prime cereal-growing country in years of good rainfall. At Rabta, 63 km from

### Berber culture in the Jabal Nafusa

The culture of the Jabal Nafusa is for the most part Berber, though Arab tribes are interspersed within the main groups. Historically, the Berbers held the lands of the Jefara Plain with their main centre at Sabrata. In medieval tiimes, they were driven back into the hills by the Arab invaders. The relative isolation of the Berber communities has meant not only a survival of their language and close kinship ties but also quite distinct urban forms and housing styles. In religion the Berbers are Muslim but follow the Ibadite branch of Islam, regarded by many Sunni Muslims as a heresy. The Berbers were aggressively separate from the Arabs on the Jabal Nafusa however much they intermarried with the Arab tribes elsewhere in Libya. The Berbers of the Jabal Nafusa participated in the revolts against Arab rule, the most ferocious of which took place in 896 AD.

More recently, the Berbers looked for the creation of a semi-autonomous Berber province. They had been a favoured group under the Italian occupation, making up important parts of the police forces in Tripolitania. On independence it was hoped that Berber cultural separateness would be acknowledged and their language given equal status with Arabic. The rise of Arab nationalism at this time forestalled any chance that the numbers of Berbers, a sizeable minority population estimated at around 150,000 at the time, could make their voice heard. The revolution of 1969 set back Berber aspirations and for some time the government in Tripoli refused to admit there was any such group as the Berbers. Despite the rapid economic changes resulting from oil wealth, the Berbers still keep a sense of cultural separateness and even superiority. Public affirmations of Berber identity are definitely no go in Libya, however, unlike Algeria and Morocco, where Berber languages are gaining a place in the media, and may eventually lead to more regional-based forms of government.

Tripoli, the checkpoint may be strict. The chemical plant where Libya was alleged by the United States of America to be producing highly toxic gases was located here. Then the road begins the rise towards the Jabal, a winding, slow climb. There is a café at the foot of the scarp on the left hand side of the road. As you climb, the old Italian road can be seen to the left. Though no longer maintained, it would be a good alternative route for walkers and more adventurous and very, very fit cyclists. At the top of the slope the roadside is built up increasingly with houses. There are numerous olive trees in the Guassem area, some 11 km before Gharyan. On either side of the road, look out for roadside stalls selling pottery, much of it from Tunisia.

## Gharyan    غريان

Phone code: 041
Population: 100,000
Altitude: 700 m

Gharyan has seen a lot of new building in recent years, reflecting its importance as a regional administrative centre. On climbing the scarp and traversing the olive groves where the road comes on to the summit of the Jabal, turn off right for Gharyan town, marked clearly but in Arabic script. Ask for *markaz al madina* – the town centre. Note that the climate of Jabal is much cooler than the plain and even in spring can be several degrees colder on the ridge than on the Jefara. **Petrol** available here.

Gharyan might make a good base for explorations into both the Jabal Nafusa to the west and the Jabal Gharyan and Jabal Tarhuna to the east. If you have time, you could try to find a guide (ask at the *Hotel Rabta*) to take you to see one of the **troglodyte homes** for which the region was once famous. There are two types: the 'crater' type, with underground rooms around a courtyard excavated 4-6 m

The Jabal Nafusa & Ghadamès

below the ground's surface; and the 'hillside' type, where the rooms are dug into the hillside and protected outside by an area enclosed by a stone wall.

Another minor attraction in Gharyan is the new traditional craft school located on a side street starting to the left of the Hotel Rabta complex. They are also very proud of their pottery and also do some carpet weaving.

**Sleeping**

*Hotel Rabta*, T31970, F31972. A recent hotel, in fair condition, clean, run in a business-like way, working lifts, 68 rooms, for the business traveller there are suites costing 35LD for single and 45LD for double, restaurant serves lunches and dinners at 7.500LD per person, modern café facing onto the street, film theatre, most modern facilities, owned by the Libyan Social Security Organisation. Try to reserve in advance, as the hotel can be block-booked. *Youth hostel*, 120 beds, breakfast included, family rooms, meals, laundry, kitchen and **camping** facilities in Gharyan at T31491, open 0700-2300, booking recommended. Information at the City Hall.

**Transport**

The main public transport hub is just 500 m from the Hotel Rabta. Mini bus and share taxi departures for Tripoli are frequent, there are fewer departures for, Mizda, Nalut and other destinations west.

## Into Berber land: a route from Gharyan to Shakshuk

Heading south from Gharyan, and then west after Abu Zayan, the Jabal Nafusa road is narrow and slow, allowing you to visit a variety of Berber centres. There are apricot and fig orchards as well as traditional terraced farmland to be seen as the highway carries the traveller along the top of the scarp slope. The real prize here are the great crumbling Berber granaries or *qsur*.

**Tigrinna**

Leave Gharyan centre and travel south via the dual carriageway, passing through housing and olive groves in rolling uplands. Shortly there is a road on the left to Tigrinna for which the Italians had great plans back in the 1930s. The *Azienda Tabacchi Italiani* experimented with tobacco growing near Tigrinna in the 1920s. It was decided to create a model village, a blueprint for future 'demographic' settlement, peopled with industrious peasants from the Abruzzi and Ferrara. Unfortunately, there was never enough rainfall, and the tobacco farming all petered out with the Second World War. Today, the old Catholic church, slowly decaying and visited only by sheep and goats is still visible to the east of the highway.

**Abu Zayan to Yefren**

After Tigrinna is a small settlement called **Abu Zayan**, just south of which the road divides with the Fezzan road leading southwards to the left (Mizda 82 km and Sabha 700 km). Carry on straight for the road running along the top of the Jabal Nafusa, which now becomes a single carriageway. You pass through the small settlement of Issabiya, with houses dispersed in the farmland. (Petrol in village centre.)

The road traverses increasingly arid countryside with light scrub and occasional olive plantations covering the hills. At Km 76 a turn to the right leads to **Kikla** 12 km away. At Km 77 there is a mosque, a café and a petrol station. Further west, there are occasional groups of houses such as at **Gualish**. There are good places for picnics on sections of the old road visible from the new highway.

**Yefren**
*Phone code: 0421*

Yefren, 52 km from Gharyan, 138 km from Tripoli, is the first main site off the main scarp-top highway, and definitely worth a visit. (Although the only hotel is now closed.) The settlement lies 20 km north of the main road. After the Kikla turn off (right) and check point, look out for the petrol station 361 on

بفرن

*The Jabal Nafusa & Ghadamès*

your right. After some scraggy eucalyptus is a used car dump. Take a right turn here. Look out for petrol station 247 on the right; 20 m further on take another right turn to get to the **Roman mausoleum of Soffit**. The road winds uphill between fields of olive trees and figs and small houses used by local residents in the summer. (If you miss the turn, you'll see the mausoleum across the fields on your right (north) next to a large water tower.) After the mausoleum, of which the history is obscure, continue via Mujarzam and Al Qala'a to Yefren.

Yefren has been much modernized. The old town, now largely ruined, was built on an easily defensible spur (altitude 680 m). In the 19th century, the region had a lively history as the Berbers fought to keep out Ottoman forces. In 1845, one Juma' ibn Khalifa led an uprising against the Ottoman presence. He was captured and deported to Turkey. However, he escaped and made his way back to the Jabal Nafusa, where he led a second revolt in 1876.

The new town spreads along the black top road. Note the house decorations on modern units. The town is very scattered around a one-way traffic system through narrow streets. It has all services, almost all clustered in the main square and the streets immediately adjacent to it and you will inevitably end up at the one and only hotel, the former *Albergo Rumia*, with its views over the region. Back in the 1930s, no doubt this was a favourite place for a break from the hot Tripoli summers. Like the *Hotel Nalut*, it was designed by Florestano di Fausto, one of the team of architects brought in by Governor Italo Balbo.

**Sleeping**  D *Funduq Yefren*. The former Albergo Rumia, named for a nearby spring, has fallen on hard times. You will have to soldier onto Nalut or back to Gharyan to find decent accommodation. There is a *youth hostel* in the city centre, just about functioning, T2394, with a lively café.

**Transport**  Share taxis for Tripoli leave from the central taxi park, journey time 1 hr 30 mins, cost 3.5LD, there are not many departures in the afternoon.

**Short excursions around Yefren**  There are good, reddish soils around the town, and there is still some sporadic cultivation on terraces and scarp-top fields. After Yefren you could continue to **Awenia** and **Aïn Rumia**. This road gives wide views across from the Jabal to the Jefara below. Some terraces cut into the Jabal face are still used for agriculture but many have been effectively abandoned. At Aïn Rumia there is a café open only in summer. The spring at the site is no longer running since the water is being used for the water supply to the town. But the plots of land there are flourishing with palm trees in the cultivated valley. This spot can be crowded on Friday and public holidays.

A visit to **Qasr Bir Niran**, below the Jabal: 5 km down from Yefren, provides a further excuse for exploring the region. There is a fork with a small mechanic's garage. Go left, pass through a settlement called **Taghma**, after which the road falls away down to the plain. About 10 km from Taghma, look out for the ruins of the granary on a rise.

**West from Zintan & Jadu**

جادو

Back on the main road on top of the scarp, the next stop is Zintan (99 km from Gharyan, 184 km from Tripoli). Before Zintan, a right turn will take you down the scarp slope to return to the Shakshuk to road. Or you can continue west along the top of the Jabal scarp. Pass through a further red soil zone with fruit tree cultivation.

Towards **Jadu** the region clearly receives less rainfall and the landscape is very arid, with few trees and little cultivation. There are a number of turn-offs right to Jadu. The town is a bit of a physical shambles since older communal and family stone-constructed dwellings have been abandoned and new individual homes are randomly scattered across the landscape. Jadu has lost its old fashioned charm but is an important town with notable tribes such as the Qabila Mizu there still. Berber is the main language in the households of the town. There is no hotel but petrol is available here.

**Transport Bus**: services to both local and inter-urban destinations run from just outside the town centre. **Taxi**: the taxi station is sited on the side of the main road at the entry to town.

Leave Jadu to head for Shakshuk at the foot of the scarp. There are two roads **Shakshuk** down the scarp; the newer one is better surfaced and maintained. Both offer a breathtaking view northwards across the Jefara plain. Shakshuk is a small settlement with animal pens and houses sited a short distance off the road. At the junction with the Jefara highway from Nalut there is a petrol station and a small general shop selling drinks and grocery items.

## West from Shakshuk to Nalut

At Shakshuk, you have a choice for getting to Nalut. You can either go on the fast road below the Jefara westwards or return to the mountain road which will take you on a more winding route to Nalut. The mountain road passes through arid landscapes and enables rewarding visits to the Berber settlements at **Tumzin**, **Kabau** (petrol available here) and other sites. Those keen to see indigenous Berber architecture should perhaps take the slow road on the scarp. The Jefara road is far quicker, though lacking the charms of remote Berber settlements. Kabao in particular has a fine ruined granary and scenic views. (Turn off for Kabao 107 km from Zintan). The scenery becomes increasingly arid as you approach Nalut.

## Nalut ‏نالوت‎

Nalut (244 km from Gharyan, 330 km from Tripoli, 310 km to Ghadamès), is a *Phone code: 047* small town with all public services near the centre. It is well provided with bus, taxi and other transport facilities, being the take off point for Ghadamès and even for the Fezzan, for those with four-wheel drive vehicles fully equipped for several days crossing the Hamada al Hamra and the Edeyen Ubari. Nalut has stores, petrol and car repair garages. Here again is a decaying 1930s hotel with beautiful views of the old village, designed by di Fausto.

Nalut may well be the Roman Tabumati. Certainly it was an outpost on the *limes*. The Berber settlement goes back to the 11th century. As at Yefren, the fortified granary was a centre of resistance to growing Ottoman control. Opposite the ruined granary (generally open, the warden lives nearby), is a small and aesthetically pleasing whitewashed mosque.

Not much choice in Nalut, which is a shame, since it is ideally placed halfway between **Sleeping** Tripoli and Ghadamès. **D** *Funduq Nalut*. Once a fine place indeed, but sadly in poor condition. (The sort of place where you prefer to sleep with your clothes on.) Horrible bathrooms. Cheap 10LD. **D** *Funduq Nasim*, on Ghadamès side of town, on left as you leave, T2816. Not terribly clean either. *Youth Hostel*, on main road out of town to Ghadamès, just before a petrol station. Prefer the Funduk Nalut.

Eateries as usual near main roundabout. **Eating**

Bus and taxi stand near main roundabout. 3.5LD to Tripoli by bus. **Transport**

### 🖐 Berber building

Building in the Jabal Nafusa was designed to deal with extremes of heat and cold, and the inhabitants' need to protect their crops and family life. Only local materials were used, and local topographic features – defensible high ground, easily excavated earth, building stone – were used to good effect.

In some areas, **underground houses** and mosques were the rule, places warm in the often bitter winters of the Jabal and cool in the heat of summer. At **Mizda** the troglodyte way of life was pursued until the 1970s so that families could escape the extremes of heat experienced in ordinary houses.

Elsewhere in the Jabal, **citadels** such as those at **Sharwas** and **Wighu** provided protection. After the Berbers were driven into the hills by the incoming Arabs, such citadel settlements became the focus of revolt against the invaders during the bitter struggles of the ninth century. There is evidence that internecine strife between powerful Berber clans at Sharwas and Wighu in the 11th century resulted in

extensive damage to their fortresses. Although eventually abandoned, Sharwas as late as the 16th century, they stand as bleak but recognizable ruins on the peaks of the Jabal.

Another effective local building system were the ksour or **fortified granaries** seen at **Nalut**, **Kabao** and elsewhere in southern Tripolitania and across the border in Tunisia. Small cells were created in the rock or built up one on top of another to accommodate stored grain and other items. These (now mainly ruined) buildings were surrounded by walls for reasons of defence. In towns such as **Jadu** another dwelling type can be seen, homes built of loosely assembled stone with a little mortaring between joints. These extended family dwellings had areas for living, cooking and keeping the animals in safety at night. Prosperity in recent years has led many residents of the Jabal towns to move into villas built in the open fields around the old settlements. The old quarters have been abandoned and are crumbling into ruin.

**Northeast from Shakshuk to Tripoli**

From Shakshuk, you may take a black top road returning to Tripoli. Roads off to the right lead back to the Jabal settlements at Kabao, Zintan, Yefren and most other Jabal Nafusa settlements. There is a petrol station at **Bir Ayyad** (turn off right for Yefren) and a roadside police control station. The control is not interested in tourists but have your passports ready in any case. At **Bir Ghanem**, the old main stopping place on the Tripoli road, there is petrol (station number 325), a café and shops. From here you are about 70 minutes' drive from Tripoli. Carry on to the north passing through Sahel Jefara, again with a café and a small market. Another road to the left immediately after Sahel Jefara leads to Zawiya, 78 km distant. Thereafter there is a slight increase in woodlands within government run agricultural projects and well-established roadside trees. Some shifting grain cultivation is visible on the plain in spring. Increasingly dense cultivation indicates that you are approaching **Aziziya**. Turn left at Aziziya (petrol available here) and Tripoli lies 38 km to the north.

**Nalut to Ghadamès**

After Nalut, you head south for Darj, an important meeting of the ways, where you either go west for Ghadamès or east to Qaryat and the main Tripoli to Sabha road. **Sinuwan** is the first important settlement, 110 km south of Nalut (and 430 km from Tripoli). An oasis located next to a *sebkha* (salt flat), it was an important source of this most valuable substance, with caravans transporting it down to Tripoli. Thanks to its plentiful freshwater wells, Sinuwan was also a key point on the caravan route from Ghadamès to the Mediterranean. Six km is a further oasis settlement, Sharwa. **Darj**, 540 km from Tripoli, has another ruined Berber settlement. From Darj east to Qaryat is around 300 km across the northern reaches of the Hamada al Hamra. From Darj west to Ghadamès is 99 km. Here you enter the easternmost part of a great dune region, the Grand Erg Oriental which extends its sandy tentacles from across the borders with Algeria and Tunisia. There is a police checkpoint halfway between Darj and Ghadamès.

# Ghadamès غدامس

*Once upon a time, deep in the Sahara, an ancient city lived under a spell, defended by high walls and tens of triangular rooftop crenellations. A deep silence held in the narrow streets, the caravans from remote Sudan no longer came … The story could continue with clichés of white-robed figures and hot winds blowing over the oasis. The desert ghost town, Ghadamès, is real enough, however, famous among architecture lovers as a place perfectly adapted to a harsh environment. Narrow alleys and courtyard homes provided protection from the sun; in the desert nights, life could be lived on the roof terraces. Although a new town, built outside the oasis, has left old Ghadamès deserted, on Fridays people return to pray in the mosque and enjoy the cool of the covered streets; tiny oasis gardens are still intensely cultivated. And slowly, old Ghadamès is achieving international recognition. In the age of the concrete breeze-block villa, its Le Corbusier-style austerity merits study and conservation. For the traveller, there are no palaces or marble monuments in Ghadamès. It is just there, to explore, to discover, rather as one might contemplate some outdated mechanical device or an Oriental curio.*

*Phone code: 0484*
*Population: 10,000*

## Ins and outs

**Getting there** Ghadamès is 640 km southwest of Tripoli. For the moment there are no flights from Tripoli to Ghadamès, although these will no doubt eventually be resumed. There are at least two buses a day from Tripoli, passing via Nalut, with stops for refreshments and police checks. In spring 2000, the nearby Tunisian border post at Dehibat was not allowing tourists through to Libya. If you do not have your own four-wheel drive, one of the local travel agencies can set up a four-wheel drive trip into the desert.

**Getting around** Ghadamès is very much the legendary oasis town, even though the population has moved out of the labyrinthine old town into new modern housing areas. Exploring the town and oasis is a pleasant day, and with four-wheel drive you could do a day trip out to the dunes.

## History

Ghadamès has the usual founding legend. The tale goes that a band of horsemen, crossing the desert, halted for the night. Back on the trail the next day, one of their number realized that they had left the cooking pots behind. He returned to their campsite and as he was gathering the utensils, his restless horse struck the ground with her hoof. Water flowed, and the place became known as Aïn el Faras, the Mare's Spring. It was to irrigate a carefully tended oasis.

Palaeolithic and Neolithic tools found in the Ghadamès region testify to a human presence in prehistoric times. In 19 BC the Romans set up a garrison in what was then named Cydamus. Under the Byzantines, the town was home to a bishopric. Columns and odd pieces of masonry recycled in the mosques and hammam bear witness to this presence. The Muslim-Arab invasion in 667, led by Uqba Ibn Nafi', passed through Ghadamès before moving northwards into

Byzantine Africa. The local Berbers are said to have resisted the Arab conquest fiercely, led by the prophetess Dihia.

By the eighth century, Ghadamès was an important port of call for caravans and pilgrims. It inhabitants preserved their independence, paying allegiance to the rulers of one or other of the powerful – but remote – coastal cities. Prior to the 17th century, the trans-Saharan trade was the main economic activity of the oasis. Ghadamès thus suffered considerably with the development of new sea-borne trade routes to West Africa. The people of Ghadamès were trading and resident as far west as Timbuktu and the Moroccan coast.

**Ghadamès & the slave trade**

In the 18th century, caravans from sub-Saharan Africa brought slaves, gold, leather, ostrich plumes and ivory in exchange for Tripolitanian horses, cotton, sugar and European manufactures: *contaria*, the glass beads and necklaces of Venice, *galanteries* and fake diamonds from Paris, Marseille linen and Scio silk, pewter bars and Venetian paper for religious texts. The profits were greatest on slaves. One 17th-century observer wrote that a slave bought for 8 piastres in Bornou was worth 24 piastres in the Fezzan, and between 40 and 60 in Tripoli. By the start of the 19th century, however, trade had started to fall off due to the abolition of slavery. The decline was erratic and the trade did not really end altogether until around 1910.

**Ottomans & Italians**

Until 1860, Ghadamès was paying taxes to the Bey of Tunis. When the Ottomans took over Tripoli for a second time in 1835, they sought to force the town to recognize the authority of the Turkish Bey in Tripoli. It was only in 1874 that the Ottomans finally managed to establish a garrison. When the Italians landed in Tripoli in 1911, tribal resistance and the great distance meant that it took them three years to reach Ghadamès and even then their stay was of short duration. The Italians eventually returned on a permanent basis in 1924. They were great admirers of Ghadamès and the area was treated sympathetically. Aviator-governor Italo Balbo would fly in, new gardens were laid out, administrative offices set up and a small but pleasant hotel, the Albergo Ain Faras was built.

During the Second World War, Ghadamès saw some fighting before the Free French Army led by General Leclerc moved in. The town and area was held under the Tunisian Protectorate until it was given up reluctantly when the Kingdom of Libya was constituted in 1951. The last French troops left in 1955.

Madraça Tilwan
Ghadamès.

• • • • • • • • • • • • • • • • • • • • • • • • • • • • • • • • • • • • • • •

## The White Fathers in Ghadamès

*Founded by Cardinal Charles Lavigerie in Algiers in 1868, the Society of the White Fathers established a brief presence in Ghadamès and Tripoli from 1878 to 1881 as part of their plan to reach West Africa by crossing the Sahara, where, south of the vast arid wastes, they intended to continue their missionary work. In Ghadamès, the small number of White Fathers eschewed overtly religious activity. Led by on Fr. Louis Richard, an experienced 32 year old veteran of the Algerian Sahara, three White Fathers set off for Ghat, 600 km to the south, on 18 December 1881, accompanied by five Touareg and*

*Chaamba guides. At nightfall on the following day, the three clerics were assassinated by a group of Touaregs. Speculation surrounds the tragic event: were the White Fathers seen as an advance guard of French penetration into the Sahara? Or did the merchants of Ghadamès fear foreign competition for the trans-Saharan trade routes? There is no way of knowing. The remains of the victims were taken back to Europe, and their remains may be found in several receptacles in the crypt of the Generalate in Rome. Hard by is the tomb of Cardinal Lavigerie himself.*

• • • • • • • • • • • • • • • • • • • • • • • • • • • • • • • • • • • • • • •

## Sights

Located close to the point where the international frontiers of Libya, Algeria and Tunisia join, modern Ghadamès has an estimated population of around 10,000. The residential area is divided into the old and new towns. The old town is situated within the oasis whereas the new town has been built on the dry slopes above the oasis. The old town has been uninhabited since 1986. The old traditional houses are not easily adapted to contemporary comforts and life-styles. Fortunately, the old town has not been simply abandoned and still plays an important role in the life of the inhabitants. The small plots of farming land around the old town are still highly cultivated. In the hottest days of the summer, the inhabitants of the new city return to their original quarters in search of shade and cool. **Modern Ghadamès**

Today, the inhabitants' only local sources of income are camel breeding and farming, the latter being very limited due to the lack of irrigation water and cultivable land, estimated at a mere 75 ha. Some Ghadamsia continue to work in long-distance trade, though lorries have replaced the caravans of yore. Others now have jobs in the petrol industry or in the administration in Tripoli. Since the construction of new housing in the mid-1980s, almost all families have moved out of the old town. Tourism is gaining some importance and the authorities are keen to promote the industry. Ghadamès now has a three-day tourist **festival** held annually in October to coincide with the date harvest. There are displays of local traditions and horsemanship.

From a difficult natural environment, the old Ghadamsia created perfect living conditions for an isolated settlement in a harsh natural environment. The houses, built of pisé bricks, lime, palm tree trunks and fronds, the only available building materials, are elegant and practical. Built on two storeys, they have a central room on the first floor acting as a kind of courtyard with all the rooms leading off it. The rooms are lit by an ingenious hole in the high ceiling, letting in sunlight that reflects off the white walls and provides sufficient illumination. The upper floors are supported by palm tree trunks covered with fronds and mud. The interior of the house would be decorated by the wife and tradition had it that this must be completed before the day of the marriage. The husband-to-be gave the key to his bride and she decorated their new home **Architecture**

The Jabal Nafusa & Ghadamès

without his interference. The decorations are very simple, generally red patterns painted directly onto the white walls, with the addition of mirrors and a few small cabinets.

The roof was the domain of the women, the kitchen being on the roof. Old Ghadamsi society was gender-separated, the women only descending into the streets just after sunrise or just before sunset when the men were away at the mosque for communal prayers. Otherwise, in the old town they were confined to the house, especially the upper floors. Thanks to the tradition of building rooms over the street, the roof terraces communicate and the women could easily move around from one roof to another. At street level, the semi-dark covered passageways give shelter from the sun and lead to small public squares, some partly covered as well. There are alleys with built-in benches for the men to sit on and socialize.

A wealthy Ghadamsi home would have a small room called the *qubba*, only used twice during the lifetime of the owners, first during the wedding ceremonies and second, when the husband died, by the widow to receive relatives and friends. The store room also has a clever system for preserving food. Due to climatic and other uncertainties, keeping a large stock of food was very important. Grain would be stocked and a wall built with a small hole remaining open. A torch would be inserted in order to burn the oxygen and the hole quickly filled enabling the contents to be stored for years. When it was needed the walls of this 'stone cupboard' would simply be demolished.

Note too the pointy corner-features on the roof terraces which give such an African feel to the Ghadamès skyline. The great mud city of Kano in Nigeria has the same decoration, too, as do the Berber houses of Tafraoute in south-western Morocco. Their role is to prevent *djinn* or other malicious flying spirits from landing on the roofs.

**Irrigation**  Vegetation and cultivable land are closely integrated with the residential part of the town. The gardens are about 5 m below normal street level in order to be closer to the water table. Within the village there are two artesian wells operating in addition to the legendary Aïn Faras. The sense of coolness given by the running water and the shade of the palm trees helps make the summer heat bearable.

# Ghadamès house

After J Martin Evans 'Libyan Studies'
Seventh Edt 1975-76 pp 32-33

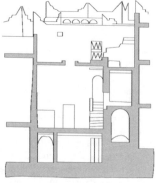

House Section

Bedroom

Store

Grain store

WC

Store

First Floor Plan

In the old town, behind the *Aïn Faras Hotel*, there is a **House Museum**, a mummified Ghadamès home. Outside the walls are plain and minimalist, inside the decoration is as luxuriant as the oasis. The interior walls are covered with red-painted motifs recalling Berber tatoos, stylized geometric flowers and stars. There is a full range of traditional bric-à-brac, cushions and carpets, mirrors, *tbak* (palm-frond couscous dish covers) and copper vessels. Though touristic, the house gives a feel for the way of life in Ghadamès earlier this century.

There is another 'popular' **museum** at the entrance to the new town with a collection covering various aspects of life throughout the region, with clothes, weapons, tools and even desert animals.

On the main square of the new town there is a large **market** every Tuesday and a small market every other day.

Museums

## Essentials

Ghadamès definitely merits (or rather requires, because of its distance from anywhere), an overnight stop. Do not however expect the high standard of accommodation you come across in Tunisian oasis resorts like Tozeur or Douz, or even in fairly remote locations in southern Morocco. Accommodation in Ghadamès is simple and in short supply, and at busy times of year, overbooking has been reported. At Christmas/New Year and Easter, if you are not travelling with a reliable agency, try to ensure you book a hotel room in advance. Otherwise make sure you have a warm sleeping bag, as winter nights can be cold in the desert. It is on occasion possible to be put up in a local's house.

Sleeping

**Visiting a house**. If you want to visit a house, contact Tayib Mohammed Hiba T62300. F021 360 1374. His Dan Do Umar House still has all its traditional contents. Recommended.

**C** *Funduq al Waha*, out on Tripoli road, 2 km or a good 20 min walk from town centre, T2569/70, F2568. Rooms around a courtyard, TV in rooms, currently clean and everything works, bargain at 25LD for double with sitting room, breakfast 3LD each. **C** *Funduq Kafila*, in new town behind mosque, T2991. Double room 40LD, single 30LD. **Youth hostel**, 1 km southeast of town centre, T2023. 120 beds, tiny 2-bed rooms, breakfast included, family room, shop, laundry, open 0700-2300, booking recommended Dec-Apr, kitchen. **Rooms in private houses**  Short lets available in private houses. Try *Uthman Al Hashash* on T62844 or 62134. Eat elsewhere. Its café is the young people's meeting point and can get lively in the evenings.

**Camping**  *Winzrik Travel Agency's* campsite, on main outer road, T2485.

There are three eateries on the main square. The Algerian-run restaurant with pool table and garden area is best of the bunch.

Eating

Once upon a time, Ghadamès had quite a flourishing **craft** tradition. Being so isolated, everything had to be made locally, from pottery to carpets and leather goods. Try the shop on the small square next to the cemetery or the reception area boutique at *Hotel Waha*. Look out for woven palm frond items, embroidered *belgha* (traditional **slippers**) and Touareg **jewellery** (most probably made in Niger, and available in tourist places throughout North Africa, but never mind).

Shopping

The recently opened *Ghadamès Travel and Tourism*, Shari'a Saydi Aqba, T/F2533 or *Cidamos Tours and Travel*, T/F2596, Shari'a Sidi Okba. Manager Mr Bashir Hammud will organize trips in the surrounding area, including complete guided tours of the old town of Ghadamès and trips into the desert down towards Ghat.

Tour operators

The Jabal Nafusa & Ghadamès

**Transport**  **Air**  Flights to **Tripoli** were not operational in 1999.

**Road**  Buses and share taxis come into the station by the new mosque. **Bus**: there are 2 buses a day to **Tripoli** (8LD, get ticket day before). Officially they leave at 0600 and 1000, but in reality they leave when full. Be at the terminal at least 90 mins before the official time as this is when the bus is likely to leave. Journey time 9-10 hours. All buses to Tripoli go via **Nalut**. The usual small 10-seater private buses do the journey from/to Tripoli. Cost 7LD, with several stops for refreshment and police checks. These microbuses leave from the Shari'a Rashid transport hub, Tripoli. If you want to head east, you may find public transport at Darj to take you across the 300 km to Qaryat on the Tripoli-Mizda-Sabha road.

**Car**: the road surface from Ghadamès to Nalut is good but attention must be given to the occasional small sand dunes across the road which can be dangerous even at moderate speeds. In more settled times Ghadamès is close to a border crossing to Algeria, currently **not** recommended.

**Directory**  **Bank** in the ground floor of block next to the *Hotel Kafita* which does foreign exchange. The bank opposite the post office (main junction north of main mosque/bus stop) does not do foreign exchange. **Communications**  Phones in post office.

## Excursions from Ghadamès

To the west of the town, the small village of **Tunine** is very similar and still inhabited, though it is much smaller and less attractive. A primitive form of water lifting, the *delu* system, was in operation until recently. Further along the road after Tunine there is a large number of sand dunes. It is particularly satisfying to walk up to the top of the dunes and watch the desert sunset. Travel agencies can also set up trips to see the **dunes of the Grand Erg Oriental**, towards the Algerian and Tunisian borders. (For this excursion you need a police permit, which the agency will obtain for you.) Out in the desert you may visit Qasr al Ghul (Castle of the Ghost), the ruins of a small Roman fort.

Another possible excursion, requiring a four-wheel drive vehicle, is **Lake Mujazin**, a brackish expanse of water out in the desert. Head back up the Tripoli road for 30 km and turn off west at the rusting signpost. Follow the dry river bed to get to the lake. The area can get crowded at weekends with picnicking families from Ghadamès.

Fezzan

8

# Fezzan

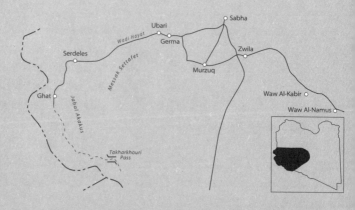

Stretching south of the Jabal Nafusa, the Fezzan, the
Phazania of the Romans, is a vast desert province
covering Libya's southwest quarter. You travel to the
Fezzan because you love empty landscape, because you
have a yen to see uninhabited sand seas, gravel plains
and dune desert and maybe because you are curious to
see how a modern nation state is trying to make use of
vast arid expanses of territory. But there is more to see
than this. Traces of more fertile, rainy times can be found
in the form of **rock carvings** and **rock paintings**. The
cliff carvings of the **Messak Settafet** and the flowing
lines of the rock paintings of the **Jabal Akakus** are
witness to the fact that the empty, pebbly plateaux you
have crossed were once grassy savannah, grazed by
elephants, elegant giraffes and curvy-horned cattle. In
fact, below the eroded cliff faces of the Messak Settafet
and the Jabal Akakus is one of the finest 'collections' of
prehistoric rock art in the world.

**Ghat**, a Touareg town, is the starting point for the
Akakus, while for the Messak Settafet, **Germa** on the
Wadi Ḥayat is the best base. Here you can also see the
remains of the Garamantian civilization. Off-road
vehicle drivers can head north into the immensity of the
**Ubari dunes**. Hidden in the miles of rolling sand is a
truly unlikely geographical event: the tiny, palm-fringed
**Dawada Lakes**.

# Ins and outs

**Getting there**  Until such time as *Libyan Arab Airlines* repairs and expands its fleet, road is the easiest way to get down into the Fezzan from Tripolitania. Distances are great: Tripoli to Sabha, capital of the region, is 758 km. Libya has put considerable investment into improving and extending the road network, however. There are regular bus and taxi services between the main settlements. Regular internal flights from Tripoli to Sabha have been resumed, but demand is great and planes fill up quickly. There are other regional airports at Ghat and Hun. If opting for public transport down from Tripoli to Sabha (journey time about 10 hrs), prefer bus (ticket about 13LD), which is cheaper, safer and more comfortable than an Iveco mini-bus (25LD). There are buses from Benghazi for Sabha, too.

Travelling south into the Fezzan, there are two main routes: from the coast at Bu Grayn via the Jufra region to Sabha, and the one you are more likely to take, the recent road from just outside Gharyan (Jabal Nafusa) via Mizda. At **Bu Zayan**, 105 km from Tripoli, you either turn off west on the Ghadamès road, or continue straight ahead for **Mizda**, 178 km from Tripoli. Musti Vecus in Roman times, Mizda was an important Berber settlement on the caravan route up from the Fezzan. South of Mizda, you hit the true desert. After a downhill run, there is a turn off for Bani Walid to the east and a check point. After this, there is not much of anything until you reach **Qaryat**, 330 km from Tripoli. (From Qaryat there is a link road to **Darj**, over 300 km away to the west, and Ghadamès.) Next stop is **Shwayrif** (petrol, stores), 50 km further on, after which there is more or less nothing until you reach **Brak**, another 200 km haul further south (petrol, stores). Brak is entry point for the **Wadi Shatti**, northernmost of the three great wadis running east-west across the Fezzan. (**NB** There is a strict check point just before Brak.)

There is not much to keep the traveller in Brak, although you might take a look at the crumbling Ottoman fort with its tiny dusty museum in the older part of town. At Brak you may chose to do a side-trip up the Wadi Shatti to **Edri**, 140 km to the west (where the road ends), or continue straight on south for **Sabha**, main town of the eastern Fezzan – and over nine long hours' drive from Tripoli. Sabha lies just 70 km from Brak. The road crosses the very eastern extremity of the **Edeyen Ubari**, the Ubari Sand Sea. Some 50 km after Brak is a checkpoint and turn off left (east) for Sukna. Sabha is only a short hop away.

Note that for the moment, entry into the Fezzan from Algeria and Chad is not an option, although numerous sub-Saharan migrants travel up to Libya on lorries from Chad and the Sudan. The frontier with Niger is subject to closure, although desert lorry-buses were running in late 2000.

**Best time to visit**  Despite (or perhaps because of) its remoteness, the Fezzan became one of the big attractions for the nascent Libyan tourist industry in the 1990s. Germans and Italians began to come in large packs of off-road vehicles, agencies in Tripoli and Ghat set up tours to view the rock art, transport being four-wheel drive or camel. Weather conditions for travel are best in the winter, from around October through to April. Such is the demand, however, that at peak times – the European Christmas and Easter holidays – hotels tend to be packed and vehicles for transport into the desert in short supply. Make sure you travel with a reputable agency, and bring a sleeping bag in case hotel accommodation is unavailable. October and February/March are said to be the best months. The days are longer and the weather not yet too hot.

**Tours**  There are three must-visits in the Fezzan: the **Jabal Akakus** (aka **Tadrart Akakus**), the **Messak Settafet**, and the **Ubari dunes** (aka **Edyen Ubari**). All three regions have truly spectacular landscape, the geography teacher's field-trip dream. The first two regions have traces of prehistoric settlement in the form of rock paintings and carvings. On a well-organized tour with four-wheel drive transport, you could cover all three areas in seven nights. Ideally, you would camp in the **Jabal Akakus** for three nights, taking in the rock art in the **Wadi Teshuinat**. Then, after the rather tedious drive up from Serdeles (Awinat) to Germa (270 km), you would make **Germa** your base for exploring north into the **Ubari dunes** and south to the **Messak Settafet**, where there is more rock art. Camping is possible at the Dawada Lakes in the Ubari dunes, although the lakes can be visited in an easy day trip from Germa. Although the rock art of the Messak Settafet merits several days, some of the most spectacular areas, including the **Wadi Matkhandush** and **In Galguien**, can be seen on a long day trip provided an early start is made. Local drivers prefer to avoid camping near the Messak Settafet because the rocky environment has lots of scorpians. A viable option is to camp near the dunes of the **Edeyen Murzuq** (the Murzuq Sand Sea), about an hour south of the Wadi Matkhandush.

For those with time, a more pleasant option is to set up a **camel safari** or *meharée*, as it is called in French, into the Jabal Akakus. Your little caravan will travel through a region of cliff-like mountains. The wadi beds are flat, essentially sand and gravel, easy going for both walkers and the camels, who will wait while you go scrambling up into the lower reaches of a cliff face to view some wonder of prehistoric art. This sort of tour needs to be booked in advance with a Libyan travel agency or a European agency working with a local operator. There are two options: camel only or camel with four-wheel drive back-up, to carry food, water and firewood. Here again, at peak times prices tend to be higher. Almost all the main Tripoli agencies have contacts in the Fezzan and can set up tours. Try the following: *Africa Tour* (Sabha office) T071-625594, *Fezzan Tours* (Sabha office) T071-627468, *Akakus Travel Agency* (Ghat) T0724-2804/2318/2938, *Indinan Agency* (Ghat) T0724-2460, *Winzuik*, (Ghat) T0724-2604, *The Dar Germa hotel*, Germa, can set up tours quickly at quiet times of year. *Al Faw Tours* Ghat T0724-2265, Tripoli T021-4802881, *Wings* (Tripoli) T021-3331855/3341655 F021-3330881,wingstravel@yahoo.com

**Off-road vehicle** enthusiasts will have a splendid time in the Fezzan. Those with GPS and solid vehicles may want to head to south-eastern Fezzan, to **Murzuq** and **Zwila**, or down to **Gatrun** on the way to the **Chad**. Although relations between Libya and Chad are now good, the Tibesti region was the scene of violent fighting, and is not for the moment an advisable area for tourism. Autonomous expeditions are however beginning to go there.

Note that off-road vehicle hire is problematic, as the Libyan government is worried about private individuals using them for contraband running. No Touareg will take you into the Akakus if he is not absolutely sure of his vehicle, however.

# Background

## Geography

One of the three great provinces of the former United Kingdom of Libya, the Fezzan lies over 600 km south of the Mediterranean coast. The province has all the main desert features, from sand-seas to rock plateaux, oases and eroded sandstone mountain massifs. Here one is acutely aware of geological time and of the great desert landforms. In fact, the dunes which are 'desert' in the western imagination only cover a small part of the Sahara. Whatever the landform, these are regions of relentless austerity. Looking down from a rock *abri* in the Akakus, a tiny rock shelter decorated with a fresco of hunters and mouflons, the harshness of it all seems unreal. (This is Keith Douglas' 'red rock wilderness' where 'the wind saws at the bluffs/And the pebble falls like thunder' where you 'watch the clawed sun/Tear the rocks asunder'.) You find yourself wondering how rock

☞ *Desertscape: key terms for the Fezzan*

*(All words in **Tamahaq** unless indicated A for Arabic)*

Abankar. *Well dug in sandy bed of wadi.*

Aqba, *pl.* aqbat *(A). Steep rock cutting leading up through a cliff.*

Adrar. *Mountain.*

Agulemam. *Seasonal lake or pool.*

Ayn, Ain, *pl.* ayoun. *(A). Spring.*

Anou. *Well.*

Bir *(A). Well.*

Barkhan *(A). Small, moving dunes.*

Edeyen. *Great sand sea.*

Erg *(A). Great sand sea.*

Feij, Feidj *(A). Corridor between the dunes.*

Foggara *(A). Tunnel excavated to bring water from an aquifer near cliff base to a settlement on lower ground.*

Jabal, *pl.* jibel *(A). Mountain.*

Gargaf. *Sandstone plateau with ravines.*

Guelta. *Permanent small pool.*

Hammada *(A). Flat rock plateau.*

Ramla *(A). Small area of dunes.*

Rejem, redjem *(A). Cairn.*

Reg *(A). Flat expanse of pebbles.*

Sabkha *(A). Low-lying closed in area where run-off water collects and evaporates, leaving salt deposits. No vegetation.*

Sarir *(A). Sandy plain.*

Tadrart. *Diminutive of* adrar, *mountain.*

Tahla *(A). Acacia radiana.*

Tassili. *Sandstone plateau.*

Tahi, *pl.* tahiwin. *Col, pass.*

Triq *(A). piste.*

Wadi, *pl.* wadyan *(A). Dry valley. Subject to occasional flooding.*

is powdered down to form thousands of square kilometres of sand hills and by what miracle the water filters up to a pool in some minute oasis.

Traditionally, the Fezzan owed its importance to its location on the caravan routes up from the Sahara. The areas most suited to human settlement are three great east-west valleys, where until recently oasis cultivation was the principle way of life. From north to south, these are the **Wadi al Shatti**, the **Wadi al Hayat** (called Wadi al Ajal on older maps) and the **Wadi Hikma**, also referred to as the **Wadi Berjuj**. In the past, one or other of these three valleys would dominate, providing a power base for local sultanates.

These slender corridors for human movement lie in the shadow of the great landforms of the desert. Centring on **Brak**, the Wadi al Shatti sits between the Hamada al Hamra and the Edeyen Ubari. Extensively settled in ancient times, the Wadi al Hayat is bounded by the Edeyen Ubari to the north and the cliffs of the Hamada Murzuq and the Messak Settafet to the south. Finally, south of the Hamada Murzuq lies a string of wells and oasis settlements sometimes referred to as the Wadi Hikma, more often the Wadi Berjuj.

Today **Sabha** is the main administrative centre. Other important settlements are **Germa** and **Ubari** in the Wadi al Hayet and **Ghat** in the Wadi Tanezzouft, close to the Algerian border. The traditional ways of life are receding. Oasis cultivation has become more difficult as the water table falls. (Within living memory, the water was only a couple of metres from the surface in the Wadi al Hayat.) The nomads, Touareg moving across their great central Saharan domain and Bedouin Arabs raising their flocks in the lands north of the Wadi al Shatti are few in number today. New activities are appearing: there are vast, artificial farms using artesian water out in the Wadi Berjuj, tourism employs drivers and guides.

## History

The Fezzan is a land of pre-history rather than written history. Scrambling up to a flint-strewn ledge in the Akakus, or gazing on some slender-limbed giraffe on a sun-saturated rock face in the Messak, the visitor is in direct contact with the

## The Fezzan discovered by Europe

It was not until the 19th century and the wave of European exploration that the first travellers reached the Fezzan, drawn by classical accounts of the lost land of the Garamantes and the great challenge of finding and mapping the great routes across the desert. The first European to journey into the region was one **Friederich Hornemann**, who left Cairo disguised as an Arab and reached Murzuq in 1789. There followed a sporadic series of expeditions into the region, many of them ending tragically.

As the Qaramanlis asserted their influence in the Sahara, the European consuls in Tripoli realized that travel was becoming possible for European scientific missions. In 1809 **Joseph Ritchie** and **Captain G F Lyon** travelled to Murzuq. Though Ritchie died on the journey, Lyon produced the first map of the Fezzan on his return to London. In 1821, **Dr Oudney**, **Captain Clapperton** and **Major Denham** travelled into the Fezzan. Travelling with an armed escort provided by Yusuf Pasha, their mission was to visit the Kingdom of Bornu. In the event, they became the first Europeans to reach Ghat. Oudney gives us the first written descriptions of the Dawada Lakes; unfortunately he died on the three year trip. The next important mission was undertaken by **Heinrich Barth**, **Adolf Overweg** and **James Richardson** in the late 1840s. Barth became the first European to observe the rock art of the Messak Settafet. His curiosity nearly got the better of him, however. Visiting Indinen, 'the mountain of the spirits' north of Ghat, he lost his way. He lived however to write an account of how he made his way out, drinking his own blood to survive.

Between 1857 and 1861 **Henri Duveyrier** put together the first maps of the Saharan routes, also writing detailed accounts of the Saharan peoples. In 1867, a German, **Gerard Rohlfs**, reached Lagos from Tripoli after a two-year journey. (In 1879, he became the first European to reach the isolated oasis of Kufra.) Among the more curious figures in Sahara travel was the Dutch heiress **Alexine Tinné**. She travelled extensively in the Fezzan, coming to know the Touareg. However, in 1869, she was killed in an attack on her caravan on the way from Murzuq to Ghat.

Conditions for European travel remained uncertain until the 1930s, when the Italians sent out the first full-scale scientific missions. A well-equipped team was sent out in 1933 to investigate the Garamantian civilization, and was able to survey the whole Wadi al Hayat from Sabha to Ubari and on down to Ghat. Of the Garamantians, considerable evidence was discovered, including kingly tombs and a stone-built Roman mausoleum, escarpment forts and water tunnels, vast necropolises and much grave furniture, from pottery to stone votive tables. After Libyan independence, this work was continued by British teams, and the outlines of Garamantian life gradually emerged. In the Akakus, the energetic **Fabrizio Mori** made the cataloguing and analysis of the prehistoric sites his life's work, rather as **Henri Lhote** had done over the border in Algeria. **Jean-Loïc Le Quellec** and others worked on the rock art of the Wadi al Shatti and the Messak Settafet. The art of the latter region was first reported back in the 1850s when Heinrich Barth first sketched 'the Apollo of the Garamantes'. Today, thousands of carvings are catalogued, vivid, vigorous, occasionally salacious, and almost always executed with brio.

artists of millennia ago. Over the last twenty years, multi-disciplinary teams of researchers have pieced together the pre-history of this remote region.

The rock art of the Jabal Akakus and Messak Settafet, like that of the Tassili-n-Ajjer and the Hoggar over the border in Algeria, has been analysed on the basis of various criteria. The archaeologists have analysed artistic styles and techniques along with the juxtaposition of different styles. The researchers have tried to interpret the symbolism of masks, magic beings and refined erotic scenes. They have looked at the patina, the surface appearance given to the rock by natural physico-chemical processes, and used carbon 14 to date remains found in the *abris*, the cliff shelters. They have also studied the tools – axe and arrow heads, grindstones and pottery – found near the sites. Years of hard physical travel and close academic work in the Sahara by the likes of Mori, Lhote and Le Quellec have given us typologies and chronologies of rock art, some highly contested, however.

**Periodizing pre-historic rock art** Simplifying heavily, the broad picture is of a once-fertile region which over the millennia dried out, eventually assuming the spectacularly arid appearance we know today. From around 6600 BC to 4000 BC, the Early Neolithic period, the region had a hot, tropical climate which gradually became drier. The round-head figures and the great carvings of savannah animals in the Messak Settafet belong to this early phase. From 4000 BC to 2500 BC (Middle to Late Neolithic), the region had a Mediterranean climate, although the mountain areas continued to have plenty of rainfall. While savannah animals no doubt survived, prehistoric people began to domesticate cows. They portrayed their daily life, leaving scenes with graceful human silhouettes. From 2500 BC onwards (Protohistoric), a dry Mediterranean climate gave way to harsh aridity. The horse made its appearance, sometimes pulling spectacular 'flying' chariots. Humans are shown as egg-timer figures with matchstick heads. And finally came the period of the camels, from 300 BC onwards with scenes of hunts and caravans accompanied by scatterings of rune-like Tifinagh characters, the earliest form of writing used in the Sahara.

**The Garamantians** The first people of the region to enter written history are the Garamantes, often held to be the owners of the first wheeled vehicle technology in the Fezzan, and indeed the central Sahara. They are mentioned by Herodotus in the fifth century BC. Their capital, modern Germa, has crumbled, but thanks to their presence in the ancient texts (there was the great legend of the Garamantian emeralds), they drew 19th-century explorers to the region. The Garamantes are thought to have invaded the central Sahara from the north, winning battles over the pastoral peoples thanks to their superior arms. They had chariots, horses, and metal weapons although, surprisingly, apparently no written language. And they also had a sophisticated system of underground water tunnels to ensure water supply for their communities.

The Garamantian realms – or at least the Wadi al Hayat – were to become a vassal state of the Roman Empire. In 19 BC, Cornelius Balbus led an expedition to pacify the Garamantes. Pliny lists fourteen cities taken by the Roman general, including Cydmus (modern Ghadamès), Garama (Germa) and Rapsa (possibly Ghat). However, the Romans realized that they would be severely over-stretched should they try to occupy the Fezzan. An alliance was made, and the Garamantians continued to play an intermediary role in the Saharan caravan trade. Ivory and gold dust, ostrich plumes and slaves were brought up from sub-Saharan Africa, as were wild animals, required by the Romans for slaughter in their great amphitheatre spectacles. Was the trade organised enough to ensure the transport of large African animals across the Sahara? It is difficult to know. It is certain however, that the Romans developed a taste for combats pitting unusual combinations of wild beasts against each other.

**Rise and fall of local dynasties** The Garamantes fade from history as the Roman Empire receded. Medieval historian Ibn Khaldun in his *History of the Conquest of Egypt* tells how in 668 Arab conqueror Uqba ibn Nafi' reached Germa – which submitted without a fight. Germa was relegated to the status of a stop on the caravan route. From the

Middle Ages, the lead city of the Fezzan shifted as local dynasties rose and fell. Under the Banu Khattab Arabs, Zwila was capital for a while, to be followed by Traghen from the 13th to 15th centuries when the Fezzan was part of the lands of the Sayfawa dynasty of Kanem-Bornu, hundreds of kilometres to the southwest (NB Banu = 'sons of'). In the 16th century, a Moroccan sharif (descendant of the Prophet Mohamed), a certain Muntasir ibn Mohamed, took control of the Fezzan. (The Knights of St John were rulers of Tripoli, so a ruler with such religious credentials had obvious prestige.) The Safyawa rulers backed the Banu Mohamed. When Muslim rule was restored in Tripoli in the mid 16th century, the Ottomans tried to impose their authority. In the end, they were forced to recognize the Banu Mohamed as rulers of the region, and settled for annual tribute in the form of gold and slaves. It was not until 1811 that Banu Mohamed rule was ended when a Qaramanli commander occupied Murzuq, and was named Bey of the Fezzan. In Tripoli's scheme of things, the region became important as Yusuf Pasha's ambitions expanded to include the conquest of Bornu to the southwest. (Control of the slave trade was the objective).

The Fezzan nevertheless grew in importance in the Ottomans' geo-political calculations in the 19th century, essentially for political reasons. In 1846, the Beylik of Tunis abolished slavery, to be followed by Algiers in 1848. Although Tripoli officially followed suit in 1857, the trade continued. In fact, the last caravan of slaves reached Murzuq in 1929. Ottoman dominance in the Fezzan was promoted in the 15th century as a way of countering French 'infidel' penetration of the Muslim Sahara.

Given the logistics needed and the presence of numerous Sanusi zawiyas, the Italian presence in the Fezzan was not consolidated until the early 1930s. In 1942, the province, along with Ghadamès, was taken by the Free French and an administration similar to that in the Saharan Territories to the west was set up, with the co-operation of tribal leaders exiled under the Italians. Elections were held in 1950, with Ahmad Sayf al Nasr becoming head of the province. Events were moving towards the creation of an independent Libya, however. (In June 1949, Britain had given Cyrenaica self-rule.) The Fezzan was incorporated into the Kingdom of Libya which achieved independence at the end of 1951. French garrisons remained until 1956, increasingly isolated as the rest of the Maghreb moved towards independence.

**Semi-autonomous Fezzan**

# Sabha and around

Capital of southwestern Libya, Sabha is a fast growing town and entry point for the Wadi al Hayat, the central east-west valley of the Fezzan. Once upon a time it comprised three oasis settlements, now submerged in the expanding Saharan sprawl of modern Sabha. As key transport centre for all road traffic between Africa and northern Libya, it has strategic importance, as the presence of large numbers of military personnel testifies. For the visitor, there is not a lot to see. (The old fort on the *inselberg* near the airport, the former Italian Fortezza Margherita, is occupied by the military, photography prohibited.) Sabha was taken from the Italians by the French in 1943, becoming the base for the Third Saharan Company of the Foreign Legion. After Libyan independence, Sabha was named capital of the new kingdom's Fezzan province. The French presence was maintained in a climate of growing tension until 1956, when they withdrew. Another interesting fact about Sabha: Colonel Gadhafi studied here. And it was on 2 March 1977 that Gadhafi made the Declaration of Sabha, announcing 'the dawn of the era of the masses' and giving Libya its

*Phone code: 071*

*Fezzan*

current, somewhat cumbersome appellation, *Al Jamahiriya al 'arabiya al libiya al sha'abiya al ishtirakiya*, the SPLAJ (Socialist People's Libyan Arab Jamahiriya). The adjective Udma (Great) was added a few years later, making the acronym GSPLAJ.

Sabha centres on two parallel streets, Shari'a Jamal Abd al Nasser and Shari'a Mohamed M'qaryif where you will find hotels, restaurants and the bus station.

## Essentials

**Sleeping**  **C** *Funduq al Fatah*, Just off Shari'a Jamal Abd al Nasser, T623951. Named for the 1st Sep Revolution. Rooms with a/c, roof-top restaurant. **C** *Funduk al Nakhil*, on Shari'a Mohamed M'qaryif. Pretty grotty but close to the bus-station. **C** *Funduk al Qala'a*, T623106/8. The best option. Rooms with a/c. Sabha also had a *Youth hostel*, which may come back into service soon.

**Eating**  Apart from the restaurant at the *Funduq al Fatah*, you have the usual restaurants near the bus-station. Try also the restaurant next to the *Funduk al Nakhil*.

**Tour operators**  *Africa Tour*, T625594. *Fezzan Tours*, T627468, on Shari'a Jamal Abd al Nasser.

**Transport**  **Air**  *LAA* offices are on Shari' Jamal Abd al Nasser, T623875. The airport is close to the town, in the military zone. If on an internal flight and asked to disembark at Sabha, make sure you have your passport and ticket stubs on you – otherwise you might not be allowed back on the plane.

**Bus** and **share-taxi** stations are close together near the mosque on the Shari'a Jamal Abd al Nasser. Try for an evening bus for **Tripoli**. It is best to reserve your ticket the day before. Share taxis and micro-buses also available for **Germa**, **Ubari** and (rarer) **Ghat**.

**Directory**  **Communications**  There are public phone shops on Shari'a Mohamed M'qaryif. As usual, the main post office building can be identified by the telecom mast.

## South of Sabha

**Murzuq**  While Fezzan's key sites are clearly the Messak Settafet and the Jabal Akakus, if you have time you might explore the regions south of Sabha. A good road takes you south from Sabha down to Murzuq, via Ghudwa and Traghen. There is a checkpoint 13 km south out of Sabha and the turn westwards for Germa and

# Around Sabha

the Wadi al Hayat. Heading south, there is a parting of the ways at **Traghen**, capital of the Tebu Kingdom in the early Middle Ages and now a poor oasis settlement. Here, some 125 km from Sabha, the road heads east for **Zwila** via Um al Aranib, or west for Murzuq. As in Sabha, the old city of **Murzuq** has disappeared, replaced by the usual 20th-century concrete. Try to visit the fort with its mosque and pointy minaret, held to be one of the finest in Libya. Should you wish to spend the night in this area you will probably have to camp. The youth hostel is generally full.

East of Traghen, Zwila is another one-camel Saharan settlement, a stop on the way to Waw al Namus. You should take a look at the much restored **tombs of the Bani Khattab rulers**, outside Zwila in the Tmissa direction. If you need to overnight, then the *Winzrik Travel Agency* (contact number at Gabraoun near Sabha T0724-2726) has a campsite on the edge of Zwila. East of Zwila, the road continues to **Timssa**, your last chance to acquire provisions and, all being well, fuel before heading down to the great volcanic crater of **Waw al Namus**, over 200 spine-jarring kilometres southeast into the Sahara. **Zwila**

An expedition to Waw al Namus is not to be taken lightly, and is a journey for those with plenty of experience of off-road driving in the desert. You will do best travelling with a guide from a reliable travel agency who has done the trip before. The description given here on Waw al Namus and the Tibesti is provided as background only for travel in a difficult region. Those with a good reading knowledge of French are referred to the following guides by desert and four-wheel drive specialist Jacques Gandini: *Libye du Sud-Ouest. Le Fezzan* (Calvisson: Editions Gandini, 1995) and *Libye du Sud-Est* (Calvisson: Editions Gandini), both of which provide detailed itineraries with GPS references for travelling in Libya's deep south. (The latter volume covers Waw al Namus and the Tibesti.) **Waw al Namus**

Heading for Waw al Namus, the military base of **Waw al Kabir** (check-point, rooms in officers' mess), is your first destination, some four hours of desert driving from Tmissa. The base was important during the Libyan-Chad border dispute. Next follows a long and dull 130 km drive east-southeast, via **Jabal Nous**, to reach the crater of Waw al Namus. This extraordinary crater, 11 km in circumference, 4 km across at the widest point, has three permanent lakes within and fresh-water wells around it. The volcano finally went out some 5,000 years ago. Nevertheless, the water in one of the lakes is distinctly warm.

## The Tibesti

Until recently off-limits to travellers, the Tibesti Massif, the largest mountain area in the Sahara, is now becoming a possible destination for travellers, although only with an organized group or else accompanied by Libyan official guides. With its labyrinthine canyons and pinnacles, the massif spans the frontier between Libya and Chad, and in fact the larger part of it is in the latter country. The original inhabitants of the Tibesti were the Tedas, an individualistic people living in scattered clans, part of the larger Tebu ethnic group. The harsh living conditions of the region have produced a nomad people extraordinarily well adapted to their environment. Fierce and tough, they are the wild men of the Sahara. (Rumour goes that an Italian tour group leader who had been running tours into the Tibesti with the help of Tebu guides switched to official Libyan guides once Libya decided to allow tourism; his onetime Tebu assistants didn't take to this kindly, and stole his four-wheel drive from an overnight camp, leaving him stuck in the desert.)

Fezzan

The Tibesti was the scene of violent clashes between Libya and Chad (helped by the Foreign Legion) over the Uzu Strip, a band of territory in the north of Chad. Unfortunately, many pistes and wadis were mined in the course of the long conflict. Although some areas have been de-mined, many remain dangerous. Journeys to the Libyan Tibesti must therefore take the form of a fully equipped expedition with the assistance of a local travel agency and official authorization.

## Sabha to Germa along the Wadi al Hayat

From Sabha, the Wadi Ajal, now re-dubbed the Wadi al Hayat ('the Valley of Life') runs west to Germa. (The new name is altogether more reassuring than the old one, *ajal* in Arabic meaning 'the appointed time', ie the hour of death.) This is the central east-west valley of the Fezzan, and the road runs through a string of small oasis settlements and irrigated fields edged with tamarisk trees. To the north lie the **Zellaf dunes**, followed by the southeastern edge of the **Great Ubari Sand Sea** (Edeyen Ubari). To the south are the high cliffs of the Hamada Murzuq and the Messak Settafet ('the Black Plateau'). The distance from Sabha to Germa is 148 km. There are the usual checkpoints. Points of interest along this route include Bint Bayya, Gabraoun al Jadid, and Tekerkiba. Strung out along the main road, the villages have the usual low yellow-washed concrete houses, all-purpose grocery shops and mechanics. Most villages have newish mosques with slender minarets in modern, pan-Islamic style. Surviving older parts of the villages are generally half-crumbling, half-rebuilt. 54 km west of Sabha, **Abyad** is the first settlement reached (petrol, road restaurants).

At 88 km from Sabha, **Bint Bayya** is a sprawling sort of place. Under the scarp of the Hamada Murzuq are numerous ancient tombs, most dating from the first century AD and later. Back in the 1930s, when Sanusi resistance had been ended, the Italians began serious archaeological exploration in the region, and more than 40,000 ancient tombs were counted. No doubt the ancient inhabitants of the region were buried away from the valley floor to avoid wasting valuable irrigated land – or to avoid cemeteries being washed away in flash floods.

At **Gabraoun al Jadid** (113 km from Sabha), the inhabitants of the Dawada villages of the Edeyen Ubari were rehoused in the 1980s. The *Winzrik Travel Agency* (T0724-2726) has an office here if you wish to set up an **excursion to the Dawada Lakes**. At **Tsawah**, there is a turn off south for Murzuq via the Bab al Maknusa pass. Next main settlement is **Fjeij**, 130 km from Sabha, where there is a well run (and hence popular) **youth hostel**, T0728-2902, with dormitory and rooms with 2-4 beds (No a/c). Shortly after Fjeij is **Tekerkiba**, where *Africa Tour* has a **campsite** close to the dunes. (Overnight 10LD a head). From here, it is a short run on to Germa where there are a couple of hotels. Both Tekerkiba and Germa make good bases for excursions to the Dawada Lakes (see below), the former being around 15 km from the lakes closest to the main road. The youth hostel at Fjeij can also put you in contact with a guide for the lakes.

# Germa

*One time centre of the remote Garamantian civilization, Germa may also have been a Roman outpost. Today, it makes a good base from which to visit the rock art of the Wadi Matkhandush and the great dunes of the Edeyen Ubari. Germa also has a fine little museum, with displays on the ancient civilizations of the region labelled partially in English and French as well as Arabic. If you are pushed for time, then Germa could be your overnight stop while you do day trips to Dawada Lakes and the Matkhandush. It also makes a more interesting stop-over on the long run down to the Akakus than Ubari or Sabha.*

*Phone code: 0729*

## History and background

Remote though it was, the Wadi al Hayat was densely settled in ancient times. Traces of human presence, of palaeolithic and neolithic populations have been found in the Zenchekra rocks above Germa, in the cliffs of the Messak Settafet. The fact that the water table, thanks to an accident of geology, is in places only a few metres below the surface, plus the construction of an elaborate system of underground water canals or *foggara*, to bring water from the foot of the Messak Settafet to the oases, made the area highly habitable. In addition, the Wadi al Hayat forms part of the easiest route across the central-eastern Sahara.

The land of the Garamantes was known to the ancient authors. The Garamantes were a warlike people, travelling across their wide domains in two-wheeled horse-drawn chariots, depicted in numerous rock paintings. They were the link on an ancient trade route between Africa south of the Sahara and the Phoenician comptoirs of the Mediterranean coast. When Rome finally destroyed Carthage in 147 BC, the question of relations between a fierce desert kingdom and expansionist imperial Rome had to be settled. Roman proconsul Lucius Cornelius Balbus Minor, conqueror of Cydamus (Ghadamès), led 20,000 men down across the Hamada al Hamra to deal with the Garamantes. One can but marvel at the Romans' logistical skills in getting such a large army across arid stony wastes and sand sea to the Wadi al Hayat. The inhabitants of Garama must have had the shock of their lives. Balbus Minor was awarded a triumph on his return to Rome, the first person of Iberian birth to receive such an honour. Roman control over the Garamantes remained precarious at best, and it was left to merchants to establish a certain Romanity in the region that came to be referred to as Phazania. Slaves and ivory, wild animals and ostrich plumes transited north via Garama to the imperial cities of Sabratha, Oea and Leptis Magna.

The Roman influence in the region began to wither in the fourth century AD, and the Fezzan remained independent until the Arab-Muslim conquest of 655 by a large army led by Uqba ibn Nafi', founder of Kairouan in present-day Tunisia. Garama lost prestige as the Arabs transferred the capital east to Zwila, ancient Cillaba. The system of underground water tunnels was to long outlive the Garamantes, however, continuing in use into recent memory.

The question remains as to who exactly the Garamantes were. Early Italian research suggested that they were ancestors of the Touareg. Thanks to research by archaeologist Charles Daniels, the Garamantian settlements are now well documented. The inhabitants of the region settled on easily defensible sites on rocky spurs on the southern side of the Wadi al Hayat. However, space ran out within the walls of these early acropoli, and the Garamantes began to develop a twin scarp fort/valley floor town pattern of settlement, probably beginning in the fourth century BC. Acropoli have been identified at Tinda, Charaig, Fjej and Chlef. The wadi towns soon took on considerable importance, overtaking the original fortified villages. There is also evidence to suggest that the Garamantes were active in the other two great valleys of the Fezzan, the Wadi Berjuj to the south and the Wadi al Shatti to the north. Unfortunately, due to later settlement, the sites of the Garamantian valley towns are not identifiable, Garama being the exception.

## Sights

Three hours will be easily enough to take in the main sights at Germa, the abandoned village of old Germa and ruins of **Garama**, and the **Archaeological Museum**. There are a number of minor ancient sites close to Germa which are worth a look if you have time, including the Roman mausoleum referred to in Arabic as **Qasr al Watwat**, ('Palace of the Bats) and the so-called **Garamantian tombs** at Al Hatya, down the Ubari road west of the town.

**Ancient Garama** Ancient Garama has been under excavation for some years now, and the metal trolley lines attest to Italian archaeological activity in the recent past. Fragments of Roman pottery were discovered, along with some fine glasswork, back in the 1930s. Under the Italians, the site was declared a national monument and the population resettled in New Germa, making fuller excavation possible. In fact, the old town of Germa, once an important caravan town, overlay the Garamantian capital. In the 1960s, further excavations revealed the foundations of a temple and dressed stone-work dating back to the first century AD and no doubt in use for centuries afterwards. In fact, the ancient settlement was much larger than early modern Germa, extending to the present day neighbouring area of Saniat Gibril, where the building spanned the first to fifth centuries AD.

The caravan town of Germa must have been very fine in its day. It was well fortified, with a kasbah on the highest ground overlooking the palm groves. The whole settlement was surrounded by a moat, filled with ground water. With towers and high walls, the kasbah must have been particularly impressive. Today, however, it is a dismal place, the rotting mud walls are slowly crumbling back to the earth from which they came, and no-one seems to bother very much with the tired palm groves. ∎ *The ruins of ancient Garama are easily reached. Take the north road from the crossroads on the eastern side of town. The road quickly gives way to piste, and after about a kilometre, the ruined adobe walls of old Germa appear on your left among the dying palms of a semi-abandoned oasis. In principle there is a 3LD entrance ticket, but more often than not there is no-one to sell you a ticket, so make your own way over the mud wall and into the site.*

**Germa Archaeological Museum** This is a good little museum which should not be missed, and in the near future it is likely to be improved considerably. The museum director, who speaks some English, may be on hand to help with explanations. The displays on the Messak Settafet and the Jabal Akakus provide a useful foretaste of these spectacular areas, and there are stones from Garamantian tombs and an ancient burial. Look out for the characteristic stone funerary tables with their hollowed out 'cups', no doubt used for placing offerings to the departed.

**Other sights** Remains of an ancient **necropolis**, below the **Zenchekra Cliffs**, can be reached by taking the road south (as if heading for the Messak Settafet), from the crossroads at the western side of Germa. After a low wall, 1 km from the cross roads, a track leads off left to the foot of the cliff. Here are the remains of what must have been a rather expensive mausoleum, built in dressed stone with carved detail. Dubbed 'the tomb of the four merchants' by Italian archaeologists, it is thought to date back to Domitian's reign (81-96 AD) and is the only Roman mausoleum still standing in the Fezzan. There is doubt, however, as to whether this was actually a mausoleum, as excavations failed to reveal any underground burial chamber. The building was dated thanks to pottery found during the restoration of the base bearing the mark of one Rasinius Pisanus, an active pottery manufacturer during the reign of Domitian.

Round the mausoleum was one of the ancient cemeteries of the region. Look out for the mortarless piles of stones which mark the burials. You could also ask in Germa for a guide to help you find the remains of the old fortified settlement of Zenchekra, high in the cliffs above the wadi. The masonry base of the ancient fortifications are clearly visible, and in the cliff-face rock carvings in the 'stick-men' Garamantian style can be seen.

Necropolis fans will also want to see the so-called Pyramids of Hatya, the **Ahramat al Hatya**, located a few 100 m south of the main road 18 km west of Germa in the Vbari direction. (There is a rusty sign in Arabic indicating the entrance to the site.) Several metres tall, the four main tombs look like nothing so much as large crumbly mud pies. The 'pyramids' are also known as the Royal Tombs of the Garamantes.

## Essentials

**Sleeping**
*Phone code: 0729*

**B** *Funduq Dar Germa*, located close to the main crossroads the western side of Germa, 2-storey concrete building visible from main road, T2396 (if in service). Built in the late 1990s, this is the better of the 2 options in Germa. Clean, plentiful hot water (all rooms with en-suite bathroom), and a/c. Camping possible in compound at the back, safe parking. Unfortunately, the plumbing is dicey and the corridors noisy. Food unimaginative, service kind and willing. Try to contact via *Al Ula Travel Agency* in Tripoli. Gets very crowded at peak times. **C** *Funduq Germa al Siyahi*, T2276, P.O. Box 53358 Ubari. 15LD per person. Older hotel set a few metres back (south) from main road behind straggly greenery, east of museum. Variety of accommodation off courtyard, not all rooms have a/c. Not as clean or spruce as *Dar Germa*, but perfectly adequate nevertheless. Willing Sudanese management. Good value. **D** *Erawin Campsite*, T2413. Almost opposite the Zenchekra cliffs. Spartan accommodation, meals available.

**Directory**

Germa has mechanics on the main road, a pharmacy and a local health clinic. There is a petrol station at the crossroads. Make sure you fill up, as petrol is prone to run out at busy times of year.

## Excursion to the Dawada Lakes

Surely one of the most extraordinary sights in Libya, the Dawada (or Ramla) Lakes are fragile oasis pools seemingly lost in the vast expanses of the Edeyen Ubari. In certain places the dunes rise to 70 m or more, and the lakes feel as though they could be swallowed up overnight by voracious masses of shifting sand. Happily for the traveller, the more picturesque lakes are not far from the main Sabha to Germa road. **Um al Ma** and **Mandala** are around 20 km from Tekerkiba, **Gabraoun al Jadid** (also spelt Gabr al Awn) is about the same distance again.

**Getting there**

If you do not have a powerful and reliable four-wheel drive vehicle, then the easiest way to get to the Dawada Lakes is through a tour agency. This could be set up through a Tripoli agency with a branch in the south or by turning up in Sabha or Germa. There are a couple of campsites on the Sabha to Germa road, close to the lakes, which run excursions out into the dunes. Try the office of the *Winzrik Travel Company*, T0728-2726, at Gabraoun al Jadid, 115 km from Sabha, or *Africa Tour* which

*Fezzan*

has a campsite at Tekerkiba, the closest settlement to the Dawada region (phone Sabha office T071-625594). Another base for an expedition to the lakes might be the youth hostel at Fjeij, halfway between Gabraoun al Jadid and Takerkiba. The *Funduq Dar Germa* can also set up excursions.

It is possible to do an excursion taking in Gabraoun al Jadid and Um al Ma in a day. However, many people prefer to camp out in the dunes. Take care to avoid camping too close to the lakes though as there are lots of mosquitoes.

**Background**

The Dawada Lakes are nothing short of a miracle. In the midst of this remote territory of sand hills, where the only living being is the occasional black crow flapping by, are the Dawada oases, tiny sheets of water fringed with reeds and date palms. Around some lakes, the dunes are so high that it looks as though the lakes could disappear in a sandsliding instant. It would appear that there are geological faults underlying the vastness of the Edeyen Ubari which allow water to well up from subterranean fossil reserves. Some of the lakes are as saline as the Dead Sea, one has fresh water. Some dry up in the summer, others have water all year round. One French Saharan expert has found over 20 lakes in the region, of which fifteen have water all year round.

Until the late 1980s, there were tiny human settlements at some of the lakes. The name given to the inhabitants of this remote territory, the **Dawada** means 'worm eaters', and refers to their odd culinary habits (see box above). Maybe the climate was more clement when the Dawada, a black Muslim people, headed out to live at their lakes. When the Italians surveyed the region, they found only a few hundred souls living in simple palm frond huts. In the 1960s, things were not much better. The Dawada, still isolated, were visited by the occasional Touareg come to barter a few cigarettes or some flour and oil for the lakes' two main products, dried crustacean paté and blocks of *natron* (carbonate of soda). Life was simple and dull, and the only buildings were the mosques at Gabraoun and Mandara. In the 1970s and early 1980s, the Dawada of Gabraoun and Mandara built themselves small houses in breezeblock. But the problems of supplying communities with growing demands were too great, and they were moved to new settlements like Gabraoun al Jadid on the main road.

**Mysteries of the Lakes**

There does not seem to be any in-depth anthropological study of the people of the Dawada Lakes. Their villages are crumbling into ruin, the odd-Jamahiriya slogan daubed here and there on the house walls a reminder of their integration into the rest of Libyan society. The origins of the Dawada remain a

abandoned mosque
Dawada Lakes

## Worm cake

The Dawada's main source of sustenance, apart from dates and a few chickens, was a sort of crustacean cake. (James Wellard, writing in the 1960s, noted that "its smell can only be described as stinking caviar"). Dawada women trawled the shallows with long-handled nets, fishing out netfuls of tiny red shrimps (Artemia salina). One visitor described the average shrimp as resembling 'a blob of red jelly'. The crustaceans were then pounded up, patted into flat cakes and left to dry in the sun. This wholesome preparation was then buried in sacks in the sand, the high levels of salt ensuring its conservation. Shrimp cake of this nature was highly valued in the Fezzan, and thought to have aphrodisiac properties. Vogel, who visited in the 1850s, describes it as 'a delicious mush'. However, today's visitors are unlikely to be served dawada delight at the little campsite at the edge of Lake Gabr al Awn.

The Dawada Lakes' other main product, natron, was harvested from the lake shores by the men. Once upon a time it was much in demand for the tanning of leather and in bakeries.

mystery. A French expedition in the 1940s surveyed the mosque at Mandara, and found that it was made of blocks of *natron*. The thinking was that it had been a fort. A German researcher reported a find of Stone Age implements in the vicinity of the fort, suggesting ancient occupation of the site.

The other extraordinary thing about the lakes is their seeming ability to change colour. The high yellow dunes, the blue sky and the green and russet of the palms reflected in the still water produce a rainbow effect. At certain times of the year, the swarming shrimps give the shallower waters in some of the lakes a reddish tinge.

# Messak Settafet

*South of the Ubari road, hidden in rocky canyons, is one of Libya's best kept secrets: the prehistoric rock carvings of the Black Plateau, the Messak Stettafet of the Touaregs. What made early humankind create these wonderful stone frescoes of African animals? Were the gorges the site of fertility rituals or initiation ceremonies? For the moment, the mystery remains.*

## Ins and outs

**Getting there** Some of the finest examples of prehistoric art are to be found on the southern side of the Messak Settafet, where the plateau gives way to a flat and stony region. Access with a four-wheel drive vehicle is relatively easy, the 150 km drive across the lonely desert spectacular. At the Germa crossroads, turn left (south) up the fine road built by the oil companies to take their survey vehicles up onto the plateau. Here the Messak Settafet is at one of its narrowest points. At its widest it reaches 60 km. The road, when complete, will lead all the way to the artificial farmlands of the Wadi Berjuj, 62 km further south. The road turns into piste which you leave some 33 km from Germa to head towards the Wadi Matkhandush, the southern limit of the Messak. You cross rough sand and sparse vegetation before you reach the stones of the hamada. This then turns into flat hard sandy gravel on which vehicles can build up a good speed. The plateau has been surveyed by oil companies, and routes across the wide, open stonebed are marked with tyres. 127 km from Germa, at N 25° 48′405″, E 12° 39′833 is the police post of In Elaluen. At N 25° 43′003″, E 12° 11′459″, you come to the track leading down to the Wadi Matkhandush. The final approach is difficult. The vehicle bumps along a well-used piste leading down through tyre-cutting stones. Then the sand wadi with its acacias and the dark cliff face of the south side of the plateau comes into view. Here you park up. Although it is possible to take vehicles down to the wadi bed, you might as well walk, avoiding any chance of getting stuck in the soft sand.

**Getting around**  Happily for the visitor, prehistoric people located some of their choicest works of art within a few kilometres of each other. The sites of **Wadi Matkhandush**, and **Aurer** are barely 10 km apart, with **In Galguien** between the two. A few kilometres further west along the valley, in the area referred to by archaeologists as **In Habeter** are further sites for another 20 km. The famous carving referred to as the Apollo of the Garamantes lies 15 km north from the In Habeter area, up the **Wadi Tilizeghen**.

A day trip allows you to visit the Wadi Matkhandush, In Galguien and Aurer. With an early start, you could take in something of the In Habeter area too. This would be a long day, however. Note that you will need to bring all your water supplies with you; there are no reliable wells and very few nomads in this highly inhospitable region. If you camp, remove all rubbish; unhappily, the growing number of four-wheel drive vehicles getting to the Wadi Matkhandush has meant a corresponding increase in rubbish. If you begin to explore, note that the topography of the region is complex. If you come across a prehistoric site, do not touch but photograph and if possible note the GPS reference.

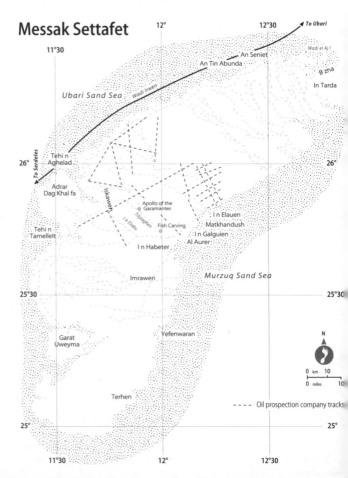

It is possible to camp in the Messak Settafet. However, you may find that that your guide will prefer to bivouac next to the great dunes of the Edeyen Murzuq, about 45 minutes' drive south from the Wadi Mathkandush. This has the advantage of having fewer scorpions. If the wind is right, you may also hear the dunes 'singing'.

## History and background

The rock carvings of the Messak Settafet mainly feature animals which are no longer found north of the Sahara. To judge by accounts from classical times, such beasts were still (relatively) numerous enough for North Africa to export them to the colossea of the Roman Empire. The carvings are much older, of course, going back to prehistory. Once upon a time, in the heart of what is now the Sahara, was a civilization which reached a high degree of artistic perfection. In the Messak Settafet, which has one of the principle concentrations of such early art, the vast majority of carvings would seem to be over 4,000 years old.

**Early explorers** The Messak Settafet was visited for the first time by a European in 1850. An expedition comprising the geologist and naturalist **Adolf Overweg**, the polyglot archaeologist **Heinrich Barth** and the experienced British explorer **James Richardson** left Tripoli in March 1850, reaching the Wadi Berjuj in late June of the same year. They headed into the Messak and on 5 July reached the Wadi Tilizeghen where "our attention was caught by some remarkable carvings, buried in the smooth, steep sandstone rocks which limit the western corner of the valley. These carvings, while not exactly perfectly executed works of art, were not just simple sketches with well-accentuated lines; they bear the mark of a strong, rested hand, well exercised in this sort of work." Barth sketched certain carvings, and in his diaries attributed them to the Garamantes; he also noted how the animals were often shown without hooves.

Barth was the first European to record the presence of ancient rock art in the Fezzan, but it was not until the 1930s that Leo Frobenius, a well-known self-taught ethnologist and pre-historian visited the region. (It is his archives and field notes which form the basis of today's Frobenius Institut in Frankfurt.) He was the 'discoverer' of a number of the great 'galleries' of the Messak, including In Habeter. Frobenius understood the importance of accurate recording, and was accompanied by specially trained artists. He was also the

Hatita, Heinrich Barth's Touareg guide. (From Reisen und Entdeckungen in Nord-und Central-Afrika in dem Jahren 1849 bis 1855. H Barth, Gotha: J Perthes)

Fezzan

first to note the importance of the dog-man figures. His findings were published in 1937, although the Second World War put an end to further exploration. In 1948, Roger Frison-Roche crossed the northern Messak Settafet, photographing and collecting material for his *La Montagne aux écritures*. Exploration was to develop slowly, however. At the end of the 1960s, knowledge of the region was still based on Frobenius and a handful of others.

**Recent archaeology**  In the 1970s, archaeology in southwestern Libya took off. Initially the field was divided by two Italian academics, **Fabrizio Mori** working exclusively in the Akakus, while **Paolo Graziosi** worked on the northern Fezzan. (Over the border in Algeria, Saharan pre-history was the preserve of Henri Lhote.) The Messak, basically ignored by the professionals, became the favourite terrain of enthusiastic amateurs, among them **Gérard Jacquet** and **Serge Berthoud, Jan Jelinek** and **Castiglioni** and **Giancarlo Negro**. The decisive step forward came in 1990 when a couple of Belgian amateur historians, **Axel** and **Anne-Michelle van Albada**, began to publish articles in *Archeologia* on their years of painstaking prospection in the Messak. In 1995 a fine coffee-table book, *The Secret of the Desert*, by R. and G. L. Lütz was published. And in 1998, **Le Quellec's** masterly *Art rupestre et préhistoire du Sahara* was published, for the first time setting the Messak rock art in the wider African context. The early explorers' knowledge of a few sites has expanded to thousands of carvings located across hundreds of sites in all the wadis of the region. It is only really today that archaeologists have had sufficient material to begin analysing the meaning of this most remote art.

**Palaeo-climates and artistic periods**  Archaeologists often refer to rock art with BP ('before present') dates, ie before 1950, the time that carbon 14 dating of material remains became possible. The theory runs that in prehistoric times, the Sahara had a damp, tropical climate. Around 8,500 BP was the height of the wet period. By 6,500 BP, the climate had become considerably drier, and by 5,000 BP, the central African lakes had receded considerably. Between 4,000 and 3,000 BP, the present climate had taken shape, with the Sahara having an extreme tropical desert climate.

Pollen analysis shows that around 8,000 BP the mountains of the central Sahara were covered with savannah. As the climate became progressively drier, the higher, wetter parts of the Sahara – the Tassili-n-Ajjer, the Jabal Akakus, the Messak – were probably a refuge for numerous plant and animal species. Although palaeo-climatic research has produced these major periods, the task of dating the carvings is not an easy one. Some writers have even suggested that the oldest carvings go back to 20,000 BP. For the moment, the consensus is that the earliest rock art in North Africa is pre-4,000 BP. The term 'recent' is given to rock art later than 2,000 BP. This date corresponds to the marked worsening in the climate.

Until recently, the presence of a patina ('desert varnish') on the engraving was held to be a good date indicator. However, incised rock in the region may acquire full patina very quickly, even in the course of a few decades, as the case of twentieth century French soldiers' carvings shows. Factors such as the permeability of the rock, the quantity of water and its pH levels are key factors. There are really too many variables for patina to be a reliable indicator of a carving's age.

**A world of hunter-gatherers or herders?**  Archaeologists and anthropologists have largely abandoned the theory that societies must necessarily move through a series of historic phases linked to available food sources, technical skill and intellectual capacity. With reference to Saharan rock art, the theory ran that such scenes – or what were held to be hunting scenes involving savannah fauna – were indicative of a culture based on hunting, while the portrayal of cattle demonstrated domestication.

Interest today has shifted to the nature of the economic cycle practised by vanished societies. Older writing on the Messak rock carvings considers that there are two discrete groups of art: the African fauna and the cattle, ie the hunters versus the herders. However, the picture is more complex. There are sites where buffalo are over-carved with large oxen. There are in fact very few sites which show humans hunting, although there are mythical hunting scenes with giant animal headed figures. There are signs showing that animals were trapped, too. All in all, in a corpus of 10,000 carvings assembled by specialist Jean-Loïc Le Quellec, only 1% of carvings feature hunting figures.

The validity of the 'two succeeding' phases approach, that is the separating of hunting and tropical fauna from herding and domestic animals, therefore still remains to be proved. The domestication of animals does, however, seem to have been well advanced: there are scenes with forked posts shown next to cattle, probably used for hanging pots of milk; there are images of women with tall head-dresses riding cattle, and a handful of milking scenes. A more curious feature are the oval shapes, generally found alongside what seem to be sheep and goats but also associated with large African fauna. Could these be placenta, a reference to a myth which gives humankind a cow-ancestor? In short, the present thinking is that there was a pastoral civilization flourishing in the Messak in 6,500 BP.

Researchers attempting to understand the meaning and impact of prehistoric rock art face considerable difficulties. Was there any specific symbolism? Is there a religious spirit underpinning this art? Despite the problems, there are a number of recurrent features for which tentative interpretations can be made.

**Rock art: symbolic communication**

On the whole, the animals tend to look towards the right; in other areas of the Sahara, animals in art look both ways. In the Akakus and the Tassili-n-Ajjer, most animal figures tend to look towards the right too. Twentieth century research has shown that when people draw profiles, they tend to show figures facing left. Examination of the horses and camels in the rock art shows 50% facing left, 50% facing right. Thus there was a taboo operating in hunter/pastoral society in the central Sahara: animals had to be shown moving to the right.

*Barth's drawing of Apollo of the Garamantes (source Barth 1857-58)*

**Masked beings** Another feature of the rock art are the animal-headed human-like beings. Masked human beings can clearly be distinguished from mythical half-human, half-animal beings. Masked men are regularly shown accompanying oxen and in pastoral scenes. The masks are often rhinoceroses or oxen, and the figures often seem to be moving, which might indicate that they were performing some sort of ritual dance.

The mythical animal-head beings are more problematic. These were noted back in the 1930s: Frobenius recorded a carving at In Habeter of two dog-headed beings, one presenting an oryx to another, holding it by the neck. Another famous example shows a dog-headed figure carrying an adult auroch across its shoulders. The animal-heads are clearly predators, and their preferred prey are rhinoceroses and aurochs. The heads are clearly not masks – and clearly have much to tell us about the prehistoric Messak's ways of looking at animality and humanity.

A close look at the actual dog-heads suggests that these are Cape hunting dogs: the rounded ears and the blunt muzzle of the mythical beings are certainly not those of a jackal or hyena. The Cape hunting dog is a nomad animal, living in packs, and, unlike the jackal, is a formidable hunter. It is ferocious, feared by the big cats, and also shares its food. An ideal hunter, it must have been considered a suitable emblem by the early inhabitants of the Messak.

Elephants are often shown in the presence of hunting-dog figures. Some scenes show a mythical being copulating with an elephant. This may be a sort of prehistoric 'master of the beasts and fertility'. The Touaregs have a legend of a mythical giant, Amerolqis, credited with inventing the main features of Touareg society: Tifinagh writing, language, poetry and music. He was also extremely promiscuous, and the only creature able to withstand his advances (and the pregnancies which resulted), was the elephant. But all female beings were fascinated by his song. The Touareg myth and the Messak carvings would seem to belong to the same cultural universe.

**Fertility** The issue of fertility is very much present in the Messak carvings. It features in
**carvings** what the archaeologists refer to as *femmes ouvertes*, sometimes associated with cattle giving birth. One theory runs that in the prehistoric mythology of the Messak, humankind was born of a cow (as is the case in certain African myths), or that humankind and cattle are of similar origin. Many of the 'open women', shown in a position recalling traditional African childbirth, are to be found in rock shelters. From this archaeologists extrapolate that such caves and carvings were part of a fertility rite. In many cases the female sex is shown as a deep hollow. As real caves are rare in the Messak, the artists had to actively seek out shelters in the rock for fertility-type carvings. The hollows are often quite deep, and

*Carvings of cattle drawn by Barth in the Telizaghen area of the Messah Settefet in the 1840s (Barth 1857-58)*

may have been produced gradually, possibly as the result of numerous visits by pilgrims carrying out fertility-related ceremonies. Given that sterility was one of the most feared infirmities in traditional African society, the Fezzan sites featuring open women carvings might have been designed to ensure effective procreation. The thinking now runs that certain sites are closely related to Messak society's ideas about how humanity came into the world.

Most of the Messak carvings belong to a style referred to by archaeologists as **The Messak** bubaline, 'the buffalo style'. The style's main features include the naturalism of **School** the carvings and their monumental nature, along with a preference for portraying large African animals, in particular a now-extinct species of buffalo, the *Bubalus antiquus*. However, thinking has moved on, and the corpus of carvings available to researchers has expanded hugely.

Critics of the traditional stylistic definition point out that many of the animals' natural activities – grazing, lying down – are never shown. Many animals which must have been present in the environment are never featured either. There are also many small carvings alongside the monumental works. The carvings are naturalistic in as much as they show the beasts in movement; there is a clear concern for detail in the portrayal of eyes, ears, hooves and muzzles. Modern conventions of perspective are present in the way legs are portrayed.

Archaeologists now distinguish sub-groups and stylistic features. There are the so-called Tozina-style carvings, with their characteristic pointy legs. Although the form of the animals is natural, certain body parts are highly stylised: tails are pointy, horns and muzzle are abnormally long, the lines are extremely fine. (Tozina is a place in the Sud-Oranais, Algeria, where the style was first identified.) Carvings in this style have been discovered across North Africa, in the Atlas Mountains and the western parts of the Sahara. Current thinking is that this style was born of technical constraints. Tozina-type carvings are generally found on flat, horizontal surfaces near the edge of the plateau, on hard sandstone. With the back-and-forth movement needed to make a line on these surfaces, it is difficult to produce a short curved line. Pulling the carving implement towards oneself, the result is a line which is deep in the middle section, tailing away towards the end.

The Tozina style represents only a tiny proportion of the Messak carvings. The vast majority have a naturalistic feel. The lines are deeply incised or smoothed 'gutters', while within the carving, the surfaces may be smoothed or worked to better suggest the form of the beast in question. There are, however, a number of outstanding technico-stylistic features in the Messak art. Particularly notable is the use of a double line defining a raised area to give definition to an image. Elsewhere in the Sahara, a simple incised line was considered sufficient. The technique is used for most of the cattle carvings. There are also a number of secondary features. A tear is often shown running from the eyes of the cattle. Sometimes a series of parallel curves can be seen on the flanks of the cattle, adding a touch of realism. Another technique, in Africa almost exclusive to the Messak, is the smoothing of the area around the image to heighten its visual impact, giving an effect verging on bas-relief.

## Messak Settafet: sites to visit

One of the finest selections of rock art is in the Wadi Matkhandush. On a 200 m **Wadi** stretch of broken rock face are samples of all the main fauna of the savannah **Matkhandush** lands: elephants and slender-legged giraffe, herds of buffalo, flocks of ostriches, hippopotami and oxen, even a crocodile and a fish. The strange round shapes next to the giraffes are thought to represent traps. One particularly fine giraffe has been superimposed on an elephant; the head is startlingly realistic, and with a gentle eye it gazes down on the visitor. High up on the cliff face is one of the most symbolic of all the rock carvings: the Fighting Cats. The 1930s explorer Leo Frobenius named these fighting lionesses the Werecats after an old German legend. Unfortunately, the rock has been scraped clean of its patina to make the beasts more visible to tourists. Human figures are present, too: hunters with dog-masks, a naked female figure.

Fezzan

## From Libues to Libyans

For ancient Greek geographer Herodotus, there were three peoples south of the Mediterranean: the **Egyptians**, the **Aethiopes** (lit: 'burnt faces'), and the **Libues**. Though the Greeks had long had contact with the Egyptians, the Ethiopians were a less well known quantity, inhabiting the edge of the earth, south of the Nile, and next to the great river ocean. With the Libues, who inhabited today's northwest Africa, the Greeks had more contact, through their five cities in Cyrenaica. Today's Berbers are no doubt the descendants of Herodotus' Libues – whose name comes from the ancient Egyptian Libu (pron. lee-boo), the name given to the people west of Egypt.

**Barbaroi** was the term given by the Greeks to anyone who babbled away in a language other than Greek. Writing in the 14th century, Arab thinker Ibn Khaldoun used the term for the mountain peoples (**al barbar**), as opposed to **al-'arab**, the nomads. The term '**nomad**' is of Greek origin as well, and gave the Romans their name for the central Maghreb, Numidia.

For the Arab writers, North Africa is the **Maghreb**, the 'land of the West', as opposed to the **Mashreq**, the 'land of the East', basically Egypt and the Near East. Ibn Khaldoun in his Ibar, a great discussion of peoples and lands, wrote that **al maghrib** "includes Tripoli and the lands beyond, towards the west: Ifrikiya, the Za'b, the central Maghreb, the Far Maghrib, the near Sous valley and the far Sous. These are the regions which formed the domain of the Berbers and the lands where they resided in ancient times."

In the 16th century, the North African coast was the setting for serious Hispano-Ottoman rivalry. The region had been referred to as **Barbary** as of late medieval times. The 15th-century traveller from Flanders, Anselme Adorne, stopped off in several cities in the region, and talks of Barbaria. In the 17th century, the Ottomans established a form of authority over the North African coast. Algiers, Tunis and Tripoli became the capitals of the **régences barbaresques**, the Ottoman provinces or ilayet of North Africa. English authors talk of West Barbary and southern Barbary.

Meanwhile, the term **Libya** as a country name only appears for the first time in the writings of Italian colonial propagandists in the early 20th century. The term was officially applied to the whole area of Tripolitania, Cyrenaica and the Fezzan in the early 1930s. (Tripolitania and Cyrenaica had been united administratively in 1928.) Ironically for a nation which until recently made pan-Arabism an essential component of its creed, Libya bears a name coined as part of the Italian colonial enterprise.

**In Galguien**  A few kilometres west of the Matkhandush site is In Galguien, (N 25° 44'389", E 12° 08'258") famed for its carvings of elephants. Here the cliffs are higher and more forbidding. (In Galguien means 'the spring of the crows'). Look out for a fabulous portrayal of a panicking elephant pursued by a tiny hunter. The enraged beast charges forward, ears flapping. It seems to be protecting another smaller elephant. (Lower down is a hippopotamus). Every wrinkle of the great elephant's trunk and ears is shown. The expression is one of fear. The hunter is there to finish it off – the animal is not far off collapse. The artist had clearly witnessed the scene: the lines flow, the trumpeting beast is rendered with economy and precision. Further along this part of the valley are other elephants, giraffes, and a procession of ostriches.

**In Habeter**  The prehistoric sites of the In Habeter section of the valley begin some 12 km west of the Wadi Matkhandush. Here the carvings are on the south bank of the wadi. A sign at GPS N 25° 42'602", E 12° 05'334" indicates the way down to the rock art. Here again you will find all the great fauna of the African plains: giraffes, oxen, antelope and elephants. Half-human, half-animal figures can be found: two strange dog-headed hunters, both brandishing a weapon of some kind, return from the hunt; they must have supernatural strength, as one appears to be dragging a slain rhinoceros along.

# Germa to Ghat via Serdeles (Awinat)

## Ubari

From Germa, the road heads west for Ubari and **Serdeles**, also referred to by the Arabic name Awinat. There is little of excitement on the Germa to Ubari section of the road (33 km), nor for that matter on the Ubari to Serdeles stretch (247 km), apart from a couple of checkpoints. Ubari is a largish, untidy sort of place. Make sure you fill up with petrol here, as the pumps sometimes run dry in the Fezzan. Ubari was once a centre for the Touareg, and has an early 19th-century mosque sometimes referred to as the Touareg Mosque. There is an Italo-Turkish fort where the *Matkhandush Tourism Agency*, T2731 has its offices. Try also *Ubari Tourism* T2950 with offices in the centre.

*Phone code: 0722*

## Serdeles

Serdeles is a possible jumping off point for the **Jabal Akakus**. Here you are at the northernmost point of the range, well placed to head south along the eastern (accessible) side in a four-wheel drive vehicle. **Al Faw Camp** on the right of the main road coming from Ubari is easily recogniszable with its palm-branch covered verandah; desert vehicles and buses of various kinds may be parked up nearby. *Al Faw Tours* has **accommodation** in simple huts (10 LD per person) and can set up **camel** and **four wheel drive excursions** into the Akakus, T0724-2265 (Ghat office) and T/F2828 (Serdeles office), or contact manager Abou Bakar on mobile T09-12140678. El Faw also have a Tripoli office, T0212-4802881. In 1999, *El Faw Tours* had a link up with Abd el Moula Voyages in Djerba, Tunisia, T00216-5651887. Camel excursions need to be set up well in advance. Budget at around £40 a day. (This figure is given as an indication, given the variations in demand and exchange rates.)

*Phone code: 0724*

# Ghat

*Situated in the far southwestern corner of the Fezzan, Ghat was the only permanent Touareg settlement in the Sahara, strategically located on the route between the Mediterranean and sub-Saharan Africa. In the 19th century, it was one of the Ottoman's Empire's most remote outposts. In the 20th century it was occupied by Italians and French. Only 80 km from Djanet over the border in Algeria, Ghat lies in the valley between the Algerian Tassili-n-Ajjer to the west and the Tadrart Akakus to the east. Once an important stopping place on the slave route across the Sahara, Ghat now functions as a base for tourist expeditions to the rock art sites in the neighbouring Akakus. Happily for those with little Arabic, lots of people speak French in Ghat, given the proximity of Algeria and francophone Saharan Africa. A small but growing settlement, it is first point of call for immigrants heading up from Niger.*

*Phone code 0724*

Fezzan

## Ins and outs

**Getting there**  Ghat is reached by road from Sabha, via Germa and Serdeles (Awinat). There is also a small airport, though *Libyan Arab Airlines* flights are irregular at the present time. At peak times, certain holiday companies run charter flights into Ghat airport, 22 km north of the town centre on the road to Serdeles.

**Getting around**  Ghat is a small place, to be visited in a short morning's meander. For excursions to the Akakus, see below.

## History and background

Little is known of the early history of Ghat, although it is thought that the Romans may have made it to the region. Certainly the Italians thought they did, and the idea was confirmed by the discovery of building remains near certain springs. Ghat occupies an important position. It has water and is located in the Wadi Tanezzouft which divides the Tassili-n-Ajjer to the west from the stone labyrinths of the Tadrart Akakus. In pre-Islamic times, the region was inhabited, as the presence of a large necropolis dating from between 500 to 750 AD to the southwest of the town shows. The Arab-Muslim conquest of the seventh century passed through the region, without, however, Islamizing the population to any great degree. The name Ghat does not appear until the 12th century AD, when the town is said to have been founded by the noble Berber tribe of Ihadjenen with the help of other tribal groups.

In the 19th century, Ghat emerges into written history. The Ottomans established a fort in 1858. A certain E von Bary, a German naturalist, visited Ghat in 1876, and found a small walled town surrounded by palm-groves irrigated with spring water. Ottoman rule was not to last, however. This remotest of the Sublime Porte's outposts was evacuated after a rebellion, and the town was not re-occupied until 1908, when Constantinople became seriously worried by French penetration into the Tassili-n-Ajjer to the west.

Italian troops reached Ghat in 1914, entering the town without a shot being fired. (The word was that the Italians would be useful allies against the French who had awarded the local ruler's land in Djanet to the Touareg leader of the Hoggar.) In the course of the First World War, the Italians withdrew as their position in northern Libya deteriorated. It was not until 1930 that the Italians finally occupied Ghat, building a strong-point on the site of the former Turkish fort on the Koukemen hill overlooking the town.

Rock arch
Jabal Akakus

## Sights

Ghat does not have too much to keep the tourist. In the winter, there is now a **Folk Traditions Festival**, generally lasting a few days towards the end of December. Otherwise, there is only enough to occupy the visitor for half a day.

The old town of Ghat, now largely in ruins, lies in the shadow of Mount Koukemen. The covered streets recall Ghadamès hundreds of kilometres to the north. Although there are only a few families still in residence, some restoration works have been carried out, thus ensuring that the picturesque old Saharan settlement did not crumble away entirely as the locals moved into new accommodation. Mud brick was the original building material. One would expect the doors and ceilings to be in palm wood, as is the case in Saharan settlements further north. In fact they are in cypress from the nearby Tassili plateau where once upon a time there were extensive cypress forests.

Behind the new main mosque, at the entrance to the madina, is the former Italian barracks. At private initiative, a house has been converted into a museum of local life. (The owner has the small souvenir shop opposite the Idinen Travel Agency.) In their remote Saharan wadi, the people of Ghat had to make things for themselves, and local craftwork includes weavings, leather bags, and basket work. Tuareg jewellery is a popular buy, much of it made in nearby Niger.

## Essentials

**Sleeping** C *Hotel Tassili*, town centre. T2560/2562. Not particularly attractive but the only option in Ghat. Restaurant and carpark. Rooms poorly insulated, cold in winter, not particularly well air-conditioned in summer. Has a branch of the *Winzrik Tourism Agency*.

**Shopping** Food market in the town centre, with the usual vegetables and some fruit, chicken. The usual stock-everything grocer shops with tinned goods. Petrol. Two petrol stations, 1 north of the town as you arrive from Serdeles, 1 south of town on the road to Al Barakat. Despite Libya being a producer country, the pumps sometimes run dry in the Fezzan, so make sure you stock up whenever possible.

**Tour operators** It is essential to use a reliable agency for setting up a trip into the Jabal Akakus (see below). Vehicle hire and agency services are payable in Libyan dinars. The following agencies are possibilities: *Akakus Travel Agency*, P.O.B. 304, Ghat, T2804/2318, Tx2938, (General Manager, A Younis, home T2938). Agency running visits to the major archaeological sites of the region. A reliable agency which works with European travel companies. *Indinan (I-n-dinane) Travel Agency*, P.O.B 60, Ghat, T2460. One of the best-established agencies in Ghat, located near the new mosque, in the town centre. Director speaks French and has contacts over the border at Djenet. Tours into the Akakus. *Tadrart Teshuinat Travel Agency*, P.O.B. 190 Ghat, T2083, F2506. Akakus circuits by four-wheel drive. *Al Ula*. Tripoli based-agency with camp in the northern Akakus. You may be given unreliable vehicles at peak times of year. *Winzrik Travel Agency* has offices in Tripoli and Ghat, at the Hotel Tassili, T2604. Head office P.O.B. 12794 Tripoli. Works with major European travel agencies.

**Transport** **Air** *LAA* has offices opposite the food market, although there are no flights for the moment apart from occasional charters. **Bus** services to **Ubari** and **Sabha**. Early departures.

**Directory** **Communications** Post office close to the *Hotel Tassili*. Phones open until late. You may be asked to show your passport before you phone. **Medical facilities** Pharmacy in the town centre, modern hospital on the eastern outskirts. **Useful addresses** Garages: Vehicle repair near the

Fezzan

petrol station on the Serdeles road. Mechanics, often Tuaregs from Mali and Niger, know names for vehicle parts and problems in French.

## Excursions north of Ghat

Some 50 km north of Ghat lies the strangely shaped **Jabal Idinen**, 'the mountain of the spirits', once upon a time much feared by the region's inhabitants as the home of maleficent beings. For years, the Touareg refused to guide anyone to this mountain with its cliff faces rising steep out of a tumble of rock. North of Ghat, the **Wadi Tanezzouft**, the region's main grazing area and several kilometres wide in places, runs between the steep western cliffs of the Akakus and the Erg Tanezzouft, a line of dunes stretching north from Ghat. In the wadi, there are acacias and tamarisks, and in some winters, good pasture grows thanks to rain water running in from the Akakus. The former caravan trail can still be seen in places on the Akakus side, too. You may also come across stone circles, the remains of Touareg mosques, the roofs of which have long since vanished. Still further north, in the vicinity of the Jabal Idinen, the road rises to run across a plateau before descending to the small oasis of Serdeles (Awinat).

# The Jabal Akakus

*The rock paintings and carvings of the Jabal Akakus are the big draw of southwestern Libya. The prehistoric rock art is located in a spectacularly beautiful, though highly inhospitable, region, reminiscent of the Wadi Rum in Jordan. The Jabal (or Tadrart, to use the Berber term) Akakus chain of mountains runs north-south for 250 km, starting from the area just west of Serdeles and finishing down at the Takharkhouri Pass. Geologically, these mountains are a continuation of the Tassili-n-Ajjer in neighbouring Algeria. The range is never more than 50 km wide, and with its steep cliffs overlooking the Ghat plain, is inaccessible to vehicles from the western side.*

## Ins and outs

**Getting there & around** Visiting the Akakus, you will drive on sandy wadi beds through canyons to reach the sites. Here and there the landscape opens up to present wide vistas of jagged mountain, gnawed by wind and sun. The predominant colours are blue, gold and shades of plum black. Centuries of sand-blasting and/or the action of micro-bacteria have darkened the cliff faces. Despite all this desolation, the sites are easily accessible for a four-wheel drive. Almost all can be approached by vehicle, necessitating a short scramble at the most to reach the cliff shelter where the prehistoric paintings have wondrously survived. (In the Tassili-n-Ajjer in neighbouring Algeria, the sites are far more difficult to access.)

A short but adequate visit to the main sites of the Jabal Akakus, using four-wheel drive vehicle, requires 5 days. As the stone labyrinths of the region can only be approached by vehicle from the east, you need a day's drive south from Ghat and then east to get within striking distance. From an overnight camp in the central Akakus, the most spectacular sites of the Wadi Teshuinat and around could be covered in a very, very rushed day. There is less spectacular rock art (but magnificent scenery) in the northern part of the Akakus, round the Wadi Awis, where Italo-Libyan travel agency *Al Ula* has a permanent tent-camp.

Another option is to rent vehicles from one of the agencies based at Serdeles, and approach the Akakus from the north. If you have time, the pleasant thing to do is to travel with camels, plus four-wheel drive vehicle to transport most of the food, bedding and firewood. If possible, avoid the crowded New Year and Easter periods. Note that nights are extremely cold in November – February, so a good sleeping bag is necessary. October and March are good times to visit.

**Permits & guides**

The Jabal Akakus is a national park, and a visitor's permit is required. The park's main office, where permits are issued, is in Ghat. The regulations also require you to have a local guide to visit the region – which is probably a sensible thing, given the absence of good maps and the nature of the landscape, a confusing jumble of wadis and canyons. If you get lost, you are very much on your own. There is no Europ-Assistance here.

Ghat-based travel agencies will deal with the formalities for obtaining the permit (10LD fee and photo required), which can be done overnight. They will also deal with passport registration (5LD, compulsory within five days of arriving in Libya) at the appropriate office, if you have not already done this in, say, Tripoli. The guide's fee will be around 80LD a day. He will have a splendid topographical memory, making sure you get to the key sites. However, do not expect any detailed accounts of prehistoric art from him. Few of the guides have more than a basic command of European languages and will not have had access to the various scholarly publications on the region. Before leaving, make sure you agree whether you are supplying the guide's food or not. It is current practice to tip the guide at the end of the trip, say 10LD per head.

## Background and history of the Akakus rock art

Unlike the rock art of the Messak Settafet, which comprises only carvings, the Jabal Akakus has both carvings and paintings, depicting the life and times of prehistoric hunter-gatherers and herders. In contrast to the Messak Settafet, the lines of the Akakus carvings are shallower and wider. The sites are different, too. While the Messak Settafet has few natural caves, the Akakus has numerous rock shelters and grottoes. While none are very deep, most would have provided perfectly adequate shelter for small groups of humans at a time when the region was wetter and more forested. Sheltered from the action of the weather, it is in these rock shelters that the prehistoric paintings have survived. The carvings tend to occupy more exposed sites. It is not known whether this was a deliberate move – or whether exposed rock faces had colour paintings, too.

**The Akakus discovered**

Heinrich Barth was the first European to record the prehistoric carvings in the Messak Settafet in the 1840s but the first European to write on the strange rock paintings of the Akakus was much later. The French explorer **Foureau** had not actually seen the sites, however. His account was based on the campfire tales of his Touareg guides as he travelled in the central Sahara. In 1910, rock art was noted by **Lieutenant Gardel** over the border in Algeria, in a region to the south of the Akakus. The *Reale società geografica italiana* funded exploration under the leadership of one Professor Graziosi in the late 1930's and discoveries were made right up until 1940.

The first serious research work had to wait until the 1950s. With a small camel caravan, **Fabrizio Mori** was the first archaeologist to venture into the region. He and his team have continued ever since, and in over 40 years of painstaking exploration, have recorded hundreds of ancient sites, from rock art to flint 'workshops' high above the valley floors. A serious attempt was made to classify the paintings and carvings into periods. It remains to be seen, however, whether archaeological research will remain an Italian preserve. Almost no Libyan specialists have been trained up, despite the internationally recognized importance of the region's heritage.

Fezzan

## Jabal Akakus rock art: the main periods

Pre-historian and Akakus specialist **Fabrizio Mori** divides the rock art of the Jabal Akakus into a series of precise periods, each lasting several millennia. Though heavily contested in certain academic circles, Mori's categories, each named for an animal (apart from the Round Head Period), give the novice a hold on the complexities of art and life in the central Sahara many thousands of years ago.

**Period and Characteristics**
(BP = before present)

**Great Savannah Fauna**, beginning 11th/10th century BP and onwards. Mainly rock carvings. Ancient ox, Bubalus antiquus, widely portrayed.

**Round Heads**, 9000 BP and onwards. Mainly painting. Early period has outline figures. Development of coloured, 'filled-in' figures. Late phase sees polychrome pictures.

**Pastoral Period**, 7000 BP and later. Mixture of carvings and paintings.

**Horse Period**, 3500 BP and later. Carvings and paintings. Stylistically cruder than the above. Images of chariots.

**Camel Period**, 2000 BP and later. Created by Garamantian/Mediterranean type populations.

Mori's periodization ends the Savannah Fauna Period at around 9250 BP. Other researchers, notably Henri Lhote and P.

Graziosi, telescope things somewhat, ending the Savannah Fauna Period in 9000 BP, and defining a different period for 9000-6000 BP, in which an Ancient Ox phase runs into a Round Head phase. (The reasoning behind this is the archaeological evidence for the extinction of the Bubalus antiquus.) In this classification, the Pastoral Period runs from 6000 to around 3000 BP. Horse and Camel Periods coincide. For Lhote and Graziosi, artistic activity thus begins in Neolithic times (10,000 BP).

These last two periods, Horse and Camel, can be dated with precision, since it is known that the horse was introduced into Africa via Egypt by the Hyksos in the sixteenth century BC. The dromedary arrived shortly afterwards, introduced from the Near East. The archaeological evidence from the central Sahara suggests that the Palaeo-Berber region corresponds more or less to that occupied by the Touareg today. Defining the earlier periods is a more problematic exercise, however, being based on the idea that as the climate grew progressively drier, there were considerable changes in human lifestyle and the fauna in the region. In particular, using 'patination' to date an item is a rash move, as even recent carvings of the Horse and Camel Periods have acquired considerable patina in certain cases.

**Scenes of prehistoric daily life** Although often faded, the rock paintings of the Akakus provide a unique record of life in the Sahara thousands of years ago. (The region only took on its present aspect some 3,000 years ago.) The visitor will see representations of animals and humans. These range from lively hunting scenes, with beasts in full flight, to stylized representations of human figures, some with little match-stick heads, others with disproportionate round heads. Some scenes are clearly narrative, depicting worship, celebration or battle. Unfortunately, even after several decades of research, it seems impossible to date the rock paintings with any degree of precision – as is also the case for the carvings of the Messak Settafet.

Italian specialist Fabrizio Mori built his academic career on an elaborate (but contested) chronological typology of the Akakus rock art, not easily boiled down for travel consumption in the pages of a short chapter on the Fezzan. Put too briefly, Mori's chronology begins towards 7000 BC, based on carbon dating of charred remains found in rock shelters containing paintings. The chronology is built on the basis of the patina acquired by the rock and what Mori considers progressive stylistic development over the millenia. See also page 234.

For today's visitor, the most fascinating scenes are those of a vivid life in a time before the desert. While both the Akakus and the Messak Settafet have rock carvings, the Akakus is unique in Libya in its rock paintings. (Over the border in the Algerian Tassili-n-Ajjer rock paintings are even more prevalent.) In terracotta red and white, the images of the Akakus are of superb visual fitness. Painted in carefully chosen rock shelters, they are delicate portrayals of a robust humankind who eventually found it more rewarding to domesticate animals than hunt them. We can see people move from being hardy predators to a less precarious way of life. Hunting continued while new ways took hold. Woven cloth arrived, pottery developed. In contrast to the Messak Settafet, the Akakus scenes are more human. There is an interest in the minutiae of a ceremony, as witnessed by the famous paintings of women dressing hair in the tiny Wan Amil cave.

Research suggests that the uses made of the rock shelters in the Akakus changed over time. Often several metres above the valley floor, they were a secure space for daily activity, the cutting, preparation and storage of food, caring for children and elders, sleeping. Archaeologists have discovered the ashes of prehistoric cooking fires and the dung of domestic animals, no doubt brought in at night in certain shelters. Elaborate rock paintings may indicate that the shelters were used for celebrations and religious rites. Here Stone Age people would have assembled to commune with their deities, deriving the cohesion necessary for group survival.

**On the cliff tops**

Besides the paintings, the region also has further fragile evidence of human settlement. It is possible to climb up onto the heights above the cliffs, and early humans certainly did. So far most of the sites studied are the easily accessible ones, located below the cliffs. Reaching the higher levels is difficult, as the rock faces tend to overhang the ground level, eroded away by the wadis. However, once up on one of the terraces, it is possible to walk for considerable distances along rock terraces overlooking the valleys. Views of the landscape are stupendous. On the upper levels, you may find traces of flint manufacture, another complex field which has been extensively studied by pre-historians.

**Making paintings**

In the early communities of the Akakus, painting must have been a time-consuming activity. All painting materials would have had to be manufactured from natural materials. Coloured rock would be reduced to powder, possibly in the rounded hollows still to be seen in certain sites. (Another argument runs that these were used for pounding grain.) Chemical analysis shows that the finely pounded coloured powders, generally red, more rarely white, occasionally black or green, were applied to the rock face mixed with egg albumen or milk. Given the longevity of the paintings, the casein in milk would appear to be an excellent fixative.

**Pressure from tourism**

The accessibility of the rock art in the Akakus has made the region very popular, perhaps a little too popular during the Christmas and Easter breaks. The sandy wadi beds are covered with the tracks of innumerable four-wheel drive vehicles, and sites can easily be identified from a distance by the number of vehicles parked up nearby. At other times of year, however, the region is empty – there are few Touareg living nomad existences here today. Large numbers of tourists create new pressures in the region. The rock art and the desert environment must be respected. In the past, tourists would splash water on the rock paintings to bring up the colours – the result being that works of art which had survived for thousands of years faded in a decade. Elsewhere, visitors have chipped images of their turbo-cooled Toyotas into the rock next to unique

Fezzan

representations of savannah fauna. The *Période des camions* is the most destructive the Akakus has witnessed to date. There is clearly a temptation to take flints and fragments of dotted-wavy-line prehistoric pottery home but it is better to leave such items in situ. Rather than gathering dust on a shelf in some European home, they are best left as clues for future archaeological expeditions. In any case, should the Libyan customs want to have a look at your baggage as you leave the country, you are for the high jump if they discover any antiquities nestling among your dirty laundry.

## Exploring the Akakus

**South from Ghat into the Akakus**
To take you into the Akakus from Ghat, your guide will probably opt for the south route. This takes you to the east side of the mountains via the Takharkhouri Pass. Heading south from Ghat, you pass through the minor settlement of **Barakat** (7 km), where there is a petrol station. The hard-top road ends some 15 km further south, turning into a track. About 1 km after the end of the road, there is a police post, and another one 30 km from Ghat at GPS N24° 43'60", E10° 12,20'. At GPS N24° 38, 74', E10° 13'35". Ignoring the track which runs off towards Tin Akoum in Algeria, you begin to follow the **Wadi Ayadhar** southeastwards. To the northeast the Akakus rises steeply to its highest point, **Anou Ayadhar**, 1,480 m. Some 65 km from Ghat, at 24° 32, 40'N, 10° 23,15', you reach the first dunes. There is a further police post 80 km from Ghat to check passports and permits, before you reach the dunes before the **Takharkhouri Pass**. A further 20 km on and you are in the Akakus proper. Here, according to the time available, your guide will choose a suitable itinerary of rock art sites to visit.

**South from Serdeles into the Akakus**
Another way of reaching the rock art is to head south from Serdeles on the Ubari to Ghat road. (This does not, of course, excuse you from getting a permit to visit the region from the authorities in Ghat.) The track runs south from the oasis of Serdeles across arid flatlands. To the left, the dunes of **Wan Kasa**, eastern outpost of the Edeyen Marzoug, appear on the horizon. (Good photo opportunities on the dunes at sunset.) To the right (west), the Akakus gradually become visible. Some 80 km from Serdeles, there is an isolated well, **Bir Talawet**, (GPS 25° 13'70', E 010° 46'60') where nomads bring their flocks to drink. The most spectacular site in the northern Akakus is the **Awis** area, with great pinnacles and chimneys of blackened rock and wadis of golden sand. It is a long day's drive from Serdeles to the Wadi Teshuinat. Ideally, you would break and camp overnight in the Awis area, about three hours' drive from the highway. There are some pleasant easy walks through the spectacular landscape here.

## Key sites in the Akakus

The guides often have their own preferred circuits, and the network of rock canyons and wadis allows all sorts of variations. The sites listed below are just a fraction of what can be seen. Ultimately, however, it is the journey through landscapes worthy of a science fiction film that make the Akakus so special.

If you are pushed for time, your time should be spent in the **Wadi Teshuinat**. Within a radius of 10 km is a major concentration of fine examples of prehistoric rock art. Key points in this area include the **Wadi Imha** and **Wan Amnal**, **Tin Ghalaga**, **Tin Taharit**, and **Azaraw**. You should also try to see **Wan Amil**, the **Wadi Kassan** and the **Wadi Kasi**. In the southern part of the Akakus, there is a spectacular natural arch at **Fozzigiaren**, and interesting hunt scenes in the **Wadi Tanshal**.

Entering the Wadi Teshuinat area, there is fine natural rock formation at **Wadi Imha**. About 7 km or so further on is the **Wan Amnal** site (N 24° 46'80", E 010° 38'75"), a large rock shelter with hunting scenes. At **Tin Ghalaga**, close to impressive rock formations, is a small shelter, for centuries home to a rather nicely painted rhinoceros. The artist either had excellent visual memory – or a rhinoceros was trundling past. Some vandal has carved their sweetheart's name in Arabic next to the splendid pachyderm. **Tin Taharit**, just under a high cliff overhang, has a fine hunting scene of men and dogs in hot pursuit of mouflons plus numerous images of savannah fauna, including some beautifully drawn giraffes. You should on no account miss the two flappy-eared elephants at **Azaraw**.

At **Wan Amil** (N 24° 50'05", E 010° 30'20") is one of the deeper rock shelters of the region. Here the rock walls are alive with some of the most amazing scenes in the Akakus. There are paintings which seem to figure preparations for a wedding. Women chat and wash hair, the bride can be seen in a long robe between two people with strange hairstyles or head dresses. Further to the right is a crowd of running archers, a scattering of cows, and also the odd giraffe. Other painted animals have faded to red stains. Visitors who have been to this site several times say that the colours are fading. Is this due to tourists 'washing' the images for photos – or due to changing climatic conditions and pollution?

**Up the Wadi Teshuinat and around**

# Serdeles to the Takharkhouri Pass via Ghat

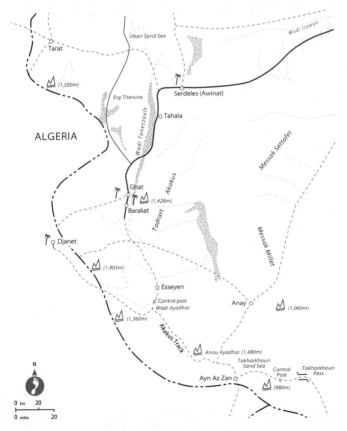

Whatever the case, Mori places the Wan Amil scenes in the Early Pastoral Period, ie between 7000 and 5000 years BP (Before Present).

The million dinar question remains as to when humankind actually first started to use the rock faces for painted and carved images. One theory runs that these images were a sudden discovery: all of a sudden, thanks to a favourable set of climatic and environmental factors, a group of humans felt the need to create. Another theory sees the rock art phenomenon as being born in a set of completely different times and places as different groups or communities reached a certain level of biological and intellectual maturity. In fact, the Saharan rock art is quite recent, the very earliest representations going back to only 14,000 years BP. The oldest cave paintings in France and Spain have been dated at 40,000 years BP.

## Libya's southwestern borders

The Fezzan has land borders with Algeria and Niger. At the time of writing, it was not possible for tourists to cross over into Algeria. Nevertheless, the southern plateaux of Algeria are open to tourism (Italian tour groups recently started to visit central Saharan sites by charter flight), and the main settlement in the Tassili-n-Ajjer region, Djanet, is barely 70 km from Ghat. As the situation stabilises in Algeria, it may become possible for tourists to visit the rock art on both sides of the border. For reference, the track for the border and Djanet via Tin Alkum turns off the Akakus piste some 38 km south of Ghat. (Distances: Ghat to the border, 60 km, border post to Djanet 210 km.)

Background

9

250

# Background

# History

A comprehensive short history of a country as vast as Libya is not easy to put together. Great distances separate regions with hugely differing, very specific social and geographic identities. In prehistoric times, the central Sahara was home to flourishing communities (see the chapter on the Fezzan). The coastal regions, on the other hand emerge into written history with Herodotus. Present day eastern Libya was important to the Greeks, and their first major colonies outside the core Hellenic lands were situated here. (This Greek section of Libyan history is dealt with in the chapter on Cyrenaica.) Under the Romans and then the Byzantines, this region continued to be important but it then faded out of written history until the 19th century.

Western coastal Libya and its hinterland achieved considerable importance as the Roman Tripolitania. The *regio Tripolitana*'s history was closely linked to that of the more northerly provinces of Africa and Numidia, roughly equivalent to modern day Tunisia and eastern Algeria. Centuries later, with the coming of the Ottomans (in the mid-16th century), this region, centering on the port city of Tripoli, began to have a geopolitical life of its own. It was here that the Ottomans sought to re-establish their waning authority in North Africa in the 19th century, and it was here that the first independent Arab republic was proclaimed. For the Italians, it was the core area of their colony of Libya. Thus, to avoid too many diversions, the focus in this section is on the history of Tripolitania.

## Berbers, Phoenicians and Greeks

Like other parts of the Mediterranean, the North African coastal regions became an area for competition between the Greeks and the Phoenicians. The power of both peoples was based on their maritime technology. In order to trade in the commodities of Africa, they established settlements on the coast of present day Libya, entering into relations with the nomadic communities of the desert, notably the Garamantes around the Fezzan. The Garamantes appear to have specialized in warfare based on charioteering and they began to raid the new coastal settlements. At the same time, they also controlled trans-Saharan commerce, one of the major reasons why the Phoenicians, at least, were so interested in North Africa.

The Greeks had begun to colonize the Egyptian and eastern Libyan coastline as part of their attempt to control Egyptian maritime trade. Cyrene, the first of five Greek colonies in Cyrenaica in Libya, was founded about 625 BC and, a little earlier, three Phoenician colonies were created in western Libya, on the coast of what is today Tripolitania, in order to exploit new commercial opportunities, for the Phoenicians were first-and-foremost traders. Eventually more important, however, was the major Phoenician settlement at Carthage, on the coast of northern Tunisia, close to the modern capital of Tunis, founded in the late ninth century in order to control access to Sicily and the western Mediterranean basin.

Greeks and Phoenicians competed for control of the coastal areas in Libya and eventually created an uneasy division of the region between themselves. The Greeks took over Egypt after the creation of the Ptolemaic Kingdom on the death of Alexander the Great in 323 BC and incorporated Cyrenaica into the new state. The Phoenicians, harried in their original Lebanese home of Tyre by the Assyrians and Persians, created a commercial empire based on Carthage, with outlying colonies to the west, right round to the Atlantic coast near Larache in present day Morocco. Traditionally, Carthage was founded in 814 BC when princess Dido led part of Tyre's population to settle in a safe place on the North African coast, founding Qart Hadasht, the 'new city', which was to become the leading maritime power in the western Mediterranean.

*Tripolis and Pentapolis*

Founded by the Phoenicians, possibly as early as the eighth century AD, the three Carthaginian trading posts of Lpay (later Roman Leptis), Uiat (Oea, Tarablus to the Arabs) and Sabratha were named the **Tripolis** by the Greeks – hence the Latin Regio tripolitana *for the area. In ancient* times, Cyrenaica was often referred to as the **Pentapolis**, the five towns being Cyrene, Apollonia (port to Cyrene), Teucheira (modern Tocra), Ptolemais (Tolmeita) and Berenice (modern Benghazi).

## The rise of Carthage

In the seventh century BC, Carthage had trading posts in the Balearic Islands, Sardinia and the western end of Sicily. In the sixth century BC, they achieved footholds in Corsica, with Etruscan aid. In 481, they organized a great expedition to extend their influence in Sicily – with disastrous results. At the Battle of Himera, the Carthaginian forces were crushed by the rulers of Agrigentum and Syracuse. It was a huge disaster for the ruling Magonid family. (Carthaginian compensation payments probably funded a Hellenic renaissance in Sicily.) Henceforth, Carthage restricted her efforts to maintaining her valuable network of trading posts. From the fifth to the third centuries BC trade flourished, with Punic merchants the link between Africa and the Mediterranean. They traded in gold, ivory (highly prized for statues of the gods), and slaves from Africa, silver from Spain, copper from Sardinia, olive oil from Sicily, exchanging them against manufactured products from the eastern Mediterranean, Greek pottery and textiles. Explorers were sent out to prospect distant coasts: Himilcon reached Finistère, while Hannon sailed along the western coast of Africa, possibly as far as the Gulf of Guinea. Commerce with remote peoples was based on barter – the Carthaginians first struck coins in the late fourth century BC.

The late fourth century was a time of internal strife in Sicily as the Syracusan state fell apart. In 310-308, Syracuse's ruler Agathocles took an army into the Carthaginian heartlands, landing on the Cap Bon (now in northeastern Tunisia) and causing considerable damage. (The Punic round town of Kerkouane may well have been abandoned after being sacked by his army.) When Carthage attempted to make the most of the confused situation, extending her hold by setting up a garrison at Messina in 270, she found herself faced with a new enemy, Rome.

## The Roman conquest

Conflict between Carthage and the expanding Roman State was inevitable. Both had interests in Sicily which, for Rome, was of vital strategic importance. Three conflicts between the two powers ensued, the Punic Wars. Although Carthage was expelled from Sicily in 201 BC, Rome still feared Carthaginian power and the city was eventually razed to the ground in 146 BC, after three years of warfare. The fertile plains around the city were then converted into a Roman province. A hundred years after the fall of Punic Carthage, Julius Caesar defeated the last of his political adversaries at Thapsus (modern Ras Dimas), an event which signified the end of the Roman republic as well as the end of the independent Numidian states. The kingdom of Juba I was annexed and renamed as the province of **Africa Nova**. Subsequently, Augustus was to rebuild Carthage as a Roman colony. The city became headquarters of the proconsul and capital of **Africa Proconsularis**.

Roman administrators in the new North African province faced a problem of border security, with nomad tribes and local dynasties constantly threatening the stability of the new province. The problem was solved by creating the *limes*. This

## Classical Libya, key dates BC

| | |
|---|---|
| **814** | Traditional date of the foundation of Carthage. |
| **753** | Traditional date for the foundation of Rome. |
| **640-631** | Foundation of Cyrene. Construction of the Sanctuary of Apollo in Cyrene. |
| **560** | Barca, modern Al Marj, founded by dissident group from Cyrene. |
| **515** | Greeks led by Dorieus of Sparta, attempt to settle at mouth of Wadi Qa'im and are driven back by Libyan tribes and Carthaginians. |
| **c.500** | Carthage turns the Phoenician trading posts of Tripolitania into colonies. Foundation of Lpay (future Leptis Magna), Uiat (Oea) and Sabratha. Greeks name these three towns the tripolis, hence Tripolitania. Foundation of Euhesperides (modern Benghazi), aka Berenice. |
| **525** | Persian protectorate over Cyrenaica. |
| **484-420** | Life of Herodotus, author of the best ancient description of Africa (and Libya). |
| **480** | End of Persian protectorate, Temple of Zeus is built at Cyrene (Parthenon of Athens built 447 BC). |
| **345** | Construction of the Strategheion at Cyrene. |
| **331** | Alexander ends Persian rule in Egypt. Foundation of Alexandria. |
| **300** | Death of Alexander. Cyrenaica becomes part of the kingdom of the Ptolemies of Egypt. |
| **300-250** | Magas governor, then king of Cyrene. |
| **246** | Berenice, Magas' daughter, marries Ptolemy III, Egypt and Cyrene are re-united. |
| **264-241** | First Punic War. Rome gets Sicily. |
| **218-202** | Second Punic War. Rome gets Spain and becomes ruler of the western Mediterranean. |
| **214-129** | Macedonia and Greek cities become Roman. |
| **160** | Construction of the Great Gymnasium of Cyrene. |
| **149-146** | Third Punic War. Carthage destroyed and her territories come under Roman control as the province of Africa Vetus. |
| **111** | Leptis signs treaty with Rome. |
| **96** | Ptolomey Apion, king of Cyrene, leaves his domains to Rome. |
| **74** | Cyrenaica becomes a full Roman province. |
| **31** | Battle of Actium. Anthony and Cleopatra defeated by Octavian, Egypt annexed by Rome. |
| **27** | Augustus sole master of Rome. |

Background

was a border region along the desert edge settled with former legionaries who formed a militarized farming population. So although the border was permeable to trade, resistance to tribal incursion could be rapidly mobilized from the resident population, until regular forces could be brought to the scene. As Roman power and influence grew, the *limes* spread westwards from Egypt as far as the Moroccan Atlantic coast. In southern Tunisia, the frontier was reinforced by a ditch – referred to as the *fossa regia*.

**From Punic emporia to Roman cities**

Under Roman rule, the towns of North Africa flourished, and Carthage quickly rose again to become one of the most important cities of the Empire. In the first century AD, the twin African provinces were a major source of wheat for Rome. From the reign of Nero, two-thirds of Rome's total grain supply came from Africa, with the remaining third coming from Egypt. Other lucrative farming activities developed, notably the cultivation of olives and vines, thanks to the establishment of irrigation programmes. Gradually, indigenous villages and Roman settlements (*coloniae*) became prosperous towns. The most fortunate became fully fledged *municipiae*, managed by Roman magistrates and embellished with fine temples, baths and market squares.

**Prominent Africans** Towards the end of the second century AD, a number of men of African origin achieved fame in the Empire, including **Fronto**, tutor to the Emperor Marcus Aurelius, and the poet **Apuleius**, author of *The Golden Ass*. Fifteen percent of the knights and senators were from Africa, and the province produced several emperors too, notably **Clodius Albinus** (AD 196-197) and **Septimus Severus** (AD 193-211), a native of Leptis Magna. Septimus was just one of a whole series of Leptis men to achieve positions of power in the Roman imperial structure.

**Rise and fall of Leptis Magna** It was under Septimus Severus that Rome's frontiers in North Africa came in for some considerable re-organization. Until the early third century AD, the region remained known as the **emporia**. Septimus Severus created a new province of Numidia, covering much of what is now western Tunisia and eastern Algeria. The area around the three cities of Sabratha, Tripoli and Leptis was dubbed the *regio Tripolitana*, no doubt a reflection of the towns' importance and the emperor's links to them. Leptis was singled out for particular attention: a lavish programme of public works was launched. The city already had a splendid selection of public buildings from the reigns of Augustus and Tiberius (first century AD), thanks to the generosity of local worthies and merchants. Septimus Severus decided to raise the city to imperial heights, making it a serious rival for Carthage in the architectural grandeur stakes. The city received a new port, followed by a vast forum complex and the famous four-way triumphal arch, regarded as a landmark in Roman sculpture.

However, though Leptis had reached the height of its power, the signs of a rapid decline were already there. In the early third century, the city's major families aroused imperial jealousy and their estates were confiscated to become part of the imperial domains. Certain leading landowners were executed. In addition, the region was sending large annual consignments of olive oil to Rome in lieu of tax. Though the frontier was essentially peaceful, the long term effect must have been a loss of confidence. There were not to be any more of the grandiose, privately financed building projects which had been such a feature of Severan Leptis. Nor were works resumed on any major scale when Leptis became the capital of Diocletian's new province of Tripolitana in the late third century.

**Cultural influences and the Mediterranean world** By the beginning of the Christian era, North Africa had been organized into five Roman provinces: **Africa Vetus** and **Africa Nova**, **Numidia**, **Mauritania Caesariana** and **Mauretania Tingitana**, the latter roughly equivalent to the northwest quarter of modern Morocco. The sedentary Berber populations were largely Romanized in the coastal and agricultural regions. North Africa in cultural terms was now part of the Mediterranean world, its gods and goddesses assimilated to imported Roman deities: Baal Hammon had become Saturn, Punic Tanit was Caelestis, and fertility god Shadrapa was the dionysiac Liber Pater.

In addition to the commercial and cultural interpenetration of North Africa and Rome, this cultural interaction was

*Leptis Magna Severan Arch*

## Classical Libya, key dates AD

**96-192** Golden age of the Antonine emperors (Nerva, Trajan, Hadrian, Antoninus Pius, Marcus Aurelius and Commodus).

**115-117** Jewish revolt causes considerable destruction in Cyrene. Revolt put down by Trajan. Hadrian gives the city new monuments.

**193-211** Reign of Septimus Severus.

**203** Grand building projects started at Leptis Magna.

**235-284** Period of anarchy following reign of last Severan emperor.

**262** Cyrene damaged in earthquake.

**284-305** Diocletian re-establishes the authority of Rome. Ptolemais takes over from Cyrene as capital of the Pentapolis. Persecution of the Christians.

**306** Earthquake in Tripolitania.

**324-337** Reign of Constantine. Byzantium, re-dubbed Constantinople, becomes capital of the Roman Empire.

**410-476** Germanic tribes ravage the western regions of the empire, Rome falls in 476 ending the Western Roman Empire.

**439-534** Vandal invasion of North Africa, including Tripolitania.

**450** Apollonia becomes capital of Cyrenaica.

**534** Emperor Justinian attempts to restore unity of Roman Empire. Byzantine general Belisarius defeats Vandals in Tripolitania. Numerous basilicas constructed.

**642-643** Arab-Muslim general 'Amr ibn al As leads campaign to Cyrenaica.

**645** Tripoli falls to Ibn al As.

**670** Foundation of Kairouan (Tunisia), first major Islamic settlement in North Africa, by Uqba ibn Nafi'.

intensified by two other factors. First, the region had long been in contact with Greek culture and, through the Phoenicians, with the culture of the Levant. Secondly, as a result of the destruction of the Kingdom of Judea in AD 70, large numbers of Jews migrated into North Africa and Judaism intermixed with Berber culture to a significant extent, as the surviving contemporary Jewish traditions in Tunisia make clear (Libya no longer has a Jewish population).

In the main, however, the culture of Roman North Africa was built on Punic foundations. Archaeological studies of the inscriptions found at Leptis Magna show that the city's aristocracy and merchants were mainly of Phoenician or Libyo-Phoenician extraction. There are bilingual Latin-Punic inscriptions which give us the names of local worthies who provided the town with fine monuments – Annobal Rufus, son of Himilcho Tapapius, for instance, who gave the town a market and a theatre in the first century AD. However, when Leptis became a *colonia* in AD 109, Punic disappeared as a written language and Latin became the sole language of inscriptions although Punic remained an important spoken language. The Roman aim was not to wipe out the local culture. Rather, the Romans wanted to create stable, well-run towns where Latin was the élite and administrative langauge – rather as the French were to do centuries later elsewhere in the Maghreb. In the interior, Roman influence among the tribes was extended via treaties, the awarding of citizenship to loyal allies, and the provision of high-quality goods from elsewhere in the empire. Though Roman religion and the imperial cult took hold in the cities, the hinterland of Tripolitania remained loyal to the cult of Libyan Ammon.

## Christian rule

The eastern part of North Africa, and in particular the provinces of Africa Vetus and Africa Nova (Byzacium in the late Roman period), was the site of major developments in the early history of the Christian church. In the early days, the church was much persecuted by the Roman emperors, who had a tendency to blame the Christians for the various problems facing their vast empire. But

**Early Christianity**

Background

Christianity spread across the empire. There were invaders constantly threatening on all sides, and the traditional gods of the Roman pantheon seemed to have abandoned the people.

By the mid-third century AD, Carthage had become the seat of an important bishopric. The forceful **Cyprian**, one of the great figures of the early church, became bishop there in AD 249. Cyprian led the African church at a time when Trajan had increased the level of persecution and he eventually died a martyr in AD 258. The church, however, continued to attract numerous new adepts and to divide into warring factions supporting different theological positions.

Under Diocletian in the early fourth century, the empire was split up into regions and ruled by four leaders, a tetrarchy. Africa Proconsularis was divided into two, the southern and southeastern areas being renamed Byzacium. The province became the theatre of the Donatist heresy – far too complicated to go into here, unfortunately. However, the emperor Constantine came to believe that the only hope for the survival of the empire was for Christianity to become the official religion – and he became the first emperor to embrace that religion. In AD 313, his Edict of Milan proclaimed religious tolerance throughout the empire. He also relocated the capital from Rome to Constantinople.

**The Vandals and the Byzantine re-conquest** With hindsight, the early fifth century was to prove the high point of the Christian presence in Africa. The Roman Empire was crumbling under external threats, and North Africa was invaded by a Teutonic tribe based in Spain, the Vandals, who by AD 429 had conquered as far as eastern Cyrenaica. The Vandal ruler **Gaiseric's** aim was clear: a rich homeland for his people and independence from the Roman Empire. The Vandals' capture of Africa deprived Rome of corn supplies – and created a dangerous precedent: the Vandal kingdom was the first independent state actually within the borders of the empire. Feeble attempts at liberating the North African provinces were launched from Constantinople in the 440s, but to little avail. The Vandals were able to use the captured Byzantine fleet for raids on Italy and Sicily, and in 455 King Gaiseric, benefiting from the chaos left behind in northern Italy and Gaul by Attila and his Huns, succeeded in looting Rome itself, carrying off empress Eudoxia and her daughters. The eastern emperors feared that the Vandals would expand into the vital corn-growing lands of Egypt. However, the Byzantine expeditionary force launched against them in 468 was a total disaster. As a result, Gaiseric was able to take Sicily, Rome's oldest province. In fact the end of the Roman Empire in western Europe was nigh, (in 476 to be exact when the heart of the empire, Italy, came under the direct rule of the Germanic tribal leader, Odoacer). Central power collapsed, and Roman populations came to co-exist with Visigoth and other Germanic settler populations.

In their new North African homeland, the Vandals, however, were not efficient managers. Although they have gone down in history as the most destructive people of the ancient Mediterranean world, certain contemporary writers left a rather different image. Wrote Byzantine historian Procopius: "Of all the nations I know, the most effeminate are the Vandals. They spend all their days in the baths and in consuming sumptuous repasts ... Covered with gold ornaments and clothed in Oriental silks, they pass their time in spectacles, circus games and amusements. They especially like to hunt. ... They like to locate their homes in the middle of well-irrigated orchards with abundant trees. Finally being lovers of the earth, they deliver themselves without reservation to the pursuit of love-making."

All of which gave time for the Byzantines to get organized. The Eastern Empire re-asserted its control under Emperor Justinian and his general, Belisarius, in AD 533. However, this was to prove unpopular, not least because of the onerous taxation system necessary to cover Byzantium's heavy military expenditure as it tried to confront the Sassanids in Asia as well as maintain its position in the Mediterranean.

A little more than a century later, when Byzantine rule in Africa was threatened once more, this time by the expansion of Islam, local populations showed little enthusiasm for supporting Constantinople's continued hegemony in the region.

Despite the supposedly destructive presence of the Vandals, there are numerous remains of the third to seventh centuries in contemporary Libya. In the ancient sites, the Byzantine presence can be clearly distinguished. Among the more magnificent remains going back to early Christianity are mosaics, notably the great Peacock Mosaic in Sabratha Museum and those from the twin basilicas at Qasr Libia in Cyrenaica.

## Islamic rule

In the first half of the seventh century, Semitic tribes of the western Arabian desert, under the sway of a new revealed religion, Islam, were able to make considerable conquests in the Fertile Crescent. The tribes' sudden unity under the charismatic leadership of the Prophet Mohamed came at a time when the two great powers of the region, the Sassanian Empire (centering on what is now Iran and Iraq), and the Byzantines in Syro-Palestine, were weak after years of fighting. The Muslim Arabs were not to stop at the Middle East, however, and continued their conquests westwards into Byzantine North Africa.

**Early Islamic conquests**

In AD 642, 10 years after the death of the Prophet Mohammed, Arab armies, acting as the vanguard of Islam, conquered Egypt. To secure his conquest, the Arab commander, **Amr Ibn al As**, immediately decided to move westwards into Cyrenaica where the local Berber population submitted to the new invaders. Despite a constant pattern of disturbance, the Arab conquerors of Egypt and their successors were aware of the potential of the region to the south. Nubia was invaded in AD 641-42 and again 10 years later. Arab merchants and, later, bedouin tribes from Arabia were able to move freely throughout the southern regions. However, until AD 665, no real attempt was actually made to complete the conquest, largely because of internal problems within the new Islamic empire. Then, after two feints southwestwards towards the Fezzan, an army under **Uqba ibn Nafi'** conquered what is now Tunisia and set up the first Islamic centre there at Kairouan in AD 670. Four years later, the Arabs in Kairouan were able to persuade Kusayla, the leader of the Berber confederation which spread right across Tunisia and modern Algeria as far as the Oued Muluwiya in Morocco, to convert to Islam. Shortly afterwards, Uqba ibn Nafi', in a famous expeditionary raid to scout the unvanquished areas to the west, swept across North Africa along the northern edge of the Sahara desert as far as the Atlantic coast of Morocco, into the land of the Sanhaja Berbers who dominated the major Western trans-Saharan trade routes. With these conquests, the process of Arabising the coastlands of modern Libya began.

These early conquests were ephemeral, however, being based on two mistaken assumptions. The first was that the new conquerors could afford to ignore the isolated Byzantine garrisons along the North African coast at places like Tocra and Apollonia. The Byzantine navy, in fact, supplied them by sea. The second was that the Ummayad Arab commanders and administrators now imposed on North Africa ignored the promises of equality of treatment given to Berber converts and thus encouraged a major rebellion, led by **Kusayla**. Arab control of Kairouan was lost and the Arabs had to re-conquer the Maghreb, 'the Land of the West', as they called North Africa.

The first Arab move was against Kusayla, who was killed in AD 688 or 689. Then after a further delay caused, once again, by unrest in the Levant, a new army moved northwards against Byzantine centres in Carthage and Bizerte, where the last remaining garrison was defeated in AD 690. The Arab conquest came up against determined Berber resistance, this time in the Algerian Aurès where the core of the Berber Zenata confederation was led by the Kahina, a Judaized or Christianized Berber priestess. Once again the Arabs retreated to Cyrenaica, returning to the attack only in AD 693. In AD 697, the Kahina was killed and her forces defeated in a battle at Tubna in the Aurès which marked the start of a permanent Arab presence in North Africa. Although the Byzantine towns of Cyrenaica declined, Tripoli emerged as an Arab-Muslim town.

**The Arab invasion consolidated**

The city of Tunis was founded to prevent further Byzantine encroachment at neighbouring Carthage and, under Musa ibn Nusayr, Arab armies swept westwards to conquer Tangiers in AD 704. There they came to terms with the sole remaining Byzantine governor in North Africa, **Julian of Ceuta**, a Christian potentate who paid tribute to the new Muslim governor of neighbouring Tangiers, **Tariq ibn Ziyad**, in order to be confirmed in his post. Seven years later, Ziyad, with help from Julian who had maintained links with the Visigoth rulers of Spain, organized the Muslim invasion of Iberia, starting at Gibraltar. By AD 732, Muslim forces had conquered virtually all of what is now Spain and Portugal and had even crossed the Pyrenees. The Muslim advance was stopped at or near Poitiers by **Charles Martel**. Although for the next four years, large parts of Provence were ravaged by marauding armies, the Muslim presence in Europe had reached its effective limits at the Pyrenees.

**Early Islamic rule**

As it was the governors of Egypt who had piloted the conquest of the Maghreb, these areas remained initially attached to that province. In 704, the eastern Maghreb was constituted as a separate province, the **wilaya of Ifrikiya**, an Arabic version of the Latin Africa. The term was initially used to cover what is now Tripolitania, Tunisia and eastern Algeria (sparsely populated Cyrenaica remained attached to Egypt). With the conquest of Morocco, the wilaya extended right across to the Atlantic, and its capital was at Kairouan. The emirs of Ifrikiya represented the person of the caliph, the leading authority in Islam, across a vast expanse of territory. Unfortunately, however, authority was not easily imposed. The Arabs imposed extensive taxes on the Berbers and created much resentment (heavy taxation was no doubt levied because of the Middle East's exaggerated idea of the wealth of the Maghreb). The inferior status given to Berber warriors in the Arab armies which conquered Spain was another factor in fuelling resentment.

**The Berbers fight back**

Eventually, major Berber rebellions broke out. In the seventh century, Islam was yet to develop the all-encompassing set of rules for an ideal, pious society which it gained thanks to the great theological and legal scholars of later centuries. A challenge arose in the Maghreb in the form of the Kharijites, who rejected the hereditary succession of the caliphate, and insisted that an imam should be chosen by the community on the basis of his learning and religiosity. They also adopted a more severe approach to sin than mainstream Muslims – the movement growing out of Berber feelings of resentment. In 741, a Kharijite Berber army defeated an Arab army in a major battle in modern-day Morocco. In 742, the position was reversed when the Umayyad governor of Egypt defeated the Kharijites in two battles near Kairouan.

**A medieval backwater: Tripolitania from the seventh to 16th centuries**

After Byzantine Africa fell to the Arab Muslim invaders in the seventh century, the coastlands of Tripolitania remained a place of passage, an alternative to the sea route between the western and eastern halves of the Arab-ruled lands. Nomad tribes dominated the vast desert expanses, while the main town, **Tarablus El Gharb**, 'Tripoli of the West' tended to come within the sphere of influence of Ifrikiya's rulers to the northwest. The vast distances involved ensured that control by dynasties like the **Almohads**, or later, the **Hafsids** was only nominal. For the record, the Almohads (lit: 'Unitarians') were the first (and last) to unite the Maghreb in a single empire in the late 12th century. This empire was short-lived, however. Tribal divisions and quarrels within the ruling group meant the Almohad state fell apart in

## Ibn Khaldoun, the first sociologist?

North Africa claims to be the home of the world's first sociologist, one Ibn Khaldoun, (1322-1406), author of a weighty work entitled the **Muqadimma** or **Prolegomena**. A man of extensive learning, Ibn Khaldoun served various courts in North Africa and Andalusia. He wrote accounts of his travels, but is best known for his theory of North African society.

Ibn Khaldoun was the first thinker to have recognized that the Islamic ideal of the State had to be adapted to the political situation prevailing in tribal societies. His theory goes that new dynastic régimes emerge through the conquest of the lands of a decadent state by a rural warrior group held together by traditional tribal solidarity or 'asabiya. But after the hardy warriors had settled in the towns, their solidarity would

weaken, destroyed by the easy living of the city. Hence they would resort to mercenaries to maintain their authority, the costs of which implied heavy taxation. Thus the régime in turn was ripe for conquest by a tougher tribal group from the steppes or mountains. And so the cycle was repeated, unless the city-based rulers could replace tribal 'asabiya with a stronger social glue, namely a government based on Islamic law and custom.

Ibn Khaldoun's ideas fitted nicely with his times which saw the rise and fall of the Almoravid, Almohad, Merinid and Hafsid dynasties. Although his theory appears somewhat simplistic today, it was based on its author's direct experience of political life in the Maghreb. Surprisingly perhaps, his merits as a thinker were only really recognized in the 20th century.

---

the early 13th century. It had proved impossible to merge the eastern Maghreb, including Tripoli of the West, into the Almohad tribal system.

In the 14th century, Tripoli was the object of power struggles between various Arab tribal groups. Hafsid rule was imposed from 1401 to 1460. In the early 16th century, the town was taken by **Hapsburg Spain**, passed on to the Malta-based Knights of St John in 1530, and was finally taken for the **Ottomans** by the former privateer Dragut in 1551.

Background

After the Turco-Spanish wars of the 16th century, a series of Ottoman provinces were established along the North African coast, of which Tripoli was one. However, direct control from Istanbul did not last long. Ultimate power was theoretically in the hands of *pashas*, sent from Istanbul. Below them came the *deys*, in charge of the permanent janissary garrisons and, in Algiers at least, the *taifa*, the captains of the privateers who continued to operate out of the North African ports right up until the early 19th century. Military councils, the *diwan al askar*, were formed to administer the Barbary regencies, as the Ottoman provinces on the North African coast were known.

**Tripoli in Barbary, an Ottoman regency**

The Ottomans imposed their authority over the Berber tribes of the Jabal Nafusa with their superior fire power, and occupied the island of Djerba using tribal warriors in 1558. In Tripoli, Dragut built a fort outside the town, and on the site of the Grand Mosque destroyed by the Spaniards, a palace complex, the Saray Dragut. He also built a mosque in which he was later buried. The Ottomans had more difficulty imposing their authority in the Fezzan, and were obliged to recognize local tribe the Banu Mohamed as the rulers of the region in return for tribute in the form of gold and slaves. Cyrenaica remained under tribal rule, outside the Ottoman administrative system, despite incursions by certain Tripoli governors. Ultimately, even Tripoli was only loosely tied into the Ottoman imperial system. The empire was too vast and communications were too slow for things to be otherwise. As an outpost with a largely arid hinterland, lacking in natural resources, 17th-century Tripoli in Barbary, had to look to the sea for revenue. Turning to piracy proved to be a profitable way of filling the coffers of the city's rulers.

*On crescent moons and the Sublime Porte*

By the mid-16th century, the Ottoman Empire, or Sublime Porte as it was known to the Europeans, was vast and sprawling. From Asia Minor, the Turks had expanded south into the Levant and Egypt, taking Cairo from the Muslim Mamlouks in 1517. North Africa followed, with Algiers falling in 1529. The Knights of St John held on in Tripoli until 1551. The Ottomans expanded eastwards into Mesopotamia, and northwest into the Balkans, reaching Budapest in 1526, and laying siege to Vienna in 1529 and 1683. Outside the walls of the very capital of the Habsburgs, the sultan's armies pitched their 30,000 tents to form a great crescent.

The flags of the Ottoman armies bore crescents (and stars) too. This symbol goes way back into history. One legend goes that a Macedonian king had prepared to take Byzantium by night, counting on the crescent moon, only to be foiled by the Moon Goddess who veiled herself, leaving the army in darkness. A later story runs that it was by the light of the crescent moon that Turkish troops found their way to the wicket gate which a traitor had left open for them in the seemingly impregnable walls of Constantinople. The year was 1453, the capital of the Eastern Roman Empire fell to Islam, and the crescent moon became the Ottoman's good luck symbol. Today, the flags of Algeria, Tunisia and Turkey still bear crescent and star. In Tripoli, great stone crescents can be seen carved above the ceremonial entrance gate to the Castle just off Green Square, while just behind the clock tower is a souk specializing in the manufacture of the great copper triple-ball-and-crescent features used to finish off any self-respecting minaret.

**Ships and slaves: the business of piracy in Tripoli**

As links with Istanbul were so weak, Tripoli effectively became an independent maritime statelet. At the top of the élite was a *dey*, who presided over the ruling council or *diwan*, assisted by a *kahiya*. Another leading figure was the *bey*, commander of the land forces and responsible for keeping the tribes of the interior in order. However, within the ruling group was an exotic mix of interests, all competing for Tripoli's rather scarce resources. The military élite was of Turkish origin, of course, and thus alien to the town's Arab ethnic base. (They also followed a different rite of Islam, the Hanefite rite, as opposed to the more austere Malikite rite of the townspeople.) Then there were the Kulughlis, the result of intermarriage between Turkish soldiery and local women, referred to as the 'Moors' by the European writers of the day. Another key group, with influence far beyond their numbers, were the renegades, Christians who after capture by a Muslim pirate fleet had been made to become Muslim, or who had renounced Christianity voluntarily. A bright renegade with advanced shipping and navigation skills might rise to become a *ra'is* or corsair with pirate ships at his command. There was a constant struggle for wealth and power between Turks and ra'ises, with the Kulughlis, Arab townspeople and Bedouin tribes taking sides as the tide turned in favour of one leader or another.

Though the political situation was unstable, occasionally a dey would emerge and impose his authority for a longer period. Such was the case of Uthman, a Greek renegade who held power from 1649 to 1672. He expanded the Tripoli fleet to 24 vessels and developed effective control of customs duties. Uthman was really an exception, however, and Tripolitanian domestic politics was a turbulent and often bloodthirsty affair.

The problem was that resources were really very scarce. Oasis agriculture was limited by uncertain rainfall and simple irrigation techniques. Tripoli in fact had little to export apart from wool, dates and, most importantly, salt from Zuwara. There was no timber suitable for shipbuilding, a serious drawback for a port city. Ships bringing in corn, olive oil, tobacco, honey and wine might leave empty. Trade with Europe was also limited by the unwillingness of European ship-owners to risk losing their boats to pirates. Nevertheless, privateering was essential to maintain the economy of Tripoli. Basically, corsairs operated out of Tripoli, preying on the ships of nations too weak to protect themselves. The booty and prisoners captured represented a considerable contribution to the revenues of the city's rulers. (Ransoms for captives could bring in substantial sums.) Yet, like farming, privateering was not a large-scale activity. Also, just like farming, it brought highly variable rewards. Small squadrons of three to five ships might be out at sea for weeks. If they failed to return with a prize, the cost of the expedition was high and ultimately, if corsair expeditions failed too often, the city's security suffered. The income generated by captured ships was essential to pay the land forces essential for the defence of Tripoli. (Salt exports could not produce enough of a return to finance an army.) There was thus a permanent tension between corsair captains and the deys in the citadel. The latter feared for their city if European powers were too angered by piracy. Yet they could not do without the revenues that corsair activity gave them. It was only with the advent of a hereditary dynasty in the early 1700s that the situation was to change somewhat.

At the beginning of the 18th century, a local leader, one **Ahmad Qaramanli**, made Tripoli independent with a power base built on the kulughlis, (the group which had arisen from the intermarriage of Turkish troops and local women). In 1711, Qaramanli took the opportunity offered by the temporary absence of the Ottoman governor and massacred the leaders of the janissaries. The new autonomous government eventually controlled Tripolitania and the coastal regions of Cyrenaica. Under **Ali Pasha** (1754-93), Tripoli grew in prosperity, managing to balance effectively piracy and trade. European Christians established a flourishing trade with Malta, while the Italian Jews handled commerce with Livorno in Tuscany.

**The Qaramanli dynasty**

The late 18th century saw Qaramanli power weakened by internal dynastic power struggles and the occupation of Tripoli by adventurer Ali Burghul. Eventually, Ali's youngest son Yusuf took control, ruling from 1795 to 1832. With Europe entangled in the Napoleonic conflict, he was able to rebuild Tripoli's strength as a maritime power. Merchant ships captured from the European powers helped to expand the fleet. Much of the seafaring know-how was supplied by European converts and Turkish captains. One of the leading renegades was a Scot, Peter Leslie, known as Murad Rais, who became admiral of Tripoli's navy in 1795. Cyrenaica and the Fezzan were brought under direct rule in the early 19th century, and **Yusuf Pasha** began to plan the conquest of the Saharan kingdom of Bornu.

Tripoli's power began to decline in the 1820s. Piracy was banned in 1818, depriving the regency of an important source of revenue. European consular influence grew, and after a tussle for influence in Tripoli between Britain and France, the Ottoman Empire reoccupied the Regency of Tripoli and ejected the Qaramanlis in 1835. This came at a time when the Sublime Porte had suffered considerable set backs in Greece and Algeria.

The re-imposition of Ottoman rule in Libya in 1835 marked an end to the corsairing economy of the Regency of Tripoli. Ottoman control was never fully applied throughout the country, however. In Cyrenaica and the desert the Sanusiya sheikhs provided a politico-religious alternative to Ottoman rule, and in effect in the 19th century, Cyrenaica was under the co-rule of Sanusis and Ottomans.

**Return of Ottoman rule**

Istanbul saw Tripoli as the base from which it might regain its waning influence in the western Mediterranean. This was a problematic strategy, given that leading Tripoli families had strong commercial links with Europe, and in any case, the tribal leaders of the interior saw the Ottomans as another group of conquerors.

The Ottomans took an interest in the trans-Saharan trade. With the abolition of slavery in Tunis in 1846 and Algiers in 1848, Tripoli increased its share of the slave trade, despite pressure from the British Anti-Slavery Society. Even after a firman

*Background*

*Recent Libyan history: main periods*

**1711-1835** *Qaramanli dynasty*
**1835-1911** *Second Ottoman period*
**1911-1942** *Italian period*
**1943-1951** *British military
administration (Cyrenaica and Tripolitania)*

**1952-1969** *Kingdom of Libya*
**1969-1977** *United Arab Republic
of Libya*
**1977** *Proclamation of the Jamahiriya,
'the state of the masses'*

(decree) was issued abolishing slavery in Tripoli in 1857, the trade continued, such was the demand in the Ottoman Empire.

On a rather different note, the Ottomans introduced the administrative reforms being implemented across the Empire. Secondary schools where sciences and European languages were taught, in addition to Arabic and Turkish, were set up. Under **Ali Ridha Pasha**, governor of Tripolitania from 1867 to 1870, a municipality was set up in Tripoli and French technical assistance brought in to dig artesian wells and improve port facilities.

**The Sanusi Order**  During the 19th century, Cyrenaica had a rather different history to Tripolitania. Peopled by tribes descended from 11th century invaders the Banu Sulaym, administered separately from Tripoli, the sub-province came under the influence of the Sanusiya *tariqa*, a spiritual movement named after its Algerian founder, **Sayyid Mohamed Ibn Ali al-Sanusi**. (The term tariqa best translates as brotherhood or order.) The main zawiya or 'lodge' of the order was founded in 1843, the Zawiya al Bayda in the Jabal Akhdar, where the order was welcomed for its piousness and for its ability to arbitrate tribal disputes. When the order's founder died, his son, Sayyid al Mahdi took over, and it was under him that Sanusi influence developed in the Sahara. Al Mahdi set up headquarters at Kufra in 1895, subsequently moving it to Kiru between Borku and the Tibesti.

Later on, the tariqa also co-ordinated tribal resistance throughout the Sahara to French colonial penetration. It came to control the eastern trade routes across the Sahara and, as a result, effectively became the autonomous government of the central Saharan region. In Cyrenaica its power was so great that, outside the major urban settlements such as Benghazi, the Ottomans accepted it as the *de facto* government and a Turkish-Sanusi condominium developed. Although the Sanusiya considered the Ottoman caliphs as usurpers, they were forced to accept their presence, as the Turks were the only force seemingly capable of countering French expansion into the Sahara.

The Ottoman administration in Tripoli had to cope with continuing European pressure, particularly from Italy and Malta. British and French influence led to the end of the slave trade towards the end of the 19th century, while the economy of Tripoli became increasingly integrated into the economy of the Mediterranean region. By the start of the 20th century Italy's intention to colonize Tripolitania, Cyrenaica and the Fezzan became clear.

**The first Arab Republic**  In 1911, the Italians finally found a pretext for occupying Ottoman Libya (and the Dodecanese Islands off Turkey, too). The take-over was to prove far more difficult than Italy had anticipated, however, despite Ottoman difficulties in the First World War and Italy being on the winning side. In fact, the outbreak of the First World War allowed the Turks to provide military aid to the resistance. However, huge changes were afoot in the Middle East. Tripoli of the West's old protectors – the Turkish army, the Ottoman sultanate, the Islamic caliphate – disappeared, one after the other. Tripolitania was on its own to face the invaders. When Turkey surrendered in 1918, Tripoli's notables met at Misrata, and on 18 November proclaimed a **Tripolitanian**

**republic**, the first in the Arab world. In fact, this was more of a coalition of local leaders, enabling them to extract concessions from the Italians. And so in June 1919, Italy, no doubt playing for time, offered a statute granting Italian nationality to the local population, an Italian governor – and an elected parliament. Later, a National Reform Party formed to put pressure on Italy to put the statute into effect.

## Colonial rule

Italy had considerable difficulties in bringing all of Libya under its control. In 1922, with the Fascists in power, Italy again decided to occupy Libya. **Marshal Badoglio**, victor of the Vittorio Veneto was sent to Tripolitania, and in 1923 the Italians entered Misrata. Cyrenaica surrendered in 1925, but a guerilla campaign continued for seven more years.

The Italian occupation

General Graziani led a cruel campaign in Cyrenaica and down into the Sahara to destroy the Sanusiya. In January 1931, the oasis of Kufra was occupied. A 270 km barbed wire barrier was set up along the Egyptian frontier to limit bedouin movement. Eventually, in 1931, Sanusi leader Umar al Mukhtar was captured and hung. In 1932, Marshal Badoglio announced the end of the 'rebellion'. Italy finally occupied the vast Libyan desert hinterland.

Italy's occupation of Libya was initially piecemeal, characterized by contradictions and ultimately short lived. It left a lasting mark on the people of what was to become an independent nation, providing a strong binding force. Italy's victory over the Sanusiya had only been achieved by coralling large numbers of Cyrenaicans into concentration camps. There was heavy loss of life during the nine year war (1923-1932), and much bitterness was engendered. For many in the Italian establishment, however, the colonization of the lands eventually named *Libia* had a strong ideological tint.

The logic of Italian colonization

In the 19th century, there was mass migration from Italy to Argentina, Brazil and the USA. The fact that the newly constituted Kingdom of Italy was unable to provide work and wealth for all her people was seen by many as a symbol of national failure. In 1906, the Italian Colonial Institute was set up, through which the colonial lobby generated a myth which saw Italy as a great nation which had been humiliated – and therefore needed to invest in colonial expansion. In the early 20th century, with the exception of Ethiopia, Tripolitania and Cyrenaica were practically the only corner of Africa unclaimed by a European power. Tunisia was a *terra perduta* (a land lost for Italy); Libya was to be Italy's fourth shore, *la quarta sponda*.

Initially, colonization was on the Jefara plain, avoiding the oases and the Jabal Nafusa to avoid upsetting local sentiment. As of 1934, **Italo Balbo**, Mussolini's one time second-in-command, headed the colonial effort in North Africa. The development of the Jabal Akhdar was to be like that of the Pontine Marshes. (In practice, it turned out to be more like Zionist colonization in Palestine, with boatloads of settlers coming in.) The colonial system was modelled on the one used by the French in the Constantine region and in Tunisia: expropriated land was given to private entrepreneurs who only gained ownership after payment and appropriate development. A reform in 1928 obliged concession holders to associate Italian peasants. In 1935, the first experimental villages were established in Cyrenaica, followed by nine more villages in 1938 to house the 'worker-legionaries'.

The Fourth Shore

Italian rule in Libya was a strange mixture of the tolerant and the cruel. The Sanusiya zawiyas were destroyed or converted to military uses, and the movement's sheikhs went into exile in 1932. But at the same time, the Italians took care to appear as protectors of Islam. No attempt was made to convert Muslims to Christianity, and Islamic personal status law was left untouched. Restoration works were undertaken

Background

## The Desert War 1940-43

*The physical marks of the destruction wrought by the Second World War are still very apparent in Libya – if mainly now in the large cemeteries of war dead.*

*Italy, the colonial power in Libya at the outbreak of the Second World War, invaded British-held Egypt in the closing weeks of 1940, mistakenly believing that the campaign there would be brief and successful. In reality, the war raged, with many changes of fortune for the combatants, until May 1943. The prize of winning Egypt from the British was the destruction of British lines of communication to the Middle East, India and the Far East, together with access for the Italian and German commands to the rich oil fields of Iran and the Arabian peninsula. Great Britain and the Commonwealth countries, for their part, desperately needed to hold their grip on Egypt, their lines of communication such as the Suez Canal and the natural*

*resources of the region. It was scarcely surprising, therefore, that the battle for control of North Africa was so protracted and bitter.*

*The local populations were for the most part unwilling spectators of the desert war, though their suffering was considerable. In Libya, the Sanusi movement backed the British against the colonial Italy, and Libyan troops did ultimately have a hand in the re-conquest of their country. In Francophone North Africa there was uncertainty and confusion in the ranks of the French colonial authorities and their colonial peoples as a result of the Pétain régime's accommodation with the Nazis.*

*Although the Italian armies made some progress in Egypt in 1940, they were soon expelled. Faced with what appeared to be an Italian collapse, German troops and armour were moved into Tripolitania in February 1941. The combined German*

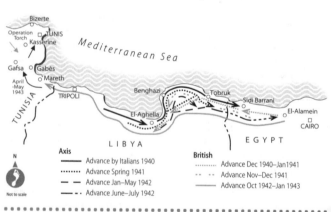

on major Islamic monuments, and arrangements for the pilgrimage to Mecca were improved. New schools for Muslims followed an Italian curriculum and provided religious instruction in Arabic. The stated aim was to integrate Libyans into Italian society. In 1937, Mussolini brandished 'the sabre of Islam' in Tripoli and inaugurated the 1,800 km coastal highway, the Litoranea, running from the Tunisian to the Egyptian frontiers.

Unfortunately for Italy, such rhetorical poses cut little ice with the growing numbers of Libyans, many in exile in Egypt and elsewhere, who felt that there was a future beyond colonial rule. Although Libya was declared an integral part of the Kingdom of Italy in January 1939, the Second World War was to provide the political opportunity for the pro-independence groups.

and Italian army pushed back the British to the Egyptian frontier by April. The Axis army was led with skill and audacity by General Rommel and was supported by a strong air force. Rommel's eastwards advance was slowed by the protracted resistance of the garrisons – first Australian, then British and Polish – at Tobruk. Meanwhile, the main armies fought pitched battles around the Libyan-Egyptian frontier until Rommel withdrew temporarily in December 1941. Once back in Libyan territory, Rommel reorganized and, taking advantage of improved lines of communication, prepared a counter attack which pushed the British back as far as Gazala, near Derna, in January and February 1942 and, after a pause, into Tobruk and deep into Egypt in June, though this advance was finally held at El-Alamein after a fierce battle. Rommel made a final attempt at Alam Halfa, east of El-Alamein, to push aside British and Commonwealth forces and break through to the Nile Valley in August 1942, but failed in the face of a strong Allied defensive effort and his own growing losses of men and equipment.

The balance in the desert war changed in mid-1942. The Allies gradually won superiority in the air and gained freedom of movement at sea. The Germans and Italians increasingly lacked adequate armour, reinforcements and strategy as Rommel's personal health also deteriorated. On the Allied side, General Montgomery took over leadership and began a build-up of the Eighth Army sufficient to overwhelm the well-trained and experienced Afrika Korps. Montgomery opened his attack at El-Alamein on 23 October 1942 and, after 11 days of hard fighting, the Axis army was beaten back and retreated by rapid stages to the west to make a last stand in Tunisia.

The German attempt to hold on in North Africa was made difficult by sea and airborne landings by Allied, including American, troops in Morocco and Algeria in November 1942. These two countries were liberated with comparative ease when French Vichy units, formerly collaborating with the Germans, were brought round to support the invasion. German and Italian reinforcements were rushed to Tunis, and a battle began to stop the advance of Allied units from the west as they fought their way in from Algeria and from the south through Libya. German attacks in the Battle of Kasserine in the hills north of Gafsa during January and February 1943 almost succeeded in halting the Allied progress. Rommel's final assault against Montgomery's advancing Eighth Army arriving from Libya failed in early March. Axis troops retreated northwards behind the Mareth Line on the Gulf of Gabès in Tunisia, before being outflanked and being forced to withdraw by Montgomery's troops. A concluding series of battles in northern Tunisia saw the Allies push through the Medjerda Valley to Tunis and Bizerte in May 1943, effectively ending Axis resistance in North Africa.

Background

The Fascist victory was short-lived, for the Italian army was forced out of Libya during the Second World War. Under the Italians, Libya had acquired communications infrastructure and the basis of a modern economy. It had also acquired a 50,000 strong Italian settler population, a substantial portion of whom remained until they were expelled by the Gadhafi régime in 1970.

**After the Second World War**

The situation of Libya posed problems. By the end of the Second World War, it had acquired strategic significance for Britain and, after the Cold War began, for the USA as well (during the Second World War, the Romanian oil fields had been bombed from bases in Libya). Britain had promised Cyrenaica that Italian control would never be restored. A series of proposals were made including Soviet Union trusteeship over Libya and the Bevin-Sforza Plan, whereby Britain would take a mandate for Cyrenaica, Italy for Tripolitania and France for the Fezzan for a period of

10 years, after which the country would be granted independence. Such proposals were clearly unacceptable to the Libyans themselves, and the whole issue was dropped in the lap of the newly created United Nations in 1949.

The United Nations' special commissioner was able to convince all the Libyan factions that the only solution was a federal monarchy, bringing the provinces of Cyrenaica, Tripolitania and the Fezzan together in a monarchy headed by the Sanusi leader, **Sayyid Idris**. In December 1951, the independent United Kingdom of Libya came into being.

# Modern Libya

Libya achieved independence in December 1951 after a 40 year period of war and violent occupation. The Ottomans had withdrawn in 1912, defeated by Italy, which during a short but brutal period of colonial rule managed to destroy the institutions left behind by the Turks. After the Axis' defeat in North Africa in 1943, the country was left under military rule. Great Britain took responsibility for the two northern provinces of Tripolitania and Cyrenaica in the same fashion as it had taken on Trans-Jordan a couple of decades earlier, while France ruled the Fezzan as an extension of her vast Algeria Saharan territories.

## The independent Kingdom of Libya

British and French military administrations withdrew in 1951 when the state became independent as a United Kingdom of Cyrenaica, Tripolitania and the Fezzan under a Sanusi monarch. The first king, Idris I, kept close links with the British and Americans, permitting the retention of British land forces and American and British airforce facilities.

In the 1950s, Libya was a poor country with one of the lowest standards of living in the world. Foreign aid supported the state, along with the profits from selling Second World War metal scrap and the rent from military bases. To the east, Egypt was undergoing a period of rapid change following the overthrow of King Farouk. A new nationalist and anti-western ideology, generated by Gamal Abd al Nasser and his companions, was eventually to spread to Libya – with serious consequences for the fragile monarchy.

Idris I had limited ambitions. (In all honesty, he would have been happy to rule his home province of Cyrenaica as an independent principality.) More cosmopolitan, urbanized Tripolitania and the remote Fezzan accepted Sanusi rule without too much enthusiasm. The king had extensive powers, and his personal cabinet, the royal *diwan* was the most important political force. Cyrenaican notables dominated in the newly created administration. The king appointed the senate, while there were elections by secret ballot for the House of Representatives, at least in the urban areas. The king remained the most important political force but he realized all too well that although he had been accepted as king of Libya, in half his kingdom the Sanusiya were at best little known, if not actually unpopular. His rule was based on a permanent balancing act, between the need to maintain the legitimacy derived from his position as head of the Sanusi order, and his status as a secular monarch as laid down in the constitution.

Idris saw himself as a mediator. He expressed devotion to the nation, but rarely took positions on specific programmes or difficult issues. He was a strong believer in neutrality in international affairs, which in practice meant continued American and UK military presence. The day-to-day running of Libya was left to prime ministers – of whom there were many. In the monarchy's 18 years, there were 25 major government reorganizations and 10 changes of prime minister.

Oil was struck in commercial quantities in 1959 and oil exports began in 1961. Libya rapidly became financially independent and initiated sensible reforms in housing, health and education. Employment opportunities improved and the first five year development plan was launched in 1963. Young Libyan technocrats were given scope to implement their policies and the country made rapid steps forward.

**Oil arrives**

Libya remained dominated by highly conservative forces nevertheless. In 1963, Muhy al Din Fkeni, a French-trained lawyer became prime minister and tried to downgrade tribal influence. However, Fkeni was dismissed after student riots in January 1964, and tribalism returned with Mahmud al Muntasir's government. Cyrenaican tribal families maintained their influence through the royal diwan and family members who had received police and civil service training under the British Military Administration and the Amirate of Cyrenaica. Nevertheless, by the late 1960s it was becoming apparent that tribal ties were weakening. There was nothing to suggest that huge changes were on the way, however.

**Conservative influence**

By the 1960s, the royal succession was looking increasingly problematic. Neither of the queens had produced a surviving heir and there had been talk of a Libyan republic with Idris as its first president. In 1964, following student demonstrations sparked off by Nasser's criticism of foreign military bases in Libya, the king had offered to resign, only to go back on his decision after hundreds of telegrams of support had been received. Eventually, in 1966, royal decree confirmed Idris' first wife, Fatima, as queen, and the king's nephew, Hassan, son of Mohamed Ridha al Sanusi, as crown prince. However, when the military seized power in 1969, Prince Hassan immediately withdrew all claims to the throne.

**The succession**

With hindsight, it was during the 18 years of the Sanusi monarchy that the bases of Libyan national unity were laid. But ultimately, King Idris had difficulty in working to build autonomous national institutions. From a deeply conservative background, he continued to operate in a way which frustrated change. The royal *diwan* functioned rather like a tribal council. There was a lack of real ministerial leadership, little real contact between parliament and the cabinet. And political parties were banned. At independence, the vast majority of the population had no understanding of the new constitution and federal system. While attitudes remained firmly rooted in the traditional community, the Palestine question and the spread of Nasserite ideas made for political instability.

**Why did the Libyan monarchy fail?**

In a region torn where almost all the monarchical régimes had been swept away by the late 1960s, it is not surprising then that the Libyan monarchy went the same way. Oil revenues were producing a new educated class – and had been used to finance new armed forces. Although the army was tiny, numbering barely 7,000 in 1967, it proved to be the force capable of generating radical change.

## The 1st September Revolution

A coup d'état by a group of young army officers took place on September 1, 1969. This was the White (bloodless) Revolution. Initially, the leaders of the revolution refused to reveal their names. Their discourse was one of liberty, justice and dignity in a country where there was still great poverty, despite the oil wealth. In January 1970, the leader of the coup emerged, one **Mu'ammar Gadhafi**, a disciple of Jamal Abdel Nasser, overtly anti-western and deeply convinced of the need to give Libyans 'lives worth living'. He was just 27, and Libya was ready to follow him.

Like his hero Nasser, Gadhafi set about reducing the foreign hold on his country. He closed down the remaining foreign military bases on Libyan soil. He abolished most private sector activities in the economy. He banned alcohol and the use of

Background

## The Gadhafis

Along with Nelson Mandela, Colonel Gadhafi is one of the most senior statesmen in Africa today. The question remains as to whom he might hand over power when he feels he is no longer able to do the job. Could it be one of his children? Libya's leader has four sons and one surviving daughter, Aïcha. His adopted daughter, Hana, was killed by the Americans in the bombing of the Aziziya Barracks in 1986. Aïcha, 22 years old in 2000, has a law degree from El Fatah University, Tripoli.

Mu'ammar Gadhafi's first wife, Khayra Ennouri, was the daughter of a wealthy Tripoli merchant. They had one son, Mohamed, aged 29, whose main interest is sport. He is an important member of the managing board of Al Ittihad, a leading Tripoli football team, and works to promote Libyan tourism, publishing Al Rukub magazine. In 1972, shortly after coming to power, Gadhafi met a young nurse from Cyrenaica, Safia, who was to become his second wife, bearing him three more sons, Sayf Al Islam, Sa'adi, and Mu'tassim Billah. The eldest son, Sayf

Al Islam (lit: 'Sword of Islam'), is a leading figure in Libyan business, having trained at an international business school in Vienna. He heads a Libyan NGO which campaigns against drug abuse, and directs a quarterly magazine, Hannibal, named for the Carthaginian general Hannibal Barca. In summer 2000, during the Jalo hostage crisis in the Philipines, it emerged that he was president of Gadhafi International Foundation for Charity, a sort of NGO financing development projects in the Third World.

The second son, Sa'adi, an engineer by training, opted for a military career. He chairs the Al Ahly football club, the other leading Tripoli side. Many Libyans seem to think that it is Sa'adi who will take over from his father. The third son, Mu'tassim Billah, a doctor by training, is also in the military, holding the rank of lieutenant. He is probably the most popular of the three sons, and is said to take after his father. The opaque world of Libyan élite politics gives no clue as to who might actually succeed, however.

foreign languages for official purposes. In this most conservative of Muslim countries, he set up a women's army corps. Perhaps the new régime's greatest success was in threatening the assets of the foreign oil companies in Libya and in helping to force up oil prices in the early 1970s. By 1974, Libya had control over 60 % of its oil industry. Living standards leapt forward, schools and hospitals went up, the people were enthusiastic.

**The Third Way?** But for many in Libya, change was not fast enough. On 15 April 1973, Gadhafi made his famous Zuwara speech, calling for a great cultural revolution in Libya. Nevertheless, there was resistance: July 1975 saw a third attempted coup d'état. Perhaps because of this, Gadhafi began to promise a new Arab socialist society under the banner of the Socialist People's Libyan Jamahiriyah. He elaborated a set of philosophies encapsulated in his *Green Book*, which set out his ideas on the nature of an Arab socialist state. He adopted the position of *qa'id* (guide) and announced that representative democracy was untenable. Political life was to be organized around 'people's congresses', set up in all administrative districts and work places, with 'committees' as their executive organs. Once a year, congress delegates were to meet for a general people's congress, whose secretaries would basically operate as ministers.

On 2 March 1977 Gadhafi declared that power had been returned to the people, and that the era of the Jamahiriya, the 'state of the masses' had arrived to replace the **jumhuriya** (republic). But in November 1977, the first **revolutionary committees'** emerged: a sort of semi-official militia established to speed up the development of the Jamahiriya system.

Colonel Gadhafi's ideal of government was expressed in the Third Universal Theory, enshrined in the *Green Book*, the first sections of which were published in 1976. Gadhafi attempted to bring together strands of his own beliefs – Islam, freedom from foreign intervention, equality of people and the welfare of the greater Arab nation – within a unified philosophy. He was never taken entirely seriously in this ambition outside the country, and it quickly became apparent that the new system had many similarities with the one-party state.

Ultimately, events were also to prove that Libya itself was resistant to Gadhafi's ideas. The old religious establishment was reticent, as were certain levels of the army – the organized military mind could not easily accept the more extreme tenets of the Third Universal Theory. Opposition centred on students overseas and former political figures. Thus the revolutionary committees' activities came to include destroying opposition at home and abroad.

**Militarizing Libya**

In 1981, Gadhafi launched a new phase of the revolution with the slogan 'the people under arms'. Schools and the work place were to be militarized so that thousands of people would be ready for action, should the need arise. (Even today, adult male Libyans in principle have to devote a month a year to military service.) The wide-scale militarization of Libyan society proved unrealistic, and the army forces' limits were demonstrated in some humiliating defeats in Chad in 1987. Further problems arose with the fall in oil prices in 1985, plus the collapse in the value of the dollar.

**Rethinking the Jamahiriya**

The régime clearly felt that single-minded expenditure of large sums of money would be enough to impose Green Book thinking. This included the devolution of bureaucratic powers to the four major regions – (Tripoli, Sabha, Al Khalij and Benghazi) – and the removal of all private privileges of ownership of goods, property and even a fully private life. However, by 1987 it was clear that the Jamahiriya dream would have to be rethought. In March 1988, 600 political prisoners were released; the role of the revolutionary committees was reduced, revolutionary courts were abolished. The State lost its monopoly on economic activity and private co-operatives were created. In June 1988, the People's Congress adopted the Green Proclamation on Human Rights, which in principle protects individuals and reduces the scope of the death penalty. The structures of the Jamahiriya persisted, however, with a Basic People's Congress still meeting to manage the affairs of state, and Colonel Gadhafi taking the position of guide to the revolution. The congress acts officially through a series of appointed secretariats, which are now, for all practical purposes, ministries in the traditional mode.

The revolutionary fervour, which characterized Libya in the 1970s and 1980s, has now dimmed considerably and lives on only in the security apparatus and military matters. Since he has these agents of political control in his hands, Colonel Gadhafi still effectively has the final say in decision-making in the country. There is no official opposition party and opponents of the régime have generally fled abroad – where many have been assassinated.

**The political system today**

The secretariats which look after day-to-day administration are located throughout the country as part of regionalization policy. Though ministries will eventually all be located in Sirte, on the coast midway between Tripolitania and Cyrenaica, key government offices and personnel remain in Tripoli. Political power remains concentrated in the hands of Colonel Gadhafi and his close associates. An annual People's Congress permits some ventilation of other ideas and apparent control of the spending of state revenues. In fact, political changes have been minor in recent years, the biggest changes taking place in the economy; the souks have been reopened, and liberalization and privatization have been extensive. In economic terms, it looks as though the 1980s, Libya's black decade, are firmly in the past.

Background

*Libya 1969-1999, key dates*

**1 September 1969**  The Free Unionist Officers Movement, led by Muammar Gadhafi deposes King Idriss.

**April 1974**  Gadhafi leaves formal political office and takes the title Guide of the Revolution.

**September 1976**  First sections of the Green Book are published, an exposition of the Third Universal Theory, rejecting Marxism and Capitalism.

**March 1977**  Declaration of the Socialist Popular Arab Jamahiriya (state run by the masses, the jumhur).

**27 December 1985**  Beginning of a long US-Libyan crisis after bomb attacks in Rome and Vienna. Tripoli is accused of backing international terrorism.

**14-15 April 1986**  American night raid on Tripoli and Benghazi leaves 40 dead and many wounded.

**March 1988**  Gadhafi limits the revolutionary committees activities.

**June 1988**  Green Declaration on Human Rights.

**4 January 1989**  Two Libyan Mig 23 are shot down by two American F-14 in the Mediterranean.

**17 February 1989**  Libya signs the Union du Maghreb Arabe treaty in Marrakech.

**April 1992**  UN declares a military and air embargo on Libya after explosion of aircraft over Lockerbie (1988) and the Ténéré (1988). Tripoli refuses to release two Libyans suspected of involvement in these explosions.

**1 December 1993**  Embargo is extended to the petroleum industry-related equipment. Libyan holdings in USA and UK frozen.

**April 1999**  End of UN embargo as a compromise is reached. USA embargo on strategic oil sector equipment and air-transport remains in force.

**1 September 1999**  30th anniversary of the revolution.

## Alarms and excursions abroad

Since 1969, the Libyan government has pursued an adventurous and often costly foreign policy which, with hindsight, has not won the country as many friends abroad as it could have, not least because of its weather-vane characteristics. Happily, the late 1990s saw a calmer, although not always more realistic approach to foreign relations.

Pan-Arabism was the main pillar of Libyan foreign policy, and the dream of Arab unity was pursued by a series of abortive unions with other Arab states, a solid pro-Palestinian stance and the creation of a vast and expensive military establishment. After President Nasser's death, the Libyan leader took on the mantle of the leading exponent of Arab nationalism. Though the results might have been spectacular, the various proposed unions had little effect. The short-lived August 1984 fusion with Morocco enabled Hassan II to put an end to Libyan financing of the Polisario guerilla movement. Libya developed an outspoken position against a negotiated solution to the everlasting Israelo-Palestinian crisis. (In some quarters, it is murmured that the UN embargo on Libya imposed in the early 1990s was a way of neutralizing any effective Libyan role.)

The Libyan régime also saw itself as leading a combat against western influences, blaming the west for the many ills afflicting the Arab and Third Worlds. Relations with the Soviet Union were established in 1973, and billions of dollars of military hardware was purchased for cash. While oil revenues remained very high, Libya attempted to influence events in countries like Northern Ireland, Lebanon, Uganda, Chad and even as far afield as New Caledonia and the Philippines. Military success, however, was denied the Libyan authorities. A war for the Aouzou Strip in northern Chad was lost and the issue taken to international arbitration. (In February 1994, the International Court at The Hague ordered Tripoli to return the Strip to Chad.) As oil wealth declined first in the mid-1970s and then in the 1980s, Libya's activities abroad ceased to be significant in terms of concrete results. Libya signed the Union du Maghreb Arabe treaty in 1989, sign of a rapprochement with its North African neighbours. In the Gulf War, Libya was critical of both Iraqi agressor and Saudi princelings, the latter seen as decadent lapdogs of the West.

In symbolic terms, however, Libya continued to be significant, not least of all for the USA. The off-the-wall rhetoric, the uniforms and public flag burnings, and the support for Palestinian radicals provided the USA with the perfect whipping boy. The assassination of Libya opposition leaders abroad reinforced the image of a revolutionary régime beyond the pale – and helped justify the USA's bombing of barracks near Tripoli in April 1986, raids which left 40 dead, including Qadhafi's adopted daughter, and 93 injured. (The Reagan administration's justification was 'self-defence', claiming to have proof that Libya was responsible for an attack on a West Berlin disco during which a GI was killed. Syria was later thought to have been behind the bombing.)

**Libya as USA public enemy**

Suspicions that Libya was involved in supporting terrorism came to a head in the late 1980s when responsibility for the destruction of a US airliner over Scotland (the 1988 Lockerbie incident), and the shooting-down of a UTA airliner over the Sahara (1989) was attributed to Libya. Sanctions were imposed in April 1992, and included a freeze on Libyan assets in the USA, a ban on civil flights into Libya, and an arms embargo. In 1993, this was extended to a ban on goods related to the oil industry, aerospace equipment and training. In the event, a compromise was reached in early 1999. Tripoli had refused to hand over the two men suspected of being behind the bombing, declaring that the Security Council had no right to become involved in matters to be settled by a court of justice. The USA and the UK thus accepted that the two suspects be tried in a Scottish court in the Netherlands, while Libya was to pay damages to the victims of the shot-down UTA airliner.

**The Lockerbie Affair**

As long as Gadhafi could play off the West against the former Soviet Union and had considerable oil revenues, he could work against the USA and the European Union, supporting their opponents. But the demise of the USSR as a world power in 1991, a massive fall-off in oil revenues in the mid-1980s and the rise of the conservative states as leading elements within the Arab world left him vulnerable to pressure to accept international legal norms for state activities. The USA and the UK were never able to drum up enough support for a fully-fledged oil embargo on Libya, however. This sanction, so damaging to Iraq, would have really hurt Libya. However, as in Iraq's case, it could well have left the existing leadership even better entrenched.

Until the late 1990s, Arabism was the driving force behind Libyan foreign policy. (A large map of the Arab world was displayed behind TV newsreaders, showing the lands occupied by *al-jins al-arabi al-kabir*, the 'great Arab race.') But when African leaders braved the embargo to fly into Tripoli, the Libyan stance changed, as did the map, to reflect a greater interest in Muslim sub-Saharan Africa. Gadhafi seems to believe that Israel can threaten the Arab lands through their (African) back door, hence the financial assistance directed at the African states. Thus as Libya's various weddings with the Arab states have failed, the régime seems to be dreaming of a new political puzzle, a sort of 'United States of the Sahara' – built (inevitably) on the strength of Libyan handouts. (Behind the newscaster's head, Libya now glows green, shedding light down across the African continent.)

**From Pan-Arabism to a United Africa**

## Economy

**The petroleum sector** Libya is an oil-based economy. Oil was first exported commercially in 1961 and output rose rapidly so that at the end of the 1960s Libya was the fifth largest Opec producer of crude oil with more than 3 million barrels per day. This expansion was based on the oilfields in the vast embayment of the Gulf of Sirte where small but prolific oilfields were found in the sedimentary rocks. While some oil was discovered by the major international oil companies (Esso, Mobil and BP), there were also many small independent oil companies involved, for which Libya was the only source of traded crude oil. By the end of the 1960s, there were oilfield installations, pipelines and oil terminals in the barren desert area between Tripoli and Benghazi.

Today oil provides the government with its principal foreign exchange income, US$7,810mn in 1993, the main source of general revenues in the annual budget (90%) and the most important single commodity for export (99%). The two areas of production are around the western borderlands and the Gulf of Sirte, the latter with export terminals at Sidra, Ras Lanuf, Al Brayqa (ex-Brega) and Zuwetina. The main oilfields are linked by pipelines to coastal terminals. Sarir oilfield and its associated installations in the extreme southeast are tied into a terminal at Marsa Hariga near Tobruk, while a small line runs on a north-south axis to Zawiya oil refinery in Tripolitania. An offshore field, Bouri, is sited on the Libyan continental shelf close to Tunisian waters in the northwest. It was won from Tunisia in a judgment of the International Court of Justice in 1982. Libyan oil reserves are only moderate, rated at around 29,000 million barrels, which would last some 52 years at present rates of extraction. Libya produces approximately 1.5 million barrels per year and exports some three-quarters of its output, mainly to western Europe. The National Libyan Oil Co owns refineries in Italy and Germany. Domestic refineries are found at Zawiya, Al Brayqa and Ras Lanuf. With prices at over US$30 a barrel in summer 2000, things looked bright for Libya on the oil revenues front. However, unlike Saudi Arabia, the country cannot quickly increase output.

**Agriculture** In the days before colonial rule, the area now known as Libya was basically self sufficient in food with small surpluses going to the many local occasional markets. The coastlands were comparatively rich agriculturally, favoured by adequate rainfall and available underground water for irrigation. Small fragmented farms were the rule on the coast, though many families had access to communal tribal lands for shifting cultivation and grazing animals to the south of the coastal oases.

Today, agriculture in Libya remains concentrated on the coastal strip. Only 1% of the country is cultivated with a further 7.6% as pasture, rough grazing or forest. The only natural woodland, mainly evergreen scrub, occurs on the Jabal Al-Akhdar, though this has been much reduced by clearances for agriculture.

**Italian influence** Superimposed on the old pattern of small-scale farming and semi-nomadic herding is an Italian colonial structure established in the 1920s and 1930s but replicated since independence. Much of the landscape of Tripolitania as it exists today is a recent creation: there are enormous areas of geometrically planted olive, almond and eucalyptus trees extending across the Jefara plain and parts of the Jabal Nafusa. Small colonial farmhouses can still be seen. The landscape east of Tripoli, between Tajura and Khums, is very beautiful in parts, with occasional lines of cypress trees and great parasol pines a reminder of some old farming estate.

The greatest single changes made by Libyan farmers, though on a model mainly reminiscent of the Italians, is the introduction of citrus fruit orchards and the intensification of output through irrigation in what had originally been dryland or lightly irrigated estates. The most important single field crop is fodder. Libyans prize their mutton enormously and sheep are reared by most farmers. There has also been an expansion of beef and dairy herding, which also requires abundant fodder production, mainly types of lucerne. On the Jabal Nafusa, there is little irrigation and the dryland crops are olives, figs and apricots.

In eastern Libya, lands in the Jabal Al-Akhdar are used for dryland cereals, some fruit and a large area of fodder. In the south, (the Fezzan and Al Khalij), oases survive using irrigation for intensive vegetable and fruit production. Libya's best dates come from the southwest, the *deglet nur* variety being the most prized.

**Agriculture today**  Agriculture remains quite important in Libya despite the economic dominance of the oil industry. In good years, rainfall turns the countryside green and the semi-desert is covered with flowers, the northwestern Jefara Plain being particularly attractive at such times. Poor rainfall means thin crops from rainfed farming and a reliance on underground water resources lifted by diesel and electric pumps. A series of dry years causes the water table to fall dramatically and leads to the excessive use of pumps.

**Disappearance of nomadism**  In much of northern Libya, across a broad zone including the semi-arid steppes and the inland *wadi* systems, various forms of pastoral nomadism were important in the past. Tribal territories spread southwards from the coast to enable seasonal migrations of the nomads. In the central Jefara of Tripolitania, the fringes of the Gulf of Sirte and much of the southern slopes of the Jabal Al Akhdar, forms of full nomadism were practised. Other parts of the north were under types of semi-nomadism (family herding movement) or seasonal transhumance (movements of flocks by shepherds). The coming of the oil era, the imposition of firm boundaries between North African states and other processes of modernization brought an end to much of the nomadic activity. Some semi-nomadic shepherding of large flocks of sheep and goats still goes on in traditional pasture areas on a minor scale.

**Changes in land tenure**  The land tenure situation in Libya has evolved rapidly through the last 100 years. Communal, tribal land ownership was generally practised in Libya except in the settled oases. The Italian colonial period saw a great expansion of state-controlled lands which eventually devolved to the government of the independent Libya in 1951-61. Government intervention in all forms of ownership, ostensibly to socialize fixed assets in the country after the introduction of the Green Book decrees of 1973/75, led to more de facto nationalization of land. However, small farmers are again being allowed to farm land in private ownership. In certain circumstances, individuals are also allowed to own more than one house. Some communal properties, mainly in the semi-arid steppes, are held by tribal groups. A gradual reassertion of private rights in land and other property began with the human rights decrees of 1988 and were reinforced by the privatization programmes implemented from 1989.

**Agricultural development projects**  Contemporary agriculture other than the private sector activities already noted has until recently been mainly state managed. Underground water resources in the far southeast at Al Kufra, Tizerbu and Sarir were developed for agriculture and new agricultural production units were created in the southwest at Sabha, Murzuq and other sites. Expensive imported technology was employed in these schemes, along with labour from Sudan, Egypt and elsewhere since Libyans were generally not prepared to move to these inhospitable regions. Despite the investment of very large resources, the majority of agricultural schemes in the south were abandoned or run down when Libya's oil revenues declined during the mid-1980s.

**The Great Manmade River** Libya's biggest and most spectacular development, the Great Manmade River (GMR), carries water in a large diameter pipeline from well-fields in Al Kufra, Serir and Tizerbu to the coast and thence to Benghazi in the east and Sirte in the west. A second pipeline, it is projected, will transport water from the Murzuq Basin in the southwest to the Jefara Plain adjacent to Tripoli. The movement of water to the north is at the cost of the closure of most major irrigation schemes in the south. Although the government has promised that the new water will be used in the coastlands for agriculture in addition to supplying industrial and urban areas, the high costs of the water delivered there make its use in irrigation questionable. The need for new water illustrates the other great problem for farming in Libya: the falling water tables and intrusion of sea water into aquifers in coastal areas. Around Tripoli, sea water has been drawn into deep aquifers more than 20 km from the coast. In the long term, the ancient fossil water reserves under the Libyan desert will be exhausted. However, the official line is that by the time this happens, desalination technology will be sufficiently cheap to enable the aquifers to be replenished with water pumped back down the man-made river pipes from the coast!

Unfortunately for the credibility of GMR project engineers, a number of severe design defects had emerged by summer 2000. Problems of pipe leakage were so severe that certain sections of the 'river' had to be taken out of use. Certain pipes had sunk badly, causing problems with pumping. It may well be that gas-fuelled desalination plants will have to be brought into use earlier than intended to ensure an adequate supply of water for Tripolitania and Cyrenaica's growing cities.

**Economic plans** The comparatively short life expectancy of Libya as a major oil exporter has given impetus to the development of alternative sources of exports for the future. A set of economic development plans have been adopted by the government, aiming to bolster self-sufficiency, create new jobs and lay the foundations for a future non-oil economy. Some successes were won, including an improvement in the country's transport infrastructure. Excellent road systems serve all parts of the country. New hospitals, hotels and schools have been set up so that even the most isolated settlements can offer good housing, health and educational facilities. However, as the visitor will soon note, much of this infrastructure is in a poor state of repair. There is little professional management, and salaries are so low that staff have little motivation to maintain facilities.

Grandiose plans for a rail system to replace the old Italian lines closed in the 1960s have been delayed. A North African link through Libya from Morocco and Algeria to Egypt is under consideration, but for the moment is little more than a pipe-dream. A mineral and general purpose line from Brak to carry iron ore to the Misrata steel plant is also somewhere on the drawing boards. For the moment, air transport in Libya only serves Tripoli, Benghazi and Sabha, although most major settlements have airstrips. The expansion of the domestic air services has been impeded by sanctions. *Libyan Arab Airways*, the national carrier, looks set to acquire as many as 27 airbuses in the near future, however.

**Industry** Economic development outside transport and other infrastructure has been expensive and limited. A series of major industrial projects were set up, including the Misrata steel works, the Syrte fertilizer factory and an aluminium

# Great Manmade River

smelter at Zuwara. However, shortages of money and personnel and distraction abroad diluted the diversification effort. Only petrochemicals, with large scale complexes set up at Ras Lanuf and Bu Kammash with a smaller operation planned at Sirte, have shown rapid growth, but they depend on the oil sector for raw materials, are highly polluting and employ few Libyans. The Misrata iron and steel mills began operations in 1989 and brought great prosperity to this old market town. How commercially viable the plants actually are, however, is uncertain.

State agencies also set up a variety of new concerns in food processing, soap making, aluminium and construction goods materials. In 1989 the socialist system of centralized national and economic management was abandoned piecemeal. As from the late 1980s, Libyan entrepreneurs were encouraged to begin work in industry on their own account, a move which saw the opening of many small scale workshops, stores and corner shop businesses.

Ultimately, Libyan economic potential is greatly limited by the constraints of a harsh environment. No more than a fragment of the land receives rainfall adequate to support agriculture; underground water reserves are slight and declining. Even the costly south to north movement of water by the Great Manmade River (GMR) project, inaugurated in late 1991, does little to mitigate the problem of water shortage. Other natural resources are scant. Oil, gas and some small chemical deposits occur. There is some potential for the development of the southwest where yellow cake (low grade uranium) is found. Overall, however, Libya's poor physical resources may restrict its future development. **Economic potential and trends**

Paradoxically, the embargo and the freezing of Libyan holdings in the USA in 1986 and the UK had positive results for the Libyan economy. More limited oil revenues forced the state to manage its resources better. Spending was slashed back – particularly on defence. Massive spending on armaments and support for liberation movements in various parts of the world has come to halt. Libya has diversified its foreign holdings, investing in the distribution of petroleum products in Germany, Italy, Spain and Switzerland. Revenues are optimized by controlling production, refining and distribution. When the embargo became a real possibility in 1991, billions of dollars held in Europe were moved to the Gulf.

The other main positive development has been the opening-up of private sector business. In 1991, Gadhafi declared himself in favour of ending the collectivization of industry, except in the case of certain key sectors. 'Lorries must not rust on the parking lots in the name of socialism', he told the nation, and a number of economic reforms were launched. In 1992, the country opted pretty wholeheartedly for the market economy. The aim was to open up company capital to individual investors, and avoid betraying the ideals of the revolution by creating a wealthy bourgeoisie. Measures were taken to encourage the retail sector and small and medium-sized businesses. Masses of immigrants, many from west and central Africa, provide the building sector with the labour force it needs.

## Future prospects

With the suspending of UN sanctions in April 1999, Libya moved into a new phase of development. There was a lot of ground to make up. Heavily dependent on oil, the economy cannot be said to be healthy. Oil prices crashed by 30% in 1998, only to rise again in summer 1999. (For investment in the oil sector to take off again, the outdated legislation will have to be redrafted.) Foreign investment in other sectors was scant, unemployment was running at around 30%, and inflation was high.

It was perhaps for these reasons that in July 2000, Gadhafi sacked his minister of finance, Mohamed Beit al Mal, seemingly a permanent fixture of the government. **Anti-corruption campaign, 2000**

### The safest car

Libya has one of the highest rates for mortal road accidents in the world, and in September 1999, Libya announced that it would be producing a car, named the **Rocket of the Libyan Jamahiriya**, to face this problem. La Presse de Tunisie (7 September 1999) reported the event as follows:

"Aerodynamic in shape, the prototype of 'the car for the 21st century' is, according to an official of the Libyan Arab Foreign Investment Company (Lafico), Mr Al Dukali Al Mugaryef, 'the safest car on earth'. It should be on sale in two years' time. The design and construction of this five-seater car, which required two years of work, was 'inspired' by Colonel Gadhafi, said the spokesman. Tripoli decided on this project because of 'the pressing need to avoid the

thousands of Libyan road deaths caused by accidents due to the sanctions imposed on Libya', which created a shortage of spare car parts and maintenance difficulties from 1992, added Mr Mugaryef. Declaring that the Libyan car had 'successfully passed all tests', he went on to mention the innovations such as special glare-free headlights, a non-reflecting windshield, an airbag capable of protecting passengers fully on all sides, bumpers capable of bearing impacts of up to a tonne, and non-exploding airless tyres.

The name of the car 'might lead to confusion, because other nations produce rockets to kill and destroy countries' said Mr Mugaryef, 'while the Libyan rocket is a vehicle designed with the safety and comfort of people in mind.'

(He had held the post since 1992.) The first indication of change came in January 2000, when Gadhafi tore up the budget document, live on television! The government was reduced to a small team, and a special commission of young officers set up to investigate the Libyan banking system. The results of the enquiry came in June 2000: the captains and lieutenants declared the banks corrupt; huge loans were being made without proper risk analysis. The newspapers reported that 2 billion dollars had gone missing. In the light of the report, a clean-up was necessary: Beit al Mal was arrested, along with 22 leading bankers, including the governor of the Central Bank of Libya, Tahar Jehimi.

Whether this anti-corruption operation means a big change in the Libyan business climate remains to be seen. It is no secret that corruption is widespread at the top of the system. Beit al Mal, however, had a reputation for integrity. He may have been sacked to provide a suitable scapegoat. Indeed, certain Libya watchers consider that as long as a number of figures particularly close to Gadhafi remain untouched, corruption will continue. It is public knowledge that when Libyan funding is made available for a major project in Africa, large sums disappear in kickbacks of various kinds. Perhaps the most important result of the affair is that it has given young officers a chance to look into the murky depths of public life. It also demonstrated once more that nobody, not even those well-entrenched at the top of the system, is safe from eventual investigation of one kind or another.

**Gadhafi, the elder statesman** Despite the occasional spectacular gesture, Libyan official rhetoric has calmed down considerably since the 1980s. Colonel Gadhafi, now in his late 50s, seems to be entering a tranquil, senior statesman phase. He is no longer the number one enemy dictator of the western states. At public meetings, he appears elegantly dressed, leaning on a stick. His image is everywhere, in traditional cloak and wrap-around shades. Sometimes he sports a turban, occasionally an African traditional toque. The ideology of a unified Arab world seems to have gone, replaced by the dream of the United States of Africa. (Libya now has a minister of African Unity, Ali Triki, former ambassador to France.) More importantly perhaps,

### Cooks and car-washers: the immigrant experience

On a hot summer's day, driving onto one of Tripoli's sweeping roundabouts, you will see large numbers of black Africans sheltering in the shade of a flyover. If you are constructing a house, this is the place to come and recruit your builder or electrician, plumber or painter. Each profession is easily identified: the electricians hang light bulbs from a tall piece of wire, you can spot the building labourers by their trowels. Tripoli and Benghazi in fact have huge immigrant populations, although no exact figures are available. There are Egyptians (dominant in Cyrenaica) and Iraqis, Tunisians, Algerians and Moroccans. There are Sudanese, many of them Christians fleeing the civil war which has torn southern Sudan apart, Malians, Nigerians and other assorted west Africans. Sometimes you will see small packs of Koreans and Philippinos in the city, on leave from some major construction project or other.

Libya must have one of the most highly qualified labour forces in the world. Sanctions have forced highly qualified Iraqis to leave home – and Libya is practically the only labour-hungry country they can go to without a visa. Chemists with MSc degrees work as cooks, engineers are switchboard operators. Most coveted are the jobs with international companies, especially those out in the desert. A sizeable chunk of a monthly salary of US$800 will help relieve hardship back in Baghdad. Many immigrants are on far less, however. The Nigerian car-washer on the Corniche, keeping Daewoo Nubiras shiny, will make 10LD on a very good day. (In all likelihood, he will have a technical diploma, too.) A builder's mate or a painter will clock up 10 to 15LD a day, the photocopy boy from Centrafrique with excellent French will make 200LD a month, if lucky. A qualified chef in a privately owned restaurant can take home up to 400LD. A female Moroccan sex worker may make 30LD per client. (To serve the needs of an immigrant population composed of single males, a sex-industry has developed behind the doors of certain Tripoli café-restaurants; trade is brisk in Ramadhan.)

The immigrants dream of better elsewheres. Life in Libya, though often better than at home, is often austere. Bachelors keep costs down by sharing flats, families squat in unsafe houses in the madina – places where the Libyans no longer want to live. Food is relatively cheap, as Libyan families sell the excess part of their monthly subsidized food handout. Not all immigrants come out of need, however. Some are people with insoluble problems in their home countries, the Algerian unfairly accused of supporting 'the terrorists', the Tunisian with a 10-year gaol sentence at home, the penalty for possession of a tiny quantity of hash. For black Africans, the immigrant experience can be particularly tough. There is a strong vein of racism towards Africans in Libya, fed by the unpopularity of the country's expensive African policy. Africans are easily accused of theft, and when a Libyan team loses to an African side, there are incidents of racially motivated violence. The question remains, however, as to the long-term future of this mix of nationalities. Are the Africans in Libya to stay? Could they be thrown out overnight, like thousands of Tunisians before them in the 1980s? Time will tell. For the moment, Libya's capital city is an extremely cosmopolitan place.

Gadhafi's very survival seems to give quite a few Libyans a feeling of pride. Other international demon figures have appeared in the US rogues' gallery. Sanctions are over, and happily for ordinary Libyans, they didn't have the crippling effect they have had on the long-suffering Iraqis.

Gadhafi's new image as a 'man of peace' takes different guises. Libya had a high profile at the 2000 Organisation of African Unity summit held in Togo, with the Guide of the Revolution driving through the streets of Lomé in a cream stretch limousine. Libya claims to have sent thousands of teachers out to work in Africa, and has financed vaccination campaigns and the construction of clinics and cultural centres in poor Sahel countries like Mali. In summer 2000, during the Jalo hostage crisis in the Philippines, Libya came forward to mediate between Islamic fundamentalist kidnappers and the western countries. Gadhafi and his team are clearly seeking to build an image of Libya's leader as a humanist senior statesman. The aim is to associate the country with something more than 'oil and terrorism', and there is no real reason to doubt the sincerity of the policy. On the home front, however, there is a feeling that domestic policy is only of secondary interest to Gadhafi. But then this is nothing new: ego and ambition have long pushed the Guide to look abroad for influence and recognition.

**And after Gadhafi?** The question of what happens after Gadhafi remains unanswered, however. There is no obvious successor, and professional Middle-East watchers in the West have a hard time knowing who actually counts in political terms in Libya. Gadhafi came to power aged just 27. Not yet 60, he could continue in power for another 15 years or so. One scenario is that he may withdraw from internal politics to focus on promoting African unity. In this case, a caucus of younger, technocrat Libyans may emerge to run the country on more modern, accountable lines. Whatever happens, developments will be watched with interest in neighbouring states, particularly Egypt. With a large and poor population, the Egyptian régime is highly dependent on American aid for survival. Some sort of union with Libya might bring considerable financial dividends. And there is the excuse that Cyrenaica is linguistically and culturally closer to Egypt than it is to the Maghreb states. At the back of the commentators' minds is the big political question: will Gadhafi leave a Libyan identity strong enough to survive? After all, this is a recently assembled country comprising three very disparate regions, with vast distances separating the centres of population.

For the moment, however, Gadhafi seems to be intent on developing relations with the other Maghreb states. This might just lead to the emergence of a strong five-country regional grouping in North Africa (from east to west, Libya, Tunisia, Algeria, Morocco and Mauritania), able to maintain dialogue effectively with the five Mediterranean countries of the EU (Greece, Italy, France, Spain and Portugal). In Europe there is a realization that Libya is too important to be left out of the Euro-Mediterranean process, whatever the Guide of the Revolution's failings.

It should be stressed that the Libyan régime is by no means 100% popular at home. Though the image of plucky little Libya standing up to the American giant is a sure winner on the domestic propaganda front, there are plenty of complaints waiting to be voiced. There is chronic mismanagement at many levels, and vital infrastructure is run down. The open-door immigration policy, which has let in thousands of Africans and Egyptians, is felt to have created a wave of petty crime, and there is resentment at the huge sums of money doled out to African states when public services at home function so poorly.

In late September 2000, feeling against African immigrants flared into open violence which left at least fifty dead and many injured. Workers from Chad and Sudan were particular targets, and many were rounded up and interned in a camp south of Zawiya, supposedly to facilitate vaccination campaigns. It was rumoured that a hepatitis epidemic had its origins in the African immigrant communities. No clear picture of the violence emerged in the international media.

Does this mean there is a loophole to be exploited by opponents of the régime? As things stood in the late 1990s, there was little sign of any major opposition movement. All significant opponents were abroad. A tiny royalist movement centres on the London-based Prince Mohamed al Sanusi. There is the Libyan National Alliance, founded by Mansour Kikhia, a former foreign minister kidnapped in Cairo in 1993 and thought to have been assassinated. Another small opposition group, led

## Lockerbie. Did sanctions work?

In 1988, a PanAm plane blew up over Lockerbie in Scotland and 259 people, including 189 American citizens and 11 people on the ground, were killed. Eventually, after enquiries suggesting that the explosion was the work of Syria, Iran or perhaps the Lebanese Hizbollah proved fruitless, responsibility for the bomb was attributed to Libya, and in particular to two Libyan Arab Airlines employees said to be working for the Libyan secret services. Sanctions were imposed on Libya by both the USA and the United Nations when the Jamahiriya. (Colonel Gadhafi did, however, suggest that the USA might like to make an exchange, sending the pilots who bombed his Bab al Azizya barracks' home, killing his daughter and wounding his wife and sons, over to Libya for trial.)

Eventually, the Lockerbie deadlock was resolved. In April 1999, the two suspects, charged with murder and conspiracy to murder, arrived in the Netherlands where a military camp had temporarily become a piece of Scotland, especially for the trial. The question was whether Libya had finally given in because of the weight of sanctions or because of the skilful diplomatic groundwork by the likes of UN secretary-general Kofi Annan. Although sanctions do not seem to work (see

Rhodesia, South Africa and Iraq), Libya might just be the exception that confirms the rule. They seriously inconvenienced the Libyan oil industry, and reduced domestic air services to a handful of flights a day. The government blamed internal problems and shortages on sanctions. However, these were probably just as much due to chronic mismanagement and a skills shortage. Libya never suffered the crippling effects of a full oil-export embargo like Iraq.

Whether or not it was sanctions that meant Libya accepted a compromise, in summer 2000, the Lockerbie trial looked like being over fairly quickly. But would all concerned be satisfied with the justice done? The question remains as to who actually ordered the planting of the bomb. Will investigations ever bring them to book as well? And what will be the outcome of the trial? Will sanctions be reinstated should the suspects be found guilty? Some Western states feel that the trial was all a sham anyway, preparing the way for business interests in what is after all a very rich country. Once the Lockerbie trial is out of the way (with an insufficient evidence verdict returned), the signing of lucrative contracts to update Libya's rundown infrastructure can begin in earnest.

Background

by Dr Yussef Maghrif, has United States' support. Within the country, Islamic fundamentalist groups may have survived, particularly in Cyrenaica. Such is the official control of information, however, that it is difficult to have any idea about what is actually going on.

For the future, Libya has many trump cards. There is a large, able and highly educated Libyan community overseas, in Italy, the UK and North America. The country is well placed to benefit from the proposed creation of a Euro-Mediterranean free trade zone in 2010. Libya has been promised full membership of the EU's co-operation programme with southern shore Mediterranean states – provided it commits itself to international human rights principles. Oil revenues may rise again, providing the wherewithal to fund major infrastructure development projects. (Above all, Libya has the third largest known oil reserves in the world – for a population of barely 5 million.) Tourism may develop too, and the numbers of westerners visiting the country rose sharply in the late 1990s, with Italians, French and Germans experiencing no particular problems in obtaining visas.

**Libyan strengths**

Whatever the changes over the next few years, one can only hope for the best for the people of this most unusual of the North African states. Despite official statements and propaganda images of Libya abroad, Libyans are a nice bunch, generally friendly towards foreigners who are clearly visitors with an interest in the heritage and people of the country. They certainly deserve better than the arbitrary government and international isolation that was their lot in the 1990s. Although few Libyans speak foreign languages sufficiently well to get into deep conversation, many relish the opportunity to chat and exchange ideas with people from abroad. Be careful however not to put a Libyan in an embarrassing position by evoking the country's politics.

# Culture

Libya is a cultural and geographic bridge between Egypt and the Arabian lands to the east (the *Mashriq*) and the territory of the extreme Arab west, the *Maghreb*. Libya also acts as a link between the Mediterranean and Saharan Africa. The Arabic spoken in Libya is generally different from the varieties of Arabic spoken in the Maghreb, much influenced by Berber and French, and is quite distinct from the Arabic of the Nile valley. Enormous oil wealth, following hard on the heels of a short (but brutal, in certain regions) period of Italian colonialism, profoundly affected the lives of a largely bedouin population, barely one million in all. Their attitudes, way of life, and political structure underwent drastic changes during the 20th century. People who have travelled elsewhere in North Africa quickly realize that Libya is immediately different to Egypt in the east, as well as to the more Mediterranean societies to the west. There the influence of France, originally established in the days of 19th-century colonization, continues to be strong through migration, education, and economic contacts.

Although Libya was colonized by Italy from 1911-1943 and was politically close to Europe under the Sanusi monarchy until 1969, the country might be said to have become detached from international values in the 1970s. In contrast to the Maghreb, Libya will often seem alien to people from western Europe. Management and administrative systems are generally slow except in the new, small but flourishing private sector. The role of the state is much greater and impinges much further on people's private lives than is now conceivable in Europe – or indeed in other North African states. Nowhere else in the Mediterranean today can the visitor experience such a totalitarian environment. Though the signboards with their propaganda slogans are rusting, the Big Brother feeling is still there. People have compared the experience of flying out of Libya to the feeling of leaving Saudi Arabia or Kuwait. However, as your plane leaves Tripoli Airport, it is minds rather than bodies which are disrobing.

## The Libyan people

The population of Libya was estimated at 5,407,000 in 1995, 3.5% above the preceding year. There is great racial diversity. The original Berber population of western Libya gradually mixed with incoming Arab tribes after the eighth century BC, though some small groups of more or less pure Berbers from the Jabal Nafusa area of Tripolitania still exist. The people of eastern Libya are proud to be mainly Arab. Intermixture through marriage with slaves and other peoples of sub-Saharan origin such as the Tibu from the Tibesti mountains of southern Libya has added to the racial variety. The coastal cities originally contained populations of diverse Mediterranean origins: Jewish, foreign Arab, Maltese, Greek, Levantine, and Turkish. Today, Libyan cities have a pleasantly cosmopolitan note due to the huge number of immigrants from elsewhere in Africa.

Background

Tribal traditions are strong. Outside Tripoli, the country was economically and socially structured on *qabila* (tribal) lines with *lahmah* (clans) and extended family sub-clans. Each tribe had a defined territory and a specific history of alliances and friction with adjacent groups. The Tripolitanian tribes are often of mixed Arab and Berber origin, and most tribes have founding myths and elaborate lineages. Some clans might claim descent from a saintly ancestor or *wali*, others claim a member of the prophet Mohamed's family as ancestor. During Italian colonial rule, the basis of rural society was changed, partly through systematic confiscation of tribal lands but also by the economic upheaval that came with colonial occupation. Nonetheless, tribal affiliation still has social importance in marriage, kinship and status, especially outside the major urban centres. Though there is no official government recognition of tribal units, a person's identity can be read in their family name, in effect a declaration of ethnic and regional origin, historical status and (possibly) current political strength.

Today, some 95% of the Libyan population people live in the narrow northern coastal strip, with 86% of all Libyans crowded into urban areas. Many of those registered as rural in fact commute to work in nearby towns. Tripoli attracts long-distance daily commuters and there are few areas of the northwest not dominated by the capital despite recent attempts to decentralize. National average population density is 3 persons per square kilometre, though in the coastal strip the densities are much higher.

It is estimated that about 46% of the Libyan population is less than 15 years old, 26% between 15 and 29 and a mere 4.1% above 60 years of age. This is a profoundly youthful population, even by Third World standards.

## Religion

The people of Libya, and of North Africa, for that matter, follow Islam in the main, a religion similar to Judaism and Christianity in its philosophical content. Muslims recognize that these three 'revealed religions' have a common basis, and Jews and Christians are referred to as *ahl al-kitab*, 'people of the book'. (Both Moses and Jesus are prophets for Muslims). There are considerable differences in ritual and the public observance of religious customs between the revealed religions, and when travelling in Libya it is as well to be aware of this. Note, however, that although the Islamic revivalist movement has in recent years been a force in neighbouring Algeria and to a lesser extent in Egypt, the situation in Libya is very different for historic and social reasons.

**Origins of Islam**

Islam is an Arabic word literally meaning 'submission to God'. As Muslims often point out, it is not just a religion, but a way of life. Called by the Arabic term meaning 'the recitation', the main Islamic scripture is the Qur'an (often also spelt Koran in English). Islam appeared in the desert oases of western Arabia in the early seventh century AD. The isolated communities of this region were Jewish, Christian or animist, existing on oasis cultivation and the trade in beasts of burden. There was considerable inter-tribal warfare. It was in this context that the third great revealed religion was to emerge. Its prophet Mohamed was a member of the aristocratic Meccan tribe of Quraysh, born c570.

**The Qur'an**

The Qur'an divides into 114 souras or chapters, placed in order of length running from the longest to the shortest. Muslim and western scholars disagree on the nature of the Qur'an. For the true Muslim, it is the word of God, sent down via the Prophet Mohamed. The Qur'an appeared in this way in segments, some in Mecca, some after the Prophet was forced to leave Mecca for another oasis settlement, Medina. The later souras tend to have a more practical content, and relate to family

*Background*

and inheritance law, for during the period in Medina, an embryonic Muslim community was taking shape. Western scholars, however, have opened up more critical approaches to the Qur'anic text and the way it was assembled. During the Prophet's lifetime, nothing was written down. After his death, fragments of the text, noted in simple script on parchment or flat bones, were assembled on the orders of Abu Bakr, Mohamed's successor or *khalifa*. In fact, the Arabic script was not fully codified at the time. The language of the Qur'an was eventually to become the base reference point for the Arabic language.

**Sayings of the prophet and the five pillars of Islam**

The Qur'an does not cover all aspects of the Muslim's life – and it became apparent to early Islamic rulers that they would need another source for legislation. The **hadith**, short statements which recount what the Prophet is supposed to have said about various issues, were assembled to provide a crucial supplement to the main scripture.

The practice of Islam is based on five central points, the Pillars of Islam, namely the *shahada* or **profession of faith**, *salat* or **prayer**, *sawm* or **fasting** during the month of Ramadhan, *zakat* or **giving charity**, and the *hajj* or **pilgrimage to Mecca** which every Muslim is supposed to accomplish at least once in their lifetime. The mosque is the centre of religious activity. There is no clergy in Islam, although major mosques will have an *imam* to lead prayers. In principle, the *masjid*, (a small neighbourhood mosque) will have someone chosen from the area with enough religious knowledge to conduct prayers correctly.

The *shahada* is the **testament of faith**, and involves reciting, in all sincerity, the statement, "There is no god but God, and Mohamed is the Messenger of God". A Muslim will do this at *salat*, the **prayer ritual** performed five times a day, including at sunrise, midday and sunset. There is also the important Friday noon prayers, which include a sermon or *khutba*. When praying, Muslims bow and then kneel down and prostrate themselves in the direction of Mecca, indicated in a mosque by a door-sized niche in the wall called the *qibla*. The voice of the *muezzin* calling the faithful to prayer five times a day from the minaret provides Muslim cities with their characteristic soundscape. Note that a Muslim must be ritually pure to worship. This involves washing in a ritual manner, either at the *hammam* (local bathhouse) or the *midha*, the ablutions area of the mosque.

A third essential part of Islam is the giving of *zakat* or **alms**. A Muslim was supposed to give surplus revenues to the community. With time, the practice of *zakat* was codified. Today, however, zakat has largely disappeared to be replaced by modern taxation systems. The practice of *zakat al fitr*, giving alms at 'Id El Fitr, the Muslim holiday which marks the end of Ramadhan, is still current.

The fourth pillar of Islam is *sawm* or **fasting during Ramadhan**. The daytime month-long fast of Ramadhan is a time of contemplation, worship and piety – the Islamic equivalent of Lent. Muslims are expected to read 1/30th of the Qur'an each night. Those who are ill or on a journey, as well as women breast-feeding are exempt from fasting. Otherwise, eating, drinking and sexual activity is only permitted at night, until "so much of the dawn appears that a white thread can be distinguished from a black one."

The *hajj* or **pilgrimage** to the holy city of Mecca in Arabia is required of all physically able Muslims at least once in their life time. The *hajj* takes place during the month of Dhu al Hijja. The 'lesser pilgrimage' to the holy places of Islam is referred to as the *'umra*, and can be performed at any time of year. Needless to say, the journey to Mecca is not within every Muslim's financial grasp – fortunately, perhaps, as the mosques would probably be unable to cope with the millions of people involved, despite the extension works of recent years.

Background

As mentioned above, Islam is a revealed religion, and God chose certain men (rather than women) to be **prophets**, his true representatives on Earth. In Arabic, a prophet is a *nabi*, while Mohamed is the messenger of God, *rasoul Allah*. The first prophet in Islam was Adam, and the last was Mohamed, 'seal of the prophets'. Major prophets are Sidna Nouh (Noah), Sidna Ibrahim (Abraham), Dawoud (David), Mousa (Moses), and 'Issa (Jesus). Yaqoub (Jacob), Youssuf (Joseph) and Ayyoub (Job) are all mentioned in the Qur'an. Prophets were recognized by their miracles, apart from Mohamed, who was to be the instrument via which the Qur'an was transmitted to humankind. Nevertheless, Mohamed's *mi'raj* or ascent to heaven on the winged horse, Al Buraq, may be considered as a sort of miracle.

**On prophets & revelation**

The miracles performed by the prophets are not recounted in detail in the Qur'an. '**Issa** (Jesus) is pictured in a particularly favourable light. While the virgin birth features in the Qur'an, Issa is definitely not the son of God in Islam. **Miriem**, as Jesus' mother is called in Islam, is held with great respect by Muslims as one of the holiest women ever to have lived. The prophet who gets the fullest coverage in the Qur'an is **Youssuf**. The story of how this radiantly handsome young man fended off the advances of Pharaoh's wife is recounted in some detail.

Like other religions, Islam has its heaven and hell, its angels and its demons. **Heaven**, *al janna*, is where all good Muslims go in the after-life. It is a place of ease, described in some detail in the Qur'an. It is peopled by *houris*, beautiful young women and a selection of graceful young men. There are rivers and springs, fruit and flowers, fine clothes and comfortable couches. In short, the Muslim paradise promises all that is lacking in the deserts of Arabia. It is *na'im*, the place of complete well-being. In contrast, Muslim **hell**, *al nar* (lit. 'fire') or *al jahanam*, is the final destination of unbelievers and all those who doubted the word of Allah. There they will be consumed by the eternal flames and be flagellated – or alternatively will consume a foul-smelling, burning drink. The Qur'an constantly reiterates that such is the destiny of unbelievers. Over a hundred of the book's souras are quite explicit on this point.

**On heaven & hell, angels & demons**

Evil in Islam is represented by a selection of **demons**. Iblis, *al shaytan al marjoum*, the 'stoned satan', is the number one devil. Iblis, who started off as an angel, was banned from Paradise when he refused to bow down before Adam, Allah's creation. Islam also has a number of more or less evil spirits, the Jinnoun. Born of fire, they are a hidden presence in the world, ever ready to perform bad deeds. Good Muslims must be prepared to fend off temptations placed in their way by such genies.

In contrast to the jinnoun, Islamic **angels** represent closeness to Allah and beauty. There are various types of angel. Some intercede between god and humankind, others note down an individual's good and bad deeds. The number one angel is Jibril (Gabriel), closely followed by Mikala (Michael). It was Jibril who brought the divine word to Mohamed. In meditation in a cave near Mecca, Mohamed was surprised by a voice telling him to recite. It was Jibril, who proceeded to dictate to him Al Alaq, the Soura of the Blood Clot, the very start of the Qur'anic revelation. In the Muslim imagination, two other angels, Nakir and Mounkir, question Muslims on their deeds on earth just after burial, while Azrafil blows the final trumpet on the Day of Judgement. However, only one angel, Jibril, he who shaped Adam from clay, will survive the end of time.

In Islam, sexuality, provided it is within marriage (*al zawaj*), is seen as positive, and there is no category of religious personnel for whom marriage is forbidden. The prophet Mohamed married nine times, so one of the best ways for good Muslims to imitate the founder of their religion is by getting married. Sensuality and seduction, between the married couple, are encouraged, without any guilt being involved. One of the best known metaphors in the Qur'an compares women to a field to be tilled by men. The Muslim male may take up to four wives, as specified in the Qur'anic

**On marriage & sex**

Background

☛ *What's in a name? Notes on Libyan first and family names*

Libyan first names are almost always of Arabic origin and as in any culture, often have a meaning. Many of the girls' names are poetic. There is Amel (Hope) and Awatef (Emotions), Houriya (Spirit of Paradise), Kmar (Moon), Leïla (Night), Noura (Light), Raoudha (Garden), Sana (Radiance), Thouraya (Chandelier) and Zahra (Flower). Some suggest desirable characteristics: Besma and Ibtissem (Smile), Emna (Serenity), Faïka (Outstanding), Latifa (Kindly), Nabiha (Distinguished), Rafia (Of great value), and Wafa (Loyalty). Another set of first names have more exotic, Turco-Persian origins: Chiraz, Narimene and Safinaz.

First names referring back to the Prophet Mohamed's family are popular for girls: Aïcha was the Prophet's first wife, Khadija his second wife, while Fatima refers back to his daughter. Meriem is the Arabic equivalent of Mary, mother of the Islamic prophet Issa, (Jesus). Other male prophets who provide boys' names are Ibrahim (Abraham) and his son Ismail, Mousa (Moses), and Yacoub (Jacob). Returning to the Prophet Mohamed's descendants, Ali was Fatima's husband, their sons were Hassan and Hussein.

Some names come in male/female pairs, as in Aziz/Aziza (Beloved), Sharif/Sharifa (Noble), Habib/Habiba (Beloved), Mabrouk/Mabrouka (Blessed), Mongi/Mongiya (Deliverer), Nabil/Nabila (Noble), Saïd/Saïda (Happy), and Zine/Zina. There are a number of variations around the root letters h-m-d,

meaning praise: Ahmed, Hamid, Mahmoud and, of course, Mohamed, for men, Hamida for women.

Men's first names often start with Abd (servant) and one of the 99 names of the divinity, ie Abd Allah, 'servant of god', Abd al Hadi, 'servant of the tranquil one', Abd al Karim 'servant of the noble one', etc. In daily life, these names are then shortened to Hadi or Karim. Another type of male name ends in 'din' (pron: 'deen') meaning 'faith', as in Shamsaddine (Sun of Faith), Qamaraddine (Moon of Faith), and Nouraddine (Light of Faith). These again get shortened (Shams, Nouri). Common men's names in Libya include Adil (Just), Khalid (Eternal), Mahdi (Rightly guided), Mourad (Desired), Naji (Close friend) and Walid (Engendered).

Another set of men's names, rather rare, goes back to ancient Arabo-Islamic tradition, and includes Kays, Kusay, and Otayil. In neighbouring Tunisia, the strong links with France influence choice of names. Families actually living in France or where the mother is of foreign origin may choose names easily pronounced in French: for the boys, Karim and Skander (Alexander), for the girls, Nadia and Sofiya, Sarra and Monia. Quite a few first names have familiar forms (tarbija): Adel becomes Adoula, Khaled = Khalouda, etc.

Family names tell a story, too. ('Ben' corresponds to the Celtic 'Mc', 'son of'). Many indicate trades and professions now half-forgotten: Haddad (Blacksmith), Meddeb (teacher in a Qur'an school), Najjar (Carpenter).

soura (chapter) *The Women*. However, the same soura recommends that the husband refrain from taking more than one wife should he feel unable to treat them all equally. This verse is much quoted by opponents of polygamy as a justification for its abolition. Islam also has a 'secondary' form of marriage, the *zawaj al muta'a*, the 'union of pleasure', which can be initiated and annulled on the wishes of both parties. Mentioned in the Qur'an, this sort of marriage is totally rejected in mainstream Sunnite Islam, (ie in the majority of the Muslim world, including Libya), but accepted in Shi'ite regions such as Iran.

In Libya, weddings tend to be between young people whose families know each other, or whose family status is clear to both parties. Parental approval is essential, and in a country with little public entertainment, weddings are major occasions for people to get together, often lasting several days. In the upper levels of society, these are costly occasions which may be held on a country estate. Note that there is no question of couples living together before marriage and the bride must be a virgin on her wedding day.

Islam has quite a small but strict selection of other requirements related to purity, some of which are close to the practices of Judaism. These are referred to as *sunna*, standard Islamic practice. Eating pork is a source of impurity, as is drinking alcohol and gambling. These interdictions are strictly applied in Libya, although alcohol, mainly in the form of *boukha* (flash) and Celtia beer from Tunisia is more readily available than one might think.

It is also sunna for boys to be circumcised. Note however that female genital mutilation, also sometimes referred to as female circumcision, is not Islamic practice, despite being widespread in certain parts of the Muslim world, notably Sudan and parts of sub-Saharan Africa. Unfortunately, this practice, varying in severity, tends to accompany the spread of Islam into formerly animist areas. Boys' circumcision tends to take place between the ages of 3 and 7. However, the Qur'an does not contain any absolute requirement to circumcise. It is a strongly recommended, but not compulsory. Metaphorically speaking, male circumcision might be said to represent the removal of impurity that might otherwise obstruct spiritual awakening. And generally a big party is held to celebrate a circumcision. Originally, this was to help take the circumcisee's mind off the operation, generally performed by the local barber. Today, as often as not, the operation is performed in a hospital under local anaesthetic.

Another area where purity is important is prayer. Islam lays down an exact way to wash in order to prepare oneself for prayer. By performing their ablutions five times a day before prayer, Muslims distance themselves from the daily routine and make themselves fit to be in contact with the divine. Ablutions involving the washing of hands, arms, elbows, face, feet and damping the hair are compulsory before prayer, while major ablutions or *ghusl* (washing the whole body) are to be performed after sex or on breaking the fast. Given that the Muslim countries are on the whole located in arid regions where water is not always readily available, Islam allows the believer to perform the ablutions with sand or with a specially purified symbolic stone.

In terms of appearance, Muslims, both women and men, have a number of requirements to satisfy. Men, if they opt to wear a beard as the prophet Mohamed did, should make sure that it is carefully barbered. In the matter of dress, maximum coverage for both women and men was the rule, though habits have changed hugely in recent years. Young women do not automatically cover their heads as their mothers did. However, the 'headscarf and long dress', the modern version of Islamic dress, widespread in Egypt, is popular. Many young women opt for headscarf with long blouse over trousers, generally worn with the trendiest shoes possible. It should be stressed that Libyan Islam, and indeed North African Islam as a whole, is a long way from the more extreme forms practised in Saudi Arabia, where women are forbidden from driving and are all but invisible in the public sphere. While in traditional families the women's domain is most definitely the home, Islam does not stop a trend for Libyan women to get themselves educated and into jobs once thought of as being exclusively for men.

In the early 1950s, following purges of the Muslim Brotherhood in Egypt by the Nasser government, some members of the movement took refuge in Libya. Later came the Hizb al Tahrir, an organization calling for a purer form of Islamic practice and the re-establishment of the Caliphate (a pan-Muslim institution, not unlike the papacy, headed by a successor to the prophet). No Islamic party has achieved the position that the FIS (Front islamique du salut) was to gain in Algeria in the late 1980s, however. The fact that a fundamentalist Islamic party, on the scale of those in Egypt or Algeria, has not taken hold is due in part to the fact that Malikite Islam is strongly rooted in Libya, and that the present régime draws much of its legitimacy from Islam. Although few details filtered out to the rest of the world, a fundamentalist uprising in the Derna region was put down with considerable bloodshed in the late 1990s. Rebels took refuge in the Jabal Akhdar and were hunted down by the regular army. Certain historic sites are said to have been damaged in the process. Note that providing assistance to Muslim African states was a central feature of Libyan foreign policy in the late 1990s.

## Language

**Origins of Arabic**

Arabic is the official language of Libya, as you will be aware right from the moment you get a smudgy stamp, translating your passport's main details, printed somewhere near the back of the document. Like Hebrew, to which it is closely related, Arabic is a Semitic language with its roots in the Arabian peninsula. It was the language of Quraysh, the Meccan tribe from which the prophet Mohamed came. The Qur'an was 'sent down' or revealed to the prophet in Arabic. Thus for the Arabs, and indeed for all Muslims, the Arabic language is synonymous with absolute clarity of meaning and beauty of form. It is not just a liturgical language, like Greek or Latin; it is the tongue chosen by God to reveal his message to humankind.

As is the case with other Semitic languages, Arabic words are based on three root consonants. Variations of the vowels accompanying these consonants are used to make words, (eg the root d-r-s contains the concept of 'study', therefore *yadrus* is 'he studies', *tudarris* is 'she teaches', *dars* is 'lesson', and *tadris* is 'teaching'; the place where you study is a *madrasa*). In theory, it is possible to coin an infinity of new terms, eg *'awlama* (globalization) from *'alam* (world), etc.

**Evolution of Arabic**

After the Arab Muslims conquered the Middle East in the seventh century AD, Arabic became the language of a vast empire – and came into contact with other languages like Greek, Persian and Coptic. After the prophet Mohamed's death in AD 632, there was an urgent need to assemble the Qur'an, the series of texts which had been revealed to him. Some sections had been memorized by members of the Muslim community, there were souras written on camel shoulder bones and parchment. It was thus essential to develop a standard writing system to preserve the divine text. Early Arabic script does not have all the dots and helpful dashes which are now part of Arabic writing. Today, Arabic script has 28 letters, including three long vowels, 'a', 'i' and 'u'. The corresponding short vowels are indicated by short strokes above or below the letter they follow, and are generally not written. A number of the consonants, including d, t, d, dh, s, and z have both weak and emphatic forms. Arabic writing does not have capital letters, and in a sense functions as a sort of shorthand; as the short vowels are not written, you have to know the vowelling to be able to read.

Literature in classical Arabic reached its peak in Baghdad in the 10th century. Poetry and rhymed prose were the highest literary forms. By the 16th century, most of the Arab world, including Egypt and the Levant, had come under Ottoman rule. While Arabic remained the language of the law and religion in those countries, the belles lettres tradition declined. In the 19th century, Syria and Lebanon were home to a revival and modernization of the Arabic language. Numerous works of western literature were translated, and the written language's vocabulary was modernized in the process. To this day, official language academies in Baghdad, Cairo, and Damascus are responsible for coining new words to ensure that Arabic has adequate terminology to deal with technological and social developments. The task is not an easy one, however, and in most Arab countries, a second language, English in the Middle East and the Gulf, French in Tunisia, Algeria and Morocco, is widely used in scientific and technical training and among the élite.

The visitor to Libya will quickly become aware of the variety of Arabic script. There are neatly carved Qur'anic verses running as a frieze in the prayer halls of mosques. There is gaudy rounded lettering on the signs of new shops, and more utilitarian script on banners announcing public events. In the early centuries of Islam, fine **calligraphy** quickly became a major art form in the Arab world. Like Qur'anic recitation, calligraphy is a means to glorify god through the endless repetition of the divine word. Schools of calligraphy arose, notably under the Abbasids in Iraq, and were promoted by governments. In societies dominated by a religion that does not allow pictorial reproduction of the human form, calligraphy came to be a major outlet for the artistic impulse. As a vehicle for State ideology, calligraphy functioned like statuary in the Roman world and the codes of heraldry of medieval Europe.

Libya came under Italian rule in the early 20th century, and was only formally part of the Kingdom of Italy for a few years in the late 1930s. Thus the Italian language never achieved the same status as French in the main Maghreb countries. With post-war British rule and the USA's dominant position in the oil industry, English quickly became the country's first foreign language in the 1960s. However, with the 1st September Revolution, the process of creating a clear Libyan identity began in earnest. Language was to be one of the main ways of doing this. The 1970s were the decade of pan-Arabism, and reinforcing the presence of Arabic was one way to dilute strong regional identities. By the early 1990s, all subjects were in Arabic in secondary schools, even the sciences that had previously been taught in English.

**Language in Libya today**

Note, however, that there is a great difference between the formal written form of Arabic, as found in the news media, and the spoken forms. A parallel can be drawn with Italian. People speak their local dialect but have to learn a formal written form at school. The differences between modern spoken forms of Arabic and the written form are great, however, and most people do not leave school with any great ability to write the formal language. In fact, they may write letters in dialect, and if they have a high-level technical job, will almost certainly be obliged to operate in English. There are considerable differences between the dialects of Cyrenaica and Tripolitania. Broadly speaking, Tripolitanian is similar to Tunisian dialect, while the dialects of eastern Libya share features with the Arabic spoken in western Egypt. Both dialects have taken on board quite a few words from Italian and English. (The visitor will find that all the car and garage vocabulary is a mixture of these two languages.)

Education has expanded enormously in Libya from a very poor level at independence. By 1990, 75% of males and 50% of females were literate. The country now has the highest literacy rate in North Africa after Tunisia. Unfortunately, however, the educational system has been the object of constant political interference. Foreign languages disappeared from the secondary curriculum for years, and Arabization was taken to extremes, with even the standard symbols for the elements being translated. Rote learning remains strongly entrenched, reinforced by importing large numbers of poorly trained teachers from Egypt; cheating in exams is said to be rife. The overall result is that standards have fallen in recent years, especially those in higher education. Even so there are 72,000 students each year in higher education. University standards, except in medicine and some other limited areas, approximate those of western European secondary schools. Apart from scientific subjects, all subjects are taught in Arabic in tertiary education too.

**Education & literacy**

Background

## Income and work

As an oil economy Libya generates an apparently high income per head at US$6,510. This figure can be misleading in the sense that the government controls and spends the greatest portion of national income. There is poor distribution of income, the isolated rural regions of the country being much worse off than the coastal cities. Between individuals, however, there is less visible difference in income than in other Arab states (a Muslim socialist ideology is still strong, the rich are discrete). Libyan participation in the workforce is low at 25% of the total population with only 10% of women taking part in paid employment. The majority of Libyans work for the government or its agencies, leaving foreigners to work in industry and provide cheap, unskilled labour.

## Daily life

In the late 1990s, the fall in oil prices had an impact on daily life. A flourishing black market developed as the Libyan dinar was kept pegged at an artificially high value. Inflation began to take hold, reaching around 40% per annum in 1996, while salaries were frozen. The impact of these factors on daily life was reduced, however, by the heavy subsidies on all basic products. Unemployment appeared, however, along with fraud and various forms of criminality. The State struck back in July 1997, introducing the death penalty for commercial fraud, currency speculation, drugs and alcohol consumption.

**Housing & income**   For most Libyans, life is immeasurably better than it was 30 years ago, on the eve of the revolution. All families are owner-occupiers by virtue of the *al bayt li sakinihi* ('the house belongs to its occupier') decree. There is education and medical treatment for all. Salaries, however, remain low, and there is no indication that they will rise. (All salaries were frozen by law 15 in 1981.) A school teacher, for example, makes around 250LD a month. The result is that a lot of Libyans on small incomes have branched out into the informal private sector part-time, opening small family-run shops selling imported household goods and clothes. Another result of the salary freeze is that those Libyans who are making good money keep a low profile. Although there are numerous large new Korean cars, the public display of affluence is not a feature of Libyan society.

However, despite low State salary levels, there is no corruption on the scale of, say, Egypt or Morocco, and practically no tipping in restaurants and cafés. On the other hand, there is said to be much theft of valuable equipment from schools and other state institutions, and no incentive to be productive in one's main job.

**Lifestyle, entertainment & holidays**   In both the cities and small rural settlements, lifestyle remains firmly family orientated. Even in Tripoli, snack restaurants and cafés close early by western standards. People watch satellite television, with Egyptian, Italian and sports channels being particularly popular. Summer is the marriage season, with opportunities for big family gatherings, sometimes lasting several days. For men, there is socializing at the café around a game of cards or backgammon, or maybe a *shisha* water-pipe. Football is popular, too, and the Italian and English leagues are followed with great interest. The two top Libyan teams are the Tripoli-based *Al Ahli* and *Al Ittihad*; Tariq Diyab, now with leading Tunisian team *Etoile du Sahel*, is the best known football hero. In the last few years, body-building clubs have opened in Tripoli. No doubt martial arts, extremely popular in neighbouring Tunisia and Algeria, will gain a loyal following as Libyan society opens up to organized sport. In summer there is the beach for those living in Tripoli and around. 'Culture' in the western sense of the term, is of extremely limited availability. There are a couple of festivals, at Ghat and Ghadamès, but these were launched for the infant tourist industry.

For a real break, all but the poorest Libyans head abroad, with Tunisia, just a few hours' drive away, and Malta being the most popular destinations. Many Libyans have family connections in the southern Tunisian town of Sfax, or rent second homes there. Others travel up to Tunis with relatives receiving medical treatment in one of the Tunisian capital's private clinics. Happily, the ending of the black market has made travel cheaper for many ordinary Libyans. However, for those on fixed salaries and no other sources of income, travel is virtually impossible.

## Music

What sort of music do people in Libya listen to? Walking past a cassette stall, your ears will be assailed by unfamiliar tunes and voices. With technology for the mass-pirating of music so easily available now, Libyan musical tastes have become increasingly catholic. Tapes are cheap too, just a couple of dinars. Among young women, top selling cassettes are by Arab singers, like the Iraqi Kazem Essaher and Diana Haddad, whose videos are shown on satellite TV. In Tripoli cafés frequented by immigrants from the Maghreb, Algerian raï music is popular; top stars include Khaled, Mami, Cheb Zahouani, Cheb Hosni, Cheb Amro and Faudel. Some sorts of western music are popular too, and not only with the urban middle classes. Adolescents and students go for Bob Marley, Madonna and various boy-bands. 'Romantic' singers like Quebec's Céline Dion and Witney Houston (whose songs also exist in Arabic cover versions) also have a following in Libya.

There is of course a more conservative taste in music. Libyan traditional urban music, sung by all male choirs, is often broadcast on local television. The combination of violins and lutes, and the mix of solo and choral singing is a little soporific, however. Also still popular in Libya – as elsewhere in the Arab world – are the great Egyptian and Syro-Lebanese singers who had their heyday in the 1950s and 1960s. Umm Kalthoum, a peasant girl from the Nile Delta who became diva of the Arab world, is popular everywhere. Her songs have probably done more for promoting classical Arabic poetry than any school book. From this period other great names you may want to ask for, if perusing in a cassette shop, include Druze princess Asmahane, Mohamed Abdewahab, Farid El Atrach, the Lebanese divas Fayrouz and Sabah, Najet Es Saghira and the brown nightingale, Abdel Halim Hafez, who died tragically young of bilharzia.

## Life in the South

In the oases of the far South and the small towns at a modest distance from the coast, there is little industry. Here life depends on earnings from agriculture, public employment, and remittances from employment on the coast. Construction of private villas and other housing is the most pronounced area of economic activity in the countryside, though farming is still a way of life for many Libyans outside the major coastal towns. The transport industry also absorbs a great deal of energy in remote desert areas.

## Libya in the media

How do Libyans see themselves? How do other Arabs view the Libyans? First of all, it is important to realize that until the advent of satellite television, the country was extremely isolated from the outside world, the only sources of information being the national media. Today, however, thanks to satellite, Libyans can see for themselves what is going on elsewhere in the world. Particularly popular channels include MBC, a London-based Arabic news and entertainment channel, and Al Jazira, a Qatari-based news channel which has taken over the niche which BBC

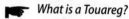 ## What is a Touareg?

The population of southwestern Libya has a small Touareg component. Some have Libyan nationality, others are Mali or Niger passport holders with many years' residence in Libya. Although the impression is of a homogeneous people, the Touareg are composed of peoples of diverse origins and cultures. In some cases, language is the only shared feature. **Imushar** is the term in the Targui language closest to the European word Touareg. **Targa**, the name of a powerful group camel-rearing of Berbers in the Fezzan referred to by Arab historian Ibn Khaldoun, may be the origin of the term Touareg.

Originally, the Touareg were a collection of semi-nomadic stock-rearing tribes inhabiting the inhospitable central Sahara. They reared camels for desert transport and raiding, while goats were the main source of food. (Unlike dromedaries, goats breed quickly and need little husbandry.) The traditional Touareg social structure was matrilineal and consisted of a dominant nomad warrior caste at the core of the system. Then there were religious specialists (inesleman), vassals, craftsmen and servile groups. The artisans (inaden, lit: 'smith'), respected for their special manual skills, tended to be of darker complexion than the nobles and vassals. Crucial to the system were the slaves, originally obtained by raiding caravans. The slave class maintained wells and the oasis gardens. Freed slaves would leave their masters to work as agricultural share croppers. Some Touareg, the eshsherifen, claim descent from the Prophet Mohamed.

In language terms, there are two main mutually intelligible dialects in the Touareg domain, **Tamashaq** in the western areas and **Tamahaq** in the north, including the Fezzan. The culture has a strong tradition of oral poetry, but no written literature. Ancient messages in **Tifinagh**, the Touareg alphabet, can be found carved or painted on the rock faces of the Tadrart Akakus.

One theory of the origin of the Touaregs is that they are a people driven out of the Mediterranean coastlands into the African interior to create strong-points in the Fezzan, the Tassil-n-Ajjer, the Ahaggar Massif, and the Ifaras Mountains. Their domain extended down to the bend of the Niger River in present-day Mali. They controlled the fertile grazing on the edge of the desert and the caravan routes to the north.

The 20th century was harsh upon the Touareg way of life. A devastating drought (1968-74) forced many to seek refuge in the Sahel countries where they settled in camps on the fringes of towns. The old social system broke down in the urban settings. Often the artisans did well, however, being less bound by tribal ties. The exact number of Touareg is difficult to evaluate. One recent estimate puts their numbers at 10,000 in Algeria, 250,000 in Mali and 150,000 in Niger.

Arabic satellite television was to have occupied before it folded. In the stodgy, State-sponsored world of Arabic broadcasting, Al Jazira with its phone-ins and debates on political issues passes for a broadcasting revolution. It even features the occasional Libyan opposition member.

There is nothing that remotely corresponds to a free press in Libya, and foreign newspapers are a great rarity. Anything which might dilute the official line is avoided, and there is no such thing as an independent opposition voice. That semi-political animal, 'the public intellectual', part of the national scene in Morocco, Algeria and even Egypt has no existence in Libya.

In Libya, the Arab identity is extremely important, and is maintained by a strain of old-fashioned nationalist rhetoric. While such language has largely declined to a ritual status in the Maghreb states to the west, in Libya it is maintained in the national media. However, the dominant theme in official Libyan imagery today is Africa, and the speeches and proceedings of major African conferences are given detailed media coverage. The African slant to State policy is not universally appreciated in Libyan

## The Fourth Pyramid

The share taxi driver has put his favourite cassette on. Who does that forceful voice, rising above the slithering quarter tones of the violins, belong to? It could well be that of Umm Kalthoum, the best known Egyptian of this century after Gamal Abd al Nasser and still the most popular Arab singer. There was nothing in her background to suggest that Umm Kalthoum was to become the greatest diva produced by the Arab world.

Born in 1904 in a small village in the Nile Delta region, Umm Kalthoum became interested in music through listening to her father teach her brother Khalid to sing religious chants for village weddings. One day, when Khalid was ill, Umm Kalthoum accompanied her father and performed instead of her brother. The guests were astonished at her voice. After this, she accompanied her father to sing at all the weddings. In 1920, the family headed for Cairo. Once in the capital, Umm Kalthoum's star rose fast. She met the poet Ahmad Ramzi and made her first commercial recordings. In 1935, she sang in her first film. She subsequently starred in numerous Hollywood-on-the-Nile productions.

In 1946, personal and health problems made Umm Kalthoum abandon her career, temporarily as it turned out. Due to her illness, she met her future husband, the doctor Hassan el Hafnawi, whom she married in 1954. She then resumed her career. Songs such as Al awal fil gharam wal hubb ('The first thing in desire and love'), Al hubbi kullu ('Love is all') and Alf layla wa layla ('A Thousand and One Nights') made her name across the Arab lands. In the 1960s, her Thursday evening concert on the Cairo-based Radio Sawt al Arab ('Voice of the Arabs') became an Arab-wide institution. During the Yemeni civil war, the Monarchist troops knew that Thursday evening was the best time to attack the Egyptian troops supporting the Republicans as they would all be clustered round their radio sets listening to their national diva. So massive was her fame that she was dubbed 'the Fourth Pyramid'.

Umm Kalthoum's deep, vibrant voice was exceptional, of that there is no doubt. Nevertheless, the music may be difficult for western ears. Though the lyrics are often insufferably syrupy, the diva's songs continue to enjoy wide popularity and her films, subtitled in English or French are often shown on Egyptian satellite channel Nile TV. In Ramadhan 1999, a TV series on her life drew huge audiences. If there is one piece of modern Arab music you should try to discover while in Libya, it has to be the Umm Kalthoum classic love song, Al Atlal, ('The remains of the camp fire'). The theme, a lament sung over the ashes of the camp fire for the departed lover, goes way back to the origins of Arab poetry.

Umm Kalthoum died in 1975, and her funeral cortege filled the streets of Cairo with hundreds of thousands of mourners. Her voice lives on, played in cafés and cars, workshops and homes all over the Arab world.

society, however, and people are heard to say that 'before the Africans, there was no crime in Tripoli', or grumble about 'all that money going to Africa.'

Elsewhere in the Arab world, off-beat political stances are the feature of Libya which is most remembered. Even after the event and details have been forgotten, the implacable logic of Colonel Gadhafi's speeches remains in people's minds. In the past, Libya's leader attracted a certain admiration for his uncompromising positions on the Israel-Palestine question. However, as other Arab states pull ahead in economic terms, his particular brand of idealism has come to seem dated, sometimes dangerous, even crackpot. In neighbouring Tunisia, the adjective 'Libyan' equates with naïve, and Tunisians tell Libyan jokes rather as the Americans tell Polish jokes. Libyans are well aware of the unfortunate image projected by the régime, and when they meet a western foreigner are keen to find out what images of Libya are held elsewhere.

*Society of slogans*

Coming into Tripoli Airport, you immediately notice the complete absence of any signs in European languages. There is no corporate advertising, either. However, a frieze of Arabic script runs round the top of the main concourse – political slogans, in fact. In Libya, slogans are everywhere: on large bill-boards by the highways, on concrete 'monuments' at traffic intersections and in hotel gardens, on posters and on the back of postcards. Al Fatih abadan, 'the Revolution forever', is the most popular, of course. All motorists coming down the winding road from Gharyan to the Jafara Plain can see it picked out on massive scale in white rocks on the mountainside. Most slogans recall the great principles of the September revolution: 'Partners not wage workers', 'Houses belong to their occupiers', 'There is no freedom in need', 'Al Fatih is an Islamic revolution', etc. Some, though quite catchy, are a little Orwellian: Al lijan fi kulli makan, 'The committees are everywhere'. Others are liberationist in tone: 'Everlasting loyalty to the breakers of chains and the destroyers of frontiers'. If you only read English, the sole slogans you will be aware of in Libya are those on the Jamahiriya Tourist Board's posters: 'The silent treasures', 'Everything you can imagine, everything you can't imagine'. The latter summarizes rather well the unpredictabilities of travel in this once most isolated of Arab lands.

Libyans have had to learn to live under a generous yet highly capricious régime. The changes imposed from above have not always been to everyone's liking, yet there is no real channel for protest or even discussion. The result has been a retreat into the family network, the only one that an individual can really trust. Libyans are used to the unexpected, and tend to deal with it well. 'We're good in a crisis', they say. And thanks to common sense and a keen realization that there is no need to make things worse than they already are, life goes on and most awkward situations get sorted out. Nevertheless, through travel and satellite television, Libyans are well aware that a number of other Arab countries, some of them with no oil at all, are doing very nicely today.

# Art and architecture

## Seeing Libyan architecture and traditional art

In certain parts of Libya, old vernacular building still survives, along with faint remnants of pre-industrial craft production systems. In most areas, however, traditional architecture, such as it was in a desert land of nomad settlement, has given way to less aesthetic – and far less climatically adapted – forms of building. As the Jamahiriya is very much a Year Zero régime, the notion of heritage along the lines of 'old things to be preserved' has not really taken root: many older mosques have been completely rebuilt and swathes of demolition have cut across Tripoli Old Town. However, collections of traditional arts and crafts from recent centuries are held at the Castle Museum in Tripoli and various smaller museums elsewhere. The Castle Museum also has the finest collection of objects from ancient times, too. Disappointingly, there is no national carpet and textile collection, nor any national gallery of contemporary painting. You will have to visit souks to see textiles, and there are one or two small private galleries in Tripoli holding occasional shows of contemporary painting. Architecture buffs are spoiled, however, and will find a huge selection of 19th- and 20th-century building styles in Tripoli.

## Apollo in England

Apollo was a popular god in ancient Cyrenaica, especially as he was in part responsible for the foundation of Cyrene. Down the centuries of Greek religion, he changed a lot, however. Surprisingly for those who have an image of Apollo as a radiant young man, Apollo started his divine career as a bearded patriarch. The handsome youth phase came later, providing a model for deified Hellenistic kings. Eventually, Apollo became rather androgynous. The powerful, over-sized marble Apollo from Cyrene on display in the British Museum (room 14) is a baroque and languishing god. An arm is raised behind the head; the long, thick hair is bound back; drapery falls in unlikely swathes across the upper thighs. The other arm balances a lyre on top of a tree-trunk around which a hissing python coils. The soft, heavy style of the figure gives the god a Dionysiac feel, far removed from the compact Apollos of classical Greece. This was an international deity, instantly recognizable to visitors from other Romano-Greek cities, and a good example of the range of figure types which Hellenistic artists could produce.

The Cyrene Apollo at the British Museum was discovered in January 1861. It was the replacement for an earlier statue destroyed in the Jewish revolt of AD 115. The temple housing it was rebuilt under Hadrian and dedicated under M Aurelius and Commodus (AD 161-192). The statue dates from this period.

## Prehistory

The earliest traces of human settlement in Libya go back to 800,000 BC. The prehistory of the southwestern Fezzan has been intensively researched by French and Italian teams, and elaborate settlement chronologies established, based on carbon dating, finds of flints, and stylistic analysis of the region's rock art. (For detail on this, see the chapter on the Fezzan.) Regarding what is now Tripolitania, towards 5000 BC, new populations, probably the ancestors of today's Berbers, are thought to have arrived. They brought with them a nomadic form of pastoralism. There are also prehistoric sites in Cyrenaica, notably the great Hawa al Ftea cave on the coast between Apollonia and Derna, and in the Wadi al Kuhuf.

### Phoenicians and Greeks

When Rome was founded in 753 BC, the coast of modern Libya was already on the trade routes of Phoenician merchants, who set up trading posts all the way through to the Straits of Gibraltar and beyond. Far inland, the Fezzan was inhabited by a people known by the Romans as the *Garamantes*. (Elsewhere in North Africa, there were a number of Berber kingdoms with zones of influence.) Important Phoenician *emporia* included the settlements which were to become Roman Sabratha, west of modern Tripoli, and Leptis. Evidence of Phoenician artistic skills is scant, but at both **Sabratha** and **Leptis**, remains of early settlement have survived beneath layers of Roman building. At the former site, the famous **mausoleum B**, dating from the first half of the second century BC, features Egyptian cornices and Greek-style columns.

Little has survived of Punic building – apart from the remains of some sturdy housing on Byrsa Hill, Carthage, and ground floor walls in the round town of Kerkouane, also in Tunisia. History has looked on the Carthaginians with a rather cruel eye, partly because of anti-Punic Roman propaganda and partly because they left little in material terms, unlike the Greeks with their temples and the elegant Etruscans. Carthaginian pottery bears no comparison with Greek black-figure ware, and there is practically no statuary. Nevertheless, Carthaginian graves have produced numerous items left as funerary offerings: small plates, jars and containers,

Background

### Architectural jargon for classical sites

**Bas-relief**. Low-relief carved feature.
**Cella**. The internal sanctuary at the heart of a temple, site of cult statue. Also referred to as the **naos** in English.
**Engaged columns**. Columns which are 'half absorbed' into a wall.
**Entablement**. The long frieze section running horizontally just below a temple's roof line.
**Metope**. Short section of the frieze,

generally featuring bas-relief sculpture.
**Pediment**. The triangular bit above the entablement, generally symbolizing the main entrance to a temple.
**Peristyle**. Colonnaded courtyard.
**Veneer**. Very much a feature of Roman temples in Tripolitania. Expensive imported stone such as marble was used to face the insides of public and private buildings.

incense burners, jewellery and amulets of various kinds. Among the more intriguing items discovered are ostrich eggshells with painted faces, probably a symbol of new life. Tiny glass pendants featuring human faces were also popular. Sacred razors, incised with varied motifs and scenes, and also part of the offerings left with the deceased, bear witness to Carthaginian skill in metal working, as does the display of Punic jewellery in the Bardo Museum, Tunis. In the Jamahiriya Museum, Tripoli Castle, look out for the small collection of Punic statuary (Punic lions and cult statues) from Leptis and Sabratha.

## Roman times

The Roman period has left the visitor to Libya (and indeed North Africa) with a wealth of sites to visit – and a fine collection of Roman mosaics and statuary, housed in the Great Jamahiriya Museum. The Romans were a practical lot, and so careful was their engineering that some of their greatest buildings have survived in an amazingly intact state down to the present day.

The remains of the Roman towns in Tripolitania are truly impressive – and there are still more across the borders in Tunisia and Algeria, (the latter for the moment off limits). To the Romans, as later on to the Muslim Arabs, the city represented the home of civilization, and across their African territories the Romans laid out new towns on a grid-iron pattern (parts of Sabratha) or overbuilt smaller existing settlements – as at both Sabratha and Leptis Magna. The typical town which the visitor can see today centres on a forum and temples, and has extensive public facilities, including baths, a circus, a theatre and basilicas. There is also generally a triumphal arch or two, honouring some benefactor or emperor. The same format can in fact be seen right across the empire.

**Temples** The temples are generally the most impressive feature of Roman architecture, and were derived from Greek and Etruscan models. Greek columns were the fashion from the second century AD onwards, but only covered the front of the temple, not all four sides, as in the Hellenic world (compare the Temple of Zeus at Cyrene with temples in Tripolitania). Accessible by steps, set at the heart of the Roman towns, the temples were extremely striking buildings, the core of a city's Romanity. Initially, temples were built to a trinity of gods, Jupiter, Juno and Minerva. Later in the empire, they were dedicated to deified emperors. When Christianity took root, they fell into disuse, as they were too small to house congregations, being built for ceremonies carried out by leading citizens and a priesthood. Great basilicas took their place, and remains of these can be seen in all of Libya's Roman sites, one of the finest examples being the Western Basilica at Ptolemaïs.

The influence of the Greek-speaking eastern Mediterranean was marked in another domain, that of statuary, samples of which (often minus head and limbs) can be seen in museums and archaeological sites across Libya. Perhaps we are a little blasé when we look at Roman statuary: but it is easy to forget that the Romans lived in a world without the instant images of today. Statuary, in stone and clay, played important social functions.

**Statuary**

The bust was one of the most widespread forms of statuary. Portraits in stone were a way of spreading one's influence, of building family prestige. It was through statues that emperors could make their authority felt. The great families of the Empire, the old and the *nouveaux riches*, kept the sculpture workshops busy: any leading member of a major family would be immediately portrayed after their death. A death mask would be made, to be carried in procession at the funeral – along with the death masks of other members of the family. Thus ancient lineage could be displayed and a pecking order of important families maintained.

The emperors used busts and other statuary for propaganda purposes. Statues of Augustus and his successors, often larger than life, showed them as athletic men in the prime of life. Growing Greek influence can be observed at work in the fashions here as well. In earlier times, emperors are shown clothed. Later, with the mode for all things Greek, they were portrayed nude, with bodies that suggest gym work-outs on a regular basis. The truth of the matter? Sculptors had a range of models, and practice was to add a lifelike portrait head to one of the standard bodies. In Tripoli Museum, see the statue of Emperor Hadrian's lover Antinous: a well-executed portrait head was added to the body of an earlier Greek statue of Apollo.

Statuary would have been displayed in niches on the honorific arches which were very much a feature of Roman towns, and Africa and Tripolitania are the provinces where the largest number have survived. At Tripoli, (ancient Oea), an Arch to Marcus Aurelius survives on the edge of the old town. Leptis Magna has four triumphal arches. Although both the Egyptians and Greeks were familiar with the arch, they made no wide-scale use of it in building. The Romans, with their well-honed engineering skills, were able to build large arches without using mortar.

**Street furniture:
the honorific
arch**

Urban arches of triumph were originally built to celebrate great military achievements. They were not related to the city walls, but were generally built on the street along which the victor's procession was to pass. Sometimes they are located outside the city. Later, arches would be dedicated by a city to an emperor who had been particularly generous. Basically, the Roman triumphal arch was a spectacular piece of street furniture – functioning rather like the Arc de Triomphe on the Champs Elysées, or the Porte de France in Tunis, an 18th-century arch which is all that remains of the walls on the east side of Muslim Tunis. One of the most spectacular arches is at Leptis Magna, a great four-way construction (early third century AD) decorated with reliefs commemorating the imperial family and military successes.

The Roman villa, built to a courtyard plan with colonnades and tiled roofs, was a cut above Phoenician dwellings in elegance and comfort. Wealthy citizens of Roman Tripolitania and Cyrenaica liked to impress their neighbours, as the mosaics and statuary found in their villas clearly indicate. They would also have had elegant furniture including couches, bronze oil lamps and tripods and *objets d'art*, some of which can be seen in Tripoli Museum. There were wall paintings, too, and some of these have survived – see the museum at Zliten with remains of frescoes from the Villa Dar Buc Ammera. However, it is the mosaics which are the clearest indication that there was plenty of disposable income for elaborate interior decoration in second- and third-century Roman North Africa.

**Villas**

Background

**The art of the mosaic**  In both Libya and Tunisia, the finest survival of ancient times is undoubtedly the mosaic. The earliest examples go back to ancient Greece and in the most primitive form consisted of pebbles which were used to cover floors. The earliest figurative mosaics date from fourth century BC Greece and the first mosaics made from specially cut stone cubes (tesselae) date from the early second century BC. The new, more refined technique – known as *opus tessellatum* – created a smoother, more compact surface and meant that objects could be portrayed in much greater detail. It quickly became popular right across the Greek-speaking lands of the eastern Mediterranean. With this popularity came increasing sophistication: fine lines of coloured stone allowed the artists to reproduce a huge range of tone and colour, to the point that certain ancient writers referred to the technique as *opus vermiculatum*, literally 'worm-style technique' (from the Latin *vermiculum*, 'little worm'), so fine were the lines.

The mosaic became popular in Italy, and fine mosaics dating from the second and first centuries BC have been discovered at Pompei. By the first century AD, the mosaic was a decorative technique to be found right across the Empire, used along with the painted wall-fresco and statuary of Greek inspiration to decorate private homes and public buildings. Local schools of mosaic-work grew up. Italy, for example, was known for its black and white mosaics. The province of Africa, however, was to develop large and elaborate multi-coloured mosaics.

The oldest figurative mosaics in Libya date from the beginning of the second century AD. The early figurative mosaics were composed by artists who were brought over from the Hellenistic regions of the eastern Mediterranean. These mosaics have a number of Hellenistic traits: they rival wall paintings in their subtle tones and detail; the themes – Nile landscapes, rural idylls, and the post-banquet 'unswept floor' motif – were popular in the East. Later, towards the end of the second century AD, strong regional schools of mosaic work emerged. New themes became popular, generally inspired by daily life in Roman Africa: hunting, the sea, the amphitheatre games and life on the farm. Sometimes these mosaics have captions. In the later third century, technique declines, becoming cruder. Mosaics become more abstract, and some, executed for early Christian buildings, have a strong symbolic charge, only obvious to the initiated observer, given that the Christian communities were initially persecuted. In the mid-fourth century, Christian mosaic-work emerges more strongly. From this period dates the **great mosaic from Qasr Libia**. From the post-Vandal revival under the Byzantines, we have the exquisite **peacock mosaic** from Justinian's Basilica, **Sabratha**. After the Arab invasions of the seventh century, mosaic work disappeared from North Africa, although the Fatimid caliph of Mahdia (Tunisia) called in mosaicists to decorate his palace in the 10th century.

## The buildings of Islam

**The mosque**  In 682, the Arab general Uqba ibn Nafi' and his army crossed the Maghreb, bringing with them a new revealed religion, Islam. This religion was to engender new architectural forms, shaped by the requirements of prayer and the Muslim urban life style. The key building of Islam is of course the mosque, easily identified by its minaret. This evolved considerably from its humble beginnings as a sort of low platform from which the call to prayer could be made, becoming an elaborate tower designed to demonstrate the power and piety of ruling dynasties.

Outside prayer times, most historic mosques in Libya can be entered by the non-Muslim visitor. The entrances are not always easy to identify as mosques are surrounded by narrow streets. Look out for minarets. Tripoli minarets are generally slender round towers with a pointy-topped roof. There are also simple square tower minarets – see the **Mosque of Murad Agha** at Tajura and the **Nagga Mosque**,

Background

## Mosque terminology

*imam*. Senior figure in a mosque, leads prayers
*jami'*. Mosque
*minaret*. Tower from which the call to prayer is made
*mihrab*. Door-sized niche in the wall of the mosque, indicating the direction of Mecca

*minbar*. Preacher's chair, often very elaborate
*midha*. Ablutions area
*muezzin*. The man who performs the call to prayer from the minaret.
*madrasa*. Institute of higher education in classical Islam.
*talib*. Student

Tripoli. Many of the original simple white-washed vernacular structures have been demolished and replaced by vast and elaborately decorated modern reinforced concrete structures. At the summit of the minaret is an ornamental feature resembling three metal spheres on a pole, topped by a crescent. This is the *jammour*, and tourist guides have a number of entertaining explanations for this. For example: that the spheres represent the basic ingredients of bread (flour, water and salt). For *jammour* manufacture, see the tiny workshops behind the Ottoman clocktower in Tripoli.

Mosques tend to have large covered prayer halls, comprising a series of narrow transepts, created by lines of arches supporting small domes. Given the lack of wood and concrete, the Muslims of Tripolitania had to solve the problem of roofing large areas of space needed for prayer in an often highly inhospitable climate. Pillars and domes was the best option, making maximum use of available ancient masonry and local building skills. The cool indoor areas thus produced were ideal for prayer. The 'forest of columns' effect is said to facilitate meditation. It also breaks the prayer hall down into more intimate units where students can sit around a venerable imam to listen to lectures on Islam. Ultimately, some mosques were extended with *madrasas* for the teaching of the religious sciences. Sometimes wealthy benefactors would put up madrasas bearing their name (see for example the **Othman Pasha Madrasa**, Tripoli).

In a typical mosque, there will be a main 'aisle' leading towards the *mihrab* (prayer niche) which indicates the direction of Mecca, and for prayer. The main nave in the traditional Libyan mosque does not, however, have the same dimensions as the main nave of a Christian cathedral. Note that Islam does not favour representation of the human form. The oldest mosques make extensive use of masonry, including columns and their elaborately carved capitals, recycled from Roman sites. Later mosques, (18th and 19th century) may have much elaborate marble marquetry, carved plasterwork and ceramic tiling. (See the 19th-century **Gurgi Mosque** in the madina of Tripoli.) There is no religious pictorial art but the same dense decoration can be found in upper class 18th and 19th-century domestic architecture too. A mosque will also have an open courtyard, occasionally provided with a decorative fountain. Modern mosques often adopt hybrid styles. At Al Bayda and Derna, for example, a sort of concrete neo-Mamluk style can be seen, with elaborate Cairo-type onion-dome minarets.

Perhaps the most easily photographed of the old mosques are the Gurgi and Sidi Salem Mosques in Tripoli, set close to the Arch of Marcus Aurelius. However, on the whole, older mosques are difficult to photograph as they are generally surrounded by buildings. In dealing with Tripoli, you quickly have to learn to navigate through the narrow streets to reach the monument or museum you want to visit.

In much 19th-century European writing, the madinas of the Maghreb – and of the Arab world in general – were seen as chaotic places, which although harbouring exotically clothed populations, were also home to disease and ignorance. The

**Background**

**Historic towns**

madina was taken as a metaphor for the backwardness of the *indigène*, the native. In fact, the tangled streets of the average Libyan or Tunisian madina are no more disorganised than many a European medieval town. Today's visitor will at first be struck by the blank external walls which traditionally would have a *pisé* (sundried clay, gravel and lime mix) or whitewash rendering. Disorientation due to narrow alleys and high walls sets in later, perhaps after leaving the main souks.

**Logic of the madina** An old madina such as that of Tripoli does, however, obey a logic, satisfying architectural requirements arising from climatic and religious factors. The climate is hot in summer, but often very cold in winter. In a coastal town, damp sea air is a problem, while in summer the hot winds blow from the desert interior. A city in North Africa, therefore, has to provide protection from this climate, and networks of narrow streets are the ideal solution. Streets could be narrow as there was no wheeled transport, there being plenty of pack animals for carrying goods around. And narrow streets also ensured that precious building land within the city walls was not wasted.

**The traditional city house** For housing the Muslim family, the courtyard house was the ideal solution. This of course is an architectural model which goes back to Mesopotamia, Greece and Rome. For Islamic family life, with its insistence on gender separation in the public domain, the courtyard house provides a high level of family privacy. In densely built up cities, the roof terraces also provided a place for women to perform household tasks – and to share news and gossip. The biggest houses would have several patios, the main one having arcades on two levels. Thus extended families could be accommodated in dwellings with large open areas. In old Tripoli and Ghadamès, a number of courtyard homes can be visited, today restored and altered to function as museums or office and gallery space. (See for example the **Dar Qaramanli** or the former French consulate in Tripoli.) You may well be invited into ordinary homes, however, where fridges and pressure cookers are in use alongside traditional braseros in the main courtyard. Thanks to the 'occupier is owner' policy, however, it seems as though much old building in the madina of Tripoli is condemned to decay. Poor families from Egypt, Chad and sub-Saharan Africa generally have neither the means nor the know-how to deal with the demanding up-keep required by traditional building.

## Vernacular architecture

The courtyard home was the most characteristic building in Tripoli, discreet and anonymous to all but a neighbourhood's inhabitants from the outside, spectacularly decorated in its patrician form on the inside. However, elsewhere in Tripolitania, there are other, more rustic, building traditions which have only recently fallen out of use, however. A **qalaâ** is a citadel, the fortified village in a mountain strongpoint. A **qsar** (pl. **qsour**) is also a fortress, the Arabic giving the modern Spanish Alcazar. In the Jabal Nafusa, the term refers to a courtyard made up of **ghurfat** (sing. ghurfa) vaulted cells built to store grain, oil and fodder. Each tribe would have its ksar, inhabited only by a caretaker and family. As times became more settled, **qsour** were constructed on the plains. (Similar villages can be found over the border in Tunisia in the Jabal Abyad and the Matmata Hills.) In the Jabal Gharyan underground dwellings, similar to those made famous by the Star Wars films, can still be found.

The nomads and semi-nomad families of inland Tripolitania would spend the spring and autumn months living in a tent (**khayma** or **bayt sha'r**, lit. 'house of hair'). In summer, when the tent was too hot, they might live in a roughly constructed hut or **zriba**. Eventually, the hut would turn into something more permanent, a **raguba**, a stone-walled enclosure roofed over with olive branches and alfa grass – preferable to the zriba as the fire risk was less.

## Dar Qaramanli, a patrician city home

*The early 19th-century Dar Qaramanli is a good example of a patrician city residence. The house now houses a museum on traditional Tripoli life. The house entrance was usually via a studded door opening into a small lobby or pair of small rooms, designed to ensure that no-one from the street could either view or easily enter the inner courtyard. All houses such as the Dar Qaramanli had a central courtyard or wast al dar, occasionally with a central fountain. Sometimes there would be colonnaded galleries on the first floor. Around the central courtyard were clustered all the principal rooms, which tended to be long and narrow. Wood was in short supply in old Tripoli, the longest planks being used for ships. Thus only short pine trunks were available for house building. Reception rooms were important in the houses of public figures, and the Dar Qaramanli was no exception with its spacious first floor sitting room. Naturally, there was a large staff with appropriate housing for it,*

*probably in a neighbouring building. In the case of the Dar Qaramanli, the house was considerably remodelled in the 20th century, and the building now houses a permanent museum with a good selection of objects related to life in the old city. Kitchens, stores, water well, storage, stables and accommodation for servants also took up considerable space. In Tripoli, the great houses of the 18th and 19th centuries would often have an upper storey. Roof areas were accessed by stairways and used for laundry, the drying of grain and fruit. Rain-water ran off the roof into cisterns under the house. Open space within the house was often generous. In lower class dwellings this same courtyard format was repeated but on a much smaller scale. Obviously, in smaller homes, the central courtyard came to have multiple functions, whereas in the more patrician residences it was merely a gracious space allowing movement from one suite of rooms to another.*

In the citadel villages, homes may be composed of a **houch** (courtyard) and a **ghar**, a cave-like inner area excavated out of the hillside. The Gharyan region has the most original form of housing in Tripolitania: pit-dwellings – a place where 'the living live below the dead', to quote the local saying.

Well adapted to austere natural environments though they are, the vernacular building styles are under threat. They are often more vulnerable to the weather than modern buildings, and despite excellent qualities in terms of temperature regulation, they need maintenance. Reinforced concrete building is becoming popular, and carries the prestige of being 'modern'. However, in the southern regions of neighbouring Tunisia, mock vernacular architecture is often used for hotel buildings. Vaults and decorative detailing of vaguely Berber inspiration can be found on hotels and restaurants. Thus Libya's growing tourist industry may yet fuel some sort of return to traditional – and more ecological – building typologies.

## Military architecture

Libya does not have anything like the variety of coastal military architecture to be seen in neighbouring Tunisia – with one major exception, the **Citadel of Tripoli**, a fortress complex of early modern European inspiration. In the 16th century, the southern Mediterranean coasts were targets for expansionist Habsburg Spain. Coastal strong-points from Ceuta in present-day Morocco to Tripoli were occupied, along with a whole range of ports and fortifications along the way. Spain was still at the height of its glory as an imperial power, and for a while it seemed that Tripoli would form part of a Hapsburg Mediterranean defence network.

Although not visitable today, apart from the area devoted to the Jamahiriya Museum, the Citadel of Tripoli is an elaborate piece of building, equipped with the

Background

most up-to-date features of the military architecture of the day. There were monumental gateways, cannons, watchtowers and sharp-angled bastions. When the Ottomans finally triumphed in Tripoli, they continued to extend the existing fortifications. In the 18th century, the citadel remained the power centre of a corsair city state, Tripoli of the West.

On a more discreet note, during the second Ottoman period (19th century), the Sublime Porte attempted to establish its authority over the Jabal al Akhdar and the desert interior in a more consistent way. Small forts were part of this strategy, and can still be seen today in Cyrenaican outposts like Gaygab and certain settlements of the Fezzan.

## 20th-century architecture

The heart of Libya's largest city, Tripoli, is very much an early 20th-century achievement, and there is a good variety of interesting styles for serious building buffs to observe. The old city walls were not totally demolished and re-used as development land (as was the case in Tunis), but kept and restyled in places. The new areas had large open spaces planted with regular rows of trees, while a system of avenues in the new neighbourhoods provided a grid for apartment building and villa developments, as well as linking into a system of highways leading in and out of the city. The Italians became interested in preserving the aesthetic face of the city – witness the rebuilding of the walls of Tripoli Castle and the re-styling of the neighbouring square, the former Bread Market. However, this operation was very much a propagandist tool for Il Duce's régime. (The tradition has continued – note the large concrete tubes commemorating the Great Man-Made River Project next to Green Square.)

**Neo-Moorish style**  In Algeria, the French had caused considerable destruction in the old cities, demolishing and pillaging entire neighbourhoods. In Tunisia, they wished to present themselves as protectors of the former Ottoman regency. Part of this policy was to display a respect for traditional building styles and crafts – hence the development of the *style arabisant* or neo-Moorish style for public buildings. The style, which involved extensive use of mock minarets, domes and horse-shoe shaped windows, originated in Algeria, were it was known as the *style Jonnart*, after the prefect who promoted it. In Tunisia, the *style arabisant* appeared in private villas, mainly the work of one Victor Valensi, and official buildings, designed by Raphaël Guy. In Libya, the style developed from 1910 to 1930, and there were some spectacular examples, including the now demolished **Gran'Albergo** in Tripoli.

**Oasis vernacular & rationalism**  In the early 1930s, under the governorship of **Italo Balbo**, a strong team of architects were in charge of seeing that Libya's infant cities got new public buildings. A vernacular building style, that of the whitewashed courtyard houses of the Tripolitanian oases, was one influence, rationalism was another. An aesthetics of smooth stucco walls and simple geometric forms took root, providing the model adopted for hotels, flats and administrative buildings. One of the team's leading architects, **Florestano di Fausto**, got most of his biggest commissions in Tripoli. He had a splendid time. The city acquired landmark monuments and elegant arcades. It seemed all set to become a fashionable winter destination: elegant visitors flew over for the grand prix racing; they could stay at the Hotel Waddan (which had a casino), the Vittoria in the old town or the Mehari, swim at the new lido, then travel down to Ghadamès to experience the Sahara. A **trade fair** was built on Corso Sicilia (modern Shari'a Umar al Mukhtar). The massive gateway was originally topped with a statue of Minerva.

For Mussolini's Italy, the base line was that Italian glory must be rebuilt. But there was the nagging doubt of persistent emigration and depopulation. The fascist state thus developed a rhetoric around the virtues of stolid rural society. To build the new Italian nation, happy country communities had to be created. In Libya, this rhetoric became a temporary reality, still visible in settlements along the great Litoranea highway in the uplands of eastern Libya.

**The minimal house**

In the late 1930s, once Cyrenaica's nomad inhabitants had been beaten and corralled into submission, Italy undertook a short-lived but intense programme of rural colonization. Each settlement focused on a piazza surrounded by carefully designed buildings in the purest rationalist style, comprising church, school, municipality, dispensary and *casa del fascio*. Villages such as **Maddalena** (Awayla al Sharqiya) and **Luigi Razza** (Al Massa) were intended to be the hubs of prosperous agricultural communities. Set at regular intervals on the roadside, the minimal houses of the immigrant farmers are still standing. Travel writer Wilson McArthur observed the arrival and settlement of the Italians, many of them poor peasants from the Veneto, in 1938. Nothing was left to chance: "The larders and pantries were stocked with food for each family for one month; in the outhouses were the implements they required and the seeds they were to sow. The land lay ready for their labour and nothing was lacking for people accustomed all their lives to privation and poverty." Journeying through Cyrenaica, some 10 years and a world war later, McArthur observed the failure of Mussolini's dream: the houses were abandoned or converted for use as stables. The peasant families had upped sticks with the war and headed back to Italy. Today, though the "neat little colonial houses" are still often used for livestock, new minimal farm houses have been built alongside.

In the 1970s, Libya was proving to itself and the world that it was a modern nation. Large numbers of new buildings were commissioned, including off-the-peg hospitals and schools. A few new hotels went up, older building suffered. Among the losses was the rationalist **Albergo del Mehari**, in Tripoli, which was replaced by an ugly tower block. Often ancient mosques were completely rebuilt, the serene austerity of the originals replaced by vast domed constructions in reinforced concrete.

**Late 20th century**

As the embargo took hold in the 1990s, investment in new official building was cut back. Mosques, however, continued to go up, often in uneasy hybrid styles, mixing hints at historic Middle Eastern religious building with petro-dollar brutalism. The simple styling of more workaday buildings which was such a feature of 1930s architecture has disappeared. If the new **Burj al Fatah** in Tripoli is anything to go by, new Libyan architecture will rely on marble and mirror glass for effect, or maybe just sheer bulk (see the **Dhat al Imad towers**). Sirte, should it become capital of a new Pan-African Federation, will doubtless see some major projects. However, in the sprawling suburbs around Tripoli, Benghazi and Sabha, very little building is architect-designed at all. Local builders use their imaginations and concrete form-work, often with surprising results – see the concrete cisterns atop suburban villas. Tripoli is acquiring some major new buildings, too. Happily for the architecture enthusiast, a certain De Chirico feel in the down-town areas survives. In nearby Italy, the fascist associations have been dusted off 1930s building; rationalist architecture is fashionable again. However, it will probably take a long time before Libya's early 20th-century heritage becomes a selling-point for the Great Jamahiriya Tourist Board.

Background

## Urban and rural crafts

Essentially a desert country, with little material wealth, Libya does not have the same reputation for crafts as its North African partner Morocco. The ceramics the visitor will find on road-side stalls in Tripolitania will be from neighbouring Tunisia. In the souks of Tripoli, pleasantly beige and cream carpets can be found, as can items of traditional dress. Basically, the traditional arts divide into two categories, rural and urban. Urban crafts are generally taken to be more refined, while rural crafts, especially textiles, are very popular with visitors.

But rural and urban crafts are in many ways very different. Rural craft items - carpets and woven items such as saddle bags and tent strips, pottery, jewellery - were produced in very different conditions to urban items. Rural craftwork had to be solid, practical, and made to stand up to long years of use in places of harsh climatic extremes. Carpets and pottery were made by women, while men made jewellery and metal utensils in small country settlements. The signs and symbols used to decorate these items are generally geometric, arranged in simple, repetitive combinations to pleasing effect. Lines, dots and dashes, lozenges and squares are combined to cover surfaces made from clay, metal and wool. Sometimes these decorative forms are linked to the tribal marks tatooed on women's faces and arms. The isolation of rural communities meant that the peoples of different areas could develop very individual styles of craftwork. This is apparent in weaving, clothing and women's jewellery. But given the fact that craft-made items were subject to tough conditions of use, few pieces can be safely said to be more than a hundred years old.

Striking colour and form are often features of rural crafts. The **bakhnoug** and the **ta'jira** were the traditional veils woven by Berber women. Dyed deep bordeaux or indigo, these pieces of textile may be decorated with dense white geometric forms or naïve silk embroidery. Flat weave carpets from the Misrata region often display strong colourful forms. The jewellery of rural communities was made by Jewish craftsmen. It is always silver; necklaces include silver tubes and spheres, mixed in with rings and sometimes amber. Pottery once varied greatly from region to region, each area having very individual forms. With the spread of hard-wearing enamelled ustensils, most of the local forms had disappeared by the late 1960s.

In contrast, urban craft items were generally produced by men, often working in structured corporations. While the women folk of nomad tribes produced for their own use, men in towns were working to sell their produce. They did not, however, build up sufficient capital to develop production on a large scale. City craftsmen produced carpets, jewellery, pottery, leather items, and metal utensils. They worked the raw materials for their production. Urban jewellery (see the souks of Tripoli) is in gold, often set with precious stones, and very finely worked. The leather workers produced footwear (*belgha*) and high quality bindings for the sacred texts. Traditional copper work included cooking pots and trays (see the souk behind the Ottoman clock tower in Tripoli). Wooden items were often very elaborate in their decoration – witness the painted marriage chests.

Within living memory, Tripoli and Saharan settlements like Ghadamès had very locally specific forms of craft production. Apart from the tailoring of traditional garments, almost all have disappeared today. The enforced closure of the souks of Tripoli from 1982 to 1987 was not exactly conducive to the survival of craft skills. It might just be possible to find the odd old item in one of the dusty junk-cum-antique shops on Shari'a Awwal Sebtambar or Shari'a M'qaryef in Tripoli. Unfortunately, there is little new craft production of any great quality – and little indication of any craft revival. (Old rural jewellery tends to get melted down to make new pieces.) However, it is a sign of the times that you may come across tailors from Chad and Senegal in the big towns who will run you up some very colourful African gear. Also look out for Tuareg jewellery, much of it made in Niger and Mali. Although available across North Africa, the simple metal forms worked with geometric designs make good (and easy to carry) presents.

Background

# Land and environment

## Geography

Libya, or the **Great Socialist People's Libyan Arab Jamahiriya**, to give the country its full title, has an area of 1,759,540 sq km, three times the area of France. The country's geography is dominated by a Mediterranean seaboard and a vast desert interior. From Zuwarah in the west to Al Bardiya in the east, Libya's Mediterranean frontage is 1,750 km long and most people live and work along this northern coast which quickly fades into semi-desert once you get inland. The southern part of the country is deep Sahara. The desert regions are lightly populated and crossed by major routes often over 1,000 km in length. North to south transport roads and tracks pass from oasis to oasis, ultimately linking with Chad, Sudan and Niger in Central Africa. For all its extent, therefore, Libya is a country where the ambitious traveller can see much of what exists simply by following the few key lines of communication.

**Borders** Libya is bounded to the west by **Tunisia** and **Algeria**, to the southwest by **Niger**, to the southeast by **Chad** and **Sudan**, and to the east by **Egypt**. These modern boundaries, running for hundreds of kilometres straight across the desert and making Libya a vast polygon, reflect the desires of European imperialism in the early 20th century. It was Italy that set up Libya as a territorial entity, after a series of colonial trade-offs with France and Great Britain. The western and southern boundaries are the result of work by the Franco-Libyan boundary commission in the mid-1950s. Libya's eastern frontier with Egypt is for the most part agreed.

In the extreme south, however, the border is not fully agreed and travellers are advised to seek authorization and a Libyan guide before venturing into the Tibesti. In fact, the entire south-central border was subject to a bitter dispute with Chad. The disagreement on the so-called **Aouzou Strip** goes back to the 1930s. The 1935 border agreed between France and Italy was more southerly than that set in 1956 by Libya and the French colonial authorities. (The story goes that a corrupt Libyan premier in the mid-1950s traded the strip for significant financial considerations, Libya at the time being one of the world's poorest states.) Fighting in the 1980s embroiled Libya in the complexities of Chadian internal politics. Through France, Reagan's USA supported one faction, while Russian logistic support enabled Libya to wage a war deep in the desert. Happily, an unpleasant war of attrition ended when the frontier was settled via the International Court of Justice in 1990.

**Natural zones** **The coast** In terms of natural zones, the area today occupied by the modern state of Libya has densely settled coastal areas contrasting with vast empty inland areas dominated by large-scale natural land forms. Along the coast, running west to east, are the Jefara Plain, the arid flatlands along the Gulf of Syrte, and the Benghazi Plain. East of Benghazi lie the limestone highlands known as the **Jabal Akhdar**, the Green Mountain. East of Derna, the land drops away again and more kilometres of stony, arid land have to be traversed before the Egyptian border is reached.

**Inland** South of the Jabal Nafusa plateau, western Libya is dominated by the **Hamada al Hamra**, a vast stony plain with no settlements and few lines of communication. To the east of the Hamada lies the **Jabal al Sawda**, 'the Black Mountains', a desolate and topographically broken area. Further south are great sand seas traversed wadis, the plateaux of the **Messak Settafet** and the **Messak Mellet**, and the **Jabal Akakus**, an extension of the Tassili-n-Ajjer over the border in neighbouring Algeria. In human terms, eastern Libya is the emptiest part of the country, dominated by the **Calanscio Sand Sea**. In the far south, an extension of the **Tibesti Massif** reaches over 3,000 metres in places.

Background

**Political regions**  The Italians divided their North African colony of *Libia* into three provinces, namely **Tripolitania**, **Cyrenaica** and the **Fezzan**. (Until 1963, Libya was a 'united kingdom' comprising these three provinces and Libyans still identify with these historic divisions.) Recent political changes brought four new administrative districts centring on Tripoli, Benghazi, Sabha (for the southwest) and Al Khalij (lit: 'gulf'), named for the Gulf of Syrte and covering the vast empty territories of the Libyan southeast.

**Tripolitania**  Tripolitania, Libya's westernmost historic province, has much in common with southeastern Tunisia. From the frontier at Ben Gardane to Misrata, the coast is a series of dune belts, coastal oases and salt lagoons or *sabkhat*. Inland lies the **Jefara Plain**, running from just south of Djerba in Tunisia to Tripoli. East of Tripoli, the plain narrows where a highland area meets the sea. This is the eastern end of the **Jabal Nafusa** escarpment, a highland area which curves round in a great crescent running up to Matmata in Tunisia.

**The Tripolitanian Jabal**  Running west to east, the mountainous areas of southern Tripolitania can be divided into four main areas: the **Jabal Nafusa** (the highest part), the **Jabal Gharyan**, the **Jabal Tarhuna** and the **Jabal Msellata**, closest to the sea. In places, the Jabal Nafusa rises to a height of 800 m, while the eastern parts of the escarpment reach 500 m in places. Between Nalut and Gharyan, the escarpment is steepest, with access from the plain by a few deep wadis. Travel is possible along both the foot of the escarpment or along the top. On it southern side, the Jabal slopes gradually down into arid Saharan lands: the dune fields of the **Grand Erg Oriental** to the southwest, the foot of the **Hamada al Hamra** plateau to the south, and the dry river basins of the wadis Sofegin, Zem-Zem and Bey al Kabir to the southeast. The Hamada al Hamra, 'the Red Table-Land', rising to 900 m in places, separates Tripolitania from the dune seas and wadis of the Fezzan. The name derives from the reddish-brown hue of the limestone rock.

**Syrtica**  East of Misrata, the desert reaches the sea, and for some 500 km, the road for Benghazi crosses nothing but barren flat wasteland colonized by salt bush and scattered grazing. This is the region which marks the break between the two great regions of the Arab world, the Mashriq or 'lands to the east', and the Maghreb or 'lands to the west', generally referred to as Barbary by earlier travellers and now known as North Africa in English, though the term 'the Maghreb', a borrowing from French, is gaining ground.

In western Syrtica, the wadis Sofegin and Zem-Zem drain down from the Jabal Msellata into the **Sabkha Taourgha**, a vast seasonal salt lake running for over 100 km along the coast south of Misrata. Inland from the Syrtican coast lie the oases of Jufra, Hun and Waddan, located on one of the major routes into the deep Sahara. Some 300 km inland is the **Jabal al Sawda**, 'the Black Mountain', a great basalt highland area situated between the Jufra oases and the Fezzan.

**Cyrenaica**  Cyrenaica's **Jabal Akhdar** constitutes something of an anomaly: an island of green highland areas and plains on the arid coast of eastern North Africa. Geographically, the region of Cyrenaica, (*Barqa* in Arabic), was once as isolated as an island: 650 km of dull Syrtican steppe separate it from Tripolitania, while there are 700 km of desert to go before the Delta of the Nile is reached. Benghazi, the main city, is located on the Mediterranean in the western part of the region. The lowland area round Benghazi is not as extensive as the Tripolitanian Jafara Plain, nor does it have the same number of coastal oases. Northeast of Benghazi, near Tocra, the plain narrows, and for the 150 or so km east to Derna, low cliffs and sand bays front the sea, south of which a narrow strip of land lies under the steep escarpment of the Jabal Akhdar, 'the Green Mountain', so-named for its evergreen woodland and juniper scrub. To the south, the Jabal al Akhdar slopes down into arid steppe lands. East of Benghazi, the first highland area is the **Jabal al Ahmar**, 'the Red Mountain' region, centring on the fertile but treeless red-soil plains round Al Marj. In the wet winters, the land here, between 200 and 500 m above sea level, gets over 350 mm of rain.

East of Al Marj, the land rises again to the Jabal al Akhdar proper, which divides into a wooded table land scattered with farmsteads and Graeco-Roman sites, and an upper level, south of Al Bayda, rising to over 850 m. Annual rainfall here can reach over 500 mm. The most spectacular natural feature of the region is the steep, scenic and generally waterless Wadi al Kuhuf.

Inland south of the Jabal al Akhdar, rainfall diminishes and the woodland fades away to brush dominated by juniper trees and then to **steppe** where there is winter and spring grazing for camels and sheep. Traditionally, this was an area inhabited by semi-nomadic tribes. In eastern Cyrenaica, the green plateau gives way to the arid coastlands of **Marmarica**, where low rolling hills run close to the coast. At Derna, the wadi runs in wet winters; it used to provide irrigation water for extensive oasis gardens adjacent to the port. Marmarica was also once an area where semi-nomads pastured their flocks.

**The southeast** Southeastern Libya, presently included along with Syrtica in the recently created province of Al Khalij, is an arid, empty land with little to offer the visitor. However, under the wastes of southeastern Libya lie a significant part of the country's reserves in oil and fossil water. Historically, the oases of Jaghbub, Kufra and Tazerbu were important for their role in the trans-Saharan trade. The most important land features are the **Calanscio Sand Sea** in the northeastern part of Al Khalij, and the remote **Jabal al Awinat**, far down on the Sudanese frontier. In the far southwest of Al Khalij are the only true mountains in Libya, part of the **Tibesti Massif** (3,000 m), which run over into Libya from Chad to the south.

**The Fezzan** Southwestern Libya is a land of massive landforms, where geological time takes precedence over fragile human history. Though dune deserts really only cover a small part of the Sahara, the visitor to the Fezzan will find some spectacular sand seas, including the **Edeyen Ubari**, south of the stony Hamada al Hamra. With the lifting and faulting of this area, underground fossil water was raised close to the surface, thus enabling the creation of the oases for which the Fezzan is famous. Within living memory, the water was only a few metres underground in the Wadi al Hayat. Oasis cultivation still remains an essential part of people's lives in this remote part of Libya.

Background

# Mirages in the desert

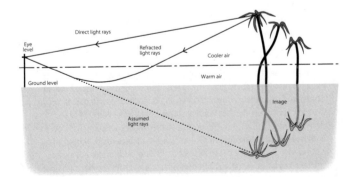

*Auto nomads in Barbary*

In 1949, Wilson MacArthur and his wife Joan set off to cross North Africa in a Wolseley 18/85, going to places "where British cars were seldom seen, where prejudice against them was deep rooted and where her appearance would create a stir". Published in 1950 as **Auto Nomad in Barbary**, MacArthur's account of a most English couple's Odyssey from Tangiers to Alexandria reflects the straitened attitudes of post-Second World War Britain almost as much as it portrays the cities and landscapes of North Africa.

In the late 1940s, Libya as a real political entity was many months of negotiations away. Wilson and Joan were travelling through Tripolitania and Cyrenaica, lands under the benign supervision of the BMA (British Military Administration) and the Cydef (Cyrenaican Defence Force). These are provinces of checkpoints and petrol chits, khaki-clad figures and the wreckage of war. Tripoli is characterized as "the city that waited for death", where food is in short supply. ("Now", said Joan, eyeing the dates and the grubby paws of the small boy with pardonable distaste, "I suppose we'll have to boil them.")

On their epic way, the MacArthurs meet with characters: the civil affairs officer at Homs, formerly in the Anglo-Egyptian Sudan, a German officer at the gate of his prison camp with an "imperious looking peaked cap", trekkers heading for South Africa in a 1928 London County Council ambulance. Contacts with locals were few, apart from the sturdy young Cydef privates and bedouins who offered tea by the roadside. (Joan, worried about the hygiene "poured hers into the sand undetected, because, in Barbary, it does not do to take unnecessary risks"). However, in Libya, a land "abducted by Italy" and then liberated from colonial rule "by the chances of war", people have "natural dignity" and "spontaneous courtesy".

Post-war ideals of being British give Wilson MacArthur's travels in Libya much of their colour. Being British is not like being Italian or French, and it is certainly not like being Tripolitanian or Cyrenaican. However, with appropriate training, the latter peoples could be redeemed. British soldiers, of course, would set the appropriate tone, walking alertly through the streets of Tripoli: "It was cheering to watch them, the conquerors of Libya, setting a model of exemplary behaviour and entirely unconscious of doing so." Forty years on, this world of salutes, Dominions and Nafi canteens, allowances of non-sterling currency and the carnet de passage seems as remote as ancient Rome. However, despite bouts of jingoistic pride, MacArthur listened to the country's political feelings, too. At least the solution of uniting the Libyan provinces under the Emir of Cyrenaica did not affront Islam or involve a European power in a North African dispute, he noted. He had no confidence in "the solution that jumps to the Western mind – a democratic republic", for "the ruler of a Mohammedan country must have absolute authority, based primarily upon his barraka and his sherifian descent." This was not a new reflection, of course. With time, however, it seems to have proved particularly true for certain Arab countries.

While some of the oases, like **Sabha**, today a large town, are isolated, others run in narrow, east-west strips along the valleys. The northernmost is the **Wadi al Shatti**, on the northern edge of the Edeyen Ubari, which runs from Brak to Edri in the west. Further south is the **Wadi al Hayat**, formerly the Wadi al Ajal. Running from Al Abyad to Ubari, this strip of oasis settlement lies between the Edeyen Ubari and the **Hamada Murzuq**. East of Murzuq lies the **Hufra** region, while south towards the Chadian frontier, to the east of the **Edeyen Murzuq** is another scattering of oases, including Gatrun and Tadjarhi. Awinat (Serdeles) and Ghat in the far southwest lie outside these oasis systems.

In the Fezzan, the influence of sub-Saharan Africa becomes palpable. A look at the map shows a different set of topographic terms to those in use to the north: Arabic place names are replaced by Touareg-Berber terms full of 't's, 'l's and 'h's. *Erg* (sand sea) becomes *edeyen*, *jabal* gives way to *adrar*; the Tuareg *taha* is a narrow passage up through a cliff, *aqba* in Arabic. Apart from the regions of massive dunes, the most spectacular landforms are the Jabal (or Tadrart) Akakus and the Messak Settafet.

Running on a north-south axis east of Ghat in far south-western Libya, the **Jabal Akakus** is in fact part of the **Tassili-n-Ajjer** plateau system, the vast majority of which lies over the international frontier in Algeria. (*Tassili* is a Touareg term for plateau). Here geology threw up a great chunk of sandstone which down the millennia, blasted by the wind and heated to furnace-like temperatures by the sun, has been eroded into corridors, canyons and chimneys of stone. The action of sand on stone has darkened the rock, the wadi bottoms are sometimes gravely, more often beach-like. But water is rare, except after occasional deluges when the *gueltas*, tiny seasonal pools fill and there is a brief flourish of vegetation. Prehistoric people once lived here, which is difficult to believe as one gazes out across another sandstone labyrinth. Their traces in the form of rock paintings are easily seen on ledges under the cliff faces.

To its east, the Akakus is separated from the Edeyen Marzuq and the **Messak Mellet** ('White Plateau') by a featureless plain, the **Reg Taita**. In part running parallel to one of the Fezzan's major oasis valleys, the Wadi al Hayat, the **Messak Settafet** or 'Black Plateau' was also home to a human population in prehistoric times. The Messak Settafet takes its name from the dark patina acquired by the region's sandstone down the millennia. Around 40 km wide for most of its length, the plateau runs northeast to southwest. The northern face is a steep escarpment, accessible via the **Bab al Maknusa** (lit: 'gate swept by the winds') pass near Germa and, to the west, by four passes or *tahi*. To the south, the plateau gives way to a vast, lifeless plain, beyond which are the great dunes of the **Edeyen Murzuq**. At its highest point, the Messak Settafet rises to over 950 m. A detailed map shows the whole plateau to be imprinted with a fern-like tracery of dry river canyons. In prehistoric times, artists chose the cliff faces of these canyons to tell the tale of their hunts and cults. In the deep stony valleys, their carved works have survived intact down to the present. The weather has changed hugely since then, however.

In weather terms, Libya is firmly in the semi-arid and arid zones, with a narrow band of coastal territory subject to a Mediterranean climatic régime. In Tripolitania and Cyrenaica, the Mediterranean coast has warm winters with an unreliable rainfall, though on average over 200 mm. Extended periods of poor rainfall are experienced even in this coastal zone. Summers are hot and often humid. Relative humidity in July can reach an uncomfortable 80% or more for days on end, especially in Tripolitania. In the Jabal al Akhdar, the rainfall is considerably more reliable in winter and early spring, while in summer the heights are cooler than the surrounding plains.

**Climate**

Further southwards the climate becomes increasingly Saharan. Low temperatures and occasional random rainfall are experienced in winter with a large daily temperature range from 15-20°C during the day to sub-zero at night. Cold nights also occur in early and late summer. Summers are hot and very dry in the south with highs of over 50°C but one can also feel cold in the night, making a sweater very welcome. Aziziya, inland on the Jefara Plain behind Tripoli, has one of the world's highest recorded temperatures, 55°C.

The *qibli* wind blows hot air from the Sahara across northern Libya and carries a large amount of dust which severely reduces visibility on occasions. Relative humidity drops immediately at the onset of the *qibli* to less than 15% and air temperatures rise rapidly. The wind is most noticeable in western Libya and is often associated with the spring solstice.

**The question of water**

The vast majority of Libya has a hyper-arid climate. There is only one minor flowing river, the Wadi Qi'am, situated in Tripolitania between Khums and Zliten, basically a small stream of no more than 2 km running from a spring source to a lagoon adjacent to the seashore. Traditionally, Libya's sparse population satisfied its water needs from wells in the oases. In the Fezzan, an elaborate system of underground tunnels, the *foggaras*, brought water from the base of nearby escarpments to the palm groves. In classical Cyrenaica, huge cisterns satisfied the needs of large Graeco-Roman cities, and in old Tripoli, many houses had cisterns kept topped up by rainwater running off the terraces. (Tripoli is located on the Wadi Mejenin, now controlled through dams in its upper reaches and partly covered over in the city).

In the desert regions, dry for almost the whole year, the wadis run in spate after heavy rains. Gathering water from vast areas, the dry riverbeds can fill at a dangerous speed after sudden rains, as campers using wadi beds have found to their cost. These violent desert rains can destroy the oasis gardens, pistes and traditional adobe homes. Rainfall comes so suddenly and in such quantities that any benefit is lost in the flooding.

With a constantly expanding population living in a hyper-arid zone, independent Libya has had to plan carefully to satisfy its water needs. During oil exploration expeditions, it was soon realised that parts of Saharan Libya were extremely rich in deep underground water, notably the Kufra oasis. Another major aquifer lies under Sabha in the Fezzan. Since the mid-1970s, policy has focused on developing these resources. Between 1970 and 1978, more than 600,000 sq km of desert land were reclaimed using underground water resources. In the Fezzan, notably in the Wadi Berjuj and Bab al Maknusa, and around Kufra, water is pumped up for vast cereal growing projects in the desert. In 1983, the Great Man Made River Project was launched, to bring fossil water from Kufra north to Cyrenaica and across to Tripolitania. Whether this is a wise use of a vast (but non-sustainable) resource remains to be seen. No effort was spared in ensuring the Man Made River's construction, however. The Korean construction company was paid strictly on time, even at the height of the embargo, and the project was never subject to budgetary restrictions.

## Flora and fauna

Libya's narrow coastal strip, plus the Tripolitanian and Cyrenaican highlands were once covered by dense evergreen forest, some of which survives extensively in the latter region. Though humankind has intervened heavily since classical times, there is quite a variety of plant life – many of the larger species having been imported from elsewhere in the world. The spring flowers which cover the fields, hillsides and ancient ruins of the Cyrenaican plateau are a particular attraction for people from lands where farming relies more heavily on pesticides.

There are few large mammals naturally present in Libya, though Roman mosaics of amphitheatre scenes suggest that the ancient Libyans were familiar with large beasts, possibly brought up from across the Sahara and shipped on to Rome for the needs of the entertainment industry. Dromedaries grazing along the verges of desert highways, oblivious to the speed of passing traffic, are the most dangerous beast you are likely to meet in Libya today.

**Trees of city and roadside**

Tripoli is the first point of contact with Libya for many visitors and much of the urban vegetation will be familiar from other Mediterranean cities. The Italians planted the avenues of their splendid new Libyan capital with shade trees which today do daily battle with growing vehicle pollution. A variety of hardy **ficus** is the basic street tree; it provides shade by being cut into a box shape when it reaches maturity. **Palm** trees are also popular for urban avenues, and both the ordinary date palm and the elegant *Washingtonia*, which grows to great heights, can be seen. In the vicinity of the Gazelle

## Islamic animals

As in other cultures, domestic animals are prized and protected by Muslims. In fact, an Islamic legend runs that on Judgement Day, they will come forward to testify against their masters. As in Europe, the **cat** (which has numerous names in Arabic) is thought to have nine lives. One of the Prophet's closest companions, Abu Hurayra (lit: 'Owner of the Little Cat'), always had a small feline with him purring in the sleeves of his ample robes. The **dog**, apart from the **slougui** or desert hunting dog, is not an appreciated animal in Islam. It is, however, permissable to eat animals caught by slouguis, provided the beast has been let off its leash with a ritual bismillah, 'in the name of Allah.'

The **horse** is most definitely a noble beast in Muslim eyes. Traditions go that the Prophet had seven steeds or five black horses. A fantastical winged horse, **Al Buraq** (Lightning), a sort of Islamic Pegasus, is believed to have carried Mohamed on his journey up to Heaven, stopping off at Jerusalem on the way. The Angel Gabriel himself is said to have brought Al Buraq to the Prophet for him to make this ascent or mi'raj. **Sheep**, and in particular the **ram** (al kibsh) play a key role as sacrificial animals, and all Muslim families will try to sacrifice at least a **lamb** (aloush) during the '**Id al Adha**, the major

religious festival which comes two months after the end of Ramadhan. (The sacrifice commemorates how God sent down a lamb for Abraham to sacrifice instead of his son.) The sacrificial animal is divided into three parts: one for immediate consumption, another for the poor, and a third to be boiled and salted.

In the Qur'an, the **bee**, **horses**, **mules** and **donkeys** all get a mention. They symbolize Allah's concern for humankind, how he sought to create animals useful in people's earthly existence. There is a mythical beast too: **al Jassassa** is a terrible animal which will rise from the earth proclaiming that many are those who failed to believe the signs of the Lord. Still on a legendary note, the **termite** reveals the Prophet Sulayman's death. When the venerable Sulayman passed away, no body realized except the termite gnawing its way through the wood of his sceptre. Finally, a number of animals get a very clear thumbs down in Islam: a saying attributed to the Prophet Mohamed runs that five harmful animals may be killed without fear of retribution, namely the **crow**, the **aggressive dog**, the **mouse**, the **scorpion** and the **sparrow hawk**. Humans must also avoid eating or drinking from receptacles which animals have touched, as these are considered impure.

Park in Tripoli, look out too for the **Norfolk Island pine** (*Araucaria heterophylla*), a relative of the monkey puzzle tree from Chile. With its distinctive frond-like branches, it gives an exotic touch to the once-elegant residential areas between the city centre and Al Dahra. This pine tree's original home, Norfolk Island, is way down in the Pacific, between New Zealand and New Caledonia.

Of the roadside trees, the **eucalyptus** is the most popular, although sadly many have been ripped out due to road widening schemes. Eucalyptus originally comes from Australia, where it grows in open savannah. In Libya, most eucalyptus are roadside trees, though they can also be found in desert plantation schemes in Syrtica and in older stands west of Tripoli. The tree grows fast, and many species have two types of leaves, broader on saplings, slender, green and dangling on the mature tree.

Another foreign plant, now firmly established in North Africa's city gardens is that great and colourful climber, the **bougainvillaea**, smothering walls with its sprays of purple, red, yellow and white 'paper flowers'. Bougainvillaea was introduced to Europe from Brazil in 1829, and in fact it is the papery bracts which surround the tiny white flowers which provide the colour.

Also supplying a note of colour is the **oleander**, (Arabic: *difla*) an attractive shrub which flowers white and pink and can grow to some height in the right conditions.

Background

*Desert beasts in Tamahaq and Arabic*

**Beetle** *khanfus (Ar)*
**Brown crow** *agali (T), ghrab (Ar)*
**Camel** *amis, pl. imnas (T), jamal (Ar)*
**Dog** *éydi (T), kalb (Ar)*
**Dorcas gazelle** *ahenkod (T), ghazal (Ar)*
**Goat** *tighsé (T), ma'za (Ar)*

**Hare** *abekni (T)*
**Mouflon** *waddan (Ar)*
**Scorpion** *tazerdemt (T), aqrab (Ar)*
**Snake** *ashshal (T), hanash (Ar)*
**Viper** *tashshelt (T), lifa' (Ar)*

It is often planted along the approach roads to towns and is highly poisonous to animals. In spring, you may notice low-growing flowering shrubs on the roadside. These may be **acacias**, yet another Australian import to the Mediterranean region. The blue-leaved **wattle** has hanging branches and strong-smelling flowers, while the silver wattle, better known as the mimosa, has long branches of tiny yellow pompom flowers. All the wattles are tough and drought resistant, and some can be found on sandy land close to the sea, like the **tamarisk**, much grown in the southern oasis settlements, too.

In parts of Tripolitania, the **prickly pear cactus** (*Opuntia ficus indica*) is much used along with the **agave** to hedge in olive and almond groves. Both are naturalized imports from the Americas. With its wide flat thorny 'leaves', the prickly pear forms great barriers that dissuade foraging goats and sheep. You may see the new plantations of prickly pear where chunks of the plant have been pushed into the earth to take root. The pear shaped fruit, an attractive yellow-orange colour, is collected by small boys with long canes. Ripe at summer's end, it is known as *sultan el ghilla*, the 'sultan of fruit', and is both delicious and constipating.

**Orchards (sweni)** In the immediate vicinity of Tripoli, on low-lying land close to the sea, are some of Libya's most fertile fruit growing regions. The orchards or *sweni* can easily be picked out: very often they are surrounded by lines of slender, dark **cypress** trees or great pines which protect the trees in blossom time from spring winds and driving rain. **Almond** are the earliest trees to flower. Then come the **citrus trees**, filling the air with fragrance. These were a 19th-century introduction. East of Tripoli, Garabulli in particular is famed for its citrus trees. In fact, oranges and lemons were unknown in the ancient Mediterranean, and were probably brought from China in the early Middle Ages. Today, Libya produces oranges for home consumption, and in orchard areas the fruit is readily available from roadside trees in season.

In older residential areas and long-established *sweni*, rarer, more interesting varieties of tree can be seen. **Mulberries** are occasionally grown: the black mulberry produces sweet, deep mauve fruit, while the white mulberry was originally planted both for fruit and as food for silkworms. The production of silk was a Chinese state secret until the mid-sixth century. Then the Emperor Justinian managed to get two Persian monks to smuggle silkworms out of the Celestial Empire in their hollow bamboo walking sticks. Silk production then took root in the Middle East and Europe.

**Tripolitania** The coastal plains of Tripolitania are an unexciting region in terms of vegetation and are characterized by salt bush. However, in the coastal oases the tier-cultivation typical of palm groves can still be found, with well-planted, irrigated plots of vegetables to be found under the palms. An area of human habitation since ancient times, the Tripolitanian Jabal has lost most of its original plant cover. However, in the 1930s large **olive** and **almond** groves were planted in the eastern parts of the Jabal. Traditionally, there was a mix of pastoral and settled tribes in the area. Tree crops such as figs, apricots, almonds and olives were important to the latter. Despite the reforestation efforts of recent years with large scale olive planting, centuries of neglect and erosion

## Islamic ornithology

*The birds of the air get quite a few mentions in the Qur'an. In soura XXVII, the troops of the prophet Sulayman are formed of djinns, mortals and birds. In the fifth soura of the Qur'an, there is a mention of the bird as a symbol of the immortality of the soul. Broadly speaking, birds are positive in the Muslim tradition. The hoopoe, nightingale, pigeon, stork and turtle dove are all held to have saintly qualities. The* **swallow** *(khutifa) is the Prophet's bird, and flies away to Mecca in the winter.* **Turtle doves** *also have a holy aura; they are the scribes of the bird kingdom and say their prayers regularly. The* **hoopoe** *(houdhoud) is the*

*symbol of mediation and far-sightedness. In the Qur'an, it is the hoopoe which carries letters between Sulayman and Bilkis, Queen of Sheba. The* **peacock** *is another positive bird, as its spread tail displays the colours of paradise, while the* **stork** *is a bird of particularly good omen. Heritage of earlier civilizations, the* **eagle** *(al nisr) was used in Islamic heraldry. In the 20th century, the proud eagle was chosen as emblem for several Arab republics, including Egypt, Syria and Libya. Heritage of an earlier ideological position, the pan-Arab eagle features on older Libyan coinage.*

in the Tripolitanian Jabal will take a long time to reverse. For the moment, much of the region remains bare steppe land with seasonal grazing after rains.

Driving up into the Jabal Akhdar, the first 'terrace' reached is the Al Marj (Barce) Plain. Here are orchards of apricots and almonds protected by stands of cypress and eucalyptus. The highest parts of Cyrenaica are covered with largely evergreen woodland alternating with open ploughed and grazing land. There are occasional stands of cedars, and impressive **Aleppo pines**. The most characteristic tree is the **juniper** bush, once much used for fuel. The bushes can reach quite a height in the more remote gorges. In many areas once covered with Aleppo pine, overgrazing and wood cutting have destroyed the forest. Vegetation becomes a dense, fragrant brush a few metres high, a sort of maquis. **Tree heather**, **lentisk** and **broom**, along with rosemary, sage and thyme are the main plants. In such dry regions, the only plants to survive have special adaptive features: some have extensive root systems; others have hard, shiny leaves or an oily surface to reduce water loss through transpiration. Plants such as the broom have small, sparse leaves, relying on stems and thorns to attract sunlight. The herbs all smell strongly, which seemingly makes them less attractive to animals. Maquis regions, Cyrenaica in particular, produce splendid honey on account of these herbs. Where the maquis is overused by people and animals, the vegetation becomes sparse, and the rocky outcrops more pronounced as the soil is eroded away. This plant cover, bright with annual flowers in spring, is an arid place in summer.

**The highlands of Cyrenaica: forest and maquis**

As the Jabal al Akhdar drops in height to the south, the sparse vegetation gives way to steppe land. **Salt bush** and the **grasses** which come up after the spring rains provide seasonal grazing for sheep and camels. In the steppes too, modern agriculture is at work. Thanks to the irrigation water available from bore holes, flocks can be watered all year round.

**The Cyrenaican steppe**

Until the advent of the pick-up truck and the metalled road, the **dromedary** and the **donkey** were the principal animals of the Fezzan. Both have declined hugely in importance. In some quarters it is still believed that the region was formerly, perhaps even as recently as Roman times, climatically more favoured than at present. In prehistoric times, if the rock paintings and carvings of giraffe, elephants, rhinoceroses and other animals of the savannah in the Jabal Akakus and the Messak Settafet are to believed, this was certainly the case.

**Desert fauna**

Background

*Look out for scorpions*

*The yellow sand scorpion, an inhabitant of erg and reg, and the large black* **Buthotis franzwerneri**, *which likes stony environments, are desert dwellers to be reckoned with. A few simple precautions should reduce the risk of scorpion stings. Preferably, wear boots covering the ankle. Watch out as you turn over rocks to make a temporary hearth: scorpions like to hide under stones. If you camp out, put your karrimat and sleeping bag on a clear bit of sand. If you need to get up during the night, take a torch with you. You don't want to be crouching down over a scorpion. In the morning, shake out your shoes and clothes. Try not to leave ice-boxes and bags open. However, there is no need to be too worried. Scorpion stings are far more frequent among locals than tourists. If you are stung, then put ice, if you have any, on the wound to stop the venom spreading.*

*Happily for the visitor, scorpions are most common in the summer months. Also, not all scorpions have a neuro-toxic sting, and the effects of the sting vary from person to person, according to age and health. The most poisonous scorpion in the Sahara is* **Androctonus australi**, *a yellow beast with a dark tail and pincers. The treatment for its sting is serum, given immediately. (Ideally, if you are stung near a settlement, you should try to capture the scorpion and take it along to the local pharmacy or clinic for identification).*

*Still on creepy-crawlies,* **snakes** *are rarely seen by visitors to the main Saharan sites as they are nocturnal and more interested in small rodents and invertebrates than anything else. They also spend most of the winter hibernating, as the cold desert winter nights do not fit with their hunting patterns.*

Today, however, the wild fauna is on a more modest scale. Given the extreme heat and luminosity of the desert, the fauna tends to be nocturnal. Marks and tracks in the sand, from the large tulip-shaped imprint of the camel to tiny paw marks, tell of animal activity. In the erg and in the dry river beds, the **Dorcas gazelle** and the shy **fennec fox** (a great scorpion eater) might just occasionally be sighted. Other inhabitants of these places include the **gerboa** and the **gerbil**. The **varan**, a large lizard which can grow up to one metre in length, is more likely to be observed stuffed in a souvenir shop. Other reptiles of the sandy places include the pinkish **Barbary skink** and the **sand fish**, also a type of skink. To be found near shrubs, living on tiny invertebrates, it burrows quickly into the sand when disturbed.

In the mountain regions, a rare beast is the **mouflon**, often hunted in prehistoric times, to judge by the Akakus rock paintings. **Porcupine** are also to be found. Raptors, including the **Egyptian vulture** and the **Lanner falcon**, are present in small numbers. During bird migrations, many small migrant birds get blown into the Sahara and even the occasional exotic species strays into the oases. The tiny crater lakes of Waw al Namus provide a stopping point for migrating birds on long trans-Saharan flights. The most easily spotted birds are the sociable **moula-moula** (Arabic *zarzur*), a white-headed variety of wheatear, the **grey shrike** and a pale, desert variety of sparrow. Flapping across the dunes, you may also see the odd crow. A careful look shows that this is the **brown crow**, so-called because of brownish plumage on the head and back of neck. A good range of larks and other wheatears can be found in wadis and stony environments. Common oasis birds include a variety of **turtle dove** and the melodious, though unspectacular **bulbul**.

The desert is also home to **snakes** of course, few of which are really dangerous. Most are more frightened of people than we are of them. **Scorpions**, however, should be carefully avoided.

## Guerrilla in the Jabal al Akhdar

Down in the gorge of the Wadi al Kuhuf, a Bailey Bridge spans the road at one of the narrowest points. And hanging from the bridge is a signboard with the noble profile of Umar al Mukhtar, a reminder that it was in this wild country that the Cyrenaican resistance's leader made his last stand against the Italians in 1931. By that year, a barbed wire fence 270 km long, monitored by armoured patrols and planes, had cut all flows of supplies and ammunition from Egypt. The Italian aim was to hunt down remaining rebel groups, now hiding out in the Jabal. Even in peace time, the bedouin were difficult to locate: on the steppe, they pitched camp on the wadi slopes, in the uplands, they were concealed by the juniper forest. Thus local tribesmen were co-opted to scout for mounted anti-guerrilla units, consisting mainly of Eritrean troops. Air reconnaissance provided the essential information on tribal movement. In the course of 1931, the war turned into a

series of fairly inconclusive skirmishes in the rough terrain of the central Jabal al Akhdar. The resistance continued, however, because charismatic Umar al Mukhtar was still active.

Then on 11 September, Italian aviation spotted guerilla horsemen on the move near Slonta. Their probable aim? Raiding for livestock near Cyrene. One small rebel group, slowed by their horses' poor condition, was captured. Eleven men were killed, the 12th turned out to be Umar al Mukhtar himself. The Italian leaders were quick to act. Wrote General Graziani in a telegram to Governor De Bono: "We shall hold a trial and then unfailingly a sensational execution." Which is what happened on 16 September 1931 at Soluq, near Benghazi, when Al Mukhtar was hung in front of 20,000 deportees. Having lost its strategist, the exhausted resistance collapsed. But overnight, Fascist Italy had turned a 70 year-old guerilla leader into a martyr for Libya and Islam.

**Desert flora**

Although the visitor is unlikely to get a glimpse of a gazelle or a mouflon, there is a sparse but interesting flora to look out for in the desert. Faced with an unforgiving environment, the Touareg inhabitants of the Fezzan had to make use of every resource available, and were well aware of the properties of every tiny ground-hugging plant and grass. Travelling with Touaregs with a little French, you might be able to pick up something of this vanishing plant lore.

The Touareg were constantly on the watch for good grazing for their beasts. *Aristida pungens* (**tullult** in Tamahaq, **drinn** in Arabic) is much appreciated by camels. The secretions of its special root hairs encase the root in sand grains and allow the plant to absorb any moisture present. As well as providing excellent pasture, *tullult* grains are also used to make unleavened bread. Dry *tullult* stalks were used to make rope.

In both the Akakus and the Messak Settafet, the largest trees are **acacias**, namely *Acacia radiana*, (*talh* in Arabic), identifiable by its spiral seed-pods and *Acacia arabica*, referred to as the *gered*. An important large shrub is a species of **tamarisk** (*Tamarix aphylla*), the wood of which was used to make well-heads and pulleys. The root systems of this tamarisk make large bushy humps in the desert landscape, while the tiny sugary droplets released in spring at the tips of the leaves were traditionally used as a sweetener.

Particularly well adapted to sandy wadis is the *akaraba* or **rose of Jericho**. In times of drought, the low-growing akaraba dries up to resemble bunches of twiggy closed claws. After the rains, the transformation is startling. The stems grow out onto the sand and longish leaves appear on the hairy stems, hiding clusters of minuscule white flowers which soon turn to tiny green fruit. However, as soon as water runs short, the plant shrinks into a woody core again.

One of the most easily spotted desert plants is the **colocynth** (*Colocynthis citrullus*, *alkad* in Tamhaq), of which the leaves and tendrils train across sandy wadis. The tiny, five-petal, yellow flower hides among dusty green hairy leaves. The fruit of the colocynth, a round, yellow and green mini melon, once had many uses. The pulp or *hendhal* was used as a cure for syphilis. The seeds (*taberka*), bitter and toxic, were used by the Tebu in times of need to make a sort of gruel.

Another useful plant is the ***tahawat*** (*Heliantheum lipii*), an unprepossessing low-growing shrub with woody stems and minute leaves and yellow flowers. The *tahawat* is much enjoyed by goats, and is a fine indicator of the presence of *terfas* (*Terfazia ovalispora*), white desert **truffles**. These are rare in the central Sahara. Some say that it needs to rain at least three times within the space of a few weeks for the truffles to grow.

When it does actually rain in the desert, much to the locals' joy, a burst of vegetation is the rule. This is the ***akasa***, (*ashab* in Arabic), the sudden carpet of green which follows the rain, providing grazing for the flocks in the wadi beds and along the edge of the dunes. With centuries worth of experience of this temporary grazing, the Touareg have a very exact idea of which areas will provide fodder and in what quantities. Even in the era of the land cruiser, this is important lore.

**Oasis flora**   Historically cultivated wherever water was near enough to the surface to be raised by primitive mechanical means, the **palm tree** is the oasis tree par excellence. In the shade of the palm tree groves grew fruit trees, including the hardy **pomegranate**, particularly tolerant of water with high salt levels. And under the fruit trees, the oasis farmers would cultivate **millet** and vegetables. Another tree much in evidence in the Fezzan oases is the **tamarisk**, which can grow to quite considerable heights. The tamarisk's delicate feathery branches are covered in tiny leaves; the flowers, pink or white, grow in attractive dense bouquets. Unfortunately, oasis cultivation has suffered with the arrival of modern life. There are easier ways of making a living than the back-breaking work of maintaining a palm grove. If you venture down to Kufra or the Wadi Berjuj, you will see the new forms of desert cultivation, great rings of cereal growing green in the desert. Several crops a year are possible, thanks to the abundance of sun and water pumped up from deep underground. A more expansive demonstration of humankind's technological capacities let loose is hard to imagine.

# Footnotes

# 10

316

# Footnotes

# Libyan Arabic: words and phrases

Arabic is the official language of Libya, a fact you are not likely to forget whilst in the country. Signs are almost exclusively in Arabic. The written form differs hugely from the spoken language, however, almost as much as medieval Latin from modern Romance languages.

Outside formal education, Libyan Arabic is the language of everyday life, and attempts to use a few words and phrases, no matter how stumblingly, will be appreciated. Those with some Arabic learned elsewhere often will not find the dialect difficult. Libyan is less clipped in quality than the dialects of northern Tunisia and regions further west. In addition, there is an admixture of Italian and English terms, often heavily 'Libyanised'. (This is particularly true of vehicle vocabulary). The following word lists might help you get started, or leave a café waiter or garage attendant totally bewildered. People working in service jobs are often foreigners in any case, and will tend to come back to you in English or French.

For the English speaker, some of the sounds of Libyan Arabic are totally alien. There is a strong glottal stop (as in the word 'bottle' when pronounced in Cockney English), generally represented by an apostrophe, and a rasping sound written here as 'kh', rather like the 'ch' of the Scots 'loch' or the Greek 'drachma'. And there is a sharp 'k' sound, (as in the word 'souk'), generally represented as 'q' or 'k', which luckily often gets pronounced as the English hard 'g', and a very strongly aspirated 'h' in addition to the weak 'h'. The French 'r' sound is generally transcribed as 'gh'. The English 'th' sound as in 'three' is represented here as 'th', while 'dh' represents 'th' as in the word 'this'.

On a grammatical note, Arabic, like English, only has one definite article ('el'), used for singular and plural, masculine and feminine nouns. There is no indefinite article. Nouns are feminine or masculine, and adjectives have to agree. Feminine singular nouns more often than not add an 'a', i.e. *sadeeq*, friend (male), *sadeeqa*, female friend. Plurals tend to be complicated, i.e. *asdiqa*, friends. You can do without the verb 'to be' more often than not, i.e. *al funduq qareeb*, 'the hotel is near'. The word *fee* will do for 'there is', i.e. *fee moyya skhouna?*, 'Is there any hot water?'

## Basic words and phrases

| | |
|---|---|
| hello | *salam* |
| good morning | *sabah el kheer* |
| good afternoon / evening / night | *tusbih 'ala kheer* |
| goodbye | *ma' assalema* |
| See you later. | *ciao, enshoufuk min ba'd* |
| how's things? | *shnee y el ahwel?* |
| everything's fine | *el hamdou lillah* (lit. Praise be to God) |
| everything's fine | *kull shay la bas* |
| Pleased to meet you. | *netsherrefou* |
| How are you? | *shniy el ahwal* |
| Fine thank you. | *la bes* |
| yes | *na'm, aywa* |
| no | *la* |
| please | *min fadhlek* |
| thankyou | *barakallaw feek / shukran* |
| excuse me | *semahnee* |
| customs | *ed deewana* |
| police / policeman | *el bouleesiya, esh shurta* |
| hotel | *el funduq* |
| telephone operator | *el shintral* |
| youth hostel | *dar esh shebab* |

| | |
|---|---|
| restaurant / fast food | *el mata'm* |
| post office | *el bousta, el bareed* |
| stamps | *twabi'; bull, ablel* |
| market | *essouq* |
| toilet / bathroom | *li mirhadh, li banyou* |
| bank | *el banka, el masraf* |
| notes / coins | *awrak / sarf* |
| Do you have change? | *'indek sarf?* |
| I do not understand. | *ma fehemtiksh* |
| Speak slowly please. | *tekellem bishweyya* |
| Do you speak some English? | *t'arif shewyya bil-inglizeeya?* |
| What is your name? | *shi-smek?* |
| How do you say XX in Arabic? | *keefaysh taqoul XX bil-'arbee?* |
| What is this called in Arabic? | *shi-sm hadha bil-'arbi?* |
| Where are the toilets? | *feen li toilette, el hammam?* |
| Excuse me, please. | *semahnee* |
| One minute, please. | *daqeeqa, min fadhlek* |
| (calling the waiter) | *ya ma'lem, min fadhlek* |

**Handy adjectives and adverbs**

(female form ends in a short 'a')

| | |
|---|---|
| good | *bahi / bahiya; kwayis/a, mleeh/a* |
| happy | *farhan / farhana; sa'eed/a* |
| beautiful | *jameel/a* |
| new | *jdeed/a* |
| old | *qadeem/a* |
| clean | *ndheef/a* |
| full (hotel) | *mu'abee / mu'abeeya, kumbletu* |
| excellent | *breema, mumtez/a* |
| excellent, well done (adv) | *brawa* |
| big | *kbeer/a* |
| small | *sgheer/a* |
| tall | *tweel/a* |
| fat | *smeen/a* |
| difficult | *sa'eeb/a* |
| easy | *sahil/a* |
| blonde, of fair skin | *byondu* |
| short-tempered | *narfuz, asebee* |
| dishonest | *falsu* |
| afraid | *khayif/a* |
| silly | *feessu* |
| light-hearted | *khfeef eddem* |
| in a hurry | *mazroub/a* |
| quickly | *bi-sura'* |
| it doesn't matter | *mish muhim* |

**Quantities**

| | |
|---|---|
| a lot | *helba* |
| a little | *shwaya* |
| half | *nesf / shtar* |

## Miscellaneous expressions

| | |
|---|---|
| Watch out! | *rud balak!* |
| How much? | *bi-kam? qaddaysh?* |
| What? | *shineeh?* |
| Look! | *shabih, shouf* |
| Please go ahead (polite) | *tafadhel* |
| Can I help you in any way? | *ayyi khidma?* |
| Please take a seat. | *stareyih; ijlis* |
| Good luck! | *fursa sa'eeda* |
| like this | *hikki* |
| always | *deema* |
| free (of charge) | *bilesh* |
| nothing | *neenti* |
| I don't know | *ma n'arifsh* |
| Keep calm! | *kalma!* |
| Go away! | *barra!* |

## At the café - handy vocabulary

| | |
|---|---|
| a glass of tea | *ka's shay* |
| teabag tea | *shay kees* |
| milky coffee | *cappucino* |
| half espresso, half milk | *nes nes* |
| bottle | *sheesha; feeyashka; gizeza* |
| a small bottle | *sheesha sagheera* |
| a large bottle | *sheesha kabeera* |
| still mineral water | *(main brand Kufra)* |
| fizzy mineral water | *(main brand Bin Ghashir)* |
| glass | *tassa* |
| Do you have change? | *'indek sarf?* |

## At the restaurant - handy vocabulary

| | |
|---|---|
| bill | *li hseb; fattoura* |
| fork | *fourguita* |
| knife | *sikeena* |
| spoon | *mu'allaqa* |
| glass | *ka's, tassa* |
| bowl | *sahfa* |

## Food and drink

| | |
|---|---|
| Please could I have … | *min fadhlek , 'ateenee* |
| beef | *lham bagree* |
| minced beef | *lham mafroum* |
| butter | *zebda* |
| bread | *khubz* |
| chicken | *djej* |
| chips | *btata* maklya |
| eggs | *baydh* (sing. baydha) |
| fish | *hout; beeshee; samak* |
| fruit | *ghilla, fwakih* |
| lamb | *alloush* |
| milk | *hleeb* |
| olive oil | *zit zitouna* |
| rice | *rouz* |
| a bottle of water | *sheesha moyya* |

## Meals

| | |
|---|---|
| breakfast | *futour es sebah* |
| lunch | *futour* |
| dinner | *'asha* |
| meal | *wajba* |
| without meat | *blesh lham* |
| drink | *mashroubet (pl)* |
| with milk | *bil hleeb* |
| without sugar | *blesh sukar* |

## At the hotel - vocabulary and a few requests and complaints

| | |
|---|---|
| Can I see the room, please? | *mumkin nshouf el hujra; medha biyya nshouf el hujra* |
| single room | *hujra fardiya* |
| double room | *hujra zawjiya* |
| suite | *jinah* |
| bathroom / shower | *banyou / douche* |
| lift | *asanseer* |
| lamp, light-bulb | *lamba* |
| switch | *takkou* |
| plug socket | *breeza* |
| with A/C | *ma' et takyeef / mkeyyef (adj)* |
| with two beds | *ma' zouz afresh* |
| with private bathroom | *ma' banyou / hammam* |
| hot / cold water | *ma sekhouna / berda* |
| to make up / clean the room | *ykhemel el hujra* |
| sheet / pillow | *el ansula, shirshef / el mukhada* |
| blanket | *el gh'ta* |
| clean / dirty towels | *fouta (pl. fut) ndheef / mwessekh* |
| bill | *fetoura* |

## Some shopping

| | |
|---|---|
| shopping | *sbeeza* |
| battery | *beela* |
| fruit juice | *aseer* |
| soap | *saboun* |
| toothpaste | *dintifreeshi* |

## More useful adjectives

NB Libyan adjectives have masculine and feminine forms, which correspond to noun genders.

| | |
|---|---|
| cheap | *rakhees / rakheesa* |
| expensive | *ghalee / ghaleeya* |
| ready | *hadhir / hadhira* |
| near | *greeb / greeba* |
| far | *ba'eed / ba'eeda* |
| hot | *sekhoun (liquid); ettaqs sekhoun (weather)* |
| cold | *berid / berida* |
| wet | *mabloul / mabloula* |
| dry | *yebis / yebisa* |
| That's great | *mumtaz / mumtaza* |

**Travelling around**

| | |
|---|---|
| on the left / right | *'al yasser / al yameen* |
| straight on | *toul, neeshan, dughree* |
| first / second stree t on the right | *awal / theni nahaj 'al yameen* |
| a long way | *mishwar ba'eed* |
| to walk | *yimshee* |
| street / avenue or highway | *shari'a / tareeq* |
| narrow street, alley | *zanga* |
| bus station | *el mahatta* |
| mini-bus/ inter city coach | *el meecro-bus / el hafila* |
| city bus stop | *el mahatta* |
| micro-bus station | *ajinseeya* |
| ticket office | *shubak al hijz* |
| airport | *el matar* |
| airplane | *et tayyara* |
| first / second class | *dereja oula / teniya* |
| ticket (return) | *et taskira (meshee ew ja'ee )* |
| boat | *es safeena, al babour* |
| hire car | *sayyara mekreeya* |
| petrol | *benzeena* |
| road | *tareeq* |
| bridge | *kubree* |
| block of flats | *balas* |
| traffic lights | *simafrou, simaf* |
| slope | *saleeta* |
| rough track | *beesta* |
| metal entrance gate | *kanseelu* |
| entrance | *intrata; madkhal* |
| the ruins | *el athar* |
| the museum | *el mathaf* |
| ticket | *tiskra, buleet* |
| sea | *el bhar* |
| wind | *reeh* |
| beach | *leedou, shatti* |
| fun | *goustou* |

**Vehicles and at the garage**

| | |
|---|---|
| There's a problem... | *fee mushkila / difeetu...* |
| mechanic | *meekaniku* |
| tow truck | *rimourk* |
| cable | *kaaw* |
| tyre | *gouma, mattat* |
| inner-tube | *kamradarya* |
| car jack | *kreek* |
| can (water or petrol) | *bidoun* |
| dry battery | *beela* |
| battery charger | *karikou* |
| pliers | *beensa* |
| Phillip's screwdriver | *kashafeeti* |
| license plate | *targa* |
| unuseable | *mfaryiz* |
| broken | *mkasser* |
| engine overhaul | *ribasseta* |

## Various vehicle parts

| | |
|---|---|
| chassis | *karkassa; haykal* |
| brake | *freenou* |
| accelerator | *shiratouree* |
| camshaft | *albroukem* |
| transmission | *kambyou* |
| shock-absorber | *mazatouree* |
| filter | *filtru* |
| clutch | *frisyouni* |
| gears | *igrineji* |
| gear | *marsha* |
| windscreen | *barabreez* |
| bumper | *barafangou* |
| headlight | *fanar* |
| gasket | *garnasyouni* |
| bolt | *ballouni* |

## Health

| | |
|---|---|
| chemist / all night chemist | *es saydaliya* |
| doctor | *et tabib* |
| hospital | *sbitar; mustashfa* |
| prescription | *resheeta* |
| Where does it hurt? | *feen youja' feek?* |
| stomach | *el ma'da* |
| fever / sweat | *es skhana / el 'araq* |
| diarrohea | *el kirsh yejree* |
| blood | *ed damm* |
| I have a headache | *ra'see youja'a* |
| condoms | *Rifel (brand)* |
| contact lenses | *el 'adasat* |

## Numbers

| | |
|---|---|
| one | *wahid* |
| two | *tnayn* |
| three | *telata* |
| four | *arb'a* |
| five | *khamsa* |
| six | *sitta* |
| seven | *saba'a* |
| eight | *themaniya* |
| nine | *tissa'* |
| ten | *ashra* |
| eleven | *ihdash* |
| twelve | *tnash* |
| thirteen | *tulut'ash* |
| fourteen | *'rb'atash* |
| fifteen | *kh'msatash* |
| sixteen | *settash* |
| seventeen | *sb'atash* |
| eighteen | *tumuntash* |
| nineteen | *ts'atash* |
| twenty | *'ashrine* |
| thirty | *tlateen* |
| forty | *'arba'een* |

| | |
|---|---|
| fifty | *khamseen* |
| sixty | *sitteen* |
| seventy | *saba'een* |
| eighty | *thamaneen* |
| ninety | *tiss'een* |
| one hundred | *meeya* |
| two hundred | *miyaten* |
| three hundred | *tult miya* |
| thousand | *alf* |
| two thousand | *alfayn* |
| three thousand | *thelath alaf* |
| one hundred thousand | *miyat alf* |

### Days of the week

| | |
|---|---|
| Monday | *nhar el ithnayn* |
| Tuesday | *nhar eth thelatha* |
| Wednesday | *nhar el arbi'a* |
| Thursday | *nhar el khamees* |
| Friday | *nhar el juma'* |
| Saturday | *nhar es sebt* |
| Sunday | *nhar el ahad* |

### Expressions of time

| | |
|---|---|
| today | *el yawm* |
| yesterday | *embareh* |
| tomorrow | *ghudwa, bukra (Egyptian)* |
| tomorrow morning | *ghudwa fi subh* |
| day | *nhar* |
| morning | *essebah* |
| in the morning | *fi es-subh* |
| midday | *el ouwel* |
| evening | *el 'asha* |
| night / tonight | *el layl / el layla* |
| hour | *sa'a* |
| in half an hour | *ba'd nus sa'a* |
| later | *emba'd* |

# Spellings of place names

Libya has two systems for spelling place names in Latin letters, the longer established Italian system and the English system, which tends to use a 'j' where the older system uses a 'gi', and a 'w' instead of 'ue'. The English system represents the Arabic letter *qaf* with a 'q', while the Italian system is closer to the Libyan pronunciation in this respect, using a hard 'g'. The Arabic *kha* (like the rasping sound at the end of the Scottish 'loch' is spelt 'h' in the Italian system. The present book uses the English system, with some exceptions. As both systems can be found in books, the following list is provided to help avoid confusion.

| Older Italian spelling | English spelling |
|---|---|
| Agedabia | Ajdabiya |
| Augila | Awjila |
| Bengasi | Benghazi |
| Cufra | Kufra |
| Derna | Darna, Derna |
| Giado | Jadu |
| Giarabub | Jaghbub |
| Gialo | Jalu |
| Gianzur | Janzur |
| Gubba | Qubba |
| Hums | Khums |
| Jefren | Yefren |
| Al Merg (Barce) | Al Marj |
| Murzuch | Murzuq |
| Sciahhat (Cirene) | Shahat (Cyrene) |
| Sinauen | Sinawen |
| Tobruch | Tobruk |
| Zauia el Beda (Beda Littoria) | (Zawiya) Al Bayda |
| Zuara | Zuwara |
| Zuetina | Zuwaytina |

# Index

# Map index

Desert adventure

330

*Right*: the all green
Jamahiriya banner
flies proud over a
tourist camp at
Mandara in the
Edeyen Ubari.
*Below*: in the Jabal
Akakus. A labyrinth
of canyons
stretching away to
the horizon.

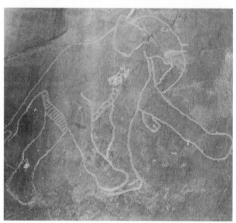

*Above and right*: Traces of a time before the
desert. Rock carvings in the Messak Settafet
and occasional acacias growing in the sandy
wadi bed.

The minimum desert adventure will take you southwest from Tripoli to the oasis town of Ghadamès, close to the meeting of the borders of Algeria, Tunisia and Libya. Perfectly possible by public transport, the journey can take you up onto the Jabal Nafusa, via Gharyan, or, more usually, via the citadel town of Nalut, described in the 1930s tourist literature as 'the Lhasa of Libya'. Ghadamès was the northernmost point of the Touareg domains, a trading town where merchant caravans arriving from across the Sahara knew that their northward trek was nearly over. The old town, now largely abandoned by its inhabitants, retains an ancient mystery. Having covered streets, tiny shaded squares and ecologically correct architecture has paid off for the locals: there is a winter festival and plenty of tourists to visit the old houses and their kitscho-rustic interiors. The oasis is still cultivated in the ancient way, though for irrigation purposes the chuntering motor pump has replaced the mule-powered delu well.

**Ghadamès, caravan town of legend**

The great sights of the Libyan desert are much further south, however, down in the desert province of Fezzan. Drawn here by arcane legends ('the emeralds of the Garamantes'), funded by scheming colonial ministers, 19th century explorers endured this desert in a way almost unthinkable today. Today, a mere ten-hour bus journey or a flight from Tripoli gets you to Sabha, legionnaire outpost turned sprawling town and capital of the Fezzan. (Distant Ghat should be possible when Libyan Arab Airlines expands its fleet). The region feels more sub-Saharan African than Middle Eastern. (The joke runs that African immigrants ask 'Are we in Libya now?', as they arrive in Ghat. 'Not yet, you've another three hundred kilometres to go', comes the cynical reply.) In these regions, where kilometres of vast horizon lie between settlements, you are acutely aware of unfamiliar landforms, of geological time. Some choose to travel south in regions without roads, taking time out to feel the empty horizons that lie between Ghadamès and Ubari. But beware. Without good navigation, this is landscape which will easily overcome the best prepared 4WD armada. The desert shows no mercy.

**Travelling into the Deep South**

Perhaps more than any other sight in Libya, the landscapes and the prehistoric rock art of the Jabal Akakus will amaze you. In golden sand wadis and hills blasted black by the desert winds, a landscape fit for science fiction, prehistoric people found a home. In the isolation of an Akakus valley, looking up at crenellated ridges and craggy bastions, the mind drifts. Is there some other presence, unseen and observant, up on the cliff? When the four-wheel drive engine is switched off, there is utter silence (apart from the odd tweet of the moula moula bird). Today, the Akakus is practically uninhabited, though within living memory there were nomad Touareg travelling the labyrinthine rivers of sand and stone. The art of existing without vehicle backup in this austere, eroded region has all but gone.

**Lunar landscapes**

In fact, current thinking runs that this uncompromising place was once a fertile savannah. Where today there are expanses of sand, camel grass and occasional scrub, there once was forest and good grazing. This was a land of game, where elephant and giraffe, rhinoceros and antelope grazed. On narrow ledges under cliff faces, our ancestors exercised their artistic talents. In red and ochre, black and white, they depicted the excitement of the hunt and ritual dances. Sometimes they carved the rocks with images of the beasts that provided their livelihood. Climbing up onto the cliff-tops, you may come across the flints of a long-gone workshop, fragments of old, old hand-shaped pottery. More recent are the traces of camel trails, smooth narrow tracks carefully cleared of sharp stones by the caravaneers. And you may come across a Touareg mosque, just a grave rectangle marked out with stones, a place of ritual purity and prayer.

**Galleries of the earliest artists**

**The Akakus, a national park** Visiting the rock art sites of the Wadi Teshuinat in the Akakus, the roar of a four-wheel drive heading up the wadi is a familiar sound. Visitors now come in their hundreds, and careful management will be necessary – the prehistoric paintings are a fragile heritage. Preserved by an astoundingly arid environment, vehicle pollution and the humidity of human breath are the last thing they need. Libya will have to take measures to protect its prehistoric past. After all, the Akakus, classified as national park and Unesco World Heritage site, contains extraordinary survivals of humanity's shared history.

**Carvings of the Messak Settafet** East of the Akakus, on the southern side of the Messak Settafet (the 'Black Plateau'), is another strange and lunar region, the Wadi Matkhandush, also a veritable gallery of prehistoric carvings. To get there from Germa, you drive across kilometres of dreary gravel plain. Away to the south, just visible, are the great dunes of the Edeyen Murzuq. Then a turn north, and you are bumping through a boulder field. Below is a dry river bed, backed by black cliffs, here and there a solitary tree and a clump of tall grass. Crossing the sandy wadi, you scan the rock face. The cliffs turn out to be a carnival of animals: there are slender giraffes, bizarre felines, parading ostriches, even crocodiles. The naturalism of the forms is striking. The artist grasped every detail of the charging elephant: the raised tail, the flailing trunk, the tiny, angry eye. Most compelling of all are the strange, dog-headed hunters. Superhuman in strength, they carry rhinoceroses on their shoulders. Are they deities of the hunt? Why make these carvings? Perhaps this was a secret site of initiation. Whatever, hidden in the vast stone wilderness of the Messak Settafet, this art was known solely to itinerant Touareg until last century. And it was only recently that its importance was realised. In the 1990s, a handful of intrepid enthusiasts discovered hundreds of carvings. More difficult of access than the Akakus, this region of toppled boulders and narrow rock defiles may harbour even more as yet unknown prehistoric friezes.

**The lost lakes** In the 1990s, the Fezzan opened up to tourism. Italian motor clubs organized Saharan 'safaris', the Germans came with desert lorries accompanied by motorcycle outriders. The biggest attraction? The great sand seas, the *ramla*, where off-road vehicles can race, dip and plunge across endless dunes, some as much as 300 metres high. Not far from Germa, lost in the Ubari Sand Sea, are the amazing Dawada Lakes. No one, not even the geography boffin in search of the oddest land-form, could have dreamed up this extraordinary sight. Kilometres out in the desert, fringed by neat reed beds and palms, the park-sized lakes are all suburban calm – if you exclude the odd cloud of mosquitoes. Under an immense sky their waters glow yellow with the reflection of huge dunes – ready to fill them in with a sand-sliding motion. Until recently, the oases close to these lakes were inhabited by an obscure people, the Dawada, 'the worm-eaters', so called as the swarming tiny crustaceans of the lake waters were their staple diet. Though the Dawada were moved on in the 1980s, in winter the lakes are more peopled than ever. That newest of nomad tribes, the Saharan tourist group, has arrived.

**Spell of the desert** Ideally, one should travel through the Akakus with camels, slowing to the pace of the beasts. (The Messak Settafet and the Dawada Lakes are really only reachable by vehicle, however). But with or without an off-road vehicle, the desert begins to work its spell. Travelling through the sunburned landscapes of the Akakus, seeing sunset on the dunes are truly unforgettable experiences. The gorges of the Messak, a russet and grey prehistoric canvas, are fearsome in their isolation – but ultimately rewarding, a place to feel a long-lost spirituality. With luck, at nightfall, backtracking to the Edeyen Murzuq to camp, you may even hear the singing of the sand sea. And when the desert night takes hold, the starscapes, far from any baleful urban glow, are sublime.

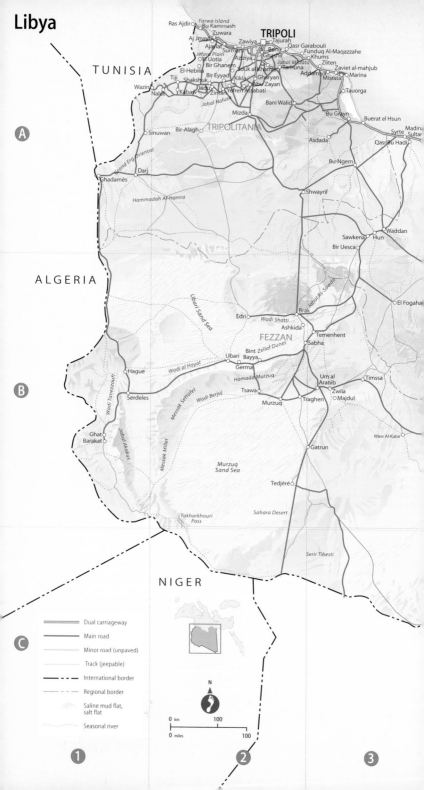

# What the papers say

*"If 'the essence of real travel' is what you have been secretly yearning for all these years, then Footprint are the guides for you."*
Under 26

*"Who should pack them - people who want to escape the crowd."*
The Observer

*"Footprint Handbooks, the best of the best."*
Le Monde, Paris

*"The guides for intelligent, independently-minded souls of any age or budget."*
Indie Traveller

*"Intelligently written, amazingly accurate and bang up-to-date. Footprint have combined nearly 80 years experience with a stunning new format to bring us guidebooks that leave the competition standing."*
John Pilkington, writer and broadcaster

Mail order
Available worldwide in bookshops and on-line. Footprint travel guides can also be ordered directly from us in Bath, via our website **www.footprintbooks.com** or from the address on the imprint page of this book.

# Acknowledgements

Credit is due to the generous help of many friends, in Libya, Tunisia, Morocco, France and the UK and USA. Nora Lafi gave important insight into 19th-century Libyan history, while the Lemaire and Baker families (in particular Zoe L. and Lucy B.) provided much-needed encouragement. Alice arrived just in time to help with the final touches. Terri White and Sarah Thorowgood were always available with advice at the end of a phone-line, ready to wrap a metaphorical cold towel round the overheated travel-author's brow. Thanks are especially due to the numerous people across Libya who shared thoughts and ideas about their country. Particular thanks go to Dr Mathias Faber and Margit Has, also Vivienne Sharp. Francis Russell was a unique source of encouragement, providing detail on marble patina, columns from Leptis and the myth of the Philaenoi and Tom Norton provided useful information on the classical sites. David Bond of the *Institut de belles lettres arabes*, Tunis, came up with many a useful reference on the Fezzan. Many thanks to Keith MacLachlan, author of the original Footprint *North African Handbook* for casting his expert eye over the proofs. Thanks also to the British embassies in Tunis and Tripoli for their support and ideas and to Dr David Snashall, Senior Lecturer in Occupational Health, United Medical Schools of Guy's and St Thomas' Hospitals and Chief Medical Advisor, Foreign and Commonwealth Office, London for supplying the information on staying healthy in Libya.

This guide is dedicated to Cathie Denham, a true Cyrenaican if ever there was one. On her Norton motorcycle, she would have roared down to the Fezzan.

## Selective bibliography

In putting together this guide, I drew on numerous academic sources. For the prehistory of the Fezzan, Jean-Loïc Le Quellec's *Art rupestre et préhistoire du Sahara* was indispensable on the complexities of Saharan rock art. The writings of Richard Goodchild on Cyrenaica and Denis Haynes and David Mattingly on Tripolitania were the primary sources for background and descriptions of the Greek and Roman sites. On Libya from the Arab invasion onwards, Jamil M. Abu-Nasr's monumental *A History of the Maghrib in the Islamic Period* was indispensable. For Libya in the early 20th century, I drew on work by E.E. Evans-Pritchard, Enzo Santarelli, Federico Cresti and Mia Fuller.

As there is so little literature on Libya, it seemed a good idea to provide a fuller (if selective) bibliography in addition to the 'Further reading' section on page 50. Note that the Fergiani Bookshop in Tripoli republishes books on Libya. The publishers and original date and place of publication are never indicated by Fergiani, no doubt due to some special exception to international copyright law prevailing in the Libyan publishing industry. In the UK, Fergiani books can be obtained from *West End Lane Books, 277 West End Land, London NW6 1QS, T020-7431 3770.*

**Abun-Nasr**, Jamil M. (1987, third edition) *A History of the Maghrib in the Islamic Period* Cambridge: CUP 450 pages of North African history from seventh century AD to present. Good balance of events and interpretation. Reveals how an entire region became involved in the clash between Christian and Islamic worlds.

**Bearman**, Jonathan (1986) *Qadhafi's Libya* London: Zed Books. An attempt to break with the simplistic portrayals of Libya current in the early 1980s. Recounts Libya's transformation from tribal society to wealthy oil state. Good account of Gadhafi's rise to power and early development of his regime.

**Berenson**, Mary (1938) *A Vicarious Trip to the Barbary Coast* London. Upper-crust ramblings in Italian-ruled Libya.

**Evans-Pritchard**, E.E. (1949) *The Sanusi of Cyrenaica* Oxford: OUP. Classic anthropo-logical study of the Sanusi movement. Useful geographic background on Cyrenaica. Unfortunately rather short on Italian colonialism, the concentration camps and how this impacted on the tribes.

**Diolé**, Philippe (1956) *Saharan Adventure* New York: Julian Messner. French Cousteau-type writer travels in southeast Algeria and the Fezzan with the help of the Third Saharan Division of the Foreign Legion.

**Goodchild**, Richard (1959) *Cyrene and Apollonia: a historical guide* Benghazi: Antiq-uities Dept of Cyrenaica. Excellent pocket guide with plenty of maps and diagrams.

**Haynes**, D.E.L. (1965) *The Antiquities of Tripolitania. An archaeological and historical guide to the pre-Islamic period* Tripoli: Dept of Antiquities Museums, and Archives. Absolutely essential reading for anyone keen on the ancient sites. Recent finds have outdated certain points.

**Jones**, A.H.M. (1937) *Cities of the Eastern Roman Provinces* Oxford: Oxford University Press. Contains useful account of ancient Cyrenaica.

**Le Quellec**, Jean-Loïc (1998) *Art rupestre et préhistoire du Sahara. Le Messak libyen.* Paris: Éditions Payot et Rivages. The best account of the prehistoric rock-art of the Messak region. Scholarly and readable, more thorough than the Italian material

**Lethielleux**, J. (1948) *Le Fezzan, ses jardins, ses palmiers* Tunis: Institut de belles let-tres arabes. Slim scholarly volume with all you need ever know about irrigation tech-niques, wells, palm trees and oasis gardens.

**Mattingly**, David J. (1994) *Tripolitania* Ann Arbor: University of Michigan Press. A truly scholarly case study on the development of the Roman province. Monumental. Lots of detail on the frontier, including isolated settlements, forts and fortified farms. Immense bibliography. *The* book on ancient Tripolitania.

**Pennell**, C.R. (1989) *Piracy and Diplomacy in Seventeenth Century North Africa* Lon-don: Associated University Press. High quality historical scholarship. Tripoli in a swashbuckling age as portrayed in the papers of a 17th-century English consul.

**Vandewalle**, Dirk (1998) *Libya since independence: oil and state-building* London: I.B. Tauris Publishers. Detailed analysis of Libya's recent political and economic develop-ment since independence in 1951. Not an easy read, but political scientists will ap-preciate the argument on oil revenues and their influence on the nature of the State. Sophisticated, takes the reader beyond the stereotypes of oil wealth.

**Di Vita**, Antonino et al (1999) *Libya. The lost cities of the Roman Empire.* Cologne: Könemann. Photographs by Robert Polidori. Coffee-table book on Leptis Magna, Sabratha, Cyrene and Apollonia. Atmospheric photographs of Leptis after rain and the theatre at Sabratha in the evening.

**Ward**, Philip (1969) *Touring Libya: the eastern provinces* London: Faber. The eastern regions of Libya, both Cyrenaica and the desert, in the years immediately prior to the fall of the monarchy. Typical quote: "Darna is a beautiful town, with palms overlook-ing the streets and the sound of water everywhere". So much can change in 30 years.

**Wellard**, James (1967) *The Lost Worlds of Africa* London: Hutchinson. Curious book, half-travelogue, half-history. Good observations and background to the Dawada Lakes.

**Williams**, Gwyn (1968) *Green Mountain. An informal guide to Cyrenaica and its Jebel Akhdar* London: Faber (republished Tripoli: Dar Fergiani). Reprint of 1950s account of living in Cyrenaica by British university lecturer. A pleasant read. Accounts of ruins and ramblings, Ian Carmichael school of travel writing.